A Life of

J.C. BEAGLEHOLE

New Zealand Scholar

all of Auchinleck, having met
the Pacific Ocean, next day called
it, & mentioned his own inclination
The Doctor ~~was discouraging~~ discouraged him. One
he said, 'till one considers how
~~casion~~ he admitted that he himself
~~itment~~. but the consideration of his
~~e~~ may, if we wish, stagger ourselves
parading the deck of the <u>Resolution</u>
not a profitable vision. I have on
~~rese~~ how profitable it would have
~~rangement~~ Boswell could have forme
~~re~~ characters just as odd, & less
improbable as sailors. How, one
~~tically~~ encouraging; if only The
Boswell should be their represent
~~ind~~ as well as of geography, & h
squared ~~Lord Auchinleck~~ the
the paternal acres at home & w

A Life of

J.C. BEAGLEHOLE

New Zealand Scholar

Tim Beaglehole

VICTORIA UNIVERSITY PRESS

VICTORIA UNIVERSITY PRESS
Victoria University of Wellington
PO Box 600 Wellington
vuw.ac.nz/vup

First published 2006

ISBN-13: 978-0-86473-535-5
ISBN-10: 0-86473-535-9

National Library of New Zealand Cataloguing-in-Publication Data

Beaglehole, T. H.
A life of J.C. Beaglehole : New Zealand scholar /
Tim Beaglehole.
Includes bibliographical references and index.
ISBN 0-86473-535-9
1. Beaglehole, J. C. (John Cawte) 2. Scholars—New Zealand—
Biography. 2. Historians—New Zealand—Biography. I. Title.
993.007202—dc 22

Published with the assistance of a grant from

ARTS COUNCIL OF NEW ZEALAND TOI AOTEAROA

Printed in Singapore

For John, Toby & Charlotte
&
for Helen

Contents

Extended Family of J.C. Beaglehole

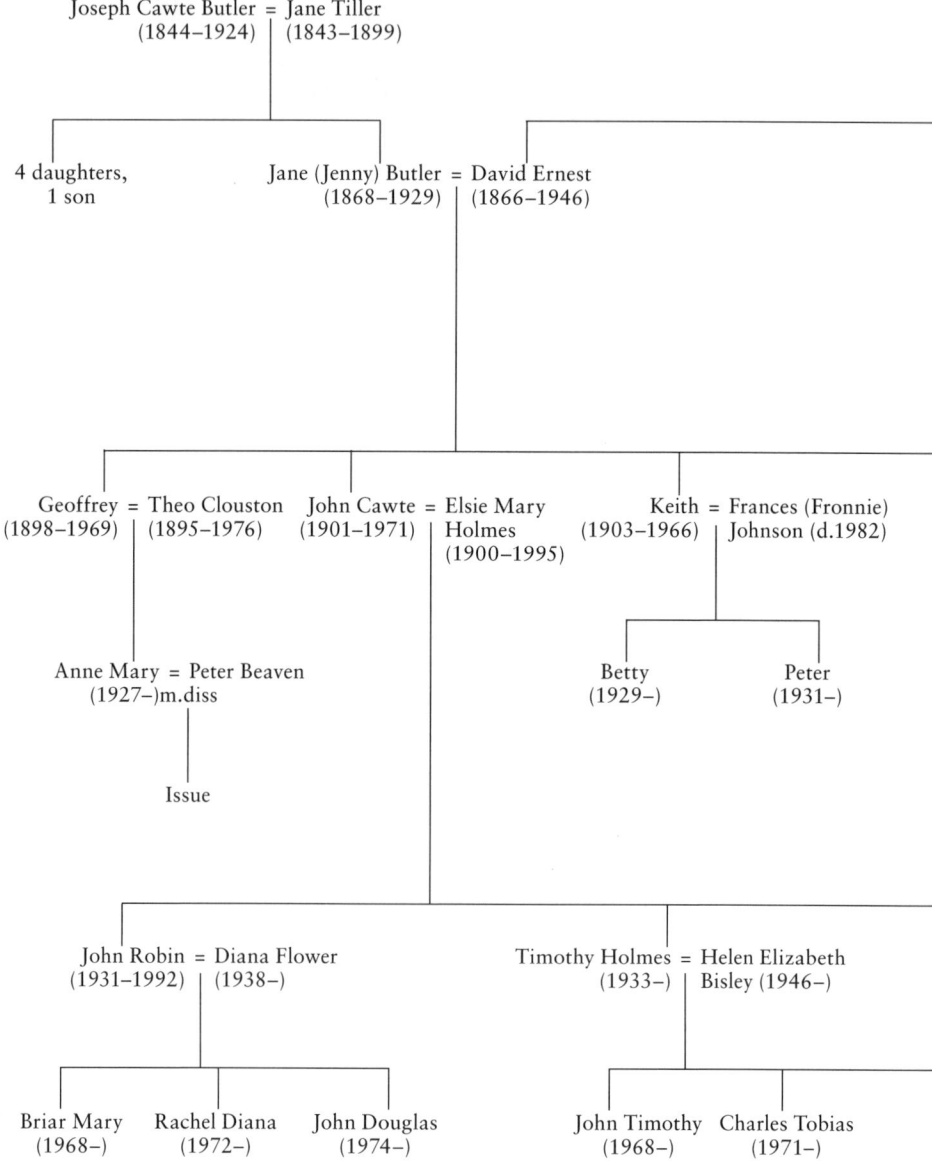

Joseph Cawte Butler = Jane Tiller
(1844–1924) | (1843–1899)

4 daughters,
1 son

Jane (Jenny) Butler = David Ernest
(1868–1929) | (1866–1946)

Geoffrey = Theo Clouston
(1898–1969) | (1895–1976)

John Cawte = Elsie Mary
(1901–1971) | Holmes
(1900–1995)

Keith = Frances (Fronnie)
(1903–1966) | Johnson (d.1982)

Anne Mary = Peter Beaven
(1927–)m.diss

Betty
(1929–)

Peter
(1931–)

Issue

John Robin = Diana Flower
(1931–1992) | (1938–)

Timothy Holmes = Helen Elizabeth
(1933–) | Bisley (1946–)

Briar Mary
(1968–)

Rachel Diana
(1972–)

John Douglas
(1974–)

John Timothy
(1968–)

Charles Tobias
(1971–)

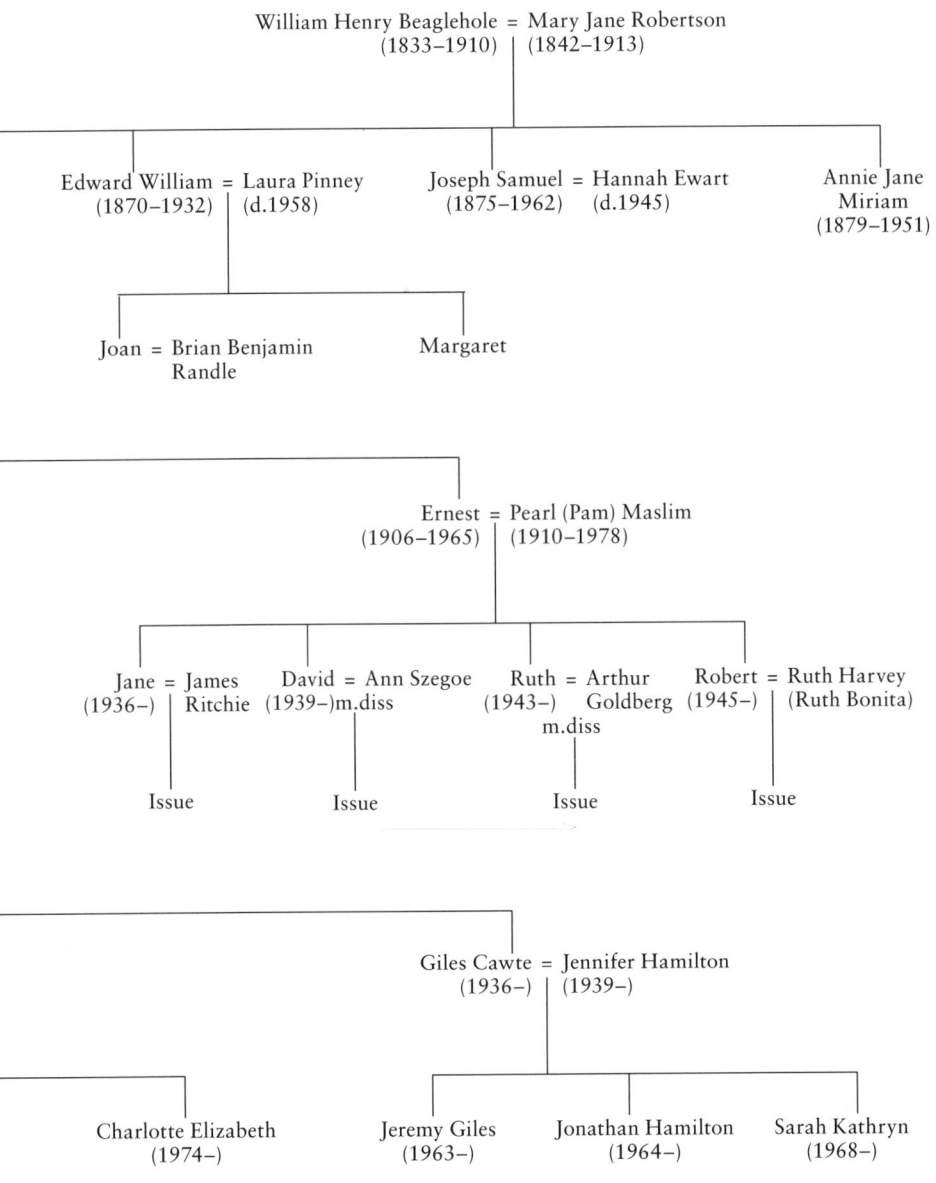

William Henry Beaglehole = Mary Jane Robertson
(1833–1910) | (1842–1913)

Edward William = Laura Pinney
(1870–1932) | (d.1958)

Joseph Samuel = Hannah Ewart
(1875–1962) (d.1945)

Annie Jane
Miriam
(1879–1951)

Joan = Brian Benjamin
Randle

Margaret

Ernest = Pearl (Pam) Maslim
(1906–1965) | (1910–1978)

Jane = James
(1936–) | Ritchie

David = Ann Szegoe
(1939–)m.diss

Ruth = Arthur
(1943–) Goldberg
m.diss

Robert = Ruth Harvey
(1945–) | (Ruth Bonita)

Issue

Issue

Issue

Issue

Giles Cawte = Jennifer Hamilton
(1936–) | (1939–)

Charlotte Elizabeth
(1974–)

Jeremy Giles
(1963–)

Jonathan Hamilton
(1964–)

Sarah Kathryn
(1968–)

Note: John's descendants beyond his grandchildren are not shown.

Illustrations

Unless otherwise noted in the captions all the illustrations are part of the author's collection.

Frontispiece

Portrait of J.C. Beaglehole by Evelyn Page.

Section One (after page 128)

William Henry Beaglehole.
Mary Jane Beaglehole.
The family of Joseph Cawte Butler and Jane Butler.
Numbers 49 and 51 Hopper Street.
David Ernest Beaglehole.
Jane (Jenny) Beaglehole.
John as a small boy.
Uncle Joe as a guide on the Milford Track.
John with curls.
The Beaglehole boys: Keith, Geoffrey, John, Ernest.
The gang of cousins.
Ern and Jenny about 1915.
Keith and John.
Thomas Hunter.
Victoria University College.
Tramping at Mount Matthews.
John is seen off by his father as he sails on the *Maheno*.

John on board the *Osterley*.

John and Raymond McGrath.

Shipboard – Duncan, Henning, Miss Rowe, McGrath.

21 Brunswick Square.

John and Lorrie Richardson on the road to Canterbury.

John at Neustadt in the Black Forest.

John, 1929.

Elsie, 1929.

John, painted by his uncle, George Butler.

Section Two (after page 256)

Title page of *Verses for my father*.

Title page of *The University of New Zealand*.

Title page of *The Maori People Today*.

Page 28 of *Introduction to New Zealand*.

Page 45 of *Introduction to New Zealand*.

Page 11 of *Tasman and the Discovery of New Zealand*.

One page in a scholarly correspondence. The Victoria University College letterhead was John's design.

The page in John's first draft of the biography of Cook describing Nicholas Young's sighting of New Zealand.

Section Three (after page 416)

John and Elsie on their wedding day.

Wedding group.

John and Elsie in Dunedin.

Norman Richmond.

John and Elsie with Airini Fisher, Muriel Billing, Geoffrey Billing and Alan Fisher.

Elsie with Robin and Tim.

Peter's Farm, 'Kowhai Flat'.

Tim, Giles and Robin.

Acknowledgements

MANY PEOPLE HAVE HELPED me as I have worked on this biography. It is a book which draws largely on the wealth of letters written by my father, and my greatest debt is to those who have given me letters or copies of letters in their care and allowed me to make use of them. They are listed in the note on the sources. I have also profited by discussions (in many cases following the reading of draft chapters) with a number of family and friends who knew John well. They included my brother Giles; my cousins Mary Beaven, Betty Beaglehole, David Beaglehole and Peter Beaglehole; Janet Paul, Nan Taylor, Bob Burnett, Frances Porter, Frank and Lyn Corner, Ester Einhorn, Jule Einhorn and, especially, my former teacher and colleague, Mary Boyd. Gary Hawke read most of the book in draft and I valued his encouragement. Alexa Barrow kindly read the chapters on editing Cook and John's working relationship with her father, R.A. Skelton. Parts were also read by Margaret Alington, Brigit Bruer (who provided the photograph of her father, Norman Richmond), Stuart Johnston, Doug Munro (who during his own historical work kept an eagle eye open for anything that might be useful for me), Hugh Price, Bill Renwick, Jack Shallcrass, Oliver Sutherland (who provided the photograph of his father, Ivan Sutherland) and Lydia Wevers. Diana Beaglehole sought out relevant material for me from the records of the New Zealand Historic Places Trust.

I am also grateful for the help I received from the staff of a number of libraries and record collections: the Alexander Turnbull Library – appropriately for a life of J.C. Beaglehole – the foremost among them; Archives New Zealand; the State Library of New South Wales (and especially to Arthur Easton of the manuscripts section); the Bernice P. Bishop Museum in Honolulu; the Hocken Library, University of Otago; the Auckland War Memorial Museum Library. The J.C. Beaglehole Room in the Victoria University of Wellington Library was invaluable in having copies of everything listed in the 1972 bibliography of John's work, as well as additional publications collected by Kathleen Coleridge during her time as librarian. I am grateful to her and her successor, Nicola Freen, for their assistance. Richard Woods, Director of Security in the New Zealand Security Intelligence Service, released material to me from the J.C. Beaglehole file in their records and allowed me to quote from it.

Sydney Shep gave me a copy of her paper on John's typographical work on the centennial publications (since published in *Creating a National Spirit: Celebrating New Zealand's Centennial* edited by William Renwick) and has generously shared her knowledge with me. I have also drawn on the work done for research essays and theses by several students, especially Chris Hilliard, Ingrid Horrocks and Sonia Reesby.

In tracing Beagleholes in Cornwall and in Australia I have been immeasurably helped by a number of Australians with a taste for genealogy: Moyston Beaglehole, Fred Begelhole, Carol Both and, above all, Betty Murdoch. In Wellington, Patricia Ramsay has been equally generous with the results of her research on the Tiller and Butler families, and Margaret Alington's work on David Robertson and his family (for her book *Unquiet Earth: A History of the Bolton Street Cemetery*) has rounded out our knowledge of my father's forebears.

At the early stages of collecting material I received a grant of $8000 from the Historical Branch of the Department of Internal Affairs, most of which was used in having letters transcribed, with considerable benefit when I came to work on them. I am especially grateful to Donna Holt and Karen Gilpin for their work on this transcription and to the Historical Branch for the grant which made it possible. For the last year of writing and research I was delighted to receive the Friends of the Turnbull Library Research Grant of $5000. In writing a book there are a succession of costs, often small individually, but discouraging if totalled. The grant has been very helpful in this respect, but perhaps even more as a recognition of the value of the project.

Andrew Mason proved an ideal editor; Tordis Flath a painstaking indexer. My gratitude to them is matched by my gratitude to the Victoria University Press, and especially to Fergus Barrowman, a publisher of taste and discrimination, and Sue Brown. They have produced a handsome volume that I believe John might have viewed with favour. Last – and first – I owe thanks to my wife, Helen.

Introduction

J.C. BEAGLEHOLE BECAME known internationally as the editor and biographer of James Cook. The four massive volumes of *The Journals of Captain James Cook on His Voyages of Discovery*, published by the Hakluyt Society between 1955 and 1967, together with *The Endeavour Journal of Joseph Banks* published by the Public Library of New South Wales in 1962, displayed his superb gifts as an historian and editor and provided the foundation for a new generation of Cook studies. In 1970 he was awarded the Order of Merit, the first New Zealander since Ernest Rutherford to be so honoured and still the only recipient to have made his career in New Zealand. At the time of his death in 1971 he had nearly completed the final touches to *The Life of Captain James Cook*. It was published just over two years later and was widely recognised as a remarkable biography, crowning his work on Cook.

Forty years earlier it had seemed far from certain whether he would have the opportunity for a career as a scholar and lecturer at all. On his return to New Zealand with a PhD from the University of London in the midst of the Great Depression, any sort of permanent position appeared unattainable. His willingness to speak out for academic freedom and civil liberties, at a time when public anxiety and economic uncertainty bred widespread intolerance of dissent, gave him a reputation as a radical and dangerous young man. This almost certainly cost him appointment to the chair in history at Victoria University College when it was filled at the end of 1934. A year later, with three books already published, he was appointed to a lectureship at Victoria. In 1948 a senior research fellowship was established to enable him to edit the Cook and Banks journals full time. Later this became a chair in Commonwealth History, in which he remained until his retirement.

John Beaglehole had left London with great reluctance. Thirty-three years later, in 1962, he was offered the Beit Chair in the History of the British Commonwealth at Oxford. He turned it down. New Zealand had changed; his relationship with New

Zealand had changed. Never the reclusive scholar, he had become involved in a wide range of activities. Working with J.W. Heenan, a remarkable public servant and Under-Secretary of Internal Affairs, on the activities and especially the publications celebrating the New Zealand centennial gave him, for the first time he later claimed (not without some exaggeration), a sense of what it was to be a New Zealander. His skills as a typographer, to which he brought a meticulous eye, had an influence well beyond the works for which he was personally responsible. The interests on which he published were legion: exploration, art, letters, architecture, music, universities, libraries, archives, politics, public taste, typography and design, as well as New Zealand history. Underlying much of what he wrote was a preoccupation with New Zealand as a society, with understanding its nature, with fostering those developments which might make it a more rewarding and civilised place in which to live.

As a public figure he was increasingly called to serve on boards and committees. He was a founder member of the Wellington Chamber Music Society in 1945. He was president of the New Zealand Council for Civil Liberties for twenty years (1952–71); for nearly as long a board member of the National (later New Zealand) Historic Places Trust (1955–71); on two occasions president of the New Zealand Institute of International Affairs (1954–55, 1957–60), in which he had been actively involved since the 1930s. He was also a member of the New Zealand Literary Fund Advisory Committee (1959–61), of the Board of Trustees of the National Art Gallery and Dominion Museum (1959–64), and of the Arts Advisory Council (1960–63). He was a long-serving member of the New Zealand National Commission for Unesco, and a member of the New Zealand delegation to the conferences at Paris in 1949, Florence in 1950 and Paris again in 1962.

Several times towards the end of his life, my father gave some fascinating glimpses of his childhood and early life.[1] Had he lived longer I suspect the biography of James Cook might well have been followed by a volume of autobiography. While he could gently mock what he styled his 'trivial self-centred' reminiscences, he was well aware that he had lived through a period of exceptional interest in New Zealand's social and intellectual history and that he had been in a position to observe and even contribute to the changes that were taking place. A biography must take the place of that unwritten autobiography, but he left a wealth of material for the writer of such a work: books, essays, reviews, which 'flowed from that seemingly inexhaustible source'[2] for over forty years, and a host of unpublished letters. Most fully, perhaps, the letters reveal the range of his interests, his wit and the sparkling and affectionate play of his mind. Not surprisingly, they were often carefully kept by their recipients. These resources have made the writing of this work very much a father-and-son partnership.

Working on the biography led me to consider a number of issues. The first was whether, as John's son, I should be writing his biography at all. The second, not entirely unrelated, was whether there were areas into which the biographer should not venture. The third, again entangled with the others, arose from the extensive use I was making of unpublished private letters, often written with considerable forthrightness and no thought of publication.

Whether writing the biography of a parent is dangerous territory for a son or daughter remains for me an open question. It may, at its worst, lead to a work of cloying filial piety or, alternatively, an attempt to explain, or reshape, a parent and a relationship that were less than satisfactory in life. My relationship with my father was, I believe, remarkably straightforward (and in writing the biography I have discovered nothing to suggest otherwise). We shared many interests, though, perhaps surprisingly for Cook's biographer, he did not share my taste for sailing, and we had something of the same temperament. We both taught history at Victoria University, and for the six years before he retired were colleagues. I decided to write about his life because I found it fascinating and, while I have not sought to disguise my feelings of affection and admiration, what I have tried to achieve is a kind of objective intimacy that will complement the public record in illuminating my father's life and the connections between his life, his work and the times through which he lived.

Inevitably, looking at the man behind the scholar – and I am looking at a life as a whole rather than writing an intellectual biography – raises the question of whether there are any boundaries. 'From James Boswell to Lytton Strachey', Michael Holroyd has written, 'British biographers have traded in gossip and bad taste – which is simply to say we are fascinated by human nature'.[3] I share the fascination; my father greatly admired both Boswell and Strachey. I am concerned more with the accuracy and liveliness of the portrait than with good or bad taste. Frances Spalding, the biographer of Duncan Grant, tells us that Grant, when he was eighty-eight, was asked whether he resented the public exposure of private lives brought about by recent biographical work on his Bloomsbury friends. 'I've come to the conclusion that it's better', Grant replied. 'Everyone's past has been revealed now, and I'm rather in favour of it. It makes the lives much easier to understand; and otherwise things would be questioned without people knowing the answer, and I think that's a bad thing.'[4] I find Grant's view persuasive and yet, as a son, I hesitate. In practice, the challenge has been to achieve a balanced perspective.

The use I have made of my father's letters – in many ways a remarkable source – raises other but sometimes related questions for a biographer. He could be cutting in his comments, not always charitable in his judgements. He was engaged, forthright; therein lies a lot of the interest in what he wrote. He made comments which could still, I suspect, cause discomfort or pain. I hope I have not quoted any such passages gratuitously; at the same time I hope I have caught his character as a correspondent. At times his language and strong feelings can mislead. What was colloquial usage at the time, would if used now suggest sexist, racist and anti-Semitic views that would be unacceptable. However, if all such language is edited out the reader loses some of the flavour of the letters. But how exactly should such phrases be interpreted? It would be rash to draw conclusions from the language of the time about the views of an individual; other evidence would be needed to corroborate what that language might suggest to a modern reader. In reading the letters, the tone – playful, gently ironical, passionate, biting – is as important as the literal meaning of the words used in conveying the writer's attitude.

I am conscious also that the reader may feel that my use of the letters leads to an uncritical acceptance of those attitudes, of my father's view of the world. There is a difficulty here, not least because of the relative paucity of historical or biographical work in many of the areas in which he was involved, which might have provided a context and a balance to what he wrote (and what I write). But I would not exaggerate the difficulty: biography is not history. I have tried to give a lively and honest portrait of the man; there may still be room for a more critical assessment of his views and what he achieved.

A further difficulty for a biographer arises from the very breadth of John's activities. The account of his early years, covered by the first seven chapters, is very much a chronological narrative. From the time of his appointment to a lectureship in history at Victoria University College at the end of 1935, and his involvement with planning for the centennial, however, a chronological account, while having the veracity of reflecting the untidiness of life itself, would be fragmented in a way that would tax almost any reader. So in chapter eight I focus on John's life as it related to Victoria University College, his home and family, and the circle of friends which he and Elsie made in these years. I then look, in chapter nine, at his work (in the same period) as a part-time civil servant and historical adviser to the Department of Internal Affairs during the centennial celebrations, the war and the early postwar years and, more particularly, at the effect on him of his work in the Historical Branch. In chapter ten I write about his growing involvement in the world of books, music and the arts in the wider community. John's work on James Cook, the crowning achievement of his scholarly career, is covered in chapters eleven and twelve. The final two chapters cover the same period as the work on Cook, to some extent dividing it chronologically, though in looking at his involvement with bodies such as the New Zealand Council for Civil Liberties and the National Historic Places Trust, both of which were started in the 1950s, I have ignored chronology and put it all in chapter thirteen. In the final chapter, which is largely on the 1960s and the first two years of the 1970s, I have concentrated more on an account of the private man, and also of the growing recognition he was receiving as a scholar and public figure. John's remarkable achievement was that the life which the biographer, for practical reasons, has to unravel into separate strands, as he lived it came together as one of extraordinary richness and achievement.

WHEN HE BECAME well known my father received a number of letters from correspondents who were Beagleholes or related to Beagleholes. He became interested enough to write back telling them what he knew of the family's history. It was not a lot. He exchanged a number of letters with an Ernest Beaglehole in Adelaide, Australia, suspecting, but not really knowing, that they were related. He knew his grandfather had left Cornwall as a youth, having already begun work as a copper miner, and after a time in South Australia had travelled on to New Zealand. The Cornish background and the remarkable change in family fortunes that followed emigration interested him, but he had little time to pursue this interest. We now know more about that background as well as that of the other families John was descended from, and can begin the story in Cornwall in the early nineteenth century.

PART ONE

The Making of an Historian

1

FOREBEARS

BEAGLEHOLE WAS A NOT uncommon name in eighteenth-century Cornwall. It was derived from *bugel hal*, meaning herdsman on the moors. As time passed, however, Beagleholes were largely found clustered in the mining villages of the county. The spelling varied; Bagelhole, Begelhole, Bugelhoal, Buglehole and more appear in parish registers, as well as Beaglehole. Christian names showed less variety: John, William, Henry, Elizabeth and Jane constantly recur. There were clearly a number of families in the west, in Helston and its nearby villages of Breage, Sithney and Germoe, and the first John Beaglehole in whom we are interested was born in Breage in 1805, the son of Margaret and William, a miner.[1] John moved from Breage to the St Austell area and became, according to family tradition, a copper miner. Most of his children were baptised in St Austell. He died in Liskeard, however, where his youngest son was born. In the 1871 death notice of his widow Margaret she is referred to as 'relict of the late John Beaglehole of St Cleer Cornwall'.

The copper mines of the St Austell district, lying to the east of the town, became prominent only after 1812. St Austell had been a tin-mining village which grew steadily in size in the second half of the eighteenth century, once china clay was discovered in 1755 and began to be mined. By the end of the century the population was just under 4000, and while the china clay industry came to dominate the town – and, in time, the huge heaps of white spoil equally dominate its surrounding landscape – copper and tin mining were significant in the first half of the nineteenth century. Copper and tin miners, indeed, regarded clay-working as an inferior occupation that called for none of their skills as miners. Copper miners from St Austell were among those who in the late 1830s and 1840s developed mines in the Caradon district near the village of St Cleer, a few miles from Liskeard. More and more miners and capital were attracted. A railway

built from Liskeard to the new mines enabled the ore to be taken by
barge down the Liskeard and Looe canal and shipped out of Looe.
By 1850 the Caradon district was recognised as one of the richest
mineral areas in Cornwall and the Caradon Hill Mine, employing
some 4000 men, perhaps the greatest of the Cornish copper mines.

John Beaglehole's initial move from Breage to St Austell and
the subsequent move to Liskeard or St Cleer, which seems to have
taken place between the birth of his son Joseph in St Austell in 1843
and that of Sampson in Liskeard in 1848, were as much a part of
a common pattern as was his family's subsequent move to South
Australia after his death. Whether there were more specific reasons
for the move from St Austell we can only conjecture. The winter of
1846–47 was particularly hard. Hungry workers believed they were
being starved in order to benefit profiteering corn merchants, and
in May 1847 there were riots in Wadebridge, in which St Austell
miners played a part, seeking to prevent the export of corn to other
parts of the country and to have it available locally at a fair price.[2]
The men did little more than threaten, but a month later a mob
of casual mine-labourers and clay-workers invaded St Austell itself
and started looting some shops. Troops eventually restored order
and ten men were given sentences of imprisonment ranging from
six months to two years.[3] It was a time when a family man might
well decide to try his luck at the flourishing new mines at Caradon,
not least because his eldest son, John, was already old enough to be
working and the second, William, soon would be.

John had married Jane Rickard on 26 July 1826 in St Austell.[4]
Both registered their names with a mark. Jane bore eight children in
fifteen years of marriage before dying of 'inflammation of the lungs'.
Only four of those children survived to adulthood: John, born in
1829, William Henry, 1833, Mary, 1838, and Absalom, born in 1840
and losing his mother before his first birthday. On 20 April 1842
John remarried. Margaret Williams was a widow whose husband,
Thomas Williams, had died nine years earlier. Margaret was thirty-
six and had two young sons of her own. She too was the child of a
miner, Joseph Watters. And if Margaret signed the register with a
cross, this time John wrote his name, spelling it Beagelhole. John
and Margaret went on to have two sons, Joseph Watters (named
after his grandfather) in 1843, and Sampson in 1848. Two years
after Sampson's birth, John died at Liskeard, leaving Margaret with
the care of eight children, ranging from her stepson John in his early
twenties down to two-year-old Sampson. The 1851 census return for
St Cleer village lists Margaret as a 'lodgings housekeeper' and her

sons Thomas and John Williams as well as John and William Henry
Beaglehole as miners. Later that year Margaret and her family, with
the exception of her elder sons and her eldest stepson, John, sailed
to a new life in South Australia.

They were but a tiny part of a great exodus of peoples from
Europe to the new worlds in the mid-nineteenth century. What
precipitated the move we do not know. Certainly, life in a Cornish
mining community was far from comfortable. Before the Caradon
discoveries, St Cleer was an agricultural parish with a population
of 984 in 1830; then copper was discovered and in thirty years the
population had reached almost 4000.[5] Mining boomed and brought
prosperity to some, but a heavy price was paid. The overcrowded,
insanitary hovels of cob and thatch thrown up by the miners
consisted of little more than walls and a roof; water supply was a
secondary consideration and sanitation came last of all. Disease was
rife. The St Cleer parish burial registers 'show an alarming increase
in the proportion of infants dying under five years, and the virtual
halving of the average expectancy of life from over 40 to less than
22 years'. Much the same tragedy is revealed in the burial registers
of other mining parishes. The miners' poverty was reflected in
their average weekly wage in the second quarter of the nineteenth
century: less than 13 shillings, a bare living wage and nothing more.
All too often meals 'consisted of sour barley bread washed down
with boiled water slightly discoloured with tea, occasionally varied
with a few turnips . . . fried in grease that had been purloined from
the mine engines'.

Margaret and her family left Plymouth, about eighteen miles
from Liskeard, on 7 May 1851 on the *Sultana* and arrived at Port
Adelaide just over three months later, on 10 August. In the shipping
list they are entered as

BEAGLEHOLE	Margaret	aged 38	housekeeper
	William	17	miner
	Mary	14	servant
	Absalom	13	
	Job	8	
	Joseph	7	
	Sampson	3	

There is a discrepancy between the ages given for Margaret and
Absalom and those recorded in the 1851 census for Liskeard (taken
in March), where they given as forty-five and ten – the ten for
Absalom being apparently correct. The differences may have arisen
from ignorance or from error. From the way she signed the marriage

register Margaret almost certainly could not write; quite probably she could not read either. Her death notice in 1871 gave her age as sixty-seven, which would give a birth date of 1804 and suggests that she was at least forty-five when they sailed. It may have been expedient to supply the younger age to meet the conditions for the passage to Australia. The Colonial Land and Emigration Commissioners in London regulated the supply of assisted immigrants by altering the terms of eligibility. Margaret got away just in time, because that year assistance was withdrawn from widows, widowers with children, single women with illegitimate children and habitual paupers.[6] The other enigma is the listing of Job. No record has been found of him being born as Job Beaglehole nor as Job Williams, so he does not appear to be a son of Margaret. After the family arrived in Australia, there is also no record of Job as a Beaglehole. Perhaps some other family asked Margaret to bring him out to relatives and he travelled under her name to make it legal.

Why South Australia? First, assisted passages were available, and without these a widow in Margaret's circumstances could never have considered making such a move. Second, it seems possible that she was following relatives who had already made the voyage. Another widow, Elizabeth Beaglehole (1801–74), whose husband William Henry Beaglehole (1800–33) may have been related to Margaret's husband John, left Helston and made the passage out with her two sons, John and William Henry, on the *Prince Regent* in 1849. Another William Beaglehole had arrived in Adelaide about 1845 with his wife and family. Maybe the two widows went out to join him; such a pattern of chain migration was not unusual at that time. The provision of assisted passages was explained by the colony's place as the first example of the Wakefield system in practice. Edward Gibbon Wakefield's theory of colonisation sought to 'synchronise flows of labour and capital with the release of land for settlement'[7] and to ensure an adequate supply of labour by funding migration from the proceeds of land sales. During the first phase of South Australia's development, 1836–57, population growth depended heavily on assisted immigration and about 160,000 immigrants arrived in the colony. A disproportionate number of these migrants came from the south of England, and for several years in the mid-century more than 10 per cent of arrivals were from Cornwall. Miners, especially those recruited from the Cornish copper-mining towns, had little difficulty finding employment at most times, and a concentration of 'Cornish' villages and towns grew about the copper fields at Kooringa (later known as Burra), Kapunda, Moonta and

Walleroo. It was widely said that, wherever in the world a deep hole was dug for minerals, you would find a Cornish miner at the bottom of it, 'highly skilled, self-reliant, with the tradition of centuries of mining enriching all his work, and most probably with the teaching and tunes of Methodism giving direction and rhythm to his life'.[8] South Australia may not at first have seemed a great improvement on Cornwall. In Kooringa, where the family first settled, 1600 out of the 4400 residents in 1851 were living in caves dug into the bank of the river, and that year there were 153 deaths from cholera and typhoid, most of them children.

Joseph and Sampson followed the family tradition and became miners, moving from the copper mines of South Australia to the silver mines of Broken Hill when the copper ran out. Sampson eventually moved to Kalgoorlie and the gold mines of Western Australia, while Joseph remained with silver. They both married and had large families, though eight of Sampson's and his wife Elizabeth's thirteen children died in infancy. Their sister Mary married William Henry Snell in 1856 at Kooringa and had a family. Absalom decided on farming and, apparently the victim of false pretences, travelled to Western Australia to take up land that proved to have no water and very little feed for stock. He returned and eventually settled on a mallee block near Tailem Bend east of Adelaide. It was an arid area of low rainfall where he and his family would have barely made enough to live on. Of what William Henry did in his first years in South Australia we know very little. Years later, in a letter to one of William's sons, Absalom wrote 'I have the Deeds of your fathers land but I think they are no good sold for rates or gone otherwise . . .'[9] The deed,[10] in which William was described as 'of Kooringa Miner', showed the land, bought from Charles Tompkins on 5 August 1852 for £18, to have been in the village of Kensington near Adelaide. Whatever his interest it was not enough to hold him and, probably in 1857,* William Henry crossed the Tasman to New Zealand.

We know almost nothing of what he did in the following eight years. Family tradition has it that he tried his luck on the Otago goldfields before moving to Wellington, where he is said to have worked on the wharves before he found a job, later a partnership, in the brickworks in Taranaki Street. The brickworks, part of the original Wellington acre 86, were on the eastern side of Taranaki

---

*   William's death certificate, dated 27 July 1910, recorded that he had been in New Zealand fifty-three years.

Street; the site, later occupied by Odlin's timber yard, is now part of the playing field of Wellington High School. The first definite date and event we have is that of his wedding on 4 January 1866 to Mary Jane, daughter of David Robertson.

David Robertson was born on 8 December 1813 and spent his early years in Fifeshire near Newburgh, a town on the Firth of Tay.[11] His father, James Robertson, was a Chelsea Pensioner who farmed at Lindores. The few surviving letters of his parents are dictated, presumably because they could not write, but David, unusually for the time, had some schooling. His father wished him to study for the ministry, but after a period of study in Edinburgh he turned to horticulture and in his early twenties went to England, where he was a gardener on a series of estates in Hertfordshire. For about seven years from 1840, David, now with a wife named Ann, was at Bedwell Park, near Essendon, apparently as head gardener. Bedwell Park was the home of Sir Culling Eardley Eardley, a religious philanthropist, friend of Dr David Livingstone and founder of the Evangelical Alliance, established to promote religious freedom throughout the world. It would have been a congenial position for Robertson, whose surviving letters and gardening diary show a thoughtful man, God-fearing, respectful of the ways of Providence, and committed to total abstinence. It was at Bedwell Park that Mary Jane (known as Jane) was born in 1842, followed two years later by a second daughter, Annie. On 24 August 1846, a few months after the birth of a son, Ann died; ten days later the baby died. The following year David married Mary Walker. There were seven children from this second marriage, the two youngest being born in Wellington.

What led to the decision to migrate to New Zealand we do not know. There are some signs of restlessness in David's letters in the years after his second marriage. He contemplated moving to Ireland, though it seems unlikely that he actually did so. Early in 1854 he was on the estate of Waresley Park in Huntingdonshire, which belonged at that time to the Feversham family. It was probably from there that the family left for New Zealand, arriving in Wellington on the barque *Alma* in May 1857. Jane, the eldest child, was fifteen, and her youngest stepsister, Helen, was born nine days after the ship berthed.

Three months later David Robertson was appointed sexton at the Wellington public cemetery in Sydney Street, a position he was to hold for thirty years. A small four-roomed cottage was built for the family, into which they somehow all fitted. David's botanical knowledge brought him into contact with Sir George Grey and in the 1860s, during Grey's second term as Governor, the two used to make collecting expeditions into the bush around Wellington. At the government's request, David classified and named many native plants, ferns, trees and shrubs. He was also friendly with a later Governor, Sir William Jervois.

Clearly an educated and thoughtful man, David was said to have helped the young with their lessons. In the case of his eldest daughters, however, what little evidence there is suggests that they had little schooling. Annie, when she married, just before her twenty-first birthday (two years before her sister Jane), signed her marriage certificate with a cross. She later learned to write her name, and she could read. She had also inherited her father's religious interests and social concerns and was one of the first converts to the Salvation Army in Wellington. As Annie Rudman, she became a prominent figure in the Wellington City Corps for over forty years and was joined there by all seven of her children. Two surviving letters by Jane suggest that she too had very limited skill at writing.

Of the circumstances which brought Jane Robertson and William Henry Beaglehole together we know nothing; in all probability it was the Methodist chapel. They were married on 4 January 1866 in David Robertson's cottage in the cemetery, and then Jane joined William in the cottage in the brickyard. There, nine months later, on 8 October, the first of their four children was born: David Ernest, always known as Ernest, or Ern to the family. There followed Edward William (Ted) on 12 March 1870, Joseph Samuel (Joe) on 24 August 1875, and Annie Jane Miriam (known as Annie, and in later life in the family simply as Auntie) on 10 August 1879. Between Ted's birth and Joe's the family moved into a new house in Hopper Street at number 49 (later renumbered 51). William and his partner in the brickworks, George Maslen,* had bought the whole section of ground from Taranaki Street, opposite the brickyard, through to Hopper Street and they built two similar small two-storeyed houses facing the two frontages. Jane, inheriting her father's gift, created a garden remembered by Ern as 'gay with flowers . . . and sweet with perfume'. William grew vegetables. The Beagleholes reached the brickyard by nipping through a gap in their back fence and then through the Maslens' section, and in his early years Ernest spent

---

*   William and George Maslen later fell out, and William seems to have left
      the brickworks. In *Stone's Directory* for 1891–92, and again in 1895–96,
      William's occupation is given as 'lumper', or waterside worker, though the
      electoral roll for 1893 and 1896 continued to list him as 'brickmaker'.

a good deal of time about the yard, often in the company of the Maslens' elder son, who was about his own age. They played hide and seek, he remembered,

about the long drying sheds, wheeled the barrows, found endless pleasure in the horses and carts, and were particularly interested in the firing of the kilns . . . Father supervised most of the kiln work and brick baking, this led to his staying up often through the night; and one of my great joys as a boy was to be allowed to go to the yard in the early evening, sit in front of the openings in the kiln through which the fires were kept up roasting potatoes with great, very long-handled shovels with much gusto and listening to the gossip . . . [of] men working in the yard with their friends [who] made a practice of assembling round the kiln in the evenings till bedtime smoking and yarning.[12]

William and Jane's was a Wesleyan Methodist household. William became a lay preacher at the Primitive Methodist chapel in Webb Street, opposite the bottom of Hopper Street, 'and would sometimes make the long journey through Karori to Makara to take his turn at preaching there'.[13] Jane, in spite of her limited education, became Ernest's first teacher of writing and reading, taking him through *Line upon Line* and *Precept upon Precept,* children's books that were based largely on incidents in the Old and New Testaments, and were popular in those days in chapel-going households. These, together with the Bible, were the first books he read. Fairy tales and nursery rhymes, he later wrote, did not come his way – only when he had children of his own did he discover such things – and he wondered if his parents had even known of their existence.

Ernest went to the Wesleyan Day School, where he received a book prize for progress in 1876, and to the Wesleyan Methodist Sunday School in Manners Street. A number of books, rewards 'for Good Conduct and Attendance', have survived, works of rather oppressive piety. 'It is a delightful employment to discover and trace the operations of divine grace, as they are manifested in the dispositions and lives of God's real children', one of these, *Annals of the Poor* by the Rev. Legh Richmond, opens. Whatever Ernest made of these particular volumes, books came to assume a place of extraordinary importance in his life. Methodism represented not simply a set of religious beliefs but also a way to self-improvement, with the printed word providing the key to progress towards that end.

Whether Ernest went on from the Wesleyan Day School to Mount Cook School, as his brother Edward later did, we do not know, but from 1879 to the end of 1881 he attended Morton's Private Academy on The Terrace. Conducted by Mr Robert Morton 'of Aberdeen

University' (simply 'of', no degree is given), this was one of a number of private schools, short-lived in most cases, that were started in Wellington in the first few decades of settlement. The academy claimed to offer 'all the essentials of a Liberal English Education' and Ernest's half-yearly reports list a formidable array of subjects: reading, recitation, spelling, grammar, composition, geography, history, arithmetic, mental arithmetic, writing, ornamental writing, drawing, mapping, Euclid, algebra, Latin and elementary science. Pupils were tested in most subjects every Monday and allocated marks for their performance every other day, as well as for attendance and conduct. By his second year Ernest was first in a class of eight in almost every subject, though a 99.6 per cent in mental arithmetic pulled him down to second. Tuition cost £4 4s per quarter, and even with a discount of 20 per cent for prompt payment this could not have been easy for the Beagleholes to pay. Secondary schooling was the exception rather than the rule for a working-class family then, and Ernest was probably lucky to have had what the academy could offer. Joe and Annie had no secondary schooling. Ted was more successful. After three years at the Wesleyan Day School he went on to Mount Cook School, and from there was awarded a scholarship which took him to Wellington College. Dux in 1888, he won the senior half-mile twice, and on leaving became a pupil-teacher back at Mount Cook School.

Leaving the academy marked the end of Ernest's formal schooling, but he left with a thirst for further education. The *Evening Post* of 14 July 1884 has a letter to the editor:

Are you aware of any classes for the study of practical chemistry, natural philosophy, or botany? Being desirous of prosecuting those studies, I should be grateful for any information.

I am, etc.,

Ernest Beaglehole

The editor replied that it was 'scarcely creditable that in a city such as Wellington we should have to answer the above question in the negative'.

By this time Ernest was deeply involved in the activities of the Young Men's Wesleyan Mutual Improvement Society, which he had joined the year after he left the academy. The society had been formed in 1869 for 'Mutual Improvement and Instruction in Theology Etc.'[14] Candidates for membership had to believe in the inspiration of the Holy Scripture, but the early preoccupation with theological questions steadily broadened and became more varied and secular. The young men met weekly, with perhaps fifteen to twenty members attending, a minister generally presided, and there were 'readings, recitations and impromptu speeches' followed by 'criticisms'. During the 1880s debating increased in popularity, both within the society and against similar societies: in 1885 there were debates on the abolition of the House of Lords, the abolition of capital punishment, and Home Rule for Ireland. As well as playing a full part in these activities, Ernest also served at different times as a member of the committee, as librarian, as treasurer, and as secretary.

Ernest read essays to the society on Gladstone and Ireland, on Charles Kingsley, Charles Darwin, Samuel Johnson and Thomas Chatterton, and gave a lecture on Lord Tennyson at a meeting open to the public at which the Wesleyan church choir sang 'Come into the garden Maud', and other appropriate songs. As editor of the society's journal (a manuscript volume in which pieces could be written to be read aloud at forthcoming meetings) he read out editorials he had written on 'Agnosticism, Positivism and Christianity' (subsequently published in the *Leader,* a newspaper dedicated to the 'interests of Christian and Temperance Work')[15] and on 'Scientific Education'. He gave a recitation of Walt Whitman's 'Hymn to Death'. He debated in favour of evolution, affirmed that 'Carlyle has had greater influence than Dickens' (losing by four votes to ten), opposed the granting of Home Rule to Ireland, and affirmed that the press 'is wielding its power for the good of the community'. In many ways the society (together with the Mechanics Institute, also active in Wellington at that time) was a precursor of the later Workers' Educational Association, or WEA, and if Ernest learned little of 'practical chemistry, natural philosophy, or botany' he was clearly reading widely and taking a keen interest in intellectual and political questions.

As secretary and editor of the journal, he was developing a fluent if solemn prose style with a distinct gift for the purple passage. Reviewing the second half-year of 1889 he concluded: 'The dark mists of gloomy anticipation, the lowering skies of chilly prognostications have given way to the brightness of summer sunshine, of realized aspirations and the fulfilment of cherished desires.' (This does not appear to have been a direct reference to the fact that following a change of rule eight young women had joined the society during that session.) Two years later, on the eve of perhaps its most successful period, he called on the flagging members of a society that 'has helped in so large a measure to keep burning the lamp of truth and learning' to protest against the prevailing climate of 'boorishness, conviction based upon ignorance or indifference, and the insubstantial pageant of passing show, the despising of all the more graceful sides of life, an utter want of appreciation of the beautiful in art and letters' – all, he asserted, 'the characteristics of present day life and thought'.

Whether or not in response to this exhortation, the society in 1892 had a number of successful public meetings and lectures, sometimes illustrated by magic-lantern slides and enlivened by 'musical selections'. These attracted large audiences and the admission charge raised money for the library. Membership rose to a high point of ninety-one. At the end of 1893 Ernest retired from the committee and as editor. He was still listed as a member the following year but there is no record of him taking part in any activities. By then he had become totally absorbed in the Forward Movement.

The Forward Movement had its origins in London, in the mixture of social work and evangelism among the working classes in east London initiated by Wesleyans in the 1880s and later centred on Toynbee Hall and Mansfield House. These were Anglican and Congregational foundations, where young graduates of Oxford and Cambridge lived and worked to promote education and temperance and the general welfare of the community. The movement in Wellington was begun by two Congregational ministers, the Rev. W.A. Evans and the Rev. G.H. Bradbury, who resigned their ministries in Nelson and in Canterbury in order to take up this work. Evans was married to Kate Edger, the first woman to graduate from the University of New Zealand. Before her marriage she had been principal of the Nelson College for Girls and on moving to Wellington she largely supported her husband (and the movement, which never had the resources to pay Evans and Bradbury adequately) by coaching pupils and opening a private school in their home.

The first meeting was held on 27 August 1893, and appointed a committee of management which included Ernest Beaglehole as well as several of the redoubtable Richmond–Atkinson clan. Among them were Arthur Richmond Atkinson, lawyer, journalist and later member of the House of Representatives for Wellington; his wife Lily, a great temperance campaigner, suffragist and feminist; and Maurice Richmond, later professor of law at Victoria University College. Within six months Ernest had become the committee's secretary.

Evans described the Forward Movement as 'a faithful attempt to bring the cardinal principles of Christianity, as conceived and interpreted by its best exponents, to bear on the complex conditions of modern society'.[16] Its purpose was at once religious, educational and philanthropic. In religion, Evans believed the movement to represent 'the expression in modern times of true Evangelical faith',[17] and in severing formal links with any institutional church he hoped it would appeal directly to those whose interest was primarily in the 'social spirit of Christianity'. In education, a number of classes were started; there were public meetings on current social issues and regular lectures on history, literature, philosophy, civics and economics. They were given by Evans and his wife, by her Theosophist sister, Lilian Edger, by Bradbury, and by other Wellingtonians of note: Atkinson and Richmond from the committee; Sir Robert Stout, former prime minister and soon to be appointed chief justice; and later, when he had moved to Wellington to become Secretary of the Department of Education, George Hogben. The philanthropic or social work of the movement was carried out largely by Evans, who became a familiar figure in Wellington's slum areas and something of an authority on charitable aid.

The Forward Movement classes and lectures in their way marked a step towards the founding of a university college in Wellington. Evans was one of its most energetic promoters and, following the passing of the Victoria College Act 1897, he became a member of the new College Council together with the college's greatest advocate, Sir Robert Stout. When the college opened, the Forward Movement largely discontinued its lectures. By this time it had passed its peak. The heady excitement of its first years was over, and in 1904 Evans followed Bradbury back into a church appointment, becoming minister at the Newtown Congregational Church.

For Ernest, the early years of the movement had been important in several ways. Fired as he was with that passion for self-improvement that was characteristic of many working-class families of the time, he can only have been gratified by his place in the movement alongside some of Wellington's most eminent citizens. For the rest of his life, while he remained a modest man, he was not one who showed undue deference towards those with greater worldly success. In material terms he had not achieved a great deal. His first job was in Brittains, a chemist's shop in Manners Street. Later, for two years, he worked for Blundell Brothers, publishers of the *Evening Post*. He was sacked from that job when one of the Blundell sons wanted to join the office and a vacancy had to be made,[18] an event which left a certain bitterness. After that he found a position as an accounts clerk with Sharlands, wholesale chemists in Dixon Street, and he remained with them for the rest of his working life. But it was not self-improvement in the material sense which stirred him.

It was through books and his reading of English literature that

Ernest sought to better himself. The intellectual life, he affirmed in an article he wrote on Matthew Arnold, 'so far from being mere elegant trifling, helps us more than all other studies to the companionship of wise thoughts and right feelings'.[19] That was the companionship he sought. Arnold, he believed, represented more than anyone else 'the intellectual spirit of the closing years of the nineteenth century', and in his poetry his 'rare and delicate genius' found 'purest and noblest expression'. Purity, nobility, beauty, truth – the words recur. Another article by Ernest, published in the Forward Movement's journal,[20] was on Robert Browning's long poem 'The Ring and the Book'. Ernest gave a straightforward account of the poem's narrative content and affirmed that the 'work contains the most beautiful and lofty thoughts nobly uttered, passages of supreme beauty and great power'. What he hoped to do in writing the article, he said, was 'simply to induce others, lovers of good books, and admirers of the great and beautiful and true . . . to turn to' this poem. Ernest does not show any remarkable insight or imagination; what he wrote at this time tells us much more about himself than the poets he writes about. As a young man, in his mid-twenties, he was discovering in literature what he had not found in the Wesleyan church of his boyhood. It was not an abrupt break, but rather a shifting balance. Sharing some of the doubts of that age of doubt, Ernest found solace in a verse by Matthew Arnold:

> Is it so small a thing
>   To have enjoy'd the sun
> To have lived light in the spring,
>   To have loved, to have thought, to have done;
> To have advanced true friends, and beat down
>   baffling foes?

It is perhaps not surprising that a young man such as this should have fallen in love, and on 23 July 1895 Ernest was married to Jane (generally known as Jenny), the daughter of Joseph Cawte Butler and his wife Jane Tiller.

Joseph, born in 1844, was one of the six children of John William Butler and Jane Cawte. Jane Tiller was the daughter of Edmund Tiller and Sarah South. The Butler and Tiller families both lived in Southampton, where Joseph is said to have worked in the timber yard owned by the Tillers. Joseph and Jane were married in 1866 and Jenny, their eldest child, was born two years later on 22 February 1868. She was followed by Ada and then by George, the only son. After George came Annie, Winifred, Amy and finally, after the family arrived in Wellington, Jessie Marian.

They emigrated in 1883, sailing from Plymouth to Wellington on the steamship *Ionic*, together with Jane's brother William (Bill) Tiller, his wife Harriet (Polly) and their young family. Polly was pregnant and had a miserable trip. During the cold crossing of the Indian Ocean, 'Polly as usual [was] groaning and bewailing her fate, expecting every minute to be swallowed up', wrote Joseph with a certain lack of sympathy in the diary he kept on the voyage.[21] The rest of the party seemed to enjoy the voyage, and Joseph was pleased to meet 'a good many Colonials who have been home for a trip and are now returning and the general verdict seems to be that if a man is energetic and sober, there is not much fear but he will do very well in New Zealand'. Arriving in Wellington, they rejoined Jane's eldest sister, Mary Tiller, and her husband James Brown, who had made the voyage out with another Tiller son, George, nineteen years before and were well settled in Wellington with three children. Joseph Butler established himself as a builder and the family settled in a house in Cuba Street. Jenny was fifteen when they arrived. She had finished her schooling in Southampton and had worked there in a bookshop. After the family arrived in Wellington she got a position in Te Aro House (the name by which the retailer James Smith's was then commonly known), but we know little else about her early years in Wellington.

It was hardly surprising that Ernest Beaglehole came into contact with the Butler family. Cuba Street was not far from Hopper Street. Bill Tiller became a prominent member of the Wesleyan church in Taranaki Street, and a Miss A. Butler is recorded as singing at an early social evening of the Forward Movement (probably Ada, who had performed on the *Ionic* on the voyage out, though all the Butler girls sang). There was clearly an overlapping of family activity. Family tradition has it that Ernest courted Jenny doggedly for years, but the first time he proposed she turned him down. She was deeply devoted to her cousin Jim Brown, a lively young man and a great sportsman, son of James and Mary, and he to her, but they believed they should not marry because of the closeness of their relationship. Ernest eventually proposed again and this time, to the surprise of her family, Jenny accepted him.[22] They were married at the Butlers' house by the Rev. W.A. Evans and moved into a house at 49 Hopper Street built for them by Joseph Butler with assistance from his son George and Joe Beaglehole. The house stood in what had been the garden of William and Jane Beaglehole's house, where Ernest had lived almost all his life.

2

CHILDHOOD AND YOUTH

JOHN WAS THE SECOND OF the four sons of Jenny and Ernest Beaglehole and was born at home on 13 June 1901. It was apparently a difficult birth; Jenny haemorrhaged badly and was said to have nearly died.[1] The family was not impressed with the baby's appearance, 'the most hideous baby they'd ever seen',[2] but the midwife, Mrs Kilfoy, disagreed and declared him to be a 'really good boy'. His elder brother, Geoffrey, had been born three years earlier, in 1898. Keith followed John in 1903 and Ernest in 1906. John, for reasons we do not know, was the only one to be given a second Christian name, Cawte, from his maternal grandfather, Joseph Cawte Butler, who in turn had been given it for his mother, Jane Cawte. Until his years as a student at Victoria University College John was always called Jack, and within the family this went on rather longer.

We know little of his early years. At seven he wrote to his Uncle Joe to thank him for a Christmas present, and continued: 'I should like to no how much money you are getting a month. I hope you are not to busy'. He ended with the news that they had been to the zoo, where he 'went on the camel three times and keith to times and ernest went on and before the ride was ended he cried'.[3] About the same time his father reported him to be very keen on marbles. 'And he lives to win too. And makes plenty of commotion whether winning or losing.'[4] It was a lively family, 'rowdy as ever', Annie wrote to Joe,[5] and Ern worried whether his salary would be enough to feed and clothe them decently. He considered trying to get a bookshop of his own,[6] but in spite of such dreams he was to remain in the accounts department at Sharlands.

Wellington, in those first years of the twentieth century, had certainly progressed since William Henry arrived over forty years earlier. Its population of over 50,000 was crammed on the little flat land there was between the harbour edge and the bare hills, stripped of the bush which once covered them, but still largely empty save for the first beginnings of the suburbs of Wadestown and Brooklyn. Te Aro flat, of which Hopper Street was a part, was a mass of working-class housing, backyard tradesmen, and local shops. The more substantial citizens lived on the western and northern sides of the city, in the more spacious houses on The Terrace or in Thorndon. Shrewd investors had built the cable car, opening up the farms of Kelburn for development. The business part of the city was still largely built of timber, the occasional building soaring three storeys skyward, with the Government Building, completed in 1876, one of the very few that had any sense of grace or fine proportion. One of Victoria's first professors, arriving in 1902, was amazed at Wellington's physical aspect. 'That agglomeration of derelict tin-shanties and pretentious pseudo-Corinthian stucco pilasters that was Lambton Quay', he described it, though he continued, 'with the harbour and sky and hills and cloudscapes more than making up for man's handiwork'.[7]

Many years later John tried to recapture something of the Wellington of his early boyhood. He was writing a foreword to a life of the forthright, Edinburgh-trained, Australian doctor Agnes Bennett,[8] who arrived in Wellington in 1905 and became a well-known figure as well as the Beaglehole family doctor and a close friend of John's mother.

Looking back on Wellington in her first years here [John wrote] I seem to see not merely a ridiculously colonial, provincial, gauche, conventional, narrow piece of society, but a sort of heroic age. There weren't the goings on, certainly that there were in London or Paris. For the dedicated painter, or the dedicated writer, there wasn't much to do with New Zealand but to leave it. For certain other people . . . there was just as much to do as in London or Paris, and they might quite well find it worth their while to come here and make of that time, quite unpretentiously, an heroic age. I, who was a small boy and neither a hero nor a dedicated anything, and never considered the merits of the place at all (though I may possibly have heard that Mr Seddon considered it God's Own Country) had no theories, no historical or geographical generalisations whatever.[9]

These were, perhaps, thoughts that John would not have until much later; for the moment the most important thing was that the Beaglehole boys were part of an extended family of formidable size, most of them living in close proximity, which provided a warm and lively base for their early years. Next door were their Beaglehole grandparents. John recalled his grandmother as 'a sweet person, with a softly wrinkled face and most often dressed in black'. She gave birthday parties for her grandchildren. Their grandfather gave them a penny and an orange on Sundays when they arrived home from the Primitive Methodist Sunday School.[10] Auntie (their aunt Annie) at times found employment minding children or in domestic service but often was living at home fulfilling the single daughter's role of caring for elderly parents. Increasingly, her life came to focus on her nephews next door and she became renowned for her fruit salads made for birthdays and other special occasions. In contrast to her brother Ern, she remained faithful to Primitive Methodism, and she and her mother were known to sweep off to revival meetings in the Town Hall in the taxi owned by Jason Cotterill, who lived nearby in Wallace Street.[11] For much of John's early years his Uncle Joe was away from Wellington. For five summers beginning in 1907–08 he worked as an assistant guide and labourer on the newly opened Milford Track. Years later his uncle George Butler told John that while Joe was a guide 'a myth grew up about him that he was an Oxford undergraduate & perhaps a remittance man, & all the young ladies were most sympathetic & reverent . . . It was because he always carried about some hefty book with him on logic or something which he read at odd times'. Even if it was never clear how much he did read, Joe, like his brother, collected books. But he was always something of a roamer and his bad stutter cannot have helped him in looking for work. After a number of odd jobs, he settled in Wellington as librarian in the Department of Agriculture.

Ted Beaglehole, having had the opportunity of secondary schooling, was to show more ambition. He was the first Beaglehole to gain a university degree, to travel back to Europe, and to have a successful career as a teacher and school inspector, including several years in Western Samoa. John always liked and admired his uncle. Ted began his career, as a pupil-teacher, in 1889; in his second year he passed examinations in Latin, French and mathematics to complete the first section of a BA degree from the University of New Zealand. It could not have been easy. As Victoria University College was not yet established, it was a case of solitary study with a textbook as an 'exempted student' – that is, one who was not attending lectures. The following year he failed the next section of the degree. Ted taught at a number of Wellington schools and in the Wairarapa until 1905, when he enrolled at Victoria – by now with a wife, Laura Pinney, and two small daughters, Joan and Margaret – to complete his BA. This was followed by an MA with first-class honours in mental and moral science (which was to become the two separate subjects of psychology and philosophy). He then went off to Germany with his family for further study at the University of Jena. At the end of 1909 Auntie reported to Joe that there were fears whether Ted's German would be good enough to satisfy the examiners,[12] and in the event he returned without a further degree. The family were once more in Wellington towards the end of 1913, living in Ngaio, with Ted back in school teaching. In 1915 he was an unsuccessful applicant for the registrar's position at Victoria College, but the same year, because of his knowledge of German, he was sent to Western Samoa as Director of Education following New Zealand's occupation of the former German protectorate. Laura and the girls, now at secondary school, remained in Wellington, though John was never as close to Joan and Margaret as he was to the cousins on his mother's side, especially the Patersons and the Osbornes.

Ada, the second Butler daughter, who had an unforgettable chuckle, had married Alexander Paterson, a draper who later became an art dealer. Joseph Butler had bought the Wellington picture framer and gallery, McGregor Wright's, when its founder moved to Christchurch in 1906. Alex ran the firm for some years and it was later taken over by his nephew, Dick Osborne, in 1932. Of the Patersons' four children the second, Alan, born a few months after his cousin, was the one John saw most of. The third Butler daughter, Annie (Aunt Nancy to her nephews and nieces), married Hezekiah Osborne (Uncle Ky). They lived in Daniell Street not far from Hopper Street. Hezekiah, it was said by his sisters-in-law, gave his wife 'a time'.[13] He was a tailor and the Osbornes never had much money. Dick and Stephen, the eldest of their five sons, were close in age to John and Keith and in their early years the four spent a lot of time together. Keith later remembered Dick as 'probably the most inventive of the bunch. At one stage he had a passion for making guns out of bits of tube much to the horror of our Mothers who doubtless expected to see us borne in as corpses one day suffering from a stray charge of shot. Then there was bicycle riding on a bone shaker around McFarlane Street.' Keith 'learned to ride on one of the tireless wonders Dick put together out of scrap iron. And the roads thereabouts were hilly enough for a turn of speed.' Later, in the years before he took over McGregor Wright's, Dick, always ingenious, 'served his time – or partly served it – as an engineer, a carpenter & a jeweller and went on to gramophone building as a hobby'.[14] Stephen, John's favourite cousin, became ill in his early teens with some kind of progressive paralysis. He was increasingly bedridden and able to communicate only by typing messages or letters on his typewriter. He was to die in his twenties, shortly after his mother.

Winifred, the next Butler daughter, did not marry. She worked for a period in McGregor Wright's and years later had memories of Kathleen Beauchamp (Katherine Mansfield) visiting the shop. Something of a stickler for the proprieties, she remained a stalwart of the established church. Amy Butler married Will Jackson. Their eldest child, Ralph, was one of the youngest of the gang of cousins. Jessie, the last of the Butler girls, was only ten when her mother died in 1899. Her father remarried (to his housekeeper, Elizabeth Holland) in 1904 and Jessie spent a lot of time at 49 Hopper Street, a youthful and very popular aunt to her four nephews. On 2 October 1913 she married a young Church of England clergyman, Harold Monaghan.

The network spread even further, mainly through Tiller relations. Many lived within walking distance of Hopper Street and before the time of the telephone they kept in touch with messages and visits. John was often the bearer of notes from his mother, and was remembered by the family of his cousin Amy Denton for such an occasion when he was ten. John was hanging around, eating apples but not saying much, while Amy's mother cooked. Finally she ventured, 'What time does your mother want you home, dear?' She was kneeling at the oven putting in a tray of rock cakes. 'What time do the rocks come out?' John asked.[15] It became a family saying. The Beaglehole boys were all said to have great appetites; none of them shared their mother's vegetarian principles, which seem to have left them feeling hungry. Large appetites may have run in the male members of the family. A story tells of someone looking out of the window at Hopper Street during afternoon tea and suddenly crying out, 'Hide the cake under the sofa, here comes Joe!'

The extended family moved around to one another's houses for parties with music or charades, occasions of great jollity and youthful high spirits. Ern showed a lighter side, teasing the girls. He clearly adored them and would have liked a daughter. A young relative met him one morning, very dapper, on his way to work. 'Whither away fair maid, whither away', he greeted her. He 'had some very flowery language'.[16] In the charades Uncle Will Jackson was a star, and Alan Paterson made his mark early, portraying a reformed sinner who had taken the pledge – a live issue, as most of the older generation were strong temperance supporters. Alan also showed an early talent for drawing, a foretaste of his career as a cartoonist on the *Dominion*. His gifts for drawing, acting and writing were all to flourish during his later membership of the Wellington Savage Club.[17] John went to dancing classes conducted by Miss Moore, 'incredibly frizzed and rouged'.[18] A cousin later recalled dancing with him 'when Miss Moore called out: "Jack and Amy, relax your muscles", and you muttered into my ear, "Good God, how are we supposed to do that?" and I said, "You ass, you know how to relax your muscles, don't you?" And your memorable reply was: "Gosh, I thought the woman said bustles."'[19] In the summer there were picnics at Scorching Bay, reached after a good walk from the end of the newly opened Seatoun tramline.

The boys went to Mount Cook School. John began in 1906, when he turned five; Geoffrey had already been there for three years and Keith started two years later. The school, opened in 1875 as a development of the Buckle Street Girls' School, was run by a Mrs Wilkinson and her daughter. The Mount Cook district was something of a social mix. The homes of the better-off were on Willis Street, where Dr Bennett lived and had her rooms, and climbed the hills to the south, where the Kirkcaldie mansion at the top of Thompson Street looked down on many fine houses. On the Te Aro flat, which included Hopper Street, the houses were the much more modest dwellings of manual workers and the unemployed. The Mount Cook School grew rapidly at first, reaching a roll of 598 in 1897, before declining to 384 in 1907 and 330 in 1913. This decline followed the suburban development that was closely linked to the construction of the new electric tramway system. In 1904 the trams began running down Hopper Street, crashing and swaying within a few metres of the Beaglehole house. Surely one day, the boys hoped and feared, one would fail to take the corner into Webb Street and would hurtle into Burbidge's greengrocery, spraying fruit and vegetables everywhere.

Mount Cook School when the Beaglehole boys were there was in three separate parts: the infants' school (under Miss Watson) and the girls' school in Buckle Street, the boys' school in Taranaki Street. By this time the neighbouring Mount Cook prison had become the home of the permanent artillery (the prison having moved to The Terrace, from whence prisoners were marched through the city each morning to work in the brickworks still on the site of the old prison). This, along with the barracks and defence stores on Buckle Street, gave a military air to the area, and created interest, particularly to those at the boys' school. This was housed in a rather forbidding Gothic building erected in 1878, which by the turn of the century was somewhat the worse for wear. School logbooks and the minute books of the school committee[20] give glimpses of the school and its activities at this time. The drains were a long-standing problem as the original ones were open and a constant health hazard; with the site subject to flooding in the winter they also occasionally overflowed. Finally in 1907, John's second year, the Education Board built a new toilet block. In 1913, his final year, the inspectors reported the rooms to be 'rather dark and badly lighted . . . the asphalt requires renewing in places, as in wet weather pools of water settle in front of the building. The floors were fairly clean but the windows more especially those at the back of the building were very dirty and some were broken.' The schoolwork done by the standard six pupils, however, was said to be very good.

There were the usual excitements that year: the annual picnic at Days Bay with the ferry trip across the harbour; school cadets for the boys who had turned eleven. There were also special events. Percy Burbidge, son of the greengrocer in Webb Street, who had graduated in physics from Victoria University College and been awarded an 1851 Exhibition Scholarship for research in science, visited his old school to talk to the boys before going off to Cambridge. He was to reappear in John's life in 1932, when they were both on the staff of Auckland University College. Ted Beaglehole, just back from Germany, taught John briefly as a relieving teacher for standard six. 'Your uncle, I believe', Mr Bary, the headmaster, said to John. 'Yessir!', replied John, covered 'in a blaze of glory'.[21]

During the waterfront strike in 1913 the school was taken over to house the special constables and was closed from 3 to 18 November, after which the rooms used by the 'specials' were scrubbed out and disinfected. The standard six classes, with exams imminent, spent some of that time working at Te Aro school in Willis Street. Even after the school reopened the back playground was kept until early December for police horses. On 27 and 28 November John sat the examinations for those finishing primary school. He was placed thirtieth on the Wellington district list, with 497 marks out of a possible 800 (top of the list was Doreen Mary Britland* with 611 marks).[22] This placing qualified him for a 'Junior free place', tenable for two years at a state secondary school. He was the only successful Mount Cook pupil that year, but his achievement was matched by his three brothers.

---

*   Doreen Britland graduated from Victoria University College with an MA in 1924 and became a secondary school teacher of classics. In the 1930s she was teaching in Hawera.

When John was eleven he produced the first number of *Smudge*, a handwritten paper with family news, stories, illustrations, quotes from other works, and jokes ('thanks to Richard Francis Osborne for jokes contributed').[23] Before long there was opposition, with the Paterson cousins each producing a paper, as well as Stephen Osborne. Such productions, while not unusual among the young, tend to be ephemeral, but there were eight issues of *Smudge* in 1913; none survive from 1914, but a further five came out in 1915. The quotes and extracts that John included suggest that for a twelve-year-old he was reading widely: Shakespeare, Burns, the *Children's Magazine*, *Chums* (for jokes), Browning, Shelley, the *London Magazine*, Wordsworth, the *Ladies Magazine* (1809) were all drawn on in early numbers. Later he twice used stories from Sir George Grey's *Polynesian Mythology*. In the seventh number he reports that he had been reading Sir Walter Scott's romances *Guy Mannering* and *The Bride of Lammermoor*. This was followed up in 1915, just before his fourteenth birthday, when he helpfully included a 'Wanted!!!' list, beginning with a watch, a fountain pen and a bicycle and continuing with a printing press and four more books by Scott. During these teenage years he collected the complete A. & C. Black edition of Scott's works. Recollecting his early passion for books many years later, John said, 'I don't mean that I had no other interest at all. I was not interested in football, but I was interested in food, and marbles, and making toy theatres. It just happened that I had a natural affinity with the printed page.'[24]

When he was thirteen John wrote descriptions, or 'Brief Biographies', of the members of his family:[25]

David Ernest Beaglehole.
Head of the family. Born in New Zealand. Exact age not known. Suspected to be about 45, though. Bookish man. Head accountant at Sharland & Co. Ltd. Dixon Street. Has a mania for pinching the Editor on the inside of his leg. Otherwise, quite an agreeable gent.

Jane Beaglehole.
Wife of D.E., and second in command. Very beautiful. Makes the best apple pies in New Zealand – best everything, in fact, in the way of scrunch . . . Been married twenty years odd. Very agreeable personality. Reads about 17 books a week. At present, fond of reading novels by Russian johnnies.

Geoffrey Beaglehole.
Motor-maniac and sparking-plug fiend. Scoffs at everything else. Is assistant assistant assistant greaser of axles and carburettor-cleaner at Norwoods Motor Agency, Thorndon and Kent Terrace. Owns a bicycle

which has always got the gripes somewhere in its inside . . . Started work and Technical School 1915.

John Cawte Beaglehole.
. . . Celebrated man of letters. Poems and articles, stories, etc. have appeared in past numbers of "The Smudge". Also famous stamp-collector. Has magnificent collection of the postage stamps of the world, which can be inspected on payment of a small nominal fee to the Smudge Company, Ltd. Aspires to be a wholesale and retail bookseller. He is the editorial staff, the printing staff, the publishing staff, and a few more staffs, of "The Smudge".

Keith Beaglehole.
. . . Fond of reading Henty's books. Has no particular ambition, but is said to have a leaning towards speculating in dentists' outfits. Very humorous lad sometimes . . . Also likes smashing up bikes, and trying to put them together again.

Ernest Beaglehole
. . . Is a foolish young spark.

There followed a more extended article on Ernest's character, which suggested that he could be a rather trying younger brother.

With pen in hand, the 'celebrated man of letters' and stamp collector was something of an extrovert and wit. Unarmed, the reality was a little different. Rather plain in appearance with a prominent nose, beady brown eyes and spectacles, John was remembered by one cousin, Amy Brown, as a funny little boy, very gauche, very shy and with a bad stammer.[26] His closest friend was his brother Keith, two years younger, who shared and was to share many of John's interests, but as a boy was more outgoing and assertive. 'Keith kicked up the Sunday before yesterday', Auntie reported to Joe, '& wouldn't go with the others to Sunday School, so Jennie bundled him off to bed, & kept him there all day much to his disgust . . . you know what Keith is when he makes up his mind.'[27] John ribbed Keith, admired him, loved him dearly, and the bond between them lasted all their lives. Of the four boys' relationships with their mother, John's was probably the most intense. She was constantly very supportive, always listened to him and encouraged his writing. John admired his father, but until her death in 1929 his mother was the central focus of his emotional life. She, without doubt, was the greatest influence on the growing boy. John 'was the creation of his mother if any man ever was'.[28]

John moved on from Mount Cook School to Wellington College in 1914. The college was not, it would seem, an important formative influence in his life. Of the masters there, only one, H.B. Tomlinson (later headmaster of Wairarapa College), who taught him English, was remembered with any warmth or enthusiasm as 'one of the few school teachers we ever came across who showed any interest in what he taught'.[29] Eric McCormick, who was at the college a little later than John, wrote in the foreword to his book *The Friend of Keats*: 'In 1923, my last year at Wellington College, I was lucky enough to have a gifted English master, H.B. Tomlinson, who was a great admirer of Keats'. Many years after his school days John recalled, 'I was soaked in Keats when I was young, from about 17. Earlier? I remember reading him when I was camping with Keith in the sandhills a bit north of Paekakariki . . . (& how my mother came up to see us, & we gave her a stew, a bit tasteless). I wallowed in the Odes. He was a sort of standard.'[30]

The headmaster, J.P. Firth, was a man of great reputation in Wellington and something of a conservative in his ideas. At the time of Firth's death, John wrote, 'I suppose he was a good headmaster in his way . . . but I never heard anybody accuse him of having taught any boy to think. Too new-fangled an idea, perhaps.'[31] By the time John was at the school Firth was past his best, and his decline was hastened by the First World War. From the back garden of 49 Hopper Street John had heard the cheering at the barracks in Buckle Street on the announcement of the declaration of war in 1914, but the initial excitement soon faded. Many old boys of Wellington College served overseas and from 1915 the school magazine, the *Wellingtonian*, is dominated by lists and photographs of the dead, the wounded and those on active service. The 'old boys' notes' consist almost entirely of letters from servicemen. Firth tried to write personally to all of the former pupils serving overseas, and he was deeply affected by the casualties among them. By the end of the war 1658 former pupils had been on active service; of this number 226 were killed and a further 350 wounded.[32] During the war years, the school, in a sense, took second place among Firth's concerns.

The *Wellingtonian* gives an occasional mention of John's activities. In the athletic sports he was second in the heat of the 100 yards under-14 but unplaced in the final. When Keith arrived in 1916, with an altogether more successful record in athletics and cross-country running, the two of them, somewhat improbably, entered the boxing competition. John was beaten in the first round of what must have been his one and only boxing match; Keith survived to the second round. The following year John was awarded his bronze medallion for life saving but, much more significant, he is listed for the first time among those winning academic honours. As well as completing the Matriculation examination, he was awarded the Barnicoat Essay Prize, the Liverton History Prize and the Navy League Essay Prize, and shared the Eichelbaum Prize for English literature for Form VIA.

MOUNT COOK SCHOOL and Wellington College in many ways were less important in shaping John than his family and the comparative richness of the intellectual and cultural life they shared. The three main elements were music, books and the Unitarian Church. From his earliest years there was music in the house. His mother 'must have sung continually when she was a girl and a young woman, and so must her sisters – their family indeed must have been a nest of singing birds', John later concluded.[33] This judgement was based on the heaps of sheet music and bound-up songs which he had found in cupboards when he learned to play the piano and was working through all the music he could lay his hands on. 'I might try out the accompaniment of some Mendelssohn duets, just discovered: "Oh that we two were maying; on the banks of some something-or-other stream!" – my mother's voice would rise like a lark: and "Oh that we two were maying!" my Auntie Nancy, who happened to be in the house, would reply; and after a time they would break down, in happy laughter.' Jenny was one of those people who could play any song by ear if she did not have the music, a gift which John very much envied. At family parties all the cousins gathered around the piano, Jenny played, and they 'roared out those lushly sentimental songs of the 1914–18 war' such as 'It's a long, long trail a-winding'.

Music was not just a family activity. It was also 'a communal exercise, a choral exercise, a public exercise'. John got to know the *Messiah* and *Elijah* as early as he got to know anything else, earlier than he got to know the piano scores of Gilbert and Sullivan operettas or saw those works on the stage. The family went to the *Messiah* every year and to *Elijah* most years. John's mother and his aunts sang in the Musical Union, conducted by 'the great, the revered, Mr Robert Parker, the touchstone of the musical art in Wellington'. John's Butler grandfather was one of the two men who played the double bass in the Musical Union orchestra – who supplied the double bass, indeed, in everything that demanded a double bass in Wellington. John understood that his grandfather was 'personally known to Mr Robert Parker' and he 'derived great satisfaction from that circumstance'.

The Musical Union also sang *Hiawatha* and *Faust* in my hearing more than once under Mr Parker, and I think they had a go at *Israel in Egypt*, and it was said that they had once done *The Bartered Bride*, and the *Golden Legend* by Sir Arthur Sullivan, and a long time back, long before I was born, even some Bach; but in my time they really concentrated on the *Messiah* and *Elijah*, the 'immortal masterpiece', as it was generally known, of Handel, and the 'immortal masterpiece' of Mendelssohn. After every performance everybody rushed to the *Dominion* to see what Harcus Plimmer said about it. Harcus Plimmer was the great critical eminence of those days. You *had* to know what he thought. You could hardly exist, if you belonged to the Musical Union, unless you knew what he thought. You should have heard another of my aunts, also a devotee of Mr Robert Parker, when as a skittish adolescent I began to cast some light-hearted aspersions on the immortal masterpiece of Handel. Well, so much was the Musical Union part of the texture of our lives that when it coalesced with the rival concern, the Choral Society – and still more, when Mr Temple White founded his Harmonic Society – I felt as if the order of the universe had somehow been tampered with.

That was John looking back many years later. In his younger days he was more critical. When in 1921 the Choral Union (the amalgam of the Musical Union and the Choral Society) published its proposals for a choral festival – the *Messiah, Elijah, Cavalleria Rusticana, Merrie England, The Golden Legend* – John, just turned twenty, offered his views to the *Evening Post*:

this list is about the worst you could possibly draw up, showing an utter and almost inconceivable lack of originality and a total absence of musical interest . . . the way to interest the musical public of Wellington is not to go on doing the same old things in the same old mediocre way, but to strike out boldly and do something new and really worth while.

And, wishing to be constructive, he went on to offer some suggestions:

First, why not one of the works of the greatest composer of all? Bach's *St Matthew Passion* was given here very successfully some years ago under Mr Robert Parker and would bear repetition; or why not the glorious *B Minor Mass*, which, so far as I know, has never been given at all? Why not Haydn's *Creation*? If we must have Handel, why not *Israel in Egypt, Joshua, Samson, Saul, The Ode on St Cecilia's, Acis and Galatea*? Anyhow, give the poor old *Messiah* a rest. If we must have operas, why not Purcell's . . . *Dido and Aeneas*, or his *King Arthur*?[34]

THE YEAR 1904, IN WHICH the Rev. W.A. Evans returned to the Congregational ministry and the Forward Movement in Wellington effectively ended, also saw the Rev. Charles Hargrove, representing the British and Foreign Unitarian Association, visiting Australasia. He lectured in Wellington and met Sir Robert Stout, now Chief Justice, who had long had an interest in liberal religion. A Unitarian Society, later the Unitarian Free Church, was formed in Wellington with Stout as an active member. At one of the first services held by the society Stout gave an address on 'Theology and the Universe' that illustrates how someone of his ideas could be attracted to unitarianism:

The immensity of the stellar universe was brought within the comprehension of the audience, and a very natural deduction was drawn that inasmuch as the ancients were unacquainted with these grand facts, it was fair to conclude that they had not said the last word on theology. The lecturer exhorted his hearers to devote their time and abilities to the search after further truths, and the service of humanity.[35]

The Wellington Unitarian Church and the Forward Movement had much in common. Again, members of the Richmond–Atkinson clan were to the fore. Miss Mary Richmond, daughter of C.W. Richmond, was among the founders, along with J. Gammell, a school inspector, and Hugh Mackenzie, professor of English at the recently founded Victoria University College. A minister was sought; the Rev. W. Tudor Jones from Swansea arrived in 1906, and immediately started to raise money for a building fund. The new church was opened in Ingestre (later Vivian) Street on 18 April 1909, with special hymns composed for the occasion by Dr Jones, Miss Richmond, Mr Gammell and Professor Mackenzie. The membership had grown to over 200.

Unitarians rejected creeds, ecclesiastical organisation, and central authority of any kind; instead, they stressed right thinking and conduct. This did not always make it easy for the church to define precisely what it was. Unitarians tended to be clearer on what they did not believe in than on what they did. For them theology was 'a Science which must be in accord with the Thought of the Day, and . . . Religion is the realisation of the highest and best in the human mind and spirit'. 'Revelation' they saw as 'the gradual unfolding of the meaning of things through the activity of man', and, above all, they believed, 'the service of God is to be found in the service of man'.[36] The confession of faith in many of their churches was 'In the Love of Truth and the Spirit of Christ, we unite for the Worship of God and the Service of Man'.

It was hardly surprising that Ernest and Jenny Beaglehole, after their time with the Forward Movement, should become involved. 'Ern . . . goes to Dr Jones every Monday and reads with him', Annie reported to Joe, 'and into the bargain has been elected secretary of the Unitarian Church, but he says he will have to resign this as he hasn't the time, and of course he hasn't, it's really madness of him attempting it.'[37] Ern does appear to have resigned on that occasion, but he accepted the position again two years later, in 1911, and became increasingly involved in the activities of the church. He took charge of the Sunday School while the minister was on his summer holiday and was 'organ blower' on those Sundays when Jenny played the organ. John, Keith and Ernest left the Primitive Methodist Sunday School and attended a Sunday morning Unitarian service for children and then Sunday School in the afternoon. Old William Henry Beaglehole, the stalwart of Primitive Methodism, died in 1910, but Aunt Annie clearly had her doubts about the family's new allegiance, writing to Joe with the news that Tudor Jones was leaving, 'and so the Infidel Church are left to mourn the loss of their beloved pastor'.[38] Jones was succeeded by the Rev. W. Jellie, who had been the founding minister of the church in Auckland. He stayed three years before returning to Auckland, and in 1914 there followed the Rev. Ernest Hale, a young Baptist clergyman from Melbourne who had 'outgrown his orthodox beliefs'. Hale stayed until 1920.

A number of printed *Calendars* of the church that have survived from these years record the family's involvement. Jenny became secretary of the correspondence committee, which sought to win friends for the church by sending 'interesting and thoughtful little books' to those known to be 'interested in Religious Freedom'. In 1915 Ern became a church warden, and for a number of years he was treasurer; Jenny was elected to the church committee and was still taking her turn at playing the organ. The following year an appeal was made for £200 to buy a new 'two manual pipe organ'. The Beagleholes gave £5. The annual report of the church committee of management for 1918–19 tells us that during the year a choir had been formed and that 'sincere thanks were due to the members of the choir and to Mr J.C. Beaglehole for his untiring zeal as choirmaster and church organist'. A year later the committee noted that Mr Beaglehole's 'fine work as organist again merits special praise' and he received an honorarium of £5. A comment in a later letter suggests that John was taught to play the organ by Bernard Page, the city organist, but we do not know when or how he began to learn. A sonnet he wrote in 1917, 'addressed to the shade of J.S. Bach' –

... thou art
The man who set the seal upon my brow
Of premature age, and broke my youthful heart.
So do I hail thee, even 'neath the yoke
Of overwork thou hast for me bespoke[39]

– suggests he was already learning at that time. After the evening service on Christmas Day 1919 he gave an organ recital with pieces by César Franck, Mendelssohn, Bach, Handel and Somervell. The choir had mixed fortunes, being disbanded the following year for lack of male voices, but John continued as organist for several years. For him, Bach remained supreme. In 1921 he bought the translation of Johann Nikolaus Forkel's *Johann Sebastian Bach* (just published in London) and the following year C. Hubert H. Parry's *Johann Sebastian Bach.*[40]

Ernest Hale left Wellington for Adelaide at the end of 1920. Ern, along with Sir Robert Stout and Professor Mackenzie, took services in the period before the Rev. Wyndham S. Heathcote arrived for what was intended to be a brief visit on his way from Adelaide to the United States. Heathcote stayed from March until August and made a great impression. Numbers increased, the church was full for the evening services, and a crowd was attracted to the Town Hall to hear Heathcote speak on 'Why I left the Anglican Church'. The Beagleholes were to the fore at his farewell (which rather overshadowed the joint welcome to the new minister, the Rev. James Shaw Brown). Ern spoke in support of the chairman's remarks, Keith sang a song and Jenny expressed the gratitude of the women's alliance (of which she was secretary) to Mr Heathcote for 'the wonderfully interesting Sundays he has given us since he has been in Wellington, and the new point of view he has helped many of us to see things from'. Brown lasted only eight months; he clearly suffered in comparison with his predecessor and was not helped by the precarious state of the church's finances. On his resignation, the committee (Sir Robert Stout, chairman; D.E. Beaglehole, vice chairman) cabled to Heathcote, who was by then in Ottawa, and he agreed to return. John marked this with a fulsome column of welcome and exhortation in the church *Calendar*:

We know we will get any amount of inspiring talk and inspiring example from our Parson. It is up to us to do something ourselves worthy of him and the Cause, which is greater than any man. We have fetched him back over a continent and an ocean to be our leader; let us see that we become worthy followers . . . Garibaldi conquered half Italy with a thousand men; can't we conquer Wellington with our small army?[41]

'We devoutly hope and believe', John wrote, 'that Mr Heathcote is
the right man in the right place', but for all Heathcote's sardonic
eloquence this, sadly, proved not to be the case. Heathcote lost
support when he spoke critically about prohibition, arguing from
his experience in the United States that it was a complete delusion
to think that prohibition would abolish alcohol. Rather, the traffic
would be 'driven beneath the surface, secretly corrupting the springs
of national life'.[42] The church was deeply divided on the issue; it lost
members and Heathcote returned to Australia (after a 'short but
brilliant ministry', the *Calendar* recorded), lamenting 'I should not
have left Ottawa [for Wellington] if I had known what was ahead.
Unitarians must learn to set the example of broad-mindedness in
New Zealand – an example which is sadly needed'.[43] Thereafter it
was downhill for the church in Wellington. Declining numbers and
financial problems led to a decision to carry on without a minister
from the beginning of 1925. John had continued to look after 'the
musical portion of the services' although, the 1923–24 report noted,
'at times of unavoidable absence, this work has been done by other
members of the family'.[44] With Heathcote's departure the family
commitment to Unitarianism began to wane. John was increasingly
absorbed by his life as a student at Victoria College; the claims of
the Tramping Club on a Sunday were coming to outweigh those of
the church.

An early short story by Frank Sargeson entitled 'Chaucerian'
begins: 'When I was a young man I used to go to the Unitarian
Church. In those days it was the thing for quite a number of young
men to go to the Unitarian Church. It was their way of letting people
know they had grown up and had independent minds.'[45] As a child
John had no choice about going. For him the church was more than
a symbol of adulthood and independence; for a decade or more it
was a significant part of his life, an important influence for both
his intellectual and musical development during his teenage years
and early twenties. It played its part in his becoming 'grown up'
and having an 'independent mind'. Although his church-going days
ended when he was a young man, the Unitarian commitment to
intellectual freedom, to reason and to the working of conscience
remained a lasting legacy.

It was also through the church that John met the Hooper family.[46]
Richard Henry Hooper, a farmer who later became a journalist, was
at this time editing the New Zealand *Journal of Agriculture*. A born
idealist with a passion for new ideas, though not very practical, he
had spent from 1902 to 1909 in England with his wife Sophia and

family on the staff of the New Zealand High Commission. While there he had taken an interest in movements for social reform. He found a home eventually in the Fabian Society, with which he kept in touch following his return to New Zealand. Sophia Hooper was a daughter of Richard Arthur Hould, an Aucklander and ardent socialist with a fixation on the single-tax notions of Henry George (a belief not shared by his son-in-law). The Hoopers joined the Unitarian Church in 1918. Their second daughter, Estelle, known as Star, taught in the Sunday School. Their elder daughter, Challis, was in Dunedin training to be a nurse and returned to Wellington in 1920.

John was drawn to the Hooper family and became a close friend of them all; with Challis, six years his senior, the friendship was to be lifelong. The families were not close socially, in spite of the church, but for John the Hoopers' ideas and their experience must have marked them as being 'a little different'.[47] For a while, during his undergraduate days, he used to have the evening meal with them almost every Sunday.[48] Challis was later to remember him as an almost daily visitor. 'He came and went. The door was on the latch for him . . . and when he didn't come he wrote, letters, verse, poems streamed from his hand . . . about the days doings, about books, and very humorously about people.' She recalled John propping up the kitchen door while her mother went quietly on with the cooking or the ironing and John talked. And he seemed so relaxed that his stammer all but disappeared. With her father, who was slightly deaf, the roles were reversed: John mostly listened while Hooper, who normally did not make contact with people easily, did the talking. The affection between them is shown in the ode John wrote to mark Richard Hooper's birthday in 1920:

> O, gentle Muse, inspire my pen,
> To sing the worthiest of men,
> To sing his virtues and his praise –
> To glorify his winning ways –
> To lay my tribute at his feet,
> Infused with all a poet's heat.
> Give me to celebrate the worth
> That rarely, on this poor old earth,
> Is concentrated in one man,
> Rarely, since earth and time began.

The ode continued, reviewing Mr Hooper's career and home life for over a hundred lines more – an indication also of John's growing facility with his pen.[49] Even more revealing, perhaps, is a letter John wrote to Mrs Hooper a year later, when she had been ill and he was recommending something to read:

How would you like Horace Walpole's Letters, in XVI vols with two supplementary vols, notes, addenda, & corrigenda etc? – my Mother has just finished them, having read with great enjoyment and advanced to the very familiar stage of referring to the Author in casual conversation, as 'Horace'. And he an Earl, too, at that! She a mere Beaglehole!! – Or how about Gibbon's Decline and Fall? If you read that you could carry it over her for a while; because She has never been able to get through more than half the first volume so far . . . Or England under the Stuarts, by G.M. Trevelyan, a standard and fascinating Book . . . Or I can recommend two books of fairy Stories – The Happy Prince, by Oscar Wilde, and Martin Pippin in the Apple Orchard, by Eleanor Farjeon. Or how about Speeches on British Foreign Policy, edited by Edgar R. Jones, M.P.? Or Bealby, a humorous novel by H.G. Wells? Or a book of Short Stories? Or Terrorism & Communism, by Karl Kautsky? . . . Madam, I have several hundred books to choose from, and my Father several thousand – all are at your service. I think perhaps a good one to start on would be The Crime of Sylvestre Bonnard, by Anatole France, which is very charming and fanciful and altogether delightful – at least I found it so . . . Perhaps, however, a Punch might be the ideal as Challis suggested – the Liquid Nourishment of Convalescent Literature? – I think I had better trust in her greater judgment and familiarity with the curious twists and turns and divagations of your Character, and send you a very light Punch.[50]

With Star, his contemporary, John shared his interest in music, and they went assiduously to concerts, especially anything free. They attended Bernard Page's free organ recitals on Sunday afternoons. John was not uncritical. 'Mr Page may be said to have three chief faults', he noted, 'over-use of the full organ, over-use of the tremulant, over-use of the 3rd movement of R-K's Scheherazade. They were all in evidence last Saturday night . . . You go to an O[rgan] R[ecital] expecting and having a right to a certain amount of intellectual enjoyment, instead of which you get an overdose of neurotic Russians forced down your unwilling gorge.'[51] Star tried to teach John to dance but had no more success than the earlier Miss Moore. He noted, at this time, 'The great sorrow of my life at present is that there is no dance music by Bach (7/6/20)'.[52] One doubts whether this would have made any difference. Coming from a family of boys, with a gang of male cousins, John was clearly intrigued by Star and may for a time have fancied himself in love. But their common interests did not go much further than music, for she lacked his intellectual cast of mind and his passion for books. 'I regret to say her taste in books was & is dreadful; & this used to give me serious qualms'.[53] As she became absorbed in her nursing training at Wellington Hospital, their paths diverged. As a confidante her place was increasingly taken by Challis, whom John came to judge 'the pick of the family'.[54]

By this time he was well embarked on his student career. University study had not been his first choice. One of his teachers at Wellington College, 'a kindly soul, whom I admired greatly', asked him, '"What are you going to do with your life, Beaglehole?" I said modestly I didn't know. "Well", he said, "you know a little about a lot of things and nothing much about anything; you might do quite well as a librarian." I thought he did a little injustice to the depth of my learning, but I was struck with his perception otherwise.' John's father consulted Charles Wilson, the Parliamentary Librarian, who was discouraging.[55]

John's second choice was to become a bookseller.[56] His father really wanted him to go to university, but, John later recalled, 'he was a wise as well as generous man, and a bargain was struck. He would get me a job in a bookshop, and I should try that for a year – my honour satisfied; and then I should concede to him a year at the university, after which I should make a free choice'. Ern saw the book manager of Whitcombe and Tombs, a Mr Cameron, and a position was arranged.

John's choice was hardly surprising. He had been brought up in a house full of books by parents for whom books of all kinds were 'precious vehicles of the mind'. Ern had been buying books since his youth and had dreamed of leaving Sharlands and opening a bookshop of his own. Jenny, for her part, 'if not exactly omnivorous, was always reading: she read while she knitted, or dressed, or did her hair; she was one of those people, as she herself said, who couldn't see a scrap of printed paper lying on the pavement without bending over to read it. As a young girl in Southampton she'd worked in a bookshop herself.' As her sons grew she developed the habit of leaving books out where they would see them, with passages marked that she believed they would find interesting – or improving.

John began to frequent the Wellington bookshops. One of the first books he bought, he later recalled,

was at Smith's (I speak as a Wellingtonian, who knew the contents of that second-hand establishment fairly well, though sometimes a bit afraid that Mr Smith might throw him out) – it was an odd volume of the *Tatler,* vol.II, a little crown octavo thing, bound in panelled leather, blind-stamped, gilded spine and (once) edges, 1733, 9d. Romance. I see I wrote my full name on the fly-leaf, and the sacred date, 26/1/1917. Just think – 1733! It may have been to make this article look even more antique that I repeated my name on the inside front cover, in my best writing, with the words 'Hys Booke'.

A year later, when he was seventeen, John produced a volume of his verse for his father's birthday, a 24-page handbound pamphlet. He had come a long way since the days of *Smudge*, having absorbed the conventions of traditional book layout, including the use of a half-title page, flyleaves, and a two-colour title page with ruled border; he also made a considered and assured use of fleurons. 'Remaining coolly classical and neither ostentatious nor pretentious', Sydney Shep writes, this slim volume carried the germ of aesthetic beliefs in typography and book design that were to be exercised two decades later. Among the assured verses, the ironically titled 'Doggerel' expresses John's ambition to keep a bookshop 'complete with leaded windows – no common banal one', in which poetry, essays, chapbooks, first editions, rare books, prints and broadsides will be his stock in trade. Was there an echo of Ern's dreams in all this? He wrote, too, of having workmen to 'execute fine bindings' and a printing press 'For printing fine editions/Of books both old and new.'[57]

Whitcombe's might have seemed something of a let-down after this, but clearly it was not, and during his year there John managed to persuade the company's book buyer to include in his orders some private press works from the Shakespeare Head Press and the Cuala Press (run by W.B. Yeats's sisters) as well as works on lettering and wood engraving by Eric Gill.[58] His official duties were upstairs in the educational department headed by H.G. Sturt, a rather small and lively man, already fighting an heroic but losing battle against tuberculosis that killed him a year or so later. He was dedicated to bookselling, and was a hard-boiled rationalist, at which John rejoiced. Sturt was devoted to the books of an American who wrote about the joys of being a small farmer in New England (a sort of watered-down Thoreau), also cultivated by John for a while under Sturt's influence. Mr Coventry, the second-in-command, in contrast, never gave any indication that he read and was a modest but solid pillar of the Methodist church. After the shop closed for the weekend, late on Friday evening, John would walk up Lambton Quay with Sturt and Coventry or Archie (one of the boys from the ground floor) and 'at the invitation of Mr Sturt, call at Gamble and Creed's for supper, tea and hot buttered toast, and listen to

Mr Sturt expatiate on life and goad Mr Coventry into argument'. Then there was Maie Ross, the sister-in-law of the manager, 'an exceedingly pleasant warm-hearted young woman from Australia' whom John liked very much. She sang in Temple White's young Harmonic Society, and John was soon her accompanist in church socials and other such festivities. Most of the staff John remembered with equanimity, even affection.

The first thing John learned was how to make a neat parcel of any size, tearing off the proper amount of plain brown paper from the roll at the end of the counter, folding it precisely and tying it up with string. It was a skill he never lost, which was later greatly admired by his sons. He had to unpack as well as pack. Large wooden cases from London arrived off the ship and on the first floor. John unpacked the books and sorted and counted them and arranged them on a long counter. From America they came in large mail bags, cardboard boxes containing two or three volumes each, cheap reprints, mainly from Grosset and Dunlap, which were to vanish completely from the market with the end of the First World War. Cameron came and stuck bits of paper in the different lots with the New Zealand price (plain figures) and the net price (secret signs) and John marked the books accordingly; he then cut the English prices off the dust-jacket flaps, and carried the general literature downstairs. That was the theory. In practice every book had to be examined carefully and dipped into or read in large chunks (another skill he never lost), John's theory being that a bookseller ought to know about the inside as well as the outside of his books – and then, of course, he had an injunction from his father to look out for his special orders. His only apprehension was the inopportune arrival of the manager. If the excitement of unpacking the books was the high point of John's life as a bookseller, it was a year which he altogether enjoyed greatly. Just before Christmas he received a rise of half a crown a week, from twenty-five shillings to 27s 6d:

I concluded that my worth as an asset to the trade was now recognised, that I was successful, and a great future lay before me. Not very long after this I was faced by the other half of the bargain with my father; and bitterly repining, but with my duty clearly pointed out by my mother, informed my colleagues that they would have to get on without me for a year.[59]

At the beginning of 1919 he enrolled at Victoria University College.

3

VICTORIA UNIVERSITY COLLEGE, 1919–26

IN HIS HISTORY OF Victoria University College John describes the
bright hopes and dreams which he found there in the first postwar
years, when more and more soldiers returned and numbers rose
again from the low of 320 in 1917 to 671 in 1920 and 750 three
years later; when the first building was finally completed with its
northern and southern wings in place, the northern one containing
the great library two storeys high with the memorial window to those
members of the college who had lost their lives in the war; when
new staff were appointed and the government grant was increased.
At first, indeed, there seemed no bounds to what was possible:

. . . when three empires had gone like wrecks in a dissolving dream, and
the intoxicating vision of Education, as the maker of all things new,
stood before the eyes of youth and age alike. So optimistic was mankind,
in that brief day. Mr H.G. Wells wrote his history, and there at the end
of it was Life, standing upon the earth as upon a footstool, stretching out
its realm amid the stars. If some of the other prophets were less ecstatic,
they could all somehow be assimilated; for faith and scepticism, Wells
and Gilbert Murray and Bertrand Russell and J.B. Bury, the League of
Nations and the Russian Revolution and the New Psychology, somehow
everything seemed capable of being sorted into a general plan, if only
human beings would consent to be tolerant, and progressive, and liberal,
and rational, if only they would think about social reform and abandon
secret diplomacy, and read *Areopagitica* and Mr Russell on Free Thought
and Official Propaganda.

But the vision blurred, optimism faded as the years passed. The
continuation of John's paragraph describes a changing mood in the
college during his years as a student:

. . . it could not last; people, in New Zealand as elsewhere, would not do
these obvious things. The student was afflicted by persons, even among
his fellow students, who betrayed a strange reluctance to be interested

in everything, and to wish to reform everything, to try everything in the light of reason and convict most of it. When these unfortunate and exasperating persons were sceptical, they were sceptical the wrong way round. They had, most of them, never heard of Bertrand Russell; and when they were told about him, they generally concluded that he should be in gaol. In spite of the wreck of empires, in spite of Education, and of the New Psychology, and of the New History, and of the obvious manifestations of the reasonable mind, it became apparent that a new world was not going to be born.[1]

John enrolled for a BA and in his first year, 1919, chose to study English, French and Latin. He did not distinguish himself. In the college examinations he was one of twenty-seven given a Class II in English; eight were in Class I, thirty in Class III. Latin and French saw the same result, with a drop to Class III for the French oral.[2] Passing the college examinations was the prerequisite for sitting the university examinations (the University of New Zealand, based on the model of London University, examined but did no teaching; that was done within the four constituent institutions) and in the university examinations John's results were similar, with French rather worse.[3] His classes were unlikely to have been very stimulating. Twenty years later he wrote an affectionate portrait of Hugh Mackenzie, the professor of English;[4] genial, expansive, boundlessly hospitable, the rationalist foe of the Bible-in-Schools League, as comfortable in the pulpit of the Unitarian Church as in the lecture room, infinitely kind and tolerant but, alas, no scholar. Eric McCormick, in a letter to John, was harsher: 'what a disaster that monument of granite was to literature and literary scholarship for more than a generation!'[5] Nor is it easy to imagine a lively course based on Seecombe's *Age of Johnson*, Skeat's *Primer of English Etymology* and Lounsbury's *History of the English Language*. French was taught by a temporary lecturer. Edwin Boyd-Wilson, appointed as professor the following year, arrived too late for John's French but in time to introduce him to tramping. John Rankine Brown, professor of classics, was a dedicated teacher and scholar, greatly admired by some of his students, but with his shyness and innate caution he failed to fire John's imagination.[6]

The courses in each subject were at two levels, pass and advanced, and an advanced subject required at least two year's study after it had been completed at the pass grade. In his second year John began the advanced course in English and added the pass courses in mental and moral philosophy and in history. Again he achieved Class II for English and for ethics, while in psychology (which together with ethics comprised the course in mental and moral philosophy) he was given Class III. Thomas Hunter, the professor of mental and moral philosophy, was to be an important figure in John's life, but his impact was outside the lecture room. For the history course, covering the development of the great powers in the nineteenth century (Hawksworth, *The Last Century in Europe*) and the outlines of English history from 1272 to 1509 (Oman, *History of England*), he was one of four in a class of fifty-one awarded Class I.[7] More important, in that year he read H.G. Wells's *Outline of History*, 'that first electrifying edition', originally published (and read) in twenty-five instalments[8] ('finished 18.1.21', John noted[9]). In tracing the rise and fall of nations, Wells 'summoned up the whole human past as an argument for his vision of the future'.[10] The destructive forces unleashed by the war threatened mankind with disaster; only the emergence of a world consciousness and a world state held out a hope of salvation. Wells, as the prophet of righteousness, had produced 'an epic that began with the Creation and ended with a vision of the New Jerusalem'.[11] There were those who willingly pointed out all the errors that Wells had made, but after Hawksworth and Oman and F.P. Wilson's lectures it must have been heady stuff.

John had found his subject. Although it meant spending two more years (four years in all) to complete the BA degree, he decided against continuing in English and in 1921 started the two-year advanced course in history. Two papers covered 'the general course of the history of Europe from the beginning of the sixteenth century with special reference to great movements and international relations'; a third paper 'the outlines of the development of the British Colonial Empire and Colonial Policy', of which at least a fifth was to be devoted to the history of New Zealand.[12] The college placed him in Class I each year, and in the final university examination, for which the examiner was Professor A.J. Grant of Leeds University in England, he was given marks of seventy, eighty-five, eighty-five. The five papers needed for his MA in history, which he completed in 1924, still concentrated heavily on British and European history. That year the first two papers were on England and on Europe in the period 1715–63. The third was on the history of the great powers, including the United States and Japan, since 1815, 'with special reference to the main lines of social and political development, colonisation and international relations'. This paper, the prescription noted, 'shall always contain one or two questions on the history of New Zealand'. The fourth paper was on the history of political ideas up to Mill,

Comte and Collectivism (Marx was not included). Finally, there was an essay or 'a brief thesis embodying the results obtained . . . in some investigation into the history of New Zealand'. The textbooks listed were: Phillips, *Modern Europe*; Grant Robertson, *England under the Hanoverians*; Graham, *English Political Philosophy*; Dunning, *Political Theories*; and Hassall, *The Balance of Power*. The college *Calendar* promised lectures only on English and European history, 'at times to be arranged'. John was awarded first-class honours (the examiner was again Professor Grant) with marks of seventy-five, seventy-seven, seventy-five, fifty, and eighty for the thesis.

In his thesis on Captain Hobson and the New Zealand Company, John sought to cut through the uncritical and widely accepted view of the Company's role in the early days of colonisation and to make a careful study of its bitter relations with the Governor. The thesis was based on printed sources: *British Parliamentary Papers*, the *New Zealand Gazette* and other published papers and books of the time. John recognised the limitations of research that did not draw on the records of the Colonial Office in London, but as an introduction to historical research, in which he was making his way with little or no guidance, the thesis served him well, and it pleased his examiner. Equally important, it introduced him to the Alexander Turnbull Library. Nearly fifty years later he recalled the dazzled awe with which he first laid eyes on the library's collections, and had 'the magical, the transforming experience of laying hands on my first historical manuscript, the brief diary kept by Colonel Wakefield on his passage to New Zealand in the *Tory*. It did not cast a flood of light on anything; but it was a manuscript, it was enchantment'.[13] He wrote an article about the diary, with copious quotations, for W.J. McEldowney's short-lived journal of 'public affairs, art and literature', the *New Nation*.[14]

When he came to write the history of Victoria University College, a work of considerable tact as well as affection, John said remarkably little about F.P. Wilson, who had taught him history. Wilson had been a foundation student at Victoria, the mainstay of the tennis team, and was described on his graduation (in the *New Zealand Free Lance*) as 'the sort of chap who is absolutely indispensable at a dance, or anywhere where organisation or social sweetness are usable'.[15] John would have met him in his first year at Victoria. F.P. was chairman and conductor of the college Glee Club, which he had founded; that year John was the club pianist.[16] In 1909, after a period of primary school teaching, Wilson had been appointed to lecture, mainly to commerce students, on history, economics, physical and commercial geography, economic history, currency and banking. With the arrival of more staff, the range of his teaching was narrowed and directed more towards students in arts than those in commerce. In 1921 a chair in history was founded, to which he was appointed: 'the genial F.P. – now with his subject at last released from the danger of mere subordination in a school of economics and commerce'.[17] How double-edged that word 'genial' can come to seem! History students could rely on 'regurgitating dictation–speed lectures';[18] John was not the only one in those years to be awarded first-class honours by the external examiners, but intellectual excitement was not something one experienced in the lecture room.

He was reading widely. He kept a record of the books he read between 1920 and 1923 and they cover an astonishing range. In 1922, the year he completed his BA, the list ran:

Jefferies	The Open Air
	The Story of my Heart
	Life on the Fields
W. James	Immortality
Thoreau etc.	In Praise of Walking
R. Rolland	Musicians of To-day
J.N. Forkel	Bach
J.L. Roxburgh	The Poetic Procession
G.L. Dickinson	Essay on India, China, & Japan
	Religion, a Forecast & a Criticism
	Religion & Immortality
Graham Wallas	Our Social Heritage
Morley	Notes on Politics & History
Conrad	Lord Jim
	A Personal Record
R. Rolland	Some Musicians of Former Days
Strachey	Eminent Victorians
W.P. Eaton	The Idyl of Twin Fires
Trevelyan	Recreations of an Historian
Willa Cather	Youth & the Bright Medusa
Stevenson	Master of Ballantrae
H.G. Wells	Washington & the Hope of Peace
J.H. Freidel	Training for Librarianship
Sir F. Bridge	Twelve Good Musicians
W. McFee	An Ocean Tramp
Conrad	Under Western Eyes
J.D.M. Rorke	A Musical Pilgrim's Progress
P.A. Scholes	Book of the Great Musicians
Seeley	Expansion of England

J.R. Elder	Age of Maritime Discovery
P.G. Wodehouse	Piccadilly Jim
L. Housman	Possession
Ramsay Muir	The Making of British India
	Nationalism & Internationalism
	The Expansion of Europe
Acton	Nationality
P.G. Wodehouse	A Gentleman of Leisure
H.G. Egerton	Origins & Growth of Br. Empire
A.C. Brock	The Ultimate Belief
C.H. Herford etc	Germany in the 19th century
J.H. Robinson	The Mind in the Making
P.G. Wodehouse	Something Fresh
F.S. Marvin	The Century of Hope
L. Binyon	The New World
J.M. Murry	The Things We Are
F. Greenslet	Walter Pater
C. Beard	Reformation of 16th Century
Belloc	The French Revolution
E.B. Bax	The French Revolution
P.G. Wodehouse	The Coming of Bill
Conrad	One Day More
A.P. Newton	The Old Empire & the New
J.H. Robinson	Readings in Eur. History vol II
Z. Kendrick Pyne	Palestrina
Eileen Duggan	Poems
Sir A. Lyall	Warren Hastings
L.P. Smith	More Trivia
H.M. Walbrook	G. & S. Opera
E. Thomas	Collected Poems
Acton	Lectures on Modern History
Bolton King	Life of Mazzini
P.G. Wodehouse	Indiscretions of Archie
	Girl on the Boat
	Jill the Reckless
Barrie	Courage
Bridges	France under Richelieu & Colbert
Egerton	British Foreign Policy in Europe
Sydney Herbert	Nationality its Problems
	Modern Europe
B. Russell	Free Thought & Official Propaganda
C.F. Warwick	Robespierre & the French Revolution
C.H. Currey	British Colonial Policy 1783–1915
Raleigh (W.)	R.L. Stevenson
Cocteau (Jean)	Cock and Harlequin
Nicholls (Marjorie)	'Gathered Leaves'

Fisher (Herbert)	Napoleon
King James I	Counter blaste to Tobacco
Collier (James)	Life of Sir George Grey
W.P. Reeves	New Zealand
Barry (W.)	The Papacy & Modern Times
Postgate	Revolution 1789–1906
Lipson	Europe in the 19th Century
Rashdall etc.	The Theory of the State
Strachey	Books & Characters
de la Mare	The Veil
P.G.W.	Uneasy Money
Guedalla	The Second Empire
Conrad	Chance
Drinkwater	Abraham Lincoln
	Oliver Cromwell
C.H. Brooks	Practice of Auto-Suggestion
Bennett	Mr. Prohack
de la Mare	The Return
James Stephens	The Crock of Gold
Mary Sturgeon	Michael Field (about ½)
Mulgan	Three Plays of N.Z.
Goldring	James Elroy Flecker
J. Stephens	The Charwoman's Daughter
Housman	Last Poem
M. Beerbohm	A Christmas Garland
J.W. Hinton	César Franck

He was also deep in the *Athenaeum* and the *Times Literary Supplement,* both in the college library.[19]

If John's reading was the most important element in his intellectual development, student life gave him a broader education. He made new friends, published verse and prose in *Spike,* the college review, and was for three years its editor (1922–24). He was an enthusiastic member of the Free Discussions Club. He developed as a writer and his MA thesis gave him that first real taste of historical research. He became a tramper, and he fell in love with a fellow tramper.

John met two students in his classes in his first year with whom he became good friends. Max Bickerton was a grandson of A.W. Bickerton,[20] the eccentric foundation professor at Canterbury College. He had been at school in Christchurch with C.E. Beeby, who described their friendship as one of 'bickering intimacy'[21] – a stimulating relationship for the young. Intellectual, quirky and, like John, from a home with books, Bickerton was also sceptical of all accepted dogmas and an unshakable atheist. He became a student of Hunter's, interested in psychology, and graduated with an MA in 1923. John clearly found him interesting and admired his outspokenness.

Harry Espiner was quite different. A returned soldier, badly handicapped by injuries from the war, he was very serious about his studies (in French and Latin) but also greatly enjoyed his fellow students. John had one memory of him, 'standing at the top of the Dixon Street steps, gazing at the lights of the town, casting some salutary pessimism into the mind of extreme idealist youth'.[22] But it was a gentle admonition, half humorous, where he might be seen to have earned the right to bitter indignation. His sympathetic open-mindedness attracted John, who had found another listener; he won John's admiration as well as his affection. After he graduated with an MA in 1922, Espiner went to France, where, eking out a small war pension, he worked for his doctorate. John was to stay with him in Paris in 1927.

At the end of 1920 John went with a group of friends to stay in a house they had been lent in the Akatarawa valley, thirty-five miles north of Wellington. His brief notes, 'Certain Memoranda made by me, J.C. Beaglehole . . .', reveal much of John at nineteen as well as recording his first meeting with C.E. Beeby (Beeb), to whom Bickerton introduced him.

Thursday 30th [December]. Great Adventure – went up bush – Glorious – cathedral dome – tapestry of moss – ferns and mosses in limitless variety – moss-curtains – enormous tree – scene for As You Like It – smoke shafts and columns – sunlight filtered through trees – early pioneers – fences – mill-busted – whitewood – Beeby's coaxing of the fire – description of climb & getting wind up – broad prospect – valley – river etc.

This reads like the jottings of an aspiring poet, but we learn more. On New Year's Day: 'Loafed. Discovered bathing-pool. Glorious day . . . Bathed and read Prometheus Unbound. Climbed hill on other side of road. Sunset exquisite.' The next day the party walked to the Waikanae Saddle: 'Argued on war, ethics, art & morality, novelists, modern novels, C.O.s, education, professors, Bickerton, words. Had tea & talked about R. Bridges, W. Watson, modern poetry, Edith Howes, songs, education. Glorious sunset.'

The rest of the party left the following day but John got ten days' work navvying in a road gang, clearing slips and digging drains. He shared a tent with a man, 'about 56–60', 'deaf as a post' and very taciturn at first, though he mellowed after three days. Others in the gang proved more congenial. At the end of the first day John counted twenty-seven blisters, but by the fourth he was enjoying the work: 'Jan 7th. 4th day of toil. Enjoyed myself immensely today. Boiling hot, Building up road, making drain, & breaking down bank. Got some butter at last, thank God! – getting a bit sick of bread & con.[densed] milk. Finished Prometheus last night. Letter from Mummy, wh. I started to answer.'

The weather seemed to get hotter. 'This is the sort of weather that takes it out of a bloke', John wrote after spending a day 'mainly quarrying metal & wheeling it to road . . . Dog tired & went to bed early.' But he was warming to the hills and the bush. After a scrub burn-off in the valley there was a 'most peculiar & magnificent' sunset, 'the sun a blood-red circle in the midst of a slowly-moving mass of exquisitely coloured clouds' above the ranks of bush-covered hills. 'A birch tree with the sun behind it had the most exquisitely delicate silhouette effect; but the whole thing was indescribable, except for Corot or Conrad or a Japanese artist perhaps. The bush grows more & more beautiful every day – one could live for ever in it & not get tired of it.'

Letters from his mother, two aunts and three friends, however, left him looking forward very eagerly to getting home. On his last day, 14 January, he got his pay sheet for £6 10s and a testimonial, and noted, 'Sorry to be leaving, but glad to be going home'. 'Going home' meant walking over the hill to catch a train. He started at 6.20 in the morning; halfway up the hill it began to rain, 'phrases for pomes began to run in my head', the rain stopped but began again. He arrived at Waikanae, soaked to the skin, at a quarter past ten to discover the morning train had left five minutes earlier. So he walked on to Paekakariki (which he had originally planned before the rain started), getting soaked through once more, and reached there about 2 p.m., having covered twenty-five miles. His Jackson relations were staying out there so he joined them, borrowed some dry clothes from his uncle, and travelled back with them in the train the next day.

SPIKE, OR, TO GIVE IT its full title of those years, *The Spike or Victoria College Review,* went back to Victoria's early days. It appeared twice a year and in the 1920s gave a lively picture of life in the college. Besides the predictable notes on student clubs·and accounts of tournaments, graduation ceremonies, capping balls and extravaganzas, there was general college news, social and political criticism characteristic of the time and the work of aspiring writers in prose and verse – it was a great age for verse. John had three poems printed in his first year and two the following year, then in 1921 he became a subeditor and began to spread his wings. For 'A Lament', a rather overwrought mixture of verse and prose on the pine trees being cut to allow the building of the new wings on the original college building ('How they are fallen, fallen, those mighty ones, those pine trees . . .'), he was awarded the first prize of one guinea for the most original contribution to *Spike* that year. There were other poems, one a sonnet published with the title 'Written During a (?) Lecture', but recorded in his notebook as 'written during a history lecture'. It suggested his thoughts were miles away.

The verse of John's student days was typical of the time. Echoes of Bridges and Hopkins and rather too much 'poetic' language for later taste make the sentiments seem very conventional. As with the less successful examples of his later verse, he often failed to find a distinctive voice. He tried the big, formal piece with his 'Ode On the Unveiling of the Memorial Window, Good Friday, April 18th 1924: Mortalitate relicta vivunt immortalitate induti'. It has not worn well. In contrast, the much less ambitious poem 'To H.G.S.' (H.G. Sturt, his Whitcombe and Tombs friend who had died not long before) is still moving in its simple directness:

> I remember the time I had dinner with you –
> How you talked and you laughed, though dying even then;
> And I remember the night (it rained like this) when
> I was told you were really dying, and it was true . . .
> How I rang up the hospital and found you were dead.[23]

Early in his Victoria days John got to know C.Q. (Quentin) Pope, another contributor to *Spike*. Pope was actively involved in the life of the college although he did not graduate – indeed, it is uncertain whether he was ever enrolled.[24] He shared John's interests in literature, in buying books – especially well-printed ones – and in writing, and had published verse in Australian and New Zealand magazines, including *Spike,* since 1917. He became a journalist on the *Dominion* and, for John, a useful source of free reviewers' tickets to concerts and theatre, as well as something of a foil for his wit in a number of his *Spike* pieces. It tells us something about college life at the time that Pope could be so involved in it, that staff members could be actively involved in student clubs and that, through his association with *Spike*, John got to know two former editors, F.A. de la Mare and Marjory Hannah (born Nicholls). De la Mare, a Hamilton lawyer, faithfully read every number of *Spike* and wrote to John with questions and comments. John was to get to know him much better in 1931 when he and Elsie were living in Hamilton. Marjory Nicholls[25] had entered Victoria in 1909 and, although she too never graduated, she was prominent in student affairs for a number of years and edited *Spike* in 1912. In 1920 she had married John Hannah, a Scottish businessman working in Ceylon, but he died of fever shortly after the wedding and Marjory returned to Wellington. For a time she taught at Wellington Girls' College (where her pupils included the young Robin Hyde), she continued to be actively involved in theatre (it was a family interest; her father, H.E. Nicholls, had been the leading member of the play-reading circle to which John's parents had belonged), and she published verse. The literary side of John found her very congenial and they became good friends.

John was in his element editing *Spike*. In his history of the college he wrote (clearly referring to himself as editor):

Spike, which was all for greater intellectual integrity and widespread denunciation ('The social condition of Wellington, if we only realized it, is ghastly'), and the editorials of which gave by copious quotation a pretty accurate index of the editor's current and dangerous reading – *Spike* lampooned the Minister [of Education] with vigour, joy and a proud sense of public duty.[26]

He went on to recall a squib of his, 'A Vision of Judgment',[27] which for its treatment of the minister 'enjoyed some passing celebrity'.

The leader of the Labour Party, Harry Holland, wishing to have the 'Vision', wrote to the editor for 'a couple of copies of your bright little paper'. The horrified editor, who regarded *Spike* as an Organ of Opinion, could only reply with noble dignity that his 'bright little paper' was already sold out but would no doubt be obtainable in the General Assembly Library.[28]

John had a fluent pen, a sardonic wit and a taste for controversy. As a writer he also had an impressive range. The news of the death of Joseph Conrad led to a perceptive and deeply felt article[29] reflecting his close reading of the novels. Very different, but possibly owing something to his reading of Charles Lamb, was a polished essay on 'Piracy as a Profession for Young Gentlemen'.[30] (He did have a footnote to the title: 'There is no valid reason of course, why any refined young woman should not adopt it as her life work as well.') He began with a reference to Tom Sawyer contemplating life as a pirate, and ended, characteristically, with a view of the future:

There are two ways of earning a living in these modern days. One is by piracy and one is by capitalism; and no young man of brains and breeding would willingly become a capitalist. So peradventure in the not far-distant future it may be granted to us to rub shoulders with swarthy seamen on the Quay, with gold rings in their ears and blood on their cutlasses; it may be our portion to hear gaudy parrots swear in Spanish and catch the glint of pieces of eight and moidores as the sailors gamble on the street outside the Duke of Edinburgh . . .
we may, some fine morning as we stand on the hills that fringe our noble harbour, see the Black Flag unfurl itself in the sun below and hear faintly the distant song of the sailors as they warp their ship out into the bay. And as we turn proudly down the path to our quiet home we will know that we have solved our unemployment problem and are a nation. We shall have found our soul.

In his first editorial John commented on the nature of university education, and it was a subject to which he returned frequently. In 1925 there was a royal commission on university education in New Zealand (the Reichel-Tate commission). John wrote to its chairman on behalf of the Free Discussions Club (he was secretary that year), asking that it should emphasise the vital importance of academic freedom:

Of all the attributes of a University, freedom, it seems to us, is of the most vital importance. If in any sense the University is to lead the community in thought or ideals, it is imperative that within its confines (as indeed without) there should be the utmost possible measure of liberty – liberty of association, of discussion, of teaching, of study. The only limit to this liberty that we can regard as valid is that of academic discipline.[31]

It was not to be the last time he expressed such a view. When the commission reported John gave it a favourable review in *Spike*.[32] Quoting the commission's view that, while the university in New Zealand offered 'unrivalled facilities for gaining University degrees . . . it is less successful in providing University education', he added that it was 'melancholy to see one's own worst criticisms endorsed – a sad triumph, a sorrowful vindication'.

Of real University teaching [John continued] there is at present, we all admit, practically none; of research (the tremendous importance of which for a University is stressed at length) we know nothing but the name; but will the Government even think of standing the expense for providing for all this? in paying an adequate staff a decent wage; in giving it the chance to do more than grind the feeblest elements of science and arts into inadequate skulls; will it, above all, give professors and lecturers the freedom of teaching, which is the point perhaps of most vital importance in the whole report?

John was not optimistic.

The Free Discussions Club filled the pages of *Spike* with accounts of its 'long grapplings with Truth'. While the Debating Society had a higher public profile – it was going through one of its great periods at that time – John by temperament was not a debater; his stutter would have made it very difficult. Only once was his participation noted. He was much more in his element in the Free Discussions Club.

Every year [Professor] Hunter opened the season with denunciations of some branch of obscurantism, a Hunter more and more indignant as the evening wore on; the modern press and democracy, Anglo-Catholicism, the part of Woman in Modern Progress, academic slavery in America (what a furore was caused by Upton Sinclair's *The Goose Step*) – all were pulled to pieces.[33]

In 1921 Hunter led off on imperialism and the self-determination of peoples; there followed the Rev. Wyndham Heathcote on the church and social reform (his views gave evidence of 'deep and original thought', *Spike* reported), a discussion on the role of women and an investigation of 'the so-called Achievements of Bolshevism' led by W.A. Sheat ('little originality of thought was displayed'). Later evenings were devoted to the white man and his rivals, and to spiritualism.[34] The pattern continued. The club had its visitors: the Rev. Dr Gibb, of St John's Presbyterian Church, tireless in the causes of disarmament and world peace; Walter Nash, Wellington bookseller and aspiring Labour politician, on unemployment; A.P. Harper of the thoroughly conservative Welfare League warning of the insidious progress of the revolutionary movement in Britain; Harry Holland, who 'laboured valorously to wreck our patriotism'.[35] Besides Hunter, I.L.G. (Ivan) Sutherland became a regular attender following his return from Glasgow, where he had gained his PhD, and his appointment as Hunter's assistant lecturer. He provided psychological explanations for the world's problems.[36] At this time John did not warm to him, finding him too pious, but that was to change greatly later on.

Among the younger members of the club, R.M. Campbell and Reo Fortune stood out. Dick Campbell was president of the Students' Association and a star of the Debating Society, with a mercurial mind and an unstoppable tongue. Even then he seemed to know everyone of importance and the answers to all questions. He also seemed destined for power and influence in the future. It was harder to imagine what Reo Fortune was destined for. John described him at the time: 'a hardy atheist of 21, the most insufferably dogmatic person I ever met in my life (I hope I never meet any more so) . . . He is a philosophy student who believes in freedom of speech & shouting down opposition; but a very friendly lad withal.'[37] Reo became subeditor of *Spike,* for which he too wrote passable verse, and was a tramper until he left for Cambridge and the study of anthropology.*

After John's response to the bush during his Akatarawa trip, it was hardly surprising that he was a founding member of the college Tramping Club. The taste for walking considerable distances was a family one, exemplified especially by Uncle Joe. John's parents walked with their young family over many of the Wellington hills and around the shoreline of the harbour. The Tramping Club was started in 1921 by Edwin J. Boyd-Wilson (more generally known as Prof), the new professor of French and a man of terrifying energies both in the classroom and outdoors: 'he built, he gardened, he slew deer and goats and fish, he had been a passionate footballer, the Tararuas were his second home . . . In the bush, some timid scholars felt, it was possible to regard him with less fear than in the lecture room.'[38]

For John, at first, tramping had to compete with harriers on Saturdays and being church organist on Sundays. He and his brothers Keith and Geoffrey had joined the Olympic Harrier Club in 1920. Their cousin Dick Osborne was already a member, as well as John's student friend Ken Griffen and a number of other Victoria College athletes. John proved a useful long-distance runner (he won the Wilson Memorial Cup for a three-mile race) and when I was young we sometimes persuaded him to show us the medals he had won and had carefully kept. Keith was a better runner and became club captain. Eventually, tramping won out. What it meant to John becomes clear in his history of the college.

. . . of all the clubs of that day, the one most touched with morning was the Tramping Club. The first Sunday afternoon excursions faded into insignificance beside the first September week-end expedition to

---

*   Fortune was to marry Margaret Mead, the American anthropologist, whom he met when they were both doing fieldwork in Papua New Guinea. The marriage did not last; he later married Eileen Pope, another Victoria College tramper. He eventually became lecturer in anthropology at Cambridge University.

the Orongorongo, when fifty students straggled over to that watery
magnificent valley, and a less number arrived at the top of Mount
Matthews; and that gentle walk itself became nothing in comparison
with snow-clad or tempest-smitten Tararuas, the exploration of lost spurs
and brown-running stony rivers. Cold words cannot register that glory.
There were cold words, such as those on a Labour Day week-end: 'some
fifty miles of walking . . . over every type of country-road, bush-track,
trackless bush, and river-bed . . . two crossings of the Rimutakas; the
first by Matthews Saddle . . . interesting enough, but not to be compared
with the second traverse, made by map and compass near Bau-Bau trig.
Ours was probably the first party since the early surveyors to cross these
bushy ridges; certainly, no woman had gone through there before.' But
the college women went, in their 'gym-frills', or, dresses relegated to
swags, in stout and well-tried bloomers. How was the elegance of the
Tararua Club despised! There were tough days that became legendary
with the participants: the descent of the long ridge from Alpha to Renata
and to the Waiotauru stream, the mist and the rain and the supple-jack,
eight miles in a twelve-hour day; crawling against the wind in Palliser
Bay; the start at two in the morning, the first steep pull after breakfast.
But oh the stars at two in the morning, the deeps of the bush, the sun in
the river-valleys, the sweep of the eye from the hill-tops. Fathers might
uneasily feel the weight of swags, but they were repulsed with contempt.
Mothers might hesitate – it was a generation ago; but it was all right,
Professor Boyd Wilson was to be the chaperon; their daughters tramped
. . . The poets went tramping, and the trampers became poets; for a
while *Spike* was redolent of manuka and wet fern and the sun on hot
hills. No one, unfortunately, kept statistics of rivers crossed, or of the
billies of tea that Boyd Wilson boiled.[39]

The club extended John's circle of friends. Among them were
Jack Yeates and Lorrie Richardson, science students who were both
to precede John in going to England and postgraduate study; Bill
Joliffe, who went on to Edinburgh to study forestry and returned
to the New Zealand Forest Service; Jack Tattersall, who became a
lawyer in Napier; and Harold Holt, who was to have a successful
career in the family timber business. The ebullient Bob Martin-
Smith they all foresaw as a future Labour politician; instead, he
made his career in adult education.

It was in the Tramping Club, too, that John got to know Elsie
Holmes. Her background was very different from his. Her father,
Robert Arthur Holmes, had left London while still in his teens for
Adelaide, where he began a career in the Union Bank and married
Mary Lucille Lamb. They were a very active couple. Mary was an
extremely good tennis player who in her youth had partnered the

great Australian player Norman Brooks in mixed doubles; later she showed the same ability as a golfer. Robert rowed competitively as a young man, and on a trip home to England had taken Mary on a holiday rowing down the Thames and camping each night. Later he turned to trout fishing. Their first two children, Edith and Charles, were born in Adelaide but, before Elsie was born (on 15 January 1900), they had come to Wellington, where in 1911 Robert became the New Zealand manager of the bank. After Elsie there was another son, Peter, to whom she was always very close.

The family belonged in that Wellington world vividly recorded by Katherine Mansfield. Katherine's father, Harold Beauchamp, was, like Robert, in banking. Charlie Holmes was a school-friend of Katherine's brother Leslie; Edith a friend of one of her sisters. The Holmes, too, had a holiday bach at 'the bay'. Elsie went to Miss Baber's school in Fitzherbert Terrace (formerly Miss Swainson's school and later Marsden) and was dux. By then Robert had retired from the bank and in 1919 he and Mary and the two daughters went on a trip to England and Europe. Charlie, who had served in the war, was working for Dalgety's, the stock and station agents, and had recently married. Peter was left as a boarder at Waitaki Boys' High School, which he loathed. In England the Holmeses took a house at Richmond and Elsie met numerous relations. For the winter of 1919–20 they moved to Cannes in the south of France and in the spring travelled to the Italian lakes and to Venice. Robert had planned to retire in England but, once there, he formed the view that the weather was not what it had been when he was a boy; the party returned to New Zealand at the end of 1920. Just over a year later Robert bought a house above the Western Hutt Road with a large garden where he could indulge his passion for roses.

He was far from happy with Elsie's decision at the beginning of 1921 to enrol at Victoria College. It was not what he wanted for a daughter of his. But she was not attracted by a life of tennis parties and bridge; she had her father's determination and forthright manner, and she got her way. He was upset again when she started tramping, later joined in this by her close friend Averil Lysaght (who was to become an equally close friend of John's) – how far Robert was mollified by Boyd-Wilson's presence as chaperon we do not know. Nor do we know what Elsie's mother thought about it. Elsie completed her BA in French in three years and graduated in May 1924. At the same ceremony John received his MA and his brother Keith his BSc. In 1924 she attended the MA classes in French, but she had been badly advised and did not have one of the prerequisites for gaining the degree, and so did not sit the final exams.

Elsie and John's relationship appears to have developed during 1924. The June number of *Spike* had an article (signed 'Viator' but written by John), 'The Truth about Tramping', which with great gusto purported to put right the previous 'extravagant eulogies' of the club's activities. There was also a touch of self-mockery:

> ... there's those two bards, R.F.F[ortune] and J.C.B., who appear
> – heaven knows how! – with such monotonous persistency in the pages
> of the Spike. They must be young and innocent. I doubt, from a perusal
> of their lines, if they have ever been on a tramp. There's that thing of
> J.C.B.'s called 'Tramping Song' . . . what does he say, in the midst of
> lines about tuis, rata, clouds, white roads, and all the conventional poetic
> appurtenances? –
> 'And praise we now the Tramping Girl, etc., etc., etc.,
> . . . and bright she trims the cheerful evening fire.'
> Absolute typical Rot! Who ever heard of a girl messing round with
> the fire at all? They sit on a good dry log and eat. That's about the extent
> of their participation in the festivities.

The article continued with an account of a poor fresher, lured out on a tramp by a charming girl (clearly Elsie), and the miseries he faced.

John provoked the reaction he hoped for. The next number of *Spike* carried an editorial statement (by John) saying what a lying wretch the writer had been. The statement about women had given greatest offence – a 'gratuitous and scurrilous attack of the most unprincipled and debasing kind on the fair name of women'. 'Not only do they on occasion tend the fire', the editor claimed to have discovered,

> but they cut bread and butter it (insufficiently to be sure) – they fetch
> water – they supply chocolate – they make tea – they deal out stew – they
> mix milk – they put up tents – they collect bedding – they scrape out
> porridge pots – their merry laughter and constant flow of wit is the life
> and soul of an expedition . . .

It was good fun, and was also intended to interest Elsie. There was a social gulf between Hopper Street and the Western Hutt Road, of which they were both conscious, and which at times seems to have left John more than usually uncertain in courtship. Gentle – or not so gentle – mockery could alternate with abject expressions of his unworthiness of her. At least on paper, however, he was never inarticulate.

For Christmas that year he gave Elsie a pocket edition of

Housman's *A Shropshire Lad*. Many years later she wrote that this was his first present to her. That Christmas too they were both members of the college party which tramped through the Urewera from Waikaremoana over the range to Ruatahuna (the linking road was not yet through) and down the Whakatane river to Ruatoki. For the time it was adventurous; the *New Zealand Free Lance* carried an account of the tramp,[40] and noted the 'remarkable feature of the trip is that several ladies were members of the party, and manfully carried their swags throughout'.

They went by train to Napier and the following day, Christmas Day, they continued to Waikaremoana by service car. After spending two wet days walking and boating at Waikaremoana they crossed the lake by launch to the mouth of the Hopuruahine river and the tramp began. From there the track, twenty-five miles over the range to Te Wai-iti and on to Ruatahuna, followed very closely the route later taken by the road. They camped near the Ruatahuna schoolhouse. Next morning they first visited Mataatua with its meeting house, Te Whai a Te Motu, built for Te Kooti; the building and its carvings had taken eighteen years to complete and had opened in 1888. They looked at it with excitement, John later commented, 'like men who saw the last flames of a dying fire – but that was before we heard of the Maori Renaissance and an art revived'.[41]

Then, in spite of warnings from the local Maori that the river was in flood, they started down the Whakatane. It was over forty miles, with four days of very tough tramping – rain every night and countless river crossings – before they emerged at Ruatoki. The Maori they met were hospitable, baking fresh bread for them and selling them wild pork. At Ohaua, on the second night, a venerable kaumatua, Te Kotahitanga, who had campaigned with Te Kooti, showed them his ancient breech-loader and told them about old battles. His stories were translated by a Maori who had settled there more recently. They arrived at the inevitable impossible ford and had a steep climb to avoid it. 'It is a painful memory, that hill', John later wrote, 'bracken probably grows that way on hills that trampers scale in Hell; it was above our heads and there was no track'.[42] New Year's Eve they camped just above Putere; a sentimental night, John remembered, with stars. The next day they reached the metalled road that took them on to Ruatoki. The storekeeper told them that Elsie and the other four were the first Pakeha women to have tramped through the Urewera – Elsie, with very fair hair, seems to have made a particular impression on the Maori they met. It was a memorable experience – the wild cherries were never forgotten. Six years later

John wrote about it for C.A. Marris's *Rata New Zealand Annual*,[43] a nostalgic piece, and a plea for preserving in the Urewera 'some last lost refuge for the spirit of [New Zealand's] native beauty'.

The next Christmas tramp was to the South Island, to the Waimakariri River with its magnificent beech forests on the river flats and the slopes above them, and encircling snow-covered peaks. Christmas Day was spent in the train from Christchurch to Arthur's Pass. John, with Jack Tattersall, Bob Martin-Smith and Harold Holt, climbed a then-unnamed peak of about 7000 feet near Mount Armstrong. John and Elsie and two others climbed another peak, probably Mount Davie, which was somewhat higher. This was possibly the first ascent since it was climbed in 1913 by A.P. Harper and his party.[44] John and Elsie had been to Ruapehu, and they climbed Egmont (Taranaki) with Averil Lysaght not long after the Urewera trip, but they were trampers rather than climbers. The Waimakariri trip did not seem to have been remembered with the same enthusiasm as the Urewera. At the time, however, John knew he would be leaving for England later in the year, and his poem 'Waimakariri (January 6th, 1926)'[45] reflects some of his feelings at this prospect:

> This is the last time I shall stand and see
> The stars above this valley and its stream –
> The last time – and this stream, these stars for me
> Henceforth will be distant as any dream.
>
> .   .   .   .
>
> I see afar in darkness whitely stand
> The unscaled peaks, the passes we have trod –
> These are the ancient dwellers of this land,
> Snowed, silent, and remote, each like a god.
>
> After this night I shall not see them more
> Like this, nor tread their snows, nor feel their cold,
> Yet will they stand, I know, and lift their hoar
> Summits toward the stars even as of old.
>
> The stars! the stars! immutable they reign –
> Thick in the eyes' full circle throb and burn
> Their million fires that stab the heavenly plain –
> O frozen peaks! O stars! grant me return!

AT THE BEGINNING OF 1924 John had been appointed an assistant lecturer in history at Victoria University College on £200 a year.

Examining was paid separately and could bring in another £50 or so. He saved all he could and was full of plans for travelling overseas and for a future with Elsie. He wrote to her at length whenever she was out of Wellington:

It's a ghastly game this saving; & if I didn't see a prospect of Cornwall for you & me I would give it best & plunge on books & records & travelling & trust to luck about getting home. Never mind, Miss Holmes, there's a good time coming in a year or two, & don't you forget it! Meanwhile the boy swots & even intends to start marking papers this afternoon, & smokes recklessly (as many as two pipes a day sometimes) & writes letters to you & poems about you & wishes for a letter from you every day & wishes to God you were back. And when he isn't doing any of these things he gazes at the rain & if it isn't raining he wonders how soon it'll start again . . . I have written quite a long poem about you saying what a fine person you are, but after the way you gloat I have a jolly good mind to throw it away or dedicate it to Florence or Lydia or Muriel Clouston or someone. It is in 48 lines, some of which are not so bad as the others, but I am stuck for an adjective of two syllables with the accent on the first in the last line which annoys me very much – indeed reduces me to frenzy at regular intervals. If I can think of anything in any way satisfactory I will send it up to you, for I must show it to someone or burst, & be patted on the head like a dog bringing in a dead rat he has found & you're the only person I can show it to.[46]

That letter ended with the news that he had applied that day, 25 August 1925, for a postgraduate travelling scholarship. He hoped to go to London University to work for a PhD, with a thesis on the New Zealand Company, in which he would follow up the work he had already done for his MA. The application was successful, and John was further awarded one of the small number of free return passages the shipping lines offered each year to scholarship winners going to Britain. The officers of the Unitarian Church wrote a warm note of congratulations: 'especially gratified . . . because of your long association with the Church as Organist and Member of Committee'.[47] Sir Robert Stout followed up with a testimonial: 'a man of high character and great industry'.[48] John did not keep papers at all systematically, but he did keep both of these.

The final months passed quickly. There was an Easter tramp on Ruapehu in which Elsie's brothers Charlie and Peter were included. John wrote a review for *Spike* of Jean Devanny's novel *The Butcher Shop*.[49] He did not care for it – 'not a great novel; it is not even a good novel; it is, in fact, in some respects an inconceivably bad novel' – but he cared even less for the action of the New Zealand Board of Censors in banning it as indecent, and he attacked the very idea of censorship in a 'modern country'. He faithfully attended the Free Discussions Club until he left. Finally, the Students' Association gave him a farewell, presented him with a college blazer, and F.P. Wilson 'expressed his regrets at losing so keen a student and lecturer'.[50] The night before he sailed, at twenty to one, he wrote a note to Elsie to say that he loved her and that he still had to finish his packing.

AS JOHN MADE CLEAR in *Spike*, he often saw Victoria University College in a critical light (though it was not the only thing he saw that way), but in later years his time there as a student and assistant lecturer took on something of a golden glow. I do not think he ever enthused about the teaching at that time and research was virtually unheard of. He remained something of a sceptic about formal courses and lectures, but he always recognised that education could be gained in many ways. Ten years later, when he published his history of the University of New Zealand, he wrote that, if such a work were to have a dedication, it would be 'to those at Victoria University College, mainly my fellow students, who . . . first taught me something of the meaning of a university; and particularly to' (and he gave just the initials) Thomas Hunter, Max Bickerton, Dick Campbell, Reo Fortune, Bob Martin-Smith, Elsie Holmes, Averil Lysaght, Lorrie Richardson, and to the memory of Harry Espiner.

4

LONDON, 1926–27

ON FRIDAY, 6 AUGUST 1926 at noon John sailed from Wellington for Sydney on the *Maheno*. Family and friends were there to see him off, but he dashed back home to pick up his toothbrush and shaving gear and just made it back in time.

I rushed on to the wharf, to find . . . Ernest & my uncle anxiously regarding the distance & my Father I suspected in a very much worse temper than he looked, loaded with insurance policies & letters of introduction from Bobby Stout; & then my Mother gave me further parcels, biscuits, lemons, & Lord knows what; & Mrs Hooper a map of London & another letter of introduction; & other people other things – heavens alive! I could hardly stagger up the gangway! . . . & then came the shower of streamers . . . & the boat began to move & I had a somewhat hard job to keep a cheerful grin on my face.[1]

Elsie had counted on the ship leaving late. She finished her morning's teaching and was driving into Wellington in her father's car (lent for the occasion) when, from the Hutt Road, she saw the ship draw out and head down the harbour. John walked the deck until he could no longer see 'the Tararuas & the road to Gollans Valley & Fitzroy Bay & the Karori Beach . . . & then went down to the Saloon & had a good meal, on the principle of getting in hard & solid while the going was good'.[2] Three days of seasickness followed. Two breakfasts were mastered but no dinners before the ship arrived in Sydney on 10 August, six hours late because of the weather experienced in the Tasman.

There John began a series of letters to his parents and to Elsie. Each generally contained from twelve to fourteen pages, though the last written from the *Osterley* to his parents ran to twenty-two pages and one to Elsie from London, thirty pages. The letters provide a remarkable record of the voyage – six weeks in which enduring friendships could be forged – and of his London years, of his introduction to things he had previously only read about.* Those to his parents (posted every two weeks) were widely shared within the family and outside, with the Hoopers and others. Yet they always began 'Dear Mummy', a sign of his closeness to her but also of his concern for her health. She had not been really well for a number of years before he left. Once a regular exchange of letters had been established, John would comment on his father's account of what the family had been up to, and make witticisms at the expense of his brothers, especially Keith, and observations which he hoped might shock his aunts. After that he would recount what had been happening. He must have been encouraged in writing by knowing how greatly his parents shared his interests – how they, given the opportunity, would have done many of the things he did. His parents replied faithfully, though there were times when his mother was not well enough to write. Ironically, her letters have more life than his father's; his father had never shaken off the solemnity of his youthful style, and they were both conscious of how confined their lives were compared with John's. Their letters reflect a deep love and great pride in what he was achieving, and at times a little anxiety about his views and actions – as well, on his mother's part, about how he was managing his clothes and what he was eating and drinking. To Elsie he wrote profusely of how much he loved her, often recalling times they had been together in Wellington and away tramping, before giving her too an account of his doings since his previous letter.

John made good use of the eleven days he had in Sydney. He stayed in the YMCA. He met with Jean Harvey, a nurse and family friend from the Unitarian days in Wellington, with whom he went to a recital by Chaliapin, 'wonderful, marvellous', and two J.M. Barrie plays, *Quality Street* and *What Every Woman Knows*, part of a season of Barrie produced by Dion Boucicault. He went out to Manly, 'pleasant on the ocean side but ghastly on the harbour side'; he walked a lot, and was alarmed at traffic going at thirty miles an hour; he discovered the most astonishing ice cream. He inspected the university library (160,000 books) and was dazzled by the lavishness of the university union building and the paintings lent by the art gallery and hung there. 'I wouldn't mind taking [it] up . . . & plonking it down in W'gton'. Sydney, he judged, 'seems pretty well to ooze money'.[3] He visited the Mitchell Library and

---

*   The New Zealand Electronic Text Centre at Victoria University of Wellington has put these letters from John to his parents on the web. They can be accessed at www.nzetc.org/tm/scholarly/name-207379.html

noted they had material relating to Cook's voyages. It was 'strongest on history & topography, travel & so on [but had] nothing like the collection of rare & beautiful things the Turnbull has'.[4] He spent some time there looking for material for his projected thesis on the New Zealand Company. On the Sunday afternoon he visited the Domain to listen to the speakers.

I never heard anything so funny. There were crowds there, all split up into groups, some big, some little; & they were being addressed – my word they were! Politics, economics, religion, debates, personal insults, mere meanderings, diagrams on blackboards, patriots, parsons, an I.W.W. man – I never saw anything like it. And there was one cheerful old unshaven ruffian lurching round, saying at intervals in a lugubrious voice (eye twinkling all the time) 'Hung by the neck! . . . Hung by the neck!' & selling ballads on recent deaths & murders & executions. I bought three (1d each).[5]

On 18 August, three days before the *Osterley* was due to sail, he was able to move aboard, 'such a swish single-berth cabin . . . on the top cabin deck, with a port hole opening on the sea; nice & white & spacious'. He wished that Elsie was with him. He added to his wardrobe, as befitted a first-class passenger, acquiring:

two prs of white trousers @ 16/6 pr; 1 pr of evening shoes @ 16/6 pr; two back studs & one front stud (in case anything goes overboard with the roll of the ship in the Great Australian Bight) @ 6d ea; 2 wing-collars @ 1/- ea; & one dress tie @ 3/6. As I had a dress tie already & also a made-up one in case of hopeless failure, you may think this extravagance . . . But the manner of the purchase of the tie was this; I said to the bird in the shop 'Can you tell me how to tie an evening tie?' And such was his willingness to demonstrate that I found myself in the generosity of my soul offering to purchase same if he could teach me to tie it satisfactorily. For he said 'Certainly; single-end or double-end?' To which I rejoined 'Search me'. And he then began to explain. It seems that a single-end is much easier to do up, is much more elegant to the view, sits on the collar with an air the older fashion never knew, does not hinder the breathing, is provocative of much less bad language & has a further large variety of virtues. Also it is as worn.[6]

In his next letter he reported 'that blasted tie is a washout. I put it round my neck & began to tie it in the most airy manner, but I'm blest if anything happened'. So he fell back on the made-up one, which seemed perfectly satisfactory, '& I shall probably continue to wear it & damn the consequences'.[7]

On board the *Osterley* were ten travelling scholars in all, four others who, like John, were travelling first class, having been awarded free passages. Three were lively young Australians from Sydney. Ian Henning, a French and German scholar, was going to the Sorbonne; 'a man of most extraordinary theories'.[8] Raymond McGrath, a postgraduate student in architecture, had already done architectural work in Sydney but his interests ranged much more widely. He had edited the student paper *Hermes*. He had shown considerable artistic gifts with a particular talent for woodcuts, having compiled a bound manuscript collection of his own poems and prose ('good prose & less good verse', in John's view) with illustrations by himself and his sister Eileen, as well as a printed book of twenty-four woodcuts – 'some of them are *stunner*, particularly some designs to illustrate W. de la Mare's poems . . . I don't know what sort of an architect he is, but I shouldn't mind getting him to design a house for me on the strength of his woodcuts'. Poems were exchanged and read; McGrath, it was agreed, would illustrate John's book of poems when it came out. McGrath, John judged, 'has very sound ideas'.[9]

W.G.K. Duncan (known by John always as Dunc or Dunkie – it was still the age of surnames) had graduated in philosophy at Sydney University with a thesis on progress and was heading for the London School of Economics. There is an unsympathetic portrait of Duncan at that time as Jonathan Crow in the Australian writer Christina Stead's novel *For Love Alone* (in her undergraduate days in Sydney she had had a passion for him). A little later, when she had followed him to London, she described him in a letter to her sister: 'He has a thorough-going indignation for (what he conceives to be) all forms of oppression, depression, impression, repression, suppression, compression and (irrational self-) expression, in short for all forms of everything which does not represent (what he conceives to be) Liberty and Justice.'[10] John took an altogether more positive view: 'We do a good deal of arguing; so much so that the place has rather the atmosphere of a miniature VUC. The Sydney lads are *right* controversialists.'[11] Duncan proved to know 'a whole lot about social problems, also has a sense of humour . . . He is mad on Bertrand Russell at present. Henning says one day "Who is this Bertrand Russell, anyhow?" Duncan looks at him wonderingly for a moment & then bursts out "Good God? have you ever heard of Jesus Christ?" He is going to London too which is cheerful'.[12]

The fifth scholar travelling first class was Olive Rowe (referred to by John almost invariably as Miss Rowe), a Canterbury classics graduate on her way to Oxford. Her fiancé, Ted Low, a Rhodes Scholar, was also on board, but not having a free passage was travelling third class. Although she had edited the Canterbury College *Review* for two years she was, regrettably, rather less of a controversialist; 'the lass lies low & says nuffin', John reported.[13] Finally, completing their table was Whinfield, the third officer, who proved well able to hold his end up against the students.

Henning, in a letter home, gave a first impression of John:

Poor old Beaglehole has a terrible time with his name. A little English lady (you know, the How long have ye been out? type) came up to him the other day and asked him: Are you Mr Begleyhole? The best of it is that Beaglehole stutters every time he tries to say b's, so it takes everyone quite a time to find out what his name really is. They generally end up by asking you after he has gone what they understood you to say your friend's name was. He is a very decent chap and plays the piano very nicely.[14]

The first-class food called forth extended and enthusiastic comment. 'It's not much use trying to be a food reformer', John told his mother, and hesitated to describe dinner lest 'her hygienic soul should shudder and wilt'.[15] The young Australians shared his enthusiasm. A week after they sailed John learned to his horror that he had missed afternoon tea every day, not having heard that it was on. Deck sports, in which he developed a taste for quoit tennis that became a lasting addiction, gave one an appetite: 'my word! you do eat on board', he wrote in a later letter, all scruples abandoned:

It gives a man a unique opportunity to get experience with food; the meaning of culinary French, & so on; & the combinations you can work out are astonishing; Potage à la Russe, Saumon, sauce Mantua, Roast Turkey, ice-cream, & coffee – there's one sample. We are experimenting a bit with liqueurs, too; each bloke shouts a round, @ 6d a head now & again. Crème de menthe & Benedictine we have tried so far, the first sickly pepperminty stuff, but the Benedictine was good. Don't tell Bobby Stout.[16]

Before leaving Wellington John had promised Sir Robert that he would keep off 'the drink'.

The *Osterley* called at Melbourne, Adelaide and Fremantle. In Melbourne John met again with Maie Ross, his old friend from Whitcombe's, now selling crockery in Myers Emporium. In Adelaide he called on Ernest Hale (the former Unitarian minister in Wellington) and his family. The chief difficulty Hale faced, wrote John, was 'contending with the excessive wealth of his parishioners'.[17] There is no mention of Beagleholes; any links between the New Zealand and Australian branches of the family seem to have long since disappeared. John checked the bookshops, reporting at length to his father (but not to Elsie, who already had her doubts about John's addiction to buying books) on prices, bargains and finely produced editions. The art galleries won enthusiastic reports, especially the Melbourne gallery:

... they have some wonderful stuff there; a magnificent Raeburn which puts all the other portraits, by Reynolds or Romney or anybody completely into the shade; about four Corots, Sargents (Landscapes), Watts (portrait of Tennyson), Burne-Jones, D.Y. Cameron, Van Eyck (a wonderful brilliant little thing they paid £21,000 odd for), Pissarro, Monet, C.J. Holmes, Madox [sic] Brown, Maris brothers, Orpen, John, Turner (great water-colour Okehampton Castle) P. de Wint, Morland, Reynolds, Romney, etchings by Rembrandt, Whistler, Mèryon, Pennell, Haden, Brangwn [sic], Durer, a lot of Australians . . . [18]

As in Sydney, he cast an envious eye over the universities.

All this for him was the 'merest fore-taste of what's to come'.[19] His mind was firmly fixed on what lay ahead: 'all these colonial towns, as towns are the same, after all; & apart from one or two pictures, none of them are worth more than a damn'.[20] As they neared Ceylon he wrote, 'it is a pleasant sensation to be crossing part of the earth that has really some history behind it & not just a few tuppenny-ha'penny scraps & tenth-rate politics', and he was thinking of changing his thesis subject to 'something in political theory; however we'll see, – the NZ Coy may still be the handiest subject to work on'.[21] New Zealand was clearly being left behind in more than one sense.

Colombo was the first place by which he felt really excited since leaving home.[22] They had twenty-four hours there and for John it was a revelation.

I never saw a place with such beautiful surroundings, such wonderful streets and avenues – trees, millions of them, lawns, parks. We passed down a great avenue with wonderful bungalows on each side – all belonging to the English civil service. But gosh, no wonder the Conquering Race doesn't want to leave. I shouldn't if I had a bungalow & grounds like that. But some belonging to the rich natives are beautiful buildings too; there was practically nothing really ugly or merely pretentious that we saw . . . We passed through a big native quarter . . . Havelock town, when all the population was coming home from work. Talk of colour! And the Buddhist priests in yellow stuck out . . . the shops [were] all open & most of the houses; every possible thing for sale, rope & lollies & coconuts & vegetables; even one or two butchers.

He visited a silk merchant with McGrath and had great difficulty in restraining himself from plunging helplessly on stuff for Elsie and his mother, 'silks & shawls & kimonos & ladies' pyjamas; finally the bloke evidently judging McG was a man of experience started bringing out garments of even more intimate intention; but we managed to stifle a blush & intimated politely but firmly that we weren't buying lingerie on that occasion'. Before their eyes a conjuror grew a mango tree from seed to flower and fruit – John sent home to Elsie the leaf given him as proof. Late in the evening the party returned briefly to the ship by rowing boat, but engaged it to call back for them at five in the morning for a final look

around the town on foot or per rickshaw to the native markets . . .
continually being rushed by diamond-merchants or bead-merchants or
beggars or small boys singing Tipperary in a way peculiarly their own or
merchants – with shops just round the corner with the most wonderful
bargains in elephants or gold rings. All of which we managed to shake
off at not much cost to ourselves.

His account of Colombo, written from the Red Sea (to be posted at Suez), ended with more excitement. 'My first sight of Africa at Cape Guardafui had me well worked up.' A little later, with the mountains around Sinai on the right and on the left the ranges of Egypt, John, as reported by McGrath, pointed towards Africa exclaiming, 'Do you realise that Cleopatra ruled over that land; that these waters are liquid history!'[23] Clearly pleased with the phrase 'liquid history', he used it again in his letter to his parents.

Passing through the Suez Canal they saw labourers working by hand to widen it. On their arrival at Port Said John was shocked when they were

immediately assaulted by thousands more niggers to do the coaling. Well,
I never saw anything more like hell. Talk of exploiting cheap colonial
labour; in about five minutes on both sides of the ship there was an
entirely black zone – the air so black that from up on the top deck you
could just see long lines of indistinct figures walked [sic] up planks to
tips in the side of the ship with no interval between them whatsoever.
The lighters were so crowded that how they managed to do any work
at all I don't know. They worked barefoot & practically naked; & how
their feet escaped the spades with which they were digging the coal into
buckets is a miracle. One poor devil got an eyeful of the stuff; & there
he stood, agonising & crying like a child, as we went past on our way to
the shore. Very pretty . . . However there were diversions for members of
the exploiting West like us; a conjuror was on board about as soon as the
ship anchored, & my word he did some clever things.[24]

After a long wait they got into small boats and were rowed ashore: 'Egypt, the land of the Pharaohs, the amorous adventures of Cleopatra, the Sphinx & Pyramids . . .' Resisting invitations to 'exhibitions of the can-can' – 'we all thought hard of our Aunties & turned these very attractive invitations down' – they examined everything else that was going on:

Antique horse-trams, sheiks, guttersnipes, what looked like illegitimate left-overs from the war, street cleaners, Arabs, Greeks & Dagos of all sorts & conditions, Egyptians, donkeys, cafés . . . We examined a Russian orthodox church, well-built, but full of shrines & a department for selling tin-pot little charms; & it was delightful to see Duncan, the hardened rationalist, who was the only lad with small change on him, tipping the man who showed us over with a couple of bob for the Church funds.

They were caught up in a great procession, with drums and incense and hundreds of red, green and white banners covered with crescents, which they discovered was part of a celebration of the Prophet's birthday. They got back to the ship just before it sailed, John having bought 'a couple of hundred best Turkish cigarettes for 5/- 100', and having had to 'repulse a bootblack with some warmth when he arbitrarily took control of my foot; for which however I was afterwards rather sorry, as I don't like behaving like the Conquering Race'.

The voyage through the Mediterranean, calling at Naples, Toulon and Gibraltar, brought more historical associations; John's admiration for Garibaldi, 'that eminent swashbuckler', grew a good deal when he saw the sort of country he fought over. At Naples 'the lads' again repelled the efforts of their guide to get them into 'the can-can'; here the promise was to be shown 'in living form the delightful poses characteristic of the wall-paintings of Pompeii'.

John continued to sing the praises of his Australian companions, especially Duncan and McGrath. 'Duncan & I indulge in the most enormous arguments; or I support him against Henning or McG.; or McG & I uphold art against the others, or I gives harangues to all & sundry'.[25] McGrath he judged to be in many ways 'the pearl of the bunch', whereas Henning was 'inclined to take life a bit too seriously'. Of Miss Rowe he rather despaired; she preferred 'not to argue at meals', and when finally roused 'called them all materialists but would not say what she meant'. She was, John believed, a 'bit mixed as to our characters though, especially mine; as she has to reconcile the vehemence of my controversial methods with the sweetly chaste character of my verse, some of which McGrath showed her'. [26]

The voyage drew to an end, and the last round of deck sports was held. John was defeated by Duncan in the final of the bucket quoits but 'won the egg & spoon race hands down, for which I got an order for 4/- on the barber's shop, & took it out in a tobacco pouch'. With McGrath's artistic talent and Whinfield's cooperation (he provided chains which they dragged, making a great clatter, as they made their entrance down the stairs and into the saloon) the four young men starred at the fancy dress ball as four ghosts. John spent one of the last days writing a

Great Epic . . . the Osterliad, in six cantos, rhymed heroic couplets, six f.cap pages of type, about 200 lines. A truly wonderful achievement . . . It is in honour of Whinfield chiefly, & ourselves secondarily. Canto I is a general description of W. Canto II is an impressive apostrophe to the hero. Canto III is the longest & a description of one of our meal-time free discussions, with W. in the chair; Canto IV is the description of a thrilling game of quoit-tennis, Whinfield & Beaglehole v Duncan & Henning; Canto V is a historical disquisition on great navigators of the past, W's superiority to them, his eminent services in the war etc, etc. Canto VI is the grand finale, summing up & driving home the lessons of the previous five, & hailing W. as the consummation of the divine purpose of the Creator. [27]

The Osterliad was an achievement, carried off in the style of a neo-Byronic Don Juan. To Elsie he wrote that it showed 'the disgraceful way in which I behaved on the voyage';[28] certainly it conveyed his high spirits as well as his fluent pen:

CANTO III

Whinfield's singular judicial detachment from common argument and error.	With what an equable and balanced mind Oh Whinfield, hast thou held the scales inclined Neither to this side nor to that, when strife Tremendous, cataclysmic, life for life Has burst upon our table! See the words Abrupt, explosive, fly like angry birds From seat to seat, the personal abuse Which custom does not stale nor over-use.
Henning lays down the law.	First Henning lays an axiom down, which seems To him self evident, to Duncan, dreams.
To which Duncan retorts that he is a damn fool.	Duncan assaults the youth, he bares his teeth He feels his native controversial heath, And "Bertrand Russell, Bertrand Russell!" shouts – Our Duncan with his philosophic doubts –

His hatchet face enlivens, rings his voice!
But who is this who cavils at his choice
Of argumentative material, who?

McGrath has still
faith in the
universe.

'Tis the respectable McGrath, and through
The mazes of his childlike faith he goes
With halting step, and frequent short repose
To show the reasons for his great decision;
For our McGrath has Ideals, Art and Vision.

To which Beaglehole
is able to give only
a qualified
approval.

Lo! rises Beaglehole and savage, hot
Throws knife, spoon, fork, self in the melting pot.
His raucous voice attacks the startled ceiling
He outrages a lady's every feeling.
He snatches words from Duncan, from Miss Rowe,
He damns all priests and parsons, heralds woe
To superstitious Mac and luckless Henning
In frightful language quite unfit for penning.

Miss Rowe seeks
peace and
quietude.

Miss Rowe assumes a headache, blanches, bites
A trifle languidly, and thinks of knights
Of ancient chivalry* who never rended
The sanctities of life, nor e'en offended
A delicate damsel's feelings of what must
Forever constitute the right, the just.

Duncan's heresy
and Beaglehole's
opinion of McGrath.

Duncan proceeds to nationalise all women
Beaglehole thinks the light of truth burns dim in
The hypocrite McGrath,† who'd sit and eat
Obliviously at Socrates' great feet.

Henning reduces
the Eternal to
a diagram.

Henning elaborates a paradox
The most appalling even of his vast flocks.
He draws a diagram‡ with spoon and fork
And steadily proceeds to talk, and talk.

Henning has no
great opinion of
human nature;
and the combat
waxes general.

'Does human nature change?' with seraph smile
He asks, and all his face expresses guile.
Duncan and Beaglehole proceed to shout,
Henning retires in psychologic rout;
Miss Rowe demands why they are not put out.
The combat waxes hotter, birth control

---

*   On the typed copy which John sent to his parents he wrote a marginal note: 'Miss R was very keen on chivalry, though she also believed strongly in the equality of the sexes.'
†   Marginal note: 'We called McG & H hypocrites because through saying nothing at moments of tension they got a reputation for politeness & perfect gentlemanliness with Miss R; but behind her back agreed that she was etc etc etc.'
‡   Marginal note: 'Henning was great on diagrams – he drew one of immortality.'

Marriage and nigger labour, how to coal
A ship, should strikers be allowed to live?
Are women worthy of their high prerogative
In being allowed to vote, if so what then?
What would you rather be, women or men?
Beagle blasphemes against the ancient Greeks

Miss Rowe is stirred to unaccustomed activity.

Shocked to the soul, Miss Rowe emerges; seeks
To slay the offender, wrath darts from her eyes
She seems a dozen times her usual size.

Duncan again attacks Henning.

Duncan with dastard economic jeer
Sneers at whatever Henning holds most dear
And now McGrath stung to the very heart
Proclaims the evangel of his conquering Art,

Whinfield's sublime detachment.

And thou, great Whinfield, what through all this
                                                    time
Hast thou been doing, Officer sublime?

He gives his judgment, which temporarily depresses the combatants.

With steady hand, full mouth, judicious brow
Thou hearest all the evidence, and now
Stoop'st from Olympian heights, and as we long
For commendation, say'st we all are wrong.
We droop, and dully think of wasted lives

But all is well.

But lo! thy magic smile our soul revives!

Duncan typed it out and they presented it to Whinfield at their last lunch with a 'magnificent box of cigars we bought at Gibraltar'. As they hoped, he gave them each one of the cigars. After a brief call at Plymouth and spending several hours fog-bound in the Thames estuary, the *Osterley* finally docked at Tilbury on the afternoon of 1 October. John caught the boat train up to London.

2/10/26 Saturday: 1st morning in London – S. Kensington: so far so good.[29]

TO JOHN EVERYTHING looked extraordinarily familiar; 'St Paul's, the Royal Exchange, Admiralty Arch, Trafalgar Square'. On closer inspection he had some reservations about the interior of St Paul's, and the Albert Memorial he judged 'a hideous abortion'. 'I'd heard that this was pretty bad, but nothing, no picture, no description, can come up to the horror of the original.'[30] Two years later Kenneth Clark put it more succinctly in *The Gothic Revival*: 'the expression of pure philistinism'.[31] There were notes of welcome from Lorrie Richardson and Jack Yeates, old trampers from Victoria, the latter 'largely condemnatory of the country'. They met the next day. Richardson had just submitted his PhD thesis at Imperial College and had been awarded a fellowship that turned into a permanent job at an agricultural experimental station at Harpenden, north of London. He seemed to like England on the whole, but he and John were silenced by Yeates's flow of invective and vituperation. Yeates was full of doubts about ever getting his Cambridge thesis finished, forthright on what a failure he was (in fact he was to finish it successfully in the minimum time), and generally down on the country and the climate. He could not wait to get back to New Zealand.[32] John, however, after inspecting the Institute of Historical Research – 'much to my liking' – and going to his first concert, informed the family in Wellington that 'this country will do me for a while, climate or no climate'.[33]

After a few days in the Hotel Madrid in South Kensington (recommended by Whinfield; 7s 6d for bed and breakfast), John and Duncan were soon settled in a large room on the top floor of a house at 21 Brunswick Square in Bloomsbury, their landlady 'a retired Indian army nurse & superficially quite decent, but with an immense contempt for the subject races'.[34] In the square: 'The houses aren't very handsome . . . though from some aspects they have a certain dignity – it's the square that makes them – the lawn & the trees in the middle'.[35] John continued:

We have two beds, one of which, a big affair occupied by me, swings back up to the wall by day. The other is a stretcher affair that doesn't occupy much room. Also a sofa, covered during the day by my rug, which at night covers me. Also two fairly satisfactory armchairs & three small chairs. Likewise a table with two extensions that drop down at the side when not required. Likewise a chest of drawers. Likewise a marble-topped sort of table for washing up on, the repose of shaving materials etc. A bookcase, divided ½ & ½ between us. A gas fire with a burner at the side for our kettle. Two cupboards for clothes just outside the door. In one of them the gas meter – one of those bob in the slot things invented expressly for the purpose of diddling coves like us, I suppose. Bathroom just across the landing.

The rent was 17s 6d a week each. Living expenses, other than lunches, proved to be five to seven shillings each with a diet mainly of wholemeal bread, raisins and marmalade, plus whatever fruit could be picked up cheap, mainly apples (4d a pound for cooking apples) and dried figs. Lunch was bought for 1s 3d or 1s 6d or even, at the vegetarian Food Reform Restaurant, for 11d. They got the *Times* and a bottle of milk every morning, the *Sunday Times* on

Sunday and the *Times Literary Supplement* on Thursday and their bill on Monday. 'So everything goes like clockwork.'[36] With £3 a week, John reckoned on '£2 for living in all its details & £1 for pleasures – or rather education in a broad sense, books, music, plays etc. What a man needs is about £1000 yr for 5 yrs.'[37] Money was to go on being a preoccupation, with the university fees of twenty-one guineas a year, plus twenty guineas for the degree on completion, being a standing cause for complaint.

London was almost overwhelming, the first months a veritable feast of music, of bookshops, of sheer intellectual excitement. Part of John's first letter home from Brunswick Square was written just after he had got back from his first promenade concert:

Well, I've been in the 7th Heaven – the London pavements were like air beneath me as I walked home, & they glistened like silver; the trees in the square as I turned the corner were the abode of magic; the street-lights sang to the policeman underneath them & I positively looked for a pavement artist to give my last penny to (I found one too, though it was after ten) . . . Bach, Handel, Mozart – you can't beat 'em; I wouldn't give two damns for anyone else . . . You never heard anything like the Bach fiddle concerto! & played by Jelly d'Aranji like a flaming angel.[38]

'Let's have some cocoa to celebrate', he said to Duncan, and they did.

In the first weeks there were concerts by the London Symphony Orchestra under Sir Thomas Beecham ('& an extraordinary spectacle he is'[39]) and Albert Coates, the New Queen's Hall Orchestra with Sir Henry Wood, the Philharmonic Society with Wood again, and with Bruno Walter. There was Gilbert and Sullivan (*Ruddigore*, 'the music is great, but a lot of the conversation terrible bunk'[40]), the Royal Choral Society singing the Verdi *Requiem* and the Philharmonic Choir in Bach's *B Minor Mass* (he heard this a second time a few weeks later). There were Saturday afternoon concerts at St Martin-in-the-Fields with no charge for admission. There he heard Myra Hess play Bach and, he assured his parents, he had put something in the collection box. McGrath booked seats for the Russian Ballet:

I have been to the Russian Ballet twice, & am going again if I can run to it . . . Some of it is great stuff . . . L'Aprés Midi d'un Faun was jolly good, & Prince Igor stunner, likewise Petroushka [sic], & some of the dancing in The Swan Lake; do you remember how we used to see pictures of all these in the Sphere in the old days before the war. I want to see the Fire Bird, so that probably means another 2/4 going plush.[41]

The problem was that there was too much to go to.

... tomorrow there are about four concerts I want to go to, & also a lecture by Bertrand Russell ... the chief concert is Kreisler playing Elgar & Brahms concertos with the London Sym. Orchestra & Landon Ronald. After a prolonged & horrible conflict of loyalties I came to the conclusion that I would certainly be able to hear B.R. again, but possibly not Kreisler or the Elgar concerto; so I went & got the last 5/9 ticket, not without a good deal of calculation & perturbation of spirit ... I am darn sorry to miss Russell tomorrow but it can't be helped. To make up Duncan hears a lot of him – he follows him round like a dog.[42]

The lecturers heard were a mixed lot: 'an astonishing number of them have been duds – Arnold Toynbee for instance one night put across the most elementary tripe about the Pacific as a political centre in the most pitiful puerile style'. Toynbee subsequently redeemed himself somewhat with a lecture in a Fabian Society series (Mr Hooper had sent over the details from Wellington) in which John also heard Sidney Webb, 'a little insignificant cove' who 'spoke in a conversational way ... with some jokes, unfortunately not loud enough to hear',[43] and George Bernard Shaw. 'Place crowded, with a good number of adorers who rippled as soon as he opened his mouth. Good stuff, but not extraordinarily out of the common for him.'[44] Shaw the dramatist won greater praise, *Man and Superman*, being 'the finest thing all round for play & acting combined I've seen in my life'.[45] This was the shortened version; John was so carried away that a few days later he and Duncan went to the full-length production. 'We got to the queue at 4, too late to get a seat, got inside about 4.30 & stood till 11.15. All for 1/6 & by cripes! it was worth it! ... I wouldn't have missed it for £25 ... Gwen Frangçon Davies did Anne, a wonderful performance, & a cove called S. Esmé Percy [played] Tanner ... a great & glorious performance.'

The bookshops were endlessly seductive, with John & Edward Bumpus's in Oxford Street being perhaps the greatest lure. There is hardly a letter among all those John wrote home that does not mention books – books read, books admired, books bought, books coveted but too expensive. Soon after arriving he bought books to send back to members of the family for Christmas, choosing a facsimile edition of Blake's *Songs of Innocence* (Ernest Benn, 1926, 12s 6d) for his father, but then deciding to keep it for himself. For his mother, something she could get her teeth into, the memoirs of the portrait painter Benjamin Haydon,[46] 'also I think it will turn out to be one of those books you will be able to quote at meal-times & put markers in for me to read selected passages if I can just spare a minute or two now & again'.[47] Then he could not resist a 'couple of little supernumerary presents', a volume of Victorian letters for his father and E.M. Forster's *Pharos and Pharillon* for his mother. 'Fair dinkum, that E.M. Forster has a style to marvel at.' For himself he enthused over the Nonesuch Milton, 'one of the best books I have ever seen', but at £4 10s he had to say 'Nuthin doin'.[48] A little later he made up for that by buying the *Selected Essays* of Edward Thomas, 'with twenty four wood engravings by R. Ashwin Maynard & Horace W. Bray, one of three hundred copies (Nos 51–350) printed on Van Gelden paper & bound in blue buckram', published by the Gregynog Press. 'I've been considering it since the beginning of December. It is a very beautiful book.'[49]

'It strikes me I am pretty heroic to get any work done under the circumstances',[50] John wrote, 'all I want to do is to sit down & read, history or otherwise, & get up & travel'.[51] No one he had seen in the university seemed very interested in overseas or research students, but John finally met with Professor A.F. Pollard, 'who is a great man . . . with the result that I shall probably be working under him on political theory of some sort, I think the idea of sovereignty [in Tudor England] . . . Pollard reckons that would be far more broadening to the mind than working on NZ history.'[52] Pollard was a great figure among the historians of his generation; he contributed 'more than any other single man or single institution to the professionalization of history in the early twentieth century'[53] and virtually created the school of history in the University of London. His historical interests were in the Tudor period and were above all political and constitutional. With a mind that was 'very good at untangling legislative and constitutional knots', he none the less lacked imagination, was neither 'sensitive nor subtle',[54] and was inclined to sniff at anything that did not fit in with his own researches. To both colleagues and students he could be thoroughly intimidating.[55]

John's meetings with him were not easy. John had heard from a fellow student that a lecturer had just finished a book on sixteenth-century political thought (J.W. Allen, *Political Thought in the Sixteenth Century*). Why would Professor Pollard not have mentioned this? John asked. Professor Pollard and Mr Allen never speak to each other, he was told. John considered switching to the seventeenth century. Then, realistically recognising that Allen could hardly have 'cleaned up the whole of the century', he went back to the Tudor idea and took along an outline of a proposal to Pollard. This Pollard 'proceeded to tear to pieces in a manner rude, if not insulting. However it is something novel for me to have a prof take enough interest in me even to tread on me; so although I was a bit dashed at first I haven't been unduly depressed on the whole.'[56]

Worse was to follow. He revised the proposal. Pollard was highly critical:

suicidal to have any sort of plan – only a rehash of other men's ideas, of no value at all; political theory all bunk; political thought of no effect at all. Suggested one or two constitutional history subjects which would be fruitful to work on. I said I had always been interested rather in the philosophical aspects of history. 'Yes' he said 'sheer drivel, in fact'. Finally I happened to mention the letters PhD & he was so horrified he nearly fell off his seat. Couldn't possibly do it – he was under the impression I was after an M.A. . . . . [57] I told him I was one already & had been accepted as a PhD student by the Univ. Homily on wonderful character of London MA. Almost superhuman character of London PhD. Well, says I, would I be wiser to get back to NZ history which I know pretty well. Finally he thought yes, I might get a PhD on that. So I have to see Newton the colonial man.[58]

In his letters to his parents John put a brave face on all this; he had worries enough with the news that his mother was ill again and confined to her bed. To Elsie he wrote, 'The main trouble about the mix-up is that it makes me horribly nervous whenever I talk to a prof; & you know the effect nervousness has on me'[59] – a reference to his stutter. Over fifty years later, Duncan still remembered how Pollard had shattered John's morale.[60] Pollard, the 'great man', thereafter became 'that swine Pollard'. A.P. Newton, the Rhodes Professor of Imperial History, 'turned out very decent'.[61] In his view the subject of research was relatively unimportant; what was needed was the most intensive grounding in historical method and research. 'But as I was a colonial student, & wd probably be occupying a colonial chair (which I thought unduly optimistic) the best thing to do would be to take a colonial subject & work under him'. They settled on the subject of instructions to colonial governors between 1783 and 1840, the years between the loss of the American colonies and the emergence of the idea of responsible government – 'I'm afraid it won't turn out to be especially readable when finished'. John then changed his registration from University College to King's, which was Newton's college. 'It is a bit of a crash to be attached to the one representative of the Church of England among the London colleges! Though as I do spend most of the time I do spend in a college, which is very little, in the L.S.E. that doesn't make much difference, except to my self-respect.'[62]

While the young colonial was being put firmly in his place by

Pollard, he found an ally – more than an ally, a friend, a hero almost
– in H.J. (Harold) Laski, newly appointed to the chair in politics at
the London School of Economics (LSE). John had gone to a lecture
by Laski and been so stirred that he wrote to him and asked his
advice about the thesis. Laski invited John to visit him and helped
him draft the second proposal for Pollard. After its poor reception,
Laski initially suggested that John should switch to the LSE and
work under him on a history of the Whig party, but he came to agree
with Newton that work on a colonial subject would provide good
training and a degree that would ensure John a career. He added
that John should come and see him at least every month and tell him
how he was getting on, and there was a standing invitation to tea at
the Laskis' 'at home' any Sunday afternoon. More than his advice,
Laski's human warmth transformed John's outlook. Returning to
Brunswick Square to tell Duncan about it, he was 'walking on air'.[63]
A little later he wrote to Dick Campbell:

This . . . Laski is a weedy undersized shrimp of a fellow, & now holding
down Graham Wallas' job. He is about 34. God! what a mind! I heard
his inaugural lecture, the finest formal thing I ever heard in my life . . .
He wrote all the editorials in the *Workers Weekly* during the General
Strike, of unhappy memory, & stands by every word of them. He is a
perfect lecturer, & friendly & companionable enough to be a colonial.
God bless him![64]

Laski's biographer, Kingsley Martin, in a phrase later quoted by
John, saw 'the clue to Harold's strength and weakness . . . in his
desire to love and be loved. His argument', Martin wrote, 'might
be derived from Marx, but at the final test he was a follower of
William Morris rather than of Lenin.'[65] At the Laskis' on Sunday
afternoons one might meet almost anyone: fellow student, cabinet
minister, trade union leader, Indian nationalist, American jurist or
playwright. And the talk! If the company was remarkable, the talk
was even more remarkable: 'I never heard such conversation before',
John wrote, though he did on one occasion report, 'I went to Laski's
on Sunday afternoon & heard some pretty good yarns – one or two
of them touched up since I heard them last'.[66] Ultimately, perhaps,
Laski was too good a talker to write the great work on political
thought that some believed he had in him. That work, however,
provided the pretext for Laski's indefatigable scouring of the second-
hand bookshops. It was another bond between him and the bookish
young New Zealander. The book collecting can be followed, the
flavour of the talk captured, from two remarkable volumes of
correspondence between Laski and the American Supreme Court

judge Oliver Wendell Holmes. In reviewing those volumes, twenty-five years after he first met Laski, John sought to sum up the man. At the same time he revealed more than a little about himself:

They [Holmes and Laski] were both, intellectually and emotionally, humanists. They inherited, they passed on, the great tradition of eighteenth century rationalism, they were men of tough and acute mind, of *esprit*; but each in his own way too was a romantic; the mind of each was touched by an enchanted music that led him beyond the efforts and entanglements of the ordinary day.[67]

Laski too was an outsider: a radical, a Jew, 'friendly & companionable enough to be a colonial'. This was to become something of a yardstick.

It was two months before his thesis subject was sorted out and John started work at the Public Record Office, 'thankful to have got something to bite on at last'.[68] He had not wasted the intervening time. As well as attending lectures, concerts and plays, writing letters and exploring London, he had spent an early weekend at Trimley, near Felixstowe, with his uncle George Butler, an artist, and his wife Jeanne, who had left New Zealand in 1905, and their two adult children, Berrie (also an artist) and Brian. He warmed to these relations and admired some of George's landscape sketches – 'a lot better than his big stuff'[69] – and portraits. He helped cut firewood and walked, 'the first time I have exerted myself since leaving home'. On leaving he was 'blowed if Auntie Jeanne didn't hang around my neck & kiss me. Which I judge, on so short an acquaintance, was taking a decided liberty.' She redeemed herself somewhat by sending him off with a pot of chutney and some cake to take back to London. A little later she followed up with a box of pickled eggs.

In the same letter to Dick Campbell in which he sang Laski's praises, John urged his friend, who had been awarded a postgraduate travelling scholarship, to come to London and to the LSE to study for his PhD:

. . . believe me, the man who gets a Travelling Schol. & does not come to the London School of Economics & Political Science has treated his lady Fortune in a shady & miserable fashion . . . My dear Mr. Campbell, come here; it is the centre of the universe. Harold J. Laski remarked to me tonight that he would rather be a crossing sweeper in London than a millionaire anywhere else, & by cripes, he's about right.[70]

It was all very well to echo Laski's rhetorical flourishes but there were things about England that John found difficult to accept. The treatment of the miners as the 1926 general strike ended struck him as 'pretty rotten . . . The way the owners are putting in the boot is sickening; & the way the Govt stands by & keeps the ring for them is disgraceful.'[71] London brought him face to face with misery and poverty, and in a letter at the end of November as winter drew in, he wrote:

We have been having pretty brummy weather lately, with a real dinkum fog on Thursday – an interesting thing for the first five minutes, but ghastly after that; the darn thing nearly chokes you & you spend half the time in blowing smuts out of your nose. Then in the middle of it a bloke sticks me up & wants me to buy a box of soap – nothing to eat since yesterday, ready to drop, etc etc. The same old yarn. So I buy his soap. The night before another washed out specimen I could have knocked out with my little finger pushed matches at me as I was going into the Institute; I said Well they'll always come in handy, I suppose; & gave him 2d for a box. He looked at me doubtfully – 'Well, it's more than they're worth you know' he said. 'But I've been in the infirmary for 15 months, & I don't know what I'll do if I have to walk round all night'. I thought a bit & then chased after him & asked him how many more boxes he had & gave him 6d for the last one, & he just stood & gazed at me as if I had been the Lord God Almighty. Fair dinkum, when a bloke gets that low it's time they had a change in the country. Another white-faced cove sits in the street down Kingsway all day with his chest covered with medals & knits kids caps & socks for a living, & a wife & Lord knows how many children. And up in Birmingham a crowd of working women got together & signed a petition for a birth-control clinic or free access to knowledge of same or something . . . & the Bishop of Birmingham rose in his blasted episcopal righteousness & damned the life out of them.[72]

He wrote of the knitting ex-serviceman in a poem, 'The veteran', published in the *New Zealand Times:*[73]

Pale face, breast medalled, ancient threadbare coat
In the wet street perpetually he sits,
While half the unheeding world roars round and past,
Moving with rapid fingers, still he knits.

Ill written sign – 'to keep a wife and child' –
This is the old unending end of man;
With sharpened anxious features strained and set
The instrument works out the given plan.

Bright-coloured wools, a red, a blue, a green,
Childs' caps and socks, the ordinary things,
With hands that may have killed he knits and knits –
A street where no one smiles and no bird sings.

Characteristic of much of the verse which he was writing prolifically – it was a more literary age than today – it lacks the life and immediacy of his letters. It provided an opportunity, however, to earn a guinea or two from the *New Zealand Times*, as had his article 'Going Home', which they had published a little earlier.[74] That opportunity disappeared with the demise of the paper shortly afterwards.

After the Unitarian Church and the Free Discussions Club, John reacted strongly to the Established Church: 'so far as I can see the only religion that will be any use in the long run will be a secular religion, if you can have such a thing', he wrote, after reading C.E.M. Joad on the subject in *Thrasymachus, or, The Future of Morals*. 'Dress it up if you like & get emotion behind it, but make it a force for & in this world & keep it in this world . . . Meanwhile about the only reason I can see for the existence of parsons is that it is a polite way of giving mental deficients the dole',[75] a comment clearly intended to shock Auntie Win. In the early months of 1927 and again the following year, the subject 'of most hectic and lengthy controversy'[76] was the revision of the Prayer Book. John followed it closely with a kind of fascinated horror – 'the most extraordinary argument! the most extraordinary people!'[77] – and cut out the reports from the *Times* to send home to his father.

For his first Christmas in England, having called off a trip to Paris with Lorrie Richardson for financial reasons, John accepted an invitation to stay with the Johnson family in Manchester – 'a filthy hole, dirtier than London'.[78] His brother Keith had come to know the Johnsons while he was working and training as an engineer in the Vickers Metropolitan factory there and had fallen for their elder daughter Fronnie (Frances), who was planning to follow him out to New Zealand at the end of February. John had already met Fronnie when she was down staying with an uncle and aunt in Rugby, and visiting them he had had his first taste of the English countryside, 'so neat & clean & trim & well arranged'. 'Father Johnson' was a Unitarian minister who described himself as a 'Christian imperialist' ('I asked him if the two things were entirely compatible, but he didn't have any doubts on the point'[79]) and had a passion for the poetry of Walt Whitman. While he did not seem 'at all backward about his own knowledge & accomplishments', the rest of the family, in John's eyes, seemed 'pretty comprehensively ignorant for such a father'.[80] John, remarkably, was almost overwhelmed with the eating and drinking: 'Christmas Eve was bad enough, but Christmas Day was disgusting', and it went on and on. Some of John's views rather scandalised members of the extended Johnson family:

I went to church last night after an argument with Fronnie of
considerable duration as to whether anybody's feelings would be hurt
if I stayed away (unfortunately went to sleep during the sermon, but I
was upstairs in a corner by myself so it didn't matter). Well, the organist
like a silly ass, for a closing voluntary played the Hallelujah Chorus &
the whole crowd stood up stock still in their pews; but I who had had
to stand while he did the same thing the morning before hopped out &
walked home. And letting this slip casually out, you never heard such
a horrified outcry! Mrs J. quite paled. F's breath taken away. Father J's
sister struck all of a heap. But this was nothing to the sensation caused
when[,] the conversation having drifted via standing up generally & God
Save the King & London customs in connection therewith, I had the face
to suggest to Father J's sister's husband, who was going off in a paroxysm
of more or less inarticulate admiration of the Br Empire that perhaps the
said empire would come to an end some day from the instability of its
social system, & added not with entire truth that I was a Socialist. They
all paled distinctly & leapt from their chairs as if I had stuck a pin in
all of them simultaneously . . . they all praise the Lord thankfully when
Father Johnson says I'll grow out of it – he was worse than that once.[81]

John was in great demand to play the piano 'as a soloist & for
songs (Watchman what of the night etc)' and learned, under protest,
to play whist. He was taken to see Heaton Hall, formerly a stately
home, now an art gallery with 'glorious watercolours of the Norwich
school . . . Cox, Cotman, de Wint etc; & a fine house'. He had a day's
tramp in the Peak District with Fronnie and some neighbours, and
had a look at Manchester University and the John Rylands Library.
'Studying the bourgeoisie' took up so much time that he was able
to read very little apart from Dean Inge's *England*; 'acute in some
places but in others extraordinarily prejudiced or extraordinarily
ignorant, & now & again both. Very rocky on imperial problems
& the dominions.'[82] After a fortnight he returned to London with
some relief and mixed feelings about his future sister-in-law.

If the account he wrote to his parents was characteristically
lively and full of cracks at almost everyone's expense, especially that
of his brother Keith, his letters to Elsie make it clear that his first
Christmas so far from home had left him very homesick. On Boxing
Day he wrote her a 'special little letter', fifteen pages devoted to
telling her how much he loved her. Their letters, in the time since
John had sailed, had left them both unsettled and anxious. Elsie, less
demonstrative of her feelings, must at times have felt overwhelmed
by John's flow of words in letters and verse. He urged her to read

Emerson's 'Give All to Love'; 'if you haven't it at home you can get it in the Oxford Book of English Verse, which is in the V.U.C. Library',[83] but he wrote out one verse anyway. She was also to read '"To Meet, or Otherwise" in Hardy's Collected Poems p 292 . . . It is a Stunner, & as soon as I read it I thought, Well, I agree with that, & not a minute I spent with E. has been wasted.' He wrote of the times they had had together, especially tramping; for her birthday on 15 January he had bought a small manuscript book at Bumpus's into which he copied all the poems he had written to her and a number of others which he believed she liked, and he had posted this early in December. He enthused about the views on love and marriage of Dora Russell (at that time married to Bertrand Russell) and urged Elsie to read her, quoting from her book *Hypatia*:

To live with vigour, body & mind & imagination, without fear or shame or dread of death; to drive these baser passions from the hold they have upon our morality & our politics – this is what we ask of modern men & modern women. They can come to it only in reckless love of one another, a passion that gives again & again without fear of hurt or exhaustion.

John found this 'very noble'. 'I should like to think we loved each other like that, & I think we could – don't you?'[84] What could Elsie have said in reply? He recommended Marie Stopes's *Married Love* and *Wise Wedlock* and sang the praises of Holland, where 'they have proper govt. teaching on birth-control; & consequently they have a much better educated & sensible & truly moral people there than anywhere else'. He was full of ideas on how much a married couple needed to live on; he was anxious that Elsie should visit and get to know his mother. He was clearly missing her dreadfully and wanted above all for some certainty about when she would follow him to England. Elsie did not find it easy to respond. She remained uncertain, conscious of the differences in their backgrounds: were they too great? could she match John's intellectual interests? was he not making new friends with whom he would have much more in common? There was perhaps nothing remarkable in this emotional turmoil for two people in love and twelve thousand miles apart. A return of letters took well over two months. What was remarkable about John and Elsie was the amount they wrote and the importance of the letters in their lives. This, as much as what was said, tells us how much they meant to each other at that time.

It is difficult now to recapture that sense of distance between New Zealand and Britain, and the dependence on letters to bridge the gap. Time and again in his letters both to Elsie and to his parents

John waxes eloquent on the shortcoming of the postal system. After four months in London, he wrote to his parents:

The ultimate mystery to me is the way the NZ mail behaves. Now if you want a fit subject on which to exercise your noble pen in the columns of the Evening Post, here is a chance for you. I don't believe I've got it on the same day in the week more than three or four times since I got here. In the first month or so I gathered that Thursday was the normal day for it to arrive, since when it has come on Monday, Tuesday, Wednesday, Friday & Saturday – once it came on the preceding Tuesday, but on the other occasions from two to five days later. What happens this week? I hadn't had a mail since my last Saturday in [Manchester]; so naturally I looks in the Times on Wednesday expecting to see 'Incoming Mails: Tomorrow: NZ' Nothing. I looks in on Thursday – Nothing. I looks in on Friday. 'Saturday Jan 22. N.Z.' Saturday morning I leap out of bed & tear downstairs to the hall table. Nothing. I get into a tube & blow down to the Bank of N.Z. (a) to draw a cheque (b) to look for mail. Notice up 'NZ mail due on Monday Jan 24'. On these occasions if Duncan happens to be with me he draws his hat down close over his ears & walks hurriedly in the other direction.[85]

In London again after Manchester, he got back to work in the Record Office and the British Museum. Newton was improving in John's estimation; 'an extraordinary range of knowledge, & he puts it across well',[86] though he lacked a sense of humour, 'a bit portentous with all his virtues, & he generally misses the point if you say anything flippant at one of his seminars'.[87] Newton had visited New Zealand and admired Dr Hight, who taught history at Canterbury, but on hearing that John had been taught by F.P. Wilson he gazed at him 'in a quizzical sort of way "I should say that you've had rather a rough row to hoe in your history" he said'.[88]

At the imperial history seminar which Newton ran for research students at the Institute of Historical Research, John was meeting a number of interesting fellow students, most of them 'colonials or yanks'; 'the English high-brow girls I have met give me the pip, & the men on the whole aren't much of an improvement; give me a Boer or an Aussie any day.'[89] The 'Boer' was Cornelis Willem de Kiewiet (de K or Dickie). Born in Holland, he spent his youth in South Africa and graduated from the University of Witwatersrand in Johannesburg in 1923. He then taught for two years in Southern Rhodesia and, when he and John met, he was already well into his thesis on British relations with the South African republics in the 1850s and 1860s. They found they had much in common. 'He has enlightened views on diet, so I gather', John reported to his parents, '& politics & quite a number of things'. 'We seem to talk the heavenly bodies in & out of the sky more nights than not.'[90] The 'yanks' were a 'charming Canadian girl of sense & intelligence', Adelaide MacDonald, who in her passion for Jane Austen rivalled John's mother and, what was more, 'she approves of buying books',[91] and an American, Helen Allen. An English member of the seminar and assistant librarian at the institute, Harry Ross, also made the grade. With Duncan and McGrath (who after a critical survey of schools of architecture had decided to study practical bricklaying and plumbing at the Brixton school of building, and in any time left over to go to a wood engraving class at the Westminster school of art), they formed a congenial and lively circle.

John and Duncan 'decided to have a party', he reported to his parents in March:

so we bought 1¾d worth of milk extra (½ pint) for cocoa & a bob's worth of biscuits & 21 crumpets; & 4 pennorth of chocolates which we ate before the party started. The personnel was my cobbers mostly from the Institute & it was a noble stroke in the cause of amity between nations; they were de Kiewiet (S.Africa) Ross (England) Miss MacDonald (Canada) Miss Allen (U.S.A.) added to which we had Duncan (Australia) & me (N.Z.) We had an uproarious time swapping national jokes; & when the time came for supper you would have been speechless in admiration at the organisation I evolved. The two girls toasted the crumpets & batted in the butter; Ross, being an Englishman & comparatively helpless watched the milk to see it didn't boil over & tried to warm a plate for the crumpets simultaneously, with the result that the milk very nearly did boil over; Duncan & I made my patent brand of cocoa, & de K, being a canny lad & a true colonial got out of the way & down on the biscuits.[92]

The socialising continued. Helen Allen, who lived in the same house as Adelaide, had a piano in her rooms. As always, John was called on to play. Helen, another great writer of verse, shared John's passion for Bach and many of his intellectual interests. The group as a whole became very close, giving one another moral support, reading one another's draft chapters, and later on proofreading theses and sharing the anxiety of all research students: would there be a job at the end of it all?

During the Easter break John and Duncan went to Bristol to a National Union of Students Congress which had the ostensible theme of the Art of Life. They were not impressed:

From the point of view of intellectual stir-up, it was a sheer wash-out . . . D & I, in our poor benighted colonial ignorance, & thinking we'd be up against mighty men if it came to a row, put in all the time we could mugging up Havelock Ellis & the Bertrand Russells . . . But jingo! a milder mannered, more conventional, stick in the mud thoroughly respectable English gathering you never saw. 350 of them there were, of whom perhaps ten had any guts. I must say these ten or so were pretty good in a way; spoke very well, & had cheerful grins, & had travelled a good bit, & could clap at the right time in a speech in French or German, but I didn't hear a single new idea there . . . Certainly I got the impression that the average English student is no more bright nor brainy nor throbbing with modernity & unplumbed depths of agonising thought than the average NZ student; though that is not to be taken as a compliment to the N.Z. student.[93]

The guest speakers were a mixed lot. Bertrand Russell was pretty good but said nothing new, Margaret Bondfield very good, Lady Astor 'a great disappointment . . . a perfectly hopelessly muddled mind'. She 'came down like a ton of bricks' on Duncan when he said his favourite form of leisure was lying in the sun – 'just pandering to the body', in Lady Astor's view. John's greatest obloquy was kept for Sir John Reith: 'if you ever want to get the real dinkum repulsively sanctimonious brand of business-success talk you couldn't apply to a better man than Sir J. Reith.'

There were social events, dances (to which John did not go), folk-dancing, 'fiercely denounced by the modernists' (to which he also did not go), a concert in which he supplied 'the brass, woodwind & percussion on the piano in Beethoven's Prometheus overture' and 'managed to start & finish triumphantly with the rest of the scratch orchestra'. Conference excursions took them to the Cheddar Gorge ('hailing too hard to see anything much'), the caves and Cheddar itself, which he thought 'hopelessly vulgarised, like every other village in this hopeless country by yellow signs & advertisements on all the houses for Pratt's motor spirit & other curses of civilization', and to Wells, Glastonbury and Bath, which made a more favourable impression.

Back in London, John, Duncan and McGrath all bought bicycles, talked of for some time, at Selfridge's: £5 7s 'for a mangle painted green weighing ½ ton, complete with bell, carrier, oil-can, pump, lamp, insurance policy & guarantee for 50 years'.[94] After several trial runs he set off at Easter for the Peak District of Derbyshire with Lorrie Richardson. They were away for eleven days, covering about 375 miles on their bikes and getting in four days' good hard tramping. 'By jingo! It was a good trip, & a great relief to get into the open & look rough again.' They slept out, pitching their tent under hedges or stone walls, selecting, on principle, spots where trespassers were firmly forbidden. John was warming to the English countryside and its villages and to Norman and Early English churches but, he sadly concluded, 'Grouse appear to be the most important thing in England, the peak & apex up to which the whole of western civilisation works'.[95] Returning south they called at Cambridge ('I never saw anything more beautiful than some parts of Cambridge') and met with Jack Yeates, who was leaving to return to New Zealand in June. 'We did our best to convince him that he was committing intellectual suicide, but in vain.' They camped at Grantchester and looked around Rupert Brooke's Old Vicarage. Then back to London, to opera, plays, concerts and work.

John's musical experience was broadening. In January he had been to a production of Wagner's *The Mastersingers* by the British National Opera Company. 'They don't go in for highly-paid stars' but 'it was good enough for me, in my first modest introduction to Wagner'. Then after Easter he went to *Tristan and Isolde* at Covent Garden, 'straight from the P.R.O. [Public Record Office] at ½ past 4 & by queuing up then got quite a good seat for 3/- in the gods. The show started at 7'.[96] He judged it first-rate, some of the greatest stuff he had ever heard. Sigrid Onegin sang Brangane – 'so there is one ambition of my life fulfilled, to hear her in the flesh' – and the other singers were mostly up to her standard. His only regret was that it was the last performance and he cursed himself afterwards for not going two or three times. 'I must get a piano score, I think, & work at it properly.' To mark the centenary of Beethoven's death, the Léner Quartet were playing all his quartets and John got to four of the recitals, 'but the music is so highbrow that it is pretty hard going when you haven't heard any of it before, especially after a series of late nights & a few hundred West Indian despatches'.[97] After a London Symphony Orchestra concert, at which he had a seat behind the orchestra, he reported on Sir Thomas Beecham's conducting:

He is a big cove with a singular assortment of mannerisms; conducts without a single score & in the slow movements without a baton; smiles in a peculiarly pleased way when anything particularly pleases him & purses up his lips & hisses horrifiedly when anything is too loud. He stops conducting altogether sometimes & just lets the orchestra go on . . . Cripes, though! he delivers the goods.[98]

The bikes continued to be put to good use as summer advanced. One Sunday John, Duncan and McGrath rode down into Kent via Greenwich, where McGrath pointed out the fine points of Wren's Greenwich Hospital which later became the Royal Naval College. After tea at Shoreham in a garden 'full of gorgeous tulips

& flowering fruit trees'[99] – but no mention of Samuel Palmer, whom John discovered only some time later – they had a three-hour ride back into London. Two weeks later it was Surrey, and then at Whitsun weekend, at the beginning of June, John and Lorrie Richardson went down to Kent again, taking Harold Holt, who had turned up in London ten days earlier after spending over a year working and travelling in North America. 'Harold hadn't been near a bike for about 10 years, & as we did about 150 miles or more in the two days we nearly killed him.'[100] They visited Canterbury and had a good look over the cathedral. John was struck by the glorious stained glass and magnificent organ, but other comments of his rather shocked his mother with their irreverence. That evening they 'hopped over a fence & camped in some bird's park' a few miles on from Canterbury. The next day they visited Dover ('a rotten place, with a notice on one side of a pier Bathing Males only & one on the other side Bathing Females only; so we spat on it & left') and Folkestone on the way back to London. 'A great trip . . . to celebrate which I had 2d of geyser & a hot bath.' John was discovering Edward Thomas's England of villages and countryside, of a man-made and age-old landscape. 'The country outside London is very beautiful . . . when you get to it; I must say I like the English civilised type of beauty very much, as contrast to the ruggedness of NZ, but the trouble is that London keeps spreading like a cancer'.[101]

The term finished at the end of May. 'Just remember', John wrote to his parents, 'that even now I am the greatest living authority on colonial governors' instructions in the last ¼ of the 18th & the first ½ of the 19th century, even if to be such is of no conceivable use whatever.'[102] On 2 June he left for Holland with Helen Allen and Adelaide MacDonald. They landed in Rotterdam, had a day in The Hague and then, met up with de Kiewiet in Amsterdam. Amsterdam struck John as the most beautiful city he had yet seen, 'full of a quiet dignity, very green & well-mannered & charming'.[103] From there they went to Antwerp and then Brussels. Everywhere the art galleries made a great impression. Early in the year he had enthused about an exhibition of Flemish art at the Royal Academy in London; accompanying it had been a small exhibition at the British Museum of Flemish illuminated manuscripts and miniatures: 'Glorious things', John reported, 'it would be worth a cove's while to take a trip to England purely to see these.'[104] He bought Roger Fry's *Flemish Painting* on its publication. Now in the Mauritshuis in The Hague he found 'some very good Vermeers . . . I have contracted a love for Vermeer, & Rembrandt's Anatomy lesson which is a great thing.'[105] The Rijks Museum in Amsterdam had Rembrandt's *Night Watch*, 'certainly one of the most magnificent things I have ever seen, & four Vermeers, some of the most exquisite, & many other Rembrandts & Lord knows what else beside – a perfect orgy'. In Bruges he was struck by Van Eyck and Memling. 'There's something very satisfying about these primitive birds, in spite of their sameness of subject; but my word, brilliance of painting!' The painters John admired were largely those he already knew from books at home; what excited him was the brilliance of the originals compared with the reproductions he had grown up with. He had yet to discover painters who were new to him, and especially those working at that time.

The group was proving very congenial. 'My travelling companions are very bright,' John reported to Elsie, 'though Dicky bores me occasionally with accounts of his soul & his views on women.'[106] He thoroughly approved of Helen's 'low-bred sense of humour highly shocking in an otherwise cultivated American lady'.

At Antwerp they had a programme of pictures and museums mapped out but, getting to the Plantin-Moretus Museum ('a wonderful place') first of all, they ended up by staying all day. It was the establishment of the sixteenth-century printer Plantin, which had continued as a family business until the end of the nineteenth century, when it was sold to the government for a museum and then restored and kept as it had been in the sixteenth and seventeenth centuries.

It is a big square, with a courtyard in the middle, two stories & three at one end; living-rooms, offices, warehouse, proof-readers' rooms, type-setting & printing rooms, the place where he cast all his own type, kitchen, library & so on. I was never in a more fascinating place in my life. One big room is kept as a small museum of printing, with the Gutenberg bible as the star item, & lots of other first-rate things. I'm beginning to believe that the first printers did the best printing. All the type-faces are on show, blocks, copper-plates, bundles of proofs, half-corrected, accounts etc, just as if the place had been cleaned up for Sunday & the family were out for the day. Marvellous place . . . very hard . . . to drag oneself away from.[107]

John's fascination with and enthusiasm for printing were a foretaste of things to come.

After Brussels (wonderful patisseries noted, and the Palais de Justice, 'the most atrocious erection on earth next to the Albert Memorial') they stayed one night in Cologne and spent all the time they had there in and around the cathedral. 'It's something to have

lived to have seen this Cathedral.'[108] For once John was at a loss
for words: 'it's simply no use trying to describe it. It's the sort of
thing you dream about . . . I'll merely remark that to visit Cologne
Cathedral is an emotional experience of the first magnitude & leave
it at that.' He was to see the cathedral next in 1955, bombed and
largely destroyed, a wrenching reminder of its breathtaking past.
They left Cologne for Coblenz with many regrets, spent a day on a
paddle steamer travelling up the Rhine to Mainz, and then caught
a train to Heidelberg. There, in a bookshop, John and de Kiewiet
discovered a great series of facsimile reproductions of etchings and
woodcuts. 'Rembrandt & Dürer & all the rest of them; absolutely
stunner reproductions, & dirt cheap . . . We got a good many
between us, but when we get to Munich we are going to have a
regular orgy.'

After a perfect day in Heidelberg, they found their way to
Neustadt, a small town in the Black Forest, 'one of the luckiest
chances of the whole trip'. The pubs were full but with the help of
'numerous bright children who tore all over the place with great
excitement & zeal'[109] they were able to get two rooms in two private
houses 'among the most charming people imaginable'. John was
totally won by the place. 'I have never seen a more pleasant, good-
natured, smiling country, & the people fit it.'[110] They spent three
nights there and left most reluctantly. 'Our two old ladies coyly
presented us with button holes of carnations & many smiles; & we
shook hands most feelingly & said Aufwiedersehen with the utmost
emotion. They were dear people & gave us bed & breakfast for
about 2/6 a time. We were slaughtering their sons & grandsons a
little while ago.' John's father was moved by the last comment to
observe: 'were they not, or their people, slaughtering *our* sons and
grandsons also a little while ago?'[111]

Then Zurich, and on to Innsbruck, which was

surrounded by the most magnificent hills on all sides; & the streets are
full of shorts & hob-nailed boots & the shops of boots & shoes & swags
& rope & ice-axes & other desirable things . . . Other things that are
cheap here are beer & liqueurs – Chartreuse 10d a bottle. But as you
are not the experts in these things that I am I shall draw a judicious &
tactful veil. I wish I could do a bit of climbing round here, but alas! &
alas! We are leaving tomorrow night for Vienna, which I am told is the
finest city in the world.[112]

Vienna disappointed – 'since the war the life has gone out of the
place'[113] – with the exception of the bookshops and the coffee topped
with whipped cream – 'perfectly marvellous, nay peerless stuff'.[114]

They visited Schönbrunn, the summer palace of the Habsburgs, 'interesting historically & for its park . . . but for sheer brutal vulgarity you never saw anything like its interior decorations'.[115] John bought a new pair of spectacles, the best Zeiss glass, for 9/-. They had horn rims in contrast to the steel rims he had worn until then. The rest of the party thought them 'very classy'. They moved on to Munich, where they spent a week and wished it was a month. Accommodation was cheap but it was made an expensive week by the price of food (3s or 3s 6d for a meal) and the opera. Beer, on the other hand, was cheap: 'you could get enough beer to drown in for a few pfennigs – gone are the days when under the influence of my Primitive Methodist aunts & other relatives I engaged with ardour in prohibition campaigns' – this was John writing to Elsie.[116] A festival of Wagner and Mozart was on. Adelaide shouted the party to *Parsifal* (magnificently done) to celebrate having got a job at Toronto University. They shouted themselves to *Tristan*, and two each went to the *Marriage of Figaro* and to the *Magic Flute*; John found the *Magic Flute* disappointing, saved in his view only by 'the overture and about three good songs'. He bought the scores of *Tristan* and *Parsifal* and *The Mastersingers*. There were more museums, more galleries. 'You can see', John wrote, 'that I am absorbing art like a sponge.' But a critical note entered:

What gets me down about the picture galleries in Europe is the vast wall-spaces they devote to Rubens. Wherever you go you find acres & acres of canvas & miles on miles of rooms devoted to his perfectly maddening facility. The man didn't paint, he spawned monsters . . . It's about time some public-spirited curator rolled up his sleeves & had a bonfire. Munich would be an admirable place to start.[117]

He left Germany enormously impressed with the country and the people. 'Of course we didn't meet any Prussians, but everybody I know who has been to Germany has the same tale to tell & the same admiration for them.'[118]

The party broke up in Paris. John stayed for a fortnight with Harry Espiner, his old Victoria College friend, who had been there for five years and was a year off finishing his French doctorate. Boyd-Wilson had offered him a job back at Victoria, but his own view, shared by John, was that he would be a fool to go back. 'The only reason any NZer I have met over here, bar Yeates & Holt, wants to go back', John wrote, 'is to see his people, & even Holt is succumbing to the attractions of civilization.'[119] They went to Rouen for three days, which they found very picturesque and full of memories of Joan of Arc, who was imprisoned and burned there.

'The oldest houses go back to about the 15th century. Not very sanitary of course, but that doesn't matter a curse to the French, sanitation being a subject to which they do not seem to have turned the national attention with any great ardour as yet.'[120] There was a fine cathedral, and some magnificent glass – '& let me tell you I have got the stained-glass bug pretty badly'.

Back in Paris, he visited the Louvre for the fourth time and discovered that he had still seen only about an eighth of it. Whistler's portrait of his mother, in John's view, 'bears comparison with anything in the whole place', Holbein's portrait of Erasmus was 'first-rate', he found more of his favourite Flemish primitives and a good Vermeer, but what thrilled him most was the *Winged Victory*. He bought some more books – though at 125 francs or just over a pound he decided *Ulysses* was too expensive – and had to borrow a suitcase from Espiner to get them back to London, together with a quarter-litre of Curaçao for Adelaide's farewell party and a little bust of Voltaire, for five francs, 'to which I pray every night'. The fares for the trip had cost just over £13.

In London, he returned to Canadian constitutional history and Earl Grey's defence of the colonial policy of Lord John Russell's administration; to the Proms, 'going steadily along with great success & biting criticism from Ernest Newman';[121] to more theatre and to enjoying life with his friends. One Saturday John visited the Wallace Collection with Helen Allen, after which she, Harold Holt, Lorrie and de Kiewiet met at Brunswick Square for tea. After a lengthy meal they adjourned to Helen's flat, where John 'performed on the piano with great vim' and they 'swapped travel yarns & sociological & political discussion & jokes & other lies'. Thrown out of there ('no noise after 10'), they returned to Brunswick Square for a 'discussion on typewriters with practical demonstrations by de K', who was in the process of typing his thesis. The next day John and Lorrie got out their bikes and 'blew down into Surrey for the day'. Two weeks before this, John and Duncan had ridden to St Albans to see the abbey. Harold left to return to New Zealand, 'cursing his fate & his lack of money'. His views had changed remarkably in the three or four months he had had in Britain.

Others were arriving, among them Bill Joliffe, on his way to Edinburgh University, and Dick Campbell, who enrolled at the LSE and found himself a room next to the House of Lords 'so as to be on the spot in moments of crisis'. He reported that the New Zealand Labour Party's great grievance was that Coates (for whom he had worked as private secretary) was 'taking away all their grievances, somewhat to the alarm of Coates' own party'.[122] Campbell was quickly absorbed into John's circle of friends, and they began their 'Winter Salon season' with a party which sparked more than any party John had ever known.

Present Miss Allen, Messrs Campbell, de Kiewiet, Duncan, Espiner [over from Paris], Ross, me. Refreshments, one large & thrilling cake provided by Mrs D.E. & Miss Beaglehole & sent over per R.M.C., wiv tuppences in it (including one Australian, therefore no good for English circulation & only good for charity); my celebrated cocoa, cider, Curaçao. Discussion: the late war, the peace, Lloyd George, dairy control, America, Dick Seddon, Bobby Stout, the weather, Pres. Wilson, presidential prospects in the U.S., foreign policy of Ramsay MacDonald, Raglan election, ducal tours, Billy Hughes, family endowment, S. African flag, Ph.Ds, the School, the Institute, distinguished profs, relative merits of lecturers, & other subjects. They are a bright lot. But these clear headed economists like Duncan & Campbell put the wind up me when they get going properly; they know everything, & they always argue straight to the point, & they have memories like magnets & they talk brilliantly. However I as host only had to sit back & cut the cake & make the cocoa & say What's yours? in an ingratiating tone.[123]

Campbell was making his mark with the New Zealand High Commissioner. 'As Jimmy Parr said to Campbell, on his return from Geneva as official NZ delegate in the cause of peace & international understanding "You know, I don't trust any of these foreigners".'[124]

The news of the composition of the party for the European tour had been received by John's parents with a certain disquiet. With his mother, at least, he had been fairly open about his feelings for Elsie, and Elsie had visited her a number of times since John's departure. Where, they wished to know, did things now stand? The reply, in John's third letter after getting back to London, was characteristic, if hardly straightforward:

Daddy wants a respectful answer to some very delicate queries as to my degree of intimacy with various ladies. Well now this subject is indeed such an intimate one that I don't know whether I am justified in answering it at all, in however respectful a manner, let alone in a letter that I suppose will be food for general consumption. I make no remark on the highly indelicate nature of the inquiry. That a father should endeavour so to tyrannise over the Soul of his son is indeed a dreadful warning of the fact that the 19th century is still with us. Turn but a stone, & start a swing. I might refer him to the Way of all Flesh & ask pertinently, does he wish to see me (a) in prison (b) running a 2nd hand clothing shop, with a wife secretly on the drink? I might ask, why should I, a man of London, Viennese, & Parisian experience, let alone Wellingtonian, be subject to the ordinary shackles of life, let alone leading questions from his parents. I might say, Is this right, is it just, is it generous? I might demand, how would you like it if your son turned round & said, What did that lady call you when you trod on her toes the umpteenth time at the Savage Club Ladies Night After Entertainment Dance? I might demur, Well, this is the sort of intimate attack on my morals I am accustomed to get from Fronnie but to think that a Father should ever treat me thus! I might plead the hot blood of youth & let it go at that, proudly & contemptuously. I might say in the sacred words of J.E. Flecker 'I am Don Juan curst from age to age, By priestly tract & sentimental stage' etc. I might lose my temper & exclaim Well upon my heart & soul this is too much! But I do none of these things. I answer as respectfully as possible, with dignity, with a certain cold reserve possibly, but as one who knows his place & how to address a Father. Let me say therefore that Yes, I am on fairly familiar terms with all my friends, including the lady ones; that the girls I have left behind me are neither forgotten nor discarded, but temporarily in abeyance; that it is off with no old loves, or alternatively, however off with old loves it may be it is on with no new ones, though possibly a more elastic definition of 'loves' might bring a different answer. To the remark on the disregarding of the usual conventions I answer What conventions? And further ask for a definition of the words 'disregard' & 'usual'. And for all further information on my philosophy of social-relationships I refer you to the broadminded tolerance & wide understanding of Auntie.[125]

Not letting it go at that, John added that he had invited Helen Allen to go with him on a visit to his Uncle George and family: 'she pointed out that on the whole it might be unwise to cause a scandal either in Trimley St. Mary or NZ, to the force of which reasoning I was of course bound to agree. But you will see that I am quite unscrupulous in intention, even if practical considerations do hold me back.' The letter concluded, 'With love from your very respectful son'. The enquiry was not repeated.

De Kiewiet finished his thesis in October. John rallied round in the last stages. 'I went up to his place one afternoon at 5 p.m. & left at ¼ to 4 next morning – we both worked straight through, he typing & I proof-reading & correcting, with 5 minutes off now & again for teas & 1.30 toast, & an occasional doubtful story.'[126] His own work was progressing well and he expected to finish at the Record Office in December and to start writing in the Christmas vacation. All his 'bright particular historical cobbers' would have left by the end of the following summer and he was thinking of trying to get his own thesis written by June; 'even if I don't put it in then, I shall have it off my mind, except for revising, & have the summer free'. Besides, he wanted to finish reading Jane Austen.[127] He had 'at last' made a start with *Pride and Prejudice* when staying with the Butlers at Trimley in September, 'after which I may say that I feel for Jane Austen almost the reverence I feel for Conrad'.[128] He told Elsie what a pleasant surprise the news would be for his mother: 'you must know that to Mrs D.E. Beaglehole Miss Austen is practically Bible, guide-book & tram ticket in one. If she was lost on a desert island she'd say give me Jane Austen & a bag of wholemeal flour & I'll be content.'

He decided that Newton was becoming quite polite to him, and

... it almost looks as if when de K goes I shall take his place as the white-headed boy. I won't mind if I can dig another schol out of it. There is stacks of work to do if only you can get the chance of doing it. I could put in about 20 years very nicely doing a history of British colonial policy since 1783; & it's easy work compared to poetry.[129]

What's more, he wrote, 'though this may be unpardonable conceit, I think I can write a darn sight better than any colonial historian I have come across over here.'[130] He had read J.S. Marais's *The Colonisation of New Zealand*, just published by the Oxford University Press, as well as A.J. Harrop's *England and New Zealand* (Methuen, 1926), and was clearly irritated. Marais had written the book that he had meant to write and, he clearly believed, 'if Messrs Harrop & Marais had got out of the way, the job would have been done a lot better'.[131]

Dick Campbell lent John a copy of the *New Zealand Parliamentary Debates* with the report of the debate on the second reading of the War Disabilities Removal Bill, which would bring to an end the civil penalties still placed on conscientious objectors after the war. John was horrified at the narrow-minded intolerance of many of the speakers opposing the Bill, especially that of the Hon. G.J. Garland, an Auckland member of the Legislative Council since 1918, who had argued that Germany remained hostile to the rest of Europe and only her circumstances prevented further aggression. With memories of his time in Germany still fresh, John wrote a 2000-word letter to the editor of the *Evening Post*. It showed his growing skills as a writer. He began with the politicians: 'On the question of the immediate or remote causes of the war it would ill become a mere historian to argue with a Legislative Councillor. And on the psychology of present-day Germany a Dominion politician is doubtless the repository of ultimate wisdom.' He continued with an almost lyrical description of the visit to Neustadt, the village seemingly growing out of the land with its surrounding hills and its cheerfully companionable people, the two charming old ladies who provided his party with rooms and were so desolated to see them leave.

Come back, they said, and we will teach you the Schwarzwald accent! There is nothing, we said that we want to do in this world so much as to come back to Neustadt! Auf wiedersehen! said our charming old ladies. Auf wiedersehen! said we, wringing their hands, and set off down the hill to the station. Neither they nor the thousands of other hardworking, modest, friendly people we met in Germany, in trains, on the streets, in parks, in galleries, in third and fourth class railway carriages, seemed to nourish any insatiate desire to fly at our quite defenceless throats.

John wrote of the German students he had met in London, 'clearheaded, unaffected, passionately interested in a more adequately organised world', before ending, rather bitterly, with a comment on the lack of understanding and imagination, of generosity, on the part of his fellow-countrymen revealed in the debate, 'which to any travelled New Zealander who has observed with candour, who has thought sincerely and dispassionately, makes any country rather than New Zealand his spiritual home'.

McGrath thought it was the best thing John had written, de Kiewiet typed it out for him and, somewhat to his surprise, the *Post* published it.[132] It was reprinted in the *New Zealand Worker*[133] and later in *Spike*.[134] John's parents reported favourable comments. Hunter thought it a 'very fine effort'; Peter Fraser, member of parliament for Wellington Central, wrote to express his appreciation;[135] and years later Eric McCormick remembered how he had read it in *Spike* and first became aware of John as a writer.[136]

John's view of New Zealand was not improved when he visited the New Zealand High Commission:

The place is full of what I will not, for politeness sake, call lying circulars, but may perhaps describe as publications projecting a rose-tinted view of life in the Britain of the South for the emigrant & retired army-officer. 'Yes', says one of the lady staff in my hearing to an anxious enquirer, 'You'll find that every town has a first-class girls' school absolutely first-class.' At which I said to myself, My oath! & left.[137]

With November, winter was closing in. 'The weather varies from bad to worse with occasional incursions into worst . . . the water in the morning pretty well gives you rigor mortis in your bath.' John and Duncan learned that they were known in the house as 'those cranky boys who have cold baths in the morning & whistle like parrots all day'.[138] The concert season began again. There were more free recitals at St Martin's. The Léner Quartet gave a series of six historical chamber music concerts for which John paid nineteen shillings for a season ticket; he once again went to Bach's B Minor Mass, this time performed by the St Michael's Singers. He heard Gustav Holst conducting the Royal Choral Society in his *Hymn of Jesus*, which John thought great stuff, and Pablo Casals play a Haydn concerto – 'he is the goods'. The London String Quartet played two of Beethoven's last quartets, which John confessed he hadn't 'got hold of yet'. The London String Quartet was a complete contrast to the Léner and pleasing for a change, 'masculine where the Léner is feminine, vigorous where the Léner is languishing'.[139] He went out to Golders Green with Helen Allen to hear *La Bohème*, and *The Mastersingers* once again, put on by the British National Opera Company. Just before Christmas he took Duncan and McGrath along to the *Messiah* 'to pump some culture into them . . . Beecham, London Symphony Orchestra, two choirs combined . . . Beecham really transforms the thing'.[140] At the theatre he saw an Old Vic production of *The Taming of the Shrew* with Sybil Thorndike and Lewis Casson, 'not a pleasant play but very well done', and also Strindberg's *The Father* which he found terrific, 'exceedingly gloomy but exceedingly good. Like other fathers.'[141] Edith Evans in *The Way of the World* proved a great actress, the play a first-rate thing.[142]

The prospect of Christmas led to a laborious morning in Bumpus's choosing books for the family. Aunts were sent Christmas cards done by Berrie Butler. John also had the idea of having his own card printed, using one of his poems and a woodcut by McGrath. The printing was done by the Cambridge University Press, McGrath now being at Clare College and 'having them well under his influence'.[143] He and John combed London to get paper they approved of, finally settling on 'a sort of Austrian semi hand made' they found at Selfridges. This cost '15/- for 100 sheets & envelopes to match. The printing only cost 8/-, so . . . I got 100 perfectly good Xmas cards for 2¾d each.'[144] John chose a poem written at Innsbruck a few months earlier, the two last stanzas being:

The hills, the hills again! I come
From peaks that cut a southern sky –
How shall I see these wind-stripped rocks
And feel no stir, nor make one cry?

They stand, they lift the heart, they stand;
There is no tide of change that kills
The passionate companionship
Of the aloof, unheeding hills!

John had worked with printers in the days of editing *Spike*, but the collaboration with McGrath marked a further step in the development of his interest in what was to become a lifelong fascination with printing and typography. His parents were delighted: 'the finest thing of the kind I have seen', his father wrote.[145]

Newton pushed his students into having a seminar dinner. Arranged largely by Helen Allen and John it was a flash affair, costing four shillings each, held in a little place off Soho Square where they went right through from hors d'oeuvres via roast chicken to coffee. John played the piano. It left him with mixed feelings. Four shillings 'would cover 4 days' lunches at the Food Reform joint. I generally get a meal there for 11d these days & spend what I save at Bertorellis on the evening meal. The soup there is the best I've tasted since I left home.'[146] Another four shillings went on Christmas dinner. He had decided to stay in London and get on with his writing, turning down an invitation to the Butlers. He and a group of young men went out to a pub McGrath was very keen on, for its architecture and situation, the Bedford Arms at Chorley Wood. Henning, whom John had not seen since they arrived in London, came over from Paris for the occasion and, as well as McGrath and Duncan, there were a friend of Henning's from Paris and three 'architectural cobbers' of McGrath's. The conviviality was such that John thought it wise largely to draw a veil over it in his letter home, 'or at least give a genteel version', while the success of the occasion led the group to gather again (at 21 Brunswick Square) to celebrate New Year's Day, to hire a harmonium for the week (a shock to John when it was delivered up the stairs), and to produce a typed programme, 'a somewhat esoteric document', which he sent home. On Christmas Day he also fitted in a 'flash Christmas supper' with Helen Allen, de Kiewiet and a Canadian student, and that completed his 'tale of debauchery – not half so long continued, solid, or wearing' as the previous year.[147] Rather, he was able to do a fair amount of work.

Helped by Christmas money from home, he bought a new overcoat (his lady friends were making pointed comments about the one he had brought with him from Wellington) and also A.V. Dicey's *The Law of the Constitution* and *Law and Opinion in England* that he had long been wanting. He went to *The Way of the World* again, with McGrath and Henning: 'I could sit & listen to Edith Evans in the second act all night'. What was more, he was able to report to his mother that he had finished *Emma* and started on *Sense and Sensibility*.

5

LONDON, 1928–29

JOBS, A GREAT PREOCCUPATION of research students, come into John's letters almost from the time of his arrival in London. On first meeting with de Kiewiet, they talked about prospects in South Africa: 'Capetown University wouldn't be a bad place for a job . . . they have a good library & a good staff there; & a good orchestra in the town, & according to de K have a good deal of intellectual stir & a pretty vigorous native culture; while the lucky blighters are only 17 days from England.'[1] He talked with Newton:

He reckoned that 2ndary school teaching in England wasn't a bad business, & gave you time for research; but I am not to [sic] keen on kid-whacking. Also that the Colonial Education Service was a good thing; it would probably be in Africa somewhere, looking after the education of little niggers – organising, not teaching, except native teachers. Rise to about £1200, retiring at end of 20 yrs on £600 yr. And of course a cove would have the opportunity of getting well browned up & wearing dinky white clothes & a sun helmet, or shorts; but somehow I don't think it's my line. He told me to write to Hight & see if he can tell me anything about N.Z. prospects . . . Of course, once in N.Z. you're dead so far as history is concerned. On most other things except books & tramping, as far as that goes.[2]

John was not alone in his view of New Zealand. A letter from Professor Hunter gave a very gloomy view of the University of New Zealand – 'In this country we might be ready for a university in 2000 A.D.' – and went on to say that the 'object of the Travelling Scholarships was to make a New Zealander . . . realise that there were other people on the globe. If they are forced by economic circumstances to come back to N.Z. that is bad luck; if they come back by choice it is a clear indication that the scholarship was wrongly awarded. The atmosphere here is stifling.'[3]

The question was hopelessly tangled for John, not only by his relationship with Elsie, his worry about his mother's health and his feelings about New Zealand, but also by his growing confidence in what he could achieve, given the opportunity. To be praised by a group of friends and by Harold Laski, people whom he admired and respected, was for him a largely new experience.

In April 1927 Elsie wrote that she and Averil Lysaght had decided to come to England in twelve months' time and planned to stay for six months. John replied enthusiastically. The news made him feel 'ever so much happier', and they should, he thought, get married straight away and have a honeymoon in Cornwall.[4] A letter or two later there was another plan: 'I really think a week or so of summer on the Thames would be a very fine honeymoon for us, even if we are not able to get married.'[5] His letters to Elsie in the following months were more settled and much happier than they had been through his first 'awful, endless' winter. There were still crises but he largely took them in his stride. Averil Lysaght changed her mind about making the trip. However, a friend of Elsie's, Kathleen McKay, another banker's daughter, took Averil's place. John had never met her and wondered whether she would approve of him. Any uncertainty produced a fever of apprehension. 'I think I must still be in love with you from the terrific ferment your news threw me into', he wrote to Elsie about the changes of plan;[6] and he worried that being so dependent on letters they were getting a bit out of touch with each other. 'It will be a terrific relief when you get here, & we can see how things really do stand . . . I wish to blazes you were going to arrive tomorrow. There are too many complications in this life & apparently it is no use trying to work them out by letter.'[7] In November came the news that Kathleen had pulled out. Elsie was in doubt as to whether she should still make the trip. Her parents would be far from happy if she travelled alone. John cabled at once urging her still to come. Elsie cabled back to say that she would stick to her plan to arrive at the beginning of June and, subsequently, Kathleen was able to come after all.

While John was in Paris staying with Harry Espiner in August they had talked about the future. John wrote to Elsie at that time:

I am going to look into the possibility of going to the States for a year . . . I am getting more & more reluctant to go back to N.Z. permanently, as every other person I know here hates the idea of going back to exile in their native countries. I am seriously thinking of trying for a job in Canada, or in the States for a while; the only thing is that I hate leaving my Mother for good & dragging you away from your people. But going back to N.Z. as an assistant [lecturer] with no prospect of anything else seems the last thing on earth . . . what's the point of going back to N.Z. & committing intellectual suicide.[8]

In his letter to Elsie after her cabled confirmation that she was coming, he wrote five pages once again reviewing the job situation.

I am coming to the conclusion that what I am cut out for is a writer & a teacher. I can teach history, of a sort, in N.Z. if I have a job in a university, though not as it ought to be taught, crippled as they are at V.U.C. both by the shocking lack of books & the shocking presence of F.P. But I am primarily cut out for a writer; & I want if possible to write on history. Well what can I possibly do in that way in N.Z. . . . If I go back to N.Z. permanently I shall never write a line worth a damn . . . [9]

And then, inescapably, he is drawn back to his mother. 'I am worried in a ghastly way about her sometimes. If she were well & strong I could propose staying away 10 years with a light heart.' He compared himself with de Kiewiet: 'Dicky is all right, as he has had the good fortune never to be on good terms with his parents; but whatever I do I'm afraid I am going to be thoroughly miserable.'[10] And his mother was far from well. From July 1927 very high blood pressure forced her to spend most of her time in bed and there were times when she could not write. John's cousin Joan, who had just finished her nursing training, came in to look after her. His father enclosed an extra note with his letter of 4 December (his parents always read each other's letters so they would not repeat the news) to say that his mother's condition was causing much anxiety and that Dr Bennett thought John should be told. A fortnight later, another special note reported that his mother was very much better. After Christmas she was able to be wheeled out into the garden on fine days. At New Year the doctor said it was possible she could go on satisfactorily for years. 'As things are now', John's father wrote, 'there is no reason for your turning anything down.'[11]

Before John received his father's first note, things had come to a head when, through Newton, he was offered a lectureship for two years at Rhodes University, Grahamstown, in South Africa. He was attracted by it; he had heard it was the best university in South Africa after Capetown and thought he 'might be able to hop into F.P.'s job after it'.[12] The catch was that it began in July. He would have a 'hell of a rush' to finish his thesis and Elsie was now due to arrive just when he would have to leave. Newton urged him to accept. Laski was away and could not be consulted. Duncan told him to accept. Helen and McGrath thought it was 'worth a gamble' to stay in London. De Kiewiet 'didn't know what to say'. John turned it down, mainly, it would seem, because of Elsie.* His parents were concerned that it was on their account and wrote to say that he must do whatever was best for his career, as long as he kept up his letters to them. The decision having already been made, the news of his mother's improvement cheered him. Then, as though that good news drew his thoughts back to New Zealand, he wrote to Elsie:

I understand you wondering about the hills & the sea & living in a place like London. I have been pretty homesick myself lately for the hills & the harbour; you know for some things I desperately want to go back to N.Z., although in other ways the thought gets on my nerves . . . however I slang N.Z., I do love it too, & love it desperately . . . If only it wasn't so far away from everything.[13]

Meanwhile his thesis was progressing. In January he typed out the third draft of his introduction, sent a copy of it to his parents, and reported that he had almost finished writing his first chapter.[14] Laski read the introduction and was enthusiastic:

No sooner do I put my head in the door than he shouts 'Beaglehole, that's a simply *corking* piece of work!' And that was only a beginning! And then he says Have you seen the new edition of Keith? (i.e. Responsible Govt in the Dominions, standard work, 3 vols, new edition 2 vols, very expensive) Yes, I says. Have you got it? Have you got the old edition? (No, No) 'Well, how would you like my old edition? – I've just got the new one' Little Johnnie goggles as if he'd been offered the keys of heaven, but at last manages to make strangled sounds of gratification. Would Laski put his name in it? Yes, give me your pen. – 'J.C.B. Amico Amicus H.J.L. 6.2.28' Well! what do you think of that from the greatest man in the world? . . . Fair dinkum, that was about the brightest spot of my stay in London so far.[15]

This letter to Elsie was written the same day: John was bubbling with excitement, and for once his punctuation, generally meticulous, was out of control.

There were more concerts to go to, although, as he pointed out, 'if you go to concerts it means the ruination of work; if you don't, you may never get the chance again'.[16] He was not deterred. He went to a harpsichord recital by Mrs Gordon Woodhouse and decided he

---

*   Thirty years later when I, in the early stages of my PhD research at Cambridge, was offered a short-term job at Liverpool University John's advice was to turn it down and to 'work like hell on the thesis'. 'I know the difficulties of making a decision', he wrote to me, 'I was offered a job for 2 or 3 years myself in S. Africa when I was doing my thesis, but I think I did the right thing in turning it down.' (JCB to THB, 30 May 1958.)

must get a harpsichord; to the Vienna String Quartet, who played a Schönberg quartet, new to John, which he found 'very good in parts';[17] to a concert of choral music at Southwark Cathedral; to a performance of César Franck's *The Beatitudes* by the London Choral Society, 'a pretty feeble thing to start with, & very feebly done'. Taking a break from Jane Austen, he had bought 'Chatto & Windus' complete Rabelais for 6/- as a makeweight against any undue refining influence' Jane might have on him,[18] and was immersed in *The Education of Henry Adams* (given him by Helen). Thomas Hardy died and John went with Helen to the funeral service at Westminster Abbey:

> by a great stroke of luck [we] got in to the Poets' corner . . . among the nobs. It was a quite simple but very impressive affair, & any cove ought to be glad to die to have such pall-bearers.* A fine looking bloke is Galsworthy, likewise Ramsay MacDonald; Baldwin short & ugly – perhaps I should say excessively homely; Low gets him well in the Evening Standard. But Shaw looks as impressive as anybody I've seen. Barrie a wee little cove . . . The Abbey was full & the choir & organ first-rate; one of my favourite Bach preludes on the organ but played too fast. I stood, of all places to stand at the burial of Hardy, under the bust of Longfellow.[19]

John sent his father cuttings from the papers and a copy of the printed funeral service, 'not over-well printed'. A little later Asquith died: 'This makes three good deaths recently – Hardy, Haig & Asquith. Duncan wants to see a great philosopher go now, after these three, & says plaintively, Why not Hobhouse? But I say firmly, No, my boy, let's get rid of the politicians while the going's good. I'm voting for Balfour.'[20]

The 'Institute gang', John reported, had been having a fair amount of fun. They had a birthday party for two of them, 'a considerable rough-house at times' and he 'nearly broke the piano'. For a change from Bertorelli's, where they generally fed, they tried a Chinese restaurant and 'had a wonderful blow-out for two bob apiece'. In early March the crocuses and daffodils were out in the squares and John vowed he must get through *Mansfield Park* and 'settle Jane before the spring is properly with us'.[21] His next letter reported that he had got to the end of volume two: 'I must say she does pick on appalling people to write about; & the tragedy of the business is that you can't stop reading about them'.[22]

---

*   The pall-bearers were Gosse, Galsworthy, Shaw, Barrie, Kipling, Housman, Baldwin, MacDonald and a representative each from Oxford and Cambridge.

John had planned a week in Cambridge but, when McGrath put it off until the next term, Helen suggested that he should go with her to the Cotswolds for a week. They took their research notes, found rooms in houses at the opposite ends of the village of Painswick, worked at their theses in the mornings, met for meals, and walked and explored in the afternoons, even when it snowed. They visited Gloucester to see the cathedral and discovered a second-hand shop with the 'biggest mess' of books John had seen in his life. Helen found a first edition of Tennyson's *In Memoriam* inscribed by the author, which she bought for 1s 6d. John was deeply frustrated by finding odd volumes of various works he coveted but not a single thing complete. The day before returning to London they went to Tewkesbury to see the abbey, which confirmed John's predilection for Norman architecture. They each bought brass candlesticks and John lamented that brass and pewter were becoming fashionable. From Painswick he wrote a long and enthusiastic letter to Elsie (she would receive it at one of the Australian ports on her way to England): the village was beautiful, it was in a beautiful part of the country, he was with a particularly charming girl, but what he really wanted, he wrote, was for Elsie to be toasting her toes at the fire next to where he was writing.[23] With this letter he enclosed his poem 'In the Cotswolds', which begins

> Yes it is beautiful, this old, old land:
> These houses root their being in the earth . . .

but goes on to conclude

> A wind strikes – and my opened eyes are blind
> With gazing on an unseen distant place;
> My deaf ears hear Orongo-rongo's stones –
> Bloom bursts on wind-swept hills within my mind.

John's father was appalled that he and a 'young lady should go off together into the country like that . . . Are all the conventions of age-long respectability being broken down . . . My dear boy, you should be careful!'[24] By the time John read this, Elsie was in England and, for once, he largely let the comment pass.

The postponed trip to Cambridge took place at the end of April. John had intended to work at the branch Record Office and to write some more of his thesis, but for four days out of the six the weather was wonderful, Cambridge at the height of spring was irresistible, and he did not do a stroke of work. After looking at 'Lord knows how many colleges', all that remained in his mind was a 'confused

vision of quadrangles & courts, fellows' gardens, huge lawns, grey
stone, bricks, punts, & the ceiling of King's College Chapel'.[25] Clare
College, where McGrath was now a research student, John judged
to have the most perfect and harmonious buildings of any, as well
as 'fine gates & a wonderful avenue & one of the best bridges in the
place'. The Cambridge trees were marvellous, they turned 'a flat fen
into a paradise'.[26] His mind went back to Wellington:

If I were a millionaire I should certainly buy up all that is left of the Hutt
Valley, & build a residential university there, in small colleges on the
quadrangle system. But it would be co-educational, with men & women
in the same buildings; & heads of colleges indiscriminately male or
female, & there wouldn't be any proctors, & very few rules; so the place
would probably be put down by the government, & the boys & girls
returned to Dick Seddon's atrocity at Salamanca.[27]

McGrath had fallen on his feet at Clare. He had already designed
a letterhead for the college stationery with a woodcut of the college
coat of arms, and had just agreed to do some typographical ornaments
for the university press. His illustrated diary of his summer trip to
Spain was to be published in the *Architectural Review*,[28] and he was
helping edit the Clare College magazine ('the best got-up thing of the
kind' that John had ever seen), for which he both wrote and made
woodcuts. 'I wish', John wrote, 'I only had half his capacity', but
noted that McGrath had yet to make a start on his thesis. McGrath
published poems by both John and Ian Henning in the magazine.
John's, 'Molecular Theory', was also published (with a woodcut by
McGrath) in another Cambridge magazine, the *Venture*, edited by
the young art historian Anthony Blunt, later to achieve notoriety as
one of the 'Cambridge spies'.

Noiseless, unnursed, the country rose
Is born, and quietly it goes:
The unheard bright anemone
Blooms for the eye alone to see.

Never a sigh, never a groan
Utters this unmarked casual stone,
There breaks no breath from this dull wood
To hear, I know, nor ever should.

Yet do I know that stone, wood, flower
Travail and sicken every hour –
Deep, deep about the hidden core
A thousand systems meet at war.

A thousand suns are brought to birth
And shattered in the very earth
Beneath my feet; without a sound
Pulses the long-tormented ground.

And yet, I think, could I but hear
Once, suddenly, with quickened ear,
Might I not start, as saw my eye
A petal fall, to catch a cry?

John used the poem and woodcut for his Christmas card for 1928.

'McGrath's Laski' (John's words) was Mansfield Forbes, a Fellow of Clare and one of the creators, along with Arthur Quiller-Couch and I.A. Richards (recruited by Forbes), of the new English tripos which, for the first time enabled Cambridge students to do a whole degree in English. Forbes himself had graduated in history; his academic interests were idiosyncratic, his lectures exciting, quirky and unpredictable.

One of his most influential courses was on romanticism, defined very widely, from William Blake to Joseph Conrad. His lectures were liable to turn into seminars, or Forbes would not turn up for two or three weeks, after which he materialized to talk enchantingly about a poem, following its ramifications into music, painting and especially architecture, his first love. Forbes did not like formal supervisions, but many testified to his readiness to talk in all sorts of places.[29]

Forbes welcomed McGrath's friends. He had splendid rooms, full of books and paintings and drawings, on a corner of the college building. On one side he looked out on the great back lawn of King's, on the other across the Cam and Clare bridge to the Clare Fellows' Garden and the trees along the Backs. It was 'as desirable a life as you could wish for', John wrote, 'bar matrimony, if your wishes run that way' (only bachelor fellows lived in college). Forbes invited him to a dinner at high table ('one of the speediest meals I ever went through') and to a breakfast to meet a man who ran a school 'on very modern lines'. The schoolmaster* seemed 'a very sound cove' but was 'balmy [sic] on libido & introverts & extraverts', which was, in John's view, all very nice but not the simple explanation of the universe that it appeared to be to its expounder. Like Laski, Forbes provided John with a model of a university teacher quite unlike anyone he had experienced at Victoria.

---

*   Theodore James Faithful, 1885– ?, author of *Bisexuality: An Essay on Extraversion and Introversion* (London: John Bale and Sons, 1927), and other works on social credit, sex education, psychology, and socialism.

John discovered the Fitzwilliam Museum, inspected the bookshops pretty systematically and bought a few books 'including a folio Hobbes 1750, for 30/- & a ditto work of James I for 21/-. A bloke must have some folios for a foundation to his library.' He went to see Charlie Chaplin in *Shoulder Arms* and with McGrath to a production of *The Devil's Disciple*. They cycled to Ely to inspect the cathedral, 'a very mixed sort of Cathedral, but a fine Norman nave',[30] and the following day, his last in Cambridge, he went and lay in the hot sun in the Grantchester meadows by the river and dreamed of the perfect university. 'What a place we could have in N.Z. if we loosened the purse strings & only tried!' – this was to his parents; to Elsie he wrote that he had been 'thinking continually' about her.[31]

Elsie and Kathleen were due to arrive in England on 4 June. John said very little to his parents about the prospect save that 'it will be pleasant to see them again',[32] but his anxiety is revealed in a letter to Challis Hooper:

The emotions in this young breast quite defy exposition; the only thing I can do is to pray (or at least to hope desperately) that the first sight of each other will clear up all difficulties . . . It will be 22 months since we said good-bye, she in despair, I in confidence; & we have been spending about the last year wondering how much we have unconsciously moved apart. You certainly can't tell much from letters. Would it be better for both of us if I decided to fall in love with my very intimate friend H. – & persuaded H. to fall in love with me (which might be difficult) – who has so very many tastes & inclinations in common with me, as well as being a historian working on the same period? . . . It's all very distracting I can tell you, to a bloke who ought to have but a single mind, & that centred not upon 20th century women, whether N.Z. or American, but upon the 18th & 19th century British Empire – a quite important subject, though one not quite so palpitating.[33]

Elsie and Kathleen moved into a room in 21 Brunswick Square and John had a break from the thesis ('Australian land instructions', with which he was getting 'fed up to the teeth') to show them around London. They went to Kew and to the zoo, neither of which he had been to before; to Hampton Court; to the opera (*Carmen* and Verdi's *Otello*); to his first revue, *Clowns in Clover*; to a second revue, *Many Happy Returns*; to the Victoria and Albert Museum, again his first visit, though it was to become one of his favourite haunts in London. Galsworthy's *Justice* he reported to be 'actor proof, always able to get its effect', but Stravinsky's *Apollo Musagetes* at the Russian Ballet he found an 'extremely poor thing'.[34] His most startling piece of news (to his parents) was that he had, at Barker's sale, bought two new suits for £12 5s. This can have been due only to Elsie's influence.* To regain his composure, he went to the Tate Gallery to look at the modern French paintings. Early in July, with no fixed plans, the three left for a holiday in France.

On the way to Southampton to catch the boat to St Malo, they broke the journey at Winchester, making a pilgrimage to Jane Austen's tomb and house. John wrote a short note to his mother enclosing a postcard of the house.[35] There was no time to look at Southampton but, John wrote, he 'got quite an agreeable thrill from being for a whole 24 hours in Hampshire, the land of one branch of my ancestors',[36] one of very few such comments in all his letters. As with his trip the summer before, he wrote a detailed account in his letters home: on food and wine and the price of everything, on French sanitation, on historic towns and cathedrals and the awful flood of development along the coast of Brittany and Normandy. He discovered omelettes and rhapsodised about cheese: 'when I think what N.Z. is & what it might be, even in such a matter as the production of cheese, I blush for the divine process'.[37] From St Malo they went to Dinan, then Mont St Michel, 'a wonderful place, now organised with the greatest energy & efficiency for fleecing the tourist', and on to Constances and Bayeux. John found the tapestry very interesting and far better than he expected, 'full of life and colour'. The weather was holding out miraculously. 'Beer good.' After Bayeux came Caen. The end of the letter John wrote from Caen is very characteristic:

In the evening of our Bayeux day we came on to Caen. For noise & dirt this is the equal of any French town I have been in, & beats anything in any other country – until you have been in France you have no conception what noise & dirt can be. There go a collection of dogs barking uproariously now, an engine has just shrieked, a tram clangs, in a minute a motor lorry will hurtle up the hill & then a sporting car with the throttle out, here comes a train with appropriate piercing whine, & soon there will be a street row; let alone the perpetual motor horns, used with enthusiasm & persistency on every possible occasion. We went down to the sea again this afternoon, for a final bathe before turning completely inland; it was by steam tram, & a filthier & slower mode of conveyance I have never tried. A most extraordinary race. There go the dogs again, & a loose cycle rattling over cobbles. Caen has some

---

*   'The news', his father wrote, 'just about knocked us out'. (DEB to JCB, 2
       September 1928.)

fine churches, the Abbaye aux Hommes & the Abbaye aux Femmes, founded by Wm the Conqueror & Matilda his wife, to appease the papal wrath at their having married within the forbidden degrees, as the guide-books repeat ad nauseam . . . The abbeys are mostly fine plain Norman work, the men's very dignified, the women's full of delicate & beautiful sobriety, which manages to make its impression even over the efforts of the Micks to ruin it. Really these Micks do not deserve to have fine churches – they have a positive genius for vulgarity which can be equalled by few non-conformist sects, however half-witted. And the way those two abbeys are built in! Compare the English cathedrals! – the C of E may be only fit for the dust-bin, but at least it has some dignity in its dissolution. But the Catholics go wallowing in the desecration of beauty to the world's end. – St. Pierre's has some fine Renaissance work, & there are some good secular buildings scattered about the town. There is a good river also, up which I rowed the party last night; we disembarked & had rolls & cream cheese & cakes & grapes & wine under a haystack – a meal of the premiere classe for about 9d each. Then rowed down again in the sunset. A great country, apart from the disadvantages retailed above.[38]

'Elsie sends you her love', he added, 'she thinks you might be interested to learn that she has had her hair cut.'

After Caen it was Lisieux, centre of the cult of the recently beatified Saint Thérèse (John was fascinated and ironic), and then Rouen, which he had visited the year before. The stained glass seemed 'even more miraculous' and the town 'even more pleasant'.[39] What was more, the place they stayed in had a marvellous supply of running water, hot and cold, in all the rooms; as against that, everything else sanitary in the house was out of order. They continued to Paris and stayed for over two weeks, meeting up with Henning, 'busting away on his thesis', and with de Kiewiet, who had recently moved there on a University of London grant, was already 'correcting Henning's French for him' and 'willing to give anybody advice on anything within the country'. They explored the sights and the weather continued to be 'unbelievably brilliant . . . [it was] the most extraordinary thing about the trip'. The second most extraordinary thing, in John's view, was an exhibition of modern painting. 'You, who have only seen reproductions, really don't know what modern art is capable of. I endeavour invariably to preserve an open mind; but this left me weak.' He does not report who was exhibiting except for the Wellington sculptor Margaret Butler, who was showing two heads: 'have you ever heard of her? not bad'.[40]

Henning joined them for a visit to Chartres, where John found the windows in the cathedral 'almost as perfect as anything could be', though he added that he did not think they had 'any individual window to touch two or three of those at Rouen'.[41] While Elsie and Kathleen were entertained by well-off relations, John joined Henning and de Kiewiet to visit Malmaison, one of Napoleon's country houses, which had become a museum of Napoleon: 'a fearful place! What an utter vulgarian he was! The more I see of palaces & emperors the more I despise them.' Fontainebleau was similarly condemned: 'the woods there are fine, the palace is another museum of junk of all periods'. Why does royalty 'reach such abysmal depths of vulgarity?' Between the expeditions they went to museums, to bookshops, up the tower of Notre-Dame to see the gargoyles, to the theatre and films – Chaplin in *The Gold Rush* again, a Buster Keaton comedy, and a new French film of Edgar Allan Poe's *Fall of the House of Usher*, which John warmly recommended to his parents: 'the best and most interesting film' he had seen since *The Gold Rush* came out.

In their last week in Paris John spent another day in the Louvre, inspecting 'Chinese gold-lacquered boxes, pottery, & French pictures'.[42] Outside the Louvre they ran into Helen Allen with her rich and talkative aunt ('she said she always had a great admiration for us in Australia because of the way we treated our women; & I agreed; yes, we were pretty good to the girls') and they were taken back for a lavish afternoon tea at the Hotel Palais d'Orsay. 'A pity we can't muster a wealthy aunt somewhere in our family', John wrote.[43] There was an expedition to Versailles and a final gathering at Henning's. Henning wrote to McGrath with an account of the party:

we celebrated Beagle's departure in sparkling wine and vodka. All went well until the time came for going, I put on the lights at the top of the stairs and Beagle tottered down and tried to get out. It was half past twelve and the concièrge must have been fast asleep. Soon the staircase began reverberating with Beagle's sonorous and stentorian roar: 'Le cordon, s'il vous plâit'. By the time the sound got to the top of the staircase it was a bit blurred, I didn't know whether to put it down to the Vodkas Beagle had had or to the Vodkas I had had, or just to the distance. Anyhow it was blurred, The roar died down by a quarter to one, and I heard some disconsolate feet pattering along the flags in Cherche-Midi and round the corner into Abbé Grégoire.[44]

Elsie and Kathleen went on to Belgium, John back to London.

THE TRIP HAD BEEN A great success in a number of ways. 'It was', John wrote in October to Challis Hooper, 'invaluable for getting in touch with E. again, which as you can imagine, was not too easy at first. But we are pretty well settled in mind now, & as soon as a job comes along, you may look for developments.'[45] The difficulty was that after Grahamstown there were no more offers. John had applied for a Rockefeller Fellowship, £300 a year for two years, which he believed would be enough to marry on. It would provide the opportunity to start on a biography of Sir James Stephen, the under-secretary at the Colonial Office (and grandfather of Virginia Woolf), in whom John had become increasingly interested as he worked on his thesis. He was encouraged to apply for the fellowship by Laski and J.R.M. Butler, the Cambridge historian and British representative of the Rockefeller Foundation. At the end of May he heard that he had been unsuccessful. 'Everybody is pretty disgusted', he wrote to his parents, 'but I have wasted no sleep on it.'[46] McGrath wrote: 'If sincere wishes could have achieved anything you should already have skipped over half the continent in a Honeymoon Chariot drawn by seven Rockefeller horses'.[47] John's later comment to Challis has the ring of truth: 'That Rockefeller refusal was a cruel blow, you know – the hardest to date in my life. It meant a complete overturning in my plans for E & everything. I didn't realise it bang off, but it becomes solider & solider every day now . . . Of course I am merely one of 1½ million odd unemployed in this country, & I can at least thank my stars I'm not a coal-miner.'[48]

Butler suggested that he apply for a studentship at Trinity College, Cambridge. A 'quaint plunge into mediaevalism it would be at the age of 27 after NZ & London',[49] John wrote to his parents, but he applied nonetheless. Laski heard of a job at Manitoba in Canada and John applied for that too. He was offered neither. McGrath wrote sympathetically about the Cambridge outcome, adding that he did not take seriously John's 'NZ and extinction', and went on: 'You see I am optimistic about the world even though Dunkie has been with me for a week.'[50] John considered a Commonwealth Fellowship to the United States, but they could be held only by single scholars, and this 'put them out of the question'.[51] He applied for the position of librarian at Rhodes House, Oxford. They appointed Vincent Harlow, an Oxford man, with two books already published by the Oxford University Press, who was eventually to become Beit Professor of British Commonwealth history at Oxford. There seemed a possibility at Manchester – 'But who wants to go to Manchester?'[52] Newton went out to India to advise the government of the Punjab; perhaps he would come back knowing of something there. Nothing.

Left: William Henry
Beaglehole.
Below: Mary Jane
Beaglehole.

Left: John as a small boy.
Above left: Uncle Joe (right) as a guide on the Milford Track.
Above right: John with curls.
Below: The Beaglehole boys: Keith, Geoffrey, John, Ernest, about 1913.

Above: The gang of cousins. Back row: John, Dick Osborne, Keith, Sandy Paterson, Tony Osborne, Ernest, Harry Osborne. Front row: Stephen Osborne, Christy Paterson, Alan Paterson, Geoffrey, Ralph Jackson, Jim Osborne.
Left: Ern and Jenny about 1915.
Right: Keith and John.

Thomas Hunter, about 1920.
Photographer unknown, Victoria University of Wellington.

Above: Victoria University College, 1926.
S.P. Andrew collection, F-18905-1/1, Alexander Turnbull Library, Wellington, NZ.

Below: Tramping at Mount Matthews, 1924. John (sixth from left),
Averil Lysaght (eighth), Elsie (ninth), Boyd Wilson (boiling the billy).

Left: 21 Brunswick
Square (the house behind
the lamp post). John and
Duncan's room was on
the top floor.
Below: John and Lorrie
Richardson on the road
to Canterbury, 5 June
1927.

John at Neustadt in the Black Forest, July 1927.

John, painted by his uncle, George Butler, July 1929.
Victoria University of Wellington.

In November a lectureship in Auckland was advertised. 'If I come back I should like to come back to Wellington; at least it has some hills.'[53] However, he applied, and was turned down.

In Wellington, his father reported, efforts were being made to raise money to revive the Unitarian Church. What about John becoming minister? 'I wouldn't give them 2d', John responded. 'I have come to the conclusion that the feather bed for falling Xians joke about sums it all up; & I am on the floor . . . I'm not likely to be standing in the queue for the job, even if I am turned down on all sides over here.'[54] Nor were his parents' suggestions that he might write historical novels or humorous sketches for *Punch* any better received. In January 1929 he wrote: 'there are some reasons why I should be very glad to go back to N.Z.; but it looks at present as if I shall have to go wherever I can get a job. If there is nothing doing at all I suppose I shall have to utilise my free passage home & trust to luck. That is about how things stand at present.'[55]

He had hoped that he might be helped in his quest for a job by the publication of his MA thesis on Captain Hobson. Laski had read the thesis during John's first year in London, been impressed with it, and suggested sending it to Professor S.B. Fay at Smith College in Massachusetts, who published a series of historical works for which it was just the right length. John spent three days bringing the references up to 'the requirements of modern historical research'. 'If that silly ass F.P. knew ¹/₁₀ of what he ought to know I should have been saved all this mucking about & probably got a good many more marks from old Grant for the thing.'[56] De Kiewiet was puzzled by what John considered some pretty good jokes in it ('he doesn't go too much on humour'). John sent it off before leaving on his first European trip and heard in November that Fay would publish it provided John was willing to cut out a few sentences which seemed to Fay 'perhaps of a facetious nature & not quite appropriate'.[57] John had the dual satisfaction of having it accepted and being able to vilify Fay for his literary judgement: 'I told [him] to fire away with his dirty work', he reported to his parents.[58] The arrival of proofs, in February 1928, produced a further burst of indignation: Fay had messed around with his first and last paragraphs, which John said he had 'worked over like a slave'.[59] After consulting Laski, John 'made a new beginning & end & substituted them for Fay's, wrote him a nice letter ordering 40 copies, & left the rest to luck'.[60] The thirty copies in addition to his ten free ones cost him $15 and there was a further $10 for the author's corrections to the galley proofs and the dedication:

To
Victoria University College
Wellington, New Zealand
this essay
written in its shadow

In the preface he thanked Duncan and Harry Ross for 'their violent but salutary criticism'.

John received his first copy of the book when he was in Paris. Copies were sent to a number of papers in New Zealand and John waited impatiently for reviews. The first, and one of very few to appear, was in the *New Zealand Worker* of 10 October 1928. It was by Harold Miller, a graduate of Victoria and Rhodes Scholar in 1920, who had just returned to Victoria to succeed Horace Ward as librarian. Miller suggested that John, whose natural sympathies, he was sure, lay with Hobson and the missionaries, had been too kind to the New Zealand Company, which, in Miller's view, had 'swindled its emigrants right and left and left them a legacy of ill-will in the native mind that finally led to war'. Miller picked gaps where he wanted more information, but concluded (having begun with a favourable reference to John's writings in the *Spike*): 'From the man who can write like this in [a] master's thesis we can clearly look for much in the future'. Looking back in the year 2000, W.H. Oliver found the book, with its limitations of focus ('Can we easily contemplate a book on the events of the early 1840s in which the Treaty was not relevant?') and its racial prejudice, still 'quite a good piece of historical writing'.[61]

In the meanwhile there was a PhD thesis to be finished (John's prediction, at the time he got back from Paris in August, was that it should be done about October, 'except for typing & indexing & adding on appendices, & all the other boring God-forsaken jobs') and the excitement of a third year in London. The house in Brunswick Square had changed hands. The room which John and Duncan had shared on the top floor had been subdivided; 'sacrilege' in John's view but 'the things they will do here to knock an extra bob out of a house are appalling'.[62] Duncan had moved to a room in Gordon Square but John stayed on in a room on the first floor, still overlooking the square but a long way from the bathroom. Once more he sent home a plan of how he had arranged the room. Over the mantelpiece he had a painting by McGrath (chosen when John was in Cambridge), below the painting 'I have got my Innsbruck medal from last year, flanked by 1 pair brass candlesticks & two pewter mugs; which I felt a sudden impulse to break off this letter after page 3 & polish, which I did . . . they look very classy now, quite a high-brow mantelpiece.'[63] The impulse to polish pewter never left him.

There were changes too in John's circle of friends. As well as de Kiewiet leaving for Paris and Berlin, Harry Ross had gone to South Africa, to the job at Grahamstown that John had turned down. Helen Allen, who had completed her thesis, went back to the States for a month, calling at Toronto to see Adelaide MacDonald, and looking for a possible job. At the end of the year she was in Florence for a month, and while she was away Elsie had her flat in London. When Helen returned she spent more time in Paris and then went to Cambridge for the summer to prepare to teach at Vassar, the notable women's college on the Hudson River north of New York, to which she had been appointed. Duncan was spending some of his time doing WEA teaching in Kent but he and John still met frequently. Newton was off in India, and while he was away the seminar was taken by J.A. Williamson, the history master at Westminster School. Williamson was a great proponent of the view that British history could be fully understood only within its wider imperial context. He had already published a lot and John knew his *A Short History of British Expansion*, having bought a copy in 1922, its year of publication. Williamson, who was to become best known for his work on Drake and the Cabots, was in John's view 'about the best bloke in England at the colonial history game'.[64] Williamson, for his part, quickly came to respect John's ability.

John's youngest brother Ernest was following in his footsteps. A student of Hunter's, he had completed an MA with first-class honours in 1928, and his master's thesis on propaganda already revealed what was to be his distinctive form of applied social psychology.[65] Ernest too was awarded a postgraduate travelling scholarship and a free passage. He decided to work for a PhD at the London School of Economics, and John met him at the Tilbury docks on his arrival in London on 21 September. That evening he wrote to his parents with a full account of the meeting: 'He looks healthy enough though wearing a very low cap that appals even me . . . I have got him parked here, in 21, for a day or two, while he looks round for a room & generally gets his bearings, & have taken him down to the Food Reform Restaurant, so you may rest in peace.'[66] Ernest, for his part, reported on John, writing most freely to his Uncle Joe:

Jack met me at Tilbury – just the same as ever. Rather untidily dressed, collar not matching shirt, long hair, ragged tie etc, but otherwise he has not changed at all. In fact, I think he has thrown off a lot of his old reserve. Probably because now he has more or less entirely got over all his stammering – speaks slowly of course still, with a certain amount of hesitation, but anyone who did not know him would merely think that he was a meditative person who had difficulty in translating his thoughts into words – not in speaking at all. Having thus conquered his stammering, he launches out quite brightly & we have great times round at B[runswick] Sq[uare].[67]

John's stammer had clearly improved while he was in London. 'It doesn't worry me a great deal now, except when I get excited or very tired',[68] he wrote to Elsie not long before she arrived. He had just started seeing a 'voice-specialist cove', who had told him that three months would make a lot of difference.* Ernest's report suggests the treatment was a success. The irony was that some months later, when John applied for the lectureship at Auckland, F.P. Wilson's comments on his stutter appear to have been a reason for his non-appointment.[69]

Kathleen left to return to New Zealand, and then go to Australia, in the middle of October. John's misgivings before her arrival had quite disappeared; they had become close and lasting friends. She took gifts from John for his family; for his father a plaster cast of a medallion of Erasmus in the British Museum that he had arranged to have made. Elsie followed Ernest into cheaper lodgings, still in Brunswick Square, a few doors away from number 21, and the three of them saw a lot of one another. Elsie and Ernest knew each other well from the Victoria Tramping Club. John was to claim he found the advent of Ernest 'not altogether an unmixed blessing. He nearly drove me mad for a time', he wrote to Challis, 'till he settled down & began to pick up some friends of his own',[70] but there seems to have been some brotherly exaggeration in the comment. They went out to Virginia Water and walked five or six miles; once again to Kew Gardens – 'Kew leaves any of these foreign parks . . . miles behind';[71] and to Welwyn Garden City to join Lorrie Richardson for a day's tramp – 'charming country England in its autumn dress', John wrote, 'copper & red & gold'.[72] There were concerts and plays. John clearly enjoyed being mentor and guide.

I don't know that I don't envy Ern his first year in London – I should like to keep on having first years for about five years, discovering fresh things every time – after a while, though you keep on discovering fresh things

---

*   The name of the specialist is not recorded. Family lore has it that it was the same man who treated the Duke of York, the future George VI.

they haven't the same shock . . . you just take them for granted, unless they bowl you over completely, like the Turkish pottery in the V. & A. Let alone the Chinese.[73]

They visited the house in Hampstead where John Keats had lived and saw the mulberry tree under which the poet was said to have written his 'Ode to a Nightingale', then went on to visit Kenwood, the house (built at the time James Cook was setting out on his first voyage) lately given to the nation by Lord Iveagh. John found it 'superb': 'Adam, brought up to date with bathrooms & new oak flooring. You can't get away from it – civilised domestic architecture is a supreme joy. Only the library there was spoilt by over-colouring – & these show libraries never seem to have enough books in them.'[74] Their interest in domestic architecture took John and Elsie to furniture exhibitions at Heal's in Tottenham Court Road and at Waring and Gillows, as well as to the Ideal Home Exhibition at Olympia. They saw elegant rooms and furniture, 'but when you come to the libraries what do you see? Beautiful furniture – wonderful writing desks, exquisitely wrought firescreens, but where are the bookshelves? . . . after you'd carried a few arm-fulls upstairs & come home once or twice on Saturdays you'd wonder where in blazes you were going to put your books.'[75] The net result of these visits, John confided to Challis, was to make him and Elsie thoroughly dissatisfied, 'disgusted perhaps', with any house or furniture they would ever possibly be able to afford. The idea of having McGrath design them a house seemed more and more of a dream. With premonition, John wrote: 'we have practically decided to make our own furniture out of kerosene & fruit cases, with which many satisfactory modern effects could be obtained . . . Ah! to be rich & furnish a house in England! . . . At least', he added, 'I shall have my books'.[76]

His book buying continued. While ransacking the shops for something suitable for his father's birthday (he was looking for a 'decent copy' of Erasmus's *Colloquies* that he could not find and had to settle for a copy of Robert Bridges's latest essay 'just by way of something to go on with'), he saw a

very good folio Clarendon 3 vols History £1.1.0 1 vol life 15/- . . . The cove said he would let me have the 4 vols for 30/- & I am seriously considering it . . . if I go back to N.Z. & don't take them I shall be sorry some day . . . Yes, I think it would be a sin to let them go at that price. I could have a lot of fun polishing up the covers with Meltonian Cream too – it would do for a change from cleaning the pewter.[77]

He bought them. The 'autumn publishing season being now in full blast', he wrote in his next letter, 'it is perfect torture to me to go into a bookshop'.[78]

JOHN'S SCHOLARSHIP HAD been £200 a year for two years. Now, in his third year, money was running very short. The final scholarship payment of £25 was to be made on completion of his thesis, though he reckoned at least £18 of this would go on the typing. Inspired perhaps by Laski's stories, John enquired from Bumpus's what they would pay him for a first edition of de la Mare's *Songs of Childhood* which he had bought for ninepence at McKay's on Lambton Quay in 1919. Bumpus's offered him 30 guineas for it.

I said I'd think about it . . . If I could only find ½ doz things like this, I could finance myself for another year. Daddy will no doubt point out that £31.9.3 is unearned increment & is therefore morally the perquisite of the state; I reply however that on the contrary it is the natural reward of the capitalist, & of his foresight, wisdom & hard-earned knowledge . . .[79]

Finally he decided to auction the book at Hodgson's – 'auction it', McGrath had written, and 'put on a reserve of £40'[80] – and it fetched £40 10s, of which John got about £35.[81] He took Elsie and Ernest to Lyons and shouted them a 2d cup of coffee each to celebrate, and then bought eleven books in the next two days, though several were remainders and only 1s 3d and 2s each. John finally accepted his father's offer of a loan, and was sent £50. In letters John referred to unnamed friends 'who would be delighted to let me have a loan for a few months or longer', but with no job in sight he felt unable to accept. What he did have, he believed, would keep him going in London for a further six months.[82] When, just before Christmas, he heard that he had not got the job in Auckland, Ernest had the impression that he was relieved and that he would just hang on until his cash gave out in the hope that a job would turn up, and that if one did not he would use his free passage to return to New Zealand.[83]

Most of November 1928 was spent in revising his thesis, 'a cruel job'[84] – which left him feeling 'in a considerable state of disgust with the British Empire historically considered, & the American elections, & the price of books & the way everything happens at once & so forth'.[85] In the United States Herbert Hoover had defeated Governor Al Smith of New York for the presidency. 'A terrible business', John wrote.[86] The American professor of economics at the LSE reckoned it was 'the blackest day in American history since the Fugitive Slave Law'. It was widely believed that an anti-Catholic vote had cost Smith the election. John's father demurred, and in a later letter John spelled out his critical view: Hoover was put up by the Republican Party – 'the biggest organisation of graft, big & dirty business, intolerance, sinister power, & filthy politics in the world . . . would you rather have a country governed by a Mick of genius & fair honesty, or by a mob of Baptist oil-kings & fundamentalist farmers'.[87] The New Zealand election later in November, when the Coates government met its surprise defeat at the hands of the Liberals, led by Joseph Ward, and Labour lost its position as the official opposition, was greeted more equably: 'it won't do the Labour birds much harm to climb up slowly, as long as they're not too slow about it. I should like to see Peter Fraser as Minister of Education for a bit – Thank God Wright's out of it now any how. That will make it a bit easier to come back to N.Z. if necessary.'[88]

The thesis was finished on Saturday 8 December, at midnight – 'at least, I finished it all except a quotation I wanted from Burke as whipped cream to top off the fruit salad with; which I couldn't find'.[89] He started to read 'all Burke through systematically' and found the quotation three days later. There was still a bit of tinkering to do and some final revision but, he was able to say, 'to all intents & purposes the thing is finished, bar the bibliography, & most of it is either typed or being typed'. Six typists were involved, including de Kiewiet, who did one chapter. John himself was to type the preface, table of contents, bibliography and index. Elsie was proofreading and Helen Allen doing all the indexing she could before setting off to Florence with her aunt. The thesis having been completed, John varied between 'thinking it a cut above ordinary doctoral theses & thinking it unutterable rot'.[90] He hoped he would now have time to 'see life a bit'.

He made a pre-Christmas visit to Trimley to see his Uncle George and cousins. His Aunt Jeanne had died some months earlier and a little later George was to remarry (John was best man) and move to a house in Richmond. John took (and read) *Northanger Abbey* and *Persuasion*, 'thus completing the corpus of [Jane Austen's] completed novels'. 'The year 1928 therefore may be accounted a notable one', he wrote to his parents. 'Finished Boswell, J.A. & govs' Insts. What other age can show such a list?'[91] Now, at his father's urging, he was considering *Tristram Shandy*, 'while the going's good i.e. before I get a job'. The difficulty was that having time to read simply brought home to him how much there was that he wanted to read. It was at this time that he recalled to Elsie an experience he had had before he left for London:

I remember once when I was at home reading a Times Litt. Supp having a curious experience – I had a feeling of utter despair & bewilderment, like being lost in a mental cyclone, at the limitless number of things to be known & books to be read, so that it seemed impossible ever to be anything but utterly ignorant or to do anything at all; & it's an experience I've never forgotten, it was so vivid. It almost frightened me physically . . .[92]

McGrath was in London just before Christmas. He, Ern and John spent an evening at Elsie's, 'entertaining & being entertained'. The next evening, with Duncan as well, they had dinner and then took a taxi to see a film with Harold Lloyd. The film was off so they saw *The Gold Rush* again – for John at least the third time. McGrath then left for Paris. With everyone scattered, the revelries of the previous year were not repeated. Nor was John cheered by the state of Britain:

Here's this Well of Loneliness suppressed with positively foully libellous remarks from the magistrates, God help them, & the coal business goes merrily merrily on, with not an effort to do anything fundamental to help it. So at Xmas we have a Lord Mayor's fund & give the miners dinner & then they starve again. Gosh, it makes me sick! I took along all my old clothes, & no doubt the Queen & the Prince of Wales & Stanley Baldwin have done likewise, & that's about as far as we get. What a govt! . . . if ever a country justified economic pessimism, it's England in 1928.[93]

On Christmas Day he stayed in bed until 11.30 and then went around to join Elsie (who was minding Helen Allen's flat) for a 'magnificent blow-out by way of Xmas dinner'. John provided balloons and red candles and a bottle of sauterne. Duncan joined them later for tea and a 'very bright evening'. At New Year they went out to stay at Lorrie Richardson's: 'Good walking there & an open fire . . . There was a fair amount of snow on the ground, & the cold bath in the morning was damnable.'[94] They also went to the circus, to the Victoria and Albert Museum again, and John took Elsie to *Peter Pan* to celebrate her birthday. They went to some architectural lectures, to a recital by the Hewitt string quartet, and a lecture by Mrs Bertrand Russell, 'which was very interesting – Ern standing by the door & guffawing in a superior way at views put forward by members of the audience – he seems to have all the amused intolerance so characteristic of the family'.[95] There was an exhibition of Dutch painting at Burlington House. John 'nearly wept tears of joy on meeting again a lot of the Vermeers I saw at the Hague & at Amsterdam, let alone the shoals of Rembrandts & all the other stuff . . . I have gone quite dippy over Van Gogh . . . very bold brilliant & swirling stuff'.[96] And he was doing a lot of reading, 'in which direction I am making up for lost time over the last 2 years as hard as I can go'. He had finished Clare Sheridan's *Nuda Veritas* (his mother, he suggested, might like to shut her eyes over a few of the pages); he was even starting to read the Bible (he had bought a copy of the new Cambridge Shorter Bible not long before) and he was immersed in H.M. Tomlinson's *Gifts of Fortune* – 'by jingo! He can write, that bloke!'[97]

The thesis was finally submitted on 1 February 1929. John offered his parents some details:

no. of pages: 726 + preface & contents pages – 7 (I mustn't forget the very classy typed title page I designed); no. of chapters: – 9, no of notes: – about 1250; weight: about 12 cwt, quantity of blood & tears & sweat involved: ∞ (that I believe is the mathematical symbol for infinity . . .); amount of disgust: ditto. However I managed to mention Jane Austen & quote Burke & Carlyle & Dr Johnson & Blake, so what more do you want in a thesis on colonial history?[98]

The same letter had news which was to shape John's future career. J.A. Williamson wanted him to do a book on Pacific exploration for a projected series on 'pioneering', 'not that I know anything about either the Pacific or exploration', John commented, though the proposal did have the advantage that he could, if necessary, do it in New Zealand using the Alexander Turnbull Library. Laski wanted him to start a book on the idea of empire. John wanted to spend a month or so on general reading, and then to have a job.

He was reading Katherine Mansfield's letters, which he had bought when they were published a few months earlier.

[I] have never been so moved by a book in my life. I had to leave off after the first volume & recover myself on Shakespeare & Sir Thos Browne. I feel I know her now better than all but one or two of my friends; but oh! how she has wrung my heart! To see her dying for 4 years & be unable to move a finger to help – frightful! It has made me want to blaspheme wholesale but what's the good? One gazes hopelessly & helplessly on utter tragedy. What a writer she was! Some of these letters are superb. And all that to come out of Karori! – as my Father said . . . what wouldn't I give to have spoken with her once! Well, no more humble, lovely, truth-seeking, generous spirit could one hope to meet with on earth, I think; I wish to God I could think that N.Z. realised it.

She – K.M. – had exactly my feeling for N.Z. . . . I wish I had a bit of her feeling for words.[99]

The thesis submitted, John and Elsie went to Oxford for a week. John thought the town magnificent, even in winter, and if he found the 'immense expanse of red white & blue stained glass' put into the cathedral by Sir Gilbert Scott in 1870 more hideous than anything he had seen anywhere, 'the Grinling Gibbons carving in Queen's Chapel; & the linen-fold panelling in Magdalen Hall & New College Hall, & the river walks by Magdalen; & the interior of St Mary the Virgin; & the quadrangles . . . & the ancient little streets everywhere; & the towers & turrets & spires & bookshops make considerable amends'.[100] Blackwell's he found about the best shop he had been in, but he could not find quite the right book to send to his father. They saw the exterior of the new Rhodes House, designed by Sir Herbert Baker and just being finished. It was to include the library – 'what a place for a job', John wrote regretfully.[101] He and Elsie were together for a week without the intrusion of anyone who knew them and were, John told Challis, happier than they had ever been before.[102]

His oral examination was on 22 March. It was, John said, 'like most oral exams – more or less of a formality & more or less of an anti-climax'. The examiners said absolutely nothing about the thesis 'as a whole either by way of praise or blame – I except Miss Penson, who did say she thought it didn't have enough dates in it, to which the others chivalrously agreed. They each asked a few tiddly winking questions . . . & then informed me after a suitable period for mutual consultation that they had decided to recommend me to the Senate for the degree'.[103] He was disappointed that they did not offer him afternoon tea. John cabled the news to his parents and was indignant when the young lady in the post office said that PhD would be charged as three words. He sent the thesis to the Oxford University Press on Laski's advice. The Press were 'very careful to guard themselves from being encouraging'.[104]

Henning had also finished his thesis, had landed a temporary lectureship at Sydney (in contrast with John, there was nothing he wanted more than to get home) and came to London for a last look around before leaving. 'A good cobber', John wrote.[105] This led to a busy fortnight with music and theatre and films, and then John took his bicycle and rode to Welwyn Garden City to stay with Lorrie Richardson. Elsie's elder sister, Edith, had arrived in England some weeks earlier, and she and Elsie were staying in a village ten miles from Richardson's place. They met several times to go exploring on foot and in the car that Edith had hired and Elsie drove. Elsie then went off for three weeks to drive Edith and her friend and fellow-teacher from Wellington, Erica Bridges, around south-west England. John rode back into London one morning to see a Russian film, *Bed and Sofa*, 'one of the best F[ilm] S[ociety] performances' he had been to,[106] and before returning to Richardson's he typed out letters (and copies of his testimonials) to seven American universities asking about jobs. The weather was hardly propitious for cycling, with gales, heavy rain, sleet and snow, but it cleared for him to ride on to Cambridge to visit McGrath.

McGrath was away. However, Mansfield Forbes was hospitable. John stayed in Clare for two nights and dined again at high table; admirable food, he reported, but 'a very low intellectual level on the whole'.[107] McGrath's life had changed. The previous August he had met and fallen for an American girl. He had reported to John at the time:

Forbes and I are in the middle of a Texan romance! Malfroy (Wellington N.Z. who knows you*) turned up the other day with a charming American girl, whom Manny singled out for his immediate blessings. So he invited them to lunch with us on the river-bank in the Fellows' Garden. I enjoyed that meal . . . This Texas girl is one of those unselfconsciously intimate people who are so refreshing. Seems to be a quality of American women.[108]

Malfroy was supplanted – 'not a bad feat over an international rugby player', McGrath judged – and Mary Crozier (or Miss Texas, as she was generally referred to) played an increasing part in McGrath's life. They were to marry in 1930. Before John arrived in Cambridge on his bicycle, Miss Texas had been 'threatened with maternal recall to Dallas' and McGrath had gone down to London to try to sort out the situation.

At about the same time as that fateful lunch took place Forbes had leased 'Finella', a late Victorian villa on Queens' Road across the river from Clare, and McGrath had been appointed as architect for its transformation. John had already heard of some of the plans:

The glass vaulted ceiling of the hall is now disturbing us. Vibration and expansion having been disposed of we are now confronted with the possibility of the ceiling resonating to some particular note and flying to pieces. We don't know whether to put in a special plant to intercept

---

*   J.O.J. Malfroy was a law graduate from Victoria. A keen rugby player, he had played for Wellington and for the New Zealand University team but was not, strictly, an international.

sound waves of the particular frequency or to insure the structure heavily against the deadly note. Any suggestions? Forbes latest request is that whenever the [door]bell is rung a musket will be fired at the far end of the hall followed by a dull thud and a sound of falling glass. On either side of the entrance door there's to be a mirror and also in a niche out of reach a brush and comb and lipstick. These are only a few of the modern improvements contemplated.[109]

And a month later: 'The latest idea for "Finella" is a mirrored glass dome 8 ft in diameter (all in one piece) for the dining room ceiling'.[110] Work had started towards the end of 1928 and John inspected the house several times, twice with McGrath when he got back to Cambridge. It 'is going to be a marvellous place', John wrote, 'plugged full of new ideas in decoration & ventilation & furniture & mirrors & patent finishes'.[111] Finally, he cycled back to London with a stop on the way after lunch to read in the sun for about four hours.

'It is satisfactory', he had written home, 'to read some real books again, & not to be confined [to those] out of which history is manufactured in the B.M.'[112] *The Brook Kerith* by George Moore he thought magnificent (he passed on a story he had heard from Mansfield Forbes that Freud thought *The Brook Kerith* 'about the greatest book in the world' and had read it twelve times) and he decided to cultivate Moore for a bit. However, he went next to *Moby Dick* and was impressed, though he thought *The Brook Kerith* had stirred him more, and between other books he finished Shaw's *The Intelligent Woman's Guide to Socialism*, which his mother had read some months earlier. A.N. Whitehead's *Science and the Modern World* he found a struggle: 'one of those confounded books which crease the brow & the soul alike of an ordinary bloke like me . . . I am coming to believe that history is a soft option after all'.[113] He read more of Edward Thomas on rural England and Wyndham Lewis's *Tarr*, 'good, but about extremely peculiar people'.[114] He recommended Gibbon's *Autobiography,* and *All Quiet on the Western Front*, 'tremendously powerful stuff' (just before he left London he heard from his father that New Zealand libraries had banned the book). He was 'lapping up' Graham Wallas's *Human Nature in Politics* and thought that, as Wallas was 'looking after Ern', his father ought to read it.

At the beginning of March John had reported to Challis on how things were going with Elsie. Their affections seemed permanently settled – with 'an occasional silent row' – but there appeared to be no prospect of getting married, and that worried John very much indeed. Elsie would not marry him until he had a job and of that there seemed little hope. It was 'a sort of constant sand in the wheels of love'.[115] John had already told his parents of the decision to marry,[116] and at the beginning of April he drafted a letter to Elsie's parents. Elsie was away touring and John wrote to tell her what a terrible job it had been and that he was sure she would get an immediate cable saying 'Disinherited'. He described the letter:

Par.1 expresses my diffidence at writing & my pride at prospect of becoming their son-in-law. Par.2 discusses briefly (very – 8 lines) my prospects of material advancement. Par.3 expresses my happiness if your happiness would make them happy. Par.4 requests forgiveness & sympathy . . . I have striven to be as amiable & modest as possible, while yet preserving a spirit of manly independence & subdued cheerfulness, I trust you will approve.[117]

With his pen in hand, no situation left him at a loss for words.

Elsie's parents took the news pretty well,* though her mother wrote that 'luckily Dad's new roses arrived yesterday so he has something to occupy him'.[118] Robert Holmes was sure he would never see his daughter again, but he put a brave face on it and cabled her £100 in addition to her usual allowance. The Holmeses were hurt that they had been told nothing earlier, though Elsie's mother said she was not surprised at the news and had been 'preparing the way with Dad', but John (who never held with formal engagements) and Elsie gave away very little to anyone. Ernest was clearly kept in the dark. At the end of March he was still writing to Uncle Joe on the 'Jack-Elsie-Helen triangle', singing the praises of both Elsie and Helen but venturing the view that it would be Elsie in the end.[119] Finally, at the end of July (a week before the couple sailed for New Zealand), he wrote that 'I understand that Jack & Elsie are engaged – officially or unofficially I don't know which, & that just as soon as Jack lands a job he will get married immediately'. About Helen Allen, he added that 'she is as nice a girl as I shall ever want to meet & I will always have the impression that she was – well – that she was very keen on Jack & would have – but what matters this now?'[120]

John had had replies from the American universities, all saying, politely, 'nothing doing'. More of a blow to him was the news that the Oxford University Press had turned down his thesis for publication,

---

*   It is not clear if John's letter was sent. Mr and Mrs Holmes's letters appear to be a response to a letter from Elsie. It is possible that John's letter was posted after the one from Elsie.

'exceedingly courteously & even complimentarily; but they think it too much of a dissertation & not enough of a book (that is the worst blow!!)'.[121] Ernest thought John was so fed up with the thesis that he was prepared to 'pitch it in the corner and forget it'.[122] Then came the final blow. On 18 May he got home from a weekend's walking with Elsie in Surrey to find a cable awaiting him with the news of his mother's death. 'I had been afraid of getting [the cable] for 18 months, & yet I never believed it would come', he wrote to his father.[123] It was a terrible shock. Through all of the anxiety about jobs and the future there had been the thought that, if he had to return to New Zealand, his mother would be there. 'I always pictured myself getting away from the wharf & springing into a taxi & leaving my luggage behind, & arriving by myself & going straight down the garden to see her.' Ernest and he were not able to help each other much – none of the family found it easy to express their feelings except on paper – but Elsie was an enormous support, and letters from his father and Keith, when they eventually came, helped John a lot. But those letters were nearly six weeks away and before they arrived there was one from his father, dated 14 April, with the news of his mother's renewed illness and his father's concern. John wrote to his father with great understanding and love, and even in his first letter was able to include comment on the British election ('the govt have come a terrible crash, richly deserved'), the English countryside in spring ('it is the ideal England') and the publication of Galsworthy's *Forsyte Saga* in one volume.

His parents had sent him two guineas to mark the PhD and 30 shillings for his birthday. He had pretty much decided, he wrote, to put the money together and get the Shakespeare Head edition of Plutarch's *Lives* in eight volumes if he could find a decent copy. 'Those Blackwell books have very often one bad fault which most books seem to have in this machine-ridden age – the pages are folded so badly that the print frequently rides up or down hill on the page, & I am getting so pernickety that these things annoy me damnably.'[124] He was also attracted by a new edition of Pepys on India paper and a new Sir Thomas Browne, though it had the same fault as the Plutarch. He cogitated for some time, almost went for the Pepys, and then in a bookseller's window in Charing Cross Road saw the two-volume Nonesuch edition of Milton's poetry. At £3 10s it seemed very cheap, less than the Plutarch at £5, and it was 'a magnificent book, a fine italic type, & with designs by Blake for illustrations, first rate most of them'.[125] 'It may be an extravagance for one in my financially very rocky position', he wrote, but he bought it. Before he left he added the Shakespeare Head Plutarch, 'to celebrate my sojourn in & departure from England'.[126]

Under the terms of John's free passage, he was supposed to get back to New Zealand within three years of leaving it. Time was running out. The shipping company stretched a point and John pencilled in a booking, once again on the *Osterley*, leaving on 3 August. He wondered whether he should borrow more money (his father offered another £50) and hang on until Christmas, but Elsie was dead against borrowing any more, nor did John feel he really could. Ernest had the impression at this time that John was now sorry in a way that he had not taken the job at Grahamstown.[127]

He and Elsie went on another tramp, in Buckinghamshire and down the Thames, 'trespassing shamelessly & sleeping out in private woods'.[128] The weather was magnificent, the best John had known in England. He went to his Uncle George's at Richmond several times to sit for his portrait. The first sitting was unproductive, Ernest told his father, as John ate such an excellent midday dinner that he could not keep awake in the afternoon, with the result that little could be done: 'typical of Jack, I fear – get a good meal when & where you can is his motto'.[129] Ernest thought the finished portrait on the whole very good: 'Uncle George has caught him in a very characteristic attitude, meditative, face leaning on his hand, unruly hair, semi-profile'.[130] George gave it to John, together with one of his watercolours.

John and Elsie saw their first 'talkie': 'an appalling thing called Fox Movietone 1929 Follies, appalling in construction, speech, song & everything else. If this is a fair sample, it looks to me as if the talkies are the worst thing that could possibly have happened to the cinema . . . however it must be admitted that perhaps it wasn't a fair sample.'[131] There was a final visit to Cambridge, with Elsie, Duncan and Ernest, to farewell McGrath and have a last look at 'Finella'. John took an involuntary dip in the Cam when Ernest leaped suddenly on to a punt on which John was standing tentatively balancing a pole. It was a very good weekend; they left reluctantly.

John was finding it difficult to accept that he was really leaving London. In the middle of July Ernest wrote to their father:

So far there is no sign of him doing any packing – he must have at least three or four cases of books to put together, not counting his clothes & other junk, so I expect a pretty hectic time towards the end of this month. I presume it is my brotherly duty to stay in London myself to do what there is to help; one thing at least, he can't be so bad now as he used to be, what with Elsie to jog his memory – though, to be honest,

Elsie told me the other day that even she despairs of getting him to do things – this in reference to seeing about his passage – sometimes apparently the only alternative to continual reminders is to let him go his own pace – the trouble being, of course, that Jack's pace in doing things is often so decidedly slow that it drives most normal people into virtual hysterics.[132]

The same day that Ernest wrote, John was writing to Challis that he was 'thinking about packing-cases, & damning the world & pretty well all that's in it'.[133]

A final possibility of a job arose. A chair in history was advertised at the new university college in Singapore. They wanted applicants aged between thirty and thirty-five; this was a snag, as John had just turned twenty-eight, but he thought that it was just possible his luck would turn. The appointment was to be made through the Colonial Office and Laski said he would put in a word with Sidney Webb, the new colonial secretary. By the time John sailed there had been no decision and there was the possibility that he would be 'hauled off the boat at Colombo or Sydney or somewhere by cable'.[134] He heard he had not been appointed only after he arrived back in New Zealand. Another unsuccessful applicant, even younger than John, was Fred Wood, an Australian who had graduated with first-class honours from Oxford the year before.

Not knowing about Singapore complicated leaving. Decisions about final shopping were difficult when he did not know where he was going to be. An afternoon was spent rushing about with Ernest choosing a wedding present for Ernest to give them; they finally settled on a table lamp that could be as useful in Singapore as in New Zealand. Ernest wrote to his father:

I think it nearly broke Jack's heart that he did not have £100 or so to spend in Heals the great furnishing shop. He took me in one day to show me incidentally what he would like to get. Not much of the stuff would be strictly utilitarian I fear, but it showed a pretty taste & no mistake. He must hope to have money to spend next time he is in London: that is cold consolation . . .[135]

Adelaide MacDonald, Helen Allen and de Kiewiet combined to present John with the London PhD robes. It reminded John of how much his mother had looked forward to seeing him in a red gown, but it was a generous gift. Dick Campbell gave a farewell party, with asparagus and ice cream. He had completed his thesis and was off to America. Elsie's father paid so she could also travel first class with John on the *Osterley*. 'I needn't say', he wrote to his father, 'what it would be like without her.'[136] On his last day in London John took a last bus ride along the Strand and up Ludgate Hill to see St Paul's as he had seen it the first time, and that night at one o'clock he and Elsie went down to Waterloo Bridge and gazed down the river.

We have no records of the voyage out. John wrote his father a brief letter from Sydney. There would be plenty of time to talk when he got home, he said. The trip had been 'middling to good' and he was in the best of health.[137] They were having some days in Sydney, meeting Henning and his family, Jean Harvey, friends of Duncan's, and Eileen McGrath, Raymond's young sister, who was training to be a sculptor. They would be sailing from Sydney on the *Makura* on 20 September and would arrive in Wellington about four days later.

'IT IS FATAL FOR YOUTHS of my temperament and tastes to come to England & Europe at the age of 25', John wrote to Challis just before he sailed for New Zealand, 'they should be set firmly to dig potatoes in the Wairarapa, with due & stringent safeguards against falling in love. Now I shall be coming back to N.Z. half-baked. Ah, well.'[138] But if the last months in London had served him up some 'solid whacks of fortune', which cast a shadow over his return home, his time there had been exceedingly well spent. He had completed his PhD and he had had that 'intensive grounding in historical method and research' prescribed by Newton, which he in his turn was to pass on to his students. But the Oxford University Press decision not to publish the thesis had been a great disappointment.

John's good fortune, far outweighing the bad, was to make a group of friends who greatly enriched his life intellectually, culturally and socially. A brighter quartet than the four young men who sailed from Sydney on the *Osterley* is difficult to imagine; and then in London de Kiewiet, Helen Allen and Adelaide MacDonald also became a part of John's world. For the first time he had fellow students who both shared his intellectual and cultural interests and matched his academic ability. Our knowledge of John's London years is based largely on his letters home, which catch only in part their high spirits and enjoyment of life. This comes out in some surviving letters from McGrath to John, and a handful from John to Ian Henning. Their affection for one another is suggested by the way they rallied around when a thesis was being submitted, by the 'violent but salutary criticism', by the gift of the academic robes, by de Kiewiet's inscription in his second book when he sent it to John in 1937: 'To J.C.B. because we loved the same things as well as one another'. Over fifty years later, de Kiewiet recalled the 'very great influence' John had had on him, 'musically and stylistically'. At eighty-two, de Kiewiet wrote that 'I still think of him quite openly, as a needed friend and a warm influence'.[139] John was always to commend de Kiewiet as an historian of South Africa to his students.

Individually, they influenced John in various ways. Duncan, the radical, with his Australian working-class background, sharpened (together with Laski) John's political interests and his contempt for the political establishment. 'As for the present [British] govt', John wrote in February 1929 in a characteristic political comment, 'it seems to consist of one brilliant man, Churchill, one very likeable personality (in private life), Baldwin, one very efficient & inhuman administrator, Neville Chamberlain, & about the biggest collection of blatant or obscure fools a country was ever cursed with'. His father had feared he was comparing Britain adversely with America. John denied it, but went on:

. . . while there are 200 tons of soot over London in the winter, while the London & Glasgow slums flourish, while the coal-mine mess exists, while the offer of men on the dole to do some public work for their money is refused 'because of some technical difficulty', while the 'Sunday Express' & 'Lloyds' Weekly News' & 'John Blunt' & Horatio Bottomley & Birkenhead make fat livings, & while a congenital idiot like Jix remains Home Secretary, & while people sleep on the Embankment in the shadow of the Cecil Hotel, then I consider I have a legitimate right to criticise . . . I'm on the side of the dissatisfied. And the same thing applies mutatis mutandis to N.Z. I believe in faith & tolerance & love & geniality. And I believe in scepticism & intolerance & hate & bitterness. And don't accuse me of lack of proportion.[140]

He was coming to recognise the growing importance of the United States in the twentieth-century world. He was also, for the first time, meeting and getting to know individual Americans, and reading and hearing more about their country.

I'm sick of these cheap English sneers at Americans; when it comes to a choice between interesting people give me travelled colonials or Americans every time . . . I'm coming to the conclusion that the States is one of the most important things to study in this here world, Babbit & Elmer Gantry ridden as it may be. It may be pretty batty in some ways, but I doubt if on the whole it's worse than England or N.Z.[141]

Raymond McGrath extended John's knowledge of the visual arts and gave him a taste of the literary world of Cambridge. He had already known about painting and printing from his reading and had some practical experience of printers from his time editing *Spike*, but McGrath made it all first hand, 'knowing' rather than 'knowing about'. McGrath's enthusiasm – for the Russian Ballet, for his discoveries on his travels in Spain (after which he became Don Ramón Majraz), for Scandinavian architecture, for his Miss Texas – was infectious. His talk of architecture and his work on 'Finella' opened John's eyes and contributed to one of his lasting interests.

With all of John's deep ambivalence about New Zealand, with his conviction that he must have more time away if he was to achieve what he believed he could, he was still thinking about what New Zealand might be. 'What a place we could have in N.Z. if we loosened the purse strings & only tried', as he said when visiting Cambridge. What is emerging is not just a dream born of nostalgia for home, but an idea of the positive qualities of the colonial mind. McGrath, Duncan, de Kiewiet were socially congenial; but, more, they exemplified the kind of sceptical yet civilised minds, the enthusiasm and directness, on which a new society might really be built. Other evidence is a comment on Henry Lawson: 'Did you ever read any of Henry Lawson's stuff? I have been reading While the Billy Boils lately & it is good stuff . . . Only colonial writing I ever read that got there; no waste words, no padding, not much description; but it couldn't have been written anywhere but in N.Z. or Australia.'[142]

The friendships of those years were given a particular intensity not just by the shared sense of discovering the world, but also by the recognition that, as on a sea voyage, this shared experience must come to an end. Adelaide MacDonald had gone by the end of John's first year, back to Toronto. Many years later, in 1958, she visited Wellington. They got on very well after thirty years: 'she and Elsie took to each other & the talk was full & free'.[143] John met her again some years later in New York, where she had become the head of Unicef. Helen Allen went on to her position at Vassar. She left that on her marriage in 1931. She and John lost touch and never met again. De Kiewiet would have a distinguished academic career. After holding positions at the State University of Iowa from 1929 to 1941, and Cornell University from 1941 to 1951, he became president of the University of Rochester in 1951. McGrath published books on twentieth-century houses and on glass in architecture and decoration. He was design consultant for the BBC from 1930 to 1935 and responsible for some of the interior spaces in the new Broadcasting House in London.[144] Later he became Principal

Architect at the Office of Public Works in Dublin (1948–68) and professor of architecture at the Royal Hibernian Academy. Henning and Duncan both returned to the University of Sydney, Henning eventually becoming professor of French.[145] Duncan joined the department of tutorial classes (university extension), becoming acting director in 1934 and director two years later. In 1951 he was appointed professor of history and political science at the University of Adelaide. John saw a little more of Duncan than he did of de Kiewiet and McGrath. Even if they had had time, it would have been almost impossible to sustain their particular friendships through letters alone. Adelaide MacDonald and the McGraths were faithful with Christmas cards. After a brief meeting in 1950 (the first since 1929), McGrath wrote, 'In future we must do a bit better at keeping in touch/Au revoir mon cher'.[146] They met only briefly in later years.

At least John was making the return voyage with Elsie, and they were determined to marry just as soon as he could get a job. But one can understand his gloom – 'We're hopelessly handicapped out there by our distance from anything'[147] – in a world where distances were still measured in terms of sea travel times, where an exchange of letters between New Zealand and London took almost three months and where one worried whether PhD in a cable was charged as one word or three. The years in London had, in all sorts of ways, developed John as an historian. Newton's seminar and his idea of an intensive grounding in historical method had played a part – though John was always to be sceptical of the value of a PhD compared with a good book – but probably this was less important than the stimulation he received from his fellow students and the breadth of his reading. He had deepened his appreciation of his British and European heritage, and through his letters as much as his thesis had developed his skills as a writer. He found it hard to believe that he would be able to work as an historian in New Zealand, but in the years ahead he was proved wrong.

PART TWO

Discovering New Zealand

6

DUNEDIN, HAMILTON, AUCKLAND, 1930–32

BACK IN WELLINGTON, Elsie went to stay with her parents on the Western Hutt hills and John moved into 49 Hopper Street with his father and Auntie. It cannot have been an easy homecoming. His father was still deeply affected by his mother's death; indeed, John gained the impression she was constantly in his thoughts: 'everything, flowers, books, house, hills, sun, air, sky, is Her to him'.[1] John visited relations, but his Aunt Ada Paterson had died a few months before his mother,[2] and cousins had married and were making their own lives. While Keith and Fronnie with a baby daughter were in Wellington, with Jenny's death the heart had gone out of the extended family. John started reading about Pacific exploration at the Alexander Turnbull Library but found it difficult to settle to work.

I started on Chapter 1 of my Pacific book the other night; but I can't even write ordinary humdrum mediocre matter of fact prose now; after a couple of hours of dreadful heartbreaking work & the completion of one foolscap page I felt like falling on the floor & crying. An impotent deadly blight seems to have settled on me; all I seem good for is teaching, or shovelling clay on my brother's [Keith's] section. Is this the influence of N.Z., my beautiful romantic homeland, or have I just come to the end of my tether?[3]

This was to Kathleen McKay early in 1930. She was back in London on another trip. 'Gawd! how your news of plays & music twists me up', John wrote, but there was one bright prospect: 'Ere you get this I shall be married'.

At one stage there had appeared to be a chance of a job at Victoria. F.P. Wilson's assistant lecturer, Winifred Maskell, had decided to leave but then said she would stay on. John was offered a job for twelve months as the WEA tutor-organiser in Dunedin while the incumbent, L.M. Ross, was on leave. With nothing else in prospect, he accepted the offer. A little later Miss Maskell changed her mind once more. Wilson, 'left in the lurch', offered John the position. Although it was only half-time with a salary of £250, he would have taken it if he had not already committed himself to Dunedin. It would have given him 'a foot in', and with Elsie's allowance from her father and free accommodation at Hopper Street he thought they could have survived. He believed he had extracted a promise from Wilson that he would do his best to get him a full-time job the following year. 'I hope to heaven the blooming luck has turned & that things will be all right next year. Otherwise we shall be well in the soup in a country like this'.[4]

Whatever it entailed, the WEA position was a job, and opened the way for marriage. The one remaining impediment was Elsie's mother's anguish at the prospect of a registry office ceremony. John, for his part, was equally determined it should not take place in a church:

I grieve to lacerate Mrs Holmes's feelings so; but some vestige of intellectual integrity we must hang on to . . . considering that her convictions are assaulted so, she stands it well, & in silent fortitude which I cannot but admire; & is going to make us a cake, even though she comes not to the ceremony . . . I go on my secular way in some distress, but hoping that I am justified. Blast these prehistoric people, pillars of the church & these ½ wits of parsons! Otherwise the Holmes crowd are behaving like angels.[5]

John and Elsie's marriage, on Monday, 17 February 1930 by the Wellington Registrar, was followed by a lunch at the Holmeses, for the immediate families. The only non-family guest was Elsie and John's old friend from the tramping club, Marjorie Wiren, with her small daughter. After lunch they left in Elsie's father's car for Raumati Beach, where they had been lent a bach for a week by another old tramper. John's 'Journal' of the week is a record of walking, bathing, quoit tennis and taking out the flounder net – and eating fish almost every day. John took *Tristram Shandy* (his intention to read it in London the year before had clearly come to nothing) but did little reading, though he and Elsie both read 'Marie Stopes' and Elsie, H.G. Wells's *Love and Mr Lewisham*. John conscientiously kept a record of their expenditure on food, which came to a total of 12s 7½d for the week, mainly on milk, bread and eggs with a 'blow-out' on the final day, when they spent 9d on a pineapple.

At the end of February John's father, encouraged by the family who hoped it would help him move on from his grieving, sailed for England. Three days later John and Elsie caught the overnight ferry to Lyttelton and from there the train to Dunedin. Accommodation had been arranged for them in a house at 34 Clifford Street (with their landlady living in part of it), 'nothing much to look at from the outside, but the rooms are big & plain & comfortable, not over furnished, & very convenient'.[6] It was on a hill, close to the northern end of George Street (Dunedin's main street), overlooking the Botanical Gardens and with a fine view of the city, the harbour, the surrounding hills and away out to sea; but, fine as the view was, John wrote to Dick Campbell, he still preferred that of Brunswick Square.[7] He had a study at the university, which was a short walk from the house.

The WEA, as the Workers' Educational Association was invariably known, had been started in England in 1903 as 'a non-political, non-sectarian, and democratic association for the promotion of workers' education'.[8] It had come to New Zealand in 1915 via New South Wales and continued to be closely linked with Australia for the following twenty-five years. At a time when opportunities for even post-primary education in New Zealand were still severely limited, many people believed in education as the key to social advancement (a belief at the heart of the Forward Movement and of the Unitarian Church of John's early years). A number of staff within the university colleges shared this belief, and Thomas Hunter, at Victoria, was one of those involved in the association from its earliest years. Sir Robert Stout, as Chancellor of the University of New Zealand, supported the WEA, and the government gave a small grant to the colleges for the teaching costs of tutorial classes, which in the early years were frequently taken by university staff members. In 1919 the government made its first direct grant to the association. From its early years it had a strong regional basis to its activities, with tutorial class committees organising the programme in each centre. In 1920 the first tutor-organiser or district organiser was appointed, in Canterbury, with further appointments following in other centres. Canterbury also held the first summer school (the successors of which were to flourish in the 1920s and 30s) over the Christmas–New Year period of 1920–21. John attended one of these two years later, and wrote a short article on it for the *Evening Post*.[9]

The association grew steadily through the 1920s, although its aspirations inevitably exceeded its resources. The original tutorial classes (an hour's lecture followed by an hour for discussion) were supplemented by correspondence courses and the 'box scheme', in which books and other written material were sent out to students who would then meet in a group to discuss the reading. Numbers grew, and in 1930 there were nearly 7500 students enrolled in 224 classes.

The director of the Dunedin WEA (a part-time position in addition to his main job), to whom John was responsible, was Dr Allan G.B. Fisher,* professor of economics at Otago University, six years older than John but also recently married. John found Fisher an admirable boss. His wife Airini had taught home science at the university, and the first time John and Elsie invited them for a meal Elsie, who had little practical experience of cooking, having grown up in a household with a cook, prepared two complete main dishes to ensure that at least one was successful. The Fishers were good company, they too were walkers, and they became lasting friends. Other new friends were the lecturer in economics, Geoffrey Billing, and his wife Muriel.

John's London premonition that they would be building their furniture out of kerosene and fruit cases was borne out when he put three kerosene cases together, 'enlarged the top a bit and put a small back to it' to make a sideboard and then put fruit cases together in the same way for bookshelves.[10] He discovered a picture framer who had known George Butler, and using wedding-present money had him frame the Cézanne print *La maison du pendu* (brought from London), a Butler watercolour, *The blue boat*, and John's portrait. John, as always, arranged objects with painstaking care: 'the Cézanne has a wall to itself; the Blue Boat just fits over the mantelpiece, flanked by those two Breton plates & the copper candlesticks I gave Elsie . . . Our other pictures are variously & suitably disposed.'[11]

Dunedin offered wonderful country for walking. Mount Cargill, the Leith Valley and Flagstaff Hill were all within easy walking distance of the house, while further away were more hills and the coast and the long, stark peninsula on the far side of the harbour. John and Elsie were out exploring almost every weekend. Elsie was always an inveterate scavenger; they carried back flowers, firewood, apples and plums from trees that she judged had gone wild, and on one occasion fifteen pounds of pears from which she made twelve pots of pear ginger jam.

---

* Fisher was a graduate of Melbourne and London Universities and was appointed to Otago in 1924. After a highly successful eleven years' tenure of the chair in economics he left to take up a similar chair at the University of Western Australia. He went on to further appointments in London and the United States. He and John continued to keep in touch.

John's travelling and lecturing ('commercial travelling in miscellaneous wisdom', he described it to Dick Campbell[12]) began at the end of March when he travelled south to Stirling, a small town on the railway near Balclutha, 'to give a kick off to a new circle starting there without a tutor'. 'Unfortunately', he reported to his father,

there were held on the same night a 21st birthday party, a meeting of the River Board, & a meeting of the local football club, which thinks it may be able to raise a team this year, so my meeting got only the residue of the population of the district, i.e. 4. Apparently however the birthday party accounted for most of the others who had promised to come, bar one gent who had a sore throat as a result of two days in Dunedin; so Stirling is going forward with fair optimism.[13]

Two days later the Dunedin WEA

had a social for the combined purposes of starting off the year with a bang, welcoming the new tutor, Dr Beaglehole, & his wife, & presenting Fisher with a Webster's Dictionary to mark the occasion of his marriage & the prevailing esteem for him etc. On walking into the hall, we found a large legend staring at us from the wall 'TUTOR NEW WE WELCOME YOU', done in crêpe paper on a spare curtain – which was staggering enough for a start. Of course there were speeches, but there was also supper; likewise a lot of jollification which I now seem to forget – folk-dancing & a play & a lady recited & so on. And I was introduced to about 50 people of whom I haven't the slightest recollection.[14]

The travelling was formidable: Palmerston on Monday night, Palmerston Sanatorium every second Tuesday, service car to Oamaru for Tuesday night as the timetable made it impossible by train, back to Dunedin for a midday meal on Wednesday and then that evening to Hampden. John could have gone directly to Hampden from Oamaru, going back to Dunedin meant six hours extra in the train, but staying away meant 'being marooned either in Oamaru or Hampden for the day, besides not seeing the missus from Monday afternoon to Thursday mid-day'. However, Oamaru was only once a fortnight. He returned from Hampden on Thursday morning and had the mid-day meal with Elsie. There was a short trip to Outram for an evening lecture, from which he got home towards midnight. On Friday there was a lunch-hour lecture at the Roslyn Mills.

As the year progressed, the train service steadily worsened as the Railways cut services in response to the economic depression. John, increasingly fed up with the travelling, began to look forward to finishing most of his classes by the end of September:

Just about time too . . . I used to go to Hampden – 55 miles – in 3 hours. Now they have knocked out the passenger trains & hook a couple of carriages on to 150 yards of trucks it takes in theory 4 [hours]. Last Wednesday it took nearly 5½. Train gets to Port Chalmers fairly well; then proceeds by a series of jolts & jerks, stopping dead in between, to within a few miles of Seacliff, when it stops altogether. It is then broken in two; some trucks to go on to Seacliff, leaving the passengers stranded for ½ hour or so till the engine comes back for them. Then we go to Palmerston at a good bat, making up a lot of time; go on for a few more miles, & wait for a goods train with no passengers; arrive in Hampden just in time for me to tear along to my lecture without any tea ½ hour late! . . . No heating of course; & after a warm springy spell, the weather has been vilely cold again.[15]

However, from the start the students he met seemed very keen and amiable. They were given some choice in the course of lectures they were to have but it could be difficult to please everyone.

I thought I had Hampden all fixed up for political science, & the meeting was nearly over on that assumption when a rebel arose & said he didn't want to hear about Plato & all those dead fellows, history was no good to him, he wasn't interested in Fascism & so on, give him literature; now what about some lectures on Galsworthy? So I said All right, but I could hardly give 24 lectures on Galsworthy, what else did he have in mind? He said it wasn't fair to ask him to make up a syllabus on the spur of the moment; anyhow he supposed I'd been to university & if I'd taken my B.A. I ought to be able to lecture on literature . . . So they took a vote, & out of 30 odd 16 voted for literature, 9 for pol. science, & the others didn't vote at all. Then they had supper, as it was the first meeting of the year, & most of them said Oh, it doesn't matter! Talk about anything you like! or Say you're going to talk about something & talk about something else! But one bloke said: Anything you like, but for God's sake no more Shakespeare! – At Outram they thought they'd like political science but also a few lectures on music. Roslyn Modern Problems – disarmament & the like. The other mobs don't seem to know what they want yet. After I've finished all the lecturing I have to write & run a correspondence course on colonial history; & finally edit & write a weekly column in the morning paper & a fortnightly one in the evening one.[16]

In spite of the vote, at Hampden as well as Outram he started with Plato and Aristotle, 'to the accompaniment of unexpected enthusiasm',[17] and given the choice between more Greek political theory and moving on everyone plumped for the Greeks. Discussion generally was on 'unemployment or coal-mining or N.Z. education' though the transition from Aristotle seemed 'quite natural'. No one wanted to learn New Zealand history. The Roslyn Mills class caused John some trepidation. He got through a discussion on disarmament but they wanted to go on to unemployment and then tariffs. 'Now no one', he wrote, 'would accuse me of being an economist; so the outlook there is not too bright'. The course was ostensibly on 'Modern Problems', but John suspected that 'even Duncan with his passion for broad views, universality & omniscience would boggle at some of it'. In the event John's trepidation was unwarranted.

By the middle of June he was looking forward to being halfway through most of the courses, and wrote to his father that things were going on pretty evenly with the numbers keeping up (this was too sanguine; the class at Palmerston had collapsed by the end of the month though not, John thought, for any failing on his part).[18] He had, however, lost the local Anglican parson from the Hampden class:

a rather loud-voiced cocksure swipe, who accused me (& wrote to Fisher behind my back) of being anti-British & socialist & disrespectful to bishops & nasty about his church to an audience of Presbyterians & disloyal to the objects of the W.E.A. & a good many other things. The rest of the class congratulated me on getting him out of the way, which was the last thing I intended to do. Fisher told him, if he thought I was so subversive, it was his duty to stay on & combat my sinister influence – so did I; but he marched out into the wilderness & respectability, taking his wife, a very meek silent damsel, with him.[19]

John confirmed that the class did have a good solid backbone of female Presbyterians, but the postmaster and the schoolteacher had 'regrettable leanings towards free thought'. There was also a former lighthouse keeper, now farming, who appeared to be extraordinarily well read and was eager to read Hobbes, never having had a chance to do so before.

Dunedin was proving very hospitable. The university staff, in John's view, were a bit more sociable than those in Wellington, though he merely raised an eyebrow politely whenever he was solemnly assured it was the only university town in New Zealand. They were entertained by the ethnologist H.D. Skinner and his wife; 'he seems to be a bit overwhelmed at times by his missus, who is pretty voluble', John wrote to his father.[20] The Beagleholes had known him when he was studying at Victoria at the same time as John's Uncle Ted before the First World War. The Bensons (he was professor of geology, she was giving some lectures on Japan to which Elsie went) invited them to a musical evening. They were an interesting pair, Quakers and ardent members of the Institute of

Pacific Relations, for which Benson got John to give a lecture on the Spanish exploration of the Pacific. 'Everybody is mad on lectures down here . . .' John reported. 'Of course, poor cows, they have nothing else to do, bar going to see one another & to the pictures. They all have a sublime faith in Dunedin & their university too.'[21] To Sophia Hooper, John was more forthright: 'Dunedin is Dead, & all the corpses walking around think it is the greatest Show on Earth',[22] and he confided that 'every now & then we get so thoroughly fed up with the place that we could break down & cry'. It was generally the English papers that set him off; with Elsie it was John's father's letters from England.

In July John wrote to him:

Work has been going on much as usual. I have nearly caused a riot at Hampden lecturing on Ruskin & Morris & civic art etc., assailing the Dunedin railway-station & N.Z. houses with much gusto. They can't see what's wrong with the Railway station. Working up this subject I read a jolly good little book by W. R. Lethaby called 'Form in Civilisation' which I bought years ago – I'm glad I waited till after being in England to read it . . .[23]

He urged his father to visit the William Morris showroom in Hanover Square, which he had missed seeing.

It was not a cheerful month. John had news that his friend Harry Espiner, who had accepted a lectureship at Victoria and was due to start at the beginning of 1931, had died at Poitiers, the result, John assumed (rightly), of his dreadful war injuries. He was 'a jolly good cobber to me . . . the gentlest & simplest fellow I ever knew'.[24] The same week John heard from F.P. Wilson that there was no hope of a job at Victoria the following year. 'This job is all right for a year', he wrote to Kathleen McKay in July,

& the hills round Dunedin are really superb . . . But the travelling is cruel, let alone absence from wife most of the week . . . The lecturing itself is quite good fun, mostly on my favourite academic subject of political theory, which can be made to involve a lot of other things. The farmers' wives & village store-keepers & railwaymen I lecture to are all good sports too, though I'm blowed if I know what some of them mean when they start arguing.[25]

He was wanting to get back to Wellington as soon as possible to work on his Pacific book.

A further blow came with the news that Marjory Hannah had been killed when she was struck by a bus in Featherston Street in Wellington. She and John had met several times in London a year earlier. She too had returned to New Zealand reluctantly, in her case to be near her elderly father. 'God! sometimes the world seems quite insane', John wrote to his father.[26]

The year's programme finished with a debate, held at Hampden, between the Hampden and Oamaru classes, with supper. 'A good deal of handshaking & speechifying & people seem to have been fairly pleased'.[27] At Roslyn Mills the chairman told John that he had greatly improved during the year and the class voted £1 to buy him a book. John chose J.B. Condliffe's *New Zealand in the Making*, which had just been published, and all fifteen members of the class signed it.

While John was thankful the travelling was over he clearly regretted seeing the last of some of the classes, and both he and Elsie 'could have stood' another year in Dunedin, where they had made good friends. John judged Fisher to have been 'an ideal boss'[28] and this regard was reciprocated. As well as expressing 'great satisfaction' with John's work, Fisher wrote to him, 'I would intensely like to have you and a few more people like you to vary permanently the atmosphere of Dunedin'.[29] John and Elsie returned to Wellington at the end of October and moved in with Elsie's parents. He finished his second chapter on Pacific exploration and wrote forty pages of an 'essay on N.Z. history' for a book of essays which he and Quentin Pope 'were proposing to edit and J.M. Dent to publish'.[30] John's salary continued until the end of January, and he had agreed to mark a thousand Matriculation history papers (such marking became a vital contribution to the family income in the years ahead). With no possibility of a university job, and some regret at the prospect of leaving Wellington just when Ian Henning was about to join the Victoria staff in Harry Espiner's place, John applied for the WEA tutor-organiser's position for the Waikato, based in Hamilton, £400 a year and permanent. His special subjects, he noted in his application, were colonial history and political theory but he also had 'a fair general knowledge of current world politics, European history and English literature'.[31]

He was interviewed in Auckland, where he met Norman Richmond for the first time and was favourably impressed. Richmond, four years older than John, was one of the Richmond–Atkinson clan; his father, Maurice Richmond, had been a barrister, and for some years professor of law at Victoria College. After graduating in mathematics from Canterbury College, Norman Richmond saw active service in France during 1918 – 'enough of war', he wrote, 'to make me a pacifist for the rest of my life'.[32] On returning to Christchurch he was awarded a Rhodes Scholarship, and at Oxford dropped mathematics in favour of modern history and political science. In 1925 he was appointed assistant tutor-organiser for the WEA on the staff of Auckland University College, three years later became director of the WEA tutorial classes in the Auckland district (which included Waikato). Richmond shared John's critical dissatisfaction with the world; for him adult education should above all play a key role in bringing about a more economically and socially just society. Their shared passion for the music of J.S. Bach proved to be an equal bond between them.

John was offered the job and told that a car would be essential for the travelling. He and Elsie bought second hand a two-seater with a dicky seat at the back, and at the end of February they drove to Hamilton, taking three days and staying a night in Wanganui with John's brother Geoffrey, his wife Theo and their small daughter Mary. Geoffrey pronounced the car, vetted by the Holmes's mechanic, to be 'lacking in some important respects as well as in most of the minor graces'.[33] Certainly, it needed attention at garages in Wanganui, Hawera and New Plymouth before they finally reached Hamilton. It was not a good start to John's relationship with cars.

They were enthusiastically welcomed, and given a bed, by the chairman of the district advisory committee, F.A. de la Mare (widely known as 'Froggy'). De la Mare had been one of the first students at Victoria University College; he had edited *Spike,* been president of the Students' Association, represented the college at rugby, cricket and tennis, written verse, and in 1910 edited a collection of verse written in and around Victoria, *The Old Clay Patch.* The college retained his lifelong loyalty. A 'reluctant lawyer',[34] he put most of his energy into public causes: penal reform and the rehabilitation of prisoners, prohibition, the ideals of the League of Nations, education and academic freedom. In his younger days he had been a member of the Forward Movement and the Unitarian Church, where he had known John's parents, but he had since become a freethinker and a rationalist and an 'anti-Bible-in-schools stalwart'. He and John had much in common, although, John reported to his father, 'my word, he can be an awful bore'.[35] He modified that judgement in a later letter: he 'is not a bore except when you are tired or in a great hurry – he only takes a whale of a time to find the right word & get his yarns off his chest'.[36]

Work began at once. John's predecessor, F.B. Stephens ('one who knows not fear in a motor car'[37]), who had been appointed lecturer in economics at Auckland University College, spent a week driving him around and introducing him to the district. John despaired of ever being on such terms of easy familiarity with butterfat and farming costs. Despite this inadequacy, during the forthcoming months he was to find the farmers generally most tolerant of his agricultural philistinism.[38]

Elsie meanwhile was looking for somewhere to live. After Dunedin, Hamilton was flat, 'flat with a flatness primitive & almost impeccable', though parts of it were 'very pretty'.[39] It was not promising for walking. They settled on a house at 6 O'Neill Street, 'the best of a bad lot'; it had the advantage of a shed for the car and was not far from the river.[40] With eight rooms there was at least plenty of space, though the wash-house and lavatory were in a shed at the back. It cost them 32s 6d a week. There was one big room that they planned to use as a living-entertaining-book-music room (John's first act was to hang some of the pictures there), and they plunged into cleaning, painting and decorating. The garden, which ran down to the railway line, was a wilderness of overgrown weeds and rubbish. They hired a 'protégé' of de la Mare's to do a lot of the dirty work of clearing it; de la Mare had saved him from gaol a day or so before, 'a very nice chap, on the mend now, but in gaol from boyhood, a regular social rebel'.[41] Inside the house they scrubbed and painted. Elsie covered a 'revolting dado' in the kitchen with orange American cloth. Coloured glass in two of the doors aroused John's ire; they covered one door with a curtain, the other they unscrewed and stored in a spare room. Elsie also pasted brown paper over two sets of offending fireplace tiles. John was not a great handyman: 'I have to do all my carpentry & constructional engineering with a hammer, a screw-driver, & a gimlet. The axe comes in handy sometimes but when used as a saw it is not highly satisfactory. We are on the look-out for a good second-hand saw though.'[42] He took to the recalcitrant lawnmower with an oil can and a hammer and, surprisingly, got it to go.

After a fortnight things were taking shape inside, and outside the place was slowly emerging from chaos. John's father sent them the family piano from Hopper Street and they found a cabinetmaker named Hodgkins to make some furniture. He was recommended by Mrs Rogers, wife of a Hamilton doctor. The Rogers were friends of the de la Mares (de la Mare's wife was also a doctor), and had a house with a fine garden stretching down to the Waikato river, which flowed through the middle of Hamilton. They too were interested in the arts and were to be very hospitable to John and Elsie. Hodgkins was set to work on a kauri dresser and a set of kauri chairs with seagrass seats for the dining room, adapted from a picture in Heal's catalogue. John wished he had some more catalogues of modern furniture besides Heal's and the *Studio Year Book* for 1930.

After sharing the house for the year in Dunedin, John and Elsie clearly enjoyed having a place of their own. 'If I had the Turnbull Library up here', John wrote to his father, 'I wouldn't mind staying for three years or so & knocking [the house] into shape'.[43] Before the end of March, however, his salary was cut by 10 per cent to £360 – a move by the government in response to the depression. They had just ordered an armchair from Milne and Choyce in Auckland for Elsie, and John had asked Hodgkins to make him a working chair – another Heal's design – from 4000-year-old manuka retrieved from the Arapuni buried forest. Should he go ahead with the chair? John agonised and decided that, if a long-promised wedding cheque did not eventuate, he would have to earn the cost of the chair by the sale of verse or by writing articles. Having made that decision, however, they began to calculate whether their remaining unspent wedding-present cheques would also run to a small settee and chair after the pattern of those they had admired at 'Finella'.

The 'minor interstices between gardening & house decorating' were filled with WEA work. John's first lecture was at the Waikeria borstal. He was driven out by de la Mare, who, representing the Howard League, took a concert and lecture party there every week – '30 miles & a rotten road. The man's a hero.'[44] John talked about the exploration of the Pacific. The audience he thought 'very acute & appreciative', and he was also roped in as accompanist for various songs. He lectured to the local branch of the New Zealand Educational Institute on democracy and art, and to the Rotary Club on historical research ('de la Mare of course wangled an invitation & was much pleased by the exhibition – he takes a very fatherly interest in all our outgoings & incomings & general performances'[45]). He was elected to the executive of the League of Nations Union.

The car continued to play up. 'We go to bed every night praying that someone will pinch or burn it. There were lots of burglaries in this district before we came; but now nobody seems to have the slightest desire to make off with a handy-sized car.'[46] It was overhauled once more and running much better, fortunately, when lectures started in the third week of April.

Debating club on Tuesday & short chat by me on oratory past and present; Wednesday address by me to Luncheon Club on Univ. of London . . . Wednesday night out to Morrinsville to start off there, on Democracy; Thursday, inaugural lecture, Hamilton, on Democracy;

Saturday, Horsham Downs, Democracy. Elsie is getting rather sick of Democracy, but I am repeating myself wherever possible. The classes are much bigger than I had in Otago. Elsie is still chauffeuring – she drove out to Morrinsville, & I drove back . . . in a frightful storm of rain.[47]

John never did become a confident driver, and after Hamilton never drove again.

In that age before air travel, Hamilton was very much more accessible than Dunedin. Elsie's father, when travelling by train to Auckland to catch a ship to Sydney for a board meeting of the AMP, entertained them to breakfast at the Frankton station (the overnight train to Auckland stopped there long enough for the passengers to breakfast in the station dining room). On his way back he stopped off for a day in Hamilton. Elsie's brother Charles and his family were in Auckland and came down to visit. At the end of April John's father came to stay – 'if you can wangle from McIntosh [in the General Assembly Library] a large folio volume of Tasman's voyage edited by Heeres (I think) & bring it I should be vastly obliged'.[48] Elsie's parents stayed in August, with 'a blow-out at the Hamilton Hotel at the Old Bloke's expense', and Keith and Fronnie, on holiday at the beginning of October, used Hamilton as a base to visit Rotorua and Auckland.

With the house and furniture in a more satisfactory state, they were also inviting people in – should they try an open house on Sunday evenings, like the Laskis? John wondered. One of their first visitors was the secretary of the district advisory committee, an Englishman named Arthur Ward. Five years younger than John, he had come to New Zealand in 1926. After a period working on dairy farms in the Bay of Plenty he had been appointed company secretary to the New Zealand Co-operative Herd Testing Association and the Auckland Herd Improvement Association. It was the beginning of an outstanding career in the New Zealand dairy industry; in 1954 he became general manager of the New Zealand Dairy Board. To Arthur, John and Elsie represented a world of books, art and music of which he knew little. If de la Mare was unstoppable on his latest enthusiasm for putting the world to rights, Arthur was insatiable for all that he had missed in his youth. He was embarking on a book-buying campaign, so John 'turned over A. Bennett's Literary Taste to him, from the W.E.A. library. He thinks my knowledge of editions etc is simply prodigious . . .'[49] John introduced him to Housman's poetry – for a wedding present Elsie had given John copies of A Shropshire Lad and Last Poems from a limited edition printed and published by the Alcuin Press the year before. Arthur recalled, forty years later, John asking him how he had liked *A Shropshire Lad*. '"Too morbid" I said. You [Elsie] sympathised with my view, but John said "No – you haven't read him properly. Read him again and if you still don't like him, then read him a third time." I did just that and . . . at one time I could recite the whole of "Shropshire Lad".'[50]

In June John reported to his father that he had been 'lecturing pretty hard'.[51] He had started a series of twelve broadcast talks, fifteen minutes every Thursday, on the local radio station, 1ZH. For two of the topics (the League of Nations and the International Labour Organisation) he used recordings lent by Henry Valder, a local businessman, proponent of a partnership in industry between owners, managers and workers, and a friend of de la Mare's.* John himself covered the other topics: the meaning of democracy, fascism, how the Soviets work, and a summary of the series, together with some words on the duty of doubt. 'A futile sort of business', he told his father. Later, however, in his annual report, he suggested that radio would be a way to extend adult education. The course of six lectures he had given at Morrinsville on political ideals had, by general request, been extended to twelve. He had started a course at Te Kowhai on contemporary problems: communism, fascism, democracy, tariffs, disarmament, and the origin of the war. Bad roads and bad weather (it was an exceptionally long and hard winter) kept away some who had attended the previous year, but he still found the class one of the best, the discussion 'always vigorous and generally to the point'.[52] Attendance was increasing at the Hamilton course, which comprised twenty-four lectures on political ideals covering 'the ideas of most of the important political thinkers from Plato to Lenin, with the object of discovering their bearing on modern life'.[53] 'De la Mare generally comes along & drags in Prohibition or Laurence Housman or both.'[54] A second course in Hamilton was on drama. John gave a number of lectures on the history of drama and there were readings of plays, including Ibsen's *The Doll's House*, Shaw's *The Devil's Disciple* and Synge's *The Playboy of the Western World*. The last was a public occasion as the main part of the final WEA social for the year.

By 1931 New Zealand was firmly in the grip of the 'great depression'. One might have hoped, John said, that this 'would lead to the stimulation of the inquiring mind'; rather, it had often

---

*   De la Mare had published a pamphlet, *A Discussion Concerning Profit-sharing and Co-Partnership* (1924), in which he discussed and supported Valder's ideas.

apparently 'caused a mood of blank despair'.[55] 'The slump & the weather combine against the adult educationalist', he wrote to his father in July (in the same letter he reported 'in another couple of days our garden will have been washed into O'Neill Street').[56] Overall in Waikato the numbers enrolled for classes were down, but among those attending interest and enthusiasm were marked. One of the brightest classes was at Horsham Downs:

The tutor had always, with town-bred arrogance, been inclined to regard farmers as a supremely conservative class, and was frankly astonished at the individuality and unorthodoxy of some of the expressions of opinion at Horsham Downs . . . Here as elsewhere there was no nonsense about an hour's lecture and an hour's discussion, and the tutor had more than once to tear himself away, not without regrets, as the time advanced towards midnight.[57]

Not surprisingly at that time, Soviet Russia was seen by some as a model for the future. 'The W.E.A. is in bad odour', John told Kathleen McKay, 'because it has been talking about Russia over the wireless & that is a thing no gentleman would do'.[58] John was reading what he could get of the books published on Russia, including *Ten Days that Shook the World,* John Reed's account of the revolution, and Maurice Hindus's *Humanity Uprooted* (recommended by Dick Campbell). He had letters from his friend Lorrie Richardson, who had done some work in Russia in 1930 and was soon to return to do six months' soil chemistry with a Russian party in the Caucasus and Crimea. But John did not find the local communists persuasive:

We had a mob of them along at a meeting about Disarmament the other night . . . & I argued the communist point with them on the pavement outside afterwards. But they are quite impenetrable. They have one particular fiery evangelist, a farmer from Taupiri who told me with passion that I was a paid agent of the capitalist state, like the whole of the W.E.A. – he'd been watching me. I was not intimidated . . . It's pleasant to have them along however, for they give fire to discussions that may otherwise languish. The trouble is the blighters can never keep to the point, whatever it may be . . .[59]

If judged by what he saw as the main test, John was certainly succeeding at his job: the students were asking for more. The local executive of the Farmers' Union, moreover, were stimulated to 'rare heights of enthusiasm for education by the slump'[60] and called on him for advice. Ideally, he said, long courses should be offered all over the district but, apart from increasing financial constraints, there was one great difficulty. All classes wanted 'their lectures at approximately the same time, i.e. when the cows are dried off, between May and July'.[61] One solution John suggested was 'to take a leaf out of Denmark's book' and run a short winter school for farmers. With his move from Hamilton early in 1932, and the growing financial problems of the WEA, the idea was stillborn.

The WEA was supported by donations from public bodies and a subsidy from the government on such donations, as well as a direct government grant. As conditions worsened many cut their donations, though the Hamilton Borough Council and the Farmers' Union were welcome exceptions. In late July John heard from Norman Richmond that the government was refusing to pay either its usual grant or a penny in subsidies:

I have had the nasty news [he wrote to his father] that after the end of November, or perhaps with great luck the end of next February, my engagement will be terminated . . . unless a miracle happens practically the whole W.E.A. in N.Z. is wiped out. In Auckland Richmond will be left but nothing else . . . I haven't heard anything formally – that will come from the College Council . . . Of course to be sacked at the end of the year is going to be damned awkward for us . . .[62]

'Damned awkward' not least because Elsie was pregnant, the child due in early November.

The news proved to be premature. The government grant was to continue, though the subsidy on voluntary donations was cut. The tutorial classes committee at Auckland University College was able to countermand its earlier recommendation to the college council that John should be sacked. There was some anxiety that Rocke O'Shea, the Auckland University College Registrar, 'the villain of the piece' who had rushed the initial recommendation through and was said to 'hate the W.E.A. like poison', might resist the change. 'Nice genial lot of enemies we have!' John commented.[63] His job was saved, but the episode clearly fed his growing disenchantment with public events and government policies in New Zealand and the world in general.

In Britain the minority second Labour government, which he had seen elected in May 1929, fell on 24 August 1931. Faced with seemingly almost insuperable budgetary problems, the Prime Minister, Ramsay MacDonald, formed a National government with the Conservative and Liberal Parties. He continued as prime minister and was subsequently repudiated by the majority of the Parliamentary Labour Party. The news left John feeling 'so sick I've scarcely been able to speak for a week'.[64] When the *New Zealand Herald* published a leading article roundly criticising Arthur

Henderson, the outstanding British Foreign Secretary, for not following MacDonald, he was roused to comment:

Why a crisis in English politics should be a signal for writers in the New Zealand press to lose touch with their senses I do not know, but to read through the recent comments on the subject in your editorial columns is to gain the impression that the Daily Mail, the Daily Express, the Morning Post and the New Zealand Herald are dwelling in Bedlam together. Nor, though it may merely be a symptom of inadequacy in myself, do I comprehend why, because the majority of the Labour Party at Westminster are opposed to a 'National' government they are necessarily and without exception knaves and fools. I do not pride myself, because I have read closely all the cables published in the Herald on the English situation, on therefore understanding that situation in meticulous totality; for, unlike leader-writers and newspaper proprietors, I do not specialise in omniscience. But I imagine, having some acquaintance with contemporary English political life, that if Mr Henderson takes a certain step, he takes it with as much patriotism, as much knowledge of the necessities of the country, as much sense of enlightened responsibility as Mr MacDonald . . .

He concluded by suggesting that the *Herald*'s criticism of Henderson was both 'grotesque and impertinent'.[65] De la Mare told him there was 'not one chance in a million' that the *Herald* would publish the letter, and he was right. 'These N.Z. papers make me sick', John wrote to his father at the end of August. It was, interestingly, a time when the *Herald* had 'no words hard enough for Forbes, for wanting to form a "National Govt." in N.Z.'.[66]

Such events were not all-consuming. In the same letter to his father John reported that Elsie's parents had paid a very successful visit for the weekend, that the fruit trees were beginning to spark up a bit, and that he had been asked to give four lectures on the growth of freedom at the Auckland WEA summer school – could his father lend him his copies of Acton's *History of Freedom* and Bury's *Freedom of Thought*? He continued:

I have my last regular lecture in the country to-night, at Matangi. Small class there, but interesting; one chap was in Russia for three years 1921–3, & has seen a good deal of the world besides. Another, one Ramstead, leaned on the car for ¾ hour after my lecture & told me all about his family – his father when in England was in with all the Labour & Socialist birds – MacDonald, Henderson, Bruce Glasier, Blatchford, etc & knew Wm. Morris. He had all the Kelmscott Press books, but sold some of them when he left England (including the Chaucer – for £80! – in 1900 though); some he still has. Apparently he has been a great book collector, & of a very lively mind. Now lives at Raglan, of all places for a bloke with Kelmscott Press books to live! I wish I could lay my hands on a few of them.

Courses came to an end in mid-October.

We brought the work of the season to a glorious end last night with the Playboy before an audience of 35 or so, with supper to follow in a simple way; & by charging 6d for the supper made a profit of a few bob. So now I am shut of lecturing for a bit . . . However I have got the Christmas business [summer school] to work up now & a series of box-scheme lectures on Western Civilisation or something equally inclusive for next year.[67]

There were also letters to write to organisations and local bodies endeavouring to raise funds for the coming year. John got back to work on the Pacific with the aim of finishing the book over the summer, but he suspected he would not make much progress unless his father could get some more books from the General Assembly Library and send them up. He was reading Chekhov's plays – 'queer things'. On 30 October the baby arrived, a boy, 'lanky rather than fat, so I hope he will turn out a good tramper'.[68] A characteristic postcard was sent to Kathleen McKay:

BEAGLEHOLE: On 30th November [October], at Waione Maternity Hospital, Hamilton, New Zealand, to Dr J.C. Beaglehole and Elsie Mary his wife, a remarkably fine son. Both well. Thanks to Marie Stopes, Bertrand Russell and Almighty Providence (in that order). Australian, English, Manchurian and Eskimo papers please copy. 'Safe in the arms of J.C.'

After protracted deliberation the baby was named John Robin, but was always called Robin.

John's reading during the year had shown all of its customary variety. He had moved on from Chekhov to Hazlitt (in the Nonesuch edition), he wrote to his father in late November – 'one of the best books I ever read' – and then J. Livingston Lowes's *Convention & Revolt in Poetry,* ('also very good'), hoping he might learn something useful for a lecture on freedom in literature planned for the summer school.[69] Before Christmas he had also read Robert Graves's *Good-Bye to All That,* Hawkesworth's account of the voyages of Byron, Wallis and Carteret, and Milton's *Areopagitica*. He had finished preparing the summer school lectures. Work on the Pacific book had progressed, and only the final chapters on James Cook and a short conclusion remained to be written.

A Christmas dinner with the Rogers fell through when Mrs Rogers suddenly got diphtheria. Elsie and Robin took the train to

Wellington on Christmas night to stay once again with her parents, and John followed on 4 January after the summer school ended. His four lectures on 'The Growth of Freedom' were said by Richmond to have been regarded 'as some of the most thought-provoking in the history of our Summer Schools'.[70] During the summer John worked not only on the Pacific book but also on 'What is Western Civilisation?' for a 'box scheme' course, to be offered to country groups where it was impossible to send a tutor. In addition to the copies of the twenty-four lectures which John was to write, the groups were to be sent books, pictures and gramophone records (it was 'assumed that at least one member of the group has a gramophone'[71]). Work on the course continued until well into the new year. John's lectures began with a discussion of contemporary civilisation, 'Civilisation or Catastrophe: Where are we bound to?', and continued with a survey of Western history up to the nineteenth century. The course was planned as the first of three, bringing the students through to the present day. Richmond later wrote of John's work as 'quite the best course of its kind that we have handled here in the last five years'.[72]

The family returned to Hamilton in late February. For reasons that are not clear they had to find another house, and settled on one further up O'Neill Street, number 30, on the corner. Once again it was 'the best of a bad lot', with 'hideous spots of stained glass here & there, but that seems ubiquitous'.[73] The outlook for the WEA was gloomy. The government had decided to cut its funding from the end of March. A grant from the Carnegie Corporation in America would give some respite, but John did not think he could count on a job beyond November.

He had again been roused to write to the newspaper, this time the Wellington *Evening Post*.[74] When the editor of the *Red Worker* had been convicted of sedition, the paucity of comment, John considered, should 'alarm anyone who has been brought up to believe in a democratic political and social system and the virtues of freedom'. He noted that the prosecution had been brought under the War Regulations, although the war had ended thirteen years earlier, and that the definition of sedition left much to the discretion of the officials involved. He quoted Dicey, Laski, and Mr Justice Holmes of the American Supreme Court: 'We should be eternally vigilant against attempts to check the expression of opinions that we loathe and believe to be fraught with death, unless they so imminently threaten immediate interference with the lawful and pressing purposes of the law that an immediate check is needed to save the country'.[75] He argued that such prosecutions did not repress and did not persuade, and were 'evidence not so much of our belief in the rightness of our social system, as of our fear for its destruction'. He concluded:

I suggest finally that though one may look in vain to Solicitors General for a grasp of elementary political principle, or to policemen for a just weighing of political possibility, one might reasonably expect from a magistrate, in assessing pains and penalties, some sense of proportion, Or is this merely the exuberant Utopianism of an academic idealist? Perhaps it is.

The *Post* published the letter but in a 'garbled, or rather truncated version'.[76] He had more luck when C.A. Marris, the editor of *Art in New Zealand*, placed his poem 'The Apple-Bough' first in their verse competition; it was published in the March number and John received the prize of two guineas. He was greatly taken with Marris's 'expounding of the inner meaning of the thing'[77] – 'The sight of the massy blossom of the apple-bough spiritualised under the moon induces in [the poet] a valid but inexplicable emotion compact of loveliness and sorrow . . .'[78] – and decided that Elsie should have a new hat out of the proceeds.

John was immersed in planning for the year's work, and in checking his Pacific chapters before they were typed by de la Mare's typist, when he heard that the professor of history at Auckland, J.P. Grossmann, had been sacked for financial dishonesty. Grossmann was a rogue, Keith Sinclair writes in his history of the university, 'albeit a remarkable one', and the events leading to his dismissal 'the greatest scandal in the history of the College'.[79] The college decided to advertise not a chair but a temporary lectureship. John had 'laughed a hollow laugh at these things for happening at the wrong time, & thought no more about it',[80] until he heard from W.T.G. (Willis) Airey (appointed to the lectureship ahead of him in 1929), who encouraged him to apply. Faced with the prospect of delivering fifteen lectures and marking fifty essays a week, Airey was clearly anxious to have assistance. John consulted Richmond and de la Mare. De la Mare insisted that he should apply, and within five days he had been interviewed and had accepted the position from 1 April.

I was in two minds whether to apply for the job, [he wrote to his father] & whether to take it when I had got it. The change from adult education to N.Z. university work has its dark side, & I don't fancy a cast-iron syllabus much after being my own master. Moreover the job is not over-permanent, but at least it may last out this one; it is temporary, to the end of December, when the position will be reconsidered. So I suppose I must make myself indispensable during the rest of the session. Airey seems a good chap, & gazes back with some sorrow at the Grossmann régime behind him – more with sorrow than with anger, I am afraid, as he is one of the principal S.C.M. boys in the place.* I warned him that I was pure pagan.[81]

The Farmers' Union in Hamilton wrote to John to say how sorry they were that he was going; once again they were packing and moving. The family stayed in Auckland with old friends from Victoria, Ken and Marie Griffen, while they looked for somewhere to live, finally finding a flat at 22 Grafton Road. It was close enough to the university for John to walk home for meals, and while it seemed expensive at £2 a week they would save on tram fares. It was also close to the Richmonds and to the WEA headquarters. Although the flat was the top floor of the house it was almost at street level, and Grafton Road at that time was 'quiet though not what you would call flash or even excessively select'.[82] There was a view of the Domain and plenty of trees, of a distant strip of the harbour and in the foreground the rusty roofs of the factories in Stanley Street and the backs of neighbouring houses – all rough as sacks. During their first weeks in Auckland it rained, at times with a 'hell-like intensity',[83] and John's impressions of the city and the university were gloomy.

The library is appalling; hardly a book on colonial history – not even a decent text-book. What there is is almost exclusively out of date. Other departments almost as bad. Political theory not taught – apparently Grossmann didn't like it. And no chance whatever of getting any books – till the Carnegie grant comes off next year. Delightful place. Really Victoria College seems a paradise compared to it . . . Bright institutions, these N.Z. so-called universities.[84]

Compared with lecturing to 'moderately good W.E.A. classes' he found the teaching 'a dud business', though one or two good students were turning up and he hoped that more might emerge as time went

---

* The SCM was the Student Christian Movement. John reported to his father that there were at the college two rival sects among the Christians: 'The S.C.M. proved too broad & modernist for some of the real dinkum Bible-bangers, so they seceded & formed the Evangelical Student Federation. Their libraries repose side by side in a sort of annex to the Univ. library, & the juxtaposition would make you laugh. The S.C.M. is very strong on the Xian life & missionaries; the E.S.F. runs to Xian evidence & proofs of the inspiration of the Bible. Gordstruth, & this sort of stuff is sheltered by the walls of a university library!' (JCB to DEB, 6 June 1932.)

on. But questions of teaching were almost at once overshadowed by questions of civil liberties and academic freedom, and John's involvement was to have far-reaching effects on his subsequent career. Writing to his father on 9 May, after a full account of the flat with a drawing of how they had arranged the living space, John continued: 'Richmond & I have got engaged in a controversy on academic freedom, to make the available time even fuller, & I don't see myself being reappointed next year if O'Shea the registrar, a swine if ever there was one, has anything to do with it – and he seems to run Fowlds.'[85] Sir George Fowlds had been president, or chairman, of the college council since 1920. In his younger years a crusader for the progressive causes of the time, he had been a capable minister of education in Sir Joseph Ward's Liberal government. Now over seventy, his age was telling, and he was to retire the following year.

Before John's arrival R.P. Anschutz, the lecturer in philosophy appointed in the late 1920s and one of the ablest of the new staff, had written a foreword to a pamphlet, *A New Zealand Woman in Russia* by Mrs H.J. Scott, a member of the Communist Party. After drawing attention to the economic progress made in Russia since the revolution, he had remarked, 'The ten years that the Russians have spent getting out of their mess, we have spent in getting into ours'. He signed the introduction with his name and gave the college as his address. Fowlds took the view that as Anschutz's comments were not based on his academic expertise he should not have identified himself with the college, and the registrar drafted a memorandum (dated 12 April) and sent it first to the professorial board and then to all the staff. It said:

There is always a possibility that the public expression of opinion upon matters of a political nature by members of the staff in their capacity as such, may tend to place the College authorities in a difficult situation. While it is in no way desired to interfere with the ordinary right of free expression of opinion, it is suggested by the Board that members of the staff should exercise due discretion in deciding whether any such statement should be made in their official capacity under the address of the College or in their capacity as a private citizen.[86]

It was a not unreasonable statement, and in normal times that might well have been the end of the matter. But the times were not normal. There were over 80,000 unemployed – in Keith Sinclair's words, 'the ragged army of men on the dole . . . architects, teachers, carpenters, chipping weeds on the footpaths; malnutrition in the schools – and children stealing lunches; ex-Servicemen begging outside a pub; the queue at the soup kitchen'.[87] The government removed the power of the Arbitration Court to protect wage levels, and government economies worsened the plight of many: public servants and teachers, whose wages were cut, and the old and the disabled, whose pensions were reduced. The misery and desperation experienced by many led to protests. Marches in Wellington and Auckland were broken up by the police, and turned into rioting, looting and the destruction of property. A blinkered government, fearing revolution, passed repressive legislation curtailing civil liberties. Public servants and teachers were threatened with dismissal for any 'public statement' by which any one of them might have 'sought to bring the government of New Zealand into disrepute'.[88] 'New Zealand', Sinclair concluded, 'had reached its nadir.'[89]

On 14 April 1932 conflict between unemployed demonstrators and police in Queen Street escalated into extensive rioting. Shop windows were broken and looting took place. 'Special police' were recruited, who included many students.* With feelings running high, a lot of New Zealanders held that the communists, who were influential in the Unemployed Workers' Movement, were threatening not just law and order but the very foundations of society.[90] 'Fair dinkum', John wrote at the time, 'the whole damn country's gone mad. The hysteria here about communists & foreigners is appalling . . . This country beats me. I gave three lectures for the W.E.A. on the Breakdown of Democracy, Dem[ocracy] & its Rivals, and the Future of Democ[racy], the first three weeks we were in Akld; I wdn't go beyond the first lecture now.'[91] The Minister of Education, Robert Masters, having seen Anschutz's foreword, wrote to the registrar on 28 April querying whether it was 'quite fitting for an Institution partly dependent on Government funds to employ a lecturer holding the opinions that Mr Anschutz appears to hold'. He further asked that the staff be informed of the 'necessity of exercising due discretion in the making of public statements upon matters of a political nature'.[92] John thought Masters should have been told 'to go to hell'.[93] Fowlds chose to reply (through O'Shea) simply, and perhaps wisely, that he had dealt with the matter.[94]

Following the riots two men, both members of the Communist

---

*   O'Shea took the opportunity to attempt to get Anschutz to join the 'specials', 'as a means of rehabilitating himself, & strengthening the college's position as a respectable institution, in the eyes of Mr Masters [the Minister of Education]. I believe on this occasion Anschutz was not polite to the Registrar.' (JCB, memorandum 'In re Anschutz' (written for de la Mare), 2 September 1932. F.A. de la Mare Papers. MS-Papers-2865-2/3/4A. ATL.)

Party, were arrested and charged with 'spreading literature calculated to cause violence'. A detective, P.J. Nalder, called on John and wanted him to give evidence in the case, as an historical expert and Crown witness, that the Russian revolution was bloody. 'I said I didn't mind telling him as man to man that it *was* bloody, but that I certainly wdn't give evidence for the Crown in a case like that; gave him my opinion of such prosecutions, etc (with which he agreed).'* The men were sentenced to six months' imprisonment. The magistrate said that such literature was 'the sort of stuff which had led to . . . the riots', whereas a 'couple of days before [he] had said they were entirely due to larrikinism'.[95]

'At this', John wrote, he and Norman Richmond 'finally boiled over & decided to write to the paper'.† John reworked the letter he had sent to the *Evening Post*. They approached a number of colleagues to see whether they would sign it too, but even the two or three who initially agreed pulled out for reasons 'which seemed sufficient to themselves'.

All right, we thought, we'll see if old Sir George Fowlds, who is supposed to be a radical, will sign it.[96] Saw him & had one of the most remarkable interviews of our lives with him & O'Shea (trust O'S to be there). Sir G. read it through aloud with much expression, carefully pointing out the sarcastic bits ('They might irritate people') & then said he couldn't agree with it. 'Why, these men – yes – these men favoured violence'. O'S shoves in his oar about people puffed up with a little knowledge rushing in etc. I really wd like a verbatim report of it all. Finally R said Well, if he thought O'Shea's conception of academic freedom represented the attitude of the Council at large, he'd be ashamed of belonging to the

---

*   Nalder's report, dated 9 May 1932, while it did not corroborate John's final comment, otherwise bears out his account of the meeting. 'I asked Dr Beaglehole whether the Russian Revolution in 1917 was not a violent and bloody one. He agreed that it was a horrible revolution and that he would not like to see the same occur here.' He records John's opposition to the government's 'repressive measures' and his belief that 'books of this class should not be repressed'. Nalder's report concludes: 'Dr Beaglehole spoke deliberately and with consideration, and as I was leaving in an apologetic way stated that "personally he would always be pleased to do anything for me or assist me".' The report was forwarded to the Commissioner of Police for his information and was the beginning of a quite extensive file on John held first by the police and later by the New Zealand Security Service (after 1969 the New Zealand Security Intelligence Service). (J.C. Beaglehole File. New Zealand Security Intelligence Service Papers.)

†   When Richmond later appeared to hold himself responsible for John's 'downfall', John wrote: 'You know as well as I do that I was at bursting point before you came on the scene. I grant that it was your idea to burst together. But I wd. have burst anyhow.' (JCB to Richmond, 7 February 1933.)

univ. I said ditto. Sir G. very amiable & fatuous throughout. Next day every member of staff gets a memorandum signed by Sir G., obviously written by O'Shea, assuring them of their determination to defend academic freedom, the most consummately insulting thing I've ever read. Must be seen to be believed . . . [97]

John and Richmond decided to go ahead anyhow with a revised letter. It was more temperate than the first draft ('mild as milk & water' in John's view), with less assertion of principle and more raising of considerations which seemed important (had they in fact been influenced by Fowlds's comments?). The letter was headed 'Communism and Hysterics' and in it they wrote:

The whole question of Freedom and authority is a difficult one, and only the person with little knowledge of the problems involved would venture to be dogmatic about it. Nevertheless we would suggest the following points as being important in any calm consideration not only of the case referred to but of the whole problem of social peace which it illustrates. In the first place freedom can never be absolute; its very existence depends upon the authority of the State being maintained (in somewhat the same way as the freedom of motorists, in any real sense, depends upon the rule of the road being enforced). And it would seem to follow that, in times when such authority is in danger, a certain curtailment of the freedom which can safely be allowed in more normal times is justified. The extreme case of this is martial law, which would be justified by most people only when the danger to the State is correspondingly extreme. Short of the extreme circumstances, however, which may be held to justify martial law, are there any principles which it seems reasonable to apply in determining the point at which the State should step in to restrain the free expression of opinions? No complete answer is possible in the present brief compass, but so far as the practice of the most enlightened countries is any guide one may perhaps take as typical an authoritative pronouncement of one of the greatest of American judges, Mr Justice Holmes of the Supreme Court bench. 'We should be', he wrote in his famous case, 'eternally vigilant against attempts to check the expression of opinions that we loathe and believe to be fraught with death, unless they so imminently threaten interference with the immediate purposes of the law that an immediate check is needed to save the country.' Now if we apply such a test as this to the case under consideration, the question arises whether the literature concerned was proved to have any connection with immediate violence. It was stated by the magistrate that 'this sort of literature leads to disturbances such as we have recently had in our city streets.' With all due respect we would suggest that no evidence has been produced which would give the colour of truth to this statement. We would go further and say that at a time when we have fifty thousand registered

unemployed whose helpless resentment at their position is sharpened by
the feeling that the world's potential wealth makes poverty inexcusable,
together with a permanent percentage of simple hooligans – latent but
nevertheless eager for activity – at such a time it is unnecessary to blame
the activities of Communists for any violence which may occur. We
would suggest in fact that the penalisation of the two men in this case is
merely one example of what can only be described as the hysteria which
is rapidly growing up in our country around the words 'Communism'
and 'Communists', words much used in this case, and apparently
unavoidably so, since both men 'admitted' they were members of the
Communist Party.

They went on to question whether such sentences had any effect
other than to 'present the social rebel with his case against capitalist
society', and concluded:

. . . we are in no sense attempting to justify violence or lawlessness.
What we do suggest is that we should be less hysterical in our search
for the causes of such violence. For it would seem to us that the attempt
forcibly to suppress opinions (however wrong they may be) which have
no proved connection with immediate acts of violence or lawlessness is
as inexpedient from the point of view of social peace as it is unjust to the
individuals who are made to suffer the penalty.[98]

Richmond took the revised version to be typed, and decided, to
John's chagrin,* to send it with only his signature, with the aim of
protecting John in view of the temporary nature of his appointment.
He sent the letter to the *Auckland Star* and the *New Zealand Herald*.
Both turned it down. John claimed that Alan Mulgan, the chief-
leader writer and literary editor of the *Star*, 'was horrified at the
mere idea of printing such a thing'.[99] John now insisted on signing it
and, with both signatures, it was sent to the *New Zealand Worker*,
where it was published on 18 May.

Before this occurred, John and Richmond had turned their
attention to the 'Fowlds memorandum', described by Sinclair as
'notorious and certainly the most famous message ever sent out in
the College'.[100] In contrast with the registrar's memorandum of 12
April, Fowlds (or perhaps more accurately O'Shea) now held that
the same considerations governed any public statement by a member
of the college staff, 'either under the address of the College, or in his
capacity as a private citizen'. Such a statement, he wrote, should be

---

*   John later wrote to de la Mare (2 August 1934), 'I have always admired
        N.M.R. for this, though I damned him heartily at the time.' (F.A. de la
        Mare Papers. MS-Papers-3865-2/3/4/B. ATL.)

a 'reasoned' one 'giving both sides of the question – all controversial questions have two sides. The University attitude should be a detached and impersonal one.' The memorandum continued (and here the tone seems pure O'Shea): 'the more fitted a man is to come to a reasoned conclusion upon any subject, the less likely he is to rush into print. The true humility of mind brought about by real learning is a definite check upon the intellectual arrogance engendered by a little knowledge.' Then, after asserting the right of 'the College authorities' to 'demand that members of the staff will not by their utterances place the College authorities in an untenable position', came the critical point: 'I regard recognition, by members of the staff, of the responsibilities referred to in this memorandum as a matter of vital importance, and as being intimately related to the question of fitness for tenure of a University post.'[101]

The college staff's reaction to the memorandum, as far as John could judge, was 'either (1) that it's rather amusing & doesn't matter much or (2) that it's perfectly reasonable. The whole place combined', he told his father, 'doesn't seem to have the guts of a rabbit.'[102] The professorial board expressed its 'sympathy' for the principles enunciated and gave an assurance of loyal fulfilment of the memorandum's terms; council approval followed. John and Richmond wrote to Fowlds about the memorandum.[103] His idea of academic freedom was so 'widely different' from theirs, they wrote, that the board's approval left them feeling 'impelled to offer a sort of minority report'. Parts of the memorandum they accepted. That a statement should be a reasoned one, giving both sides of the question, seemed to them, however, a 'maxim needing fairly liberal interpretation, for it might easily deny the University teacher the right to express any opinion of his own whatever'. The edict against statements which might place the College authorities in an untenable position clearly depended on what constituted an untenable position. They continued:

It would seem to us that though the community has a right to expect that a University teacher will arrive at his views only by the fullest, most rigid and most honest thought of which he is capable, the nature of those views is of no concern to anyone but himself. It would seem also that his method of expression of such views in public is equally of no concern so long as that expression is equally honest and capable. In our opinion, that is almost all that need be said. Reasonably interpreted this would mean that no College Council could consider itself placed in an untenable position by any utterance of a member of the staff unless that utterance and the thought behind it had been put to this test and had failed.

They hoped, they concluded, that the setting forth of their views would not convict them of 'that intellectual arrogance which is referred to in the Memorandum'. The whole issue, in their view, affected 'the innermost and essential principle of university life. If our attitude', they wrote, 'unfits us for the tenure of a post at Auckland University College, we must express our regret'. Fowlds replied to John, saying that he hoped no one who was acquainted with his past would think he was in favour of repressing free speech.[104] 'Blow his past', John commented, 'it's his present that worries us.'[105]

A few days later a controversy developed in the Auckland papers on 'liberty and licence'. Anschutz had a letter published in which he claimed that the limitations on free speech should lie in the laws of libel, slander and sedition; unsettled times did not justify further limitations. Nor should there be additional limitations on the rights of particular people, such as university staff or public servants, because of the nature of their employment. John wrote to both papers – 'on the same lines as usual', he told his father, 'mainly pinched from Laski's Liberty in the Modern State'[106] – largely in support of Anschutz' argument.

If written or spoken words can be proved by the ordinary rules of evidence, in ordinary law (not under the specially designed provisions of war regulations and the like) to have been the immediate cause of unjustifiable violence, obviously their employment has been an abuse of the liberty of the citizen. Farther than that we cannot go without lending ourselves to the institution of tyranny. Apart from the highest ranks of the Civil Service, there seems to me to be no special case of professional or academic freedom involved, to which we can rightly apply a different rule; we are all citizens whether we dig drains or sit in a professorial chair. We may be guilty of errors of tact; but I am not aware that tactlessness is a criminal offence.[107]

Neither paper published the letter. The editor of the *Herald*, R.M. Hackett, claimed (inaccurately) that John's letter suggested 'that the force behind the law has no better sanction, and is entitled to no more respect, than the force which may be used to overthrow the state' and that this made it 'impossible to publish'.[108] John replied that if he had propounded that theory it might be worth examining; why it should make the letter impossible to publish he was at a loss to understand. He added that he was sending the interchange of letters to the *New Zealand Worker* and he trusted that Hackett had no objection. Hackett wrote back that he did object.[109] The editor of the *Worker*, however, had too much 'copy' to print the letters.[110]

It is clear that for John these were serious issues. His correspondence confirms this, but it also suggests that he relished the excitement of the controversy. If he were a man of means, he wrote to his father, he would

write a red-hot pamphlet on things in general, publish it at my own expense & then vastly enjoy the ensuing row & dismissal. There doesn't seem to be anybody in the university who has at once the guts or the security to stand up to Masters & Co. & tell them off as they deserve. By gosh, a man with nothing to lose could have a good time giving N.Z. all the political theory it wanted, & a damn sight more.[111]

Copies of all the correspondence were sent to Fisher in Dunedin, Hunter in Wellington (now vice-chancellor of the University of New Zealand as well as professor at Victoria University College), and de la Mare in Hamilton. Hunter, who was sure the 'Fowlds memorandum' would never have got past the Victoria professorial board without a protest, spoke to Fowlds about it and was reluctant to believe it really expressed his views.[112] Fisher thought Hunter had been too easily satisfied by Fowlds' explanations, but that it would do Fowlds good to know that Hunter 'thought it worthwhile to enquire about the matter'.[113] De la Mare entered the controversy and collected everything, perhaps already planning his pamphlet, *Academic Freedom in New Zealand, 1932–34*, which was to be published two and a half years later.

By the middle of June the subject of academic freedom had, publicly at least, 'lapsed for the time being'.[114] John did lecture the local Fabian club on 'Liberty in the Modern State' but the members appeared unlikely to 'bring the New Jerusalem along with a rush'. He led off the college's winter public lectures 'with a few remarks on the exploration of the Pacific' and received a warm note of thanks from the registrar. His book on the same subject had finally been completed and posted to England at the end of May. In July he 'went to lecture to a mob called the Labour Defence League on Freedom of the Press, its dubious merits, & had every word taken down by a couple of detectives. Very gratifying for a univ. lecturer to have any notes taken at all at a lecture, I thought. But you can see that the police are leaving nothing to chance.'[115]

The police report, dated 30 June 1932, was again by Detective Nalder. Only fifteen people were present at the meeting, which was chaired by Thomas Stanley, said by Nalder to be a Communist Party member. The closely typed account of John's lecture suggests that it was largely historical – one wonders what his audience made of it – though towards the end he is reported as saying that 'Society to be decent at all must allow for freedom. It is difficult but must be prepared to pay the price of freedom or inevitably pay the price of repression. The speaker did not believe in repression'. Detective Nalder noted finally (in what can only have been a reference to his report when he asked John to give evidence for the Crown on the Russian revolution), 'Dr Beaglehole was previously reported on by me owing to his sympathy with the Communist Movement' – a judgement which, whatever its truth, was hardly justified by the earlier report. In a later report (14 October 1932) on 'The Labour and Liberty Defence League', Nalder reiterated his view that John was 'a man of strong socialistic tendencies'. Norman Richmond he thought 'undoubtedly' the same, 'but like Beaglehole, owing to his position, and the presence of the Police, he has been wise enough to restrain and control his remarks'.[116] The detective's views seem to have owed more to the heightened political emotions of the times than to objective reporting,* but they almost certainly had their effect on John's future fortunes.

Life was not all politics. John exchanged letters with his father on what was available in the Whitcombe's sale in Wellington. Had they still the Shakespeare Head edition of Bede's *Ecclesiastical History of England*? What price? Could he afford it? Of course he could not afford it! Anyhow, don't let C.Q. Pope beat him to it. In the next letter, John would take it – as well as Keith, *The Sovereignty of the British Dominions* and Webster, *The Foreign Policy of Castlereagh*.[117] For his birthday he had bought himself Herbert Read's *The Meaning of Art*; he and Elsie had both read Aldous Huxley's *Brave New World* in spite of the *Star* telling them that most of its New Zealand readers regarded it as 'horrible & disgusting. How the Star knows I don't know, but I dare say they do.'[118]

The respite from controversy was short lived. On 18 August John wrote to his father:

The news of most moment is that it looks as if I'm going to lose my job again at the end of the year. A tangled story & a dirty one. However in a way it has been so amusing that we have not had time to feel depressed yet, & as the forces of the righteous have won what is anyhow

---

*   Nalder's imaginative powers were shown again in a 1940 report on two young German refugees who had had some contact with John, when he wrote, 'While at Auckland University in 1932 Beaglehole frequently wrote articles of a revolutionary nature for publication in the "Phoenix" magazine'. This is a very odd statement indeed, as the only thing of John's published in *Phoenix* was his poem 'Decline of the West'. (J.C. Beaglehole File. New Zealand Security Intelligence Service Papers.)

a temporary victory, it is possible that we may be all right in the end. The intriguing has been going on for about six weeks now, but I only came into it about a fortnight ago. It looks like a political business & the result of the letter Richmond & I wrote to Sir George. The yarn is of course economy – but as the council is spending money right & left on extra help in other directions & giving O'Shea £200 above & beyond his salary & Carnegie grant to study university administration abroad (what for only O'Shea & Heaven know) that doesn't wash too well.[119]

O'Shea had proposed,* ostensibly for reasons of economy, that John's temporary appointment should not be extended after its initial year, and that F.B. Stephens (John's WEA predecessor in the Waikato), who had been lecturing in economics (also on a temporary appointment) and whose BA had been in both economics and history, should give half his time to history. Both Willis Airey and Horace Belshaw, the professor of economics, protested at the proposal, but their objections were not reported to the education committee of the college council, which accepted O'Shea's proposal and recommended it to the full council for approval. Before the council meeting took place on 15 August, members of the education committee, most importantly H.J.D. Mahon, the headmaster of Auckland Grammar School and not an admirer of O'Shea, had learned of the 'pocketed' objections and the council agreed to refer the whole matter back to the education committee. In spite of opposition from Mahon and T.U. Wells, the committee, after a 'very fiery meeting',[120] held to its earlier decision.

Before the matter came back to the council on 19 September, there was intensive lobbying. Richmond and Anschutz were very active.[121] John regretted that his role had to be limited to gathering in the news and making suggestions. De la Mare wrote to Fowlds, saying that Auckland could 'ill afford' to lose John, who was an 'independent and extremely intelligent and useful spirit',[122] and added that if they sacked him, his prayer would be 'Father forgive them for they know not what they do'. 'Too right they do', John commented, 'at least those two b's O'Shea & Fowlds do. The amusement doesn't come out in all this', he added, 'but it has been there all the same – talk of international politics & secret diplomacy! They have nothing on A.U.C.'[123]

---

* It is an indication of O'Shea's power at Auckland (and the weakness of the professorial board) that the registrar should have decided on such academic arrangements. De la Mare seems to have been almost alone in arguing that O'Shea should have said how much must be saved, and the board should have determined how it was to be saved.

Airey and Belshaw sent in further strong protests.[124] Airey drew attention to the very adverse staffing situation in the history department, which had the largest advanced classes in the college, and stated unequivocally that the removal of a full-time teacher would seriously endanger the standard of work. Stephens's qualifications, in Airey's view, were 'beyond question considerably less' than John's. Belshaw, for his part, wrote that 'at no time have I stated that I thought the curtailment of the staff in History was wise, or that the financial aspects of the proposals were altogether fair'. Both Airey and Belshaw suggested other ways of making economies, with Airey offering to take a cut in his own salary if John could be kept on, and also suggesting that both John and Stephens could be offered half-time positions. Belshaw pointed to other funds that might be drawn on. A delegation of history students met with Fowlds and O'Shea to present a memorandum protesting at the proposed changes – the department would lose 'a valuable lecturer whose influence has been and would be in the future a keen stimulus to critical and thorough work'[125] – and came away from the meeting believing that the points they had made had not been answered. The professorial board added its protest, resolving, on Airey's initiative, that the difficulties the history department already faced were exceptional and urging the council not to make any changes in its staffing.

It was all to no avail. When the council met on 19 September, Fowlds read, in a voice 'trembling with emotion', a prepared statement[126] in which he reiterated the college's financial difficulties and repeated the earlier arguments for Stephens to teach both economics and history.[127] Airey's and Belshaw's letters had been sent to council members before Fowlds wrote his memorandum, but he ignored their suggestions and protests, as well as those of the history students. Mahon later told Richmond that 'Airey's arguments were not answered and were unanswerable'.[128] Discussion went on for more than two hours, with Mahon and Wells again arguing that John should be retained. Only P.W. Burbidge, the professor of physics (whom John as a schoolboy had heard speak when Burbidge visited his old school, Mount Cook Boys, before leaving for Cambridge on a postgraduate scholarship), and S.I. Crooks, formerly a lecturer in engineering, supported them.[129]

Fowlds then and later firmly maintained that the economic arguments were the sole reason for retrenching John's position, and it would not have been unreasonable at the time to have concerns about the level of future government funding. John's political views were not mentioned at the council meeting, although in private one council member was said to have described him as a 'dangerous young man',[130] and Richmond was told by two members (Burbidge and MacKenzie) before the meeting that there was a prejudice in the council against John, the letter to the *Worker* being apparently the reason.[131] The reasons why members of councils vote the way they do are not always revealed in debate, and as Mahon said, 'The trouble was half the Council was there to vote blindly with Sir George'.[132] Burbidge wrote to de la Mare that, while the council had made a bad error in terminating John's appointment, for which he thought 'it did not have a leg to stand on . . . There was, of course, absolutely no evidence of any motive and consequently none can be imputed . . .'[133] This may be a little ingenuous. The proposal clearly started with O'Shea and, in Sinclair's words, 'O'Shea greatly disliked the left-wingers';[134] and he shared his views with Detective Nalder.[135] In May O'Shea had written to the editor of the *Herald* saying that 'the University as a whole frowns very strongly upon dabbling in foolish subversive criticism'.[136] He had no time for Airey or Richmond. His view of John is not recorded and must be inferred.[137] When O'Shea first raised with Airey the need to economise in staffing, he referred also to John's exchange with the editor of the *Herald*.[138] Airey made no comment on this, simply saying the proposal for a part-time assistant would be entirely unsatisfactory. When John later wrote, 'in the general alarm [of those times] even persons trained in an older tradition of liberalism were liable to lose touch with reality',[139] he may well have been thinking of Sir George Fowlds. At the time Hunter wrote: 'I am inclined to think that Fowlds is quite honest in his opinion that he acted solely because of economy, for he does not realise that "though the voice was the voice of Fowlds the hands were the hands of O'Shea".'[140]

The evidence does not allow us to state with absolute certainty why John lost his job. His friends at the time, however, believed the conclusion to be irresistible: that he was being retrenched, consciously or unconsciously, because he had shown too much independence of mind. Viewing the process as a whole it is difficult to disagree.

As far as John's appointment was concerned, that was the end of it. His friends, led by de la Mare, decided to assemble a full statement of what had happened, with copies of the relevant letters and papers. De la Mare worked assiduously, but his pamphlet, *Academic Freedom in New Zealand, 1932–34*, took more than two years to appear. The Auckland papers showed no interest in reporting the controversy. The *Waikato Times* and the Christchurch *Press* both published a number of articles on it. *New Zealand*

Truth sensationalised it with a front-page article headed 'Auckland University Students on the Warpath', but it rather lamely concluded that 'Council's decision appears beyond doubt to have been made on grounds of economy alone'.[141] The student press showed an interest in the issues raised. At Auckland the disputes over academic freedom were far from over,[142] but while John continued to take a lively interest it was as an observer rather than as a participant.

The controversy had made his name well known. The arguments he had put forward were far from revolutionary, and almost academic in their expression. But at that time to argue at all, even if it was to urge careful reflection on the causes of the problems facing New Zealand, was not well received. John too became the object of the 'hysteria' against which he had warned. Whatever the reasons for his 'retrenchment', many accepted the view of him as 'a dangerous young man' with 'advanced views'. The consequences for his future would become clear later.

The excitement over, John still had the year's teaching to complete. With pressure easing, he had time 'to read a book or two'. He started with Leigh Hunt's autobiography, which he thought very good, then went on to Dean Church on the Oxford Movement:

Funny lot of birds that crowd – what a pity they couldn't have worried about something fundamentally important . . . What beats me about all these brilliantly clever blokes like Newman & Froude & W.G. Ward is that they did all their arguing within narrow intellectual limits – they never questioned anything that might have busted up the whole show . . . It was just as well Darwin came when he did! England had need of him.[143]

DURING THE TIME IN Hamilton and Auckland John showed the first signs of an interest in New Zealand painting that was to increase steadily as the years passed. Mrs Rogers had asked him to go on a committee 'to run an offshoot of the Akld Society of Arts exhibition' in Hamilton. The reason for the invitation, he gathered, was because his Uncle George had taught painting to Mrs Rogers in her maiden days in Dunedin, and also because

we possess the Cézanne & Van G. prints, which indeed give us considerable standing. It wouldn't be a bad idea to startle the local cognoscenti, connoisseurs, intelligentsia & arty birds generally with an exhibition of [Christopher] Perkins' stuff, I suppose the stuff is all too expensive to buy. If the Wgton birds have any sense, they'll get that Silverstream Brickworks one for their permanent collection, but I dare say it is still about 50 years or so too advanced. I'd like a drawing or two myself.[144]

In Auckland he saw one of the visiting shows of British art brought out by Murray Fuller, 'some quite good stuff . . . along with a lot of mediocre . . . It was decent to see some professional painting after the tripe turned out by the local talent anyhow'.[145] Then, shortly before he left Auckland, John met the painter John Weeks. Weeks, like John, had returned to New Zealand in 1929, to paint and to teach at the Elam School of Art, after spending a number of years studying and painting in Europe and Africa. John visited his house at Northcote to see his work and was enthusiastic about what he saw:

The bloke is an artist all right & knocks C. Perkins sky-high. Hundreds of beautiful drawings from Morocco (he went for a fortnight & stayed 15 months) & then ripping paintings of Paris & then this more abstract pattern stuff he has been doing since he got back. He worked under a modern bloke called André Lhôte in Paris & got bitten properly by the idea . . . Stunner still-lifes & N.Z. landscapes & figure designs . . . I was wildly excited.[146]

He was a great deal less enthusiastic about having once again to pack all their possessions. They would, he told his father, be leaving the flat 'with many regrets'.[147] Elsie and Robin took the train to Wellington in mid-December to join her parents for Christmas. John stayed on once more for the WEA summer school. He was making enquiries about possible jobs: he wrote to von Zedlitz about work in his coaching school and to Scholefield about the General Assembly Library, with no luck in either case. With no idea what he would be doing, he was able to store their packed possessions in the WEA rooms until the future became clearer.

He was cheered by the expressions of sympathy and regret from students at his departure. He thought he might print them all and send a copy of the pamphlet to each member of the college council. A nun in Hamilton whose thesis he had supervised said that she was sending him and Elsie 'a small piece of hand-work for the house'. After much speculation as to what it might be, it arrived: 'An immense cardboard box . . . disclosed a yellow lightshade of the largest size & complexity of shape – God knows what we are going to do with it. Elsie pronounces it a marvellous bit of work technically & the most expensive materials; but somehow it doesn't seem to fit our style of furnishing, & nobody seems to be getting married at the moment.'[148] John took it to a lampshade shop and was offered 18s 6d for it. He wondered whether he should try to push the price up to 26s 6d so that he could buy D.H. Lawrence's letters,* but decided the day was too hot to bargain and took the price offered.[149]

Until the summer school began John stayed for ten days with Lascelles Wilson, who had led the history students' protest at his retrenchment. Wilson was working as a cleaner at the university while he completed his degree and was also involved with the WEA. He was to make his career in adult education, later becoming (in succession to Duncan) director of tutorial classes at Sydney University. 'A very decent fellow', John wrote to his father, 'with a very varied experience of life, so that what with yarning after meals & late at night, the past week has been rather like the Duncan-Beaglehole ménage in London again'.[150] They both spent Christmas day at the Richmonds', and the summer school, again held at Wesley College in Paerata, began the next day.

There were nearly a hundred at the school, a remarkable variety of people, and testimony to the liveliness of the WEA in those years.[151] John gave lectures on Germany, and on literature and morals. Von Zedlitz was up from Wellington – 'all very charming, but there are times when he wanders from the point a bit too much' – Allan Fisher was 'very good', Anschutz 'very good indeed'. John Shearer, another young economist, gave 'an absolutely masterly lecture' and was 'easily the outstanding man at the school'. Owen Jensen, later to be a well-known music critic in Wellington, lectured on music and organised record recitals using the 'stunner' gramophone of the college headmaster. Forty years later Jensen still remembered a passionate debate on Bach between John, Richmond and Shearer. 'For wit, erudition and sheer enthusiasm, it was a discussion of aspects of Bach's music and its interpretation that would have been unmatched in any company.'[152] Arthur Ward was there, and other friends from Hamilton, de la Mare and his son, Henry Valder and one of his daughters. Walter Nash and his wife arrived, driven by Dick Campbell in his car. John indulged his enthusiasm for quoit tennis at all opportunities (beating Nash and being defeated only once, by Ward) and played Bach on the piano. Finally it came to an end, and Campbell drove John down to Wellington to an uncertain future.

---

*   He bought the letters anyway. 'I added the 7/6 which I have not yet received from the Akld Star for a poem; & so made up the requisite sum.' He and Elsie both read the letters 'with riveted attention'. (JCB to Kathleen McKay, 6 February 1933.)

7

'UNEMPLOYED AND ODD JOBS', 1933–35

JOHN DESCRIBED HIS occupation during the next three years (in *Who's Who in New Zealand*) as 'unemployed and odd jobs'. While that was literally true, it was at the same time a period of great achievement and, in spite of some financial difficulty and disappointment over jobs, considerable personal satisfaction. He read widely; he completed his short history of New Zealand, wrote the greater part of his work on the University of New Zealand, and published a lot of verse. Domestically it was a very happy period. John greatly enjoyed his young sons, while Elsie established the pattern of running the home and family in a way that gave him sustained support for his scholarly activities.

On arriving from Auckland they once again stayed with Elsie's parents in the Hutt while they looked for somewhere to live. In January 1933 John poured out his feelings in a letter to Norman Richmond:

I feel that my friends, cobbers & comrades-in-arms are now in Akld. rather than anywhere else so far as N.Z. is concerned, & I do not like being cut off from them . . . what I mean to say is that I hate leaving you all, blast you! That you are the best cobber I have in this loathly country . . . or perhaps anywhere else . . . Damn it all, this outpouring must be the effect of reading Lawrence's Letters. I thought that after being sacked & having looked at houses – shacks – heaps of wood & corrugated iron – bloody bungalows – for three weeks I was incapable of further emotion. But apparently I was the victim of my own misjudgment.[1]

They had decided to stay in Wellington, John explained, for two reasons. One was a 'certain duty' to their parents, and the other that, failing a job, he planned to 'read history systematically for the first time in my life' and to 'revise and boil down' his PhD thesis for publication, 'when if ever publishers publish again', for both of which the General Assembly Library and his father's books would be useful. He had started reading seventeenth-century English history and thought he 'could cheerfully stay there for the rest of the year'.[2] It would give him the opportunity to read his folio volumes of Clarendon's *History of the Rebellion and Civil Wars in England*, 2000 pages in all, which he had bought in London. Elsie was anxious to get settled (she was expecting a second child); he more interested in 'writing about Bach'.[3] He was referring to his poem 'Considerations on Certain Music of J.S. Bach', which he had just completed.

In the middle of February they moved into a small house at 82 Marsden Street, Lower Hutt. They had hoped not to have to pay more than twenty-five shillings a week, but had to stretch to thirty shillings. It was on the flat below the Holmes's house on the Western Hutt hills, and a few minutes' walk to the railway station for the Wellington train. The small garden, with room for a good plot for vegetables, extended back to the stopbank which ran along the Hutt river. The river had pools with just enough water for a bathe, and the river bed was a good source of firewood.

John kept up a lively correspondence with Norman Richmond that was to continue for several years and to embrace a remarkable range of subjects. They continued to plan WEA courses; Richmond agreed to pay John £40 (£2 a lecture) for writing lectures for the next stage of the European civilisation course. They reported on books read, on people, on further developments at Auckland University College and Victoria's fall from grace, on politics, poetry, babies and birth control, the prospects for jobs and for revolution, and the virtues of the film star Jessie Matthews. They took a particular delight in what they saw as pompous inanities in the speeches of the Governor-General, Lord Bledisloe.

They continued what was clearly an on-going discussion of Marxist ideas and Soviet Russia. Governments in the capitalist world seemed unable to take any effective steps to ameliorate the impact of the depression; Hitler's rise to power was destroying the bright hopes once held for the Weimar Republic. However misplaced in the long run, a belief that the Soviet Union might represent a new kind of society attracted many who despaired at the failures of the established politicians. The intemperate reaction to any whiff of communism by those in positions of power gave the ideology an attraction it would possibly otherwise never have had.

Richmond was readier than John to accept the ideas of Marxism and Leninism.[4] He read more in the field, and lectured both on Marxist ideas and on the Soviet Union. For John, Richmond was more a stimulus than an influence. An acute observer of human failings and human folly, John remained sceptical about all-embracing answers. 'I object intellectually to anybody swallowing anything whole even Lenin', he wrote to Richmond, reporting on his reaction to John Strachey's *The Coming Struggle for Power*, in which he thought the last section, on communism, the weakest part of the book.[5] His view at this time comes out clearly in his letters to Richmond:[6]

. . . remember that revolutions must become fashionable to succeed . . . [yet] I must admit that people like M[iddleton] Murry make me want to be a die-hard Tory, a blood & iron man, a keen hard ruthless captain (or even brigadier general) of finance, a Sacco Vanzetti slayer & a shooter-down of strikers. Have you read M. Dobb's Soviet Russia & the World? He has some good stuff in that. The thing that holds me up is the question of liberty, & he has a few pertinent words to say about that. But as things are, you have the state claiming as complete an allegiance in the U.S.S.R. as in England or N.Z. And by now I am a convinced political pluralist. Of course the withering-away of the state wd. solve that question all right, but damn it! is the state really going to wither away? That's what I want to know. Anyhow when the revolution comes I don't think I'll carry opposition to it so far as to be shot for a reactionary, though I may be despised for a Laodicean*.[7]

. . . what the hell do Marxian economics matter anyway? I mean as Marxian economics? The class-struggle seems to me the essential point. I found when I woke up the morning after Hitler began slogging the other side that I had definitely turned Communist – at least I had all the sensations of a painful intellectual struggle, & that seemed to be the cause. Can you be a Communist without swallowing the whole bag of tricks? Need you spout the jargon like my young brother [Ernest] in the States? The trouble is I want to be a Communist & a Laodicean at the same time. So I dare say I'll face the firing squad yet. All right; but when I die note that my last words will be 'Comrades, I die in the faith of Voltaire & Bertrand Russell &' – the volley crashes.[8]

If the bourgeoisie jails me first, & I am asked what turned me Communist, I answer from the dock succinctly, 'Sir George Fowlds & Hitler'. My God! aren't the newspapers awful to read these days? My heart bleeds over poor old Germany. It's one damn thing after another. Here's the chief theoretical point about Com[mun]ism that sticks me

---

*   Laodicean: 'Having the fault for which the Church in Laodicea is reproached in Rev.iii. 15, 16: hence "lukewarm neither cold nor hot", indifferent in religion, politics, etc.' (*Oxford English Dictionary*.)

up at present – assuming that I swallow the personal liberty camel as
being no worse a beast than ours & perhaps a better one: here's the
sequence – dictatorship of proletariat, withering-away of state, perfect
socialism. Yes, but if history is 'dynamic', why stop there, or how can
you stop there. If you stop even in theory, doesn't that make the process
meaningless. Is the world to remain permanently without classes?
Do dynamics become statics? It may be argued that the contingency
not having arisen, the point is of academic interest only – but then
I'm interested in points of academic interest. For all I know the great
communist theoreticians may have settled it – ask [R. A. K.] Mason will
you? It doesn't seem to be altogether negligible.[9]

In many ways John seems to have been more absorbed by D.H.
Lawrence's letters, which he and Elsie were both reading, than any
of the volumes on Marxist theory. You must certainly read the
letters, he told Richmond. 'But', he went on to confide:

I really can't make out what he [Lawrence] was after, even with the help
of Aldous Huxley's introduction . . . But they certainly bear out what
H. Nicolson said of him in those broadcast articles – a new faith after
the 19th cent. scepticism of Huxley & the rest. But what the devil is the
new faith? No use asking you, for you like me are quite 19th century.
Why have a new faith anyhow? Won't it do more harm than good? You
can't put machinery up against faith & say there's the antithesis. I wish
to God I knew what L. was driving at. You can analyse up to a certain
point, instinct, etc., but then you, or at least I, come up against a blank
wall. These favourite words of his, darkness, the blood, dark sex, & so
on, mean nothing to me except in a vague emotional way. But we don't
want vague emotion. Anyhow what is the matter with conscious sex in
daylight? It is all wrong, according to L. Still I like him a damn sight
better than most people I have met or heard of. Guts.[10]

John had sent his poem 'Considerations on Certain Music of
J.S. Bach' to Richmond (to whom it was dedicated 'as by right')
in January 1933, with the qualification that it probably had not
reached its final form, but he 'couldn't wait for the tinkering of
months before sending it'. 'Perhaps it is no damn good at all', he
added, 'perhaps it is merely the lingering after effect of the S. School
. . .'[11] To Kathleen McKay he expressed some of the same doubt: 'It
is mainly about Bach – about 150 lines, some good, some bad'.[12]
Richmond liked it, though John agreed with his comment that 'I
don't say quite the things you wd. say if you had the ability; but then
neither do I say quite the things I wd. say if I had the ability'.[13]
The poem opens:

Meditating in silence after the last note
I consider old John Sebastian
cantor and capellmeister, official writer
of Leipzig anthems, player in court bands,
chief of the sons of God, by his music divine
in his own right beyond the Lutheran God.
He was twice married, had eighteen children . . . he was
twice married, had eighteen children; mark that
my soul: the genius philoprogenitive,
historical instance for once; was, too,
a model of conjugal stability; prayed
piously; quarrelled with his churchwardens;
taught Latin. Colossal! – and lived to sixty-five,
producing and teaching all those small Bachs –
must have lost count of children and anthems alike!
Regularity did it; punctual
to the Sunday Bach with his anthems; punctual
I suppose with his offspring: man must work,
his days are numbered, the old cantor must produce.
And his works were good – his Wilhelm Friedemann,
young Johann Christian and the rest, good musicians,
and his anthems that outlasted them all.
So I consider in front of the clavier
old John Sebastian tempered so well,
playing his forty-eight preludes and fugues, sublime
manifesto: more final than that later one
of communist Marx. The fugue that I played –
it closed on a cadence like the hours of his life,
when the old man lay dictating that last
choral-prelude, last elaboration of faith
and dying humbleness before his God.
Wenn wir in höchsten Nöthen sein – troubled those words
but how transfigured, in trust glorified.
And yet consider that annoyed fierce cantor's face
of his portrait, the just indignation
of a virtuous man affronted with a false note,
with a choir attacking at a wrong angle
some *Sanctus* or *Kyrie;* John Sebastian,
master, I much prefer your Forty-eight;
your face for the excellent Leipzig musicians –
out of strength sweetness: give me the honey! . . .
That prelude flowed like a spring of consolation
in a hard southern land; come, my fingers,
over the page, forget the multiplied children,
that severe Leipzig physiognomy,
court bands, conjugal stability and Latin;

to it again – to the tenderness, sad
beauty, to the firm exquisite line, the lovely
pulsation and triumph of order: turn,
this next is John Sebastian himself, cantor,
his soul and mind; then to our fifth French Suite.

The poem was in five parts. John saw the first as the prelude and
the second as a fugue – 'so far as I was thinking of any particular
prelude & fugue, I was thinking of the 6th in Bk 1; one of the first
I ever got to know'. The third section, the gigue, 'is the 5th Fr. suite
one'. John was least happy with this: it 'seems to me the weakest
part & very weak at that'. In the fugue and the gigue he sought
most directly to find a kind of verbal metaphor for the music, and
they are less successful than the first and last two parts, where his
historical imagination is more immediately involved. In the fourth
part, 'J.S.B. Loquitur *Vor deinen Thron tret' ich*', Bach, old and
blind, praises God for his mercy in giving him 'great power/among
all men to sing unto his greatness'. The poem ends with the 'great
gates' of heaven opening for Bach to meet his God. John 'wrote the
last section first, & then the first, & then thought well why not a
whole blooming suite?'[14]

'Considerations' was followed by another longish poem, 'Decline
of the West', which John sent to R.A.K. Mason to be published in
Phoenix.[15] He thought it had one or two good lines, but admitted
in advance 'that its heredity is by T.S. Eliot out of Spengler'.[16] The
admission is hardly needed and the poem seems strangely lacking
in personal emotion, oddly unrelated to experience. It is perhaps
significant that John was unsure whether to call it 'Decline of the
West' or 'Decay of Capitalist Civilisation'. He thought it was 'rather
good', but admitted to Richmond that people 'who deign to read it
at all regard it merely as an academic exercise'.[17] It was reprinted
the following year in *Art in New Zealand*[18] as the first section of
a longer poem, 'Meditations on Historic Change'. Although John
claimed that the longer poem finished 'on a note of bright optimism
and the forecasting of the transformation of society on a Planned
Basis' he confessed that he found it 'not either Very Original or
Very Good'.[19] Only in the last section, in which he contemplates his
sleeping son Robin, thinks of him in a line of fathers and sons and
foresees him growing to build 'the thing that's yet undone', does the
poem really engage the reader.[20]

Since returning from London John had written a considerable
quantity of verse. By the end of the 1920s he had shed the Georgian
style of his early years and, influenced by his wide reading of

recent English poetry, had moved to a studied engagement with the modernist style; echoes of Bridges and Hopkins gave way to Eliot and the later Yeats. He was far from happy with Quentin Pope's choice from his poems for the much-vilified anthology *Kowhai Gold*, published in 1930,* a group which reflected his earlier work. What he felt about Quentin's dedication of the volume to him is not recorded.

Norman Richmond's wife Larry (with whom John was never very comfortable), a daughter of Arnold Wall, professor of English at Canterbury College, approved of 'Considerations'; John's other verse she thought 'ingenious but derivative'. John did not defend himself: 'Alas! I thought, she has summed me up in one, & all my works & mind; sometimes I admit it, I am ingenious, but Oh God in heaven how constantly derivative! I have the perfect academic qualifications in fact, & yet academe eludes me. Extraordinary fate!'[21] He conceded too readily and too much.

Roger Robinson, in *The Oxford Companion to New Zealand Literature,* writes that John's poems 'are characteristically metaphysical, meditations on often commonplace experiences like riding a bicycle, listening to music or visiting a cathedral or museum, which turn the poet's mind to the universal, the meaning and processes of life'. [22] His poem 'Lighting My Pipe'[23] opens in a matter-of-fact way:

> Lighting my pipe in the road this late afternoon
> I see the sombre evening close round the houses . . .

Twenty lines later his thoughts are far from the wet road and falling darkness:

> . . . suddenly I think, as I fling down my match
> and the rain thickens, and I look at the near trees
> black-clustering, of men my remote ancestors,
> shaggy and ape-like forms, gathered in winter's cold
> crouched close in a rough circle, while the terrible
> primeval all-embracing forest gathered night,
> holding out famished hands to the new-found magic
> wonder of warmth and light burning red among them
> sending contentment or strange-felt uneasiness

---

* In Eric McCormick's view, '[Rupert] Brooke was in effect the chief contributor to that ignoble collection'. (E.H.McCormick, *An Absurd Ambition: Autobiographical Writings*, edited by Dennis McEldowney (Auckland: Auckland University Press, 1996), p.41.)

on those scarce-dawned minds, while inarticulate sound
murmured around the group with comforting assent.
And still they crouched and gazed, fascinated beyond
all knowledge: as I a moment gaze, and then walk on.

John was, in a sense, a classic colonial modernist, asking 'What
does it mean that I am here?' And 'here' not only in the immediate
physical sense but also in relation to the whole Western intellectual
and cultural tradition. Written in an 'intellectual-contemplative
mould',[24] his verse sometimes lacked spontaneity; it could be laboured and show an odd mismatch between language and subject, and
even a clash of language within a poem. The most successful poems
are those where his personal feelings are involved as well as the
intellect; as when he was writing about Bach rather than the decline
of the West, for example, or the poems 'You were standing' (1932)
and 'After Dinner' (1933), which both express the love and delight
he felt at becoming a father. 'After Dinner' begins:

'You funny little rough!' she said. There was
poetry in that, I thought. Smilingly
she stood and gazed at him, laughing himself.
He was sitting in his chair, fast gripping
his crust, looking upward with ecstasy
of inborn merriment, the little sinner,
as if the world were only cause for laughter . . .

During the 1930s John's verse was widely published, in *Art in
New Zealand, Phoenix, Rata* and the weekly journal *Tomorrow.*
He was included in every anthology for three decades: Alexander
and Currie's *Treasury* (1926), Pope's *Kowhai Gold* (1930), Marris's
Best Poems (annual volumes during the 1930s), Curnow's *Book of
New Zealand Verse* (1945) – though Curnow seemed unable to work
him into the argument of his influential 'Introduction') – through to
Chapman and Bennett's *Anthology* (1956). 'You were standing' was
included in Lauris Edmond's 2001 anthology *New Zealand Love
Poems.* On a number of occasions John considered bringing together
a collection of his verse for publication. This finally happened in
1938 with the Caxton Press's *Words for Music*, a slim volume of
fourteen pages which included 'Considerations on Certain Music of
J.S. Bach' and five other poems written between 1926 and 1937 on
musical subjects.

Robin Hyde judged John to be 'one of the finest verse-writers
in New Zealand';[25] in 1935 Denis Glover ranked him together
with Fairburn, Mason and Curnow as 'younger writers . . . who

have been influenced by a new freshness in English poetry';[26] and a reviewer of *Verse Alive*, a 1936 Caxton Press anthology of verse first published in *Tomorrow,* wrote that he stood 'head and shoulders . . . above any other practising New Zealand poet'.[27] Later judgement would suggest a more modest place; at his best an able poet but not in the front rank. Allen Curnow, writing at the same time and subject to the same modernist influences, mastered these to forge his own distinctive voice. This was something John failed to do. From the late 1930s the flow of verse almost ceased, though he continued to buy and read poetry. The practice of writing poetry, however, and the ruminative spirit that characterised much of his best work, helped to shape the prose of his mature years. The love of language and fascination with words, the concern with balance and with rhythm, which underlay his insistence that reading aloud was a vital step in the craft of writing, mark the essential link between the verse and his later prose works.

AT THE BEGINNING OF March 1933, F.P. Wilson had become ill with pleurisy and John was hired by Victoria to do his teaching. He was paid £40 a month and hoped, before Wilson's return, to make enough to pay the year's rent. The college staff were welcoming but he was 'overwhelmed with advice' to hold his tongue on the state of the world until he had a permanent job there and 'then to let it wag as freely as it will', advice which he tried to follow but found hard when lecturing on the revolutionary spirit in the nineteenth century.[28] The job was frustrating. No one knew when Wilson was likely to come back and John could not plan anything more than a week ahead. When Wilson finally returned at the beginning of July, John was rather sore at having to get out.

I was born on 28 April and provisionally named Tim, which met with universal hostility. After protracted deliberation (at the end of May John suggested to Norman Richmond that I should be Timothy Norman Lenin Marx John Sebastian[29]) I was finally registered in late June as Timothy Holmes. John and Elsie had hoped for a daughter, to be called Jane after John's mother. Nevertheless, John reported me to be fairly satisfactory, 'if we smother up the unfortunate matter of his sex in a judicious blanket of silence'.[30] Within weeks I was showing 'all the signs of developing into a man of sterling character'.[31]

Life in the Hutt had its pleasures. In spite of their limited means John and Elsie seem to have been very happy and clearly enjoyed their growing family. John's brother Keith (working as an electrical engineer for the Railways), Fronnie and their two small children were living nearby.* John Reid, a young lawyer who was assisting Walter Nash in his campaign for the Hutt seat in parliament, and his wife Aileen, also with two small children, became close friends and the three couples met often, at times to play ping-pong or indulge John's enthusiasm for quoit tennis. Elsie's parents were welcoming and generous in lending their car for outings and in helping feed a hungry family, sometimes sending down a pudding to Marsden Street, or having John and Elsie or the whole family to their house. In July Ernest Beaglehole and his wife Pam were briefly back in New Zealand from Yale, before going to the Bishop Museum in Hawai'i to work with Peter Buck. John was still rather ambivalent about his young brother; he found it difficult not to envy Ernest's success in finding both publisher† and employment. 'He is a Very Superior bloke . . .' he told Richmond, 'Both [Ernest and Pam] are intense American university communists as far as I can gather, with all the lingo & no doubts of their own correctness'.[32] Friends from earlier days at Victoria reappeared. Ivan Sutherland (a source of coffee beans and oranges, both of which he imported from the Cook Islands), Alister McIntosh (after his return from Carnegie-funded library studies in the United States), Dick Campbell (now private secretary to Gordon Coates, the Minister of Finance in the coalition government) and others were regular visitors and kept John and Elsie in touch with what was going on. Sutherland brought out the painter Christopher Perkins (down from Rotorua to see his pictures hung in an exhibition), who turned out to be an enthusiast for Bach. So he returned a day or two later for an evening of talk and John playing. It was a memorable meeting, but the Perkins family were to leave New Zealand to return to England at the end of 1934.

The winter months of 1933 saw an outburst of dissension within Victoria University and attacks on the college from outside.[33] In some ways it was not very different from the early 1920s; Victoria remained in the eyes of conservative citizens a hotbed of Bolshevism and immorality. But the frustration and tensions resulting from the depression – now at its worst – sharpened differences. The college's

---

*   Keith saw little hope of advancement in the Railways during the depression years, and the following year the family left for England where he was to have a successful career working for English Electric.

†   Ernest's London PhD thesis, supervised by Morris Ginsberg, had been published in 1931 by George Allen and Unwin as *Property: A Study in Social Psychology*.

government grant had been savagely cut, teacher training colleges had been closed, and it was recognised that the government might have to go further. The situation was more complicated than that in Auckland the year before: 'everybody was involved in struggle – student with student, students with [Professorial] Board and with Council, students and Board and Council with the press, the gutter-press, and correspondents of the press. Never had there been such dissension; never did the official representatives of the college cut a less happy figure.'[34]

The trouble began in April when the Debating Society (following Oxford's lead) passed a motion 'That this house will not fight for King and Country'. The next month the Free Discussions Club issued *Student,* 'a poorly cyclostyled, militantly left-wing'[35] paper, its first number edited by Bart Fortune (Reo's brother), the second and third by Gordon Watson. After two numbers the Students' Association executive banned the paper on the grounds of the blatant inaccuracy of much of its content; when a third was issued, the club was disaffiliated from the Students' Association. The professorial board reprimanded the editor and the college council approved the measures taken against the publication. All of this coincided with a public attack on the college by the New Zealand Welfare League for allowing teaching that was against the Empire, against British ideals, against religion, against the family, against 'nearly everything our civilisation is based upon'. The league's attack, while unsigned, reflected the views of its secretary, A.P. Harper, a great mountaineer and explorer, but a man 'whose dicta on education and politics', John thought, 'come as near imbecility as anything uttered in this unfortunate country'.[36] The league was supported, in the correspondence columns of the *Evening Post,* by Canon Percival James, 'a rather foolish person with an ecclesiastical talent for overstatement',[37] who enlarged on the 'haunting dread' that Victoria College inspired in a great number of parents for the effect it could have on the immature minds of their children. The canon demanded that the college give an assurance that it accepted an obligation to ensure that the conscientious convictions of decent youth would not be outraged.[38] Other correspondents joined in. John wrote opposing any such assurance: 'Does Canon James imagine that education comes essentially from anything else but the clash of conviction on conviction, and meditation over the results?' The Welfare League he dismissed more summarily:

As for the New Zealand Welfare League, that dubious institution, whose cause Canon James has adopted, and in whose extraordinary asseverations the present controversy began, one need waste no words on it; for it has lived so long on the borderlands of defamation and libel that to introduce it further to the geography of truth would serve no good purpose.[39]

John was rather pleased with that sentence, and pleased also that for the first time he had had a letter published 'verbatim & in full by one of the great metropolitan dailies of this country; a fact which I think entitles me to couple with my name the concept of SUCCESS'.[40]

In face of the attack, the college wavered. Professor Gould, chairman of the board, invited James and others to make their complaints specific and to name the staff involved. The invitation was not taken up. After an acrimonious discussion, in which one of its members, the Hon. Robert McCallum, was said to have named Hunter as one of those staff from whom students were getting their opinions, the council set up a committee of inquiry. Their report, a revised version of one from the board, which the council thought too critical of the college's critics, represented, in John's view, 'a pattern of abasement, an exemplar of flunkeyism, a model of treachery to the most elementary principles of university life'.[41] The 'most noisome, crawling bits' of the report were, he understood, the work of Arthur Fair KC, the solicitor-general.[42] The report expressed regret that debates on sexual and religious subjects had taken place (the board moved quickly to forbid further debates on these topics), asserted that the religious faith of students was immune from assault and that disloyalty was under supervision, and went on to assure the public that 'the very small number [of students] whose conduct and beliefs are in conflict with the great majority of the community attract attention entirely out of proportion to their influence in the college. Their influence must, and will, be restrained within reasonable bounds.' The report concluded with an expression of confidence in the academic staff. That too riled John: all 'thoroughly, utterly, completely and damnably respectable'.[43] Fifteen years later, when he wrote his history of the college, he dismissed the report briefly: 'It is an ignoble document, but it is one the faithful historian cannot pass over.'[44]

Before that matter had run its course, there was further excitement when *Spike* appeared in September. A member of the council, Justice Ostler (who had himself edited *Spike* in its early days), took strong exception to three articles; two he saw as seditious, the third because it very persuasively attacked the law teaching in the college. The editor, and writer of the law article, was I.D. Campbell, later to be a colleague of John's as professor of law at Victoria and deputy vice-chancellor. The board directed that the magazine should be withdrawn. It was later reissued with the three offending articles removed. John reported to Richmond that Ostler had behaved diabolically, he 'nearly had the poor devil of an editor sacked from his job, telling his boss he was a Communist – which was quite untrue'.[45]

All of this left John in a fury. He wondered if one could any longer trust Hunter; he 'has gone the politician altogether . . . all very excited over the Akld. row; but when it comes to a show-down down here, his stock remark is the one about "choosing our own battle-ground" – with the result that he's never in the scrap at all'. John thought the tactics of those behind *Student* 'were rotten, & that young Watson wants to be booted out of the college just to prove that it is a bourgeois institution (& it always amazes me how eager the communists are to prove the obvious)'.[46] His strongest views were kept for the council: 'there was a mad race between the Council, Prof. Board & Students' Assn. to see who could be the most thoroughly & nastily reactionary. Things seemed very even for a time, & then the Council drew away in a burst of quite remarkable speed & finished (if it really has finished) with the rest nowhere.'[47] 'Your Victoria College', he wrote to de la Mare, '& my Victoria College exist no longer . . . they have knuckled down to all the demands of the Rev. Canon Percival James, that muck-raking notoriety-seeker, & of Mr A.P. Harper, of the Welfare League, & boast about the number of parsons Victoria College has given to the world! Well, it's about the only thing they can boast of now.'[48] John felt deeply frustrated and would have liked 'to flay the swine alive',[49] but he looked to F.P. Wilson's retirement as probably his only chance for a job: 'here I now pin all my hopes, however distant they may be'.[50]

WHEN THE TEMPORARY work at Victoria came to an end, John revised and added to his 'little history' of New Zealand. 'With revision it has turned into a little essay in Marxian interpretation', he told Richmond, 'though the holy Name is only mentioned once, & then without praise'.[51] He sold the 'serial rights' for £20 ('privately thanking God, because I wd. have taken £10'[52]) to *National Opinion*, the journal of the New Zealand Legion. It was published as 'Youthful Nation: History of New Zealand' in sixteen fortnightly parts beginning on 19 October 1933.[53] The legion was a conservative political movement, born of the Depression, which opposed party politics and made vague appeals to patriotism and old-fashioned individualism. In John's view it was 'developing in a way more futile than sinister . . . the moneyed men who were financing it at the start, Beauchamp etc., have withdrawn their support,* & it's hard up. Besides it temporises with things like socialism, & Campbell Begg [its leader] is a friend of Walter Nash'.[54] Its membership peaked at about 20,000 in late 1933; twelve months later it was finished. *National Opinion* was not consistently right-wing (it carried, among other things, complaints about censorship, and contributions by W.B. Sutch[55]) but John thought selling the essay to it 'one of the best jokes of modern times'.[56] Harry Tombs had turned it down for publication but John still had hopes he might find a publisher in Britain.

With Christmas coming there were again Matriculation history papers to mark: 'those bloody papers kept me cloistered for a month, with the exception of Xmas Day, when I cut the number corrected down to 10, & spent the rest of the day gorging & sleeping'.[57] This brought a cheque for £56 13s 8d: 'I must say . . . we have not had half so black a year as we anticipated. In fact in one way or another I made upwards of £250'. He had to add a note to his letter: 'E points out, that to be exact, it was £218'. Elsie always had a rather better head for money. Without her modest allowance from her father, life would have been difficult indeed. The lectures on Western civilisation, which Richmond had commissioned the year before, had been postponed for a year so there was still the prospect of £2 a lecture: 'I am rapidly becoming unemployable & really don't want to do any work at all', he wrote to Richmond, 'only read books I have been hankering to read for years; but your letter is so pitiful, & my sense of duty to wife & family so profound that I suppose I must sacrifice myself.'[58] Richmond's formal offer, when it came, was accepted by Elsie, 'on account of the rate at which Tim is wearing out his trousers'.[59] The Wellington WEA also employed John for £75 to look after its correspondence courses, with up to £25 more for travelling expenses when visiting groups outside Wellington, and he agreed to give eight lectures at Lower Hutt on 'Social and political science' for £16.

WEA work once more brought him into contact with an

---

*   John did hear that Beauchamp 'was very scared lest the preliminary finance he gave [the New Zealand Legion] would do him out of re-appointment to the board of the Bank of N.Z. by the govt, & wrote to both Coates & Forbes to say he had nothing to do with it'. (JCB to DEB, 16 November 1933.)

interesting range of people. There was a group of unemployed men at Titahi Bay who seemed to be very keen. He had a week's tour of Taranaki, 'tiring but amusing':

the Hawera group-leader is also Adjutant of the N.Z. Division of the League of Frontiersmen, a great admirer of [Bledisloe], & treasures a letter from Bled's private sec. Curiously enough, he is also quite convinced of the rottenness of our newspapers, & of the capitalist system, & appears to be an efficient W.E.A. secretary! There were some other funny birds too – A Russian Jew at Levin who made some £thousands in N. York & lost it all poultry farming in N.Z. . . . This bloody Douglas credit is still a menace though. People solemnly discuss whether they'll 'have a W.E.A. group or a Douglas credit study circle this year', & so on.[60]

Later, he had a week in Hawke's Bay. He was able to stay with Elsie's brother Peter, who was farming near Hastings, to meet with Harold Holt and see over the Holt family timber business, and to go to a rugby match – 'an odd game, but not without its sporadic excitement'.[61] Quite possibly it was the only rugby match he ever saw. The Wellington WEA, in John's view, could not compare with that in Auckland in either the way it was run or the quality of the material it provided to students. 'God preserve me from being a permanent tutor-organiser for the Wellington district'.[62]

Early in 1934 he reported to Richmond that the focus of his reading was now the nineteenth century: 'I'd like to devote about three years (for a start) to the study of England in the 19th century'.

When I was marking papers I read, & re-read in parts, [Morley's] Politics History & Oracles on Man & Govt in the collected ed. . . . just to keep myself in touch with some sort of balance & sanity. I like the way he tears up Maine & Lecky, their lucubrations on democracy – it's very thorough. But doesn't it all seem simple & idyllic & remote from the problems of democracy circa 1934? I think I could be a really good Liberal, no Radical, of the late Gladstonian era. However no doubt the simplicity is chiefly apparent to us, & the conscientious Radical had to do a certain amount of soul-searching even in those days. But contrast Maine for an antagonist with Lenin – or Hitler . . . my God! those do seem halcyon days. I am reading his Recollections now: or rather I have finished one volume & have the other ready for when I have got through a Life of Blake [by Mona Wilson] now in progress, a Xmas present from my Missus.[63]

Three weeks later it was John Stuart Mill's letters. 'Some good stuff . . . But the more I read of the Great Victorians the more I realise how deep Marx went'.[64] The breadth of John's reading, recorded in his letters, is more impressive than its focus. At this time he was also reading Donne's poetry, E.M. Forster's *Howards End* and his life of Lowes Dickinson. A little later it was Croce on history: 'he is a tough nut to crack. The second half of his book is easier & more interesting, being more about history & less about the identity of history & philosophy'.[65] He generally read for several hours after the evening meal, often going to bed well after midnight, and he was never an early riser.

THE AUCKLAND HISTORY chair had been advertised in August 1933 and John had applied.[66] He did not expect to be appointed and applied 'as a strategical move, hoping to be highly placed by the English committee, which would give me a push somewhere else'.[67] Professor Newton was a member of this committee, which advised the college on the applicants. 'Unaccountably', Sinclair puts it, John was not included in the shortlist of four,[68] though there is no evidence that he ever knew this. Did his application reach the English committee? He had heard from de Kiewiet that Newton had asked him to apply, and he had no doubt that de Kiewiet would get the job. De Kiewiet's appointment was announced in the middle of November and John, greatly amused, reported to Richmond that he 'is quick-tempered, obstinate as a mule, & can out-bluff twenty O'Sheas'.[69] His delight increased when he heard that Isobel Airey (whose husband had also applied) was at a public luncheon in Auckland and sitting next to Sir George Fowlds:

Sir G. tactfully waxes enthusiastic about this man de Kiewiet – marvellous record, wonderful scholar, nobody in N.Z. to touch him etc. So Mrs A., getting her own back, fixes him with her most charming eye, & says with deathly sweetness, 'Yes, indeed, not only is he a great friend of Dr B's but seems to share his ideas & outlook exactly.' Poor old Sir G. turns quite white & doesn't say another word.[70]

De Kiewiet turned the job down. John was not the only one who had warned him about Auckland,[71] and it may well be that he was hoping an offer from Auckland could be used to increase his salary at Iowa.[72] The chair went to James Rutherford, a young Englishman with a doctorate from Michigan, who had published one short paper. John wrote: 'I should feel very insulted to have been passed over in his favour if I had stood any chance on grounds other than qualifications'.[73] Sinclair, a little ingenuously, found it 'difficult to see' why Rutherford was ranked ahead.[74]

Early in 1934 the history chair at Adelaide was also advertised when W.K. Hancock, whose book on Australia John had read and admired, left after a short stay to go to Birmingham. John applied, but without 'even a sneaking hope' of getting it. 'We just apply for jobs these days on the principle of here's a job, let's apply for it. It doesn't do any harm or cost over-much . . . & it gives a minor interest to life'.[75] His application was unsuccessful. There was also a job in Tasmania but, as he wrote to Richmond, 'we draw the line at Tasmania, having still some money in the bank'.[76]

In June 1934 came the news that F.P. Wilson had given notice that he would retire the following January. John refused to believe it until he actually saw it 'in print & irrevocable'.[77] He wrote that 'I shall be annoyed, but certainly not surprised, if I don't get it'.[78] As the closing date, 31 August, approached and he organised testimonials for his application, however, it became difficult to think of much else. He asked von Zedlitz if he could 'stick his name down as a referee'.* Von Zedlitz agreed but left John with a 'very empty feeling in the stomach' by saying that he thought his chances were pretty thin, as 'The Council is much more concerned about what Canon P. James or the Welfare League might possibly say than anything else'.[79] As September stretched into October, John and Elsie went from waves of optimism to troughs of pessimism. There was a pleasant distraction when the first copies of *The Exploration of the Pacific* finally arrived – and wry irritation that it was Elsie's father who picked up an elementary mistake in Spanish geography. A further worry was Elsie's mother, with whom John had come to have the best of relations. She had had an operation for cancer and, while she was back home and taking a lively interest in the family, the outlook was not cheerful.

On Friday, 26 October John sent his father, who was staying with John's brother Geoffrey and Theo in Hamilton, a telegram:

Job not announced but definitely have no hope confidential

The council had met the evening before and made its decision, but before this could be made public the recess committee of the university senate had to approve the appointment. Five days later

---

* The testimonials he submitted, which strongly supported his application, were from Newton, Laski, Williamson, Allan Fisher and a joint one, covering his work in Hamilton and Auckland, signed by W.H. Cocker (an Auckland lawyer closely associated with the WEA, later a long-serving president of the Auckland University College Council and then chancellor), de la Mare and Richmond.

John wrote to his father and to Richmond with accounts of what had happened. He had hesitated, as the appointment was still in theory confidential, but it was 'surprising how many unauthorised people know these confidential things – including Mr Masters',[80] the Minister of Education – so he did not feel too constrained in what he said. He had had 'the whole story' from Professor Gould, a council member, and it was, in John's view, 'the dirtiest piece of business I ever heard of in the N.Z. university, & I've heard of some choice specimens'.[81]

A council committee of three – Phineas Levi, the council chairman; Gould, chairman of the professorial board; and Hunter, the second board member on the council – considered the applications for three chairs: history, mathematics and law. For the first they recommended unanimously that John should be appointed. F.L.W. Wood, a young Australian with a BA from Sydney University and an Oxford MA, who had been lecturing at Sydney since 1930, was ranked second, the rest nowhere.

Gould told me before the [council] meeting that they had picked me [John wrote to Norman], thought there wd. be some opposition because of the Auckland business from swine like McCallum etc, but couldn't see how the recommendation could fail to get through, Hunter told Sutherland it was all right for me, & the expectation down here was so general that I would get it that that bloody fool & little swine Cornish the Sol Gen. even told Coates that a Communist had got the history chair at V.U.C. Luckily Dick Campbell was there & when Coates said 'I didn't know Beaglehole was a Communist' Cornish was settled. He's a damn sight worse than [Arthur] Fair, & I didn't think that was possible.

Council met Thursday night. I cdn't get Gould that night, but next morning he cd. hardly speak, he was so overwhelmed . . . Hunter, who seems to have come very well out of this particular business & to have fought for me like a tiger, told Sutherland he cd. have vomited. Three chairs to be filled, History, maths, law. Cttee's recommendations challenged in each case but maths & law got through easily enough . . .

As soon as my name was mentioned two members brought up the Akld business & were squashed by Ostler & Atkinson. But if they brought it up they voted against me & so did others who hadn't the guts to mention it. The struggle then started. Wood had a very long & extraordinarily detailed testimonial from his boss S.H. Roberts . . . praising him to the skies – even saying he had invented a new system of marking papers! And that was what the majority grabbed & hung on to. Hunter got busy on the Pioneer Histories – B[eaglehole] asked specially to collaborate with all these distinguished knights & professors – yes, they said, but – look at this chap's testimonial, he's invented a new system etc. And so on . . . I gather in fact that although they didn't so much want Wood as be determined they wdn't have me Wood was strong enough to be an arguable alternative – if my books were ignored, plus the facts that they didn't know me, hadn't read my testimonials properly, & ignored Gould & Hunter, who were the only ones who did know me & who had considered all the applications thoroughly, & were also the only ones who knew anything about univ. teaching . . . And they were determined not to have me because of the Akld fuss – though they had no idea what the fuss was about – except that I had 'advanced views'. Ostler pointed out that Wood's views might be as 'advanced' as Beaglehole's; but that possibility was brushed aside.*,82

Since John's time as assistant lecturer, ten years before, the idea of succeeding Wilson in the chair had never been far from his mind. If he had taken the job at Rhodes University in 1928 and applied from there it is very hard to imagine him being turned down. Unlike in Auckland two years before, when the excitement seemed to buoy him up and he still had something to look forward to, this was a devastating blow. 'I had some minutes of complete & dreadful breakdown on Friday & two days' utter depression; now I have a normal depression & a tendency to lose my temper on the slightest provocation, so that I have to hold on to it consciously all the while, which is a damn nuisance. Elsie is magnificent.'83 Ivan Sutherland and other friends did what they could to soften the blow, and von Zedlitz wrote in sympathy:

2 Nov
I have just heard the lamentable & horrifying action of V.U.C. Council. I am more disgusted than surprised – have known McCallum for years, an odious drunken swine. The rest are just spineless, only 2 or 3 have honest convictions. I hear Hunter & Gould did their best. I don't know

---

*   Some time later (6 March 1935) John reported to Richmond that he had worked out how council members voted:

For B	For W
Hunter	McCallum (odious drunken swine)
Levi	Huggins (City Council – retired builder, I think)
Gould	O'Leary (lawyer, keen on testimonials)
Ostler	Bakewell (v. aged)
Parkinson	Cresswell (b[loody] f[ool])
	Valentine (b. f. probably, Harrop's father-in-law)
	Atkinson (Oxford man, so's W.)

John was almost, but not quite, correct. In the critical vote, to amend the committee's report by placing Wood first, those who favoured Wood were as John listed, with the addition of Duncan Stout (son of Sir Robert Stout and later a long-serving chairman of the council and Chancellor of the university), who had moved the amendment, while Huggins is not recorded as voting. The chairman, Levi, did not vote on the amendment. (Minutes of the meeting of the Victoria University Council, 25 October 1934.)

what to say to you about it, I have suffered too & know what it feels like. That sort of thing creates a revulsion of feeling & may serve you yet, if only a chance opens again. Alas, all our sympathy & indignation won't help you now. No answer. I'm only letting off impotent rage.[84]

On 5 November the matter was raised in parliament, during an appropriation debate,[85] by M.J. Savage, the leader of the Labour opposition, Walter Nash and Harry Atmore, the independent member for Nelson. Savage put the issue succinctly: 'Dr. Beaglehole is recognised as one with outstanding qualifications; and, because he is alleged to have advanced ideas,* the recommendation of the committee, the members of which have also a good grasp of the subjects they are handling, is vetoed by others who are less qualified to form an opinion.' He asked the government to look into the matter and see that justice was done, arguing that 'men with advanced ideas are the very men we are looking for'. Nash followed with a fuller account of John's career: as a young New Zealander he had extended his experience and gained his doctorate in Britain and then returned, 'as he should do, to give us the benefit and the knowledge of the experience he has gained overseas'. He had been denied that opportunity. Atmore added the information that the English committee advising on the applicants from Britain 'informed our committee that in Dr Beaglehole there was a more brilliant applicant in New Zealand than any applicant' they were considering. 'But this distinguished young New Zealander may have given utterance to some new thought, which in some quarters in New Zealand, is the unpardonable sin.' The explanation for Victoria's decision, Atmore suggested, was that John had a testimonial from Laski, and 'that made him suspect' in the eyes of the council. In reply, Gordon Coates agreed that Beaglehole was 'very able and a very excellent lecturer on history', but while he would 'be glad to see that the questions raised . . . are passed on to the proper quarter' he did not see how the government could act to adjust the matter.

The parliamentary action made the whole thing public, and the *Dominion* and the *Evening Post* the following day both carried reports of the parliamentary speeches, though they concentrated on those by Savage and Nash.[86] The *Post* also reported a statement by Levi which claimed that what Savage and Nash had said had been misleading, and added: 'the question considered by the council of the college in committee was the respective merits of two candidates each with very good qualifications and supported by excellent

---

*   'Query: What *are* "advanced ideas"?' (JCB to DEB, 7 November 1934.)

testimonials'. All this would, John wrote to his father, 'give me once again all the pains of notoriety without any of its pleasures'.[87] On 7 November the *Post* carried, without comment, a report of the appointments to the three chairs.

The decision stood. John had lamented that Gould, 'the typical Liberal . . . sees nothing to be done . . . but to fold the hands & regret the nature of mankind', but John conceded that he too could not see how anything could be done.[88] Rumour and conjecture on why the council had acted as it did and whether it had been subject to outside pressure continued. In the days after the parliamentary debate John drafted a letter to the chairman of the college council – feeling free by then to refer to matters which had been discussed in committee because they had become so widely a matter of public knowledge – in which he set down some of the reports he had heard. Some time before the council met, he wrote, the director of education, who had no formal connection with the college, had stated that John 'had not a hope' for the chair, and immediately after the council meeting the Department of Education, and the minister, knew all the details of the discussion that had taken place in committee and its result. John understood that Fair, the former council member and Solicitor-General, now a judge, had warned councillors against appointing him on the grounds that he had seen files which proved John's unfitness to occupy the post. Further, McCallum had been heard in Parliament Buildings expressing great satisfaction at having 'blocked Beaglehole', and the circumstances of the appointment appeared to have been generally known to members of the government parties in parliament for some time before the Labour members raised it in the House. Information such as this, John suggested, called for some investigation, 'if only as a means of restoring the confidence of university circles in the Council itself'.

John went on to point out the extremely difficult position in which he was placed, subject to hurtful and even slanderous charges with no opportunity of defence against them and no means of redress if they happened to be made public. As to 'advanced views' – which involved, he suspected, views on social and political reform but he could not be sure – he wrote that

as an historian I have considerable admiration for the principles of freedom and toleration and general human decency that are said to lie at the root of British ideals of social organisation. On the one or two occasions when I have sought publicity (with little success) for any controversial words of mine, it has been solely to give expression to such ideals; and to be the recipient of considerable abuse and enmity for doing so has, I admit, surprised me. I can only assert again now, in agreement with these ideals, that I do not know that such general orthodoxy should make me either fit or unfit to occupy an academic chair.

Finally he adverted to his personal situation: 'It may possibly be a cause of pride and joy to certain councillors to have "blocked Beaglehole"; but to me, with my whole academic career at stake, and as it seems at the moment, ruined, and with the future of my dependants gravely jeopardised, the transaction does not appear in quite so entertaining a light.' The letter, of which there is a typescript carbon copy in John's papers, is undated but refers to the parliamentary statements 'on Monday last'. The copy has corrections in ink in John's hand, and corrections and comments in pencil in two other hands, one of them Ivan Sutherland's – Sutherland noted that the report of Fair's intervention 'definitely cannot be used'. John wrote in the letter that he was sending copies to the Vice-Chancellor of the University of New Zealand (Hunter) and the chairman of the professorial board (Gould), but we do not know whether any copies, with or without amendments, were sent.

The evidence does not enable us to say beyond question that there was outside pressure on the college council, and that the council made its decision as a result of that pressure – councils are never immune from making inexplicable decisions. Three months later John heard that some council members were assuring people 'that the matter was decided purely on testimonials – which wd. only make them fools instead of knaves'.[89] It does appear, however, that there had been political pressure and it is difficult to avoid the conclusion that it had had some effect. It was widely believed to be so at the time and Dick Campbell, from his vantage point in Coates's office and with an acute ear for what was going on, had absolutely no doubt.[90] However one explains the decision, it was a very low point in Victoria's history.

The immediate result for John was that once again he had to take on Matriculation marking. The rates of pay had gone down; he earned only £31 for a month's work, whereas the first Christmas he was back in New Zealand it had been £75.[91] He also accepted another year's work with the Wellington WEA. More important, C.E. Beeby became foundation director of the newly created New Zealand Council for Educational Research (a further example of the beneficence of the Carnegie Corporation of New York) at the end of 1934. At John's suggestion,[92] Beeby contracted him 'with some trifling financial assistance from the Council',[93] to work full-time on the council's first and, in Beeby's view, 'arguably . . . finest' major publication. Proposed as a study of the working of the University of New Zealand, what was intended as an historical introduction to the book grew to 400 pages and was to be published in 1937 as *The University of New Zealand: An Historical Study*. John and Beeby (always known as Beeb) had last met, briefly, in London. Now a warm friendship developed between the two men and their wives.

The hunt for a job continued. John wrote to Professor Roberts in Sydney to see whether he was looking for someone to take Wood's place, but Roberts replied that when appointing lecturers they considered only their own graduates. J.A. Williamson wrote from London sympathising about Victoria – 'Even if your views were of the luridest scarlet that is your own affair and ought not to make any difference in an academic appointment' – but went on to say that 'I wish I could see a chance of a job for you here, but in truth there is not one, apart from the precarious venture of journalism'.[94]

A long letter to Richmond in February, however, suggests that John had largely recovered his spirits. They had had plenty of visitors: Anschutz and Rutherford down from Auckland, the Billings to stay a night on their way from Dunedin to England. Lascelles Wilson came and stayed for four or five days, a time 'which might approximately be described as wild but profitable – we make all our visitors who bathe bring back wood for us from the river, & by developing a healthy spirit of competition between Lascelles & Arthur Ward (not to speak of a certain amount of wise & able team-work), I got the wood-pile to hitherto unimagined proportions'.[95] One weekend in February Ivan Sutherland took John out to a bach he rented at Golden Gate on the Paremata harbour. They lay in the sun and bathed and were taken for a sail by Ivan's landlord: 'I thus realised one of the great ambitions of my life – I have never been out in a sailing boat before. The water went past & the breeze freshened & the boom came over & we ducked & it was all very romantic.'[96] Sutherland was at this time warden of Weir House and the matron, who had a very tender spot for him, had sent him off with enough food 'for an army for a week'. They did not even start on the chicken, and Sutherland insisted that John take it home. He and Elsie ate it to celebrate their fifth wedding anniversary, together with some 'personally selected' Adams Bruce chocolates – by choosing your own selection you could concentrate on 'the booze-filled kind'.

Once the marking was finished John got back to reading – 'Did you ever read *Clayhanger*? Magnificent thing'. He discovered G.M. Young and his essay 'Portrait of an Age':

. . . who is he? Very good on Evangelicalism & Utilitarianism. And was it he who told me of the man who said 'What we want is less chastity & more delicacy', or who was it. I also learn that James Mill once got into trouble for poking pamphlets on contraception through area railings in London. A long struggle, isn't it? Also I am on Jane Austen's *Letters*, which I like. I should like to have known her.[97]

Young's essay always remained high on his list of recommended reading. A little later he was rereading Milton's *Paradise Lost*. At this time also he was 'wading through' the sonatas of Beethoven, as a change from 'the greater Bach', but he had some doubt as to whether he found the romantic temperament really congenial – 'too many superfluous notes'.[98]

John met Fred Wood soon after he arrived to take up the history chair. Wood had known of the circumstances behind his selection and had wondered whether he should accept the appointment. He confirmed to John that he had talked to his vice-chancellor in Sydney about it and had taken the job only after being told that John would not be appointed under any circumstances whatsoever.[99] The meeting with Wood cannot have been easy. For a time John's gloom returned, but in May he wrote to Bill Airey:

I like Wood as a person considerably – which is another blow to me; because . . . I haven't even the satisfaction of making nasty remarks about him behind his back. I have no idea what he is like as historian or teacher, but I shd. think he could hardly help impressing students, or the best of them, favourably . . . He has a nice lot of books . . . inherited from his father, Arnold Wood, who was prof. at Sydney. Oh, another reason why he disarms me is that he shares my enthusiasms for Erasmus, Milton etc. Cd. anything be more irritating? His wife is rather rushing things & putting her foot in it accordingly . . .[100]

Hunter's first impression of Wood was 'a nice chap but not nearly as strong a personality as J.C.B.',[101] but Ostler's comment to the council that Wood's views might be just as advanced as Beaglehole's, was justified. 'It was the college's good luck that they did not get what they expected'; Wood, who while at Oxford had taken an active part in the British general strike of 1926, matched John in his dedication to social justice.[102]

Meanwhile, *The Exploration of the Pacific* was being very well received and widely reviewed. 'I had a column review in the *Sunday Times*', John wrote to Richmond, 'which causes even me, with an insatiable lust for applause & capacity for swallowing it, to blush.'[103] The British *Sunday Times* reviewer wrote:

Dr. Beaglehole, as a New Zealander, takes the history of Pacific exploration seriously; no man who had not put heart and soul into his work could have written so brilliantly. To skim lightly yet vividly over 260 years of international exploration in the greatest ocean, so as to leave the reader with a sense of fulfilment, from blank ignorance to complete knowledge, is an astonishing feat.[104]

The book was a history of the European exploration of the Pacific. This was the editors' decision and reflected the prevailing Eurocentric view of history. John, at that time, had read little about the earlier Polynesian voyages and discoveries. Having set the scene for his account with a discussion of the idea of the *Terra Australis Incognita*, the great southern continent, the search for which underlay Pacific exploration until almost the end of the eighteenth century, he went on to trace the narratives of the various voyages from Magellan to Cook. The book was praised for the breadth of its scholarship, for John's remarkable gift of bringing his characters alive – 'from the narrative gradually emerges a splendid gallery of portraits as the character of the discoverers is revealed in their actions or etched in a few incisive phrases'[105] – and for his vivid picture of the horrendous difficulties of maritime exploration. Ships were small and often ill-found; until Cook's time there was no adequate method of establishing longitude, and scurvy was a constant threat. The *Sydney Morning Herald* reviewer commented: 'We are gripped and held fascinated by shipwreck and mutiny, by alternate fraternising and fighting with the natives, by old-world tragedies of cruelty and treachery, sickness and starvation.'[106] The *New York Times* reviewer wrote that the book proved that 'sound and thoroughgoing scholarship and notable writing ability know neither latitude nor longitude'[107] – though we should note that this was the only historical publication in a field other than New Zealand history by an historian working in New Zealand between the wars. Edward Thompson, in the *Spectator*, on the other hand, suggested that as a New Zealander John was writing 'out of familiarity with the seas and lands where his voyagers pass, which books can never give and which the writer who has it need never obtrude'.[108] Thompson's suggestion cannot be sustained, as John had virtually no first-hand knowledge of the Pacific and at that time had yet to visit Ship Cove in Queen Charlotte Sound.* Rather, the book represented a triumph of scholarly work on the published sources and of the historical imagination.

---

* The previous September John had made a WEA visit to Marlborough and wrote to his father (18 September 1934): 'Now I want to get a launch & spend a good holiday in the Sounds & follow up Cook. I wanted to get to Ship Cove but there was no launch going.'

Nearly a third of the book is given to the three chapters on Cook's three voyages. Some memorable phrases emerge: 'The study of Cook is the illumination of all discovery';[109] 'To dogma he opposed experience; to the largeness of faith the hesitations of the enforced sceptic; to enthusiasm he presented the cool passion of unsatisfied enquiry';[110] 'He was the genius of the matter-of-fact'.[111] John's portrait of Cook concluded:

To measure the stature of Cook . . . one needs no recourse to legend or controversy; to compare his voyages, not in the mass of their result but individually, with the achievement of other men who were deemed with justice to have made contribution to geography, is its adequate realisation. Chance might enable the most ignorant man to discover islands, said La Pérouse, but it belonged only to great men to leave nothing more to be done regarding the coast they had found. Yet one thinks of Cook, not only as he who would be in the eyes of that immortal Frenchman 'the first of navigators', or as the scientist for whose safety the governments of France and America and Spain took such honourable thought, but also as the tall smiling figure who on the beach at Ship Cove, in Queen Charlotte's Sound, threw trifles for naked Maori urchins to scramble for, laughing and fearless, till his pockets were empty. For the rest, the map of the Pacific is his ample panegyric.[112]

The portrait was, perhaps, a little more effusive than it was to be later and some shadows were missing, but John's Cook of *The Exploration* 'was to shape appreciations [of Cook] for the next forty years'.[113] A. & C. Black brought out new editions of the book in 1947 and 1966; the third edition was published in the United States by the Stanford University Press and was kept in print until the end of the century.

Edward Thompson wrote that John brought out 'the achievement of Cook as I have never seen it brought out before', but what John had recognised in writing the book was just how poorly served scholars were in the study of Cook. The printed editions of his journals were far from accurate and the journals of Joseph Banks and others who sailed with Cook remained largely unpublished and unknown, so that those biographies which had been written, as well as having other limitations, lacked scholarly foundations. The appearance of *The Exploration of the Pacific* seems to have sharpened John's idea of pursuing further work on Cook. Early in 1935 Dr Frederick Keppel of the Carnegie Corporation visited New Zealand, and John talked to him about the possibility of getting support to spend a year in Sydney working on the Cook material in the libraries there. 'I propose to write the standard life', he informed

Richmond, adding, 'it is a bit early yet to make any suggestion about presentation copies'.[114]

There was further excitement in August with the publication of Ivan Sutherland's 123-page pamphlet, *The Maori Situation*. For John this was important, as it marked probably the first real thought he had given to the place of the Maori in New Zealand. From the late 1920s Sutherland, whose lectureship, as assistant to Hunter, was in the old field of mental and moral philosophy, had become increasingly interested in Maori affairs. He formed a close relationship with Apirana Ngata, whose policies for land reform captured his imagination, and also visited Te Puea Herangi to study her land development projects in the Waikato.[115] Christopher Perkins's daughter remembered Sutherland at this time as 'a lively person of great charm', but also 'an intense, emotional man, who could easily be roused to fury by injustice and bigotry'. She recalled him 'holding forth . . . with great passion on the plight of the poorer Maoris'.[116] The spur to his pamphlet was the commission of inquiry into the administration of the Native Department that followed political attacks on the administration of Ngata's schemes. The report largely exonerated Ngata of wrongdoing but he resigned from Cabinet in 1934. The whole situation, in Sutherland's view, reflected a woeful lack of understanding between Maori and Pakeha; the pamphlet, he hoped, would do something to increase that understanding on the Pakeha side.

Something of Sutherland's intense involvement is suggested by John's gently ironic report to Richmond at the time of publication:

You must understand we have been on the highest pitch of excitement, about twice as high as Everest – or anyhow Mt. Hobson – for the last few weeks, & I have fallen into the position of literary adviser, proof-reader, publicity writer, show-card expert, & general friend rock & stay. The tension has been Awful, & the booze has flowed freely. All at S's expense. The day of publication we met in Beeby's office, & as S. insisted on driving us both down to the printers afterwards to take *him* out for a drink I had serious thoughts of my children's future. However all's well; & we are now engaged on various newspaper controversies of a mild nature arising out of the reviews, which have been very good on the whole.[117]

John added that Sutherland had 'proved a good & generous friend to us, & I have dedicated a poem to him* (not as good as the Bach one, of course)'.

---

*   'Chinese Plate', published as the first of 'Three Poems of Escape' in *Art in New Zealand*, vol.8, no.2 (December 1935).

John reviewed the pamphlet in *Tomorrow* and, more briefly, in *Pacific Affairs*.[118] He was enthusiastic, but could not resist a critical crack in opening:

One had so long abandoned hope of vivid and original thought emerging from the University of New Zealand that, now that it has come to pass, one feels somewhat confounded . . . *The Maori Situation* will be taken very seriously by everyone in New Zealand with a sense of responsibility, a respect for logical and lucid argument, and an appreciation of good writing.

Sutherland had argued that there were two races in New Zealand and that it was likely there would be two for a long time to come, that the cultural inheritances of the two races were different, and that an expectation that the minority would in a short time die out or be swallowed up by the majority had not been and would not be realised. The primary reason for this, in his view, was the leadership provided from within Maori society by the Young Maori Party. The responsibility of the Pakeha was to understand what was happening; the failure of the commission of inquiry to understand properly was caused by its implicit acceptance of a rigid European set of values. This failure was shared by the Pakeha politicians. As John summed it up:

. . . what we have, primarily, in this book is a plea for Maori individuality, as opposed to the Europeanisers of the older generation, the philanthropists who wanted to redeem the Maori from barbarism by turning him into a white man. You can't do it. The plea seems to me to be convincing. Maori nationalism can either be worked into, or rather allowed to grow into, the general pattern of the country's life, as an enlivening and broadening factor – perhaps for later generations as a factor of seminal social importance; or it can be scorned and exacerbated.

John fully accepted Sutherland's estimate of Ngata's importance: 'one of the key men in New Zealand'. 'It seems absurd', John wrote, 'that such a man should not be returned to the position of highest executive importance in native affairs as soon as possible', and he went on to raise the problem of reconciling leadership such as Ngata's with New Zealand's party electoral system. With a general election due later that year, he suggested that such leadership should really be a non-party question: 'Has the Labour Party anyone to put in Ngata's place?'

John's growing friendship with Sutherland led him to consider the Maori and their place in New Zealand in a way that he never had before. Sutherland was to move to Christchurch in 1937, on being appointed to the chair in philosophy and psychology at Canterbury University College, but he continued to be a regular visitor to the Beaglehole house, generally as he passed through Wellington on his way from Christchurch to further fieldwork with the Ngati Porou or other Maori people.

In July John heard from Sutherland that Wood had succeeded in getting a full-time lectureship in history established for the following year. He was anxious to appoint John to it, but was plagued with diffidence and found it difficult to speak to him about it. Sutherland and Hunter had to act as intermediaries. 'Apparently I can have it if I want it', John wrote, 'McCallum now being off the Council & Atkinson dead & everybody else suffering badly from conscience'. He appreciated Wood's move, but at the same time was irritated by the position he was in:

all I have said is that my economic position is such that I wd. have to apply for a hangman's job. In the meanwhile we haven't heard from Carnegie & hope that will release us from the indignity of asking for a job at V.U.C. – & Beeby has offered me £100 a year with him as long as I care to take it, if all else fails . . . If I could see a casual income ahead for two or three years of £400 I certainly wdn't apply – but the utmost I seem able to make is about £250.[119]

He fairly quickly came to the conclusion that it was best to take the job, 'unpleasant as it was to apply for it, as a possible jumping-off place for something else',[120] and sent in his application at the end of August.[121] The college council made the appointment on 28 November, the day after the Labour Party under Savage had swept into power in the general election. A telegram from Fred Wood was the first John heard of his appointment, and the two met shortly afterwards. 'It looks as if Wood & I will get on all right', John told Richmond, 'At least he is not a 2nd-rate schoolmaster, as Rutherford appears to be,* & has the instincts of a scholar & a gentleman. A little less gentleman might be an improvement.'[122] They were to get on remarkably well for the next thirty years, to the inestimable benefit of the college and of their students.

---

*   This may be a little unfair to Rutherford. In his early years at Auckland, at least, he worked hard to collect manuscript sources for nineteenth-century New Zealand history which he used as the basis for an MA course. He was later to publish *Sir George Grey K.C.B. 1812–1898: A Study in Colonial Government* (London: Cassell, 1961). His relations with his colleagues were, however, far from happy. (Chris Hilliard, 'Island Stories: The Writing of New Zealand History 1920–1940', pp.94–5.)

John 'had a lot of congratulations, generally couched in tactfully modified terms',[123] including some from his WEA students. Boyd-Wilson wrote welcoming him 'as a trusty colleague coadjulator [sic]* & co-conspirator in the damnation of all duds and the glorification of all bright intellects',[124] and the news gave pleasure, and must have been a great relief, to Elsie's mother, who was now very ill and losing ground. The salary was to be £457 (and the college agreed it would start at the beginning of January rather than mid-February as advertised), and John and Elsie, with a secure future for the first time, decided they should pay John's father £60 for the family piano, which they had had since their time in Hamilton.

After Mary Holmes's death on 2 January, John and Elsie moved in with Elsie's father for three weeks. This gave Elsie's sister Edith, who had given up teaching to run the family home when her mother became ill – the expected thing for a single daughter at that time – a chance for a break. At the beginning of February John and Elsie left for a celebratory holiday; first to Hamilton for a day to see friends and then on to Auckland. They turned down an invitation to stay with the Richmonds:

We have never stayed in a hotel together in this country, & feel it would be fun for once . . . we (or anyhow I) have come to the point where it is necessary to spend some money, with a certain lavishness (for us) or be forever lost, spiritually. I have become positively mean in the last three years. We conclude that we must be deliberately extravagant. Hence hotel. Hence 1st class on train – anyhow as far as Hamilton. Hence parking kids out at Worser Bay with professionals. Hence general feeling of let 'er go, boys, & to hell with the overdraft! No doubt you understand the feeling. We may never do it again; but we've got to do it now.[125]

It was an uncharacteristic ambition for them both, and a measure of the impact of the previous few years, as a result not just of having to make do with very little money, but also of the growing concern as to whether John would ever get a university appointment, or indeed any sort of satisfactory employment at all.

After a few days in Auckland, they went on to Coromandel for a week of tramping and camping. From Coromandel they tramped over the range to Kennedy Bay and on south around the coast and over the hills again to Whitianga; then on to Cook's Beach (off which

---

*   coadjutor: 'An assistant, *esp.* one appointed to assist a bishop' (*New Shorter Oxford English Dictionary*). Boyd-Wilson did note that he had 'just had 2 snifters'.

Cook had anchored in the *Endeavour* 166 years before). Over thirty years later John remembered the spot:

we . . . dossed down for the night on the verandah of somebody's untenanted shack. Next morning was one of those mornings we get sometimes, absolutely pure and crystalline, the sea and the sand as pure as the air and the early sun; and I walked along the beach by the side of the sea, round the magnificent curve . . . up to the edge of what Cook called the Oyster river. On the other side of the stream two or three Maori figures appeared and looked at me: otherwise the whole bay, from the sea in to the hills, was empty and silent. And yet I felt something. It was nothing to do with a half-stirring breeze, or the gradually warming sun, though it was a sort of faint tingling of the mind . . . I don't want to use that old expression, 'the trembling of a veil', but it really was as if a veil had suddenly trembled, an invisible veil; and on the other side, just outside my vision, was a ship, and a boat rowing towards the shore; and somewhere or other, just floating beyond the reach of my ear, was the sound of words. I almost, before I turned back, caught sight of the *Endeavour*: I almost heard the voices of eighteenth century sailors.[126]

From Coromandel it was back to Hamilton, the overnight train to Wellington, and the new term at Victoria College.

IN 1936 THE ESSAY ON New Zealand history was finally published as *New Zealand: A Short History*. Bob Lowry, who had been a student of John's in Auckland ('a jolly good one too, when he had time to do any work') had been very anxious to publish it, and John had thought he would let him have it,[127] but nothing eventuated. He sent it to J.A. Williamson to see if he could find a British publisher. Williamson tried it on the Oxford University Press but Kenneth Sisam,* the assistant secretary of the press, returned it, saying that John's politics were too evident.[128] Williamson then tried J.D. Newth at A. & C. Black (who had published *The Exploration of the Pacific*). Newth too turned it down but suggested George Allen and Unwin, 'whose general tone is politically advanced'. By this time the Labour government had been elected in New Zealand; Allen and Unwin believed that this would give the book topical interest and accepted it, asking John to send by airmail an additional chapter bringing the story up to the election.[129] The book was dedicated to Duncan, 'For a memorial of Brunswick Square', and John wrote to him that he

---

* Sisam was a New Zealander, an Auckland graduate who had been a Rhodes Scholar.

hoped that Duncan at least would 'recognise the occasional deliberate parody of the style of . . . our common master, Harold J. Laski'.[130]

The short history was topical; John's contemporary concerns shaped both the proportions of the book and its content.[131] This was enough to upset some readers, and one reviewer, A.B. Chappell, in the *New Zealand Herald*,[132] complained at the summary dismissal of the pioneering period, with everything up to 1890 being crammed into fifty pages, less than a third of the book. Alister McIntosh, writing in *Tomorrow*,[133] recognised what John was doing: Dr Beaglehole's essay, he wrote, 'for essay it is rather than a book', is 'essentially an interpretation of this country's development in the light of the present phase of our political and social life'. The interpretation reflected John's view that New Zealand history since the European arrival could best be understood as an example of the expansion of British or Western capitalism. As the creature of British expansion, New Zealand was at that time inextricably linked to British markets for its produce and to British financial institutions. When the great depression hit Britain, New Zealand was lost; there was little the politicians could do.

The thesis now seems unremarkable, hardly as provocative as it was seen at the time, although it then represented something new in New Zealand historical writing. Its impact owed as much to the brilliance of the writing – 'brilliantly savage', one later scholar has put it[134] – and its epigrammatic quality (though Chappell put it more sourly: the 'constant indulgence in smart quips'). Nor could the vivid sketches of political leaders be fully explained in the terms of the basic thesis. Rather, they pointed ahead to John's growing interest in what it meant to be a New Zealander. Seddon earned the fullest picture:

Inescapably genial, inexhaustibly itinerant, expansive in body and in claims, with an unrivalled capacity for identifying the workings of the Deity with the politics of New Zealand, radical with a real sympathy for the oppressed under his eyes, and imperialist with a vulgarity noisy and flamboyant, devoid of theory but shrewdly apprehensive of the concrete fact, an astute manager and a good administrator, he united within himself a whole orchestra, or, rather, brass band, of achievement; and as a performer on the big drum he was without a peer. Yet the noise did, it must be noted, signify something. If the corruption of his 'roads and bridges policy' was so open as almost to lose the savour of iniquity, if he stormed the defences of a sensitive mind with the rush of a barbarian on Rome, at least he did in some sort fairly represent the colonial mind. True, he liked his empires big. But his humanity was fundamental, if unimaginative, and in the colony itself his disregard for the rigours of ceremonial was over-balanced by the passion of his unforgetful friendliness.[135]

The legislation produced by Seddon's governments, in John's view, called for less comment. Lacking any large philosophic basis and owing much to trial and error, it was seen by some, then and later, as an approach to 'state socialism'. John disgreed:

The intrumentality of the State was certainly exploited: the socialism, generally speaking, was a label affixed either by external observers who took an imperfect deed for a will enlarged beyond recognition, or by the astonished conservative who could express his surprise and displeasure only by the simple exercise of recrimination in terms incompletely understood.[136]

Other figures were dealt with more summarily. Ward: 'a good administrator . . . though his acquaintance with principle perhaps suffered from his willingness to close his eyes to the inevitable consequences of gambling in futures'.[137] Massey: 'a laborious farmer and a laborious politician, successful in both rôles, dividing a faith as massive as himself between the Scriptures and the British Empire. Precipitate in patriotism and inaccessible to subtlety, he was the epitome and exemplar of the country he led . . .'[138] Forbes: 'The personal integrity of Mr. Forbes was unimpeachable, but honesty has never been a compulsive rallying-cry . . .'[139] Downie Stewart: 'wise with all the wisdom of a world that had ended'.[140] And Ngata: 'one who brought something like genius to the office of Native Minister'.[141] John added that 'it was evident that the lapse of a century had not lessened the need for adequate interpretation between the two races'.[142]

Coates clearly intrigued him: he would have had first-hand information on his work in the coalition government from Dick Campbell.* John judged him 'the most considerable figure in New Zealand politics' of the previous ten years;[143] one for whom the 1935 election was 'a personal and shattering defeat, an individual judgment' as well as the judgement of 'a system'. John's summing-up was nonetheless sympathetic:

. . . without Seddon's popularity or bluster, or Massey's fundamentalist and competent obstinacy, more subtle, more imaginative, and more

---

*   Alister McIntosh, also in a good position to observe, wrote: 'The estimate of Mr Coates and his achievements in bewildering difficulties are based on what I know to be facts and should appeal to all fairminded people as thoroughly just.' (*Tomorrow*, 22 July 1936.)

unhappy in his *milieu* than either; where they inherited from the past a
calm and certain strength, the child of perplexity and divided worlds;
torn where they were unitary; driven, like his age and unlike theirs, to
ambiguity – to the expedient, but not the solution, of compulsory and
painful compromise.[144]

On whether the new Labour government would bring about
fundamental changes, John did not express a view. He did describe
Walter Nash as 'the party's most persuasive intellectual force', which
Nash never forgot (though he always remembered it as John having
said that he was the party's 'coming man'); he was to remind John
of this a number of times in later years,* and he told me more than
once when we met at graduation ceremonies.

Although the book was organised around recent politics, John's
underlying interpretation, in his view, explained much about New
Zealand's intellectual and cultural life. If he argued that the country's
development was essentially 'only an episode in the expansion of
Western civilization',[145] he also conceded in the final chapter, where
he focused on questions of identity, that it was perhaps in its isolation
that one discovered the secret of 'the national life'. This argument
he did not develop, simply suggesting that New Zealand 'pastures
its soul impartially in fields classically English and delightfully
American'.

The tenderness of place, the *genius loci,* in no large sense it appears, is
part of the life of the European born in our country – for the Maori,
the ancient conqueror, it is different – the sense of intimacy, quietude,
profound and rich comfort is not yet indestructibly mingled with the
thought of a native soil, an habitual and inseparable surrounding.
There is glad recognition, there is love even; but there is not identity.
Not enough men have died in this land. Not in letters nor in art has
life crystallized and ennobled itself. But where lakes and torrents rise,
where in the far gullies and on unscorched hills the bush perpetually
and in silence renews its green† inviolate life, it may be that the spirit of
man also will find renewal – not as a thing sought, not with travail nor
born from an old despair, but quietly and unconsciously as the spring
seeps from the moss, or the *rimu* roots itself in the mould, or the fragile
clematis appears starred over unattainable slopes.[146]

---

*　　Perhaps the final occasion was when Nash wrote to John to thank him for
　　his congratulations when Nash received the KCMG; he appreciated the
　　'generous nature of your message – which follows on the prediction made
　　in your essay Short History of N.Z.'. (Nash to JCB, 1 September 1965.)

†　　The published book had a comma at this point: in the copy John had
　　corrected before sending to Duncan, he took it out.

This reflective brooding has led John far from his political analysis; his view of New Zealand identity, as Chris Hilliard suggests, is related to those of his contemporaries – Brasch, Curnow and other writers of their generation. 'For them, "identity" resided in the future, to be anticipated with guarded hope or sometimes resignation'.[147] John was later to write of the period in which he worked on the *Short History*: 'to be candid, I was not interested in New Zealand – except in so far as I had to be'.[148] The *History* itself is evidence that we should not take this at face value. It may have revealed little love for New Zealand's past; it could not hide a concern for New Zealand's future. Its publication coincided with the turn for the better in John's fortunes and marked the beginning of his own intellectual and emotional discovery of New Zealand.

8

VICTORIA UNIVERSITY COLLEGE, FAMILY AND FRIENDS, 1936–49

WITH THE YEARS OF UNCERTAINTY at an end, John and Elsie looked forward to getting a home of their own for the growing family while John, admittedly with mixed feelings at first, could look to a secure future at Victoria. The house they bought in Karori John lived in for the rest of his life. Fred Wood and he were to create a history department probably unmatched in quality for its size in New Zealand and Australia in the 1940s and 50s, and John became almost at once a figure of note and of influence in the college community and beyond. Within a short time he was drawn into the planning for the New Zealand centennial, and within the Centennial Branch and subsequently the Historical Branch of the Department of Internal Affairs he, together with Joe Heenan, the departmental head, formed a kind of embryonic ministry of culture. Here, in a very practical way, he developed his interest in typography and book production, making a major contribution to the standard of commercial printing in this country and becoming so interested that at one time he even wondered whether he should not consider becoming the Government Printer. Increasingly, he was recognised in the community as a critic with a concern for the quality of life in his country, a man of considered views who was not afraid to express them. As early as 1938 William Downie Stewart, the scholarly Dunedin lawyer and politician and former Minister of Finance, wrote to him: 'I judge from letters I get from some of the younger generation that you are exercising an influence that is greater than you may be aware of'.[1] In the postwar years we can see him as an intellectual mentor not only to government departments but to a growing number of public and private institutions and to young New Zealanders engaged in the creative and performing arts.

FOR THE FIRST TIME A NEW job did not mean immediately packing and finding somewhere new to live, and while the family remained in Marsden Street there was always the possibility of a lift home in Walter Nash's ministerial car when he and John had been at the same meeting. With the prospect of a third child in August 1936, however, the cottage there came to seem decidedly small. John and Elsie considered building and talked to Cedric Firth about plans. Firth had trained as an architect at Auckland University College and then travelled in Europe during 1931–32, where he visited new public housing schemes and absorbed modernist ideas. On his return to New Zealand he spent some time in Auckland, where John and Elsie first met him, before moving to Wellington, where he contributed both to the Labour paper, the *Standard,* and to *Tomorrow.* At John's suggestion, he was writing a series of articles for *Tomorrow* on the problems of working-class housing.[2] Firth's plan for their house was 'about as plain and simple as anything could be without vanishing into string and brown paper';[3] most of the rooms were small but the cost, with a section, looked to be about £2000. It seemed an awful lot and, with great reluctance, they abandoned the plan. The alternative was to buy a house. They heard of one in Karori, 'on the old side' but very roomy.[4] The owner asked £1550, they offered £1400 and the offer was accepted.* In the same week, on 24 August, another son, Giles Cawte, was born. 'Poor Girl', John reported to Kathleen McKay, 'she [Elsie] wanted a Girl, & so did I. But we go forward to met the Future bravely, nerved proudly with the thought that the Empire . . . needs all her Sons, & that the Revolution needs a lot more.'[5]

The house, one of the earliest in Macdonald Street (later given the name Messines Road after the south Belgian town taken by the New Zealand Division at the cost of high casualties during the First World War) had been built in 1901–2 for Robert Hayes, a clerk in the Post Office, who eventually became Secretary of the Treasury, and his wife Ellen. A roomy villa typical of its time, it had had a large sitting room added about fifteen years later. Some years after Hayes's death his widow decided to sell the house. When the Beagleholes moved in in November there was a lot of work to be done. John reported to Richmond:

---

*   I have always understood that my grandfather, Elsie's father, paid for the house but I can find no written confirmation of this. John wrote to Richmond, 'It is [Elsie's] house, & I am merely providing the furniture' (JCB to Richmond, 29 December 1936). The certificate of title does show that on purchase the house was transferred from Ellen Hayes to Elsie.

We had a lot of inside painting & papering done & a concrete yard laid down for the kids & odd verandas & outhouses knocked down & the maid's room converted into a wash-house . . . & though the bathroom is too small the sitting-room is about 21x21. And of course it is all in a Very Nice Locality. We can get anything on tick anywhere in town by just mentioning that we live in Messines Road.[6]

Cedric Firth gave advice and designed a wall of cupboards for the kitchen. Bookshelves began to creep up the walls of John's study. The Van Gogh and Cézanne prints were hung in the dining room. It was hardly Finella – there was very little money and Cedric was a more austere modernist than Raymond McGrath – but it was 'really thoroughly satisfactory'.[7] The verdict was prophetic. Over the next thirty-five years the house remained at the heart of John and Elsie's life; for family, students and a growing circle of friends John and Elsie and 6 Messines Road seemed inextricably linked. John's study became the hub of his working life; it was there that he wrote, there that he read late into the evening.

The garden too needed a lot of work. It was surrounded by overgrown hedges; three pines in front of the house were whittled away over the years. John bought a pair of hedge clippers and a stepladder and each year spent several weekends in early summer cutting the hedges. Apart from this and lawn mowing (until we boys took that task over), the garden was largely Elsie's domain and she looked after it with a skill and enthusiasm inherited from her father.

John quickly settled comfortably into his study, although it was on the southern side of the house and always a cold room. Here, with his books around him and the little bust of Voltaire bought in Paris on one of the shelves, he worked at his desk or read in the armchair next to it. The year 1936 was very full. John wrote to Richmond:

We seem to have been in a jam from one end of the year to another, with the result that during 1937 I absolutely decline to write any books, build, buy, rent, or demolish any houses, have any babies, run any printing-works, make any promises, carry out any contracts, give any interviews, pack or unpack any books, apply for any jobs, stain any floors . . . reform any universities, save any student's soul. What shall you do then? you ask . . . I shall read the Left Book Club books, & Mehring's Marx, & Laski's two last books, & Paradise Lost, & play Bach, & look at prints of Cézanne, & lie in the sun, & occasionally deliver a lecture . . . I think I might continue my study of Voltaire too. Or, I don't know, I might go to Spain & shoot a few fascists. Or go to Austria & lay my services at the feet of the Dook of Windsor.[8]

The constitutional crisis caused by the decision of the new King, Edward VIII, to abdicate from the throne in order to marry Wallis Simpson had led John to discover, with some interest, that instinctively he 'was a Royalist, & to hell with Parliament'. He could hardly support the British Prime Minister, Stanley Baldwin, and the Archbishop of Canterbury. Alister McIntosh took the same view but Hunter, 'after meditating over the matter for some days, decided that two divorces were a bit too much'.[9]

To celebrate the end of the teaching year, John read the novels of Thomas Love Peacock: 'very amusing, sort of ancestor of Aldous Huxley in manner . . . long conversations & a good deal of omniscience'. He had also just finished Geoffrey Faber's *Oxford Apostles*, which he judged *'very* good . . . [it] gives a more reasonable account of Newman & all that gang than anything else I have read. Incredible people! Incredible controversies! Incredible agonies of soul!'[10]

Completing his book on the University of New Zealand had had to compete with the new job. By July John had finished a first draft and was 'adding bits' and 'putting in the style'.[11] The manuscript went to Beeby, who has described what followed:

I had the temerity to edit his draft, and never did editor learn more from the edited. From him I got my first insight into the techniques and standards of educational research at their most scrupulous . . . I felt more assurance on the writing of English prose than I did on historical scholarship, and we argued endlessly, and sometimes vehemently, on the structure of a sentence or the precise meaning of a word or phrase. In our more heated moments the difference between a comma and a colon could threaten a friendship . . .[12]

As director of the fledgling Council for Educational Research, Beeby also had a diplomatic eye, while John, 'where a pompous bubble could be pricked by an apt phrase . . . would fight to the death to retain it, no matter who might take offence'. Beeby checked even the page proofs of John's index.

It was a beautiful index, with not an idea missed or a word wasted, and I was full of admiration till I came to 'O'. There I found an entry, 'Ostler, H.H., improper costume of, 161'. It had a spicy flavour, and would have been acceptable if the man in question had been a nonentity long since dead. But he happened to be a distinguished member of the Bench, the Hon. Mr. Justice Ostler. The sartorial incident had occurred in 1902, when Ostler, a law student of independent vein, had appeared for his examinations clad in 'a sweater or white football jersey', and had been told by the supervisor that it was not proper attire for a University occasion. After the third day on which the young rebel defied his authority, the supervisor reported the offence to the Senate, which had a solemn debate on 'the improper costume of H. H. Ostler'. John was tilting at the Senate for wasting its time on trifles, and not at the learned judge, and could see no point whatever in my objection. After days of intermittent argument I had my way, and . . . the item now reads, 'Ostler, H.H., inappropriate costume of'.[13]

Peace was made, friendship maintained, and Beeby judged the finished work, which appeared early in 1937, 'a magnificent piece of scholarship, which established the NZCER's scholarly reputation with even the most critical of academics'.[14]

John, however, wondered why he had devoted two years of his life to the history of an institution for which he had so little respect. The subtitle, he concluded, 'should undoubtedly be A Study in Futility'.[15] It was a story of provincial discord and parochial rivalry, but a story in which, he admitted, 'in spite of myself, I got interested'.[16] 'Though one tends to rise from the study of our University with exasperation ever renewed', he wrote in the preface, 'there have been men, there have been ideas, within the University, for whom and for which one can record only unqualified respect'.[17] More significantly, he had sought to portray the university's development in relation to its environment:

There have been examining universities, and federal universities, and colonial universities, and quarrelsome universities, before; but nothing, in all respects, quite like this. For New Zealand, as the naturalist has so often assured us, is a museum of rare and astonishing things. And our University: is that not too, for the curious student, both rare and astonishing? . . . The environment, in its uniqueness, conditions the institution, its product; and no study of an educational institution, above all, can be highly fruitful, that does not recognise this premise. A history of this University, therefore, is a study not altogether of education, though the bounds of education are wide; it is also a study of colonial history, a study of political science, a portrait of the colonial mind . . . If the student and the teacher, for whom the University allegedly exists, seem to get surprisingly little notice, that is in the nature of the case. They are none the less in the background, a cloud of embarrassing witnesses, acquiescent, puzzled, confounded, impatient, obstreperous; waiting – can it be? – for a true epoch to be marked in the University's life; and the historian must, at least, not be unaware of their existence . . .

John began with the premise that a university, simply stated, 'is an association of teachers and students, with this characteristic, that the teachers do not cease to be students'.[18] In contrast, the University of New Zealand was primarily an examining body; teaching was the responsibility of the affiliated colleges. With wit, scholarship and at times a biting irony, he explored the disastrous effects of this division – already spelled out by two royal commissions as well as by Hunter, T.H. Laby (the first professor of physics at Victoria University College) and other members of the university reform movement in the years before the First World War. John quoted Thomas Huxley's devastating observation on the dangers of the examination system for students: 'They work to pass, not to know; and outraged Science takes her revenge. They do pass, and they don't know.'[19] Unfortunately, the voices of those who believed that a university was significant primarily for the standard of its teaching were drowned by those who elevated its examining to a pre-eminent place. The result, John suggested, was that its mission 'has not been to facilitate the diffusion of that culture which its founders sincerely desired to see spread from one end of the colony to the other; but to provide cheap professional schools for the supply of duly certificated lawyers, doctors, bank-clerks, dentists and teachers'.[20] The history of the university explained both the genesis of that mission and the price paid for failing to advance beyond it:

Professional competence . . . if it has any meaning beyond acquaintance with the baldest tricks of a trade, is allied with an indispensable closeness to the disinterested pursuit of knowledge. To 'teach' law without ever-renewed scrutiny of the origins of law, the roots of justice, is no teaching . . . to 'teach' medicine or engineering or history without returning continually to the laborious and galleried mine of research is to run to meet frustration. And the man or woman who comes from the university – in turn to teach or practise – with no realisation of this primary and fundamental thing . . . may flourish, with pride or cynicism, a certificate; but has a competence the limits of which are severe and inelastic. This primary and fundamental thing also it has been the business of New Zealand, in effect, to deny. Our country has been primitive; it has been rough and ready; it has had – but too long – the pioneering willingness to make do. It has sought and ensu[r]ed mediocrity with unusual success.[21]

The book was enthusiastically reviewed: an 'eagerly awaited work' and a 'model of how history should be written';[22] 'a remarkable and delightful book';[23] 'witty and inspiring'.[24] Von Zedlitz, in one of the few signed reviews, praised it warmly, 'few more intelligent books have been written'.[25] Arthur Sewell, the lively and radical professor of English at Auckland, found John's conclusions 'exhilarating – if only for the fact that one can enjoy on every page the thought of the particular person who is bound to disagree with him'[26] and wrote that John's 'final word . . . should be inscribed in a prominent place in every University College in the Dominion':

As the court of justice should be no respecter of persons, so the university should be no respecter of ideas; as we do not seek to intimidate the majesty of the law, so we should recoil with equal repugnance from the intimidation of the intellect. For the intellect is by nature critical, and only in the free functioning of intelligence is there hope either for the university or for the world.[27]

In contrast to the sparkling essay on New Zealand, the 'historical study' of the university was a more substantial and scholarly work. Grounded in the records (which John found 'like our colonial records generally . . . in a shameful state of chaos'[28]), it reflected not only 'his matchless capacity for transforming a mountain of arid documents into readable prose'[29] but also a critical engagement with the idea of the university which had begun in his student days, when it found expression in *Spike*. The writing has worn well and, even if we can no longer share Arthur Sewell's particular exhilaration, the cogency of argument, the wit and the lively portraits of the protagonists such as Tancred (the Canterbury politician and first Chancellor of the University of New Zealand), and Robert Stout have lost none of their force.

VICTORIA WAS ALL VERY familiar in spite of some staff changes. At the end of 1936 Hugh Mackenzie retired, 'which cost us all a few bob in luncheons & travelling rugs – but well worth it',[30] leaving only Rankine Brown of the original staff. Mackenzie was replaced by another Edinburgh man, the energetic, ambitious and scholarly Ian Gordon. The demands of the expanding public service, which followed economic recovery and the change of government, led to the School of Political Science and Public Administration being established.[31] John had put the case for it in his pamphlet *A School of Political Studies*,* something of an appendix to his history of

---

*   JCB, *A School of Political Studies*, (Wellington: New Zealand Council for Educational Research, 1938). At a time when almost all public servants were first appointed straight from school and very few had a university education of any sort, John argued for an education for a selected group 'that will be not merely technical but, in the intellectual sense, liberal and humane . . . [the public servant] needs to be acquainted not merely with office-files and the peculiar mode of prose-composition they breed, but with literature . . . he should know *Paradise Lost* and *Hamlet*; he should know James Joyce

the university, in which he described what would be at once a school of political studies and a 'staff college' for public servants. The new chair was filled by Leslie Lipson, a twenty-seven-year-old graduate of Chicago and Oxford, but John found the young Australian Robert Parker, who lectured in public administration, more congenial. In spite of the changes that were being made the college was hardly a place of intellectual distinction;* most of the teaching was at best adequate, and with one or two exceptions, such as the geomorphologist C.A. Cotton, staff did very little research. In both respects the history department, with John and Fred Wood, rapidly made its mark. A real blow to John was Ivan Sutherland's appointment to a chair at Canterbury in 1937, 'my only intellectual stay on the staff being removed'.[32] Ernest Beaglehole succeeded Sutherland and the two families saw much of each other, but, for John, Ernest never really took Sutherland's place.

The college in the late 1930s was still a small community. Although student numbers were climbing after the trough of the depression years, they had yet to reach a thousand and, except in science, the students were mostly part-timers. A lively minority among the students were still caught up in social and political discussion. A Labour Club was started in 1934, in time to keep the new government on the rails. The Debating Society was more and more political. John went to the visitors' debate in 1936 when Gordon Coates ('quite good') moved a motion of no-confidence in the government; John A. Lee, who was 'expected to clean him up' was shockingly bad, obviously hadn't troubled to prepare a word'.[33] The same year the society, not for the first time, had a majority

---

and Eliot and D.H. Lawrence, and later men even than these'. Downie Stewart, to whom John sent a copy of his lecture, was unconvinced: 'you will say I am an antiquated fogey suffering from induration of the mental arteries if there are any but *please* explain why public servants must study James Joyce, Lawrence & Elliott [sic] – I always regarded these first two as pathological sex maniacs & no brilliance of style seems to warrant asking a lady public servant to study Ulysses where the talk is between girls in a brothel &c. if I remember – & will she have to study Lady Chatterley's Lover?' (Downie Stewart to JCB, 22 July 1938.)

*   Leslie Hearnshaw, who lectured in psychology at Victoria from 1939 to 1947, when he returned to Britain to take up the chair at Liverpool University, wrote of Victoria at this time (in an unpublished memoir, kindly shown to me by his son, Professor John Hearnshaw): 'With one or two exceptions I don't think that most of my colleagues at Victoria University College could be regarded as more than very moderately distinguished academically.' John he judged as 'unquestionably the most eminent member of the staff academically'. The Hearnshaws found 'numerous compensations in the friendly and close-knit community of Victoria', however.

disinclined to fight for king and country. The Student Christian Movement (SCM) began a study circle on communism and joined with a number of other clubs in starting the Victoria University College Anti-War Movement. Increasingly, events in Europe and north Asia were casting a shadow. The radicalisation of student opinion in the late 1930s owed less to the world economic crisis and the abject performance of conservative politicians in dealing with its impact than to a dawning realisation that the advance of fascist dictatorships carried the inescapable threat of another world war. The Italian consul spoke to the Free Discussions Club on Abyssinia, the German consul on the Nazi movement. They were critically received, 'the meetings . . . went on far into the night',[34] and the German consul walked out because of the reception he was given.* The student weekly paper, *Salient,* which first appeared in March 1938, argued passionately against academic isolation and for linking the university 'more closely to the realities of the world'.[35] There were appeals for Chinese university relief† and for children in Spain. John's book of poems, *Words for Music,* published by the Caxton Press in 1938, carried a note, 'profits from the sale of this book will go towards Spanish Medical Aid', and he was involved with the Wellington Spanish Medical Aid Committee.[36] The next year came the Munich crisis. In his history of the college John is clearly writing autobiographically when he mentions the silence and tension 'that waited on a lecturer who had been asked, suddenly, on that most fateful night, to waive his usual subject – was it responsible government in the British Commonwealth? – and speak on the antecedents of the crisis'.[37] It is telling that he should have been asked, as an indication of his reputation among his students and of the way in which he saw his job as a university teacher. Student life, however, was not all politics and world events. The short-lived Phoenix Club was devoted to all the arts. John invited its members up to Messines Road for a talk on printing, 'with a small exhibition'. 'I hope', he wrote to his father, 'they won't seem

---

*   Over thirty years later one history student could still remember the questions that John had suggested he should ask the consul (and that Hunter had tried to persuade the newspapers not to mention the incident). (J.W. Davidson to EMB, 9 November 1971.)

†   At this time Reo Fortune was associate professor of anthropology and sociology at the American Lingnan University in Canton, where he and his second wife, Eileen Pope, were visited by Robin Hyde in March–April 1938. (Derek Challis and Gloria Rawlinson, *The Book of Iris: A Life of Robin Hyde* (Auckland: Auckland University Press, 2002), pp.548–9.)

as paralysed as students generally do when you ask them out.'[38]

In January 1938 John and Elsie went to Sydney and Canberra for a brief visit. It was a chance to stay with Duncan and his wife, who had a 'nice spot of hillside' at Chatswood 'where Dunc devotes himself to the cultivation of the native bush with national enthusiasm',[39] and the Lascelles Wilsons, to catch up with Kathleen McKay and with friends of Duncan's whom they had met on their way back to New Zealand in 1929. John visited the Mitchell Library to look at Cook material (he was already corresponding with the Argonaut Press in London on a proposal that he should edit the journals for them). They drove to Canberra in the Wilsons' car for the two-day summer school of the Australian Institute of Political Science. Canberra was still tiny, with about 8000 inhabitants, but John thought the site 'really marvellous' and was deeply impressed that the federal government cut the residents' hedges for them – a 'great place'.[40] We have no record of the proceedings of the summer school but John again had a chance to look at Cook material: the holograph copy of his *Endeavour* journal in the national library, which had been bought in 1923 for £5000. 'I was left alone in the strong-room with keys & Cook's own original *Endeavour* journal ... & told to help myself, as it were.'[41] Back in Sydney, they went with Kathleen to inspect Cook's landing place at Kurnell. John would not have minded staying for a few months and starting work then, but it was to be ten years before he was able to make that start.

To many students in the late 1930s and early war years, John seemed to embody Victoria's radical tradition. It was there in his teaching: 'He talked with irony and humour but with an undertone of involvement and of passion. He was an older man who shared our indignation with the stupidity and corruption of the mediocre and powerful – though he expressed it more moderately – and who cared about the causes we had at heart.'[42] The involvement went beyond the classroom. *Salient* and *Spike* both sought his views on matters as diverse as modern jazz, *Salient* itself, and the New Zealand centennial. He featured as a character, 'Dr Weevilbole – the eternal historian', in the student extravaganza 'Centennial Scandals'. When a student international relations club was formed amid the rising world tensions of July 1939 he and Fred Wood took an active part in its discussions.

The two of them shared an interest in international affairs and the evolution of the British Commonwealth. Wood's centennial survey, *New Zealand in the World*, was a pioneering study that was to be followed (in 1958) by his masterly volume in the official war history,

The New Zealand People at War: Political and External Affairs. Both
men were members of the New Zealand Institute of International
Affairs (NZIIA), which had been established in 1934 by a group
of prominent people including Downie Stewart and Walter Nash,
notable among their parliamentary colleagues for their interest in
world affairs. Downie Stewart became the first chairman, Alister
McIntosh (a member of the General Assembly Library staff and a
close friend of both John and Wood) the first secretary-treasurer. In
its membership the NZIIA overlapped that of two existing bodies:
the Institute of Pacific Relations (IPR) and Round Table groups.
The New Zealand branch of the IPR, founded in 1926 with J.B.
Condliffe and Nash among its original members, was absorbed by
the NZIIA. Round Table groups had been originally organised in
Britain and the dominions by Lionel Curtis in 1910. Fred Wood
became a member of the Wellington group. All three bodies had
affiliations with their parent organisations: the Royal Institute of
International Affairs (Chatham House) and Round Table in London,
the IPR in Honolulu. Membership of the NZIIA branches was small
but included prominent professional and business men and women
as well as academics, journalists and public servants.[43]

In its early years the NZIIA had been a rather conservative body,
but by the late 1930s it was clearly changing:

Can you . . . picture me as a member of the I.I.A. [John wrote
to Richmond in December 1939] discoursing on war aims & the
desirability of all-round revolution to a select audience including Alan
Mulgan & C.H. Weston in the front row, with H.F. von Haast in the
chair?* . . . But the I.I.A. in W'gton has worse blokes than me in it
– Sutch & young Milner & that bunch. By the way, Mulgan is going
very red – in private life, not as talks-director – it is a fair treat to hear
him hailing the revolution & talking about state-action & the sins
of Chamberlainism. Apparently his son's letters from England have
switched over that humane heart. I got an awful shock when I first heard
him give utterance on the subject. As if the milkman had left four pints
of beer in the morning.[44]

---

*   Mulgan, the father of John Mulgan, had in 1935 left his position as chief
      leader-writer of the *Auckland Star* and moved to Wellington to the newly
      created position of supervisor of talks for the New Zealand Broadcasting
      Board. Weston was a prominent Wellington lawyer, a stalwart of the RSA
      and Judge Advocate-General, who served for three years as president of
      the National Party following its formation in 1936. Von Haast, too, was a
      pillar of the Wellington legal community who became best known for his
      biography of his father, *The Life and Times of Sir Julius von Haast.*

Contemporary New Zealand: A Survey of Domestic and Foreign Policy, published by the institute as a set of background papers for the British Commonwealth Relations Conference held in Sydney in September 1938, nicely illustrates the change. Nearly half the volume was written by Alister McIntosh and W.B. Sutch, while among the contributors to other chapters, in addition to John, were von Haast and the ardent imperialist Frank Milner, rector of Waitaki Boys' High School. John's opening chapter in the volume, 'New Zealand in the Commonwealth: An Attempt at Objectivity', raised some eyebrows: it was 'by far the most provocative of the sections', one reviewer wrote, adding that while the tone of the *Survey* was on the whole judicious, in that first chapter 'the judicial atmosphere is charged with a certain archness, which some will find stimulating and others, possibly, a little flashy'.[45] In seeking to assess the advantages and disadvantages to New Zealand of its association with the British Commonwealth, John had sought to cut through the 'generalities which have been in recent decades the stock-in-trade of politicians, leader-writers, and other dealers in optimistic superficiality'. He could be sharp on the views of the 'average New Zealander':

British foreign policy [in the early 20th century] . . . was British foreign policy, and therefore right, and New Zealand sealed its approval with the gift of a battleship. Nor did the war seriously affect this devotion. It was rather, in spite of the cost, an opportunity for congratulations all round. The lion-cub had rushed to the side of its dam. The empire had stood the strain. Mr Massey had sat, and [Augustus] John had painted. And after all, the war had been won – at least, New Zealand thought so in 1918 and for some years afterwards.[46]

Flashy? Not really – a little sardonic, even caustic, perhaps, and certainly distasteful to 'dealers in optimistic superficiality'.

The chairman of the editorial committee (and a foundation member and secretary of the institute) was G.R. (Dick) Powles, a young liberal-minded Wellington lawyer and teritorial soldier.* He was to have a distinguished military and diplomatic career during and after the Pacific war, in the occupation of Japan, decolonisation of Western Samoa, representing New Zealand in India, and service as New Zealand's first Ombudsman. In these years his 'humanitarian instincts, curiosity and sense of fairness led him to become a

---

*   Powles had studied law and been a prominent debater in his student years at Victoria College.

liberal activist, a characteristic that prevailed as he grew older'.[47] He and his wife Eileen were to become close friends of John and Elsie.

When the *Survey* was reprinted the following year, Fred Wood added a chapter 'N.Z. in Crisis' which brought the story up to the outbreak of war.

In 1943, on Hunter's suggestion, the College arranged five public lectures on the Statute of Westminster. John gave two and Fred Wood, Leslie Lipson and R.O. McGechan, professor of law, one each. The statute had been passed by the British parliament in 1931, with the advice and consent of the dominions, in order to remove the *legal* obstacles to their equality of status with Great Britain as defined in the Balfour Declaration of 1926. It could have no effect on New Zealand, however, until the New Zealand parliament itself passed legislation adopting it as part of its own constitutional law. This it had failed to do. For practical purposes this failure to ratify did not make very much difference as to what the country did or did not do except that it was unable to exercise extraterritorial powers – for example, in the Pacific. At times it became the focus for political debate that owed less to the statute's legal provisions than to political point scoring between those who thought they had all the autonomy they wanted and those who wanted the New Zealand parliament to have full legislative power internally and extraterritorially. For John and Wood, New Zealand's reluctance to ratify the Statute of Westminster seemed symptomatic of a national unwillingness to stand on our own feet, evident in the continued use of the word 'Home' for England. New Zealand, John had written in *Contemporary New Zealand*:

is a 'Dominion' in spite of itself, it has not pursued, with passionate experimentation, the idea of equal nationhood; in the imperial family it is the daughter-nation, that preferred not to smoke and drink with its emancipated sisters, that shuddered a little and drew its garments somewhat closer when Canada and South Africa began to saunter on the boulevards of the world . . .[48]

For Fraser in the war years, there was the fear that ratification would be interpreted as disloyalty to the mother country. But it is difficult now to understand the strong feelings that the statute provoked.

The course of the war raised crucial questions about the deployment and control of New Zealand forces. Especially after the disastrous 1941 campaigns in Greece and Crete, Fraser was determined to have a voice in these decisions. He was equally determined that New Zealand should have a voice in the direction of the Pacific war and in the political decisions that would shape the postwar world. The role he played at this time did much to clarify the concept of dominion status in wartime. The logic of Fraser's leadership pointed to what he later described as 'independence plus'* for New Zealand – that is, in stature as well as status – but, although there was talk of the statute being ratified in 1943 (hence the lectures), it finally happened only in 1947, after Fraser had taken his place among world statesmen at the founding of the United Nations Organisation in 1945 at San Francisco.

While it is not clear whether the lectures, published by the college in 1944, had much public impact, Peter Munz has written of John and Fred Wood at this time, when the postwar aims of the Allies embodied in the Atlantic Charter, the Australia–New Zealand agreement of 1944 and the United Nations Charter seemed to hold out so much promise: 'the two men created an atmosphere in which we were all persuaded that nationhood and independence, self-government, responsible government and an independent foreign policy were all linked together as part of the great battle for freedom which was being waged for social justice in every country and against Nazism and fascism in the international field.'[49] One could argue with some justice that John and Wood were among those who helped change New Zealand attitudes in a way that meant that New Zealanders could move on from the question of their country's international status to other issues. John, with his slightly mocking self-perception, recognised that he could 'go on a bit' about the statute. 'Could we work in a mention of the Statute of Westminster?' he enquired of his niece Mary when she sought advice on an English essay, or, 'Why not start with Who has not heard of the Statute of Westminster?'

JOHN VOTED FOR THE Labour Party in elections. He had got to know both Walter Nash and Peter Fraser but he was not a member of the party and tended to view all politicians with a critical eye. He had not really believed that Labour would transform New Zealand politics and New Zealand society, but he was still disappointed with many aspects of its performance in office.

The government had been re-elected in 1938, increasing its share of the popular vote to 56 per cent from the 46 per cent it had won in 1935. This was the first clear majority vote for any party in

---

*   He was referring to Indian independence in the Commonwealth.

thirty years, and was to prove the peak of its electoral support. This popularity with the voter owed much to the Social Security Act, which came into effect only after the election. The government's outward strength, however, was increasingly threatened by internal divisions. John's reservations come out clearly in a letter to Richmond at the end of 1939:*

Politics. If I can bring myself to write on the subject . . . Melancholy outlook. Do you still see Tomorrow? Walter [Nash] very bitter about its criticism of the Govt. & especially about an article by Jack Lee published in its last number† – & about Jack Lee that ambitious & turbulent man himself. It looks as if we're not far off a split, I mean an overt snorter historic split big enough to swallow an army – or the Labour Govt. The Govt. won't do anything socialist, can't think ahead (except Walter who like Downie Stewart sees only horrific consequences), spends all its time placating its own opponents (who won't be placated) & either ignoring or blackguarding its supporters. Semple's exhibitionism is getting beyond all bounds. He is now running a campaign against left-wing ('Communist') influences in his best style of gutter-eloquence . . . this fatal Macdonaldism that attacks Labour in office! Meanwhile Savage appears to be, ill or well, now just a bloody nuisance, & ill certainly touches the depths of fatuity; & Peter Fraser, who might pull things together, is over in England pledging our last shilling & drop of blood to Chamberlain . . . Gawd, if the Party only had a Coates somewhere in the cabinet instead of all these nitwits; if only Nash could transcend his function as a bottle-neck; if only they could use a bloke like Jack Lee; if only they would ditch H.G.R. Mason & ½ dozen others; etc; etc; there might be a bit of hope in life.[50]

Within months Savage was dead and Fraser was prime minister.

Before this, on 21 February 1940, the government had brought in the Public Safety Emergency Regulations, 1940/26. These defined subversion in very wide terms, banned strikes, restricted the holding

---

*   At the beginning of 1938 Norman Richmond moved to Australia to head the Queensland WEA. It was not a happy move. The following year, despite a positive report on the organisation from a state government commission of inquiry, government funding was terminated and the University of Queensland withdrew its support. Richmond was appointed to a full-time position at the university, but his best work was over and during the war years he suffered the first attacks of the depressive illness that was to haunt him thereafter. The correspondence with John changed (though not the affection between them); letters became infrequent, though when John wrote it was sometimes at considerable length: 'Beaglehole & Family Annual Report', he headed his letter of 10 December 1939.

†   This was Lee's barely veiled attack on Savage, 'Psycho-Pathology in Politics', *Tomorrow*, 6 December 1939.

of meetings and processions, and greatly extended the powers of
the police to prohibit meetings and processions, to search premises
for subversive persons or material, and to make arrests without
warrants. Fraser, introducing the regulations, clearly referred to
recent pacifist meetings but subtly linked them with 'persons, some
openly agents of a foreign Power'.[51] The regulations were much
more severe than the corresponding British ones, which, after being
strongly criticised in the British parliament, had been considerably
amended. John was one of a group of Wellington citizens, which
included Bishop St Barbe Holland, Walter Scott, lecturer in English
at the Wellington Teachers' Training College, and Dick Powles, who
tried to persuade Fraser to modify the harsher clauses.[52] It had seemed
to them necessary, John wrote in his draft of their memorandum,[53]
that private persons should protest because little criticism could be
expected from parliament; indeed, it was likely that there would
be no criticism at all, and 'certainly not the informed & analytical
criticism members of the Govt, when in opposition, would have
brought to bear on regulations such as these'. There followed a
careful critical analysis of the regulations and their drafting, and
a strong plea that they should more closely follow those introduced
in Britain (a comparison between the two sets of regulations was
prepared as part of the group's submission). John concluded:

We ask members of the Government to read these Regulations, & our
analysis of them, carefully & in cold blood. They are inequitable. They
are, in the highest as in the lowest sense, inexpedient. They are wrong
in principle. Reluctant as we are to oppose a Government of men with
whom we are in such general sympathy, we do regard it as our duty
to oppose with all our resources of argument, & all possible vigour,
regulations which seem to us the denial of everything for which the
Government has hitherto stood, for which its members have individually
suffered, & for their defence of which we have admired them in the
past. We cannot concede that circumstances have changed so much as to
warrant this change.

Fraser met with the deputation on 17 May. Nothing was changed.

In 1941 the government finally succeeded in breaking an
impasse with the medical profession and passing a bill to implement
the general medical benefit promised in the Social Security Act.
Richmond had asked John for information on the new benefit; John
was unable to find anything useful as the government publicity was
'appallingly bad':

It makes me sigh for the days of Dick Campbell & the pamphlets he
wrote for Coates. There wasn't even a handbill distributed to say what

it was all about; & out of all the mess of misrepresentation & lying on either side . . . I'm damned if I could make out a sensible statement for you, or find a single honest analysis of either the govt's case or the doctors'. I'm opposed to the B.M.A.* of course, but it is very hard to sympathise with the govt. Indeed when you work it out, there are precious few Good Things this Govt hasn't gone about the wrong way . . . The final struggle over the bill, by the way, resolved itself into one between Peter Fraser & the B.M.A. on the one hand, & the Labour Party on the other, & P.F. managed to get amendments that made the doctors purr over him like a lot of over-fed cats . . . as time marches on P.F. is less & less highly thought of by the workers & the intelligentsia. And not very popular with the others either I should think . . .[54]

Much later, in a brief but eloquent biographical article for *The Dictionary of National Biography 1941–1950,* John gave a more favourable picture of Fraser, and especially of his role as leader of New Zealand at war and in the early postwar years, saying that he was 'first-rate in a crisis'. John also brought out the complexity of his character, his capacity to exasperate as well as to inspire.

MESSINES ROAD WAS proving a very good base for the family. The pattern of life that John and Elsie established there changed only slowly over the coming years. It was an informal age; doors were not locked, friends dropped in. Social life by and large was local, and visits were generally made on foot or by public transport. Relations and old friends were not far away and new friends were found both in the college and outside.

Not long after the family moved in, Elsie's brother Charles was posted by Dalgety's from Hamilton to their head office in Wellington, and bought a house two doors away. He had a tennis court much used by Elsie and the boys. John did not join in the tennis (apart from quoit tennis he was not a games player) but over the years, especially after Charles's death in 1948, he became a great confidant of his sister-in-law Norah, who had long been an invalid. His gentle nonsense over a glass of sherry invariably reduced her to giggles. In 1941–42 Ernest and Pam Beaglehole were nearby in Shirley Street, before they moved into 22 Messines Road. After years of helping Ernest in his fieldwork among the Hopi Indians, the Tongans and Pukapukans, and the Maori at Otaki, Pam was not taken with

---

*   The British Medical Association (New Zealand Branch), possibly the toughest union in the country.

domesticity. Their two eldest children, Jane and David, spent a lot of time at 6 Messines Road and looked to Elsie for practical advice. David learned from her how to sew, and darn his socks; Jane called on her for help in making a frock for her first school ball. Grandfather Beaglehole was a regular visitor for lunch on Wednesdays; Uncle Joe could be rather less welcome. On one occasion John was interrupted in the middle of writing to Richmond by Joe's arrival 'in a burst of rain to ask me the questions he has asked me 17 times before about the centennial publications, their value, price, binding-cases, usefulness to himself etc. The outside public who know him only as a genial eccentric, little guess how we of the inner circle suffer from his thirst for useless information among other things.'[55] For some years John's brother Geoffrey, with Theo and their daughter Mary, were living in Kelburn. Mary, at Wellington Girls' College, regularly called in to get her uncle's advice on her English homework. She and Keith's daughter Betty were both invariably John's 'favourite niece'.

Elsie's father and Edith had moved from the Western Hutt hills to Eastbourne, where the family visited them regularly, often crossing the harbour on the ferry, the *Cobar*. We continued to do this even after Elsie bought a car, a Vauxhall 10, because very shortly the war came and with it petrol rationing. From Eastbourne we walked and picnicked around the coast towards Pencarrow, or over the hill into the bush-filled valley known as Butterfly Creek.

Cedric Firth and his wife Bobbie (their marriage on 7 January 1938 had been celebrated with a party at Messines Road, 'a hogshead of beer . . . going down with remarkable celerity'[56]) were nearby in Vera Street, in a house Cedric had designed and built in 1941 to put his own ideas on low-cost, good-quality social housing into practice. Next door were Arthur Ward (by then in the Dairy Board's head office), his wife Jean and their growing family, in a house for which Cedric, a year after his own, had produced a more refined design. A little further away, but still (in those years) in Karori, were Tom and Sylvia Smith. Tom had left school at twelve to look after the family farm when his father drowned while fishing from a Northland beach. Later, after completing a master of commerce degree at Canterbury College, he had come to Wellington to a position in the public service and was one of the first students to gain the Diploma in Public Administration at Victoria. Sylvia, as outgoing as Tom was laconic, was English and had been a postgraduate student at the Institute of Historical Studies not long after John had left London. She had written a thesis on international rivalry in Samoa and come out to Wellington to teach at Marsden School (where Edith Holmes had taught), and she and Tom had met in the Tararua Tramping Club. For a few of the war years she was a part-time assistant lecturer in the history department at Victoria. Nearby, in Kelburn, were Jim Campbell, lecturer in mathematics and a remarkable teacher, and his wife Margaret. Jim, like John, was one of the new generation of Victoria staff with a postgraduate qualification, in his case a PhD from Edinburgh University; he also resembled John in his addiction to his pipe. He was to share his expertise in statistics with Arthur Ward, to be applied in research on breeding in the dairy industry. Margaret played the viola; music was the interest the Beaglehole 'crowd' almost all shared.

It was shared too with new friends made from among the refugees from Nazi Germany. Joachim and Gertrud Kahn were two of the first John and Elsie met. 'Poor blighter,' John wrote to Richmond, 'he is a Harvard as well as a German univ man, who quotes Greek as well as Latin French German & English, & now he has to help his father-in-law in some dud chemical factory at Miramar.'* He also sang very well and was an accomplished actor. They all seemed to speak three languages and 'make us feel very inferior & uncultured & raw, damn them'.[57] The architect Ernst Plischke, who arrived in Wellington from Vienna with his wife Anna in May 1939, designed a house for the Kahns in Ngaio in 1941. It was remarkable for its time: flat-roofed, with some walls largely of glass and a big glass sliding door.[58] The large living room was on two levels; the raised dining area was wonderful for parties, serving as a stage for charades and other theatrical performances. Plischke, who became one of the foremost early exponents of modernism in New Zealand,[59] designed a set of dining chairs for John and Elsie in 1948, but their structural integrity did not match the elegance of their appearance.

Peter Jacoby, who arrived in July 1938 with his wife Ilse, was the son of a distinguished German classics scholar, who had himself found refuge from Hitler when he was offered a position at Oxford. With a doctorate in law, Peter spent his first years in Wellington washing bottles in a glass factory before eventually becoming a research officer in the Department of Education. Ilse worked as a secretary-typist; later, when John began work on Cook's journals

---

*   The factory proved far from dud. As Ados, it became a leading manufacturer of adhesives. After the war, Joachim Kahn became a lecturer in political science at Victoria College. He returned to Germany in the early 1950s, but Gertrud and their son Claude remained in Wellington.

he turned to Ilse, with her painstaking accuracy and lively interest, to do all the typing. The Jacobys were able to buy a tiny house in Tiro Street, off Messines Road, where they transformed a piece of gorse-covered hillside into a garden of New Zealand native trees and shrubs.

Marie Vanderwart was another to arrive in Wellington in 1939. She had grown up in Berlin, where she studied the cello, but finding work as a musician was frustrated by the anti-Jewish restrictions. Her fiancé, Alfons Blaschke, a pacifist who escaped to England just before being conscripted into the German army, planned to join her in New Zealand but was foiled by the outbreak of war and restrictions placed on aliens. It was to be seven years before she was able to return to England to join him. She was rescued from a position as a domestic servant by a Karori couple, May and Walt Long, who took her into their home and gave her the family support she desperately missed. In one way, perhaps, Marie was more fortunate than others, such as Peter Jacoby or Joachim Kahn, who for years were unable to get work which matched their professional training. She found eager listeners. It was music that brought her together with John and Elsie; she played for them and their friends in the sitting room, and introduced John to the Bach cello suites. With his encouragement, she formed a trio with Dorothy Davies and Erica Schorss. They too played at 6 Messines Road and then in a number of recitals in Nimmo's small concert hall in Willis Street (with any profits going to the Patriotic Fund). From this beginning, in 1945, grew the Wellington Chamber Music Society.

Helmut and Ester Einhorn also arrived in 1939 but did not meet John and Elsie until a little later. Helmut was an accomplished architect who, after serving in the Royal New Zealand Air Force, was to make his career in the Government Architect's office. He designed a house for his family which, in striking contrast to its neighbours on a steep Karori hillside, was modernist in style; the furnishings, a mixture of antiques and pieces designed by Helmut himself, had 'a definite intellectual European flair'.[60] John and Elsie admired his design sense. Ester won renown for her coffee and bread rolls and, with Ilse Jacoby, became one of the group of women that Elsie led out walking on the Wellington coast and hills every Wednesday for over three decades. Barbara and Jule Einhorn, both born in New Zealand, became the daughters John and Elsie had always hoped for.

At a time when New Zealand society was remarkably homogeneous (and the Maori population still largely rural), such newcomers were to make a striking contribution to intellectual and cultural life. Yet they were met with suspicion and even hostility. New Zealand was not generous in making a place for refugees. John and Elsie, in contrast, were warmly welcoming and the friendships they made at this time were long lasting.

The sitting room at 6 Messines Road was the scene of some memorable parties. Elsie would make a fruit cup with cider – they were an abstemious as well as a hard-up crowd in the 1940s,* though after the war a little gin was sometimes added – and they had a weakness for charades. Certain scenes were always remembered: Beeb as Eros in Piccadilly Circus, perched on a stool and clutching a coat hanger, though what word he was acting out is long forgotten. On a later occasion, after I had taken up the sitting-room carpet for a school class party, Elsie, with a marked lack of cooperation from John, decided to have a dance and, what was more, that the men should be in dinner suits. Afterwards John conceded it had been a great success: 'There wasn't too much formal dancing. I managed a vertiginous waltz with E[lsie], and fended off grimly the other ladies, even the ones I loved best, like Ilse Jacoby; but after supper the fun started & we had some riotous special performances & ballets'.[61] John himself was the highlight, leaping in through the window from the verandah, clad in long pink underpants and a wreath of roses to dance the *pas de deux* from the *Spectre of the Rose* with the young wife of his cousin Alan Monaghan.

Almost all these family friends shared a taste for the New Zealand outdoors. Day tramps were a regular activity and some of them became institutions: the annual outings over the Makara hills to Te Ikamaru Bay with the Campbells and the Jacobys ('the annual pilgrimage' Jim Campbell later called it) and over the hill from Kaitoke into the Tauherenikau valley with the Firths and Morva Sutch. Elsie organised everything, but John invariably set the fire and boiled the billy. Everyone was expected to collect firewood, but he alone, with great deliberation, arranged stones to make a fireplace and the supporting branch to carry the billy; once it had boiled he made the tea. The postwar years brought excursions further afield

---

*   Although the foundations of New Zealand viticulture went back to the 1890s, wine of any quality at a reasonable price was not readily available and not widely drunk at this time. Arthur Ward was one of the first of John and Elsie's crowd to buy locally produced wine; with his Dairy Board connections he got it from the Department of Agriculture's experimental vineyard and winery at Te Kauwhata. John and Elsie did not drink wine regularly until the 1960s, beginning with the ubiquitous McWilliams Bakano.

but did not alter John's quiet satisfaction with being by the sea or in the hills with family and friends.

In January 1939 we had a holiday in Queen Charlotte Sound with Tom and Sylvia Smith and their two children. We had a one-roomed bach and tents in Cherry Bay, a tiny bay which we had to ourselves. There was a dinghy to row and Tom led us in fishing. I caught a large snapper (alas, now rarely there for five-year-old fishermen). John got to see Ship Cove at last. The Cook monument on the foreshore, he confessed on his return to Wellington, had not been as bad as he expected, though some attention to details ('lettering very bad') would be worthwhile. If we must have monuments, he concluded, 'we should do our best to avoid converting our historic sites into third-rate grave-yards [with lettering] in what might be called the Karori-tombstone style'. It was held to be impossible to make any changes while members of the original memorial committee were still living.[62] The following summer John 'did a bit of Cook looking round' when the family had a holiday in Hawke's Bay at Mangakuri, a wonderful open beach with abundant crayfish among the rocks. He and Elsie, having abandoned me and my brothers with farming friends, then drove up the coast towards East Cape, discovering Anaura Bay, and then Waipiro Bay on Elsie's birthday, both superb beaches. The weather was very hot; Maori on horseback flourished; most places seemed to have ice cream.[63] There were no more such holidays until the war and petrol rationing came to an end.

In 1939 Elsie's brother Peter bought a farm in Wairarapa just north of Featherston, and for a number of years we went to the farm every holiday. If Elsie turned off the car engine and coasted down all the hills, we could just get there on the petrol she had carefully saved; Peter squeezed a bit from his more generous farmer's ration to see us home. Peter's marriage had broken up, and we went to the farm partly to provide more of a home for his son Mike when he was on holiday from boarding school. Furthermore, at a time when labour was difficult to get and Peter was working enormously hard breaking in a farm that had become very run down, we could help a little with some of the work.

For John, it was a new experience, a side of New Zealand that he had not known at first hand. Although he always made sure of a plentiful supply of books, he took a hand in clearing water races and working the sheep for dipping, and he designed a name plate for the front gate – Kowhai Flat – and the stencil for the wool bales. He went to the races for the first and only time, the New Year meeting at the Tauherenikau course,* and on the strength of its name put some money on a horse rather improbably called Voltaire, but it finished well back in the field. The Tauherenikau river marked one boundary of the farm and most summers we found a good swimming hole. John cultivated a suntan; he was always passionate about getting into the sun and at home on sunny days he would lie outside in his shorts for a spell after lunch. Beaglehole friends and relations visited and often stayed at the farm. When the eminent American historian Alan Nevins visited New Zealand, after the United States had come into the war, Joe Heenan (who looked after official visitors) sent him up to the farm in a government car to spend the day with John (later John travelled with him to the South Island). An English representative of the Oxford University Press made a similar visit. After Peter remarried in 1944, our visits continued but were less regular. Peter let us use a one-roomed shack with a little wood stove and we usually put up a couple of tents. As long as the weather was fine all went well, but I suspect John missed the comfortable reading chair in his study where he had his half-hour snooze after lunch on days unsuitable for sunbathing.

AT THE HEART OF JOHN'S life was his position at Victoria, his teaching and the history department. He soon found, however, that Tommy Hunter (from 1938 part-time principal of the college and the following year, Sir Thomas Hunter KBE) had 'taken to consulting me on odd occasions'.[64] One such occasion, some years later, was when he was primarily responsible for the appointment of Frederick Page as lecturer in music. He redesigned the college *Calendar* for 1939, and was increasingly drawn on for typographical advice with college printing. He played the Town Hall organ for graduation ceremonies. The effective partnership which he and Fred Wood quickly formed only deepened as the years passed. They had much in common in their liberalism, their tolerance, their regard for other people as well as for each other, and notwithstanding their very different postgraduate studies – Wood an Oxford BA following his Sydney degree, and John a University of London PhD – in their methods of teaching.

---

*   There was some feeling in the country that racing should not be allowed while the war was on. After Japan entered the war, midweek meetings were stopped but meetings on public holidays continued. (Nancy M. Taylor, *The Home Front*, vol.1 (Wellington: Department of Internal Affairs, 1986), pp.306–9, 321–2.)

The structure of the history courses they had inherited – prescribed by the University of New Zealand and difficult to alter – had changed somewhat since John's time as a student. Three stages – History I, II and III – required to major in history for a bachelor's degree had taken the place of the pass and advanced stages, though their content continued to be largely British and European history, together with the expansion of Europe. The three stages each included a paper on European history and a paper on the expansion of Europe in the same period. For History I the period was 1815–1914, for History II 1494–1715, and for History III 1715–1815. 'The outlines of the history of Australia and New Zealand' were included in the second paper for History I. The books listed in the college *Calendar* were very much the standard texts of the time. For History I they included Grant and Temperley on *Europe in the Nineteenth Century*, Moon's *Imperialism and World Politics*, the first volume of J.A. Williamson's *A Short History of British Expansion*, Muir's *Expansion of Europe*, and Condliffe and Airey's short text on New Zealand. In 1937 John's *New Zealand: A Short History* and Reeves's *The Long White Cloud* were added to the list. For three years in the late 1930s some choice was given in the second and third years – in 1937, for example, the second History III paper was either the expansion of Europe or Burke and his times. This was not continued, but Wood and John seem never to have accepted the prescription as the straitjacket that it might have appeared to be.

There was more room for change and flexibility in the MA and honours course, although it included one compulsory paper on the constitutional history of modern Britain. In teaching this, Wood always found it difficult to resist edging into questions of social history. Students could then choose their other four papers from a wide range of subjects, including the 'Great Powers' from 1815 to 1914, with special reference to international relations; colonisation and colonial policies of the nineteenth and twentieth centuries; a period of political ideas; and a special topic for the year, such as puritanism or the causes of the Great War. In some years, as a substitute for one of the papers, students could elect to write a three-hour essay in the final examinations on a subject chosen from a list previously provided by the supervisor – an attractive choice for part-time students interested in the nature or philosophy of history or historiography, and an option that was linked to some of the discussions at coffee evenings. In addition there was a thesis, which until 1949 was required to be completed in the same year as the papers. The 1945 Victoria *Calendar,* under MA and honours, noted that a short course would be given at the beginning of the session with special reference to thesis work. This was the first formal mention of John's 'footnotes' course, which he had been teaching more informally in a wider historiographical context for some years.

In dividing the teaching, Wood generally took the British and European courses, John those on the expansion of Europe and colonial history. But this was not always the case. For example, John always taught the political ideas course for MA and at times taught on eighteenth-century France and Britain. Neither he nor Wood seem to have been too constrained in their teaching by the formal detail of the syllabus, though they did have to prepare their students for examinations based on it. Neither attempted to cover everything in their lectures or read from a prepared text or handed out lecture notes. Both talked about topics that interested them and were happy to recommend reading for parts of the course they were not covering in lectures.

As a lecturer, John was something of an acquired taste and many first-year students were baffled by what they heard. He spoke as if he were thinking out what he was saying in the lecture room, often burrowing into detail and unravelling the arguments of individual historians. There were pauses – one was never quite sure whether it was for further reflection or a lingering effect of his earlier stutter – but when he was really wound up the words would flow easily in a style uncannily close to his written prose. For some students, his critical and analytical approach could be unsettling. He described and illustrated the difficulty in a letter to Downie Stewart:

I talk about E.G. Wakefield. I say 'Now I want you to put behind you the usual schoolroom dogmas about Wakefield as an unblemished saint who saved the British Empire from the twin devils of the Colonial Office & the French, & consider him simply as a man who played an important part in history; & as a man who had certain grave defects as well as certain virtues. His historical importance was determined by his defects as well as his virtues.' Immediately an awful hush falls over the class, the most conversational back-benchers look pained, & some one bursts out 'But how can you say that Wakefield was such a complete scoundrel when he saved the British Empire?' And then I carefully explain again that Wakefield was not a complete scoundrel & that I didn't say so, & that he didn't save the British Empire or even New Zealand. It seems to me that my job is not to talk like Mr Frank Milner, but to try to understand & explain the British Empire as an historical phenomenon. Somehow that sort of approach seems blasphemous.[65]

His style was appreciated increasingly by students as they progressed through to stage III and honours. J.W. Davidson, a student in the late 30s, gives a picture of John teaching, thinking his way through an argument or an historical situation, 'thinking because the question he was discussing was of absorbing interest to him, and it was important to try and get the answer right'.[66] Davidson came to judge him to be, while not a good lecturer in the formal sense, the 'most influential teacher' he ever had. His lectures, another student recalled, were 'working illustrations of thinking historically. A sentence marked in a book, a few points jotted down on a half sheet of notepaper, a sharp question or a comment were sufficient to launch him into a masterly unravelling of complicated problems.'[67] He very quickly made it clear that he was not impressed with copious note taking: 'there would be a long pause and he would make a comment such as "a comma or a full stop Miss or Mr So-and-So?"'[68] At the same time you were expected to remember what he had discussed. 'Now what was I talking about in the last lecture?' he was inclined to ask at the start of the next one. It could be quite intimidating. What he taught owed less to the prescription than to his own intellectual curiosity – indeed, he could be thoroughly cavalier about the prescription. He would lecture on what interested him; if students wished to know more he could suggest a book or two.

For Frank Corner, later to have a distinguished career in the New Zealand Ministry of Foreign Affairs, one of the most enriching experiences of his student days was to be in a class when John was teaching a new course on the colonial, prerevolutionary, period of American history while still in the process of mastering the subject for himself.* He involved the students in grappling with some of the same major works as he was reading.[69] Turner on the American frontier, Perry Miller on New England puritanism, Samuel Eliot Morison on the founding of the Massachusetts colony – these were the kind of books that really interested him, as well as the multivolume collections of printed documents on the American colonial period that he found in the college library. Textbooks he had very little

---

*   Corner's study of this period of American history, 'as immigrants strove to establish themselves in a new country, maintain life, set up democratic systems of government to serve their needs, move the frontier westward and settle a continent', gave him an admiration for America and Americans that 'remained strong enough to withstand the questionings provoked by later nineteenth and twentieth century developments' and, in his view, became part of his mindset throughout his career.

time for, though he made exceptions for Curtis P. Nettels's *Roots of American Civilisation* and Morison and Commager's masterly two volumes on *The Growth of the American Republic* (one of very few works in his collection that he replaced with a later edition, passing the earlier edition on to me).

The English eighteenth century was a period that came to fascinate John greatly. He hated its wars, he neglected its politics and diplomacy, and was never a follower of Namier, but he loved its music and architecture, its painting and its literature, men such as the Adam brothers, Capability Brown and Horace Walpole. Even in the early 1940s he was beginning to explore its scientific and philosophical thinking, the background to the voyages of exploration – A.N. Whitehead's *Science and the Modern World* caught his attention at this time. But it was far from being an exclusive interest. He was excited by an honours special topic on English puritanism that he taught in 1943 – R.H. Tawney's *Religion and the Rise of Capitalism* was a book he always admired, not least for its prose. His lectures in 1942 on the eighteenth century as an age of form and enlightenment made the greatest impression on Mary Boyd, later a colleague of his in both the Historical Branch and the Victoria history department. Once again it was a new course in the sense that he was grappling with what he was currently reading and relating it to what he already knew; he could go on teaching the same course without losing his critical engagement with the questions it raised. Some of his greatest scorn was reserved for colleagues in other departments whose lectures were written out like chapters in a textbook, especially for the professor of economics who even wrote in the jokes.

When I did history honours in 1954, John was called on to teach the paper on American history in place of Winston Monk, his colleague who had just died in an air crash. He had read Arthur M. Schlesinger Jnr's *The Age of Jackson* not long before and we argued about Schlesinger's revisionist views on the relationship between the frontier and democracy. Another book he had discovered was Walter Prescott Webb's *The Great Plains,* a pioneering study of the impact of the environment on human settlement, both Indian and European. Webb wrote about transportation, barbed-wire fencing and the Colt revolver, about the search for water and making new laws to govern rights to that water. It was very different from most of the history books we had read. Again, the books John suggested were those with an argument, an introduction and a conclusion, to be read in full and considered critically. He also suggested autobiography and novels that might increase our understanding of American life: Hamlin Garland's *A Son of the Middle Border,* O.E. Rölvaag's *Giants in the Earth: A Saga of the Prairie* (first published in Norwegian) and Sarah Orne Jewett's *The Country of the Pointed Firs.* It was exciting stuff. He never taught a separate course on maritime exploration, though he was a great admirer of Samuel Eliot Morison's *Admiral of the Ocean Sea: A Life of Christopher Columbus.*

He did not believe in exhaustive reading lists and was averse to anything he saw as 'spoon feeding'. He would suggest a 'boiled down' list of books and some broad but thought-provoking essay topics and encourage students to follow their interests, to use the library, to read and to go on reading. 'God bless you if you have read all these books', he wrote at the bottom of one student's essay.[70]

Until the classes were swelled by returned servicemen the number of students majoring in history was not great, especially during the war years, when John taught honours classes in his study, a narrow and rather dark room on the top floor of what is now the Hunter building.[*] It was close to C3, the main lecture theatre, and next to a physics store room where water could be heated on a Bunsen burner to make coffee in a 'Black and White' whisky jug, to be served in bakelite mugs that smelled when hot.[71] His bookshelves were full of books, carefully arranged (as were those at home) and lined up with the edge of the shelf. A Frances Hodgkins lithograph of jugs and vases[†] brought a splash of colour. More books were stacked on the desk and, in time, there were stacks of papers on the floor. It was a cold room, like his study at home, but he made an effort to warm it for students. He was remembered by one for the occasion when he was taking trouble with a heater and, when the students demurred, he said, 'Well, perhaps in after years you'll say "he was a lousy lecturer, but at least he kept his students warm"'.[72] He did not talk a great deal and was not troubled by silence, but he had a knack of getting others

---

[*]   John actually occupied two different rooms in the same part of the Hunter building, moving in 1948 into the room that Ernest Beaglehole had been occupying when Ernest moved into Hunter's room, on being appointed professor of psychology following Hunter's retirement and the division of his chair in mental and moral philosophy into the two chairs of philosophy and psychology. For a brief period before he retired John moved with the history department into the top floor of the newly opened Rankine Brown building.

[†]   *Arrangement of Jugs* is Frances Hodgkins's only surviving print. It was published by Contemporary Lithographs Ltd, London, in 1938. We have no record of how John and Elsie acquired it.

to talk. Peter Munz, recently arrived as a junior lecturer and sitting in on the class, recounts an occasion when the group was immersed in a long debate on Marx. John 'kept sucking at his pipe, trying to persuade us to be reasonable'. Munz continues:

On these occasions he was always very sceptical about abstract arguments and his artistic sensitivity made him uneasy in face of the cold logic of theory. I think that he also disliked theory because he considered metaphysics part of obscurantism, but to the present day I have never been able to decide whether the irony with which he treats abstraction is due to cold contempt or bemused puzzlement.[73]

With honours students and those starting on theses he 'was a brilliant expositor of the intricacies of research and writing, one who insisted on accuracy and lucidity, not out of pedantry but because error or ambiguity could lead us away from the truth we were seeking'.[74] While a stickler for the niceties of footnotes and bibliography, and for systematic note-taking – preferably on cards five inches by three as recommended by Sidney and Beatrice Webb (advice greatly at variance with his own habit of making notes on whatever paper came to hand, often used envelopes) – he made it clear that the historian also needed other qualities, 'the mingled endowments of the scientific detective, the poet, and the navvy'.[75] He was fond of quoting Tawney: 'What the historian needs is a stout pair of boots'* – though in his own case it would be rather a 'well-found vessel'. He saw the exploration of place as a vital complement to the documentary record in establishing what happened, as well as being a spur to the historical imagination.

Discussion went far beyond the classroom. Honours classes spilled over into coffee evenings in John's study to which young graduates, interesting visitors and an occasional a third-year student were invited. If Wood was there, he and John would spark each other off. Both invited senior students to their homes, introducing them to a world of manners, ideas, books, music and art very different from their provincial homes in Taranaki or Hawke's Bay. Frank Corner remembers:

John Beaglehole would include us in an evening of discussion and argument with some eminent visiting professor from the United States.

---

*   The Tawney quote is as I recollect hearing it from John. Ross Terrill gives it as the 'historian needs . . . not more documents but stronger boots'. (Ross Terrill, *R.H. Tawney and His Times: Socialism as Fellowship* (Cambridge Mass.: Harvard University Press, 1973), p.7.)

On some occasions he would play Bach's preludes and fugues, share his delight in newly acquired paintings of John Weeks or Woollaston, or pewter plates, or great examples of typography, or would introduce us to the works of E.M. Forster, or Virginia Woolf and the Bloomsbury set.[76]

As a research supervisor he expected students to work with a minimum of direction and left them to contact him if they needed his help or advice. He had ideas on suitable topics but did not press them. When I came to look for an idea for my master's thesis (though this was some years after he had largely withdrawn from teaching to work on Cook), he suggested working on de Bougainville, the French explorer and contemporary of Cook. He must have viewed my knowledge of French a great deal more optimistically than I did, and I found another topic, on Maori schools. It might have been a mistake to work in a field so close to his own. Students remember him for his readiness to talk about their research – or perhaps for his way of getting them to talk about it – and 'for raising questions that led [us] along paths to see important issues and make significant judgements; he was somewhat Socratic in his approach'.[77] He was both appreciative and encouraging, reading draft chapters with care and pointing out anything that was poorly written, but he expected the student to deal with it. One bit of advice he gave was to listen to what you had written, read it aloud and hear how it sounded – a practice he followed himself. Very rarely did he suggest how a passage or a chapter should be written, though he did insist that J.W. Davidson remove the final pages of his master's thesis, 'a typical indiscretion of a budding poet'.[78]

John had written on New Zealand history, and working in the Centennial Branch, as we shall see in the next chapter, extended and deepened his interest. Yet in 1946 he wrote: 'It is not, paradoxically perhaps, the duty of a New Zealand university to devote a major amount of its attention to the history of New Zealand.'[79] He conceded that if the resources were there it should be taught, and certainly not condemned 'as too pitiful or . . . lacking in dignity' to be given attention. When the history department was asked to teach New Zealand history to Diploma in Public Administration students, John drew up a list of subjects for a half-year weekly seminar and taught a number of them. Masters' theses, most of which in these years he supervised, were almost all written on New Zealand topics because of the ready availability of research material, and he recognised that many of the department's graduates would find themselves teaching New Zealand history in schools. But the practical difficulty, in both John's and Fred Wood's view, was that the published literature in the 1940s was inadequate to support a full undergraduate course. They also felt that it was better for students to read history written by leading scholars rather than the work being produced in New Zealand at that time.* Nor could the syllabus, until 1955† still set by the University of New Zealand, be easily changed (almost the only opportunity for looking at New Zealand was in that part of the stage one course dealing with the second British Empire and colonisation). But John's view was a much wider one. The university, he wrote, is 'the guardian of the great, the whole, tradition in civilized thought, and it is bound to see the parts in relation to the whole . . . the ideas by which we live have no limited ancestry'. He was not arguing that the university must teach everything, must cover all history – he hardly could, with the way he treated the formal syllabus. Indeed, suggesting a further paradox, he added: 'We might almost say that it does not matter what the university teaches, as long as it teaches in a certain way . . . The university's duty to its students, when history is its concern, is to teach the validity and importance of historical thinking, to preserve the integrity of historical thought.'[80]

When one of his graduates, about to spend two years in Oxford where her new husband was doing postgraduate research in physics, asked John's advice on how she might spend her time there – should she embark on some kind of research? – his advice was clear:

What I incline to think is, that you could have a really interesting time (& education, & all that) by getting down to a really solid course of reading on European, or English, history – or American, or all, if you like: something I wish to God I had two years for. And read the classics, Gibbon & Clarendon & Lecky, as well as the modern stuff. Or you could do something I once planned to do during the 1930's slump, only I got shunted. Take the English 17th century for a start, & read Trevelyan's *England under the Stuarts* for a general guide (I got as far as that) & then do Clarendon, & then read everything you can lay your hands on – there's God's plenty on the 17th century. And read all the 17th century prose & poetry & political pamphlets & so on that you can, & see all the 17th c portraits, & all the contemporary houses, big & little – which you couldn't do in NZ. And then you really would have done something,

---

*   When the undergraduate course on New Zealand history was first offered at Victoria in 1960, taught by Mary Boyd and W.H. Oliver, Keith Sinclair's Pelican *A History of New Zealand* had just been published, and Oliver's *The Story of New Zealand* was about to appear.

†   The colleges were given the power to make course regulations that replaced the statutes of the University of New Zealand under the New Zealand University Amendment Act 1954 and regulations made under it.

& furnished your mind much more than by digging up something about the NZ Company. You could take in the colonies & N. England Puritanism as well, & all that. There wouldn't be too little for two years. Think about it, anyhow. And then think what a seminar you could run for us at VUC! Anyhow, read the Verney Memoirs! & Paradise Lost.[81]

It was a very characteristic comment, though more suggestive, perhaps, of his own interests and experience and a certain ambivalence about the value of his own PhD study than of the increasing postgraduate work developing in both New Zealand and in Britain in the postwar years.

John's period of full-time teaching lasted just over ten years. From 1948, when he was appointed to a research position to work on editing Cook, he generally taught only a little at honours level, and sometimes an undergraduate seminar as well, until his last three years before retirement, when he again taught a third-year course on the development of responsible government in the British empire. In those earlier years, especially, he had a lasting impact on many of his students. It was significant that classes were small, and with the war they grew smaller. In 1939 the college had almost 1100 students; in 1942 there were only 750 and, John recalled, 'an arts professor or lecturer, gazing out sometimes over his class, might be pardoned for thinking it contained, besides women, nothing but the halt and the blind'.[82] The prewar years of conflict in Spain, Abyssinia and China and the war years were a time when few could ignore the world beyond the college walls; for a long time the future appeared, at best, grimly uncertain. The men students he knew most intimately, he reported to Richmond at the end of 1941, were not anxious to get into camp or get killed, but seemed 'to accept it as a sort of inevitability'.[83] If, as it seemed, New Zealand was caught up in a worldwide struggle for civilisation, then an understanding of what that civilisation was all about was all the more important.

When the war ended the numbers immediately grew. The returning servicemen, or 'rehab students' – assisted by bursaries for full-time study and 'war concessions' that reduced the number of units required for a degree – brought a maturity to their study and a new spirit to the campus and the classroom. History numbers shot up; honours classes rose from about ten students to as many as thirty, and were filled again mainly by men, 'with sports coats and cheerful grins'.[84] Additional staff were appointed. John's teaching style by this time was largely formed. He appreciated students who were thinking; they were always welcome to knock on his door. His course on 'footnotes' for thesis writers had quickly become something of a legend – it was remarkable how a discussion starting with the nature of a footnote could open up the widest questions of evidence and of writing history.

What effect did teaching have on John? He clearly liked students.

They seem to have all the virtues of open-mindedness & tolerance & straight thinking that their elders on the staff so conspicuously lack; they're 'free' & unprejudiced in a way I don't remember my contemporaries as students to have been, except a very few of them – & then we were deliberately struggling to be free, on a basis of Bertrand Russell & Wells. This lot seems to have grown into it naturally . . . it will be interesting to see what difference if any there is post-war.[85]

University teachers, John held, never cease to be students. He met his pupils as men and women who, he assumed, shared his interest in history as well as a lot of other things and, while knowing he had much to teach them, he remained conscious of how much he had to learn. Those uninhibited discussions at honours classes or coffee evenings epitomised his idea of education, and help explain why 'the relationship between teacher and pupil often passed imperceptibly into enduring friendship'.[86]

As departmental colleagues, as well as teachers, John and Fred Wood had complementary strengths and generally saw eye to eye. In their early years, as we have seen, the curriculum and examining were matters for the University of New Zealand rather than the individual institutions. The examining would be divided up so that a staff member would be responsible for marking all the papers for a particular course regardless of where it had been taught. This gave an insight into the teaching in other colleges, and John and Wood were often critical of what they saw.* Furthermore, it led to a certain amount of sparring in which they were willing participants.

Last year in my report on Stage I [John wrote to Richmond] I made a few remarks about candidates who had been carefully fed on the right questions & Elder [at Otago] was going to bring a libel action against Freddy Wood & me. The correspondence on his lawyer's side was simply fierce & we were all looking forward to the libel action, but the University lawyers took a hand & it rather faded out in legal correspondence. A great shame. We have another huge argument on now, but this time it is Rutherford [at Auckland] & Elder insulting each other, & everybody refusing to accept Elder's marks. If only Hight [at

---

*   The examiners' reports were published in *University of New Zealand Reports of Examiners* each year.

Canterbury] wouldn't insist on pouring oil on troubled waters! but we may succeed in setting fire to the oil yet. Elder becomes more intolerable every year. Half the year we are quarrelling about setting examinations & the other half about marking them.[87]

Whether this helped their relations with the other departments is a moot point. Bob Burnett, a student at Otago in the late 30s, recalled Elder making disparaging remarks about John, but that was 'probably for [his] touch of pinkness as much as anything else'.[88] Time brought retirements and new appointments, as well as a great deal more autonomy for the departments in their teaching and examining, and the relations between them were transformed.

In many ways Fred Wood was excellent at running the department: thoughtful, considerate, always ready to listen and consult, but inclined to be indecisive – as Peter Munz put it, 'Fred Wood's decisions were never *made*, they evolved; he was for ever "shaping up to them"'.[89] He invariably consulted John, often phoning on a Sunday evening. 'God dammit', John would comment ruefully, 'why can't Freddy make up his mind?' In the long run, in spite of temperamental differences that may have inhibited close personal friendship (though in this respect the temperamental differences with Joan Wood were probably of greater significance), they were bound by a deep mutual esteem.

In 1940 the journal *Historical Studies Australia and New Zealand* was first produced in the history department at Melbourne University. Fred Wood was the New Zealand member of the editorial board. In the third issue they published John's article 'The Colonial Office, 1782–1854'. It drew on the work he had done for his PhD but also on the research of the American historian Helen Taft Manning* (eminent both in her profession and as a daughter of President Taft; John and Elsie entertained her many years later when she visited New Zealand) and of E.T. Williams. Bill Williams was a very bright young Oxford graduate who had spent some time in New Zealand as a Harmsworth Scholar in the mid- to late-1930s doing research on British colonial policy of the 1830s. He and John had much in common, starting with a shared admiration of Sir James Stephen, and Williams became and remained both a friend and a great admirer of John's scholarly work. If John was 'running the show', Williams wrote at one point, he would not mind coming out as his assistant lecturer. But an Oxford fellowship and then the

---

*   Helen Taft Manning, *British Colonial Government after the American Revolution* (New Haven: Yale University Press, 1933).

war changed all that. There was talk of Williams writing a volume for the planned centennial publications and he sent a draft out to John early in 1940. He was already in the army, a subaltern in a mechanised cavalry unit:* 'please get this thing published as I have been writing for weeks after military duty and I just couldn't face the notion of it all being wasted. I know it's overclever and underwise in places. But I trust you to cut out that stuff for me . . .'[90] The work did not fit the pattern for the surveys, but from it (or possibly from other material Williams had sent him) John produced an article on the Colonial Office for *Historical Studies*.[91] Williams discovered that he had the publication to his name only after he had returned to Oxford and was looking through a bibliography of historical writing for 1940–45.[92]

John published two further articles in *Historical Studies* during these years. Of the first, 'Some Philosophies of History',[93] he noted 'These very summary and inadequately documented reflections were in the first place delivered as a lecture, and their sole virtue may be that they helped me to get my own scattered reading and thinking into some sort of order'; his judgement is not unduly harsh. He had not long before read Isaiah Berlin's Home University Library volume on Karl Marx, which he thought very good, the 'sort of book I should like to write myself; but I understand from one of the pure milk of the gospel boys at college who is very thick with the Party that it is no bloody good. He hasn't read it of course.'[94] He had also been impressed by Edmund Wilson's *To the Finland Station*, 'one of the best approaches to [Marx] I have read'.[95] John's discussion of Marx is interesting in revealing where he stood after his reading of the previous ten years:

There is this to say of Marx; he realises and asserts the historical nature of any philosophy of history, including his own. As a philosophy of history it works a good deal better, I think, than any other yet recorded . . . And his philosophy, like those of the eighteenth century Frenchmen and of Mill, is not a closed system. It leaves room for the future. It is hardly final; class-struggle we may accept, with modifications, while having the very gravest doubts about the dialectic.

It was not quite his last word on Marx, though in the years ahead his interest waned. But if Marx had little relevance for the study of

---

*   Williams was to have a war record of exceptional distinction, becoming Montgomery's chief intelligence officer and attaining the rank of brigadier. After the war he returned to Oxford, where he became warden of Rhodes House, a Fellow of Balliol, editor of the supplements to the *Dictionary of National Biography* and, in time, Sir Edgar Williams.

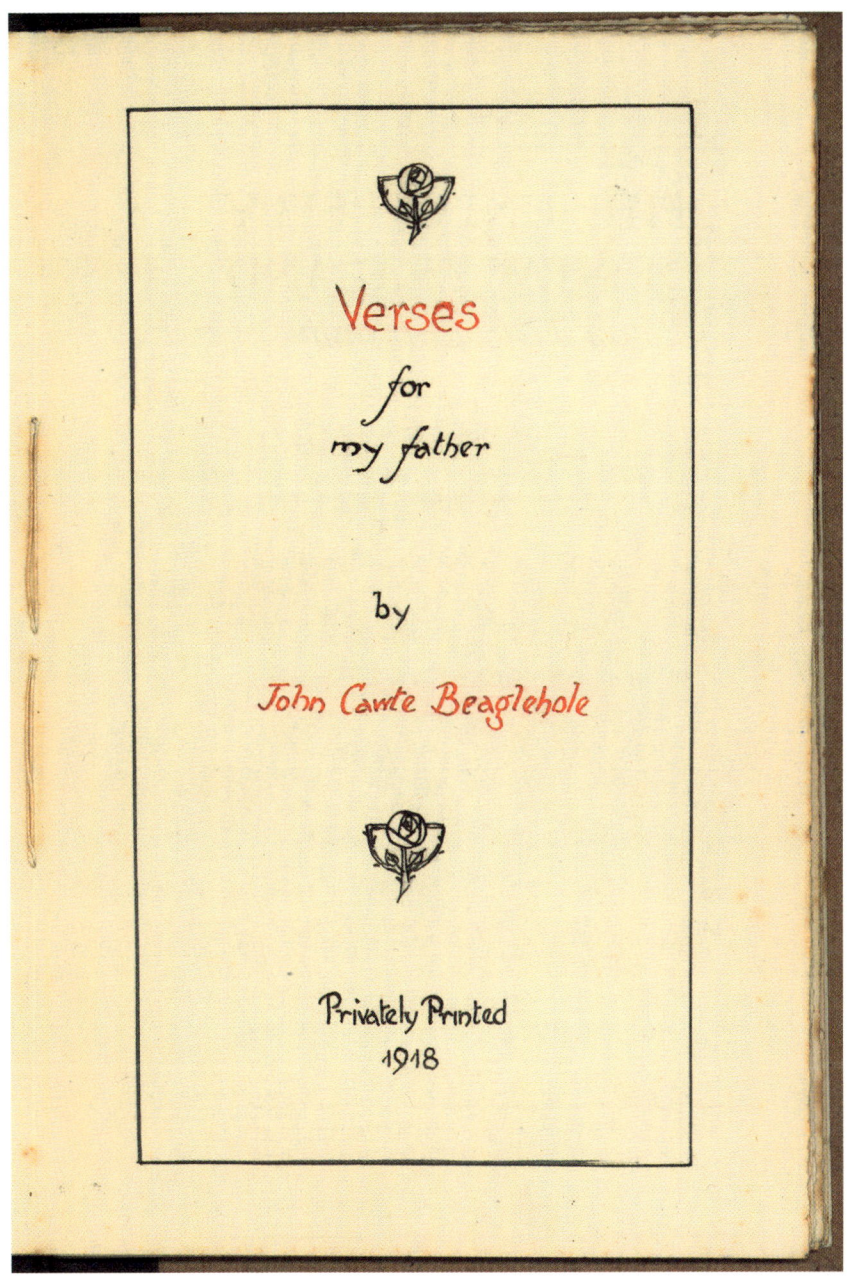

John's *Verses for my father* showed the 'germ of aesthetic beliefs in typography and book design that were to be exercised two decades later'.

THE UNIVERSITY
OF NEW ZEALAND
an historical study

by

J. C. BEAGLEHOLE, M.A., Ph.D.

*But where shall wisdom be found? and
where is the place of understanding?*

NEW ZEALAND
COUNCIL FOR EDUCATIONAL RESEARCH
1937

John's typography – Title page of *The University of New Zealand*, the
first book John designed and the beginning of his long typographical
association with the New Zealand Council for Educational Research.

THE MAORI PEOPLE
TODAY

a general survey

edited by

I. L. G. SUTHERLAND

issued under the auspices of

THE NEW ZEALAND INSTITUTE OF INTER-
NATIONAL AFFAIRS & THE NEW ZEALAND
COUNCIL FOR EDUCATIONAL RESEARCH

1940

John's typography – Title page of *The Maori People Today.*

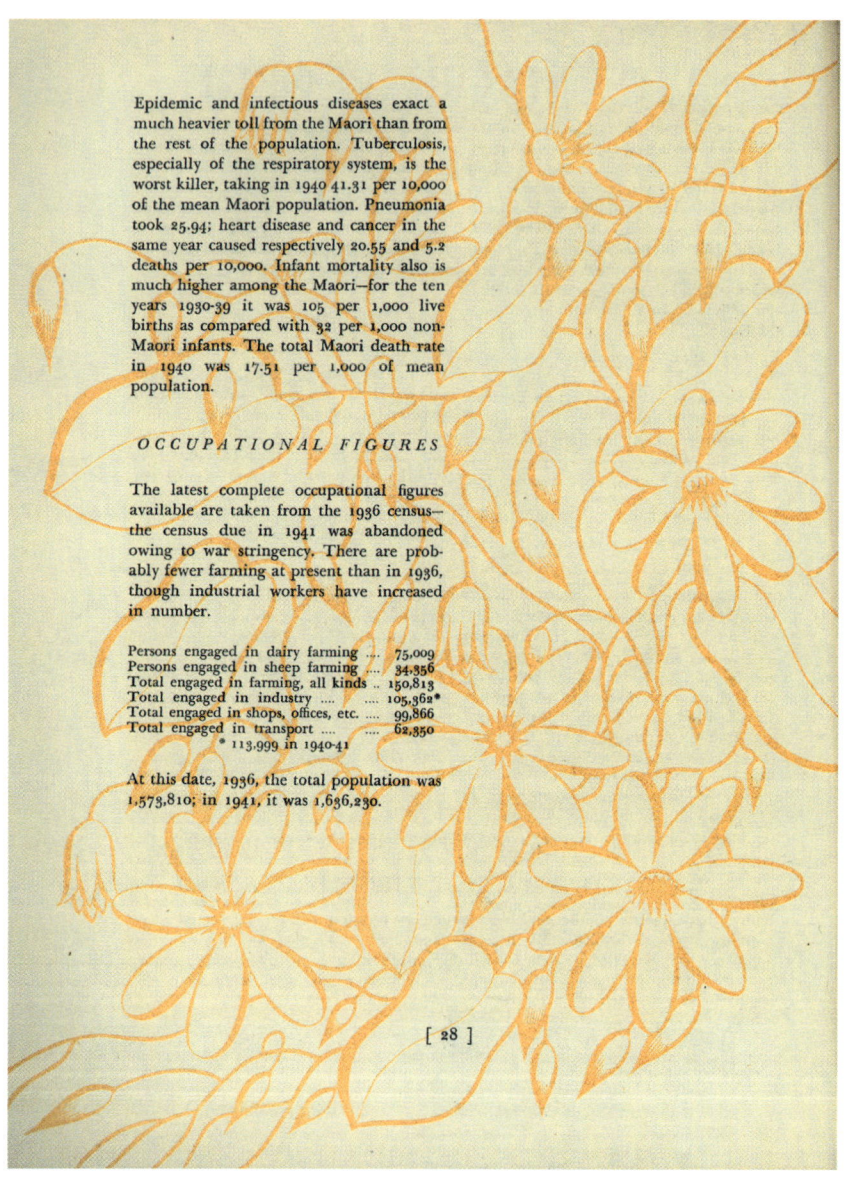

Epidemic and infectious diseases exact a much heavier toll from the Maori than from the rest of the population. Tuberculosis, especially of the respiratory system, is the worst killer, taking in 1940 41.31 per 10,000 of the mean Maori population. Pneumonia took 25.94; heart disease and cancer in the same year caused respectively 20.55 and 5.2 deaths per 10,000. Infant mortality also is much higher among the Maori—for the ten years 1930-39 it was 105 per 1,000 live births as compared with 32 per 1,000 non-Maori infants. The total Maori death rate in 1940 was 17.51 per 1,000 of mean population.

OCCUPATIONAL FIGURES

The latest complete occupational figures available are taken from the 1936 census—the census due in 1941 was abandoned owing to war stringency. There are probably fewer farming at present than in 1936, though industrial workers have increased in number.

Persons engaged in dairy farming 75,009
Persons engaged in sheep farming 34,356
Total engaged in farming, all kinds .. 150,813
Total engaged in industry 105,362*
Total engaged in shops, offices, etc. 99,866
Total engaged in transport 62,350
* 113,999 in 1940-41

At this date, 1936, the total population was 1,573,810; in 1941, it was 1,636,230.

John's typography – Page 28 of *Introduction to New Zealand* (1945). 'The design of the book more than matched the exuberance of the text.'

HOW WE ARE
GOVERNED

New Zealand is a Dominion. What does that imply in the field of government? The answer to the question may be given broadly and dogmatically so far as the outlines are concerned, but beyond a certain point it tends to become subtle; for this Dominion is a British Dominion founded on the principles of the British

constitution, and no one has ever been able to define the British constitution in a few well-chosen words.

One may perhaps best begin with a negative. New Zealand is not a colony. It began its constitutional life as a colony, but it is a colony no more. In the nineteenth century the British Empire took a curious twist, and invented 'responsible government'. If responsible government had been invented in the eighteenth century, constitutionally it would have been possible for the American colonies to remain within the empire; indeed, some of the definitions given by delegates to the Continental Congress, around 1776, of the reality of the constitutional relationship between England and the colonies, describe pretty well the reality which has now become known

as 'Dominion Status'. Consider this for example: 'All members of the British Empire are distinct states, independent of each other, but connected together under the same sovereign, in right of the same crown'. That's James Wilson of Pennsylvania. Or this: 'The Britannic Dominions constitute an imperial state consisting of many separate governments, in which no single part, though greater than any other part, is by that superiority entitled to make laws for any other part'. That's Stephen Hopkins of Rhode Island. Are not those statements echoed by the famous definition of the nature of the Dominions made one hundred and fifty years later at the Imperial Conference of 1926?—'*They are autonomous Communities within the British Empire, equal in status, in no way*

[45]

John's typography – Page 45 of *Introduction to New Zealand* (1945).

ON THE PLACE OF TASMAN'S
VOYAGE IN HISTORY

THE SEVENTEENTH CENTURY HAS A GLORY OF ITS own. Our popular conceptions of historical periods are apt to conform but little with what the scholar would regard as justice, or what the men of whom we talk would take for truth. We think of the sixteenth century as a feverish burst of activity, wherein the full European intelligence burst at last into flower, and burst with it the old structure of western civilisation, secular and religious; as a century of heroic hopes and high devotion and desperate adventure, when new worlds were entered and new seas explored, when by land life moved in a pageant of music and poetry, and on the ocean armadas went down before the breath of God. We think of the eighteenth century as a calm and ordered age—'the peace of the Augustans'—static and hierarchic, before it was plunged into the industrial revolution of England and the political revolution of France, the infernos from which emerged our own contemporary world. Between these two the seventeenth century presents an aspect somewhat indefinite—sober certainly, not ruffling its way with extravagant gesture and mounting affirmation, nor proceeding with an aristocratic and dignified air to the coffee-house or the tumbril; the century of Cromwell, yes, of an English revolution; we may even think of it as the century of Newton; but it is not commonly lit up for us by any striking characterisation. Yet it is a century of cardinal importance for the modern mind; it is (there is almost no extravagance in the assertion) the one century we could not do without. 'A brief, and sufficiently accurate, description of the intellectual life of the European races during the succeeding two

11

John's typography – Page 11 of *Tasman and the Discovery of New Zealand* (1944). Heenan thought it 'the best bit of book production we have yet achieved'.

Victoria University College

Telephone 46-546

28 May 1954

P.O. Box ~~1580~~ 196
Wellington
New Zealand

My dear Skelton,

A number of matters in your recent budgets seem to call for attention, though not entirely ~~are~~ all connected with C.C. First let me warn you that it is all up with us — i.e. you & me. I was incautious enough to read some extracts from yours of 20 April to my wife, including a reference to your wife, & she (i.e. my wife) said H'm, I'd like to meet that woman, we seem to have a good deal in common. Now it looks as if we shall be coming to England again next year — in fact most of my family seem to be thinking of invading your unfortunate country — & once those two women get together, I fear the worst. I note how yours terrorises you — same on this side. I used to get a bit of support from my youngest son, Giles, who was willing to risk ganging up with me; but he has now left home to go farming (very appropriate with his name), & I am left defenceless & alone. I will do Tim (2nd) the justice to say that when it comes to book-buying he is on my side, & frequently buys books himself, but otherwise he is a broken reed. The only remedy I can think of, tentatively, is for each of us to take the other's wife aside, & say Look, Mrs {Skelton / Beaglehole} I do hope you appreciate at its full value your great good fortune in being married to so noble a character as {Skelton / Beaglehole} a man who unites talent & virtue in so unusual a degree; a man whom any woman, really, would break her neck to get hold of; modest & unassuming but manly; reasonable, charitable, tolerant; yes, essentially a Good Man, though suffering much from the iniquities of others; a man whose life it should be a delight to ease — & anything else in that line of talk you can think of. The idea being that once a proper amount of admiration has been instilled they will be unlikely to enter into an

One page in a scholarly correspondence. The Victoria University College letterhead was John's design.

If friends of Cook could have invoked this magical glass they might have wondered if he whether he retained any nights in his own cabin.

'Our old enemy Cape fly away entertained us for this hours this morn': it is Banks again, 5 October, about latitude 38°, & some were sure the clouds were land. A paler sea had for some days again caused frequent sounding, without bottom. The 6th came with ~~gentle settled weather south gentle settled breezes settled weather~~ ~~the ship was working her way slowly~~ settled weather & gentle easterly breezes, before which the ship sailed slowly, making once more a little northing. At 2 p.m. a boy at the masthead, Nicholas Young, ~~looked out~~ shouted Land! – & by sunset the land, no bank of cloud or fog, could be seen from the deck. At noon next day it was still about 8 leagues away, high land; below the heights smoke was rising; the weather was still clear; before nightfall a bay ~~was descried~~ ~~exposed~~, & the inland ~~mountains~~ ranges, it appeared ~~descried~~ higher than ever. 'Much difference of opinion & many conjectures about Islands, rivers, inlets &c, but all hands seem to agree that this is certainly the Continent we are in search of,' are the words Banks commits to his journal that night. In the morning Cook stood in for the bay, where canoes, people, houses could be seen; the sailmakers were busy making covers for the 'blunderbusses' – no doubt the swivel-guns – for boat service, so that he was taking no chances with these potentially difficult inhabitants; & in the afternoon he anchored on the north-east side of the bay before the entrance of a small river, & immediately went ashore with Banks, ~~Solander~~ Solander, & a ~~party of~~ ~~armed~~ landing party in the yawl & pinnace. They landed on the east side of the river.

§

'Certainly the Continent we ~~ar~~ are in search of'? Were these, then, the first steps, or the first European steps, on that fabled shore? Banks might think so. Others, even if not all hands, thought so. The titling for number 4 of Pickersgill's charts begins, 'A Chart of Part of the Southern Continent'. There is nothing to indicate that Cook thought so. Not having discovered it or any evident signs of it in his run south – & he had found 'no prospect at all then of meeting with land – he was to turn west until he discovered

James Cook, he still did for John's teaching on colonial history and on political theory.* J.A. Hobson's *Imperialism,* influenced by Marx and widely read in its time, was a book he admired. Mary Boyd, in John's classes in 1942–43, remembers him discussing Hobson and Marx and referring to various Left Book Club books on India and Africa as well as to *To the Finland Station,* a book he recommended to honours students as well as to Norman Richmond and Downie Stewart.

The second article was a review article on 'The Writing of Imperial History',[96] a discussion of the American scholar Paul Knaplund's general history, *The British Empire 1815–1939,* and of de Kiewiet's *A History of South Africa, Social and Economic.* It is an impressive display of John's knowledge of the field – of a breadth to rival that of Knaplund himself – and of his measured criticism. A little later he told Downie Stewart about how he wished he could get time to

write something rather detailed on the early beginnings of responsible government. I have one or two ideas which do not seem to have been worked over by anybody else, about the constitutional & psychological background. I wish I could find out more about not so much Robert Baldwin as about his father William Warren Baldwin who seems to have hit on the idea first somewhere in the 1820s. The underlying unity of intention between the American constitution of 1787 & the Canadian constitution of 1791 is interesting too. There are quite a number of footnotes to constitutional history lying about waiting to be picked up & fitted into place.[97]

We are reminded of what he might have written had he found a way to stay in Britain in 1929 instead of returning to New Zealand.

In 1941 the Staff Club at Victoria was formed and a room above the front steps to the College building became the common room.† Furniture was almost impossible to get, upholstery fabric unobtainable. John had seen the flax wool bales at Peter's farm and suggested using the same material to cover armchairs and couches.

---

*   At the end of 1941 John wrote to Richmond that he had a 'remote ambition' to read all the *Selected Works of Marx and Engels* 'but 12 volumes are a hell of a lot'. He was also thinking of starting on the twelve volumes of Proust. (JCB to Richmond, 21 December 1941.) We hear no more of the Marx and Engels but six years later he reports finishing the last volume of Proust: 'One gets the feeling, on coming to the end, that one really must belong to a pretty exclusive set of intellectual snobs, because after all, twelve volumes are twelve volumes, especially when so much of them is devoted to the unrelenting analysis of jealousy & to the outside aspects of homosexuality.' (JCB to Richmond, 12 January 1948.)

†   Now the Victoria Room in the Hunter Building.

He had it dyed dark blue (Plischke's dark blue and terracotta were becoming ubiquitous colours in those years) and it was a great success.* The first club committee in 1942 put aside £1 to hire suitable pictures for the common room and agreed that John should act as selector. The desirability of buying paintings was regularly raised at meetings, but in those days of rationing had to compete with investing in cups and saucers and ensuring adequate supplies of tea and sugar. It was not until the sixth annual general meeting, in June 1947, that a motion was carried that 'at least 5/- of the customary annual levy [of 10s] be spent on the purchase of original New Zealand pictures for the Common Room'. John was appointed convenor of the selection committee, and Frederick Page, just arrived as lecturer in music, a member. They were to be responsible for most of the purchases for the next ten years or so. Their first choice was a still life of daffodils by Sam Cairncross. The next was *Mountain Stream* by John Weeks which cost thirty guineas. There was only £19 in the fund, so John paid the balance and said the club could pay him back. There was muttering on the club committee and the view was expressed that more liaison between club committee and picture committee would be a good thing. It was not the last over-spending John was responsible for.

In the immediate sense the war did not have a great effect on him. He was one of the fortunate generation just too young to be called up in the First World War and just too old for the Second. He and Elsie were lucky and did not lose any close friends, though two of his cousins, David and Gerald Monaghan, died overseas. They were much younger than John and he had not known them well. That he was not entirely unmarked is suggested by a passage in his poem 'Draft Song for Victory: To John Mulgan and other New Zealanders', published in the *Listener*[98] at the end of the war in Europe:

We have known
  The safe, the waiting part,
We have known the dart
Of private fear; we have known
The hammer-blow on the heart.†

---

*   The fabric proved remarkably tough. When the Staff Club moved to new accommodation in the Rankine Brown building in 1965, I was warden of Weir House, the men's hall of residence. I got hold of the old common room couches for Weir and they had several more years of life in them.

†   Mary Boyd remembers how very upset John was when he arrived at the Historical Branch after hearing of Mulgan's death.

During the blackout and firewatching days he was a fire warden at
the College and had to spend some nights on duty. He very briefly
served in the Home Guard, but for reasons that are not recorded
was exempted from further duty. A young American naval man,
Ensign (later Lieutenant) W.J.L. Parker, who was deeply interested
in maritime history and exploration and a book collector, found his
way to John when his ship was in Wellington. After a number of
visits to Messines Road he left his books there for safe keeping. 'My
recollections of Wellington', he wrote at the end of the war, 'and
most especially the evenings spent by your fire-side learning about
New Zealand, Cook, and the Pacific islands remain the happiest by
far among those of my service years'.[99]

THE END OF THE WAR led to a period in which John was clearly
unsettled. Soaring student numbers increased teaching loads even
with the appointment of additional staff; his activities outside the
college made increasing demands on his time; he was just emerging
from a love affair that had moved him profoundly (see chapter nine);
he was anxious to start work on Cook but seemed unable to make
the first step. During 1946 his father's health was failing. On his 45th
birthday, 13 June, John wrote sombrely: 'The only moral reflection
I can get out of it is that I have a hell of a lot of work to get through
in the next 25 years, & it's about time I started'.[100] His father died in
December. It was the final break with 49 Hopper Street, the house
built for Ern and Jenny when they married just over fifty years before.
It brought back memories to John of his mother and of the family
when he was young. He was 'tired to death of examination papers',
he wrote, and just wanted 'to sit & potter round in my father's room
a long while & feel the past . . .'[101] Auntie, too, was very ill. John
hoped she would hang on until his brother Keith arrived in New
Zealand, on a business trip, at the end of January.

   In the middle of all this John was asked whether he would
consider a job in the School of Pacific Affairs and Diplomatic Studies
in Sydney 'with . . . a chair to follow in the National University at
Canberra when they get it going . . . I just sort of sighed. People
want me to write books & take jobs now. Ten years ago I would
have rushed them . . .'[102] Ida Leeson had been asked to write to
sound him out, and John responded: 'I hope you won't mind if by
way of reply I do some thinking on paper'. He said that he found
the idea attractive, particularly when he was in the middle of
marking examination scripts, then listed some 'buts'. He doubted

whether his academic interests, which he gave as Pacific exploration and Cook, development of responsible government, seventeenth-century puritanism, and American history, were what they really wanted. The combination of jobs he had in Wellington, though very demanding of time, he found fairly satisfactory; there were 'House, wife, children, friends, and all that'. Then, at greater length, came a revealing paragraph:

I don't know quite how to put this without a terrific lot of explanation, but I think I am becoming a New Zealander. That is part of the fact that a good many other people are becoming New Zealanders. Is it just that I am sinking back into a middle-aged coma and don't want to try anything new, whereas in 1929, when I came back from England, I would have given anything to get out of N.Z.? I don't know, but don't think so. I desperately need to get out of N.Z. for a while, to shake up my mind before I go completely stale; but I think I should come back. I think that in the last ten years we have proved that we can think for ourselves in N.Z., and do some interesting things; and I think that we are beginning to find that life as New Zealanders can be worth while. It seems to me that our foreign policy is worth while, and a good deal of our domestic policy, and some of our poetry and some of our art, and some of our history; and we're learning how to print books. Our university is getting a bit better, and we're just starting a University press. And I think we're going to get an archives system going. Admittedly everything is a hell of a struggle, and the dead weight of the philistines is pretty heavy, and sometimes good things break down badly. Somehow I don't feel I can say To hell with it all, and up and leave. Maybe I am taking it a bit too seriously. Maybe I just don't think the country can do without me. But I don't know. In some ways it would seem a sort of cowardice to go. I know I can help some things, and I sort of feel that I should stay on and help. Perhaps as a New Zealander born I am a bit sentimental about it; but also I am in the show, and the show is a live one, not just imitation as it used to be.

Well, that's about all I can say, and perhaps it's too much. I don't like to show a lack of enterprise, but there it is. Perhaps I'm mad. I know I'll miss a lot.[103]

He went on to say that, now the war was over, he really meant to get on with Cook. He was going to get lots of microfilms and do a lot of the work in New Zealand.

Having turned down Sydney, he was then pressed to apply for the political science chair at Victoria following Lipson's departure for the United States. This too had its attraction. Tom Smith had just come from the Public Service Commission to be senior lecturer, Joachim Kahn was there, there were no honours students whereas in history the class had reached thirty. But 'How would it match with Cook? I ask myself . . . I don't, as far as I can see, seem to have any ambition working in me at all – I shd get no kick out of being called professor'.[104] He decided he was really an historian rather than a political scientist and let it go.

In September 1947 he was tempted once again. The Mitchell Library, a part of the Public Library of New South Wales, had in its collection a lot of the papers of Joseph Banks, including his *Endeavour* journal. They wished to embark on a programme of publication of some of this material, and having advertised for an editor and received 200 applications, all of which they turned down, they invited John to accept the position with a professorial salary. He made a quick trip in early November to Sydney, Melbourne and Canberra and discussed the proposal with the trustees of the library, floating the idea of an edition of Banks and Cook sponsored jointly by them and the New Zealand government. He told them he 'certainly couldn't do [Banks] as a full-time job, but would be willing to do as they then urged, & consider a part-time arrangement, if the College would allow' him.[105]

Barely a month after the approach from the Mitchell Library he heard indirectly that the Hakluyt Society in London was proposing an edition of Cook's journals. Assuming that they had arranged British editors, he was shocked and disappointed* – 'I felt as if somebody had kicked me very very violently in the stomach & wouldn't stop'[106] – and wrote at once to J.A. Williamson. They had not corresponded since before the war but Williamson, who had moved to Looe in Cornwall at the end of the war and was out of touch with the society of which he was a former vice-president, replied immediately. 'On the face of it the Hakluyt Soc. has committed a crime and a blunder in not coming to you to edit Cook',[107] he wrote, though he was sure they must have done it 'quite unwittingly'. He got in touch with the new president, Edward Lynam. It transpired that, while planning had begun (under the great Cook collector and bibliographer Sir Maurice Holmes), editors had not yet been appointed.

On receiving Williamson's letter, Lynam wrote to John at once to ask for his collaboration in the project; they had not yet reached the stage where he could make any definite proposal, but he was interested

---

*   John was told of the proposal by C.R.H. Taylor, the Turnbull Library chief librarian, who was the New Zealand representative of the Hakluyt Society. Just after getting the news he called on Nan Taylor, who lived close by in Aitken Street. Almost fifty years later she still remembered how upset he had been.

in whether there was any particular work which John would like to undertake.[108] John's situation was getting remarkably complicated, apart from the inescapable fact that he could not possibly commit himself to anything unless he could reduce the commitments he already had. He 'put the whole extraordinary position [he] was in' to Hunter, who at once had the idea of a research chair.[109] Shortly after that John replied to Lynam's letter. 'It is of course a great pleasure to me to know that Cook is to be properly done at last. At the same time I cannot help feeling a trifle rueful to see a castle in the air of my own blown to bits, which, the war being over, I thought I had at last managed to get tethered down to hard material foundations.'[110] He went on to say that he 'would very much like to edit the material for the first voyage'. Lynam wrote back, in early February 1948, a very conciliatory letter, with a firm invitation to be the editor for that voyage.[111]

The research chair took somewhat longer to finalise. The college was in no position to fund it and an additional grant from the government was needed. A new chair also had to be approved by the university senate. However, the college council was supportive and Hunter discussed it with the Prime Minister himself, who was 'all in favour'.[112] The Trustees of the Public Library of New South Wales approached the premier, who approached the Prime Minister of Australia, Ben Chifley, who in turn wrote to Peter Fraser asking that the New Zealand government should approve of John's services being made available on a part-time basis to work on Banks.[113] But things moved very slowly: 'It seems that when the Minister of Education was approached for money he didn't see why there should be a chair, & if there was a chair why the university shouldn't pay for it out of existing funds, & anyhow all chairs should be advertised . . . All I ask of life is time, not chairs.'[114]

In May the Hakluyt Society asked John to edit the material for the third voyage as well as the first. Heenan told him that the Prime Minister was quite prepared to give the society 'all the financial backing it wants'.[115] In early June he heard that the Minister of Education had agreed to a senior research fellowship, but there had been no official word when, in the middle of the month, he had a letter from Williamson with the news that the Rhodes chair in Imperial History at King's College, London, once held by A.P. Newton, was becoming vacant. Vincent Harlow, who was moving from London on being appointed to succeed Reginald Coupland in the Beit chair in Commonwealth History at Oxford, told Williamson that he believed John would be a strong candidate if he applied.[116]

What should he do? His initial reaction was not to apply, although Elsie thought that this time perhaps he should, though she did not really want to go.[117] He clearly thought quite a lot about it. 'I sort of don't want to walk out on NZ. Is that only a sort of conceit on my side, a foolish unseemly persuasion that I matter?'[118] He talked to Hunter, who told him 'there were things in New Zealand that only [he] could do'.[119] An added complication arose as Fred Wood was 'trembling on the verge of applying' for the vacant chair in Sydney. John thought that job needed 'a man with more guts and less charm',[120] but if Wood did go the Victoria chair would be vacant and there would be a wide expectation that John should succeed him. 'I don't want it', he said, 'I'd rather be a research fellow'.[121] But there was still no firm news of a decision.

The Prime Minister, however, took a hand and on 29 July wrote to Chifley to say that Cabinet had just approved the establishment of a research fellowship, and that he understood that Victoria University College was quite prepared for John to do the work on Banks as the Australians wished.[122] The title finally agreed to (there had been some discussion in the university senate over nomenclature) was Senior Research Fellow and Lecturer in Colonial History; it carried a professorial salary and John's appointment was from the beginning of October 1948. In the meantime, Wood had not gone to Sydney and John finally decided not to do anything about London.* Ian Gordon, just back from a university conference there, had told him that financially 'it would be a hell of a swop', besides which, as John wrote to Richmond, 'I'd have teaching to do, & with this new job here I've practically retired from work'.[123] The establishment of the research position, as John recognised, owed a great deal to the strong support and political adroitness of Hunter and to Heenan's masterly handling of Fraser. The College, John wrote at an early stage of Hunter's successful campaign, 'has gone faster & certainly much farther than I suggested or dreamed possible, but it seems that sometimes agreeable miracles happen'.[124] The debt to Heenan was acknowledged in the dedication of the first of the Hakluyt Cook volumes.

---

*   A further complication had been when the Carnegie Corporation offered him a year in America. 'I'm damned if I know what to do. It all just makes me tired now. To get Cook & Banks & England & America & writing books & articles & univ press & I.A. sorted out is getting beyond me.' (JCB to JEP, 15 September 1948.)

BEFORE HE COULD GO ON leave and start work on Cook in earnest, John's immediate task was to finish the history of Victoria University College he had been asked to write for its fiftieth jubilee and get it through the press as early as possible in 1949, the year of celebration. It was not a job that he had really wanted, but there did not seem to be anyone else to do it and, once he had started thinking about it, it began to get more interesting – and somewhat more of a challenge:

I can't make it a thorough formal history, with footnotes clustered thick & all that – partly because it would take too long, but mainly because I don't think it's what is wanted. I can't hope to tell the whole unvarnished critical truth – I don't have to varnish, but I must be reasonably discreet here & there, because it is a jubilee celebratory thing & we don't want too many rows, & also it mustn't be too long.[125]

He cross-examined people on the 'intellectual & social & moral life of students', wanting to give a picture of the changing student over fifty years, which he found 'very interesting indeed, but also a little hair-raising . . . when it comes to the American invasion period'.[126] He began to write at the end of May, hoping to finish in three or four months. By the middle of August he was halfway through, and by the beginning of October there were only two or three chapters more to do.

It has been hard work, [he told Richmond] but amusing. As I said to Sir Thos [Hunter], it would be easier to write the history of the whole British Empire than of this place. There are too many things One Can't Say . . . I have just finished the Twenties, & am coming this week on to the Thirties. Joyful decades. One ends with a depression, & the other with a war. And then these Respectable Bastards have the bloody cheek to run down university students. Do you think I could use the phrase Respectable Bastards in an Official History? Maybe in a footnote.[127]

The final revisions to the last two chapters were completed only early in the new year. He had some doubts. 'I'm afraid [Eric McCormick] is going to find [it] facetious. I can't help it.'[128] A little later, when he had almost finished the first draft:

I wish there was time to put it aside & give it a thorough re-drafting . . . You know I'll never write, really. I'm getting all sorts of new mannerisms ('really' is one). The other night I was reading Virginia Woolf's *Common Reader* (wonderful book) . . . When I read her essays, I wonder if anybody else has ever been able to write. Well, I can't write, I just have a certain facility in multiplying words.[129]

John called the finished work *Victoria University College: An Essay Towards a History*. It might just as aptly have been called a memoir. John's knowledge of people and events went back over the whole fifty years (had not Robert Stout written him that glowing testimonial when he left for London in 1926?); he had been taught by a number of the early members of the staff and some among them became good friends. He was remarkably successful in giving a picture of student life over the fifty years, though a careful reading shows that some of his most vivid writing is on those times when he was a member of the college, as in the striking paragraph which opens his chapter on the 20s: 'the intoxicating vision of Education, as the maker of all things new, stood before the eyes of youth and age alike' (quoted in the account of John's student years); or the account of the Tramping Club and Boyd-Wilson (again quoted earlier). But there was more than this. His account of the 'Von Zedlitz affair', written with a barely concealed emotion and almost an essay in itself, was judged by one reviewer to be 'perhaps the finest thing' that John had written.[130] He gives an exhilarating account of skirmishes with cabinet ministers, city dignitaries and clerics – exhilarating at least to those who shared John's view of the world – and from this raised the question of the place Victoria and the other colleges had played in their communities. In writing about Victoria, he was again facing questions on the nature of university education which he had first written on in *Spike* and later in his history of the University of New Zealand.

But first and last, as Leicester Webb wrote in his review in *Education*, the history was 'an act of piety, a tribute rendered in affection to an institution and the men who made it'. Webb continued: 'affection is a difficult emotion to sustain over nearly 300 pages without lapsing into sentimentality. Beaglehole has succeeded (where no other New Zealand writer could have succeeded)'. A similar point was made by Eric McCormick in his review in the *Listener*.[131] He confessed that he had not been able to share the general enthusiasm for the article John had written on the college in the *Listener* at the time of the celebrations in May,[132] when, he suggested, John had 'appeared in the role of ardent lover celebrating the charms of his mistress, a difficult and even . . . embarrassing part to sustain in public . . . to win credence it has to be amplified, analysed, perhaps qualified'. This, he believed, John had achieved in the history where 'in 300 pages he has been able to make his devotion wholly credible', and in a 'coherent narrative in a prose that is sometimes overwrought but never undistinguished'.

McCormick was more critical in a second review he wrote later, this time for *Landfall*.[133] His major issue was 'the methods' John had used in portraying certain figures in the history. Rankine Brown (the only teacher McCormick had had at Victoria for whom he had any real respect) had been introduced by John thus: 'Brown with his suppressed emotions, his shyness, his Scots mingling of caution and ambition . . .' McCormick bridled, believing that this was tagging Brown with a label – 'cautious and ambitious' – that we would never be allowed to forget, the portrait being added to with 'tasteless trivialities' reminiscent of Lytton Strachey. But Strachey, McCormick said, at least had the merit of consistency. He had no heroes. In contrast, John, in portraying Hunter, was positively reverential as he 'proceeds to the election of a patron saint' for Victoria College. In portraying these two men, indeed in most of the portraits in the volume, McCormick suggested that John 'has used two distinct methods, one tending to deflate, the other to elevate, one veering towards contempt, the other towards adoration'. He then shifted his analysis to a broader field:

. . . we now perceive that Dr Beaglehole is not only a gifted historian but an imaginative writer of romantic disposition. And – the inspiration flashes on us – perhaps he has written the Great New Zealand Novel. Here in *Victoria University College,* is the saga we have yearned for – the epic of small beginnings and bitter reverses, of conflict with man and with nature, of plot and counter-plot, of cosy domestic hearth and proud vice-regal hall, of villainy dethroned and virtue finally triumphant – all founded on fact (but not too pedantically anchored thereto), all based on documents (with only the detail and the dialogue invented).

John thought the review 'pretty good', though McCormick 'is a wrong-headed cuss over some things'.[134] Elsie, he reported to McCormick, 'thought it an extremely good article indeed, & high time that someone took me to pieces, as I have had quite enough praise'.[135] He added that he just could not 'see this Lytton Strachey business'; none of the people who had read his drafts had suggested he had been 'unjust or flippant'. The 'trivialities' about Brown that McCormick had objected to all seemed to John 'to throw light on Brown's character', which he found 'very interesting, but by no means "great". I had a sort of affection for him myself', he continued, '& I should never have dreamed of guying him'. McCormick replied with a rather tortuous account of his state of mind when he wrote the review, but he held firm on Rankine Brown, before concluding: 'In spite of everything and without any important qualifications, I do admire you and your work . . . you are really the only one of the lot of us who amounts to anything outside our own parish'.[136] The distinction between the 'telling detail' and 'tasteless triviality' is perhaps not quite as clear as McCormick implied, but John's impressionistic portraits, however brilliant, were not always persuasive to those who did not share his views. The same point might have been made about some of those sketched in *New Zealand: A Short History,* and later a similar comment was made, with perhaps less justification, on his depiction of Johann Forster, the German naturalist who sailed with Cook on his second voyage.

For the Victoria jubilee John had organised Evelyn Page to paint Hunter's portrait – and raised the money for this from council members, staff and former students. It was a great success and is a fine painting, though perhaps not fully capturing the sparkle in Hunter's character. The celebrations took place in May 1949:

people have been running joyously into people all over the place whom they haven't seen for 19, or 34, or 48 years; & even I met the bloke who was business manager of the Spike when I was editor in 1922. Wonderful reunions; & the old groups of hockey players & execs & graduates & so on . . . have been one of the staggering successes of the week.[137]

In addition to the college history there was a golden jubilee number of *Spike,* edited by R.W. Burchfield, and a third edition of *The Old Clay Patch: A Collection of Verses Written in & Around Victoria University College* (the first edition had appeared in 1910), with contents ranging from Seaforth McKenzie's 1904 'Ode on the Laying of the Foundation Stone of Victoria College' to work by the young W.H. Oliver, Alistair Campbell and Hubert Witheford. Among them were seven poems by John, five of them from the early 1920s.

Oliver Duff, in one of his last editorials in the *Listener* before he retired after ten years as editor, warmly praised the article John had contributed for the jubilee and went on to say of him:

he is the eloquent and generous answer to his own question about the meaning of Victoria College to the community. It has focused the light in him and enriched the feeling; made him in short a truly educated man . . . When a University brings one first-rate mind to full capacity it brings many more to a point only a little below that, and in those two ways abundantly justifies its existence.[138]

And while one can perhaps understand why a critic of McCormick's temperament should have reacted as he did to the article 'A College Jubilee', as a celebratory paean it was appreciated by many readers who, moved by the occasion, found themselves agreeing with John when he wrote of the college:

it has had one capacity beyond all riches – the capacity to call forth affection from a continuous stream of students . . . this sort of personal feeling, this odd but not fantastic warmth, this sense of life lived in common in a particular way, which has meant not merely mechanical existence, not merely teaching to a programme and learning by rote, but something that has affected the heart as well as the mind.[139]

For John and others there was another side to the celebrations. Von Zedlitz, a member of the staff for only fourteen years but figuring so largely in the college's history, was dying. John was grateful that he was able to give him a copy of the history and farewell him not long before the end came on 24 May. He had no doubt that 'Von' was a great man: 'great not for what he did, exactly, not for making an undue noise in the world or for imposing himself here and there, not for shouting any particular gospel at people; but great for what he was as a personality, as a man of a peculiar and persuasive quality of mind – humane, stoical, wise, of a most noble sense of honour, and always kind'.[140]

9

'A PECULIAR SORT OF NON-CLASSIFIABLE PART-TIME PUBLIC SERVANT',[1] 1938–51

JOHN'S LIFE AT VICTORIA and in the circle of family and friends based on the college and on his home in Karori was remarkably full. Yet he came to have a parallel, almost separate, life based on the Centennial Branch (later the Historical Branch) of the Department of Internal Affairs. How this began he recounted in his 1954 lecture *The New Zealand Scholar*:

Some time in the late thirties I met a very remarkable man, and I became involved in the work of a government department and the preparations for celebrating the New Zealand centennial. I did not want to be involved; I regarded the whole thing as indulgence in a series of fatuities, all of them depraved, from which a sensible person ought to be exempt. I ended by undergoing a process of conversion, slow and awkward, into a conscious New Zealander. It was very largely, though not entirely, owing to the remarkable man. Let me be precise in my memory. I was coming out of a side entrance to Parliament Buildings one day when a stocky figure in an overcoat and an old cloth cap, who was going in, stopped me and without preamble said, 'I agree with you in every judgment you made in that book of yours [the *Short History*] except about Massey; there was a great deal more to Massey than people think; I could tell you a lot about Massey' – and immediately passed on. This was my first – I cannot say introduction to – experience of Joe Heenan.[2]

One of Heenan's moves, in fact, related to Cook rather than the centennial celebrations. John had approached the Education Department and its director, N.T. Lambourne, seeking funding for the college so that he could be freed from some of his teaching to start the work on Cook. He could get no reply from them and he suspected they had simply lost his memoranda. This was the opportunity for Heenan, 'our priceless Undersec. for Internal Affairs', to act. As John reported to Richmond, Heenan said:

'I had an idea just as I was washing up the breakfast dishes on Saturday

& I rushed straight to the phone & rang up Peter Fraser but he was out of town.' However Peter Fraser was very sympathetic when back in town; I'm Peter Fraser's white-headed boy, just now, says Joe. Joe's idea was to take advantage of the late demise of Lindsay Buick . . . who had a sort of pension-salary of £275 at the Turnbull Library* . . . & give me the money to do Cook (pay for substitute at V.U.C. part of the time etc) by appointing me Research Adviser . . . to the Turnbull Library at £300 p.a. He actually wrote a memorandum & took it to Cabinet & even got it past Walter Nash. Walter wanted to be certain they would get . . . value out of me. 'Oh, he'll have to write his own schedule of duties, I can't do that' says Joe airily. I am supposed to advise people & so on, whatever that means, & generally do any damn thing I like.[3]

The brief John drew up was 'to carry out historical research and to supervise the publication of material in the library', to assist students, and to advise the government on historical matters generally and on subsidising research and publications.[4] The Victoria council approved the arrangement[5] and on 1 July 1938 John was offered the appointment.[6] In the event he made little use of the office (with new nameplate) provided. The Turnbull Library was under the Department of Internal Affairs, and Heenan was happy to view John as a 'somewhat unclassifiable . . . part-time public servant'[7] in his department rather than in the library[†] (John's brief could apply almost equally to both). Moreover, by this time he had already been drawn into the centennial plans.

Officially, the centennial, to be celebrated in 1940, 'was about honouring the pioneers, celebrating a century of material progress and government, and about fostering "a proper national pride" in time of war'.[8] There was to be a re-enactment of the signing of the Treaty at Waitangi, a Centennial Exhibition in Wellington, literary competitions, an art exhibition and a host of other public events. Heenan was enthusiastic about them all and in charge of the whole operation, but his particular brainchild was a programme of historical publications. A National Historical Committee was appointed to advise the government. It was chaired by the Labour MP James Thorn (Heenan had suggested John A. Lee but had been overruled, though

---

*   Buick had retired from journalism in 1933 to devote himself to history. A 'compiler and recorder of historical facts', he had already produced a number of books based on material in the library. His position in the Turnbull was vaguely defined: 'to write up the history of N.Z. in a popular way'. (Rachel Barrowman, *The Turnbull: A Library and Its World* (Auckland: Auckland University Press, 1995), pp.34–5)

†   Formally, his appointment was to the staff of the department, as were those of the other library staff at that time.

Lee was a member of the committee), and its members included the professors of history from the three university colleges and the University of Otago (Rutherford, Wood, Hight and Elder), a number of others with historical interests, and representatives of government departments. John and Bill Airey were included, both having been suggested by Walter Nash.[9] The secretary was Eric McCormick, who had moved to the department from his part-time position at the Hocken Library at the end of 1936. McCormick's brief had been to spend half his time assisting Dr Guy Scholefield with the government's archives, which were under his control as Parliamentary Librarian. Although some records were in the attic of the General Assembly Library, departments still housed most of their records, while the governor-general's were still held at Government House. The remainder of McCormick's time was allocated to Centennial Branch work but increasingly Heenan called on him for more work in this area. The committee met for the first time on 18 June 1937 and considered a wide-ranging list of projects: historical surveys, a national bibliography, an encyclopaedia, volumes of historical records, restoration of historic buildings, a fund for the endowment of historical research. The list was 'more imaginative and extensive than time, resources and political sensitivities in the end allowed'.[10]

Most of the decisions were effectively made by the standing committee, which consisted of the Wellington members of the committee: Scholefield, Alister McIntosh (who had moved from the General Assembly Library to the Prime Minister's Department), Fred Wood and John, with Heenan in the chair. John's influence came to the fore when Wood was away on leave later in 1937.[11] The staff members, John Pascoe (a Christchurch mountaineer and photographer with historical interests, happy to escape an unpromising legal career when he was appointed in August 1937) and especially McCormick, played as active a role as the committee members in making decisions. John's position was a little ambiguous. A member of the national committee, he was also, as we have seen, a part-time adviser to Internal Affairs. At the first meeting of the standing committee, Beeby, with the example of *Building America,* a publication from the Columbia University Press, sold them the idea of a set of brief 'pictorials' on New Zealand history and life. This developed into the series *Making New Zealand.*

The proposed historical surveys raised a number of questions besides those of topics and authors. On certain points Heenan was clear. To Dick Campbell, now deputy to William Jordan at the New Zealand High Commission in London, he wrote, 'With regard to size, style and method of treatment I have taken Beaglehole's "Short History" as a model for the series'.[12] McCormick was anxious to give them some kind of intellectual coherence. He set down his ideas in a letter to Heenan dated 11 October 1937. The books, he said, 'should be bound together by some common idea, they should exemplify in all its ramifications some general thesis which is applicable to the whole field of New Zealand history'. In McCormick's view that general thesis, should be adaptation, an idea he had developed as a research student at Cambridge:

Now the idea which seems to me to be of fundamental importance in any consideration of New Zealand history is this; that 100 years ago a sample of nineteenth century society and civilization was transferred to New Zealand and has since been reshaped and adapted, with varying degrees of success, to conform to the conditions of a new environment – i.e. natural surroundings and climate, a new order of society, special economic conditions, a native people and all the other elements which constitute environment in its widest sense.[13]

The idea, he suggested, was simple, 'so simple and obvious that one finds scarcely any mention of it, either implicit or explicit, in the vast mass of New Zealand writing'. Two notable exceptions he allowed were Guthrie-Smith's *Tutira* and 'Dr Beaglehole's work, particularly his *History of the University*'.* It was hardly surprising that John told Heenan that his views coincided with McCormick's and he thought that 'the guiding thread he [McCormick] suggests should be brought very emphatically before authors as our ideal'.[14] McCormick's own survey, *Letters and Art in New Zealand,* exemplified his idea admirably but was one of the very few that did so. In writing on the discovery of New Zealand, it was not an approach that John could follow.

It was a time of ideas, 'a fruitful period of planning and preparation', McCormick recalled, 'when, at meetings of the standing committee or in many informal meetings among the members, the nebulous proposals for commemorative publications began to take on substance and form'.[15] John was asked in October 1937 to write a general survey of political ideas in New Zealand.[16] Early in the new year a history of the discovery of New Zealand was added.[17] The Dunedin members of the National Historical

---

*   Adaptation, as McCormick explained it, was essentially a one-way process. The Maori came into the story as one of the influences on Pakeha society but he did not recognise how Maori society itself underwent a process of reshaping and selective adaptation, that there was a two-way process of social change.

Committee* reacted strongly to the assignment of two surveys to one author,[18] though their reasons for objecting were not made very clear. John was the only writer in question. It was the volume on political ideas to which they seemed to take exception, and it is possible that this was more of a personal objection than a matter of principle. 'Dunedin seems to be the place where most disgust at my existence is expressed at present', John reported to Richmond,[19] though what he was particularly referring to was the reaction to his contribution to the NZIIA's forthcoming volume *Contemporary New Zealand*. Dunedin members of the institute said that they would not subscribe to that book if John's chapter was included ('apparently I was disloyal & think there is something to be said for Mr Jordan'). The NZIIA editorial committee, which included W.B. Sutch, 'said All right, don't; & Dr Butchers said he'd resign from the editorial cttee, & the rest said All right, do; & he did'. John decided that 'pressure of work' made it impossible to write both books[20] and the political ideas volume was dropped from the series.

Out of continuing discussion, ideas emerged for two more publications: a biographical dictionary, a project on which Scholefield had been working for many years; and an historical atlas, suggested by Professor Rutherford, which would be a joint project with the surveyor-general and his department. Early in 1938 the committee's final recommendations for twelve 30,000-word historical surveys, thirty pictorial surveys and a literary competition, as well as the biographical dictionary and the atlas, were approved by Cabinet after Heenan had beaten back a Treasury protest at the cost involved.[21] In March Oliver Duff, formerly editor of the Christchurch *Press* (1929–32), latterly struggling to make a living from a Canterbury smallholding, was appointed editor of the publications. The staff was established in a rather decrepit former boarding house in Sydney Street East, grandly named Centennial House, and their numbers grew. J.W. Davidson, a history graduate from Victoria, was briefly a research assistant until he left for Cambridge. His place was taken by R.I.M. (Bob) Burnett, a history graduate from Otago. John Pascoe was made illustrations editor. David Hall, a New Zealand Cambridge graduate (married to a von Zedlitz daughter) was appointed publicity officer and 'proved to be a most versatile writer . . . willing to tackle anything'.[22] Heenan

---

*   Professor Elder at Otago University, and J.T. Paul, the veteran journalist and Labour Party stalwart, who was deputy chairman of the committee. In 1939 Paul became the government's Director of Publicity and, in effect, chief censor.

was never far away. He 'was like a ballet impresario', McCormick recalled, 'a Diaghilev. Our jobs had not been advertised: we were his choice, and he liked to show us off. The old faithful people in the department were sometimes resentful of the favours these newcomers received.'[23]

When Duff left in December to become first editor of the *New Zealand Listener*, McCormick succeeded him as editor and John was given the title of typographical adviser; 'nominally typographical adviser', as McCormick recalled it, 'but oracle in all matters'.[24] Why 'typographical adviser'? His interest in printing and book design went back to his boyhood and student days, but he had really begun 'his typographical apprenticeship in earnest'[25] when Beeby gave him the responsibility for planning and printing *The University of New Zealand* and for similar work on subsequent publications of the New Zealand Council for Educational Research.[26] He would have had some involvement in design decisions from the early days of centennial planning and he clearly shared Heenan's determination to have the printing done outside the Government Printing Office,[27] which, in John's view, represented the worst in New Zealand design and printing at the time. To Heenan, at the beginning of 1939, he wrote that 'the printing practice of the Government Printing Office is so deplorably old-fashioned and its equipment in type so entirely inadequate* (judged by contemporary standards) that there is some question how far it is competent to print a book at all'.[28] Before Duff left it was decided that the pictorial series should be printed by Wilson and Horton in Auckland. John's first approach to its design was that each survey should have a distinctive format to reflect its individual content; he was 'steered away' from this to a standardised design.[29] John Pascoe was hard at work collecting illustrations and working on the layout.

Scholefield's biographical dictionary was said to be finished and ready for the printer and research had begun for the atlas. John offered to design the dictionary and see it through the press. He was now effectively in a position to make decisions himself. He wrote to Heenan and sent him a specimen page:

---

*   In a slightly later memorandum to Heenan, 'Shortcomings of the Government Printing Office' (1 March 1939), John wrote that the office 'should have a fundamental outfit of standard type-faces such as Caslon, Baskerville, Bell, Aldine Bembo, Perpetua Titling. If it has not some such types as these, it simply has no pretensions to be considered a modern printing office at all.' (J.C. Beaglehole Papers, 73-004-01/10. ATL.)

After getting a good many specimens set up we have settled on this for the D.N.Z.B. It is 9 point Baskerville, the black type is Cloister. The price per page is 19/3; 800,000 words would work out at 1087 pp; say 2 volumes of 544pp. & total printing £1047. This is about £120 cheaper than the page in Garamond first quoted on, at 15/3 a page, & will give a better-looking job. If they use Baskerville, they can start setting right away . . . [30]

The printers were Whitcombe and Tombs; their composing room manager and later works manager in Wellington, with whom John was to establish a warm friendship, was L.G. (Lance) Davison.* Producing the two volumes took over fifteen months. John not only designed the book and supervised its production, but acted virtually as editor. Getting the dictionary ready for the printer meant 'wrestling with an untidy and tattered manuscript';[31] later he read galley proofs and page proofs with a wary eye for factual errors. McCormick thought he should be officially recognised as editor but John was unwilling.[32] When the job was finished John drafted a letter, which he hoped the Prime Minister might sign, to be sent to the manager of Whitcombe and Tombs:

The task of producing the Dictionary has been a long and arduous one and has, I know, called for a great deal of patience and care, in type-setting, correcting, paging, printing, and binding, and I know too that Dr. Beaglehole, in charge of the production, has not been remarkably easy to please. But the interest taken in the job by your people, as well as their solid work over a long period, has been a very pleasant feature of this phase of the Centennial. It is perhaps invidious to particularise, but your linotype operators certainly have had a difficult task; and I think also that the work of the apprentice who, I understand, paged practically the whole book, calls for special mention. The result on the production side is, I think, the finest set of volumes on this scale that has ever appeared in New Zealand.[33]

John was anxious that not only the manager but the men and women who did the work should know of the government's appreciation, and asked that the letter be sent on to Davison and be circulated among the staff. He did not get the Prime Minister's signature. Heenan sent it to his minister to sign, and in doing so commented on John's 'remarkable work as our typographical adviser' and on the dictionary's 'outstanding excellence as a piece of book production'. What John had learned was that to achieve the

---

*   Davison subsequently moved to Christchurch on becoming Whitcombe and Tombs printing works manager there.

results he wanted he needed to get into the printing works and talk with the men directly involved in the job: 'except where the printer's every page, line and word is supervised and virtually designed for him', he told Heenan, his work is deplorable.[34] However, he found he liked 'the blokes who do the actual work at Whitcombe's, works-managers & machine-men & comps. & so forth'.[35]

'Printing is an interesting game', he wrote to Richmond at the end of 1939, '& I should like to be Govt printer for a couple of years . . . it has been the main occupation of my life this year'. But he wished 'all the stuff' they were 'turning out was worthy of the pains'.

> I do not think that Dr G.H. Scholefield's Dictionary of NZ Biography is a monument of accuracy & judicious comment; & I would not advise you to buy even vol ii, where a constellation of Richmonds blazes away like the tropic sky . . . To say nothing of Atkinsons & Hursthouses & the rest of your Ten Shining Tribes. I do not observe any great redeeming vice in the midst of your virtuous ancestors; they seem to have pinched a lot of land from the Maoris, but all in the most improving way, in the highest interests of the res publica & with the aid of much ethical statement. But our Dr Scholefield is not the man to soil a tomb with ambiguous flowers; he lays the pure lily; no weed of criticism enters into his wreath; our Great it seems were all Good, or if not good then Misunderstood . . . He seems to feel a hint of something lacking when he remarks in his preface that he aims only at giving Fact & not Comment. I.e. to say that a man arrived in 1840 is a Fact (even if he didn't); to say that he murdered his grandmother or swindled the Poor is Comment. But this is all very small beer, who the hell is interested in Scholefield anyway? He is only one of the curses that have afflicted me since April, when we started printing his damned book.[36,]*

Before Oliver Duff left for the *Listener,* the printers (Whitcombe and Tombs in Christchurch), typeface, binding cloth and paper for the historical surveys were decided – was it from this period that Eric McCormick later recalled a great many arguments between Duff and John about the specificities of type, paper and binding cloth?[37] John then became responsible for the design of the individual volumes. He had persuaded Whitcombe and Tombs to import monotype moulds of Aldine Bembo, an 'elegant and robust Italian

---

*   Scholefield's volumes had been compiled mainly from newspapers in the General Assembly Library and in the course of his other duties as Parliamentary Librarian. With all their shortcomings, they did temporarily fill a gap until the publication of the five volumes of *The Dictionary of New Zealand Biography*, produced with infinitely greater resources, during the 1990s.

type designed by Francesco Griffo of Bologna for the great Venetian printer-publisher, Aldus Manutius, in the late fifteenth century'.[38] When the third survey, *The Women of New Zealand* by Helen M. Simpson, was published, an anonymous reviewer in the *Listener*, while praising aspects of its production, was critical of some of the design decisions on the three volumes which had by then appeared:

The title-page on all three volumes is so weak that it ought to be changed even at this late stage. It is, of course, as difficult for a typographer as for anyone else to make bricks without straw, but there are some good substitutes for straw available. Also, there is no justification for untrimmed edges on a machine-made book. To trim and stain the top end of the volume and leave the bottom just as it happens to fall is to forget that we are nearly half-way through the twentieth century.[39]

John welcomed a typographical critic and, in his explanation of the two points of which the reviewer was critical, he revealed 'an intimate and sophisticated knowledge of the principles of design as well as a recognition of the realities of book publishing in New Zealand at this time'.[40]

Your reviewer deplores the title-page . . . So do I. The difficulty here is one of balance. If the frontispiece is covered with a blank sheet, you will find that the title-page doesn't look so bad after all – perhaps a little too restrained, but not so bad. Unfortunately the unit in book printing is not the single page but the two-page opening; and in these surveys the frontispiece badly overweights the title-page. The obvious remedy is to make the title-page heavier – i.e., to use bigger type on it. But at present we have no bigger type of the right sort – Monotype Aldine Bembo – to use on this page, though it has been on order for more than three months. Why not use a different sort of type then? Because a whole book should also be regarded as a typographical unity, and we have, I think, no type that would fit in well with Bembo. That remedy would be worse than the disease . . . We can only watch and pray for the arrival of the right sizes of type.*

John was not concerned about the 'slight irregularity' in the length of the page at the bottom; it was, he claimed, 'quite a standard practice in book production'. The 'dignity of a double-page of type', he argued, depends on its margins and particularly on its bottom margin, and to take off 'an arbitrary quarter-inch . . . for the sake of

---

* The bigger type arrived and was used for the title page of Eric McCormick's *Letters and Art in New Zealand*; and a bigger size again for Leicester Webb's *Government in New Zealand* and Oliver Duff's *New Zealand Now*.

mechanical regularity' quite unnecessarily diminished that margin. (Appropriate margins, whether he was designing a book or writing a letter, were always a central element in John's sense of space and right proportion.) He concluded with a plea for more criticism:

We are just beginning in New Zealand to produce books of tolerable appearance, and there is no reason why in a matter that demands craftsmanship and taste rather than genius we should not reach a relatively high standard. But to become complacent at this stage, to lavish indiscriminate praise, would be disastrous. I hope therefore that those of your readers who are interested in typography will regard these Centennial books as a starting-point, not as a final achievement.[41]

John's response reflects a modest satisfaction with what had been achieved, and this is echoed a little later in a memorandum to Heenan:

I don't think the jobs are by any means perfect, but taking all the circumstances into account, perhaps they may be called quite reasonably good. We have got on good terms with the printers anyhow, and I even think convinced them that we are not mad. At least we have set up a standard, and this Government work has knocked anything ever done in N.Z. in the commercial line into a cocked hat (not that that would be difficult anyway). It seems to me important that the Government standard shouldn't be lowered; it seems important that it should even be raised.[42]

John's taste as a typographer was relatively conservative. He had a high regard for eighteenth-century typography and a preference for 'unobtrusive simplicity'.[43] With the centennial publications he was already, in Sydney Shep's words, showing 'some of the typographical trademarks which he would flourish through the next decade – classic typefaces such as Monotype Aldine Bembo and Baskerville, swelling rules, centred title-pages, meticulously letter-spaced titles, the use of a fixed grid, and insistence on wide margins'.[44]

When John described his role to Richmond he left out of the list 'author': 'I've turned into a sort of printing hack; with jurisdiction over all govt. historical publications, & a sort of supplementary editor to be consulted on spelling, punctuation, copyright, treatment of authors, treatment of Under-Secretaries, price of fish, & other details impossible to reduce to classification'.[45] He did mention in the same letter, however, that he had got an advance copy of his own volume in the centennial surveys. He had finished writing *The Discovery of New Zealand* in September 1939 and it came out in December, the first to appear.

John's object was to 'give an account . . . of the process by which

New Zealand was "discovered" – that is, by which its coastline and its extent became generally known'. Much of the story was familiar to him from writing *The Exploration of the Pacific* but there was one significant difference. 'It would have been both unjust and absurd,' he wrote, 'to enlarge on the achievements of European discoverers, and exclude all mention of the remarkable voyages of the pre-European centuries'.[46] His training and his inclination as an historian was to look for written records. He depended, therefore, on the accounts of Kupe's discovery and of the Great Fleet handed down in Maori tradition and interpreted and published in English by S. Percy Smith and Elsdon Best. These were the orthodox views of the time, but since he first wrote they have been greatly revised in the light of later scholarship. When John prepared a second edition of the book, published by the Oxford University Press in 1961, he confessed he had given much thought to what to do with that first chapter; in the end he decided to leave it much as it was.

The discussion of Maori, and of Polynesian, origins is a battlefield, littered with gashed theories and not a few dead bodies of speculation; and tradition is obviously open to destructive attack. We cannot ignore the fairy-tale quality. A different sort of treatment of this chapter, however, would inevitably have meant analysis and argument at second hand (for I am not an expert in Polynesian history); and the Maori traditions, whether we believe in a historical 'Fleet' or not, have a value in themselves. They were part of the land that the European navigators discovered – even if the 'Fleet' itself was a European invention.[47]

There was a question not only of content, but also of style. John wrote a first chapter that, stylistically, is in marked contrast with what follows. 'Extravagant and ornate', as Chris Hilliard judged in 1996, 'with dramatic rhetorical questions and "picturesque" passages in the absence of quotable documentary sources',[*] it had the effect that, while he attempted to take Maori traditions seriously, his chapter created 'an aura of stylized unreality about "Polynesian history" compared to the lively European-centred narratives that follow[ed]'.[48, †]

The later chapters provide a straightforward narrative with the

---

[*]   John's prose style in this chapter was 'taken off' in the 1940 student extravaganza, *Centennial Scandals*.

[†]   Whatever the style, Maori had a greater presence in John's survey than in any of the others. McCormick's guiding thesis in practice seemed to provide little room for a consideration of the Maori part in New Zealand history, and those authors who went their own way saw New Zealand history as a Pakeha story. Apirana Ngata was commissioned

best identification then possible of the places mentioned by the early explorers. For some of this John was able to draw on work already done for the historical atlas. Cook, inevitably, takes centre stage. John wove his material together with the same unerring sense of proportion that marked his typographical work and wrote with a lively eloquence, though the romantic touch (and lack of a sailor's eye) could let him down. To describe Ship Cove in Queen Charlotte Sound as 'a calm and lovely little bay' gives little idea of what it can be like in a nor'westerly gale with williwaws tearing off the hills and whitening the sound.

In his role as 'oracle in all matters' John was involved in the controversy over the survey that W.B. Sutch was engaged to write on social services in New Zealand.[49] The manuscript was finally produced in April 1940 and criticised by staff for its 'alleged bitterness, bias, irrelevancies and clumsiness'.[50] McCormick, McIntosh, Hall and John met with Sutch, who agreed to make revisions, but the revised version still failed to satisfy the staff. McCormick and Hall then worked on the long final chapter, but Sutch would not accept their suggestions. John did further work on the chapter, but this was still unacceptable. Walter Nash, for whom Sutch worked as a private secretary, was drawn into the discussion and, at a meeting in late November with McCormick, Sutch and John, he said that approval could not be given for publication until Peter Fraser had seen the book. At that point Sutch proposed completely rewriting the survey, and he was released from his normal duties to do so. McCormick and Heenan recommended publication of the new manuscript, though Heenan thought it gave 'a rather bleak impression of New Zealand life throughout the century'.[51] However, Fraser, who by this time had read both manuscripts, would 'not have even the second version at any price'.[52] He 'turned it down', John told Richmond, 'because he didn't like its "tone". God knows what he meant.'[53]

John had little patience with Sutch – 'I shouldn't myself object to Bill Sutch's writing the nastiest minded stuff of the century, if only he'd write it and not chuck it together with a bloody shovel'[54] – but the decision not to publish was clearly Fraser's alone.[55] Sutch was hardly a popular figure with the Labour leadership; his close links

to write a volume on the Maori, which would have done something to restore the balance, but it was never written. Maori history would have been much more adequately represented in the historical atlas, for which Ngata was deeply involved in the work on the Maori maps.

with *Tomorrow* and with its publication of John A. Lee's attacks on Savage and the government, especially Lee's article 'Psychopathology in Politics', would have added to Fraser's deep distrust of him. He was paid for the survey (£100), however, and given permission to publish it elsewhere and use government photographs for illustrations. His second manuscript was the first to appear, published by Modern Books,* 'with guarantees from Sutch & Scrim[geour] & one or two others'. John thought it 'a damned bad book & from B.S. a disgraceful production'.[56] The earlier version was published the following year by Penguin Books.†

Well before the centennial year was over, John was thinking about the future of the historical side of the Centennial Branch. The war had brought uncertainty and he was anxious that work on the historical atlas and plans for the archives, among other planned activities, should not simply be put on hold until hostilities were over. This was due partly to his belief in the uniqueness of the group of staff that had been brought together, in 'its special experience, capacities and accumulated knowledge', and partly to a recognition of how the work already started could be built on and expanded; but underlying both was the change that was taking place in his relationship with his country, 'the process of conversion, slow and awkward, into a conscious New Zealander'.[57]

The historical atlas clearly was not going to be produced by the end of 1940; it had become apparent that 'war or no war it would have been physically impossible to do the job'. With time no longer a particular object John believed that it could be made a 'fine and exciting, as well as a useful volume', and he hoped that if work continued they could be ready to produce it at the end of the war, when Lands and Survey staff were again available for drafting, paper supplies were restored and new type for printing had been purchased. He also urged the importance of continuing work on the archives; a start had barely been made on gathering together, sorting intelligibly and making available for consultation the records in the country, and a successful centennial project had been the collection of further primary source material relating to New Zealand, especially from Britain.

Looking ahead, John saw further possibilities:

---

*   *Poverty and Progress in New Zealand* (Wellington: Modern Books, 1941).
†   *The Quest for Security in New Zealand* (Harmondsworth: Penguin Books, 1942). The Oxford University Press published a new and enlarged edition of the book in 1966 in which the original work made up about the first third.

Our archives department ought also to act as a Historical Monuments Commission. There may not be many old buildings &c. that we can hope to preserve indefinitely, but there are many the memory and picture of which should certainly be preserved. What we need is a photographic survey of the country before decay and demolition goes any further. Cottages, shacks, farmhouses, churches – they should all be photographed and when necessary made the subject of measured drawings . . . We want, too, as complete a photographic record as possible of historic spots; and when it comes to the question of marking these, the archives department ought to have the final say. One thing more in this connection: if we photograph at all, let's photograph also from the air . . . what mayn't we expect to get . . . for pre-European history by an expert air-survey of the whole extent of Maori settlement? Take even the pa-sites of Taranaki or the East Coast – we might get results of astonishing interest.

There were projects that had been considered by the National Historical Committee but not found a place in the centennial programme: the production of volumes of historical documents that might include things of a general, not merely a New Zealand, interest – we 'could start with a grand flourish and do Cook's journals and earn the gratitude of people all over the world', the publication of books such as Charles Cotton's *Geomorphology of New Zealand*, a scientific classic but of little interest to a commercial publisher. New Zealand museums and art galleries were a worry to him: as part of education, 'or if you like art and culture and N.Z. nationalism and sensibility . . . we could do first-rate coloured reproductions of Heaphy and Buchanan that would make the kids realise N.Z. and art and history at the same time . . . I was reading McCormick's survey last night and got more and more excited. When I think of what we *could* do I get so excited I could run round and bang my head against the walls . . . if we can seize the chance we might really in time touch the mind of the country.'

The case for the government being involved at that time was simple: without it, little if anything would be done. What was needed was a 'sort of archives plus historical publication plus historical manuscript and monuments commissions plus Tolerable-Printing-and-Graphic-Art-education department . . . all in one'. If, during the war, the preliminary work of 'organising and collecting and planning and experimenting' went ahead something could be done without delay that would 'increase our self-knowledge and power of self-criticism, which will be as much part of our self-respect as Social Security or the Government [state] houses'. What he argued for proved a remarkably accurate indication of where his main interests would lie in the next three decades, although his ideas did not work out in quite the way he foresaw.

By the end of 1940 John was coming to recognise how his view of New Zealand and its history had changed from that of only a few years before. Of that earlier period, after he first got back from London, he later wrote in *The New Zealand Scholar* that 'I could not see much point in New Zealand.'[58] New Zealand history, he had thought,

was interesting chiefly as an example of what happened when capitalist civilization in its heyday stretched out and started to interfere with a land and a culture hitherto untouched by this dubious way of life. It wasn't particularly interesting in itself, and it was the duty of the New Zealander to step outside his narrow experience, contemporary and historical, and become a citizen of the world, in history and in his own life. I still believe that, except that now I think New Zealand in itself is thoroughly interesting, and that one does not get at its real significance for ourselves or the wider world of history without a good deal more attention than I have been prepared to give to it.[59]

To that history he now allowed more complexity: 'a history of the conflict of men and their environment, of the conflict of races, of the conflict of classes', as he put it in a review article, 'The New Zealand Mind', published in the *Australian Quarterly* in December 1940. It was a history, however, that New Zealanders had yet to assimilate, to make part of a tradition 'in which and from which only, a great piece of significant creative work could emerge – itself to illustrate and strengthen the tradition'.[60] Hence the importance that John gave to Frank Sargeson's first book of sketches and stories, *A Man and His Wife,* 'something as native to our scene as the work of Henry Lawson to Australia'.*

Mr Sargeson is important, and he is important because he represents a certain idiom of thought. It is an idiom of thought we have been waiting for. Obviously it cannot be an exclusive one; yet in other, and related idioms, part of a general cast or scheme of mind, we must learn to express ourselves in New Zealand, mastering our medium and being tinged in it, if we are to be ourselves, and not merely an offshoot of England.[61]

---

*   His support for Sargeson took a more practical form when he joined with Eric McCormick and a small group of anonymous Sargeson admirers in Wellington to send him £13 (a not insignificant sum for that time) as a gesture of esteem. (Michael King, *Frank Sargeson: A Life* (Auckland: Viking, 1995), p.201.)

The way in which such a tradition might work, John suggested, could be learned from the symposium edited by Ivan Sutherland, *The Maori People Today*.* The ongoing life of Maori customs and traditions was the key to Maori survival. 'It is an astonishing story', John wrote, 'this Maori renascence, instructive alike in its successes and its limitations; it is the story above all of the utilization, the working-out, the logic of a tradition maintained with the tenacity of despair, realized anew with the tenacity of hope.' There was 'comparatively little, in the realm of the spirit' that the Pakeha New Zealander could place beside that. 'New Zealand is in my very bones', Katherine Mansfield had written. 'That is true, no doubt of an increasing number of us', John commented, 'but it does not show itself in a great many of our minds'.[62] But there were grounds for hope.

How do we explain the remarkable changes in John's views? They began, I suspect, in those very years which he referred to so bleakly in *The New Zealand Scholar* (and was a more complex process than he there suggests), when through his work for the WEA he discovered parts of New Zealand he had not known before and in his classes and the summer schools met a remarkable range of New Zealanders. In its way, debating J.S. Bach with Norman Richmond and John Shearer was a step towards discovering the New Zealand mind, as was finding the paintings of John Weeks and, a little later, T.A. McCormack. The *Short History* proved to be something more than a study of the extension of capitalist civilisation. In the later 1930s John began reading in the history of colonial America, especially Virginia and the New England colonies, which, as we have seen, became one of his great interests and a field in which he did some of his best teaching during and after the war. He recognised that to view such colonies simply as the products of England's commercial capitalism of the seventeenth century gave little real understanding of what they were and what they were to become. Did this not suggest that there might be more to New Zealand history than he had earlier allowed? His teaching, especially the supervision of theses, and working in the Centennial Branch greatly increased his knowledge of New Zealand and New Zealand history; greater knowledge led to greater interest.

These intellectual changes did not occur in isolation. Marriage,

---

*   I.L.G. Sutherland, ed., *The Maori People Today* (Wellington: New Zealand Institute of International Affairs and New Zealand Council for Educational Research, 1940).

a family, a permanent job and a home played their part. Davidson, who as one of his students and as a colleague in the Centennial Branch came to know John well in these years, suggested something more when he wrote of the time after John's return from London:

> Gradually . . . the magic of the land of his birth reclaimed him, and it had a new potency for him because he now savoured it as a man who had drunk at other wells . . . Wellington, in particular, where he had been born, was important to him. The windy hills, the clear light on the harbour, the clanking trams, the tension between the small but lively intelligentsia and an establishment inclined to interpret the words 'Man Thinking' as a warning of imminent danger – all these were parts of his heritage. He made Wellington his Athens.[63]

In John's view, however, unquestionably the most important influence in his engagement with New Zealand was Joe Heenan.* Heenan, as we have seen, was extraordinarily adept at getting things done.[64] He had the continuing support of his minister, Bill Parry, and a remarkable gift for winning the ear of Peter Fraser and, if necessary, Walter Nash as Minister of Finance. Fraser had a weekly meeting of the Executive Council in the wooden Government Building in which Heenan's department was housed. Almost invariably, the offer of a cup of tea after the meeting lured Fraser into Heenan's office for a chat and, for Heenan, the chance to float his latest idea. But there was a great deal more to Heenan than being adept at handling ministers. John wrote of

> that passionately informal, that impulsive, generous, quick-tempered, wise, imaginative, romantic, pig-headed, enthusiastic, hard-boiled, sentimental, gullible, sceptical, prejudiced and tolerant man . . . [with his] extensive and peculiar knowledge not merely of the public service and of politics and politicians, but of racehorses, footballers and athletes . . . [and] detailed familiarity with some tracts of literature, though at modern poetry he stopped dead.[65]

Heenan's enthusiasm for Conrad was matched if not exceeded by his enthusiasm for H. Guthrie-Smith; he judged *Tutira* to be New Zealand's greatest book and John's 'Considerations on Certain Music of J.S. Bach' the greatest poem written by a New Zealander.

---

*   This was how John put it in his brilliant portrait of Heenan in *The New Zealand Scholar*. He gave the lecture in April 1954, just two and a half years after Heenan died and at a time when he was very conscious of what Heenan had done to support his work on Cook. Whether he would have put it in quite such striking terms had he looked back again fifteen years, later we do not know.

Heenan's papers, now in the Alexander Turnbull Library, show the astonishing range of his correspondents; their contents bear witness not only to the breadth of his interests but also to his ability to establish and maintain warm friendships. Winning the affection as well as the admiration of those who worked for him, he was a man quite unlike anyone John had met before. Heenan, both by example and in his enthusiasms, helped shape John's idea of what it was to be a New Zealander. Their association was to continue through the 1940s and to have a significant impact on John's career.

As the centennial year drew to a close Heenan sought John's and Eric McCormick's advice on the future of the Centennial Branch and its staff. Confident that Fraser and Nash would give him every support 'in anything that tends to add a cultural side to our activities',[66] he had been plotting for some time to have the staff retained as a permanent acquisition to his department. He was even hoping that 'Beaglehole's own life job, the edition of Cook's Journals may be one of the works ultimately to be carried out by this Department'. McCormick left to join the army at the end of 1940 and Heenan, having known McCormick's intention, had suggested to John that he might consider heading an Historical Branch within the department. John demurred. He did not think he had any particular qualifications for the task of building up the archives – on the importance of which he and McCormick were agreed. The other task envisaged, working 'quietly on plans for further historical publications and the publication of historical records after the war',[67] interested him more but he had 'no wish to abandon the relatively agreeable life of a university lecturer, even partially', unless he could do 'really good work' – which he thought possible only if a regular publications fund was built up.[68] However, he suggested a twelve months' experiment with him in charge, and with this information Heenan carried his proposal through with his political masters. John was to occupy the position for eleven years.

An immediate difficulty was staff. Heenan increasingly used John Pascoe for tasks unrelated to the branch, in 1942 appointing him official war photographer with the job of recording New Zealand life during the war. In late 1941 Bob Burnett and Frank Lingard were still working on research for the historical atlas, but both were gone within a few months. The Lands and Survey draughtsmen had all been diverted to wartime tasks and Ruth Fletcher (later Ruth Allan) was the only one left of the Centennial House editorial staff. She had developed, John wrote, 'into a very highly-skilled historical odd-job woman to whom are referred all questions that can't be answered easily and immediately'; without her, he added, he could do very little indeed. She left shortly afterwards to take charge of the broadcasts to schools, which were just beginning. In suggesting the appointment of two of his students from Victoria, John wrote that 'It is no use appointing anybody but hand-picked people . . . and if I am in charge I want to do the hand-picking myself'.[69] The two appointed from the beginning of 1942 were Janet Wilkinson (later Janet Paul) and Ruth Guscott (later Ruth Burnard, then Ross). Janet had trained as a teacher and had taught for two years, including a year's 'country service' in a tiny, isolated one-teacher school up the Mokau river, while completing her BA in English and history. At the beginning of 1941 she had returned to Wellington to enrol in history honours and, a teaching position not being available, had found a job as a plan tracer in the Railways. While Ruth had passed three years of history she had not yet completed her degree, but John judged her one of the ablest students they had had.

Before Ruth Fletcher left, she introduced Ruth Guscott into research for the atlas – knowledge and skills were passed on to later recruits in the same way – and Guscott from the start showed herself to be a 'passionately devoted researcher',[70] making her mark with her work for the map of early European settlement. Janet was less of an historian but wrote well, and quickly proved an able assistant to John on typographical matters. In this he found her 'an absolute Godsend'. She showed a great capacity for picking up technicalities and an ability in design and lettering; she also got on well with the people involved – printers and blockmakers, managers and foremen alike.[71] Her experience with the staff in the Railways drawing office clearly stood her in good stead. Later in the war there were more appointments, among them further history graduates from Victoria: Nan Taylor (late 1942), Mary Boyd (the end of 1943), and Frances Porter, who joined when Mary left in 1945.

The branch had moved from Sydney Street East into a former ministerial house in Molesworth Street, before moving into one crowded back room in the Government Building.[72] About the end of 1943 it was moved downstairs to two rooms immediately to the north of the main entrance – with a box-seat view of comings and goings for the weekly Executive Council meetings that took place upstairs. The main office was spacious with a very large table and chairs in the middle. John Pascoe and his boxes of photographs and files occupied one end of it. Other staff had desks by windows or in the smaller room. Heenan, who had a remarkable fund of anecdotal stories, would call in regularly on his way to his office upstairs. It was understood that no one should ring John at home before 9.30 a.m., when he had finished drying the breakfast dishes and practising Bach on the piano. He was in the branch several mornings a week for morning tea or to visit Heenan (in those years teaching at Victoria, other than in science, was almost all in the late afternoon or early evening). He was largely preoccupied with publications work, and the staff working on the atlas were left very much to their own devices. He would catch the tram back to Karori for lunch, after picking up a loaf of wholemeal bread from the dairy in Bowen House next to the cenotaph.

There was a continual stream of visitors to the branch: authors, historians, artists, public servants involved in wartime publicity, ex-Centennial Branch staff. It was a lively place to be, in some ways more like an extension of John's honours class than the public service – the group were viewed with some bemusement by other staff in Internal Affairs, who referred to them as 'the Beaglehole kindergarten', a name said to have been bestowed by Graham Bagnall. John kept them up to date with the worlds of music, art and writing; opinions were very forthright and not always very tolerant. He recommended books they should read, and introduced them to the American Information Library in Woodward Street, run by the redoubtable Mary Parsons. Mary Boyd remembers the talk at morning tea as far more interesting than any she experienced later in the university common room.

Heenan was never content with his initial thought that the branch should work quietly on plans for publications after the war. As John recounts it: 'The telephone would ring: "Have you got a minute to spare, boy? Just slip upstairs and have a cup of tea – I've just had an idea."'[73] One such idea was that they might have a number of sets of *Making New Zealand* and the biographical dictionary specially bound to be presented by Peter Fraser to President Roosevelt, Secretary of the Navy Knox, Secretary of War Stimson and Secretary of State Cordell Hull, as well as to the Canadian Prime Minister, McKenzie King, when Fraser was in North America in August 1941.

So I had to turn to & design a lot of gold-tooled morocco bindings & supervise the job – not without some preliminary horror from the boss binder in the Govt. Printer's at such outlandish designs as I put forward. Luckily there turned out to be a very good & very keen young finisher there who got thoroughly excited & worked overtime, & we managed to have a little exhibition in the Turnbull & get the damn things packed & away . . . The leather was certainly beautiful stuff, & it was certainly instructive to watch the way in which Joe H. called in Walter Nash to disorganise the whole Govt Printer's works to have the job given top priority. You can do things in the govt all right if you can make enough noise & go to the right people – & if the matter is trivial enough.[74]

Heenan thought the bindings 'marvellously done' and John's designs, simple linear patterns done in gold, 'admirable'.[75] They failed to reach Washington in time for Fraser to present them but were still well received.

Public relations at a very different level inspired the 36-page booklet *Meet New Zealand,* produced by the branch to explain some of the mysteries of New Zealand to the 50,000 American servicemen who arrived in the country from mid-1942. Heenan believed it created 'something in the nature of a sensation' with its descriptions of New Zealanders' drinking customs, road rules and work habits.[76] Rereading the booklet now leaves one a little sceptical about Heenan's enthusiasm.

The same year the branch produced a commemorative booklet to mark the tercentenary of Abel Tasman's voyage. John suggested that Allen Curnow be commissioned to write a poem for the volume (he judged Curnow's poetry 'about the best stuff turned out in NZ'[77]), 'length to be agreed, intelligibility to be a pre-requisite, and editor to have power of rejection'.[78] The result was one of Curnow's best-known poems, 'Landfall in Unknown Seas', with its striking opening lines: 'Simply by sailing in a new direction/you could enlarge the world'; while its sobering reference in the last line to 'The stain of blood that writes an island story' introduced a new note into a celebratory occasion.* John contributed an introductory essay on 'The place of Tasman's voyage in history'. In a way a reworking of material from *The Exploration of the Pacific* and *The Discovery of New Zealand,* it was a fresh and vigorous piece of writing, beginning with a wonderful sweep across Europe in the seventeenth century and then narrowing in focus to the Netherlands, the Dutch East India Company and its voyages and, finally, to Tasman and his voyage with the *Heemskerck* and the *Zeehaen.* The volume was completed by a new translation of that part of Tasman's journal covering his time on the New Zealand coast. John told Heenan that he had 'one or two fancy ideas floating around in my mind, involving a severely limited edition on Dutch hand-made paper', and 100 of

---

*   The poem was included in Curnow's *Sailing or Drowning* (1943). John, reviewing the volume in the *New Zealand Listener* (3 March 1944, p.10), said the poem 'gives exhilaration both to our history and to our literature'.

the 1000 printed were on handmade paper (the Treasury raised no objection to releasing Australian funds up to a limit of £3 to pay for suitable paper, available in Sydney) and a number leather-bound with a gold linear decoration similar to John's design for *Making New Zealand*. Printed by Whitcombe and Tombs in Christchurch in 14 pt Monotype Aldine Bembo type, the volume was illustrated with coastal views taken mainly from J.E. Heeres's facsimile edition of the journal. Each section begins with a striking hanging capital letter (printed in red) designed by Janet Wilkinson, who worked closely with John on the volume.* Heenan thought it 'the best bit of book production we have yet achieved',[79] and a recent scholar agreed, calling it 'Heenan and Beaglehole's finest collaboration',[80] though Denis Glover was not impressed at the time: 'I can't honestly say I find that kind of typography is my piece of cake, but there are points on which one may meditate'.[81]

The Curnow commission had a further happy outcome. Curnow wrote to John to say that Douglas Lilburn was 'keen on the idea of writing some music for strings round the Tasman poem' and asking if he could get backing for its performance. 'It would have to be 2YA in fairness to Lilburn. He has had his music badly hashed by the local strings here' in Christchurch.[82] John took it up with Heenan, Heenan with the Director of Broadcasting, James Shelley, and the music was broadcast by 2YA on 13 December 1942. The Broadcasting Service string orchestra was conducted by Andersen Tyrer; the poem was read by a young Wellington lawyer, A. Eaton Hurley.

There were other ideas to mark the tercentenary: the establishment of the Abel Tasman National Park, and a memorial in Golden Bay close to the spot where Tasman first anchored in New Zealand waters. John was wary. The plans for the centennial had included marking Cook's principal landing sites. We have seen how John reacted to the memorial at Ship Cove. A year later, after he and Elsie had seen the East Coast anchorages, he wrote again on marking historic spots:

A material monument must be conceived not merely as an act of piety, and therefore praiseworthy in itself, but as an addition to the landscape . . . it should therefore above all be in key with the landscape, as well

---

*   To mark their collaboration he gave her the two volumes of the 1927 printing of Daniel Berkeley Updike's *Printing Types: Their History Forms and Use: A Study in Survivals* (Cambridge Mass.: Harvard University Press); a little later he bought himself the new edition.

as reflect the simplicity and solidity of Cook's own character . . .
My opinion remains that for the purpose of memorial nothing could
more effectually serve than to keep these lovely bays as unchanged as
possible.[83]

On John's suggestion Paul Pascoe, the Christchurch architect,
designed a simple granite cairn to which a plaque could be attached.
Government funding was approved, but with the war the plans
barely got under way. The only memorial erected was at Kopu bridge,
marking a spot near which Joseph Banks and Daniel Solander landed
while exploring the river Thames in the *Endeavour*'s boats. The job
was left to Public Works Department workmen with instructions to
have it ready to be unveiled on the anniversary of the landing and
to keep costs down. When John saw a photograph of the unveiling
in the *Auckland Weekly News* he was horrified. The 'monument
bore little resemblance to the original Paul Pascoe design; it was an
aesthetic disaster'.[84]

Mr Heenan
This grotesque outrage is the essence & summation of all we have been
struggling against ever since this matter of memorials came up for
consideration. It would be difficult to imagine anything 9 ft high which
more completely ignored Pascoe's design. I have delayed commenting for
some days because I have wished to employ only scrupulously moderate
language. It is very disheartening indeed.
J.C. Beaglehole
12.xii.41[85,*]

When the Tasman memorial was proposed in Golden Bay, John
took a very close and continuing interest. The site, on a hillock between
Tarakohe and Ligar Bay,[†] was selected by him and Ernst Plischke,[86]
who had been chosen to design the monument, as the nearest point of
vantage to Tasman's anchorage.[‡] The structure was very simple: a tall,
slender concrete obelisk and next to it an inscribed marble slab. This
time James Fletcher was called in by the Prime Minister to build it on
time for the anniversary. John wrote the inscription; Janet traced the

---

*   John first saw the memorial twenty-five years later when he and Elsie
       were driving to Coromandel: 'all the rage & despair I felt in the Historical
       Branch rushed up at me again'. (JCB to JEP, 21 December 1966.)

†   The site with its surrounding land was given to the dominion by its owners,
       the Golden Bay Cement Company.

‡   Grahame Anderson has shown that John and Plischke did not get the spot
       quite right. (Grahame Anderson, *The Merchant of the Zeehaen: Isaac
       Gilsemans and the Voyages of Abel Tasman* (Wellington: Te Papa Press,
       2001), pp.93–8.)

lettering for it from the Gill alphabet onto the stonemason's plaque. The memorial made, in John's words, 'no attempt to compete with the magnificent and dramatic qualities of the coast on either side; rather it draws down and concentrates into its austere structure of white concrete and local stone the tremendous vertical lines of the cliffs past which one comes to approach it, and the horizontal lines of the great outcrops of limestone in the massive rise which backs it'.[87],* John was there when the memorial was unveiled on 18 December. The following day wind and heavy rain prevented the party from getting to Torrent Bay for the planned opening of the national park, and the ceremony had to be held at Kaiteriteri.

Once the Tasman booklet was finished work started on a handbook on New Zealand, intended as publicity material for the newly opened diplomatic office in Washington.[88] When it appeared in 1945, *Introduction to New Zealand* was quite unlike any previous official publication. It includes much of the statistical data one would expect in an official publication such as a yearbook, but it is accompanied by a text that is not only full of information but often positively engaging. Much of the text was drafted by Nan Taylor, though John was responsible for the whole. The tone is set in the foreword, which is unmistakably his work:

Here is a book about New Zealand. It is not, we hope, a superfluous book, or a vainglorious book, or a flowery book, or a contentious book. It aims at plain and modest statement. Nowhere in these pages will you find New Zealand confused with Paradise. We don't make absurd claims for our country. It is a little country. It is a young country; in terms of Western culture, it is no older than the states of Iowa or Wisconsin. But it is, we think, an interesting country . . . It is like America. It is unlike America. It grows things. It makes things. It conserves and it wastes things. It has party conflicts. It assails itself. It admires itself. It tries to learn through experience. It is noisy. It is subdued. It is the usual bundle of contradictions that make up a democratic society. It has a certain unity. We think it is a beautiful country. We don't say that it is more interesting or more beautiful than the United States. We don't want to seem conceited; but we don't want to be too absurdly humble either. And as we think our country is beautiful and interesting, and as we have

---

*   At some later date the marble slab was repositioned so that it rests vertically on one of its sides, quite altering the original design. John and Elsie saw it in 1967 and he wrote gloomily to Janet: 'The Tasman inscription has been reset by an unskilled hand – Oh God, some of the letters – & the table all upended & the pavement all irregularly sunk & unlooked after . . . but it still looks good from a distance. Don't you ever go & look at it again.' (JCB to JEP, 6 March 1967.)

written this book in answer to suggestions from our American friends, we think Americans will probably be interested in it.

The voice, with its echoes of Whitman, carries through in the introductions to each of the eleven sections which make up the volume. The eighth, introducing 'Manly and Womanly Sports', begins: 'Sing, muse! of mightiest deeds of heroes, and of the sons and daughters of heroes, locked in grim struggle on the field of sport! But sing also of our ordinary selves at play. Of how we leap and run and propel balls. Of how we ascend great mountains and plunge gladly into the waves of ocean, or glide in boats upon the deep . . .' John was a master of the ironic baroque; at times, perhaps, it came a little too easily.

The account of New Zealand history reflects his interest in both the differences from and similarities to America's experience as well as the volume's intended readership. It is also very different from the history portrayed a decade earlier in his *New Zealand: A Short History*. There is a greater appreciation of the part played by the Maori, 'who had done much of the work of colonisation' and had 'been the basis in fact of early colonial agriculture and trade and prosperity'. The meeting of two races and two cultures, he wrote, did result for the time being in a tragic mess, but 'the tragedy was by no means final'. This section, indeed the volume as a whole, suggest the extent to which he was growing to appreciate the complexities and character of New Zealand.

The design of the book more than matched the exuberance of the text; its intended purpose gave John the opportunity to break out from the rather restrained elegance of much of his earlier work and to try out all sorts of bright ideas. The typefaces were still the distinguished traditional ones that he had battled hard for but were now used with more variety and imagination. To succeed as a piece of publicity the book had to attract readers, but it is not pushing conjecture too hard to suggest that John planned it, as a physical object, to exemplify that adaptation of a tradition, which he valued, into something distinctively New Zealand. A number of artists were used for drawings and decorations in the text (many of them John had already encouraged the School Publications Branch to use to illustrate the *School Journal*): George Woods, a polished draughtsman and illustrator with a strong decorative sense, who did most of the drawings, and Nancy Bolton,* who, among other jobs,

---

* Nancy Bolton was married to Robert Parker, John's colleague at Victoria College.

had illustrated *The Book of Wiremu* by Stella Morice, a children's book that John had designed for the Progressive Publishing Society in 1944. The cartoonist A.S. Paterson, John's cousin, illustrated the sections on sport, and two of Mervyn Taylor's wood engravings were also used. Many of the headings were printed over a background monochrome image, sometimes of an appropriate object, often adaptations of koru designs. Photographs, most of them by John Pascoe, illustrate the land and the people, and there are also photographs of a number of New Zealand paintings, from Charles Heaphy to T.A. McCormack, M.T. (Toss) Woollaston and Rita Cook (later Angus).

Seeing the volume through the press took much of 1945 and there was a final delay of some months at the beginning of the following year in producing a map, although it is not clear whether this was finally included. There were frequent visits to Whitcombe and Tombs and constant conferring with artists (John found George Woods difficult to pin down and get work out of), and production was not helped by the almost proprietorial interest taken by Walter Nash. The volume was extremely well received in the United States. Two years later, with stocks dwindling, an embassy officer in Washington wrote: 'Without the slightest hesitation I can tell you that I think the book was, and is, the very best publicity material that has been released in this country by any nation in the world'.[89] The possibility of an English edition was discussed but nothing came of it. The book was not released to the public in New Zealand and the final copies were distributed to those who enrolled for the Pacific Science Congress held in Auckland in January 1949.

From the time when the centennial publications were being planned, Heenan had enthusiastically shared and backed John's determination to have them and later departmental publications well designed and well printed. His own interest in typography was long standing and with his support the branch built up a library of reference works. He was a great peruser of booksellers' and publishers' catalogues, asking Dick Campbell in London to keep an eye out for any prospectuses from 'the Golden Cockerel or any other private Press that may still be functioning', adding that we, 'and when I say "we", I mean J.C. Beaglehole, Janet Wilkinson and myself',[90] were particularly interested in these as specimens of good typography. An earlier Golden Cockerel Press prospectus had announced the publication of *A Voyage Round the World with Captain James Cook in H.M.S. Resolution* by Anders Sparrman. Heenan thought it would be just the thing to give John to mark his 'admiration for all that he has done for this Department over the past six years'.[91] Campbell discovered that the book had been over-subscribed before it appeared, but managed to winkle a copy out of the press and sent it out in the diplomatic bag. Heenan reported its reception:

I asked Beaglehole to come in in the course of his morning visit to us and sprung the whole thing on him suddenly. It would hardly be correct to say that J.C.B. is a sentimental bloke, but he definitely is an emotional person, and the little gift rocked him right back on his heels . . . The measly £350 a year we pay him represents only a fraction of his worth to us over the past six years. He has placed New Zealand on the typographical map, and our departmental standard of book production has earned a mild form at least of world fame.[92]

IN MUCH OF THE WORK being done Heenan sang the praises of the 'Beaglehole–Wilkinson combination': 'as a typographer she is, today in New Zealand, one in a class with Beaglehole himself and a few others of consequence not overlooking Denis Glover'.[93] John and Janet worked closely together and he clearly delighted in having a colleague with whom he could discuss the finer points of printing and book design and plot their joint offensives against the Government Printer. She was also extremely well read and articulate. Did she in her intellectual gifts remind John, perhaps, of Helen Allen? At some stage she and John began an affair.

These were the war years, Janet had had no close men friends, and the few with whom she had had even a slight acquaintance were soon in the armed forces and overseas.[94] She had joined a small friendly group of students, almost all women, enrolled for history honours, where they had got to know Fred Wood and John more personally. Both of them were interested in and concerned about students and invited them to their homes, where they also got to know Elsie and Joan Wood and their circles of friends. Both men epitomised a lifestyle and values that fascinated the young. Moving to the Historical Branch brought Janet and John more closely together. She responded to the affectionate and at times bantering manner he had with young women. He fell for her completely.

From the days of his courtship of Elsie, John had pitched his affections at a level of intensity that she, with her less demonstrative nature, found difficult to match. Elsie was an extremely able woman: a founding member and early president of the Family Planning

Association, the first woman member of the Karori School Committee, later a Justice of the Peace, with much more voluntary work in the years ahead. She read widely, mainly contemporary fiction, and shared many of John's interests in the arts, but her interest was not historical or theoretical; she would not have read Herbert Read or Berenson or Gombrich. In their early days together she was inclined to depreciate her own ability (not helped by John's mocking of what he claimed was her background of bridge and tennis parties) and she never saw herself as an intellectual. At the same time she could be forthright, practical and down to earth. Her views of John's book buying when she believed there were more pressing needs, which went back to their student days, became something of a family joke but at its heart it may epitomise a difference of values between them. For John, like his father, books (and, for John, music) were at the very heart of civilised life; for Elsie they were part but only a part of it. After twelve years of marriage they were both probably settling a little into their own ways. John did much of his work at home, but he kept it to his study and talked very little about it either to Elsie or, later, to his children. Elsie, for her part, was always concerned to support him in his work and, taking on the role of women of her time, became remarkably good at organising and running the home and family and shielding John from interruptions.

To John, his relationship with Janet was clearly enormously important: for a time they were deeply in love (and a part of John was in love with her for the rest of his life), but he made it clear to Janet that he was not going to leave Elsie for her. These were, in a sense, parallel relationships, with Janet at the centre of one of John's worlds, that of books and printing and literature, while Elsie remained the centre of another world, that of home and family, Victoria College, and a wide circle of friends. He brought her a bunch of red roses every anniversary of their wedding. Although it may now seem extraordinary, my brothers and I had no idea of the situation – indeed, I learned of it only after I began work on this biography. This may say something about a child's lack of perception or self-preoccupation (I was nine or ten at the time), or it may be testimony to Elsie and John's determination to keep their marriage and the family intact. Looking back now, my memories of those years are of family activities, of farm holidays, of school days, with no sense of imminent crisis. How Elsie and John worked it out we can only conjecture. It says an enormous amount for her forbearance and her strength, and for their underlying loyalty and unshakeable commitment to each other, that they stayed together.

My impression is that not many people at the time were aware of the relationship. It was to continue until Janet married Blackwood Paul in April 1945.* For a wedding present John gave them a copy of John Milton's poems with illustrations by William Blake, published by the Nonesuch Press in 1926. He found it very difficult to let her go. During the time she was on her honeymoon he wrote a daily diary for her – a strange gift to someone just beginning her marriage. He at least half-recognised this when he wrote at the beginning that she should perhaps destroy it without reading it. It was thirty-five pages, a mixture of the most intimate expressions of longing for her, of hopes for her happiness, and detailed accounts of each day, with a great deal about the production of *Introduction to New Zealand* and other printing jobs he was involved in. After Janet and Blackwood moved to Hamilton they added publishing (as Paul's Book Arcade and, later, Blackwood and Janet Paul) to the business of bookselling, and Janet had full scope for her exceptional skill as a book designer. John wrote to her regularly, for long periods almost every week: at other times, especially if he was travelling, much less frequently. His deeply affectionate letters, about 500 in all, are full of news about books and printing, art and music, family, friends, and what was happening in Wellington, and form a remarkable record of friendship and of the last twenty-five years of John's life. However, reading them through reminded me of just how much letters were, for him, always something of a literary artifice, of how far, once started or when his emotions were involved, his pen could carry him away. Janet became, and remained, a friend of the whole family, coming to stay on numerous occasions. Elsie, while despairing of Janet's lack of practicality, enjoyed her company and lent her a helping hand when she needed it, and would do so until the end of her life.

IN THE MID-1940S JOHN must have felt almost overwhelmed by questions of typography and book design and seeing volumes through the press. In 1943 the branch had brought out *The Price of Citizenship* by Apirana Ngata, a tribute to the gallant service of the Maori Battalion and especially to that of Lieutenant Moana-nui-

---

*   As a student in Auckland, Blackwood had been part of the group around *Phoenix*. He had subsequently run the family bookshop in Hamilton, Paul's Book Arcade. The war brought him to Wellington as part of the army education and welfare service, and he met Janet through their common involvement in the Progressive Publishing Society.

a-kiwa Ngarimu, killed in action and awarded the Victoria Cross. Ngata inscribed a copy for John:

You, I know have understood the spirit of Polynesia, even as reflected in the cooler environment of Aotearoa under cover of a modern mufti.

Among the other volumes he saw through the press for the department were K.B. Cumberland's *Soil Erosion in New Zealand* (1944), and Ernst Plischke's *Design and Living* (1947), a persuasive introduction to modernist ideas based on material Plischke had prepared for the army education and welfare service. These were followed by G. Leslie Adkin's major study, *Horowhenua: Its Maori Place-names and Their Topographic and Historical Background*. This proved a protracted undertaking of which there is a fascinating account in Anthony Dreaver's biography of Adkin.[95] Publication of his exhaustive work by the Polynesian Society, which Adkin had expected, was caught up in an intense controversy over the spelling and capitalisation of Maori names, in which Adkin was in heated opposition to Johannes Andersen, the editor of the society's *Journal*. In May 1944 J.W. Butcher, a tramping friend of Adkin's who worked in the Statistics Department and knew both Heenan and John, suggested approaching them with his manuscript. Adkin took it in to show John, and later described in his diary the 'warm welcome' he was given:

I laid myself out to impress [Beaglehole] with its authenticity & value, & when he saw the maps and drawings, he seemed quite convinced and decided to push for publication . . . JWB[utcher] had informed me of the process involved: first Dr. B intimates his approval of the material to Mr Heenan; Mr Heenan then recommends publication to Minister of Internal Affairs (Mr Parry); Mr P then submits the matter to Cabinet. If Cabinet sanctions publication, the Publication Board, of whom JWB is a member, proceeds to authorize the printing. The question of the spelling of Maori place-names & of the use of caps. in geographical and other terms . . . came up & I was pleased to find that Dr Beaglehole considers Andersen's rules 'preposterous' in most cases and had told the Poly. Soc. so when they applied to the Dept. for a ruling, following on my objections & the subsequent controversy.[96]

John was impressed with the work, 'a model . . . of its kind', and wished 'it could be paralleled for every other part of New Zealand where there is a like richness of Maori remains'.[97] His initial plan was to persuade the Polynesian Society's council to publish the book with the aid of a government subsidy, though the Historical Branch would have total editorial control. He got a quote from Whitcombe and Tombs in Christchurch: £1000 for 750 copies. The Polynesian Society had pledged £300. With the government baulking at the remaining £700, the society suggested that he was insisting on too extravagant a design and that the printers they normally used in New Plymouth, Avery's, would do the job for £650–700. John stood his ground: 'Avery's were just not skilled enough, nor did they possess adequate bold or italic typefaces; and a good clear type giving 500 words to the page was essential'.[98] Adkin got his friends to lobby Parry. In May 1946 the government approved going ahead using Whitcombe and Tombs (at the same time also approving Plischke's book and Roger Duff's *The Moa-Hunter Period of New Zealand History)* and the book, published by the department and distributed by the Polynesian Society, finally appeared in December 1948. The author's impatience, Dreaver writes, 'was moderated by the charm and courtesy of Beaglehole'.[99] Plischke's book had appeared the year before. *The Coming of the Maori* by Te Rangi Hiroa (Sir Peter Buck) came out in 1949 and Duff's volume a year later.

In 1945 John designed and saw through the press Downie Stewart's little book *Portrait of a Judge,* a memoir of Sir Joshua Strange Williams, whom Stewart had greatly admired when he was a young Dunedin lawyer. John's letters to the elderly Stewart,[100] gentle and respectful, give a glimpse of how he approached such a task. John had made it clear that he was doing the job in his private capacity and Stewart was worried that he would not accept any reward. John was firm: 'I've had my fun . . . & after all, I've had the pleasure of playing around with your money. You're the only Elder Statesman who's let me do that.'[101]

The branch was also called on for many small printing jobs, often for special occasions, which could present interesting problems that John relished. He designed a service sheet for the memorial service to Brigadier James Hargest, member of parliament, soldier and writer,* killed in action on 12 August 1944, and an 'elegant order of service'[102] for the funeral of Janet Fraser, the wife of the Prime Minister, in August 1945. His first reaction on hearing of President Roosevelt's death was that Heenan would want something printed in an impossibly short time, but the fear proved groundless. His tasks extended to other questions of design: 'Peter Fraser has got me designing a war-medal now [John reported to Janet], and I have got M[ervyn] T[aylor] drawing it. When I say designing, I mean that

---

*   Hargest's book, *Farewell Campo 12* (1946), is a classic account of his escape from incarceration as a prisoner-of-war in Italy.

Cabinet says it doesn't like the Army's idea, what Cabinet wants is a fern-leaf like on the All Blacks' jersey, & Peter asks me to arrange it accordingly.'[103]

In 1944 the Department of External Affairs, acting on Fraser's belief that New Zealanders should be interested and well informed about the world outside, inaugurated a series of publications beginning with the Australian–New Zealand Agreement signed on 21 January. Frank Corner, who had joined the department the previous year (strictly, he had joined the Prime Minister's Department, as External Affairs came into being only later in 1943), persuaded John to advise on the typography. The Government Printer had at last acquired some new typefaces. John even produced a simplified and more modern version of the New Zealand Coat of Arms, which fitted more naturally with the new typefaces. 'The result', Corner writes, 'was so good that in due course the style devised for the Department's series was adopted for Parliamentary publications.'[104]

Meanwhile John continued his typographical work for the Council for Educational Research, treating each annual report as a discrete exercise in design, while the research series through the 1940s carried his characteristic printed label pasted on the spine (one of the techniques he had picked up from Francis Meynell, the publisher and director of the Nonesuch Press). He also redesigned the Victoria College *Calendar,* and later the college's letterhead and its degree certificates. He arranged for the artist and engraver Mervyn Taylor to redesign the college coat of arms and heraldic crest. When the Chamber Music Society began he designed its programmes, as he had those for the Nimmo's hall concerts that preceded its formation.

John's interest in printing and publishing did not flag in spite of the frustration which seemed inescapable at that time. Wartime paper shortages continued. The New Zealand industry in general still lacked the skills and equipment to do first-class work. The Government Printing Office seemed as bad as ever. John had good relations with Whitcombe and Tombs, especially with Lance Davison in Christchurch, but even with them he felt he needed to be watching closely to be sure of getting the results he wanted. Nor was this a guarantee of success. When Whitcombe's in Wellington were producing *The University and the Community,* the 1946 festschrift for Hunter, there was a problem with the binding. They rang John up 'in such a tone of agony that I thought the factory must have burnt down. I did some mild complaining. Well, said Athea, the fact is, if we know it is a Beaglehole job we get so nervous the whole bloody thing goes wrong.'[105]

Nor did ministerial involvement in the work of the branch make for efficiency. Each volume had to have ministerial approval. Heenan's way with Fraser and Nash certainly enabled things to be done that otherwise might not have been done, but there was a price to be paid. Nash's close interest in *Introduction to New Zealand* did not hasten its production. When John reported to Janet that Plischke's book was out, he continued: 'Of course Peter Fraser doesn't like the binding, or the lettering, or the colour, or the title, but who cares? At least McIntosh got him to agree to a price, 6/- paper 10/6 cloth, a decision which Joe was too weak & tired to make on the one day he was in town. Oh send it to the PM, he said wearily about the memorandum.'[106]

Heenan was due to retire from the Department of Internal Affairs in 1949 but he effectively handed over to his successor the year before when he was appointed manager of the 1949 Royal Tour. He made a two-month visit to England, via the United States, for discussions with Buckingham Palace, and while he was in London he met with the secretary of the Hakluyt Society and committed the New Zealand government to a grant of £3000 to help with the costs of producing the Cook volumes. It was his first trip out of New Zealand. He met a wide range of people, some of whom he had corresponded with for many years, and he returned with a new fund of stories. 'Well', John said to him, 'do you still have the common touch? Too right, he said. But I knew', John wrote, 'that corruption had set in, or he would have said Too bloody right.'[107] To Heenan's relief, as it turned out, the tour did not take place, and one of his final actions was to write formally to Peter Fraser recommending that, when John went to Britain on his forthcoming refresher leave, he should be given leave on full pay from the branch* and an additional grant towards his expenses. Heenan confessed that it was a mystery to him how John had managed both his jobs and 'a tribute to his genius that he has been able to combine the two offices with complete satisfaction' to both his employers. 'At no time', Heenan continued, 'has he ever been paid by us in a manner commensurate with the worth of his work to the Government and to the country'.

---

*   When John was first appointed he was paid £300 per annum, which was subsequently increased to £350. Following his appointment by Victoria to the research fellowship it was reduced to £175. The additional grant, which the government approved, was £500.

John, he stated, 'had made an indelible mark on the standard of printing in New Zealand' while his work for the Hakluyt Society would be itself 'work for New Zealand'.[108] John, for his part, wrote to Heenan from Auckland before the ship sailed, taking advantage of the fact that Heenan could not interrupt him to say how much he had valued working under him, in 'an atmosphere that few other heads of departments can ever have created', and how he had valued doing the things that Heenan had made it possible for him to do.[109] He recognised that it was the end of a chapter, but hoped that, if there was ever a ceremony to celebrate the production of the first map of the historical atlas, they should both be there.

This was not to be.[110] Although during the war work on the atlas had never stopped, for some time the number of staff involved was down to one. However, after he came out of the army, Bob Burnett resumed his position as secretary of the atlas in March 1946, and one or two new young graduates were recruited as research assistants. It had become clear that a good deal of the early work, hurried over, had not been done well enough, and had to be checked, updated or redone. To this Burnett, in John's view 'born for the job', brought the most meticulous scholarship (as had Ruth Ross in her time) but, looking back, one wonders if he had the temperament to push the project through. By 1948 the point had been reached where a great deal of preliminary drafting was necessary. But at that time the Lands and Survey Department (with whom the atlas had from first planning been a joint project) was suffering from both a grave shortage of staff and great demands for its services. Although it promised to get on with the work, the drafting of historical maps was never given sufficient priority and nothing was done. There was also one series of maps, on the economy, for which the research remained to be done, and it was proving extraordinarily difficult to get people with the right qualifications to do it. In spite of these difficulties, John went off on leave still expecting that the job would continue to completion. He visited the British Ordnance Survey to seek advice on technical questions about paper, drafting and inks, but the report he sent back to Internal Affairs was not acknowledged.

While he was away there was a general election and a change of government. The National Party came to power determined to cut government expenditure, 'especially on such fancy luxuries as education and culture'.[111] And in Internal Affairs they had a willing accomplice in G.H. O'Halloran, the assistant under-secretary, who took the atlas within his province. To save money and because government historical work was no longer regarded as desirable, with the possible exception of the work being done by the War History Branch under Sir Howard Kippenberger, it was decided to end work on the atlas project. It was saved at that point only by the Public Service Commission, which insisted that nothing should be done until John got back to New Zealand and had been consulted, but essentially the die was cast. He arrived home in July 1950 and from then until the end of 1951 did his best to ensure that the work would be completed. Shortly after John's return Burnett, 'goaded by pin-pricks and insults to despair', resigned from the public service and took a job in an insurance office. A little later Nan Taylor, too, left the Branch. Work on the atlas virtually ceased.

John's memoranda, reports and meetings, his argument that 'so much work has been done that it would be tragic now to leave it unfinished',[112] if they achieved anything, simply put back the final decision. Some time after a meeting with the minister, W.A. Bodkin, he wrote to him to ask once again if any decision had been reached: 'You will remember that you said you would discuss it with some of your colleagues, and see if you could put in a united recommendation to Cabinet'.[113] The reply, two and a half months later, said nothing about the atlas but told him that the 'present arrangement' concerning his engagement would be terminated from the end of the month.[114] John's immediate reaction was regret that he had not got in first. He thanked the minister for 'releasing' him 'from a disagreeable and embarrassing situation', and continued:

I had already come to the conclusion that if the Government were not going on with the Historical Atlas, then there was no justification for my remaining connected with the Department, and I was on the point of resigning the rather indeterminate post I have held. I should be still glad if you would consider my resignation immediate – i.e., as from the date of this letter.[115]

As for the atlas, he was eventually told, in terms of pure formula, that it was hoped to complete it ultimately, 'probably in a modified form'.[116] The head of the department told him privately that he was quite certain nothing further would be done. Before giving up completely John approached the Carnegie Corporation. If they provided the money and the government made available all the material, Victoria College might be persuaded to take over the responsibility for the work, which could be housed in the History Department. He would need sufficient funds for two research workers for two years and perhaps £30,000 for the costs of producing 5000 copies of the maps (by this time he was thinking of a box of maps and letterpress rather than a bound volume). Nothing came of the proposal.

Joe Heenan had always recognised that the work of the Historical Branch, together with his other schemes for supporting the arts, depended very largely on the continuation of the Labour government in office, as 'the re-acquisition of a true-blue farmers' Government would, I fear, write finis to this particular chapter'.[117] The Historical Branch of the 1940s, carrying out work for which the new government had little understanding, and run in a way (if 'run' is the right word) which made it an easy target for an unsympathetic public servant on the make – 'the enemy of everything Joe Heenan stood for and had done'[118] – could not survive. Nor could the individual style that Heenan had brought to the patronage of the arts survive him – the times were changing as well as the government – but the way in which the atlas was brought to an end left John feeling exceedingly bitter. Not long before he received the minister's letter sacking him, he wrote to Janet: 'Cook continues to be a great comfort when things go wrong, & people don't write to me, & Bob resigns, & Mr O'Halloran weaves his plots. And in the interstices of life I manage to read a bit. I have nearly finished Ivor Brown's Shakespeare . . .'[119]

10

PUBLIC LIFE, BOOKS, MUSIC AND ART, 1936–50

IN WRITING *NEW ZEALAND: A Short History* John revealed an interest in the ways in which life in New Zealand was shaped not simply by the nature of expanding British capitalism but also by the isolation and hostility of the land. It was an interest he shared with a number of the poets of the time, especially Charles Brasch and Allen Curnow. Curnow prefaced his book *Not in Narrow Seas* (1939), an exploration of this theme, with four brief extracts from John's *Short History*, among them, tellingly: 'in the midst of converging cables, shipping and wireless communication, it has remained always isolated; and in that verdant isolation perhaps lies the remote secret – if there is one – of the national life'. John favourably reviewed the collection in the *Press,* 'a warm and welcoming notice by a man whose intellect one deeply respected', Curnow was later to describe it.[1] His next collection, *Island and Time* (1941), again showed John's influence. In his notes Curnow 'mentions *The Exploration of the Pacific,* but the *Short History* is also evident'.[2] John, for his part, once again reviewed the volume warmly, as deserving 'the attention of everybody interested in poetry, or the poet's mind, or the mind of our country':

He does in fact show us the spectacle of a poet and a highly intelligent man approaching and rendering New Zealand and the history of New Zealand really imaginatively, with strength and with pity. Nothing like his 'Unhistoric Story' or 'A Victim' or 'House and Land' has, as far as I know, ever been done here before. And it is not perhaps too lavish praise to suggest that as Mr Curnow finds himself we may find ourselves.[3]

In his study of New Zealand literary culture in those years Lawrence Jones argues that the writers he focuses on – Curnow, Brasch, Glover and Fairburn, with Mason and Cresswell lighting the way – were attacking the familiar myths that New Zealanders lived by: pioneering families building a pastoral arcadia while sustained by the values of an idealised Britain. In its place the poets were constructing an 'anti-myth' with a number of elements: the relation to the land, to history, to the Maori, to England, to puritanism. It was, in its way, their contribution to the centennial. That anti-myth, Jones writes, 'was aimed at removing a false consciousness, to clear the slate for a true consciousness on which a genuine New Zealand culture could be built'.[4] John echoed their aim in his 'Centennial Meditations' in *Spike* when he wrote that a genuine 'national culture' could 'only come from the free intelligence working on its environment and its history'.[5] The poets did not get very far on just what that 'national culture' might be – though Glover was clearly at one with John in holding that decent printing was part of it – as they recognised more clearly what they were against than what they would put in its place. 'Probably necessarily', Jones writes, 'their expressed sense of any positive hopes was less specific and usually metaphorical'.[6] For John it was very different. We have seen his response when Heenan sought his ideas on the future role of the Centennial Branch. While he did not often talk in terms of 'national culture', in the late 1930s and the 1940s he not only established a place as a critic in the arts but, adding to his activities in the Historical Branch, he was directly involved in a number of initiatives to do with books, reading, music and the visual arts that he believed would make New Zealand a better place to be. It was, perhaps, not surprising that, when in 1949–50 he revisited England for the first time since he had left in 1929, he came to realise that he was first and foremost a New Zealander.

Towards the end of 1938 he was one of the group who began the Wellington Co-operative Book Society as a way of raising capital to start a new bookshop. Such societies were very much a part of the Popular Front politics of the late 30s – the short-lived attempt by the parties of the left to work together against the Nazi threat, an attempt bedevilled by internal divisions and ended by the Hitler–Stalin pact of August 1939. Auckland's Progressive Books was the first such bookshop, opened in 1936 by Jack and Doris Basham; a Christchurch shop with the same name followed the next year. The initiative for the Wellington shop came from Bart Fortune, who had left Victoria College in 1933 after his experience editing *Student* with the desire to 'get down to working class level',[7] and had briefly run the International Bookshop that sold, or sought to sell, mainly Marxist material.* It went bankrupt in 1934. Fortune joined the

---

*   Bart Fortune and the International Bookshop were the subject of
      correspondence between the British Security Service and the New Zealand
      Police. The director of the British service (Colonel Sir Vernon Kell) wrote
      (26 April 1938) that 'A new shop is to be established which will be "generally

Communist Party in 1935. With the new shop he wanted 'to draw together people of liberal and leftist persuasion, irrespective of party affiliation, to create a body of opinion in opposition to the trend towards fascism and war'.[8] W.B. Sutch, whom Fortune looked to to draw in the intellectual liberal left, chaired the inaugural meeting on 28 November 1938.

The society's aims, less overtly political and distinctly high-minded, were adopted at the meeting on the motion of John and Walter Scott, who was greatly influenced by the Cambridge critic F.R. Leavis:

Recognising the difficulty of training and preserving a sound judgement of literature and art in a world in which so much of it has been debased for profit, the members of the Society look to their Bookshop to help them and the public generally to this end; they regard it as a means of developing the critical intelligence that the understanding and treatment of human conditions today so urgently need.[9]

From the beginning, the Wellington shop would have less of a political emphasis than those in Auckland and Christchurch, though the balance was always controversial. In part this reflected differences among the three cities; the Wellington society had a higher proportion of academics, civil servants and professional people among its members and the majority of them were to show a greater interest in books than in political pamphlets.

The first meeting elected a management committee that included John, and when the committee met it made him president. He had already designed them a letterhead. A possible manager was in the offing. A young Londoner employed in the Westminster Bank, Roy Parsons, and his wife Nan, both members of the Fabian Society, had been attracted by what they had heard of New Zealand under the Labour government and were thinking of migrating to start a progressive bookshop. Roy was interested in the Wellington position. Indeed, Nan had already arrived in Wellington, where John and Elsie were among the first people she met.[10] A.G.B. Fisher, then in

---

progressive but non-sectarian", and will work in conjunction with an organisation called the Wellington Left Book Society', and he named John as one of its sponsors (along with a number of other 'prominent lefts'). The New Zealand Commissioner of Police, D.H. Cummings, in reply (21 June 1938) suggested that it was 'the intention of the Communist Party to conceal their identity with the shop in bringing it before the public', an odd suggestion because, even if they had wanted to conceal their identity, most of them were well known to the non-Party Left. (J.C. Beaglehole File. New Zealand Security Intelligence Service Papers.)

London, and Victor Gollancz were asked to report on Roy Parsons's suitability for the position. Fisher cabled 'Not bad', Gollancz 'Parsons suitable', and on that advice he was offered the job. He arrived at the end of May 1939; the shop (named Modern Books) opened shortly afterwards in the Dominion Farmers' Institute building in Featherston Street. Just over a year later it moved to Woodward Street.

An immediate difficulty facing the society was the government's restrictions on overseas funds. Responding to a letter from John asking for an import licence for £1000, Walter Nash had written, characteristically, 'as long as there are funds there will be no restriction on the issue of licences for books and medicine – both essential to the mind and body'.[11] The difficulties continued for some years, however, even though John met Nash several times to put the society's case. A second problem was the continuing lack of agreement about the shop's purpose. In July the committee, after discussion, had reiterated that 'it was necessary to preserve a balance between stocks appealing more especially to people of purely intellectual interests and those people whose interests lay primarily in left wing political publications'.[12] That did not settle the matter. The non-aggression pact between Hitler and Stalin, signed in August 1939, put an end to the Popular Front, and the controversy came to focus on the newly appointed manager. John reported on the shop's first six months in a letter to Richmond:

. . . we tried to mobilise both the Left & the intelligent book-buyer (I don't mean what that says); we sell both Lenin & Eric Gill's 25 Nudes & poetry & books on Cézanne etc & Left pamphlets & so on. I am president of the committee, on the score of being acceptable to both wings of our supporters – both a literary man & of approved political views! We're not doing badly on the whole, in spite of import licences (if we can't get one for 1940 we're sunk) & the war. I don't worry about the finance – I mean I worry about it but I make no attempt to understand it; my chief duty is to try & keep people sweet to & about one another & it isn't always easy . . . Our greatest current controversy is whether [Parsons] is the right bloke or not; & discussions which are supposed to be extremely confidential & in committee have a way of getting broadcast all over the place. God knows how – or at least I think I know how as well, but not so certainly as to stage a show-down. But I find some people extremely irritating in the virulence of their instinctive dislikes . . . Certainly . . . Parsons is a New Statesman sort of bloke rather than a die-hard Moscovian – & that is hard for some people to follow.[13]

The shop, however, made a good start. Christmas trade boomed.

They tried to build a stock of good children's books. The first book tokens were introduced to New Zealand – an elegant design by John with decorations from sixteenth-century French woodcuts. The society had a social committee chaired by Elizabeth (Gran) McGowan, a working-class stalwart who had joined the Communist Party in 1936, and the shop was the venue for meetings and lectures on literary and political topics.

John later confessed that he had become president of the management committee on the understanding that he was to be 'only a presiding officer; but [I] soon found I had to work damn hard, & have done so ever since', he wrote two years later. 'In fact we all have except the Left Wing/C.P. boys, who have talked a hell of a lot but done damn all beyond that. There are times when one becomes heartily sick of the C.P. – & even understands Mr Peter Fraser's feeling about it.'[14] The most talkative member of the left wing was R.F. Griffin, a publisher's representative and a communist since the 1920s, who had been expelled several times by the Party: 'a loquacious Irishman with strongly held opinions – turbulent, thorny but talented'.[15] He was a member of the management committee from 1938 to 1944. Fortune and Sutch both resigned from the committee within the shop's first year, but at the annual meeting in October 1940 they led the attack: 'after Dr Sutch, Dr Finlay [Martyn Finlay, later a Labour member of parliament], Mr Southworth and Mr Fortune had spoken criticising the bookshop and the management of the Society a motion was carried that future speakers be limited to 3 minutes'.[16]

John gave Richmond a long account of these happenings – 'the story of how I lost the confidence of the Left Wing, & part of the story of Uncle Scrim & of Bill Sutch & all sorts of other things' – though he added he could never tell it properly in less than 140 pages, and even then 'it would be but a bare & brief summary, so much are lengthy & analytical character sketches called for'.

. . . before very long we had two parties, the anti-Parsons, who regarded themselves as the sole representatives & patrons of the workers (Griffin, Sutch etc) – & the not exactly pro-Parsons, but pro-square deal, pro-original purpose of the shop, intelligent books in general & not just C.P. pamphlets & little Lenin Library. In other words I, for one, was not content just to be a stooge. The storm burst at the Annual General Meeting last year [October 1940] when the Left having insisted that all others were reactionaries, packed the meeting & had a lovely time getting their hatreds off their chest. Scrim was put up for the committee but didn't get on. I was accused of speaking in favour of censorship, because I had said that in a war I was afraid we must regard censorship as inevitable, & I was accused of organising a ticket & so forth. I got on to the committee again, & we had the devil's own job to keep Parsons from resigning (he is an excellent man on the financial side, by the way). However I was to be tolerated no longer as president; one Finlay, a new member, was immediately made president, & when he resigned on becoming Nordmeyer's private sec., Scrim came on & was made president, at once also. Well, the amusing thing is that Scrim has been a very good president of committee, has adopted precisely the attitude I always adopted in general (glaring differences of detail of course) & has been far more crudely rude to C.P. ideas than I ever thought of being.[17]

The wartime censorship, introduced by regulations on 1 September 1939, was not only a bone of contention in the society but a real practical difficulty in running the shop. The Controller of Censorship, who came under the prime minister, took a wide view of what was 'antagonistic to British ideals and of a subversive nature',[18] and customs officials detained a large amount of material. At first booksellers were not told what had been withheld and had no way of knowing why orders had not arrived. In July 1940 importers were told that books and periodicals deemed subversive would not be delivered and must not be purchased under import licences but at the same time they were refused a list of the proscribed works. Parcels were piling up in censorship offices. Walter Nash took charge and established an ad hoc and invisible advisory committee that included Alister McIntosh and John Reid (by now a private secretary to Nash). The committee's recommendations led to the immediate release of a number of publications, including the *New Statesman and Nation* and *New Republic*. From the booksellers' point of view, however, the situation remained exasperating. They repeatedly asked to be told what titles were proscribed; the censorship authorities, 'showing much skill in dodging questions',[19] avoided giving an answer.

At the society's annual meeting in 1940, at which John battled so royally, the incoming committee was instructed to work with trade unions and other bodies to mobilise opinion against the censorship. Parsons drafted a statement on the difficulties and anomalies in the system and suggested that the level of censorship in New Zealand should never exceed that in force in England. In forwarding a copy of this to Nash on 21 November,[20] John explained that the committee had preferred to 'go a bit more quietly for a start' and that the letter had 'been sent to a few Labour M.P.'s, four or five in all I think (none of the wild men) in the hope that the matter may be brought up in caucus in a reasonable way'.* There was little change. Even after Hitler's attack on the Soviet Union on 22 June 1941 and the Soviet Union's entry into the war as an ally (and the New Zealand Communist Party's reversal of its opposition to the war), works on communism or Soviet Russia were still treated with suspicion, as Peter Fraser remained wary of anything which might stir up 'undesirable feeling in the community when unity was all important'.[21] As the war moved on the forbidden list was shortened, and by the end of 1943 its contents were made known, in confidence, to 'responsible persons'. John, who had never liked censorship, recognised that there were circumstances in which it was inevitable but wanted it limited as far as possible and open to 'reasonable' discussion.

John felt that the annual meeting at the end of 1941 was similar to that held a year earlier:

Another nasty annual meeting last month; but as there was nothing for the Left to complain about, they invented things & refused to accept the committee's recommendation for a dividend (we had a profit of nearly £150). Bill Sutch acts as their main mouthpiece now – he is getting pretty intolerable, with an almost pathological need to talk. He has made a mess of his own job, P[eter] F[raser] hates & distrusts him (the feeling is returned) & yet he is too Lucifer-proud to take anything else. Awful psychological maladjustment which has become too too apparent. I just crawl on to the committee this time at the bottom of the list; meeting again packed & a C.P. ticket – the argument being that if Beaglehole organises a ticket & packs a meeting the workers have got to do it too in self-defence. And nothing will convince them that I am not a sinister sort of Algie-plus, going around organising this & that & generally behaving as a bloody reactionary. C.P. arguments against the shop – it sells too much poetry, art, expensive books, high-brow books, Virginia Woolf & such-like tripe, it's too pansy, Parsons is rude to the workers, he deliberately refuses to sell pamphlets, it isn't enthusiastic in the workers' cause, its site (Woodward St) is too near the Wgton Club. But every now & again will come a sort of startling unpremeditated admission that it's very well run, that it's sold far more left-wing stuff than the Christchurch shop with all its millions of pamphlets, that it really is not in league with the censor, & so on. Taking it all in all, we really have lived up pretty well to our United Front ambitions – & that is the root of the trouble. For a while the C.P. made things very difficult for us with the Govt – some fool reported to the Party last year that they had captured our

---

committee, the police of course got hold of the report, we had our import licence cut by more than half, & I had the devil of a job straightening things out again with Walter Nash. I didn't know the reason of course – I only found that out a few weeks ago. The conclusion I have come to is that the C.P. people are damned hard to work with – & that is putting it pretty mildly. But my God they can gas – particularly if they don't know what they're gassing about; & the atmosphere of petty & gratuitous intrigue in which they live seems to make it impossible for them to conceive that everybody else isn't doing the same.[22]

Through all of this John showed remarkable patience. Roy Parsons, however, had finally had enough. He wrote to R.H. Griffin in June 1942 in reply to criticisms about an alleged lack of left-wing pamphlets. Having dealt with the specific complaints, he continued: 'your ceaseless criticism during the three years . . . has accomplished the not inconsiderable task of killing my enthusiasm for the shop and the Society. There may be those who do their best work under the spur of unremitting attack, though I doubt it'.[23] Later in the year he left the job to join the air force, where he spent the next three years. John stayed on the committee for one more year, becoming president again briefly when Scrim was called up, and continued loyally to support the shop. Parsons, on being demobilised, resigned from Modern Books in February 1946 and started his own shop, first upstairs at 288 Lambton Quay and a year later back in Woodward Street (Modern Books in the meantime having moved to Manners Street). John gave him unstinting support. Nan Parsons later recalled Elsie scrubbing the floor of the Woodward Street shop before they moved in, and John and Roy Parsons on a trestle painting the high ceiling.[24]

The Progressive Publishing Society, or PPS, grew out of moves to coordinate the work of the cooperative bookshops, each of which had independently published a small number of works.[25] The new society got under way in 1941; John feared that the same divisions were going to take place as they had already seen over the bookshop: 'The first wrangle has been over a pamphlet of Sewell's – "full of historical generalisations, & they're all wrong" said Mr Griffin of the C.P. to me; the publishing soc. doesn't exist to publish that sort of thing, only fit for the intellectuals. Luckily I've kept out of that.'[26] He did not keep out completely. He went to a number of the conferences of representatives of the three cooperative shops, and in 1944 the society established a typographical panel that he chaired. It does not seem to have been very active. That year the society brought out its most substantial publication, *Islands of Danger,* a popular account by Ernest Beaglehole of the time he and Pam had spent on an ethnological study of Pukapuka, an atoll in the northern Cook Islands. John spent many hours preparing the manuscript for publication[27] (he retained an older brother's critical view of Ernest's prose style) and arranged both the typography and design of the book, which was printed by Whitcombe and Tombs in Christchurch. John, rather charitably, described the PPS style as 'straightforward and workmanlike and decent'.[28]

From an early stage he was concerned that the publishing society should be kept quite separate from the cooperative book society: 'if once things get really mixed we shall be in for a hell of a time'. 'Our first duty to our members, I think, is to make sure that the future of Modern Books will not be imperilled. Of course I am a member of the publishing society and I want that to go ahead – but it must go ahead under its own steam.'[29] His caution was justified. The publishing society, always undercapitalised, went into liquidation after three years and the three book societies were responsible for its debts. In that time the society had published sixty-five works, including the popular *New Zealand New Writing* – much criticised by some members for its lack of social content and summarily dismissed by Denis Glover: 'I begin to suspect that we do right to take a proper pride in our footballers'.[30]

One might have thought that John had had enough of publishing but in 1945, after a thirty-year campaign by Sir James Hight of Canterbury College, the Senate of the University of New Zealand agreed to take 'initial exploratory steps' towards establishing a university press by voting £500 for preliminary expenses and appointing a provisional board that included John. The following June he reported to Janet on a meeting of the board: 'I threw my weight around somewhat scornfully & disgustedly & intolerantly for about three hours, & as a result had to miss two lectures. But at least I got them to consider low & mundane things like money & time & punctuation & editing. Apparently the idea now is that I am to see to all these things, plus typography . . .'[31] The following year the senate made a grant of £7500 for working capital, John succeeded Hight as chairman, and the power to act was essentially in his hands, together with those of Ian Gordon, who was at that time vice-chancellor of the University of New Zealand as well as professor of English at Victoria. 'It's the only way the damned affair will get anywhere',[32] John commented. For the following fifteen years the press was sustained by their enthusiasm and John's hard work, supported by the registrar of the university, who acted as secretary. The first book to appear was P.S. Ardern's *First Readings in Old*

English – 'God what a thing it was to do',[33] John wrote – followed by Ian Gordon's *English Prose Technique*. Both texts for university classes, they sold well and went to second editions.

In the first years John actively canvassed the idea of setting up 'a real university press' with its own printing house. He asked Harry Tombs, the printer and publisher, who had a long interest in the arts and was by then in his seventies, if he might be interested in selling his business. Lance Davison came up from Christchurch to cast a critical eye over the works and machinery with John, who clearly had the idea of bringing Davison into some kind of partnership as manager of the printing works. While the plant was 'better than [Davison] expected',[34] Tombs was very vague about financial details. Davison decided against leaving Whitcombe and Tombs, and Harry Tombs's offer to sell, when it came, included a provision that he should be kept on as manager for three years. 'Quite inadvisable', John noted on the letter, and nothing came of the idea. The university press remained, as J.E. Traue was to describe it, 'from beginning to end an unwanted child'.[35] After the initial capital there was no continuing grant; with no staff, office or sales organisation, it remained 'a part-time enthusiasm'.[36] During its sixteen years of existence thirteen books were published, with over 24,000 copies printed and almost 20,000 sold. Notable among them were Eric McCormick's *The Expatriate: A Study of Frances Hodgkins and New Zealand* (1954) and Keith Sinclair's *The Origins of the Maori Wars* (1957). The major undertaking was *The Buttermakers' Manual* by F.H. McDowall of Massey Agricultural College, already accepted when John took over the press and finally appearing in 1953. The *Manual* incurred 57 per cent of the total costs of the board's operation and produced 56 per cent of its receipts; the author contributed a substantial portion of the costs himself. Its production in two volumes with 1590 pages of text plus notes and appendices nearly drove John to distraction, and telephone calls from Dr McDowall for a time seemed a constant part of family life. The ever-rising costs of printing and binding and the problems of distribution continued to plague the press, but by what John called 'a policy of worried caution' it managed to keep its original capital intact and when, after several years of progressive devolution the University of New Zealand was finally dissolved into its constituents in 1961, the press disappeared with it and the board returned £8500 to the new University Grants Committee.

'Though as an organ of the University of New Zealand', John wrote in his final report,[37] the press 'has not captured the approval of the separate universities . . . it has not wasted the money of the

University'. He regretted that the universities had no interest in keeping the press going as a collaborative venture, choosing rather to enter into publication ventures separately. In the circumstances in which it worked, Dennis McEldowney considered the press's achievement impressive. 'Its list was small but uniformly high in quality; the typography . . . distinguished. Its weakness was in distribution.'[38] The achievement was almost entirely John's work.

John's interest in books led to his involvement with the newly formed New Zealand Library School. This had started its teaching in 1946 under the directorship of Mary Parsons, the much-travelled American who had come to Wellington to establish the United States Information Service Library, having previously taught in library schools in France and America.[39] John and Elsie had got to know her well, and John gave a number of lectures on the history of the book, on printing, illustration and publishing. He reported to Janet: 'I've done four of my six lectures to the Library School. Are they worth while? I don't know. The kids sit there as dumb as a lot of new students in Stage I'.[40] Mary Parsons left in 1948 when she retired home to the United States (where she had a house designed by Plischke built at Ann Arbor in 1955–56[41]), but John continued with the lectures for a number of years.

IN A TALK GIVEN IN 1968 John recalled the beginning of the Chamber Music Society,[42] how it followed from the decision of the pianist Dorothy Davies, cellist Marie Vanderwart and violinist Erica Schorss, towards the end of the war, to play together in public, 'consistently, seriously, regularly, and not to let their public down'. John, in Fred Turnovsky's words 'their guiding spirit and promoter',[43] was one of those who managed the recitals (and, needless to say, designed the programmes), which were held in Nimmo's hall, a rather cramped upstairs space (long since gone) in Willis Street.

The performers never got much out of it, in cash, [John recalled in his talk] beyond a pound or two each, and then only because, somehow, we got amusement tax waived. They said they had fun, as well as the agony of conscientious performers . . . and on the last night of the last season we ever had, someone said to me, look don't you think it would be a good idea if we could get other musicians in New Zealand into this sort of thing, and get various groups co-ordinated, and start a chamber music society with subscribers?

Fred Wood organised a gathering on 9 November 1944 in the studio of Spencer Digby, a well-known photographer and great record collector, a temporary committee was chosen and four months later, on 6 March, a meeting was held to form the Wellington Chamber Music Society. Two thousand invitations had been designed, printed and sent out, and about 180 enthusiastic people filled Nimmo's hall. The evening began with music; the Broadcasting Service quartet (Vincent Aspey, leader, with May Hyam, Frank Hoffey and Molly Wright), having been given special permission to appear out of the studio for possibly the first time, played quartets by Dvořák and Haydn. John moved the motion to form the society, and it was seconded by E.C.(Ted) Simpson. The subscription, fixed at one guinea per person, was intended to cover six concerts – 3s 6d for each one. John had thought they might get 200 or 250 subscribers, but within the year the society had grown to over 600, filling the Town Hall Concert Chamber, and there was a waiting list for membership.

The first committee was chaired by Simpson, managing director of Kodak, a mild man who was passionate about the arts; he had lectured on art for the WEA for many years and had a remarkable collection of both records and books on art – of which John was deeply envious. John was a member of the committee, along with Spencer Digby, C.R. Straubel, a journalist who later worked in publishing for Whitcombe and Tombs, W.B. (Walter) Harris, a member of the Education Department and a pioneer in the use of films and film strips in education, and Fred Turnovsky, the young refugee from Czechoslovakia who was to become the driving force of the newly formed society, with R.C.G. Weston as secretary. The committee was notable for the work its members shouldered. They divided among themselves all the tasks involved in planning and managing the concerts, and early committee meetings, generally held at either Ted Simpson's or 6 Messines Road, could go on well after midnight. John designed the programmes until he resigned from the committee in 1949 when he left for London on sabbatical leave. He also acted as doorkeeper for the concerts, which proved unexpectedly hazardous. At the annual general meeting held in February 1946, at the beginning of the society's second year, after a member had commented that Wellington audiences were 'diabolically dilatory' and recommended that latecomers should not be admitted until the end of the first item, John 'spoke of the difficulty of keeping the door closed during playing. He had actually had the skin torn off his knuckles when acting as doorkeeper'.[44] When he resigned from the committee, the secretary wrote to him: 'We have valued especially the high standard you have always set in supervising the Society's printing. Mention was also made at the meeting of the loss which will be immediately apparent to a great many members of the chief guardian of the portal at the Concert Chamber'.[45]

The first concert, on 1 May 1945, was given by Maurice Clare, the distinguished English violinist who was at that time living in Christchurch, and pianist Frederick Page, 'already noted for his espousal of new music, a passion which [had] brought him into deadly conflict with the more conservative musical forces of Christchurch'.[46] On the committee's recommendation they included in their programme Douglas Lilburn's sonata for violin and piano in C major. The first season was inevitably somewhat ad hoc as the committee explored the availability of performers, sought to reach agreement on fees (the £75 paid to Maurice Clare, while justified for him in the committee's view, created difficulties when they sought to negotiate much lower sums with other players), and reached agreement on programmes. Some groups had firm views on what they would, or could, play; the committee considered that it should make those decisions and seems to have succeeded in making what John Thomson described as 'musically intelligent and individual programmes'.[47] Looking ahead to the second year, John suggested to the committee that they should consider a programme devoted wholly to a particular composer; it might be 'worthwhile sounding out Mr Douglas Lilburn as to what he contemplated in chamber music and get a line on anything he might compose in the next few months . . . he felt it desirable that the Society should encourage the composition of music as well as performance'.[48]

Some difficulties were hard to resolve. In those immediate postwar years there was scarcely one good piano available in any public hall in the whole of New Zealand, and this remained so for many years. The Town Hall Concert Chamber was the only venue for the concerts; it had the feel of a rather unloved and shabby school hall, and the lack of soundproofing between it and the Town Hall itself was especially trying when concerts coincided with professional wrestling, then in its heyday and filling the Town Hall with large and enthusiastic crowds. But despite the difficulties the society flourished.

The sensation of 1946, the society's second year, was the pianist Lili Kraus. Born and trained in Hungary, in the 1930s 'she won an international reputation as a soloist for the lucidity and stylishness of her Mozart, Haydn and Beethoven'.[49] During the war she was interned by the Japanese in Java, and following the end of hostilities she made her way to New Zealand via Australia, arriving with her husband, Dr Otto Mandl, and their two children, in June 1946. James Bertram has described her 'magnetic appeal to war-worn New Zealanders'.[50] She won applause for the quality of her playing, but the impact she made drew as much on her exuberant and exotic style, fiery temperament and effortless self-promotion, which led A.R.D. Fairburn to write to John suggesting that he should join those poets, the hard-boiled Denis Glover among them, who were saluting her in verse.* John thought he had better hear her play first. A little later he did, at Dorothy Davies's studio, and was favourably impressed: 'she really can play, it's true, but whether she calls for a book of verse I'm not convinced yet. We'll see'. And he continued, 'Fred Page says when he heard her play Schubert, she smeared the first movement all over with sex'.[51] Whatever the final verdict, Lili Kraus clearly came at a good time both for herself and for New Zealand music. The following year there was further excitement with a tour by the Boyd Neel String Orchestra from Britain. John was bowled over: 'They are miraculous. I've never heard string-playing like it, & you could tell after two notes of God Save the King what it was going to be like . . . I finished up completely exhausted, I didn't have a clap, or a stamp, or a bravo left.'[52] The Chamber Music Society's third season, John Thomson wrote, was 'artistically successful beyond measure'.[53]

That same year the advent of the National Orchestra held out the possibility of an even richer musical life. The idea of a professional symphony orchestra in New Zealand went back many years. It had taken a step forward with the formation of the Broadcasting Service string orchestra in 1939 under the direction of Maurice Clare; 'the step from amateur to professional had been accomplished'.[54] The following year Heenan's National Music Committee, on which he and James Shelley, Director of the National Broadcasting Service, were the key players, brought the Centennial Orchestra into being. The conductor (and musical organiser) of the Centennial Orchestra was the English musician Andersen Tyrer, pianist, conductor and composer, readily available for the position as he was in New Zealand on an examining tour for the Trinity College of Music, London. The war ended plans to continue the orchestra on a permanent basis, but Tyrer, who had stayed on in New Zealand to conduct the Broadcasting Service string orchestra, was assiduous, not without self-interest, in keeping the idea alive. When the plans were revived,

---

*   Poems to Kraus by Bertram, Curnow, Fairburn and Glover were published in the second number of *Landfall*, June 1947.

after the war, John was one of those who, unimpressed by Tyrer's ability, were alarmed by rumours in early 1946 that he was to be appointed conductor of the new orchestra without the position being advertised. He became part of a loose group from several centres, which included Professor A.C. Keys in Auckland, Frederick Page and Stanley Oliver in Wellington, and Dr Vernon Griffiths, Douglas Lilburn and Ngaio Marsh in Christchurch,[55] who lobbied the government both directly and through the press to ensure, among other things, that the post of conductor was advertised in order to attract the widest possible range of candidates.

John, Stanley Oliver and L.D. Webster (also a member of the Chamber Music Society) had a long interview with Peter Fraser towards the end of April:

. . . the Hon F. Jones [Minister of Broadcasting], the fool, was there, & Shelley. All about our efforts to keep Andersen Tyrer from being appointed conductor of the National Orchestra. Peter was visibly shaken, but I'm afraid the thing has gone too far to be stopped. Dammit I really haven't got time for this sort of thing, but people seem to expect me to do it. It was funny, Jones started to make a personal attack on me and Peter leapt to my defence like a knight errant to the side of Beauty; & Jones bade me a most effusive farewell.[56]

John had been willing enough to take part in the agitation, but was less happy to be 'pushed into the forefront of battle'.[57] The controversy brought him into direct conflict with Heenan: 'I believe Joe is very wrath with me, & has referred to "Beaglehole & his gang going around stirring up trouble" – in other words spiking one of his plans'. Not only was Tyrer one of his centennial stars, but he had also 'been of use' to Heenan in helping his musician son, Ashley, and 'Joe thinks that Tyrer is a great man'.[58] And yet John felt he had to do something. 'There seem to be so few people with the guts to say Here come off it Peter to his face.'[59] There is no evidence that he gave any thought to the fact that he was a part-time employee in Heenan's department.

The battle was lost. Fraser, backed by Heenan and Shelley, could not be moved. Tyrer was not only to conduct the orchestra, but to organise it as well, auditioning and selecting players, and choosing programmes. The orchestra met for the first time for a week in October 1946 after which they dispersed, to reassemble in February 1947 to prepare for their much-heralded first concert in the Wellington Town Hall on 6 March. John was asked to review their performance for the *Listener*.

Apart from all the ballyhoo and build-up we may, I think, be pleased.
And one wants to be a Builder and not a Wrecker. But probably the time
has come for a little cold – well, temperate – appraisal, rather than build-
up; it may be, indeed, that they also build who only raise objections.
The great occasion is past. The National Orchestra of the New Zealand
Broadcasting Service has given its first concert . . .

He suggested that it was the duty of the critic 'to examine with
coolness, and what knowledge he has', and that the orchestra should
be able to stand any amount of criticism: it should 'be so constituted
that controversy is its stimulant and attack its challenge'. He
continued:

In the light of which preamble, let us consider the Sixth of March. The
orchestra really did very well indeed . . .

   It could have done a great deal better still, I feel, if the programme
had been better chosen. I suggest very modestly to Mr. Tyrer that it was
badly chosen. Dvorak's Carnival, Brahms's Second Symphony, Enesco's
second Rumanian Rhapsody, Butterworth's Shropshire Lad Rhapsody,
Strauss's Till Eulenspiegel, the Prelude and Liebestrod from Tristan,
plus some other quite gratuitous encores – what can you make of that as
an exercise in programme-building? The romanticism is all too thickly
spread. Wouldn't a Haydn Symphony or an early Beethoven, have been
better than the Brahms; and would it have been any less popular?

   Let's go back to the actual performance. It was more notable for
hearty goodwill than for refinement. Mr Tyrer has trained his team
to play pretty well together, they attack well; and that is something
considering the circumstances – considering the fact that some of these
people have never heard an orchestra before, let alone played in one, or
probably in any concerted music at all . . . There was a lack of balance
. . . In the middle of the row, downstairs, close to the front, the brass
nearly lifted us out of our seats. The trumpets really had no need
to anticipate the day of judgment. The horns rather exploded at the
beginning of the Brahms, but it looks as though they will work up a
good tone. Thanks largely, it seems to the Air Force Band, the woodwind
section is both adequate and potentially very good, and it gave us some
very nice bits of playing when left to itself. The strings have so far
worked up a fair measure of precision but little delicacy. The general
uproar in the early part of the concert left me wondering whether the
whole orchestra, or any considerable part of it, could produce a piano at
all; but the strings managed to show promise of this in the first bars of
the fast movement of the Brahms; and it is to be hoped that in time Mr.
Tyrer will get his people to whisper as well as to shout. They let go with
the utmost enthusiasm . . . but how much more thrilling, how magical,
the perfectly controlled whisper, the really angelical syllabling!

After strongly criticising the playing of encores, an 'abuse of time and tolerance' (equally his view at chamber music concerts), John concluded:

Well, that's how one person at least reacted to the show. I've tried to be honest. The very fact that the orchestra is at last in existence and giving concerts is important. For bringing it into existence the Government deserves all our thanks. Whether its existence is going to be of profound importance is a question to which an answer is not possible just now. The answer will depend partly on us – on our ability to give it support continuously, but critically . . . To crab for the sake of crabbing at this moment would be both churlish and silly. Mr. Tyrer, as a conductor, has been the subject of considerable controversy; I must confess that for me (and I am pretty certain for the players also) some of the emphatic patterns he wove in the air were devoid of significance. But it would be both churlish and silly also to deny him credit for bringing the orchestra as a combination to the point it has reached. What I wonder now is how much further it is going to go? How much better is it going to be? In a year or two we will know more about that.

Looking back twenty years later, Owen Jensen judged John's review 'well-informed, thoughtful, and certainly . . . honest', and written 'perceptively and intelligently'.[60] At the time it was followed by an outburst of bitter controversy. John was taken aback. The review had been a Sunday's work which he had not wanted to do:

And now the orchestra is up in arms, & my name stinks . . . Do you know that the orchestra held a meeting & decided that none of them would play for the CMS [Chamber Music Society] until I resigned from it* (or from the Committee? – it's all very confused). And I thought I'd done a fairly reasonable piece of work that couldn't possibly hurt anybody's feelings. But no – I have even received an anonymous communication – a copy of a little book entitled 'How to listen to the Orchestra' with an inscription 'With the compliments of one of the brass players (?) . . . Why do you think people are so fantastically absurd . . . ? Or am I the fantastically absurd person, just for trying to be reasonable?[61]

Two weeks after John's review appeared the *Listener* published a lengthy response to it by Dr H.J. Finlay,[62] a scientist and keen amateur musician (and brother of the young Labour MP and one-

---

*   The first programme of the year was 'scuppered by . . . some b-s of string players who won't play because of my article. Can you beat it? We really are in an awful crisis.' Dorothy Davies saved the day by stepping in at short notice. (JCB to JEP, 16 April 1947.)

time chairman of the Wellington Progressive Book Society, Martyn Finlay). Finlay argued that the appropriate yardstick for judging the orchestra was what had existed previously in New Zealand, but in his rebuttal of John's criticisms he actually went much further than John had in criticising the orchestra, and the comparisons he made were with 'any good recordings'. Other correspondents, in the same issue and the next, were largely content to question John's musical qualifications, to suggest that 'a more authoritative critic would have dealt firmly with shortcomings without dealing in malicious verbosity', and to assert 'that in his rush to demonstrate his own aestheticism your contributor has merely revealed his lamentable inadequacy as a critic'. A.R.D. Fairburn agreed with John on the programmes: 'the music that was played was nearly all marginal stuff'. Joe Heenan, however, after suggesting that the *Listener* had been a 'party to an unfair attack on fellow workers in the NZBS', went to what he believed to be the heart of the matter:

What I do assert is that it is difficult to read Dr. Beaglehole's article as written in good faith. Not all his capacity to handle the language as an artist in words can conceal the venom of chagrin in what he says. It is his own fault if those who know the history of the Orchestra believe that he is still smarting under the defeat he and those associated with him suffered in their campaign against the appointment of Andersen Tyrer to organise the Orchestra and be its first conductor.[63]

Three weeks after Finlay's article and Heenan's letter appeared the *Listener*'s billboards announced A CRITIC REPLIES TO HIS CRITICS. In his reply John wrote that he had 'in reality paid the orchestra the highest compliment in my power, and treated it seriously'.[64] Having noted that he and Finlay seemed to 'occupy a good deal of common ground', he considered Finlay's criticisms tougher than his own:

Dr. Finlay . . . is a critic who may well be feared. If I had said about the bassoons what he said about them I should probably be lying a cold assassinated corpse by now; but I wouldn't have the courage. It reminds me of that excellent proverb that one man can steal a horse while another can't look over a fence. I peer gingerly over the fence, to the accompaniment of roars of indignation; while Dr. Finlay, in the most charming and deprecatory fashion imaginable, to general applause, walks off with the noble animal – slinging a brick at me on the way.

John's final words were a heartfelt plea to Heenan:

One correspondent I cannot leave unnoticed in the crowd is Mr. J.W. Heenan. Mr. Heenan makes the serious charge against me that I have written not in good faith but with the 'venom of chagrin'. I feel some embarrassment. There are few men for whom I have a higher admiration than for Mr. Heenan; there is no man whose judgment in many things I respect more; there is no other man to whom in many things I owe so much; there is no man with whom I should be more unwilling to enter into public controversy. To Mr. Heenan therefore I can only say, borrowing those words of despair which Oliver Cromwell addressed to the Kirk of Scotland, 'I beseech you in the bowels of Christ, think it possible you may be mistaken'.

Heenan's letter had also drawn a response from Ormond Wilson, the Labour MP for Palmerston North, later to become a close friend of John's when they were both on the Historic Places Trust. He found it alarming that Heenan, unable to confute John, had chosen to slander him. 'The real question', he wrote, 'is whether Dr. Beaglehole's article is correct or not. This is the question Mr. Heenan runs away from'.[65] A careful reading of John's review shows that what he criticised mostly were aspects of the performance directly under the control of Tyrer: the programme and what might be termed 'the interpretation'.[66] Nowhere did he directly criticise the actual quality of playing of orchestra members. Yet, if such an emphasis might be seen as giving grounds for Heenan's comment, a concert later in that first year, when guest conductor Eugene Goosens drew a performance from the orchestra quite unlike anything achieved before, seemed to bear out John's analysis. Before the year was over a number of the players, too, were growing increasingly unhappy, and John heard that 'there is a great anti-Tyrer revolutionary movement going on in the orchestra, & . . . they are all saying By gosh, Beaglehole was right'.[67] Alex Lindsay, who later formed his own string orchestra modelled on that of Boyd Neel, and who contributed significantly to New Zealand's musical life, was one of a number who left at that time and made no secret of the fact that it was because of Tyrer. Nor have later judgements been particularly kind. Owen Jensen, in his history of the orchestra, writes of Tyrer: 'He was not, by any means, a first-rate conductor . . . his knowledge of the orchestral repertoire was limited. His tastes, too, leaned towards the flamboyant, and there was an element of vulgarity in his interpretive approach. Nor was his ear for the niceties of orchestral tone the most sensitive.'[68] Fred Page needed fewer words: 'a fearsomely bad conductor'.[69]

This was not the only occasion on which John, writing in the *Listener,* was caught up in controversy. The first had been two years earlier with a review-article, 'Lots of Poetry'.[70] Faced with C.A. Marris's anthology, *Lyric Poems 1928–42* he was critical, characterising the work as 'poetic', 'palpitant', 'lavender scented': 'we get the "grey waters of oblivion" and that sort of thing'. *Poems* by the Labour MP Clyde Carr was dismissed in similar terms: 'like Mr Marris's lyricists . . . [Carr] is well in touch with God' and 'is appallingly sentimental and completely uncritical of his own words'. In contrast, John praised three recent Caxton Press volumes: Basil Dowling's *Signs and Wonders,* Denis Glover's *The Wind and the Sand* and James K. Baxter's *Beyond the Palisade.* Two weeks after his review appeared, the correspondence began. Allen Curnow, while conceding that the critical judgements were 'fairly well-considered', took issue with the tone of the review, 'the mess of facetious by-play, the knowing winks, the girlish mincings'. The editor, Oliver Duff, would have none of Curnow's criticism, suggesting that a 'very slight capacity to take himself less seriously would have saved our correspondent from such solemn nonsense'. Curnow was back a fortnight later, chastising Duff and taking further issue with John for 'the passages in which . . . [he] discusses himself, not the books, and the references to God' which, Curnow claimed, might be taken to rule out all devotional poetry. Others wrote of John's 'savage tearing to pieces and throwing to the winds' of the Marris volume, or suggested some political bias in his comments on Clyde Carr. Gordon Ingham, however, congratulated the editor on 'the most refreshingly candid book review', and one of the last letters printed, in the fourth week of the controversy, said the review was 'lively, provocative, and a pleasure to read'. John replied to his critics, claiming that he did not understand Curnow's assumption that he was 'guying' poetry, adding that he liked Curnow's poetry and concluding, not without irony, 'I have, I trust, rigidly excluded any note of levity or inelegance from these remarks'.[71]

Some years later he again obtained a lively response with a critical review of T.S. Eliot's *Notes Towards the Definition of Culture.*[72] This time the onslaught on John was largely deflected on to his young colleague Peter Munz, who had written a full-blooded attack on Eliot's views in a letter of support for John. Nor did the correspondence have quite the heat of another at the same time over the merits of a prize-winning Royal Ode by the writer Ruth France. John never hesitated to say what he thought; perhaps, however, there was an element of truth in what some of his critics claimed. The terms in which he expressed those thoughts – partly because of the imaginative fluency of his writing – could provoke those accustomed to more solemn discussion.

Underlying John's critical writing in these years, including his review of the orchestra and the further note on the orchestra he wrote for *Landfall* the following year,[73] was a consistent evaluative stance. 'New Zealand', he had written in 1946, 'has reached a stage when one of its principal needs is a fine and disinterested critical integrity',[74] and he developed this further in a review of the 1946 *Second Yearbook of the Arts in New Zealand*:

. . . to realize its greatest potential value, [the book] needs to be firmly grounded on a set of clearly thought out critical convictions; those critical convictions should be explicit as well as implicit, frank and all-pervading, quite willing to damn as well as exalt, and to damn with force and comprehension . . . If the arts in New Zealand are to flourish in an adult way, then we desperately need criticism as a working partner of creation – as a partner working hard.[75]

To Janet he wrote, 'We'll just have to keep banging away in NZ until criticism is accepted as a normal part of life . . . God knows how long it will take'.[76]

NOT LONG AFTER THEY moved to the Hutt from Auckland, John and Elsie had got to know the Wellington painter T.A. McCormack. McCormack was born in Napier and began his career there, but in the 1930s and 40s he was hardly known outside Wellington. New Zealand in the 1930s was still divided into communities of astonishing parochialism in their activities in the arts, a condition that changed only very slowly. To see McCormack's work in Wellington, other than the small number of paintings included in shows of the somewhat mistitled New Zealand Academy of Fine Arts, one visited the painter at his studio in Hill Street, where he would 'cautiously bring out [paintings] one at a time to place on an easel. If he found the viewer unresponsive and uninformed, he would not continue.'[77] John was responsive. In 'A note on T.A. McCormack', published in *Art in New Zealand* in June 1936, he singled him out as 'one of the two really good and original artists in New Zealand' and compared his sincerity and seriousness with Cézanne's, 'the same devotion to the technical problem of the realisation of the idea'. He concluded, characteristically: 'I wish some rich man who wants to do the country a service would present half-a-dozen of these pictures to the National Gallery; and I wish he would give me the job of selecting them'. He and Elsie bought a painting of the Hutt river, the first of a number of McCormack's they acquired, and the beginning of their collection of New Zealand art.

During the 1940s John and Elsie got to know well Sam Williams, a New Zealander who had trained and worked in London as a stage designer, and his English wife Liza, who had come to New Zealand hoping to make careers here. They built a house in Karori, designed by Cedric Firth, and having shared interests in the arts, and young families, John and Elsie saw a lot of them. Sam Williams had considerable talent; he both designed and played a leading part in Maria Dronke's 1947 production of T.S. Eliot's *Murder in the Cathedral* in St Paul's Cathedral Church, a high point in the postwar renaissance of amateur drama in Wellington. But there was no living in the work he could get at that time; the family returned to London in 1948, where their home at 4 Markham Square in Chelsea became something of a base for Beagleholes in future years.

The renewed activity in music and drama which came with the end of the war was matched in the other arts. In 1946 the Wellington Public Library held the first of a number of exhibitions of painting. It was of work by James Coe. Writing about it in the *Listener*,[78] John suggested it was worth seeing not because the paintings and drawings were all brilliantly successful (they were not) but because they were 'by a man young, vigorous, experimental, seriously thinking in terms of paint . . . There is not, thank God, one well-bred water-colour landscape here at all.' Through Heenan, John persuaded the government to buy for £40 each two large oils that Coe had painted of New Zealand troops in the Pacific. Two years later there were exhibitions by both Toss Woollaston and Colin McCahon. The Woollaston show included *Edith Knitting*, the portrait of his wife that I think John and Elsie already owned at this time* – it hung in the front hall at Messines Road for as long

---

*   In a letter to Woollaston, on 31 March 1942, John told him that he had already bought a postal order to pay him for a painting when he received Woollaston's letter suggesting he had set too high a price: 'Personally I think that most NZ artists ask too much for their pictures (not all); but I also think that this one is worth its price to me, & looking at it again last night after getting your letter I agreed with myself. I don't want to do violence to your conscience; but on the other hand I don't want to do violence to my own. Couldn't you smother yours in paint for further pictures? I suppose I have got to let you have the last word, as you will no doubt take it in any case; but you would really leave me much happier if you let the price be. I enclose the postal order on the assumption that you will.' (Toss Woollaston Papers. CA 457/2, box 2. MONZPT.) *Edith Knitting* was the only Woollaston John and Elsie owned until much later, so it seems very likely that it was the painting in question. In the same letter John asked Woollaston if he would provide work for the picture rental scheme being started by Modern Books.

as I can remember. McCahon's work John already knew from the dark, brooding landscape *Otago Peninsula,* commissioned in 1945 by Mario Fleischl and his wife Hilda (another refugee couple who were friends of John and Elsie's) and hanging in their Karori home, and it was Hilda who persuaded John to open McCahon's library show. He was impressed by it: 'not a brilliant technician, in the academic sense', he wrote (again in the *Listener*), 'yet for us he is one of the important people. He is a serious artist. His pictures are open to criticism but they can take criticism.'[79] And in a letter at the same time: 'By golly, he's got something'.[80]

Another public library exhibition, of original drawings that had appeared in the *School Journal,* John hailed as representing 'the first major and consistent effort in this country to link illustrations to the printed word . . . and very often the effort has been brilliantly successful'.[81] He did not mention the close association he had with School Publications* under the able leadership of Thelma Maurais, giving advice on typography, writing school bulletins and encouraging the use of New Zealand artists as illustrators, including Russell Clark, Yvonne Bendall, Juliet Peter, Nancy Bolton, Mervyn Taylor, Sam Williams, George Woods and many others. Mervyn Taylor (always called Merv) was for two years (during 1944–46) on the staff of School Publications as illustrator and art editor. It was during this time that he found he liked working on wood rather than on metal (he had trained originally as a jewellery engraver) and he developed his skill at making wood engravings for illustrating the *School Journal* and other school publications. He looked to John for advice – one of his questions was what should he charge for his prints?[82] – criticism and moral support. When Taylor resigned and became once more a freelance 'artist-designer', John continued to support him, Taylor frequently walked over to Messines Road from his Karori home in Hatton Street, where he had his studio, to talk. In the next dozen years he engraved more than two hundred wood blocks and made his name, publishing a collection of his work, *Engravings on Wood*, in 1957.

John's interest in art was never simply a private pursuit but something to be shared; artists were to be encouraged to create, the public to open its eyes. There was always the teacher in him, the enthusiast delighted to share his enthusiasm, and working with Heenan had led him to think about ways in which worthwhile

---

*   The School Publications Branch of the Education Department, at this time an almost autonomous branch of the department.

developments in the arts could be nurtured and supported. In 1947 he was behind a plan to commission Eric Lee-Johnson to make a series of drawings and watercolours of old New Zealand buildings for the Historical Branch;[83] he admired what he had seen of Lee-Johnson's painting, and early the following year he and Elsie bought *Kohu kohu*. The plan fell through but John's support for Lee-Johnson continued, particularly during the two years Lee-Johnson was editing the *Arts Year Book* (for 1950 and 1951). In the late 1950s, John was also involved with the National Council for Adult Education, selecting a collection of New Zealand paintings to be sent to centres that would otherwise have little chance of seeing such things.

Wellington was beginning to get more places where paintings could be seen, and McGregor Wright's (run by John's cousin Dick Osborne) could still come up with something interesting. They had a show of Raymond McIntyre's work in 1946; John had not known of him before and was very enthusiastic, lamenting only that the Auckland City Art Gallery had got the best three in the show, the National Gallery being hopelessly slow to act.[84] The French Maid coffee shop had exhibitions; Gordon Walters had four shows there during the 1940s before he went overseas. In June 1947 an exhibition by Sam Cairncross created a stir. 'Plenty of stiff duds', John wrote to Janet, 'but some corker things, brilliant colours, laid on with a trowel. He seems to be a natural genius . . .'[85] The wife of the French ambassador took Cairncross up enthusiastically and arranged a scholarship for him to go to Paris. The Victoria staff common room committee bought the first painting in its collection. Two years later Helen Hitchings opened her dealer gallery with pottery and furniture (designed by Ernst Plischke) as well as paintings and drawings. It was a short-lived but courageous venture. There was, John wrote, 'a sort of creative air in the Hitchings gallery, not phoney'.[86]

A sign of the slow recovery of British publishers from the grey austerity of wartime production came with the Penguin series *Modern Painters*, offering (for the time) good quality colour reproduction at a low price, and including Frances Hodgkins among its subjects. John bought the slim volumes as they appeared. Early in 1946 there was more excitement:

. . . I walked into Modern Books just as Jean [the manager] was unpacking some parcels from Faber. She showed the stuff to me. I'll take those I said. I don't know what the price will be, she said. I don't care what the price is, I said. THE FABER GALLERY!!! Degas, Blake, Florentine Paintings . . . I nearly went mad with excitement – so much so that when I got home in the evening I displayed them in the most brazen way . . . . the Degas is really exciting, & I am living in a fever of expectation for the number entitled Homage to Venus to appear.[87]

A month later, having brought home 'rather a heap of books lately', he thought it prudent to put the Phaidon Press *Augustus John* into a drawer of his desk 'until later'.[88]

Even if by the late 1940s John found he could not continue as late in the evenings as he once had, he was still reading as widely as ever. He began 1946, for example, by reading on holiday at the farm Hamlin Garland's *Son of the Middle Border*, Marie Kimball's *Jefferson, the Road to Glory*, Norman Douglas's *Together* ('very amusing'), Una Pope-Hennessey's *Charles Dickens*, half of Collingwood's *Autobiography* and Perry Miller's *The New England Mind: The Seventeenth Century*.[89] Back home he read Joan Bennett on Virginia Woolf (which made him want to reread both Virginia Woolf and Jane Austen), Douglas Cotterall's *Some Notes on Bookbinding* and George Dyson's *The Progress of Music*. Later in the year he noted Sassoon's *Siegfried's Journey*, *The Odyssey* in the new Penguin translation, and David Matthew's *Acton the Formative Years*; he had been 'going through Shakespeare's sonnets again', reading 'Donne and others' in Grierson's *Metaphysical Poets*, and a bit of Christina Rossetti. It was at the end of that year that he finally started on Proust; he read three volumes while the family was on holiday in the Bay of Many Coves in Queen Charlotte Sound – the weather was not good – finished volume six in mid-February and completed the last volume in December. Many books John read right through, sometimes making notes and listing page references in pencil on the endpaper inside the back cover. He was also a practised 'dipper' into books. Sorting out his father's library gave great scope for this. He and Ernest both chose books they wanted (more bookshelves had to be added at Messines Road) and 2000 volumes were given to the Victoria College library in memory of David Ernest and Jane Beaglehole. John brought home the complete edition of George Moore, but his George Moore days were probably over. He did read some novels by Mark Rutherford: 'the morality of people, as well as the theology, is so interesting. A good observer of small local snobberies too . . . I can see how he was important for my father. I find him fascinating.'[90]

ONCE THE VICTORIA COLLEGE jubilee celebrations, in 1949, were over, John and Elsie turned to preparing to get away on sabbatical leave. Leaving the country was much more complicated than it is today; in those days before PAYE the Inland Revenue Department had to be satisfied that one's tax payments were up to date, and there was a complicated process for getting the overseas funds needed for the trip. Amid everything else, John was running late with a chapter on the Commonwealth which he had been asked to write for the *New Cambridge Modern History*. There were several farewell parties. The departure date from Auckland kept being postponed, but they finally sailed on 25 July. The ship, M.V. *Condesa*, of the Houlder Line, was about 10,000 tons; it carried refrigerated cargo and 24 passengers.

The voyage to England on the *Condesa* through the Panama canal took five weeks. John kept a journal to send home to the family, a record of deck games, meals and the foibles of the other passengers. He completed the chapter he was working on for the *New Cambridge Modern History*. They looked forward to the refuelling call at Curaçao, with the prospect of buying the local liqueur and nylon stockings (still unobtainable in New Zealand's persisting postwar austerity) but arrived in the late afternoon, after the shops in Willemstadt had closed, and left again in the early hours of the following morning. On 29 August they docked at Liverpool. John and Elsie stayed for three days with the Hearnshaws (with whom they had become good friends while Leslie was lecturing in psychology at Victoria, before he returned to the chair at Liverpool in late 1947), then going on to Keith and Fronnie Beaglehole's at Baildon, just outside Bradford, on the edge of the Yorkshire moors. They had seen Keith when he visited New Zealand on a business trip at the beginning of 1947, but it was fifteen years since they had seen the rest of the family. John's relations with his sister-in-law were prickly (fortunately, she and Elsie always got on well) but he fell for his niece and nephew, Betty and Peter. After ten days in London (staying with Averil Lysaght in her tiny house near King's Cross), during which he met a number of the Hakluyt Society people and made a start on looking at Cook material, John flew to Paris for the fourth Unesco general conference, at which he was one of the New Zealand delegates. Elsie joined him there a little later.

John's involvement with Unesco had begun in 1947, a year after its first general conference, when Heenan nominated him to represent Internal Affairs on the New Zealand interim committee, chaired by C.E. Beeby, who also had led the New Zealand delegation to the first conference in Paris. For eighteen months from the middle of 1948, Beeby was on leave from his job as Director of Education in New Zealand while he served as Unesco's Assistant Director-

General with the task of establishing a new international education secretariat to implement the organisation's education programmes. New Zealand's National Commission for Unesco (which grew out of the interim committee) had pushed for John to go to the third conference, held in Beirut, but the government, keen to save money, looked around for people already overseas 'quite irrespective of whether they know anything about it or not'.[91] Now he and James Shelley, who had just returned to Britain after retiring as Director of Broadcasting, filled the bill. The arrangement was far from ideal. A delegation of two was too small; it was the first conference for them both, and in John's view some continuity in the membership of delegations was desirable if they were to play an effective role.[92] Nor did he have much time for Shelley: 'a two man delegation with Shelley as one of the delegates – impossible! There were times when I despaired.'[93] It was very hard work. He was elected chairman of the procedure committee, which proved very interesting as it grappled with the question of whether Spanish should be adopted as a working language by Unesco, carrying on an argument that had been in full flood at Beirut. With passions still running high, John judged it a 'great achievement' to have had the subject discussed in an atmosphere of moderate calm.

The conference members also devoted three evenings to a series of addresses on the question: what are the duties of the state in regard to education, science, and culture for the purpose of ensuring a better understanding between peoples, and what practical steps should it take in order to discharge these duties? Initially twenty-six speakers were listed and, when it became known that a number of them had prepared speeches of up to an hour in length, alarm set in and the list was reduced to three speakers each night who were given twenty minutes each, with provision for others to make short statements. 'Surprisingly enough', John wrote in his report, 'this experiment in international co-operation was not entirely unsuccessful',[94] and it attracted widespread public interest. The expectations held for Unesco were still remarkably optimistic. Among the speakers were Georges Bidault, the French Prime Minister; Bertrand Russell; the American theologian Reinhold Niebuhr; Jean Piaget, the Swiss educationist: and John himself. John thought that a New Zealand audience would have found the most interesting contributions to be those of Russell, 'for amusement', and Piaget and the Australian, Professor Stout, 'for instruction'. 'One or two other contributions, no doubt, would have struck it with blank amazement'.

The speeches were recorded and extracts from those of John

and Bertrand Russell were sent to America for broadcasting. John's speech, opening with a felicitous tribute to the civilised virtues of Paris, continued with a measure of scepticism: 'I am going to ask myself as many . . . awkward questions as possible. I do not really know what will be the outcome'.[95]

. . . are the main things we need for better understanding more education and more science, or, more accurately, better understanding of education and science? And should I now proceed to ask what is education and what is science? Heaven forbid. I must pass on. But before I pass on I suppose I should add that the notion of better understanding between peoples carries with it the feeling that thereby international peace and security are visibly strengthened. That is the feeling, at any rate, on which Unesco is founded. From what we know of human psychology, the feeling has something to recommend it; exactly how much I do not know.

In the end he came to echo Voltaire's Candide: 'as well as being world travellers (at least in the spirit), we should cultivate our own gardens . . . education has for one of its main purposes the strengthening of a society's own individuality. That is the best gift we can give to the international family', and 'if the state educates well, understanding between peoples will look after itself'. It was a conclusion to which he returned some months later when he was asked by the BBC Third Programme to talk on the question: 'Is International Understanding Possible?' Again he questioned what exactly was meant by international understanding and just what the relationship was between it and world peace, whether 'the amount of understanding between peoples which is humanly possible is ever going to be of much account for the mutual relations of those people?'[96] He very much doubted it. A multiplicity of well-educated minds might, however, at least provide for 'sensible judgment when the necessity for judgment arises', but what is 'really important for us all . . . is to get on with the life of our own community, and to make that as rich and strong, as intellectually alive and emotionally satisfying as possible'. 'As a New Zealander', he said,

I want New Zealanders to work out something of their own, however long it takes us. I do not, of course, want any more politically sovereign states, each yelping passionately about its immortal and idiotic rights: that is a different matter. In the end I think about the best thing any of our people can do for the family of nations is to make as good a job of ourselves as we can.

It was a belief to which, over the preceding decade, he had become deeply committed.

Whereas John had thought that London was looking 'dirty & down at heel'[97] – though a lot of refurbishment was under way – Paris, or at least the part he saw, 'was just as good as new, all trees & fountains & hurtling traffic & some wonderful food'. He walked up the Champs Elysées every morning to the conference and back 'under the twinkling lights at night' and decided there could not be another street like it in the world. One Sunday Beeby drove them down to Chartres to see the cathedral again, and another Sunday through wonderful woods to the Chateau of Chantilly and the little old town of Senlis. John wished that his sons

could see some of the streets, both in Paris & in the small towns & villages, or some of the village squares; what makes the difference from New Zealand, apart from age, is that everything is not merely well designed but in such good proportion with everything else. But I don't think the French know how to design a small house standing on its own. Something big – a large house or a small chateau – yes, but the isolated small house is generally horrible.[98]

Both he and Elsie got some excitement out of the social events that went with the conference and the champagne which flowed freely. There was a Chopin centennial concert and a wonderful party late one night in the sculpture galleries of the Louvre, when the lights would suddenly go out and an individual statue be breathtakingly floodlit. The film star Myrna Loy was a member of the United States delegation as a special adviser on films: 'I don't ask you to believe this', John wrote to Richmond, 'but I drank champagne, as well as conversed, with Myrna Loy. Nice Person. People kept on introducing me to her, & finally she was driven to say that she knew me.'[99] He managed to find time to go with Elsie to see the permanent exhibition of the Impressionists, 'the Degas pictures especially beautiful', and a big centennial exhibition of Gauguin, which was a 'real knock out'.[100] At the end of three weeks' hard work, they flew back to London. There was still the report on the conference to be written. Shelley left it almost entirely to John, writing only four of the thirty-eight pages. 'The man is completely useless', John told Janet.[101,*]

He got back to work on Cook but there was also time for some travelling. They went down to Cornwall to stay with J.A.

---

*   John had never had much time for James Shelley, but Shelley's biographer suggests that at this time, after the death of his wife and his retirement, he was depressed and missing the sort of public recognition he relished in New Zealand. (Ian Carter, *Gadfly: The Life and Times of James Shelley*, (Auckland: Auckland University Press, 1993), pp.251–5)

Williamson, who was living at Looe – it was John's first visit to his ancestral county – and spent a week walking in the Cotswolds with Keith and Fronnie. England was ruined for walking, in John's view, as all the roads were now tar-sealed. They fell in love with Bath. They had a weekend in Cambridge, which moved him to several enthusiastic letters:

you should have stood on King's bridge with me [he wrote to his niece Mary] & seen Clare bridge all weathered silver white shining in the cold autumn sun with the great copper beech behind it lifting into the air & all the greens & browns & russets behind that receding into the distance; & you should have been in King's Chapel yesterday evening with us at Evensong, with the long lines of candles burning yellowy bright & brighter as the day turned to dusk & the lovely white fan-vaulting dissolved into mist . . . And the pure voices of the angelic choirboys . . .[102]

The Fitzwilliam Gallery he thought the most perfect he had ever seen. His enjoyment at being back in England and France was such that, inevitably, his mind returned once again to the question of where he really felt at home.

Did I tell you [he wrote to Janet] about the floodlit Winged Victory at the Louvre party? – never have I had an aesthetic sensation like it . . . that & the west front of Chartres Cathedral, the very texture of the stone, & the Sanctus of the B minor Mass in Southwark Cathedral, have been the three things. No, there are others to add to them . . . Oh dear you know I could write a book just like Alan Mulgan's* all about the Right Things. The fact is, that so many of the Right Things are the right things, there's no way of getting away from it . . . And yet with it all . . . I haven't been permanently captured – anyhow yet. My heart kept on rising within me at Cambridge, at times leaping, but what I want to do is to get an art gallery, however small, at Victoria College, to do something to the library there, to build something of some sort in NZ. I want to go back to places, to Bath, to the Fitzwilliam, to afternoon tea with the Master of St John's – but after twenty years am I a New Zealander? I dunno. Perhaps I am.[103]

Elsie was to fly back to New Zealand in time for Christmas. Before that she and John had a weekend in Oxford staying with Bill Williams, whom they had not seen since he left New Zealand before the war. John dined with the select Ralegh Club, where 'the

---

*   Mulgan's *Home: A New Zealander's Adventure*, published in 1927, was generally reviled by the younger generation as hopelessly sentimental and pro-English.

drawcard was not the food but the quality of the speakers',[104] and addressed it on New Zealand foreign policy. He and Bill talked long into the night about the war, about the end of Bill's marriage to his first wife, Monica, the daughter of P.W. Robertson, the professor of chemistry at Victoria College, and about John Mulgan, who had been a close Oxford friend of Williams's:

> Bill could understand the suicide, but not the poison – 'I should have thought he was a revolver man'. Other chaps committed suicide under the same conditions – left too long in the same place, under awful conditions of mental stretching & strain, until their last nervous reserves were used up, there seemed no possible solution for anything, personal or political, & absolutely no hope for the world, & no way out but death.[105]

For Elsie's final weekend Keith and Fronnie came down to London and they went to see Ralph Richardson and Peggy Ashcroft in *The Heiress*. Her flight back to New Zealand was hair-raising, with the plane twice having to turn back with engine faults, but was redeemed by breaks in New York, staying with Cedric and Bobbie Firth (Cedric was then working for the United Nations) and San Francisco, where she stayed with the New Zealand geologist Frank Turner, who was teaching at Berkeley, and his wife Esmé, whom they had got to know during their year in Dunedin.

For the rest of his time away John wrote home every week, generally to Elsie and sometimes to 'My dear Wife and Children'. Like his family letters from London twenty years earlier, they were a great mixture: family badinage (this time generally at the expense of his sons, whose spelling, especially, caused some anguish, while the possibility that they might add to the growing misuse of 'disinterested' in place of 'uninterested' led him to threaten not to come home at all), reports on concerts and plays and other outings, people met and, occasionally, work on Cook and Banks. 'I am getting on with checking Captain Cook's journal now,' he wrote just before Christmas, 'working quite hard though you mayn't believe it. I should really have gone to Chelsea to hear the Boyd Neel Orch. last night, but I did Cook instead, indeed I don't think I'll hear another concert till tomorrow night'.[106] A week later he wrote, 'I am getting fonder & fonder of Capt Cook & grudge every hour spent away from him. So he may prove a preservative from dissipation'.[107] A sign of the times and the extraordinary restrictions of the New Zealand system of import controls was just how much time he and Elsie had to give to getting approval to buy a car 'on export' and have it sent out (cars were almost impossible to obtain in New Zealand at that time), to deciding on curtain fabric for the sitting room, a carpet and two comfortable chairs from Heal's and an automatic washing-machine.

At Christmas John went again to Baildon, staying a week to see a bit more of Keith, but taking some work with him. He and Fronnie 'were going all out to be on [their] best behaviour to each other; polite, not to say cordial, the whole time'.[108] He went on from there for a wet and grey day and a half in Whitby, the tiny Yorkshire port inextricably linked with James Cook's life and career (his first visit), exploring the town and the museum and talking to the local historian. The weather deterred him from hiring a car to explore Cook's villages and instead he went on to Durham about which he had mixed impressions. 'A good deal of it looks like hell now, though there are some very pleasant . . . streets, Georgian brick & earlier' and the cathedral 'stood up magnificently'. The hotel the taxi took him to was said to have been built in 1630; the bed was absolutely first-rate, 'snowy clean, but everything else grimy, & smuts coming in the window all the while, even the hot water ran brown, food awful'.[109] In a second-hand shop he found three large pewter plates, 'chargers rather than plates', which were to find a home on the sitting room bookshelves in Messines Road.

John and Elsie's twentieth wedding anniversary occurred on 17 February. Elsie wrote that she was prepared to take on another twenty years if John was (this was squeezed in at the end of two pages on no remittance licences for cars and carpets, and how much money there was to spend).[110] John had settled on exactly the same message for the cable he sent her, while in the letter he posted a few days earlier he wrote that, as it would no doubt be read by all sorts of people, he had decided to merely say 'thank you again, & remark that the original scene, as well as a good many others bearing on the subject, is still vividly painted before my eyes. It is a pity that a marriage that started off so well should have to proceed in company with three such rough types as we have to live with.'[111] The comments of each were characteristic; the letters between them during these months reflect a warm and settled relationship, a shared involvement with family and friends and with all that was going on. On the wedding anniversary Janet happened to be staying at Messines Road on her way back to Hamilton from a trip to visit family in the South Island. She wrote to John: 'I did enjoy my two days with Elsie – we talked & talked & talked & looked at all the things she had brought back. I still think it curious, odd – comical that after everything E. is the one woman with whom I feel most completely at ease & happy.'[112]

John was getting a great deal of enjoyment from outings with his niece Betty. She was in London training to be a ballet dancer, and most of his letters recounted an outing with her and the amusement she gave him:

I have rung up Betty, & after due consideration we have decided, or rather I have decided, because she never decides anything, being helplessly immobile between the alternatives, to go to the Wigmore Hall this afternoon & hear Beethoven's three Rasumovsky quartets, rather than to the Albert Hall to hear a lot of Sibelius. It is certainly difficult to choose sometimes, so I generally go on the principle of specialising in chamber music; & Betty on whether it is easier to get tea after the Albert Hall or after the Wigmore Hall. Last Sunday we didn't do any concerts, & the movies didn't start till about 4.30, so we had a good afternoon at [the] French landscape [exhibition] instead, & then coffee and meringue (for her) at Forte's, & then dinner at Golders Green, & then she stooped to darning two or three socks for me. She also brought along a few pieces of birthday cake to eat with the wine & coffee & Benedictine I so kindly provided for an after dinner snack.[113]

A number of his former students also turned up in London and John took a particular delight in showing them his favourite Bloomsbury squares and the British Museum, as often as not with a meal at what had become his almost habitual Swiss restaurant, the Maison Suisse at St Giles Circus. By the end of February he had exhausted all the Cook work he could do at home and 'could afford to be social' in the evenings.

He was booked to return home on the *Akaroa,* due to leave in late April, and packed a great deal into the weeks he had left. The Williamsons had moved from Looe to Chichester. He went down to stay with them, was very taken with the town and had a good walk with Williamson, ten miles through woods and over the Downs. The next day they went to Portsmouth to see the *Victory* and he was impressed with the remarkable job that had been done to restore the vessel to exactly as it had been at Trafalgar in 1805. 'We talked about Cook in the evenings', John wrote, '& lamented the decay of our civilization & the growth of bureaucracy at every opportunity & on every subject, whether the price of milk, civic & domestic architecture or second-hand bookshops in Charing Cross Road.'[114] They had remarkably little in common when it came to politics but a great deal in their historical interests. John's admiration for Williamson went back to his student days when he first discovered his *Short History of British Expansion* (a book that John observed would have been more popular if it had been decently printed), and while he might have been sharply critical of Williamson's deep conservatism he invariably showed him an affectionate respect.

On 24 March Harold Laski died suddenly. John had talked to him on the phone some time earlier, receiving a welcome 'like a long-lost brother'.[115] He had seen him briefly in January, when he found him looking 'terribly older',[116] and had been promised a dinner invitation after the general election. Laski, as the party's chairman, campaigned hard for Labour, which was returned with a greatly reduced majority. Shortly after, he caught flu; exhausted, 'he just seems to have gone phut', John wrote, 'as he was bound to some day, without any reserves'.[117] He was fifty-six. John was very depressed, and disappointed by the *Times* obituary, which he considered was 'without any understanding of the man at all'. Had he been in New Zealand, he said, he would have written an article for the *Listener*. Two and a half years later, his feelings about Laski were still very close when he reviewed the *Holmes–Laski Letters*, edited by Mark DeWolfe Howe, and Kingsley Martin's biographical memoir of Laski for Roy Parsons's publication *Parsons Packet*.[118]

John went down to Chessington in Surrey to see the Ordnance Survey people and discuss historical atlas production, and to Dover to see a paper-mill. He spent a day at the Monotype works and found them 'very distressed at the determined conservatism of the [New Zealand] Govt Printer, who keeps on ordering the type they prefer to forget about. So I said I would do what I could.'[119] He visited Oxford again to see the Oxford University Press; he got a good reception from the University Printer and saw all over the works – a staff of six working on typographical design alone. He went back to Cambridge for a weekend, going to the wedding of one of his students in the chapel of Trinity College, and visiting Ely, before calling on the Cambridge University Press on the Monday. At Easter he was again at Baildon with Keith and Fronnie.

A few days later he met Raymond McGrath and his wife and son. They had crossed from Ireland and were driving through to pick up the ferry at Newhaven on a trip to Europe. He stayed with them at a little village called Alfriston, in a fold of the Downs about ten miles from Lewes, 'in a 15th century pub, all oak beams & wonderful views from the windows of gardens & fields & village street, & drank half a bottle of Irish whisky, & chin-wagged pretty late'. He thought Raymond more 'aged in appearance than any of us' but healthy and cheerful, the son a 'long gangling oaf' much the same as his own.[120] The McGraths went off the next morning and John went on to Rye and Winchelsea and was carried away. 'Gosh, I wish you had been there', he wrote to Elsie, 'I've never seen such places, & now I don't know whether to retire to Bath or Rye or Winchelsea or the Bay of Islands'.

Rye seems to have been restored a good deal, but very intelligently . . . it's half really beautiful ½-timbering & ½ Georgian & plaster; there's a suburban bit or two, but really very little, I never saw so much good blue & white china in windows, private as well as shop – & you were obviously supposed to look at it, so I did. Henry James lived there for about 18 years in a Georgian house which caught a bomb, but the National Trust is doing it up. A big parish church, wonderfully weathered stone, at the top of the little hill, & a little churchyard full of daffodils & crab-apple among the tombstones. And all around the Romney marshes, where the sheep come from, with the river Rother winding through it . . . Winchelsea is a much smaller place, not much more than a big quadrangle of churchyard with a double row of houses round it, & almost all perfect, only one short row (& that in the background) of fake half timbering. It is on a little hill like Rye, you look from one to the other over the meadows, & the farm-lands wash up to Winchelsea like a sea round an island. Rooks cawing away like mad, rushing backwards & forwards to their nests. Big trees still bare but little ones all in leaf. More old stone gone beautiful colours, & good brick . . . Really quite staggeringly beautiful.[121]

In the middle of April the shopping was coming to a head: 'I have spent so much on household goods', John wrote to Elsie, 'that any books I may have bought look the merest chicken-feed, a candle-flame in the sun, a push-bike by the side of a Rolls-Royce'.[122] Cedric Firth, now in London for twelve months after finishing his job in New York, was a willing accomplice: 'he goes round saying Damn it, I'll only be here once, why not buy it & damn the expense'. He was talking of buying a 1680 pewter plate. John had come to much the same view: 'If we can't have one of those Regency houses in Alexander Place,* or Mrs Piozzi's in Bath, well we'd better try & make the house in Messines Road as good as possible & damn the expense'. So he and Firth looked at carpets and furniture and dinner sets and wondered if they should start a contemporary art society in Wellington and how could they get exhibitions of prints, and carpets and rugs, and pewter.

If only I could go round buying the things that I see that are really good, [John lamented] & not worry about the things that we desperately need,

*   John had not long before discovered, and been very taken with this group of Regency houses just off Thurloe Place, close to the Victoria and Albert Museum.

life would be much simpler. E.g. I have now seen a set of six completely beautiful & strong high-quality Swedish glasses & decanter; but if I brought out those you would go right through the roof & never come down again & your children would be left motherless. Let alone me being wifeless.[123]

On Elsie's instructions he was also buying some clothes. 'I bought a new pair of shoes, after having scrutinised a good many . . . They were called Aquatite. Will these really keep out the water? I said to the bloke. He was quite shocked. Oh, they won't keep out *water*, he said, they'll keep out the damp. But nobody else's shoes will keep out water, they say, they're all quite frankly & cheerfully defeatist about it.'[124]

In almost every letter John reports on concerts. His greatest excitement was hearing the Stuttgart Chamber Orchestra in London for two Bach concerts, the best string playing he had ever heard.[125] When there was a break in the concerts he went to see Michael Redgrave in *Hamlet,* and to *Love's Labour's Lost.* It was all reminiscent of his first stay in London. What was different were the lunches at the Athenaeum and the Reform Club and dinners at High Table.

The work on Cook took him to meet Rex Nan Kivell, the urbane art dealer and collector, managing director of the Redfern Gallery.[126] The gallery had been a significant force in introducing to England European artists such as Bonnard, Picasso, Rouault and Vuillard, and in promoting the work of British modernists, among them Barbara Hepworth, Henry Moore and Graham Sutherland. From the late 1920s, Nan Kivell had also built up a remarkable collection of books, manuscripts, maps, and historical and documentary art from the period of early European contact with New Zealand, Australia and the Pacific. He sent the collection to Canberra for safe-keeping during the war but had photographs of it all, and John was interested in using some of the works to illustrate the Cook volumes. He described his visit to Nan Kivell's flat 'in a rather grubby street east of Portland Place':*

But there is nothing grubby about Mr Nan Kivell's flat; not very big; but he is I gather unmarried, & inherited money from an aunt, & must do pretty well out of the Redfern Gallery; so he has most of his books leather-bound; & hanging on the walls a beautiful little sketch by Manet of Berthe Morisot walking on the sands, & a Cézanne water-colour,

---

*   He also had a country house in Wiltshire and a villa in Tangiers.

small & unfinished, & an early Van Gogh of which he is part owner, & a Matisse, & a small Italian Renaissance portrait, & a few more things like that; & a few odds & ends of Chinese pottery & Egyptian basalt, & old navigation instruments, not in the least like a museum & not too much. Plenty of coffee to drink. He had a book illustrated with engravings by David Jones I'd wanted to see for a long time, The Ancient Mariner, by Samuel Taylor Coleridge, & when I admired it said Oh, I've got two or three more of those, I'll give you one. And when I said Don't be silly, you can't do that sort of thing, he said No I'd like to, I helped to publish it, they're no good to me. Then when I asked him where I could get some engravings of D[avid] Jones for M[ervyn] Taylor, who desperately wants one, said Oh come down to the gallery, I've got loads of those things left over from the wood-engraving rage of years ago, they won't sell now, take as many as you like. So now I've got a heap of Claire Leightons & Agnes Miller Parkers & Gwen Raverats . . . I'll have to sort them out & bestow them where they'll do most good.* He certainly is a most generous chap. Anyhow I gave him an Introd to NZ & a Dictionary of NZ Biog in return as he collects NZ stuff too . . . I forgot to mention his beautiful Christopher Woods.[127]

John must have been largely unaware of Nan Kivell's extraordinary life. Born in Christchurch, he began life as Reginald Nankivell. Until he escaped New Zealand by enlisting to serve in the First World War, he was a bookbinder. Once his war was over, there followed the remarkable invention by Nan Kivell himself (beginning with the name) of the personality he became: 'the archetypal outsider – illegitimate, homosexual, self-educated, an Antipodean colonial' became 'the urbane dealer and collector who threw off his modest origins to emerge as a man of wealth, a knight of the realm, a connoisseur and collector of all manner of fine, beautiful and historic objects'.[128] What John did become aware of was Nan Kivell's interest in finding a permanent home for his collection and his initial thought that this might be in New Zealand. Just after this visit John wrote to Heenan blasting the timidity of New Zealand House:

The damned place needs the Heenan touch . . . Now, if you were High Cmer, & I one of your off-siders, we could really have some fun, besides turning Treasury pale with anguish & white with rage . . . the things we could do here for NZ if we had a bit of money – not merely in publicity, but in gathering things to send back – pictures, books, – well, I won't say any more; but it goes to my heart to watch the opportunities passing by.[129]

---

* Most of the engravings John passed on to the New Zealand National Art Gallery.

With Nan Kivell the motivation was not just money. He had come
to feel that such a munificent act might be a means of his securing
a title. When the offer of a knighthood from New Zealand, which
had seemed possible in the 1953 Coronation Honours list, failed
to materialise, to John's intense disappointment the way was left
open for the Australians. The Australian government eventually
purchased the collection for £70,000, but were rather slow with the
knighthood, which was bestowed only in 1976, the year before Nan
Kivell's death.

At the end of April John heard that the *Akaroa*'s departure was
delayed indefinitely because of a dock-workers' strike. A day or
two later the news came that he was to go to another of Unesco's
general conferences, this time in Florence, beginning in the middle
of May. Parsimony, it would appear, had finally prevailed with the
new National government, so that R.M. Algie, the Minister of
Education, was prepared to accept John as one of the delegates. In
some ways he was ready to leave and was unhappy about the delay
in getting home. 'Perhaps because it is Home', he wrote to Elsie,
admitting that he was 'rather anxious' to see the faces of his three
boys again, although he supposed the novelty would soon wear
off.[130] To Heenan, he said a little more:

curiously enough I am quite eager to get back. You know I was almost
afraid to come to England, I thought I'd like it too much, & would get
into the most frightful psychological tangles. But now as far as I can see,
I really don't want to stay, I want to get back home & get on with the job
– or jobs. Whether I'll feel like that when I do get back & look around I
don't know, but I'm willing to try it.[131]

JOHN FLEW TO ROME ON 16 May and caught a train from there
to Florence. It was daylight and the sun shone and the country was
very beautiful, 'haymaking going on all over the place . . . whole
families out hoeing, ploughing going on till dark; olive trees, that I
had always wanted to see, on the slopes, towns & castles on the hill-
tops, everything came true out of the books again'.[132]

This time the New Zealand delegation had three members: Beeby,
John, and Wynne Mason from the New Zealand Embassy in Paris.
During the conference they were able to recruit a young English
woman as secretary. The delegation, finding itself hard put to
cover the necessary meetings, reckoned that four, with a delegation
secretary, was the minimum for really efficient participation.[133] John
clearly enjoyed working with Beeby. 'B & B arrived yesterday, still

co-operating', they cabled to the Education Department. The acting director thought that could not possibly be right, and passed it on as 'recuperating'.[134] The conference was 'on the whole . . . a hardworking and even at times rather pedestrian meeting'. This they saw as a good sign. The 'lack of debate at a lofty intellectual level' could, in some measure, be seen as 'a reflection of . . . hard-won wisdom'.

The argument about Spanish, that had begun at the Lebanon conference, and had taxed John's chairmanship at Paris, was resumed, with the Latin Americans, most of whom were heavily in arrears in their contributions to Unesco, again making the pace: 'the Cuba bloke screaming & howling & yelling away in a dreadful harsh voice as he insists on the beauty & the music of the Spanish tongue', John reported to Elsie.[135] This time, with the backing of the Middle East and China, the advocates of Spanish won the vote in the procedure committee. The New Zealand delegation had been instructed from Wellington not to oppose it, but John was 'damned' if he would vote for it and he abstained, 'much to the surprise of all our friends, & not noticeably to our increased popularity with S. America'.[136] In spite of the extra cost to Unesco, there did not seem to be any argument remaining to withstand any proposal for an additional working language if it was spoken by a large number of people. John was involved with redrafting the rules of procedure and also some preambles to resolutions:

The French text is alleged to be all right, though I can't see how it can be, if it is as repetitious & nonsensical as the English. – An English professor of education from Leeds & I have been working on the English text so far, & there is an American involved too, but also a Frenchman put on for liaison with the French text; & his idea is simply to have a literal translation from the French – that being the way to perfect English prose apparently. So if he insists on that, & . . . the Englishman & I insist on writing English – & perhaps the American will want to write American, we shall be having a first-rate row . . . [137]

Whatever the trials of the conference, and John seems to have taken them in his stride, they were almost insignificant next to the excitement of being in Florence:

it was a bit unreal to walk into one thing and another that I'd known for thirty years or so in pictures – Donatello's St George & the Palazzo Vecchio & palazzo after palazzo & S. Maria Novella & Benvenuto Cellini's Perseus & Ghiberti's doors. And I knew I wouldn't be able to settle down till I had seen the Botticellis; so before the meeting this afternoon I went into the Uffizi & there was the Birth of Venus on one wall & Primavera facing it. I never knew there was so much gold about the B. of V., or how blue the cornflowers were on the figure on the right. The Primavera badly needs cleaning, as indeed most of the pictures in the gallery do . . . And then as I was coming out what should I run into but a room full of Bronzinos, & there, newly cleaned & reframed, was our little Marie de Medeci,* you never saw anything lovelier – certainly the best thing in the room. In fact it's probably the thing I'd pinch if I had the chance – too many people know the Botticellis.[138]

He was staying in a hotel in the Piazza de Santa Maria Novella, near the railway station; the conference was held in rooms in both the Palazzo Vecchio and the Palazzo Pitti and John explored the narrow side streets – 'they're all narrow & almost all side, as you might say'[139] – as he walked to and from the meetings. The noise was remarkable. The place full of motorbikes of all sorts; he saw policemen just sitting on their stationary bikes and racing their engines at any hour of the day or night. Then there were the church bells and the usual high-spirited shouting and singing, 'with a good deal of loving Italian dwelling on the last note'.[140] The traffic rules appeared to be open slather, though astonishingly no one seemed to get killed. John decided that on the whole he liked the Italians. The place was full of wonderful things to buy for presents, leather and silver and pottery and prints, but as he would be travelling home by air he resisted being carried away. There was a conference excursion to Siena to see the Palio, the ancient horse race around the square. The place was crammed with people mad with excitement, with a parade first

of groups representing all the various parishes, with the jockeys in armour riding on cart-horses with the race-horses led behind, men-at-arms & pages & standard bearers & flag-bearers & marshals & halberdiers & special champions, all clad in the most gorgeous 15th century dress, you never saw such colours or combinations, gorgeous beyond your wildest dreams.[141]

On the way there they went to San Gimignano, 'the little hill town with all the towers', with a beautiful Romanesque church, and another church with wonderful arcading – John decided it was really the arcading that he 'liked best of all in the architecture' – and texture in all the stonework of the towers and walls. But the countryside, with its slopes bursting with crops and vines or olive trees and with villages or castles or villas on top of all the hills, he found 'almost

---

*   John and Elsie had a number of favourite paintings of young girls – the daughters they would have loved to have.

too lushly romantic' – he had earlier wondered if one had to get rid of a lot of English puritanism to really appreciate the pink and green marble of the Duomo and the Campanile. There were trips as well to Ravenna and to Rimini and a wearying round of cocktail parties, but the champagne did not flow as it had in Paris.

The conference finished on 17 June, and the next day John flew back to London. The city was a bit of an anti-climax at first but he decided that Bedford Square would 'stand up to anything' he had seen in urban architecture, 'apart from single buildings like the Palazzo Vecchio, which are just individual bits of supreme genius'.[142] There was time to do a little more work, and the president of the Hakluyt Society 'turned on a very good & amusing lunch . . . at the Athenaeum to celebrate the launching of Cook' and to farewell John.[143] On the morning of 3 July he left London on the five-day journey that it then took to fly back to New Zealand.

PART THREE

Scholar and Public Figure

11

THE SCHOLAR AT WORK: I

Editing the Endeavour *Journals of James Cook and Joseph Banks*

JOHN'S LEAVE IN 1949–50 was an exciting period. Back in London for the first time since he had left, despondently, twenty years earlier, he began the real work on editing the journals of James Cook on his three voyages and Joseph Banks's *Endeavour* journal. Editing the journals, he had long said, would be but the preliminary step – and how lightly that was once viewed – towards the biography of Cook. This work on Cook and Banks, on which rests John's enduring reputation as a great scholar, occupied him until his death in 1971, though, single-minded as he was in his dedication to Cook, other activities continued to take up a good deal of his time.

As each volume of Cook's journals appeared, in 1955, 1961 and 1967, together with the Banks journal in 1962, readers came to appreciate the magnificent achievement they represented – the sequence of introductions and explanatory notes, carefully annotated text, appendices, maps and illustrations – and the extraordinary scholarship that underlay all of these. John's organising skill and architectural sense informed the whole work, reducing a vast array of documents and commentary to order. Possibly less obvious was what lay behind the printed page: the immensity of the labour expended in the whole undertaking, from the tracking down of material in archives, libraries and private ownership in many parts of the world and the painstaking decisions about spelling and punctuation in eighteenth-century documents to the innumerable hours spent collating and checking texts against the originals or photocopies of the originals, even more time in research for the introductions and explanatory notes, and an almost interminable process of proofreading and correcting. This chapter and the next are intended to give the reader some understanding of how John did this work, to provide an account of the editor, historian and biographer – already an accomplished scholar and writer – discovering the full extent of the task he had taken on, and mastering the additional skills it required.

John's ideas about how Cook's journals should be edited go back to his recognising, when he was writing *The Exploration of the Pacific,* that they had never been printed as Cook wrote them. For more than a century knowledge of the first voyage had been based on Hawksworth's volumes, published in 1773. Hawksworth – in John's words, a 'miscellaneous writer' – not content with drawing on both Cook and Banks without distinguishing between the two, also added a polish for public consumption to the unpolished seaman's journal, losing its matter-of-fact vividness, and contributed his own sententious observations. Admiral Wharton's edition of the *Endeavour* journal, published in 1893, was an immense step forward but was still not a literal transcription of his sources. There were facts he felt it necessary to spare the reader; he was, John wrote, 'an awful prude'.[1] The published journals of the second and third voyages, edited by Dr John Douglas, the Canon of Windsor, were essentially Cook's in spite of Douglas's 'improvements' to their style. But as a basis for scholarship they were hardly adequate. Thus John came to nourish what seemed at first a very simple ambition: to print the journals as they had been written.

I had seen the original of the first journal at Canberra [he wrote in 1957, after the journal of the first voyage had been published], and photostats of the others in the Mitchell Library at Sydney. The writing seemed plain enough. What indeed could be simpler than to have them typed out, and to print them as a plain text, on which anybody could work? They could be paper-bound, and sell cheaply. Some way could surely be found of raising the money to pay for such an edition, and the chances were it would pay for itself in the end. Simple, straightforward; you see I was not going to worry about things like annotation – why annotate when the thing was so well known? – or textual introductions – why make difficulties unnecessarily? How naive – how staggeringly naive – I was.[2]

During his leave in London, as he began work on Cook, 'the realities of the situation began to dawn on me'.[3] For a start the idea of 'a plain text' proved illusory; his first task was, rather, to establish an accurate text. It rapidly became clear that there was no single original journal of the first voyage – indeed, such a document probably no longer existed (if it ever had), though what appeared to be fragmentary drafts were in a number of collections. The Canberra journal was, at least, in Cook's hand; three other 'copies' existed, one in the Mitchell Library, one in the British Museum

and one in the National Maritime Museum at Greenwich.* Before
he left for London John had a photostat copy of the Canberra
manuscript (the Australian government had given this to the New
Zealand government, it was then passed on to John and, when he
had finished with it, it went – together with other photocopies of
material he had collected – to the Alexander Turnbull Library).
From the photostats he had had a typed copy made. His first task in
London was to complete 'the painful process'[4] of going through the
photostats and typescript, checking on every letter in the 200,000
words, a far from mechanical exercise. Working so closely on the
documents brought him closer to their author, 'even his character
begins to emerge', though he still judged him a 'damned hard person
to know'.[5] To Kathleen McKay he confessed that he was 'getting
an awful crush on Capt. Cook'.[6] His letter to her, characteristic in
its quizzical wordplay, reflected his preoccupation at the time with
spelling and punctuation:

Really that voyage makes most of the other Great Occasions of the
18th century seem pretty silly. What is Dr Johnson, what is Voltaire,
what is Burke or Pope or Chatham by the side of Cook? . . . Now I
want to plunge immediately – or emmidiatly, as the gallant capt. spelt
it – into Banks. We must confess one thing, indeed, even in our
bemused state of Hero Worship, a dreadful blot – no two things
indeed, which sully the shining record; the gallant capt., the distinguished seaman, the calm astronomer & mathematician, riding the
whirlwind & directing the storm – or at any rate riding the waves &
getting off the rocks – he the Nonpareil could not spell, he had no
more idea of punctuation than my foot. Such a welter of ei & ie you
never saw. Has any other seaman ever wieghed anchor? Has any other
journal writer written seven foolscap pages without a paragraph &
without a capital letter† & without a full stop or a comma? Ought this
to be allowed even in the Navy? Are there not some prerogatives that
a decently considerate Providence would forbid even Genius? . . . But I
will say this for the Capt., that he is legible, vile spelling & all, & does
not descend into the hopeless scrawls of Sir J Banks when that Gt. Man
was President of the Royal Society . . .[7]

Cook's spelling, John decided, should be kept as it was, but what
was the answer with capitals and punctuation? John had a 'sort of

---

*   John was to write a fascinating account of the four copies of the journal
     in his textual introduction to the *Endeavour* journal. (*Journals*, vol.1,
     pp.cxciv–ccxxv.)
†   His capitalisation, John later wrote, 'we may call unsystematic eighteenth
     century, modified by ambiguity; for it is frequently uncertain whether
     Cook is writing a capital letter or not'. (*Journals*, vol.1, p.cciii.)

sentimental feeling' that there was a 'lingering flavour of the author, or at least of the period, about capitals that one should retain if possible'. 'But of course as soon as one drops a cap one is open to the charge of inconsistency & illogic; & too many caps spoil reading. As a matter of fact, this last consideration depends, somewhat subtly, on the face of type the thing is printed in – is it an old face type, with caps not as high as ascenders, or not?'[8] Adding to the problem was the difficulty of knowing whether Cook (or Banks) was using a capital or not. Cook, John noted, had a 'most peculiar large r, – or is it R? – ʔound = round, in a number of different sizes & slight variations of shape'. He had noticed the same thing in one or two other eighteenth-century manuscripts but when he asked a Public Record Office official about it, 'he merely asked wearily "Does it matter?"'.[9] Later, when the journal was in proof and John was checking it against the photostat rather than the typescript, he had a dreadful feeling that he had got it wrong – 'how in God's name did I come to put in so many capital letters' – and he was panic stricken at the thought of the printer getting the corrected proofs back and 'bracing himself to curse adequately'.[10] He had been told that Dom David Knowles, the great medieval scholar, held that to print a text accurately was beyond human capacity, but he could not accept that as an explanation for his 'virtual invention of capitals'.*

Punctuation caused less worry. Cook almost habitually used a full stop where twentieth-century writers would use a comma, and often used a dash, like many eighteenth- and nineteenth-century letter writers, simply as the full stop. John believed his task was to make the text intelligible, 'so one must punctuate or re-punctuate to that extent; & that involves a certain amount of translation'.[11]

Once these decisions had been made and the typescript had

---

* This experience with Cook's Journal led John, when he came to work on Banks's Journal to draft a note on spelling and punctuation. An editor's duty, he wrote, was to give a readable as well as an accurate text, which pointed to a compromise between printing exactly what was written or reducing it to a 'flat twentieth-century normality', for 'I am not an 18th c. editor, a Hawksworth, imposing orthodoxy, and I want to give as much of Banks as possible, his peculiarities as well as his abilities.

Therefore (1) normal capitalisation for names, persons, peoples, and countries, either as nouns or adjectives.
(2) retain caps for nouns, when Banks clearly has caps.
(3) retain caps otherwise when they do not clutter up the page, or present the reader with a shock that there seems no justification for. What this means in practice is elimination of a great many E's, C's, S's and a smaller number of L's.'
(Undated note. J.C.Beaglehole Papers, 73-004-01/05. ATL.)

been checked, it was then collated against the two journal copies in London and a microfilm of the Mitchell copy in Sydney. It was a tedious task but one with some surprising rewards for Cook's future biographer:

By the time we have finished our collating, indeed, we have found out some interesting things. One of them is that Cook was not altogether the simple sailor that one is accustomed to think him. I would not call him a conscious literary artist, but it is clear that he did not write his journal straight off and let it go at that. He did a great deal of drafting and re-drafting, and luckily we have a few bits and pieces of manuscript in which we can see this process going on. We can see as it were, the growth of a mind. We can see an increase in elementary education, we can see the widening of the interests of a very able man, we can see a process of moral struggle, we can see an enlarged appreciation of the possibilities of description. We are rather getting away, in fact, from our old idea of the plain text.[12]

What also became clear in this process of collation, and from John's study of the logs and journals of other men on the first voyage (most of them held in the Public Record Office), was that Cook, in that drafting and redrafting, had been ready to use the work of others, especially Joseph Banks. On board the *Endeavour,* John surmised, journals were common property. The borrowing and rewriting, as he disentangled it, revealed a good deal about Cook, the unpractised writer learning his craft, and about his relationship with Banks. It was, John judged, 'an interesting study in the way a great man learns from one less great'.[13]

IN LONDON JOHN HAD got to know R.A. Skelton, the honorary secretary of the Hakluyt Society and newly appointed Superintendent of the Map Room in the British Museum. It was the beginning of a scholarly partnership that would prove enormously important to the success of the whole enterprise. Before the war Skelton had been an assistant keeper in the Printed Books Section of the British Museum, where he had laid the foundation of his deep knowledge of explorers' maps and cartographic history.[14] After the war he joined the Map Room as assistant to Edward Lynam, 'verse writer & Irish nationalist . . . as well as [an] expert on maps',[15] who had been secretary of the Hakluyt Society since 1931. Lynam then became the society's president and Skelton soon succeeded him as honorary secretary. Early in 1950 Lynam died of cancer and Skelton was appointed Superintendent of the Map Room. Subsequently he won an international reputation in the history of cartography.* As editor of the Hakluyt Society's publications, he showed a remarkable capacity for quickly learning the background of the areas covered by the books he was seeing through to publication; the breadth of his knowledge came to reflect the wide historical and geographical range of these volumes. His work on Frank Debenham's edition of Bellingshausen's voyage to the Antarctic, published by the society in 1945, was his introduction to the Pacific Ocean and the Antarctic. Working with John saw Skelton become an established authority on both Cook and the exploration and charting of the Pacific.

Their association had begun with an exchange of letters in the months before John left New Zealand for London. (In one of his first, Skelton reported that he had met with Joe Heenan,† who had promised £3000 from the New Zealand government towards the cost of the Cook project.) In a letter to Heenan from London, John judged Skelton 'a most admirable person, with whom I have got (almost) to swearing terms'.[16] While John was in London, in 1949–50 and again in 1955–56, Skelton became absorbed in Cook to such an extent that, belatedly, the society had to appoint a second secretary–treasurer to share the work of producing the society's other volumes.[17]

Before he left London in July 1950, John had established a text of the journal which was sent to the printers (Robert MacLehose and Company Ltd in Glasgow) for setting in type. They had already produced specimen pages that met largely with his approval. Again, as with capitals and punctuation, there were questions – partly scholarly and partly stylistic in nature – to be settled. They decided to retain superior letters for Mr Lieut^t and such terms, 'to retain the 18th century note as far as possible'. Whether that was 'the ultimate wisdom', John later confessed, he was not quite sure, but in practice the result did not 'look bad'.[18] He had also nearly completed work on the text for the third voyage. At that time, before he inherited the work on the second voyage from J.A. Williamson, he believed that the

---

*   Of his many publications, Skelton became possibly best known for his work in rewriting and developing Leo Bagrow's great *History of Cartography*, so that Bagrow–Skelton remained the standard work in the field, (Leo Bagrow and R.A. Skelton, *History of Cartography* (London: C.A. Watts, 1964), and for his part in the publication on the Vinland Map (R.A. Skelton, Thomas E. Marston and George D. Painter, *The Vinland Map and the Tartar Relation*, (New Haven and London: Yale University Press, 1965), which became the subject of considerable scholarly controversy.

†   It was Skelton's suggestion that the first volume of Cook should be dedicated to Heenan's memory. (JCB to JEP, 13 February 1952.)

first journal presented many more textual problems than the others, and he sometimes felt 'a bit like a harassed classical scholar working on the text of Homer or Euripides'. He had a growing feeling that the whole job would take a good deal longer than the four or five years the society originally hoped.[19] Galley proofs of the journals were to be posted to John in Wellington, where he planned to do the rest of the editorial work. In contemplating what this would involve, the 'realities of the situation', once again, had struck him:

. . . an eighteenth century document, if it is to be made plain, needs annotation. It was essential to be a historian as well as an editor. My texts had a history as well as the voyages. The journals were part – certainly a large part – of a highly complicated story. It became necessary to find out everything that could possibly be found out about Cook's voyages: about Cook, his companions, the sciences of the age, the administrative background, innumerable personal relations and tensions as well as matters of geography, navigation and handwriting. The problems did not merely rise, they proliferated. Nothing was as simple as it seemed . . . [20]

Back home in Wellington, John resumed writing letters to Skelton. These grew into an extensive correspondence between Wellington and London that continued through the 1950s. As well as providing a record of a remarkable scholarly collaboration, the letters reveal much about the two men and their growing friendship. Until his return to London in 1955, however, when they moved on to first name* terms, their letters invariably began 'My dear Skelton' and 'My dear Beaglehole' – not uncharacteristic of the English at the time, but it was unlike John not to have broken through the formality somewhat earlier. His appreciation of Skelton's work grew steadily, and the discussion of the whereabouts and history of manuscripts, the foibles of scientific experts, footnotes, muster books, graphic records, introductory essays, illustrations, corrections to proofs and innumerable other questions were intermingled with family news and comment on public events. 'My room at home is a shambles at the moment with Cook & Banks stuff', John wrote a few months after his return, 'photographs, photostats, microfilm, typescript, books, notes etc. My intolerant wife sighs deeply, & wanted to know how long this was going on. I told her about 20 years. That is, of course, I said, till I've finished my life of Capt. Cook.'[21] It was to prove

---

* Skelton's initials, R.A., stood for Raleigh Ashlin with which he had been baptised. He had been registered, however, as Peter and, perhaps not surprisingly, this was the name by which his friends knew him.

a remarkably accurate prediction. This letter went on to suggest that he should write a general introduction to all three voyages, 'on Cook's place in the exploration of the Pacific, & the significance & interaction of the three voyages'; each volume would still have to have its own special introduction. (The suggestion was adopted.) The letter ended with a request for a copy of 'just one other thing I want from the BM – Add. MSS. 33,979/29, a letter from Matra to Banks, some yarn about a threatened general mutiny on board the Endeavour, under the impact of Tahitian delights. – My God,' he concluded, 'how I keep worrying you.'

In annotating the journal John set out first to answer the question: why did Cook say what he did say? Some of the answers, as already noted, he found in his work on the texts.[22] Second, he sought to explain Cook's experience in the light of later knowledge – scientific, geographical, historical, ethnological. He tried to work out, as precisely as possible, where Cook went, and to account for the observations of men and all manner of other things that he made in those places; to identify the native place names Cook had picked up and the plants, animals and sea creatures he had recorded. He sought to explain Cook's allusions to different facets of Polynesian and Australian life, particularly for the Tahitian and New Zealand portions of the journal. This led not only to a large number of footnotes but also to his twenty-one-page 'Note on Polynesian History'[23] in the introduction to the volume. Paying such attention to the indigenous people, whose worlds were to change dramatically following their contact with Europeans, marked something quite new in writing about Cook.

Many years of historical reading had given John a remarkable range of knowledge, but there were gaps – 'in matters of navigation and eighteenth century shipboard practice and language it has seemed wisest for an editor to regard himself as a representative creature, and to annotate for his own ignorance'[24] – and in this area, as well as others, he drew on the knowledge of experts in many parts of the world, not least on Skelton in London:

. . . you know all about maps, & therefore all about the names on maps. Well, tell me, why the devil did Cook call a small group of islands and rocks off the E. NZ coast the Poor Knights? He generally gives reasons, but here gives no reason, so I assume the reason was obvious – but it beats me; & everybody nautical, Yorkshire, literary I have consulted. I have been to Shakespeare, the Bible, Brewer, guides to Yorkshire, the Pilots for the English coast, N America, Newfoundland, Ency. Brit., cookery books. I have found out (a) there is a rock in the Bristol Channel called the Poor Knight singular (why?) (b) there is a crack in King Lear about 'a poor knight' (no caps) (c) Poor Knights was the alternative name for the Knights Templars – but what would Cook know about the KT's? (d) there is a traditional German or central European or Polish dish called Poor Knights, bread fried in egg or something. Now does the BM or the RGS or the University intellect of the UK know of any natural feature, legend, story, nursery rhyme, popular 18th-century ballad, local landmark, tragedy, comedy, tragico-pastoral comedy, proverb, sentimental song, piece of cooker, part of a ship's furniture, botanical nomenclature, legal terminology, sea-shell, or nautical jargon or nickname for any admiral or member of the Royal family that has anything to do with Poor Knights?[25]

Clearly his pen warmed to the inquiry, but the humour should not mislead; John was tenacious in pursuing the information that he thought the reader needed to understand Cook and the voyage properly. Skelton, at that time, was unable to add anything to John's list.[26] The Royal Geographical Society was similarly gravelled, though the secretary of its Permanent Committee on Geographical Names, Marcel Aurousseau (who was later to index the first two volumes of the *Journals*), wondered if there was some link with the Three Kings. A close reading of the journal, he wrote, 'gives one the feeling of the way in which [Cook] looked continually ahead, and, while beating up the North Coast of your North Island, he clearly had Tasman's Three Kings continually in mind . . . worried about how to get around the cape, I should think'.[27] While an interesting observation, this did not really advance the question of the name. Skelton, however, did not give up, and three years later he wrote that he had at last an alternative explanation:

The military knights of Windsor (see Whitaker's Almanack) were until 1833 known as the Poor Knights of Windsor . . . What more likely than that Cook, who no doubt read newspapers & anyway inherited a tradition of giving placenames with a Royal or Court association, had them in mind? I can't suggest why, unless the islets looked like gentlemen in cloaks marching in procession . . . If you think there is anything in this, please send me quickly a revised footnote for transmission to MacLehose . . . [28]

The volume was already in page proofs; changes at that stage were costly and difficult to make. 'I may manage the guts of the Poor Knights one with a bit of surgery & careful counting of spaces',[29] John replied. The footnote as printed reflects both his initial research and Skelton's suggestion.

In Wellington his great resource was the Alexander Turnbull

Library with its rich collections, especially of material on exploration and the Pacific. The ideal, he wrote in 1952, 'would be to work at home & at the Turnbull on the ordinary things – we really are very well off for printed material, & I can treat the Turnbull practically as if I owned it – & hop over to London fairly frequently for two or three months at a time for the MSS & the maps & charts. However there's no millionaire in the business yet.'[30] But not everything could be discovered in the Turnbull. Wanting something on the Portuguese governor and viceroy at Rio (with whom Cook had an interesting encounter), he asked Skelton if 'some expert could provide a line or two on both men'; as 'when the details of Portuguese colonial history are concerned we are up against it in NZ'.[31] For further searching or checking in the archives, the British Museum or the Public Record Office, the Hakluyt Society employed a researcher, Stella Campbell.

For the zoological annotation, John involved his and Elsie's old friend Averil Lysaght. Since their student days at Victoria, Lysaght had spent much of her time in England. After three years' postgraduate research at the Rothamsted Experimental Station she was awarded a University of London PhD in 1935, and went on to a number of short-term academic and scientific jobs. In 1947–48 she was employed as assistant editor of the zoology section of *Chambers Encyclopaedia* and met Norman Kinnear, Keeper of Zoology at the British Museum of Natural History. He suggested to her that working on the birds of Cook's voyages could be a worthwhile project and offered her space to work at the museum, with its great collection of Sydney Parkinson's paintings and drawings. It was an example of her habit of 'constructing private empires in obscure corners of learned institutions',[32] and with no formal position, let alone remuneration, she dug in there for more than twenty years. Her work on the zoology of the voyages led to an interest in the artists and she did useful work in identifying drawings by Banks's assistant, Herman Spöring, that had previously been attributed to others.

Lysaght provided much of the material for the zoological notes for both the Cook and Banks journals (though John also consulted scientific colleagues in New Zealand) and she drew on experts in the museum when she felt it necessary. John had considerable respect for her scholarship, but did not always find her easy to work with. She became very proprietorial about her material, indeed about all Cook and Banks material, and could become rather excited about the necessity of outwitting other scholars, especially Americans, who might (quite legitimately) wish to have access to it.[33] She could also be very forthright to John when she considered that he fell short of her scholarly standards, but her denunciations were generally followed by a letter restoring peace. She is a recurring subject in John's correspondence with Skelton:

At the moment I'm in one of those ghastly complacent moods; but I think this is probably due to the fact that I've thrown away one obviously absurd note contributed by a bright boy at the BMNH through AML & substituted another more in accordance with the dictates of Sound Sense & Natural History on this side of the World. I am standing on my editorial dignity & last word over this, so you'd better not tell AML or she'll rend me limb from limb. If I can work up the courage I'll write to her about it myself. If I can't work up the courage we'll just sneak it in unbeknownst, with a desperate sense of adventure.[34]

In a later letter, having commented on a fresh outburst by Lysaght, John added, 'Dammit, I'd much rather talk about all this than write about it. She has done such first-rate work too.'[35]

Many inquiries to the scientists produced straightforward answers; identifying a plant or fish from Cook's or Banks's comments and Parkinson's paintings and drawings was generally not too difficult. This was not always so, however. The photocopy of the Banks journal which John was working from, in the section describing Tahiti, had two blanks with faint and indecipherable pencillings in them. A member of the staff at the Mitchell Library had scrutinised these for him. The first did not present any difficulty. It was the second, John wrote to Phyllis Mander Jones, the Mitchell Librarian, that caused him all the trouble:

Miss Sherrie thought the words were possibly 'Eng mallow'; & for a while I rested on that. But it just doesn't make sense in relation to the fruit 'reckoned most delicious'; which I have otherwise identified as the *ahia* or jambo. I happened to take another look at Hawksworth last night, & the relevant bit reads 'a fruit known here by the name of *Jambu*, & reckoned most delicious'. Now what is jambo in Latin? – Answer, *Eugenia malaccensis*. Well now, is it possible that the pencilled words are 'Eug malacc' (or 'mallacc')?

If that is so, it all makes sense. – even if Cook did copy the words as 'Eag melloa', & almost drive me mad trying to make out what he meant until I realised he had been using Banks.[36]

Further scrutiny of the original journal confirmed John's hunch and illustrated the benefit of working on both the Cook and the Banks journals at the same time. He wrote footnotes on the plant for both volumes.[37]

By May 1952 John was feeling increasingly uneasy that he knew nothing about the Pacific islands except from books.[38] He had a horror 'of making the same sort of bloomers about (e.g.) Tahiti as some people make about NZ'[39] and, when the regional airline TEAL* began its service to Tahiti at the beginning of 1952, he and Elsie decided to go. 'Of course nobody will believe that it's anything but an expensive holiday,'[40] he wrote to Phyllis Mander Jones. He found the trip enormously useful:

Really it has been worthwhile coming here & treading in the sacred footsteps [he wrote to Skelton from 'somewhere outside Papeete']. I must have trodden in some of them in covering so much ground; & I have carefully collected a tridacina shell for you from Point Venus, to be delivered I don't know when; it would make a nice romantic ash-tray in the B.M. The only trouble about footsteps is that the local historians are so dogmatically & scornfully divided about where they were. The Point Venus stream has apparently changed its course more than once, so has the one at what Cook called Ohitepeha Bay. We, by the way, have been camped down in the bungalow of a hotel not far from Matavai Bay, so that now I know that bay fairly well. But where the hell did the Dolphin water? The streams seem to have got filled up, as well as having moved. They're not unlike NZ streams in that way. And the streams have different names from the valleys they run through. Well, I've got some light on place-names, & promise of any further help I need from the leading bloke in that line. I am a bit stricken with the sheer complexity of that matter, but at the same time I feel a lot safer than I did before. There is going to be an awful bunch of footnotes as a result of all this. – For sheer romantic scenery give me Cook's two harbours in Moorea/ Aimeo/Eimeo – there's no word really which hasn't been rather overused already. I've seen other islands, Raiatea, Huahine etc fairly closely from the air, but haven't been able to get to them by sea – plenty of time for a round trip on a trading vessel if I had known when I came what I know now; but it takes you such a hell of a time to find out anything here, so that it's quite impossible to plan ahead until you come on a second visit . . . Anyhow I have seen reefs, & streams, & volcanic peaks, & bathed off Point Venus, & tried to place the fort, & climbed over the sorry remains of Amo & Purea's giant marae, & observed the constancy of some Tahitian habits, such as sitting around in picturesque attitudes doing nothing, & I don't want to go home just yet.[41]

He thought he could now 'turn out a purple patch or two', but where should he put them – in an introduction as a relief or rather a variation, from pedantry, or in 'the Great Life'? There was only one, which appeared, unmistakably, in his description of Matavai Bay in

---

*   Tasman Empire Airways Ltd.

the general introduction in volume one of the *Journals*:

. . . its long curve of black volcanic sand backed by the tall innumerable pillars of coconuts with their wild crowns, immobile and sculptured in a hot still noon or moon-charmed night, streaming like vast bunches of pennants on a rising wind; given sobriety by the deep green of the sand-haunting myriad fingered casuarinas; while further back the bread-fruit and the ancient buttressed *mape* or chestnut rise into splendid benedictions of plenty . . .[42]

In Tahiti he met an American, J. Frank Stimson. Attracted to the South Seas after reading *Typee* and *Omoo*, and disillusioned with American life ('simply a nightmare'), Stimson had settled in Tahiti in 1912 and for forty years devoted himself to acquiring a remarkable understanding of the language and culture of ancient Polynesia.[*] He had come to have possibly a wider knowledge of the islands and their speech than any Polynesian had ever possessed.[43] John warmed to him at once, 'bursting with enthusiasms & volubilities', and was charmed by his Tuamotuan wife and his daughter – 'he keeps a very tight hand on her morals & won't let her dance at the fête'.[44] John drew on Stimson's deep well of philological knowledge and was clearly fascinated by the man:

One of the most vivid experiences of my life was the first afternoon I spent with him – he was reading out some of his translations of ancient Tahitian chants, & I said, Now do it in the original, & he did; & it was electrifying. He suddenly became old Tahiti, & I was back in the 18th century before the discovery. His linguistic learning seemed to me to be immense . . .[45]

The Peabody Museum of Salem, Massachusetts, had sponsored a project to capture Stimson's knowledge, and sent out a young anthropologist, Donald S. Marshall, to work with him. John met and got to know Marshall, as well as James and Suzanne McConnaughey, rich American writers and benefactors of the

---

[*]   Stimson was a controversial figure in anthropological circles owing to his long and bitter controversy with the Bishop Museum scholar Kenneth Emory. They had worked together on two prewar field trips to the Tuamotu archipelago and from the same material reached diametrically opposite views on the question of whether there had existed in former times in the Tuamotus a cult of a supreme god, called Kiho-Tumu or Kio-Tumu. Stimson said yes, Emory no, and Emory appears to have carried scholarly opinion with him. (Bengt Danielsson, 'Kia Ora Keneti', in Genevieve A. Highland et al., eds, *Polynesian Culture History*, (Honolulu: Bishop Museum Press, 1967) pp.23–4.) John knew of the controversy but kept out of the argument.

project, who had a home in Tahiti (which they visited every second
year) as well as one in Ohio. They were very hospitable, and drove
John and Elsie all around the island. Another 'most charming'
couple who entertained them were the van den Brucks, who, John
believed, 'must have staggering wealth'. They 'gave us a wonderful
earth oven-cooked traditional lunch, sucking pig, taro, plantains etc
– he French but Cambridge educated, she English & quite dazzlingly
beautiful; spending money in an apparently quite disinterested effort
to break some of the high-lands into farming, with a wonderful . . .
collection of Chinese jade'.[46] 'I wish I were still in Tahiti', John wrote
to Suzanne McConnaughey soon after he got back to Wellington,
'I hope I'll be there again – & when the McConnaugheys are there'.
He remembered their house '& the cliffs, & the sea, & the reef, &
the breadfruit trees, & the coconuts'.[47] In Tahiti he had frequently
been asked what he thought of Captain Bligh, and he had responded
that you did not need a tyrant to account for the mutiny on the
Bounty, 'you don't need anything more than Tahiti'.[48]

The visit to Tahiti left him impatient to see Tonga, '& every other
place Cook went to':

Damn it [he wrote to Skelton], even in NZ I haven't been to Dusky
Sound yet. The fact of the matter is, that there is no one place in which
you can edit Cook properly. One thinks of London as being central &
having all the logs & journals & charts & so on; but Tahiti & NZ, to be
done properly, mean actual physical presence in NZ & Tahiti, & I'd be
better for being wrecked somewhere on the Great Barrier Reef, or sailing
round the SW coast of New Guinea – for part of which there doesn't
appear even to be an Admiralty chart, by the way, so far as I can find
out. Lot of work in my half-dozen N Guinea footnotes.[49]

Some time later he heard that the McConnaugheys were planning a
trip in their yacht 'around the various outlying islands'. Heavens, he
wrote, 'how I want to do that. If only they would sail to Tonga &
the Marquesas & the New Hebrides & a few other places I'd pawn
my soul to go with them.'[50] In time, he was to see most of these
places, but not under sail.

After returning from Tahiti John had written the 'Note on
Polynesian History' for the introduction. 'Polynesian society &
notes & reading on same now seem a bit more real, & I even begin
to think I am making sense out of it.'[51] By the end of 1952 he had
finished annotating the first voyage – typed, there were about 400
pages of notes – or, rather, he had almost finished. He had just
written to Phyllis Mander Jones asking her who would be the best

person to consult about Australian aboriginal language, 'to see if any useful deductions about anything can be made from Banks's and Cook's vocabularies', and to ask her to vet two footnotes on Australian trees.[52] And he was still trying to solve one or two problems about obscure Maori place names, and asked Skelton if he could track down in the British Museum Manuscript Room a chart or plan by Cook of Mercury Bay on which Cook said he had put all the native names. However, there was a note of achievement in his letter: 'Skelton, do you mind if I skite? – I think I have done a bloody good job'.[53] He took that back at once ('it must be the influence of the New Year') but continued:

I have just gone on trying to make the voyage clear & vivid & comprehensible to myself. Now & again I've thought I've been getting somewhere, & the Soc. need not necessarily be ashamed of me; & then I've been covered in shame & depression, reviling myself as a worm & a pedant . . . [however] I think it will now be possible to follow the voyage pretty exactly, & know why Cook said whatever he did say. I don't think it will have to be done again in a hurry.

After working on the first Cook voyage for over three years, he had found himself 'more and more drawn to individual character'.[54] It was not the first time. This interest had surely been there in his pen portraits of politicians in his *Short History* of New Zealand; he had found it again while he was writing the Victoria College history, especially as he contemplated Hunter; and now, as he worked on the annotations to Cook's journal, it was as much as a biographer as an editor. He 'wished he could start on a biography . . . at once'.[55]

This first voyage is taking a hell of a long time [he continued in the same letter to Skelton]. But the more I study it the more important it seems in the whole scheme of things – the more important for Cook himself. It seems to me he came into it more or less by chance – i.e. when the Admiralty & the RS were casting around for a man it looked as if he might be the right sort of man, but there was no ransacking of 'available' men to pick out the absolutely best one; & by great good luck he turned out to be a positive genius. But apart from being a good seaman & surveyor & knowing a bit about mathematics & astronomy he was an uneducated man, & he started off by being a bit puzzled by Banks's enthusiasm for plants. He hit it off with Banks & Solander, thank God, & on the Endeavour he got his education: he learnt that exploration was not just getting the right latitude & longitude & charting coasts, or even keeping your men healthy & off mutinous thoughts & saving your ship, but beasts & bugs & plants & mankind as well. He sort of did his post-graduate work as a seaman & surveyor; but coming up against the minds of Banks & Solander, who were animals of a sort he'd never encountered before, he got his real undergraduate widening of mind as well; so that the great cabin of the Endeavour was really his university, but he had all the practical work he needed too. At the beginning of the 1st voyage you have unknown genius inadequately equipped – or perhaps we had better say inadequately exercised – at the end of the voyage you have genius completely mature & ready for anything – except perhaps the elder Mr Forster. I can't help damning Banks for his conceit [footnote in letter: I mean the conceit that kept him from going on the 2nd voyage]; Cook gave him an education too, but couldn't keep him from thinking that the voyage was in a way all his own work, so that when he got back to London he thought he was an expert on everything, & acted the insufferable aristocrat. Though dammit he was only a gentleman. Apparently he was thoroughly content to have the newspapers treat the voyage as 'his' voyage, & finished up by believing it. And thought he could run the Resolution as if it were part of his personal estate. Silly ass. Never mind, he did a lot to make Cook Cook, & for that purpose no one could have been better. With which profound reflection I leave you, with best wishes for the New Year . . .[56]

LOOKING AHEAD, JOHN planned, once he had sent off the corrected text and footnotes of the first volume ('as soon as possible'), to draft the general introduction and the introduction to the first voyage, and to get all the 'introductory stuff' to the printer. Then he thought he should 'knock off Cook for a while & clean up Banks's journal'.[57] Banks had, indeed, been on his conscience for some time and he rather expected the Australians to start asking embarrassing questions, but they appeared to accept his view that 'the only way to make a real job of the Banks journal is to edit it in conjunction with Cook'.[58] He was regularly in touch with Phyllis Mander Jones about both Cook and Banks material and kept her posted on the work, adding on one occasion, 'Next time anybody complains about slowness of progress on my part you can say I keep on turning down very agreeable offers of contracts from publishers* so that I can get on with the job'.[59]

---

* He had turned down four, including one from the Oxford University Press, who wanted a book on New Zealand for their Home University Library; one from Penguin Books to write a short history of New Zealand, despite a very persuasive approach from Sir Allen Lane, who was visiting New Zealand and came to dinner at Messines Road (John suggested to him that he should ask Keith Sinclair to do the job); and one from Fabers to do a similar volume (they then turned to W.H. Oliver).

He had started writing the general introduction in November 1952. 'I have done 6 pages in 4 days', he told Janet, but added, 'unfortunately a purple patch crept into the second page. I suspect Tawney's influence, but it gave me awful trouble.'[60] Everything took longer than hoped – 'what interminable trouble small points give' – and, although at the beginning of the following August[61] he said that he had just about finished the work on the first voyage apart from revising the introductions, three months later, in November, he reported to Skelton that he had received some further notes from Averil Lysaght. A lot of them were identifications he already had, but there was still some 'valuable stuff' that he had incorporated. He was just waiting for some further documents that Stella Campbell had found which would affect the textual introduction and might affect the notes.

As he revised the general introduction, John was 'appalled at the slovenliness of the writing . . . I am crawling through the wretched thing', he told Janet, 'trying to do away with the repetition of words – my God when I repeat I do repeat'.[62] Once it was revised, he gave it to his colleague Winston Monk to read. Monk 'went through it like a hawk': he 'picked on innumerable things', John reported, '& almost always, blast him, he's dead right . . . at this rate I'll be rewriting till the end of the year'.[63,*] He confessed to Skelton that he 'could brood, & play around, & put & take indefinitely over this first voyage' but recognised he had 'got to make an end somehow, even at the risk of making a fool of myself in some way or other'.[64]

Lord in Heaven [he wrote to Kathleen McKay in December 1953], how this so-called research stretches out if you want to make an honest job of it. The dreadful lust to be complete, to leave no stone unturned, smites one & tortures one in the still watches, so that sometimes a cold sweat breaks out, & one thinks Alas alas I have done wrong not to get a microfilm of that copy of Cook's log that bloke in London owns. The only refuge I have is to say now & again Here I shall be deliberately inconsistent just to show that I am not the victim of my own pedantry . . .

---

* At the end of July he wrote to Janet: 'Well I've been all through that wretched Introduction, & tidied & tightened, & dragged out all the damned sibilants I can, it's astonishing how they cluster constitutionally & essentially into cussed clots of exasperation. But I find that sometimes I can get a run of l's & r's instead, which gives me pleasure, though when I read it through they'll probably irritate me equally. You see. The language is really quite unmanageable . . . I think with about a year's tinkering maybe it would be all right. But still not as good as K. Clark, blast him.' (JCB to JEP, 29 July 1953.) John had just read Kenneth Clark's *Landscape into Art* and greatly admired Clark's writing.

And all those damned introductions have been rewritten & rewritten & rewritten. And a good proportion of those notes have been ditto.[65]

Finally, early in March 1954 he sent off 'all the copy for Cook vol I', with a final word: 'All I can do now is to pray that I haven't simply provided irrefutable proof of being a half-wit'.[66] Ernest Beaglehole, flying to Geneva for a meeting at the International Labour Organisation, took the four parcels and posted them surface mail when he arrived, greatly saving on postage. John never forgot that the costs of the project would inevitably be reflected in the price of the published volumes, even if further grants of assistance could be found.

Skelton's reaction on receiving the material would have delighted any author:

I have read your introductions (couldn't go to bed last night until I had finished) & skimmed a good part of the notes. You are entitled to all the skiting you like for this is plainly a magnificent job noble in conception & proportions & enthralling in detail. In precision of scholarship, in analysis, in range of reference, & – not least in mastery of the English language it makes your 'Exploration of the Pacific' (which I always thought a jolly good book) look like juvenilium. This is a job worthy of Cook in workmanship.[67], *

A few days later he had a further comment on the textual introduction; it seemed to Skelton that John's 'meticulous collation of the MSS . . . had led [him] right into Cook's mind' and that this might well 'appear to many people the most subtle & original contribution to the study of Cook in a volume which is nowhere short on subtlety, or originality'.[68] Skelton's response was a foretaste of the reception the volume received when it finally appeared eighteen months later.

J.A. Williamson, on hearing from Skelton about the work, wrote to John telling him that he must take on the second voyage as well and make it his. 'I want to see those three volumes all with your name on the spine – Beaglehole's Cook. If you never did anything else it would make you memorable'.[69] Williamson was facing domestic difficulties: his wife had suffered a cerebral haemorrhage in 1950 (her last outing before this had been when they went with John to see the *Victory* in Portsmouth) and she was very dependent on her husband's care. He was also recognising that he was less at home in the eighteenth century than the sixteenth, the period of his

---

*   John's pleasure, and relief, at Skelton's reaction is suggested by the fact that
        he copied this paragraph into a letter to Janet. (JCB to JEP, 7 April 1954.)

most scholarly work. For some time he had been showing signs of wanting to involve John more in the work on the second voyage. Now he was quite firm about handing it over completely, and the society accepted his view. If Skelton was right in suspecting that John had always wanted to take on the second voyage,[70] John had never said a word against having Williamson as co-editor.* When the galley proofs of the journal of the second voyage arrived with Williamson's work on the transcription and notes, however, John had to conclude that he had simply given up and that most of the job remained to be done. 'Well, I'll do my damnedest to fill the gap'.[71]

John still had a great deal to do before publication of the first voyage, quite apart from the continuing work on Banks, the third voyage, and now the second voyage. In the sixteen months between sending off the first voyage material and leaving for London in July 1955 on his second period of leave, John wrote frequently to Skelton – about sixty letters survive, some of them very long – and this was only a part of his extensive correspondence during the period. The letters covered many questions and are a striking testimony to John's determination to do full justice to Cook's achievement. Skelton, at his end, wrote frequently. 'I have been getting some lovely wads of letters from Skelton', John told Janet, 'draft notes on graphic records, & lists of charts, & announcements of microfilms & photostats to come; it keeps me in a perpetual simmer of excitement'.[72] He was developing confidence in MacLehose's work as printer but still took a very close interest in what was proposed and done. A typical comment to Skelton was:

I am quite agreeable to Appendices going into 10 pt – in fact, rather expected it, but preferred to leave the decision to you & the typographers. I think however that on a royal 8vo page & in 26 em measure they will need to be leaded 1 pt, or will be a fearful mass of print to wade through – I mean if set solid, in fact I'm sure of this. Same thing will apply to bits of 10 pt in text of journal.[73]

His interest – and expertise – was quite unusual in an author.

The selection of illustrations for the volume became a recurring

---

* Williamson, writing to Skelton to welcome the news that John was to take over volume 2, said: 'I always believed that his work would be first-rate, and I wish that the Council would have believed it more whole-heartedly when I said so years ago. However by taking on Vol. II he has made it evident that his name must stand on the whole work. It is his due, and I know that he must have felt disappointed at the editorship being divided, although he never gave any hint of it.' (Williamson to RAS, 13 April 1954.)

topic. While both men drew on the work done by a young Australian art historian, Bernard Smith, in listing the graphic records of the voyages, Skelton was to be primarily responsible for the introductory note on these. A surprising number of portraits that were said to be of Cook, turned up in likely and unlikely places. Phyllis Mander Jones sent John a photograph of one, purportedly by Gainsborough. His reaction was immediate:

> I have just got to College & opened the photograph. It may be by Gainsborough, & it may be Captain Cook, but by no possibility in creation, by not the remotest slinter, sliver or shaving of a possibility, by not the least possibility of the shadow of a shaving of a ghost of a possibility, can this elegant young beau, with all those gold buttons, & those shirt-cuffs, & that heavy dangling seal, & that etc., be our Captain Cook.
>   But thank you very much for it.[74]

Although he eventually came to the view that the portrait by Nathaniel Dance, while conventional, was 'probably as good a portrait as we could hope to get of a man not self-conscious enough, or knowledgeable enough, to oversee his own depiction',[75,*] no Cook portrait, he felt, revealed much about its subject. 'Damn it', he wrote to Skelton at the time, 'I wish I could have a good look at him in the flesh'.[76]

Decisions on illustrations also involved considering maps and charts. The more work John did, the more convinced he became that the charts were 'just as essential as the journal for the analysis of a voyage', and he agreed with Skelton that they should be the nucleus of the illustrations. The size of the original drawings made it difficult to reproduce them satisfactorily in the book. Perhaps, Skelton suggested, they should reconsider an idea, discarded earlier on the grounds of expense, for a separate atlas or portfolio for the larger charts?[77] The main advantages he saw were avoiding too much reduction in size, keeping folding to a minimum, and helping reduce the bulk of a volume which already promised to become unwieldy in its fatness. John had a more radical suggestion: why not 'dump everything' already decided about the size of the volumes and start again? 'What we want is a series of folios, & none of your fancy slim Golden Cockerel folios, but the real noble 18th century touch,

---

*   The portrait by William Hodges, missing since the early nineteenth century and now in the National Maritime Museum at Greenwich, reappeared only after John's death.

a foot & a half high & thick in proportion; then we really could do the maps & charts properly, & have a text worthy of them.* If you think we have gone too far to retrace our steps, then let's consider the portfolio question . . . '[78] They reached agreement on a portfolio (somewhat smaller than John's eighteenth-century ideal); the society accepted the idea, with its extra expense, and the selection of charts and coastal views entered into the correspondence. It was complicated in that the portfolio was to include material for all three voyages, but Skelton, consulting closely with John, saw the project through.

The portfolio was published at the same time as the first volume, as *Charts & Views Drawn by Cook and His Officers and Reproduced from the Original Manuscripts*, edited by R.A. Skelton. John was delighted that Skelton was named as editor; he believed that his considerable contribution to the first volume should be given some formal recognition, but saw little chance of this being done: 'your name ought to go on the title-page of this book as co-editor, but I suppose if I make that suggestion there'll be another long & bitter controversy'.[79] 'I doubt', he wrote a little later, 'whether you will ever let the Cook committee know how much you have done positively & negatively, as it were, to make me look knowledgeable & to keep me from looking an ass, but the fact, the multitudinous facts, is – are – very much alive within me.'[80] Skelton viewed John's compliments as undeserved, though 'extremely cheering & encouraging', and added that it was 'a pleasure & a privilege to devil for you (which is all I'm doing) by digging up the dry bones of facts which you so beautifully bring to life'.[81]

As the date of John's departure for London grew closer the correspondence increased in volume. On the sixth page of a letter in April Skelton had a heading, 'Notes on your notes on my notes on your Notes', and he then continued for several more pages.[82] Later, he wrote: 'When we get to the stage at which letters cross I begin to feel that this correspondence is gaining momentum, in fact running away with us'.[83] John wrote: 'Haven't had a communication from you for a week, & feel famished.'[84] Skelton confessed that 'Your handwriting on an envelope on my desk in the morning at once

---

*   When the Hakluyt Society, over thirty years later, completed the publication of the records of Cook's voyages with Andrew David's three superb volumes of *The Charts & Coastal Views of Captain Cook's Voyages* (London: 1988, 1992 and 1997), volumes dedicated to the memory of J.C. Beaglehole and R.A. Skelton, they were indeed noble volumes 'a foot & a half high'. John would have been delighted.

raises my spirits & gives me some hope for the day'.[85] 'Do we really need to publish this book?' John wrote in September. 'It would be much more agreeable just to keep on as we are doing for a few more years, you plunged in detective work, & me picking up odds & ends & discovering from time to time what an ass I am – no I can't say this last is an agreeable process, but at least it is salutary'.[86] Family news found a place. 'You have often asked (& I have never answered) about my daughters', Skelton wrote,[87] and then produced a rather glowing page about them: Charmian, who was almost seventeen, and Alexa, fifteen. John responded in his next letter: 'It looks as if Charmian must be ruled out for Giles owing to incompatibility of temperament, but Alexa will be ideal if she can get her mind off criminal detection. Consider her booked.'[88] John, for his part, painted a picture of himself domestically as the defenceless scholar. 'I note how [your wife] terrorises you', he wrote, 'same on this side. I used to get a bit of support from my youngest son, Giles, who was willing to risk ganging up with me; but he has now left home to go farming . . . & I am left defenceless & alone. I will', he continued, 'do Tim . . . the justice to say that when it comes to book-buying he is on my side, & frequently buys books himself, but otherwise he is a broken reed.'[89] His pen ran on in the same vein. These passages, often witty and sometimes with a grain of truth, are rather less convincing evidence of the nature of his family life than of the warmth of the relationship with Skelton at this time.

John was caustic about some of the books on Cook that were appearing. He was horrified by a work by Christopher Lloyd, senior lecturer at the Royal Naval College, Greenwich – 'How anybody could possibly do, let alone get published, such an outrageously bad piece of work . . . I simply don't know' – but more amused by an American life called *Great Sailor*. This, he thought, had its moments.

You must allow for my blowing off by the written word [he wrote to Skelton] which is so much more dreadful than the spoken. I have as a matter of fact ripped off stuff to you in the most disgraceful way, envisioning you on the other side of the table at that pub near the BM, & left you to make the necessary modifications as I have thumped the table.[90]

Another time, having apologised for being 'quite foolishly loquacious', he added, 'I do too much thinking with my pen'.[91]

More than once John wrote about the business of writing:

A damned, cold, rainy, unpleasant Saturday afternoon – I don't know why I tell you this, but I have been reading Virginia Woolf's *Writer's Diary*, & she often tells herself about the state of the weather. She makes me, with all her conscience & rewriting, think with horror & remorse that I ought to do all my introductions over again: to make them hard, & solid, & muscular, & all that. I keep on telling myself I must be concrete, & yet have rhythm & elasticity, & get rid of all these bloody metaphors. Shouldn't I ditch my purple patch? I ask myself – I rationed myself to one purple patch, the bit about Tahiti, & Winston Monk wanted me to cut that out;* & I clung to it grimly, but cut out some of the adjectives & the sentiment, but finished up by making it longer. Blast the English language . . . I hate writing, & yet it fascinates me.[92]

'Don't you really mean "I love writing & yet it infuriates me"?'[93] Skelton perceptively asked.

A number of people in London read the draft introductions and the notes. Helen Wallis, who had joined Skelton in the Map Room in 1951, where she completed an Oxford doctorate in geography with a thesis on early European exploration of the Pacific, thought his references to Pacific winds were inadequate. 'Those confounded Pacific winds & currents', John confessed, 'have been gnawing at me for years'. He saw them as 'the great omission' in *The Exploration of the Pacific* and welcomed her work and comments – 'the toothcomb is a most valuable instrument'.[94] 'I am going to add that HW girl to my admirations',[95] he told Skelton. George Naish, at the National Maritime Museum at Greenwich, was the expert on eighteenth-century ships and seafaring, but John admitted that some of Naish's stuff got him 'all tied up'. For example, Naish's note on the jib traveller finished up, 'the whole outfit can be inspected on the bowsprit of my old fashioned Pilot Cutter but gets rarer as bowsprits go out of fashion'; John was puzzled as to how he could include that in a footnote. Naish also provided some 'interesting stuff' on crossing the line which John used for a footnote in the Banks volume. Averil Lysaght's comments were more temperate than John had feared they might be.[96] Skelton politely called his corrections 'queries' and John happily incorporated them.

Skelton had further done some fascinating work on the history of various Cook manuscripts that had originally been in the hands of Cook's widow, before passing on to relatives of hers, and later being dispersed by auction. 'You & I', he wrote, 'will have to put on sackcloth & walk barefoot from Mile End to Clapham & on to

---

*   Monk told him that 'the novelists have used up a good deal of this currency'. (JCB to JEP, 14 October 1953.)

Marton as a penance for some of the half-truths, mis-statements, & rash guesses which we (mostly I) must now unsay . . . on the history of Cook's MSS'.[97] 'You certainly have knocked the Textual Introduction sideways', John replied[98] and, with 'profound & endless gratitude', set to to boil down Skelton's discoveries into a paragraph and other interpolations and footnotes in the introduction before returning it to him for checking.

In late September 1954 John wrote, 'Now all I have to do is to get down and rewrite the Introductions',[99] but that was far from all. Compiling an accurate list of the ship's company, as an appendix to the volume, proved surprisingly complicated. The *Endeavour*'s muster books, in the Public Record Office, were the main source, but there were some discrepancies between these and information in the journals – for example, on dates of death. John attributed this muster book 'mess' to Cook's clerk, Richard Orton, 'careless & inefficient as well as drunken',[100] and in these cases he gave the date recorded by Cook. He also gave the place of origin and date of joining the ship, where these were known, and any other information which could be hunted down. But the light thrown on the ordinary seamen and marines was fleeting:

Stainsby, Robert. Darlington, 27. A.B. Joined 11 June [1768]. Tattooed at Tahiti.

Simpson, Alexander. A.B. Joined 17 June. Punished 2 December 1769 for stealing rum; died 21 February 1771.

Stephens, Henry. Falmouth, 28. A.B. Joined 22 June. Punished for refusing his ration of fresh beef, 16 September 1768; and for stealing potatoes, 30 November 1769.

John was unable to explain satisfactorily the history of the boy Nicholas Young ('young Nick'), who first sighted New Zealand and appeared for the first time in the muster book at Tahiti on 18 April 1769 as a supernumerary. How he was accounted for before that date John could only surmise.

Two further appendices, the second especially, drew on Stella Campbell's archival work: a calendar of documents that listed all those that could be found bearing on the voyage apart from logs and journals, together with a few private letters written on the *Endeavour* or after its return, and a collection of newspaper extracts, 'printed not for the light they shed on the voyage of the *Endeavour* – a questionable illumination – but for their place in what has come to be called "public relations"'.[101]

Once the introductions were in page proofs, there was little opportunity for rewriting, yet John was clearly very reluctant to let them go. Before posting them off he returned once more to his description of Matavai Bay. 'In the end', he told Janet, 'I left "utter"' – this was in a phrase 'the utter point of Point Venus' – as 'I just couldn't think of anything' else.

> But I changed 'narrow line of whiteness' to 'white line of foam', & I rehashed the previous sentence to make it run better & fill up the spare space, & now I have done my damnedest. And as the stuff went I said Well there goes my assault on English literature; I don't suppose it will stir a ripple, but I can't complain I've been rushed over it, I've had ample time to think & to revise, it's all my own fault, but still it would be nice if it did stir one ripple. Now I've only got two lots of proofs to come, Ship's Company & Calendar of Documents.[102]

He knew he should get straight on with work on Banks but decided to take a day or so off to read a life of Abraham Lincoln (he was teaching the honours course on American history) and reread Kenneth Clark's *Landscape into Art*.

AT THE BEGINNING OF 1955 Skelton wrote to say that all his other commitments had been held up while he 'struggled with (a) the illustrations & (b) the general problems of publication & finance'. He thought daylight was 'leaking in on both now'.[103] The whole undertaking had grown considerably in size since it was first planned in 1948–49; the portfolio of *Charts & Views* had been added and the first volume, with the introductions and appendices, was promising to be nearly a thousand pages. The officers of the Hakluyt Society decided that the Batchworth Press, which had originally been contracted to publish the volumes, did not have the resources for the job. The president, Malcolm Letts, managed a very diplomatic switch to the Cambridge University Press.[104] John was delighted. The society had hoped that the New Zealand government's grant might be matched by Australia, but nothing was forthcoming. Help came from the distinguished New Zealand scholar and benefactor Esmond de Beer, who since the end of the First World War had made his home in London, where he lived with his two sisters, Mary and Dora. For over twenty years he had been working on the first full edition of John Evelyn's *Diary* for the Clarendon Press. He had become a member of the Hakluyt Society in 1946; he knew of John's work and admired his scholarship. De Beer's quiet determination that the journal should be fittingly published led to a guarantee of £2500 if needed towards the costs. In the years ahead de Beer and his sisters were to contribute unstintingly to the publication costs of the entire work.[105] In May 1955 the Pilgrim Trust agreed to a similar guarantee.

The passage of printer's proofs between Glasgow, London and Wellington continued over many months. These were subject not just to the correction of printer's errors but also, as with the material on Mrs Cook's papers, and Skelton's idea about the Poor Knights, to revision if additional material or information was discovered or turned up. 'Did you know', John wrote to Skelton in March 1955, 'about the Nautical Almanac error referred to in new fn, p.cclxxv? I only picked [it] up by chance, as I picked up that volume of sailing directions by chance in the Turnbull as a result of their re-shelving some of their books'.[106] It was a not unimportant point, as it showed that Cook's apparent error of thirty miles in placing the island of Savu was due not to shortcomings on his part but to an error in the almanac. It also showed how John's inveterate book-browsing could pay off.* Aurousseau, working on the index, also provided queries and suggestions. There was an explosion, however, when Averil Lysaght started to correct and alter proofs beyond those of the notes on natural history for which she had provided the material.

I have just got & read a letter from AML, & if I don't put something down on paper (even if I don't post it) I'll blow up. As it is I am trembling with fury so much I can hardly hold the pen . . .

I will *not* have her inserting 'screwpine' for pandanus 'in all the obvious places' because some stray American botanist tells her it is the most commonly used name. 'He thinks that mapé should always have an accent'. The hell he does – perhaps he'd like to re-spell the whole Tahitian language. I will *not* have her cutting out notes because she thinks 'Gadwalls do not occur in that part of the Pacific at all'. I will *not* have her 'correcting' the 'spelling of Georg Forster's name'! – because I call him George.[107]

And it was, he continued, 'such a blithely amiable letter too, as if it were the most natural thing in the world to take to a man's proofs'. Skelton replied at once: 'Believe me, she hasn't been half so much a nuisance to you as she has to me . . . she has just about as little tact & *savoir faire* as any woman I have ever met'.[108] Three days after Lysaght's first letter another arrived, 'withdrawing completely &

---

*   The book-browsing could also work less productively: 'I have just read Day Lewis's translation of the Georgics. I was looking up a translation of two or three lines some correspondent of Cook quoted, & I thought By jove, this is very good, I'd better read it all, particularly as I've had it a couple of years. And it is really very good indeed . . .' (JCB to JEP, 11 July 1951.)

very charmingly previous dogma on pandanus – on the authority of another American!'[109]

The size of the volume, the complexities of correcting the proofs and the vagaries of the post between Britain and Wellington were clearly a challenge to John's scholarly standards, not to mention his equanimity. He was finding out that he was by no means as good a proofreader as he had thought he was, '& dammit, was once'; he was very aware of the repercussions for the printer of all the corrections and changes, especially in the page proofs, and was beginning to feel that he was giving Skelton 'far too much gratuitous trouble'.[110]

There are moments when I think perhaps I am being too fussy, & other moments when I am haunted by an awful sense of your report on the excellent dummy that MacLehose supplied – guaranteed to last for 100 years. If this is going to last for 100 years then it seems essential to get things dead right – the idea of some awful bloomer being revealed in 100 years, or some crashing grammatical error, makes my blood run cold: on the other hand I find I don't worry so much about the effect on my contemporaries. Perhaps you can explain this psychological oddity. I am haunted by another awful sense from time to time: a cloud in the sky follows me round, & a large dread finger points at me with unerring aim, & the Voice of God utters the single word 'Careless!'. Sometimes it seems to be the voice of AML, & perhaps even her finger, but generally I know it's God, & I wish he wouldn't do it.[111,*]

Did he really mean this? It is a question which recurs when reading his letters. Is the elaboration driven by the need to explain in detail how he felt, or is his pen following his lively imagination and ironic sense of humour. My feeling is that at this time, as indeed at most times, his underlying concern about getting things right was very real. The literal truth of passages such as this one is another matter, though in this case he did include a careful drawing of the 'large dread finger'.

---

*   As John wrote in his lecture 'Some Problems of Editing Cook's Journals' (1957), one does what one can. 'And then the ghastly thing happens'. When he was writing the lecture he was looking over the pages of the first volume of the *Journals*, 'pages irrevocably, irretrievably printed and bound'. He came on a reference, his own reference, to 'Mount Egmont in the Bay of Plenty'. 'Now,' he wrote, 'I know perfectly well where Mount Egmont is, and I know it is not in the Bay of Plenty. I have had ocular demonstration of it, I have stood on top of it, I have slid down it. And yet there is that awful, that appalling phrase, with its air of quiet and casual certitude . . . There it is. And the frightful query arises, to haunt the watches of the night – how many others, in 970 pages, are there like it?'

Nor did John find it easy to stop polishing the introductions:

J.C.Beaglehole crawls into the presence of R.A.Skelton like the Duke of Monmouth before James II, & asks R.A.S. if he will alter p.xxi as follows:
(1) l.17 change 'expanded' to 'enlarged'.
(2) last sentence of para.1, change to 'Energies were bursting, thought was expanding; and misery was deep-rooted with complacency, squalor with magnificence; there was obscurantism' etc.
Why? Because (1) there is altogether too much expanding in this paragraph (2) the construction 'While' etc is repeated in the sentence immediately following in para. 2, & this won't do.

By May 1955 most of the outstanding points had been settled, John had carefully drafted a 'Formal Charter of Authority' giving Skelton 'full complete and total rights power and authority to make and assign all proper and necessary corrections to the final proofs . . .', and was looking forward to seeing the half-title and title-pages – they 'make publication seem quite near'.[112] He had revised Skelton's draft portfolio title-page, changing the title *Hydrography of the Voyages* – 'Hydrography doesn't seem to me to be a handsome word typographically' – to *Charts & Views* . . . (with a preference for the italic ampersand rather than the roman one 'for display'), and suggested filling some of the white space with a drawing, for which he enclosed a rough sketch, of 'the Muse of Hydrography conferring a wreath of South Pacific Seaweed on Skelton'.

WITH THE WORK ON THE first Cook volume winding down, John was increasingly engrossed with the Banks journal. He and Elsie were planning another trip to London, leaving in mid-1955, and in February he wrote, 'I *must* get Banks done before I leave NZ, though loose ends will undoubtedly hang out'.[113] He conceded that he had 'mercilessly exploited' the New South Wales trustees in favour of Cook, 'using soft words to the effect that all this Cook work is essentially Banks work, which is only half-true'. By this time, however, he believed that he had broken the back of the annotation to Banks, while warning Phyllis Mander Jones that he had 'learnt from Cook that it's no use making a dead-line or announcing that the work will be finished on such & such a date, for that is an invitation to disaster, & things keep on cropping up . . . long after one thinks one is finished'.[114] He was hoping to get started on the introduction and to have a draft finished before he left for England, though he was still puzzling over what form it should take: 'life of

Banks, Banks in relation to Cook, The Young Banks, or whatever?'[115] It worked out as a study of 'The Young Banks', taking him up to his election as president of the Royal Society and his marriage. It was to be one of John's finest pieces of writing, an essay of lively erudition, warm humour and wide-ranging imagination, judged by Averil Lysaght to be far and away the best thing he had done.[116] John was inclined to agree.* He had begun the draft early in March and finished it at the end of May, though there were still gaps to be filled; he also planned to add more from Banks's Newfoundland and Iceland journals (which no biographer had used before) when he had access to them. He had become fascinated by 'the development & character of Banks as a part of the English 18th century non-literary intellect, & his place, both typical & untypical, in that particular society'. The biographers, he wrote, 'have all been so amateurish & superficial'.[117] Although the amount of material was terrifying, he thought that perhaps he would devote his declining years to a 'real life of Banks', if he lived 'long enough to have a decline'.[118]

Near the end of 1954 John had asked Skelton, 'Are you feeling exhausted as the year draws to an end?'; he confessed that he was, but did not 'intend to die till Cook is done'.[119] Six months later, apologising to another correspondent for his long delay in replying to a letter, he wrote, 'I have never worked harder in my life than over the last couple of years . . . & I must say I am ready for the break I shall get by going to England next week – thank God by ship & not by air'.[120] After a 'damn sight too many' farewell parties,[121] he and Elsie left Wellington on 5 July. They flew from Auckland to Sydney, where he had a meeting with the library trustees, before they sailed on the Italian Flotta Laura ship, the *Sydney*, through Torres Strait, calling at Djakarta and Singapore before continuing to Genoa. After two or three days there they went overland to London. John had hoped to see something of the east coast of Australia and Torres Strait but was largely foiled by darkness:

We did Whitsunday Passage & all that part in the dark. We did the Endeavour River & all that critical part in the dark; & this morning there wasn't the tiniest bit of surf to indicate the reef & whereabouts of Providential Channel. Heart breaking. But I have seen enough coast to realize that Cook was a damned good hand at a coastal profile. I have

---

*   When he later read it in proof he wrote to Janet, 'I have a feeling . . . it's the best single lump of writing I've done, though when I read the cold proof of the specimen galley my heart fell & I thought This needs a bit of rewriting to improve the logic . . . the prose was not effortless. Blood sweat & tears.' (JCB to JEP, 16 July 1958.)

seen with my own eyes Mount Warning, Cape Byron, Cape Grafton, Cape Grenville, the Frankland Islands, Fitzroy Island, Cape Direction, Home Islands, Palm Islands, lots of bits of reef & 'sandy cays'. The hell of it is that on this 20,000 tonner with radar & all mod convs you don't get any idea of the real nature of the case . . . Too easy. Not fair on the Capt. Crumbs! how I admire his charting.[122]

My brother Robin and I travelled to England at the same time as John and Elsie. We went via Panama on the old Shaw Savill ship the *Mataroa*. They had given us each £100 when we turned twenty-one to pay the fare (it cost £92) on a trip we had long planned. Robin had qualified as a primary school teacher and was to spend a year or so teaching in London. I had just completed my MA thesis and been awarded a studentship by King's College, Cambridge. John was very pleased by this – not least, it emerged, because Trinity College, Cambridge, had turned him down for that research studentship many years earlier. He had hopes too, that Cambridge would help to civilise me. We all joined up in London. Elsie bought a car and, together with Ilse Jacoby (making her first visit to Germany since she left as a refugee in 1938), we drove through much of West Germany and Austria.

John had not looked forward to this tour. After the sea voyage the idea of another month away from his work horrified him. Nor did he find driving with the family a relaxing experience. He would rather have spent a little more time in Italy with Elsie before coming on to London. But the tour turned out to be a success: lunches in pinewoods or by lakes, mountain roads, flat roads, Cologne, Frankfurt, Salzburg, Vienna, Munich, Innsbruck, The Hague. John was struck by the 'miraculous restoration of churches, the beautiful simple graceful Austrian furniture, heartbreaking little memorials to young soldiers killed in North Africa'.[123] He discovered new things: Ernst Plischke had provided us with a list of superb Austrian baroque churches to visit; John was bowled over by 'a wonderful and lovely Vermeer' he had never seen before, *Diane and Her Nymphs*, at the Mauritshuis in The Hague. On getting back to London, Elsie found a flat for them at 164 Goldhurst Terrace, close to the Swiss Cottage underground station, and John resumed work on Banks.

He had gone to London as a Carnegie Commonwealth Fellow at the invitation of Sir Keith Hancock, the distinguished Australian historian whose work John greatly admired and the Institute of Commonwealth Studies at the University of London. He was given a room overlooking Russell Square and left to get on with his work. When he could, he attended Hancock's path-breaking interdisciplinary seminars, which he found extremely interesting, but he resisted making any large contribution to the discussion. He was very conscious of just how much work there still was to finish Banks and to get ahead with the next two volumes of Cook.

He was interested to find that his first reaction to being in London was to wish that he was back in Wellington, 'working properly'. It was partly the nature of the work required to finish Banks: interminable checking and visiting numerous libraries – 'messing around', as he put it. 'London used to excite me', he told Janet, 'but now, even on a fine day, I don't feel very excited.'[124] He found it 'so huge, so overcrowded with traffic, that God ought to smite it'. There were some good things, however. Standing out among all the dreary postwar rebuilding, which he gloomily compared with what we had seen in Germany, was the Royal Festival Hall, which he found admirable. Within two months his feelings were changing: 'the wicked old temptress is getting her insidious fingers around me again, & probably by June I shan't want to leave'.[125]

The first Cook volume, *The Voyage of the* Endeavour *1768–1771*, was published in November 1955. The High Commissioner for New Zealand, Clifton Webb, gave a lunch at the Devonshire Club (masterminded by Dick Campbell) to mark the occasion. John was disappointed at one or two typographical particulars,* but he thought the portfolio of charts 'a truly magnificent thing'.[126] The reviews his volume received, in a variety of languages, gave a 'good deal of relief to an anxious editor's mind', he was later to report.[127] The first appeared the following January. It was a full page in the *Times Literary Supplement*,[128] but it focused almost entirely on an account of Cook and the voyage. There was no direct discussion of John's work save for the phrase 'this monument of minute scholarship'. The following day the *Illustrated London News* had a full page 'appreciation' by Sir John Squire, the well-known 'bookman' and reviewer, with reproductions of three illustrations. Squire was lavish in his praise: 'a very impressive monument to a great and good man, a model of research and of textual criticism and collation which emulates the greatest performances of scholars in the classical field,

---

* He was critical of the space at the top and the margins of the title page, and thought the title page itself looked insignificant against the frontispiece – he considered the type to be too small with that frontispiece (an interesting echo of the discussions over the centennial surveys). Two of the folding maps had been pasted in so that they folded out the wrong way. But there was also praise for the printers: 'most of their typesetting & press-work really is good, & they are excellent at adjustments of text & footnotes on the page . . .' (JCB to JEP, 15 October 1955.)

and a work fascinating on every page, both from the human and from the scientific point of view'.[129] An enthusiastic review by Oliver Duff appeared in the *New Zealand Listener*,[130] which would have given John especial pleasure for two reasons. First for singling out the footnotes for praise: Duff made it clear that he was not a footnote man, but continued – comparing John with Gibbon – 'I expected the notes to be scholarly, I did not dream that they would be so wise, so judicious, so illuminating, and often, very often, so amusing.' Second, for his tribute to Heenan (to whose memory the volume was dedicated) as 'the creator of a mood in Ministers and a tradition in the Public Service that made assistance to such projects [as this one] possible'. John had enormous regrets that Heenan's death meant he could not present him with a copy of the work, which he had always supported and done so much to make possible.

More academic reviews, which appeared later, continued the praise. Skelton and John agreed that the best of them was by Professor Morrell of Otago University.[131] His one criticism, echoed by other reviewers, was that the book was too bulky and would have been better in two volumes. But as an edition of Cook's own text, he wrote, 'this is unlikely ever to be superseded'. Eric McCormick's six pages of praise in *Education*,[132] however, was almost too much for John. He explained to Skelton that McCormick had always dealt very faithfully with his failings in the past. 'This time it is such staggering praise' that he wanted 'to go away & hide in a hole for six months'.[133]

JOHN'S FIRST THREE OR four months in London, apart from the excitement of publication, were devoted to completing the introduction to Banks's journal. In a letter at the end of November 1955 he gives a picture of what was involved:

I have almost finished revising the introduction to Banks, with consequent huge expenditure of pins & little bits of paper, & time spent in the British Museum tracking down quotations that other people have misquoted & given wrong references for, or no reference at all. The trouble is that every stone turned entails the turning of other stones, & every avenue followed opens up a vista of other avenues, & every correction means other corrections, & footnotes begin to bristle as if I were writing of early Greek historians.[134]

The textual history and annotation of the journal also needed a good deal of work that was impossible to complete in Wellington. Apart from that in New Zealand and Australia, which he had already looked at, the material lay in the libraries of the British Museum, the Natural History Museum in South Kensington, the Herbarium at Kew, the Royal Society, McGill University in Montreal, and the collections of several private owners.

There had been some discussion about printing the volume when John met with the Mitchell Library trustees on his way to London. They believed that the New South Wales Government Printer would do a satisfactory job at little or no cost to them. In March John sent out a layout and some text to set it up from, suggesting that if the printer had any worries or queries he should look at a page of the Cook journal.[135] The results horrified him: 'this all-done-for-free-by-the-Govt Printer plan simply won't work', he wrote to Phyllis Mander Jones, 'the total hopelessness of it must be clear from the latest proof. I really believe I'd go clean off my head if I had to see Banks printed in this way'.[136] Three days later he reiterated his view of the work of the Government Printer, and suggested that they should 'go all out to make a really first-class piece of book production, & get the Cambridge University Press to do the job'.[137] The trustees were firm about printing in Australia; John was equally firm about not handing over his material without an assurance that the work would be decently printed and produced. A further 'alleged specimen page' from the Government Printer, and the news that he had 'turned hostile' after John's comments, left him at something of a loss as to what to do – 'I suppose I've just got to go on creating hostility.'[138] Eventually, however, the Trustees accepted his view and, to his great relief, reached an agreement to publish jointly with Angus and Robertson, using the Halstead Press as printers. John found their specimen page 'Infinitely superior to the Govt Printer's – some portions quite admirable',[139] and sent everything over to Sydney in May 1957.

In October he told me that he had not heard a word, except a casual one that the material had arrived. 'If I hadn't got enough on my plate with Cook', he wrote, 'I should be raising hell with them, but as it is they can take as long as they like.'[140] Progress would prove preternaturally slow. A year later, in September 1958, he heard that they were 'starting to set Banks up in type . . . but maybe they are just beginning to talk about it again'.[141] The following June he was just about losing hope of ever seeing the volumes all set up in type, let alone published, before he died. 'The only thing is, it gives me limitless time to play around with the proofs of my introduction'.[142] The situation got worse. Angus and Robertson were taken over by the Australian Consolidated Press and the new management reduced it to chaos. In October 1960 John, desperate to know what was happening, wrote to A.G. Cousins, the works manager at the Halstead Press:

... can you tell me what is wrong? I have been dealing, so far as correspondence goes, with Angus and Robertson. I know that Angus and Robertson are in some sort of mess, but this Banks mess has been going on for a long time. I have been connected with printing and book production for about twenty-five years, in more than one country, and to tell you the honest truth, I have never experienced anything so preposterous as the production of this Banks book in my life before. There may be some perfectly good reasons behind it all; but what are they? Is the book just laid aside for months at a time? Is there some secret bottle-neck? Is someone sabotaging the job? Are proofs put in a safe and forgotten about? Is it just that nobody gives a damn? I simply cannot understand, and am given no means of understanding.[143]

Cousins's reply confirmed the problems Angus and Robertson had faced – 'you cannot possibly realize the frustration and the disorganization that has resulted from extraordinary interference' – but assured John that the problems had been overcome and that the press looked forward to making the work 'a publication of the highest standard'.[144] But a further letter to Cousins the following June suggests that John's patience was running out:

will you get your comp *for God's sake* to place the three words of the running heads of the left hand pages, 'Banks's *Endeavour* Journal', in the proper place, centred over the type beneath? I have given instructions about this twice already, and the last two lots of proofs I have had are completely haywire ... These proofs are revises of revised pages, and should be perfect – instead of which, so far as these running heads are concerned, they are perfectly preposterous.[145]

In the meantime the work on selecting the illustrations and having them printed in Holland had been completed. In this John was greatly helped by Phyllis Mander Jones, who had moved from her position as Mitchell Librarian to be Library Liaison Officer at the New South Wales Government Office in London.

The work, in two very handsome volumes, was finally launched in Sydney on 13 February (Banks's birthday) 1962 at a ceremony attended by the Governor-General of Australia and a cluster of distinguished Australians. The Sydney *Daily Telegraph* reported that book-lovers there had queued for the release and that more than a hundred copies, at six guineas a set, had been sold on the first day. John had received a letter at the end of January from the Principal

Librarian of the Public Library of New South Wales telling him that the ceremony was to take place and asking him, as 'cost and distance' would no doubt rather stand in the way of his being there, if he might think it appropriate to send a special message.[146] The only message John could think of, 'after prolonged meditation', was 'Thank God' – and that, he feared, was hardly usable. Nevertheless, he hoped a good time would be had by all.[147]

Marcel Aurousseau was at the launch, and reported that honour had been done to Banks and to John in a fitting manner. He had started to read the book at once with great enjoyment, and was 'continually struck with the fact that Banks, for all his position and his enterprise, his courage, and his indefatigable interest in so many things, seems . . . to show up as a much less distinguished man than Cook'.[148] Having commented on the book's production, he added that John 'might have done something towards the raising of publishing standards in Australia'. He made much the same points in a very favourable review published in *Meanjin Quarterly* – his only criticism being one or two aspects of the index![149]

There were other favourable reviews.[150] John's reaction on rereading the introduction, however, was 'I shall *never* learn to write'. Always the perfectionist in writing as in so much else, he was appalled by the endless repetition of the words 'extreme' and 'extremely'.[151] For him, publication could hardly be other than an anticlimax. The work belonged with the first volume of Cook, published six years earlier. The second volume of Cook, itself the subject of interminable delays in printing, had appeared the year before, and by this time John had nearly completed his work on the third volume.

12

THE SCHOLAR AT WORK: II

The Journals of the Second and Third Voyages and the Biography of Cook

AFTER COMPLETING THE work on Banks in the first months of his leave in London over 1955 and 1956, John turned to working on Cook's second and third voyages, searching out all the manuscript material in Britain and arranging for much of it to be microfilmed to take back to Wellington. He extended his contacts with scientific and museum experts and worked closely with Skelton. He also met David and Alison Quinn, with whom he and Elsie were to form a close friendship. David was professor of history at the university college in Swansea (he would shortly be appointed to the chair in history at Liverpool) and already widely known for his immense knowledge of British expansion and the American colonies in the seventeenth century. He was Irish and Alison was a forthright Scot who shared David's scholarly interests; their three small children, at that time, were Welsh. They were a warm and lively family.

John and Elsie, from the base in Goldhurst Terrace, took up once more their London life of concerts and plays and exhibitions. They saw a good deal of Sam and Liza Williams, of Averil Lysaght, and other friends. With the car they did some touring in England. On a trip to Cornwall John was disappointed to find no traces of any Beagleholes in St Austell; he mistakenly believed that this was where the family originated, and had he found his way to Liskeard he could have met another John Beaglehole, a cousin, descended from William Henry's older brother John. They saw more of John's brother Keith and his family. John represented the University of New Zealand at the ceremonies for installing the Queen Mother as the Chancellor of the University of London. He and Elsie were very taken with the champagne at St James's Palace, and as he walked in procession at the Royal Festival Hall to a fanfare played on silver trumpets by six trumpeters from the Horse Guards, and listened to the University's Public Orator, he wondered what might be done for the graduation ceremonies at home. He interviewed a number of applicants for university positions in New Zealand; he attended the Home Universities Conference of the Association of Universities of the British Commonwealth, and 'was not entirely overwhelmed by the amount of wisdom there current'.[1] He also wrote a lecture 'On the Character of Captain James Cook',[2] which he delivered at several universities.

The passage home on the *Rangitata*, leaving on 31 August and sailing via Panama with a brief stop at Curaçao, was uneventful. John shared victory with 'a young & charming female' in the mixed doubles quoit-tennis, and did his duty to the Commonwealth by appearing as quiz-master in a twenty-questions session. 'It is curious what a vast amount of entertainment the British need, whether UK or NZ citizens'.[3] There proved to be absolutely no spot on the ship where he could work on his proofs, so he had 'a mild orgy of miscellaneous reading, the first for years', but found it very demoralising because, having started, he wanted to keep on. He read 'George Moore & Sydney Smith's letters, & Hoskins on the English landscape & Sir W. Ralegh's Poems & a life of Mark Rutherford & a life of Martin Tupper & Geyl on history – it was wonderful'.[4] They arrived in Wellington to find Giles 'on the wharf, down from his farm, leaning over a railing as if he were inspecting pigs, & with a grin as wide as the ship, so parental happiness was complete'.[5]

JOHN HAD ONCE THOUGHT that establishing a text for the journal of the second voyage would be more straightforward than for the first, but soon found that 'the more it is scrutinised the more complicated it becomes'.[6] There were several copies of the journal of the first voyage, but they were all essentially copies of the same thing; the many variations in detail could, if significant, be recorded in footnotes. Among the records of the second voyage (to simplify a complicated story of which John gives a fascinating account in his textual introduction to the volume) were two copies in Cook's hand of a journal, both in the British Museum but neither complete, (John refers to them as A and B), a number of holograph fragments in various libraries, and two other copies of the journal, one of which was made by Cook's clerk, William Dawson, during the voyage (referred to by John as G).

[our] stated objective [John wrote] is to print from Cook's manuscript. But there is in fact no complete manuscript that one can print. We are confronted with two: one of these [A] . . . stops with the final departure

from New Zealand; and B . . . is so chaotic and has lost so many of its
pages that we are in no better case here. An easy way out, if we merely
wanted a text, would be to print G, a highly legible, quite admirable
copy, quite complete, of B before B began to be worked over in England
[by Cook preparing it for publication]. But G has the disadvantage that
it is in William Dawson's hand, not Cook's; it is indeed too perfect. We
miss the process of growth; and to annotate a copy from an original is
not a process one cares to contemplate.[7]

The plan he adopted was to use A as far as it went, and to complete
the journal from B, the latter part of which was less broken than the
earlier. Where there were significant differences between these two,
or with G, John would record them.

It was a painstaking process, but there was a further complication
in finalising the text. J.A. Williamson's typescript of the journal had
been used by the printer to produce galley proofs. When he got back
to Wellington from London, John began work on these proofs and
wrote to Skelton with some anguish:

you know the affection & respect I have for that great & delightful
man, so I can tell you that I am appalled. He simply couldn't have had
the faintest idea of the nature of the beast he was dealing with; & he
could never have compared a page of his proofs with the photostats. I've
corrected the galleys from the photostats. When I corrected the
vol I galleys, you will remember, I went into a cold sweat over some
of the things I had done myself, but I was the Pedantry of Exactitude
compared to this . . . Funny thing is, that you told me that Wmson was
coming to regard every letter of Cook's as sacred. He can never have
read what Cook wrote.[8]

Skelton found it extraordinary: 'you'd think that a man who
managed the Cabot documents so skilfully could cope with Cook'.
He continued: 'Nobody but you could have tackled all the problems
of Voyage II.'[9]

Once the text was settled John continued work on the annotation.
As with the first voyage, this involved studying carefully all the
surviving published and unpublished accounts in addition to those
of Cook himself, together with extensive research in libraries
and, where necessary, recourse to various experts. Many of them,
Skelton especially, had helped with the first volume. In April
1957, John wrote that he should have the back of the annotation
broken in another month, 'having had a real hell of a time with
Easter Island, text as much as annotation'.[10] In the twenty-three
pages relating to Easter Island in the published volume,[11] there are
eighty-nine footnotes. In them John gives significant variations in

Cook's accounts and quotes from the journals of Charles Clerke and William Wales, and from George Forster's *Observations made during a Voyage Round the World*, as well as the published accounts of the island by earlier explorers. He used the work of modern scholars: Alfred Métraux's *Ethnology of Easter Island* (1940) and *Easter Island* (1957), Thor Heyerdahl's *American Indians in the Pacific* (1952) and *Aku-aku* (1958), Peter Buck's *Vikings of the Sunrise* (1938). His notes elaborate, identify, comment and explain, adding greatly to the reader's interest and understanding, making the voyage (to repeat John's words quoted in chapter eleven) 'clear & vivid & comprehensible'.

The second voyage was notable for Cook's three great ice-edge cruises, during which he circumnavigated the globe in high latitudes, demolishing any lingering hopes of finding a great southern continent. They were, perhaps, the most remarkable part of what is generally recognised as the greatest of all voyages of maritime discovery, and both Cook's observations and the latitudes he reached raised many questions about the nature and the extent of the Antarctic ice. John sought advice from Dr H.F.P. Herdman, of the British National Institute of Oceanography, who had published work on the Antarctic ice, and Herdman wrote for him a long discussion of the Antarctic portions of the journal, on which John drew for both the introduction and the notes.

At the end of May 1957 he went to Tonga, hoping to visit all the Cook anchorages and the islands where Cook called on his second and third voyages. The New Zealand navy gave him passage on their survey vessel the *Lachlan*, under Commander F.W. Hunt, and when he arrived at Nuku'alofa he was invited to stay for a few days with the British agent and consul, 'a very nice chap called Reid', and his wife, who gave him kava for morning tea and took him out in their car and the consular launch to show him all he wanted to see of Tongatapu.[12] Before he got to Tonga John had suspected that 'everybody goes round in long trousers & Mother Hubbards like a lot of broken-down market gardeners',[13] and he had written to Prince Tungi suggesting that he might revive the eighteenth century. But when he got there John discovered that the Mother Hubbard was on the way out. He was left with mixed feelings. Even that garment, he decided, if clean, would have looked better 'than some of the rags they wear, gaping at the seams; they look a bit like the reef when the tide has gone out'.[14] The little boys and girls, however, he found charming.

From Nuku'alofa he went by launch to the island of Eua where

Cook had made his first landfall. It was only about ten miles but he got 'half-drowned' on the way. There was some mistake or muddle about the launch and

instead of staying the night as I had been told it was to come straight back with 20 passengers & a load of cargo. I didn't go crook but said I was a bit disappointed. While I was eating a banana preparatory to looking at the landing place the launch-owner came over & said 'Look, it's a pity if you can't see this place, not enough people come here, it's very much neglected; I've spoken to all the people & they'll all go away & come back tomorrow morning, so we'll start at seven.' 'Crumbs,' I said, 'You can't do that sort of thing with a crowd like that.' 'Oh,' he answered, 'they're all perfectly happy; I said you were an important man from New Zealand come to look at their island, they've all got friends here they can stay with, you can make them a speech in the morning.'[15]

He made the speech and was presented with a piece of tapa cloth. He concluded that Cook was not far wrong in calling the group the Friendly Islands, 'even if they did hatch a plot later on for doing him in & getting down on the ship'.

He travelled north to Lifuka in the Ha'apai group, where Cook spent time during his third voyage, and hoped to visit Nomuka on the way. He did not get ashore there – it was the one island he wanted to see that he failed to get to, and he had to content himself with views of the coastline and with cross-examining the public works foreman at Lifuka, who claimed to know the island well. From Pangai, the capital village of Lifuka, 'with a jetty & a Burns Philp warehouse & the residence of the governor of Ha'apai', he visited a number of other islands. On Foa, the next island to Lifuka, he admired the women's weaving and 'was entertained to what was alleged to be very strong homebrew – one of the few English words the maker of it knew', as well as being prevailed on to ride one of the local horses, behind its owner, to see the island. Never a horseman, he decided that this was the only instance in which the Tongans carried their friendliness too far. The public works man took him to Moungaone, a little island ten miles west of Lifuka, to take a new tank to the schoolhouse. They went in a cutter and drifted rather than sailed across, but had an exciting hour on the way back at night with a good breeze, tearing along in a flurry of phosphorescence before being struck by a rain squall, and then having the wind drop right away and being left drifting for several hours. From Lifuka he went to Vava'u to join the little interisland steamer, the *Tofua,* to go on to Niue and Samoa. Elsie was already in Western Samoa, with Tom and Sylvia Smith.

When John arrived they had ten days with Dick and Eileen Powles*
at Vailima. 'Such luxury & comfort I've never known', Elsie wrote
to Janet, '& the whole place just so beautiful'.[16]

At the end of 1957 John got the text and annotations of the
second voyage away by air at 'vast expense', and wrote to me in
Cambridge that I might get the volume 'next Christmas, or maybe
not'.[17] Skelton judged the notes, which he 'read carefully', to be 'a
real triumph – both as a remarkable feat of textual collation, & as
a brilliantly illuminating commentary on the events, the Journal, &
Cook himself . . . I feel sorry', he continued, 'for those reviewers who
used up all their superlatives on your first volume'.[18] The following
April John sent off the calendar of documents, the last appendix to
the volume (the introduction still remained to be written). He was
not too happy about the calendar as it seemed 'devilish long', and he
could see no chance of the volume being less than about a thousand
pages:

I have boiled down where I could: perhaps I should have boiled down
more. If I could put the thing away for three months & have another go
I should feel more certain about this; but as you know my experience of
calendars is limited. The Clerke letters to Banks I think are worth giving
in full. But I have also given in full, or near full, some from Solander.
They seem to me to be very good, & ought to be printed somewhere;
I am a bit uncertain about the long one about Omai, but Omai, or the
talk about Omai, has to be documented somehow. I have not listed other
letters of Solander that exist. Once one steps outside the purely official,
& the voyage itself, there seems no end to it all for this voyage – & so
much good stuff. I have deliberately excluded everything bearing on the
publication of the voyage & the Forster row – it would take a calendar
in itself . . . anyhow I am quite prepared for all sorts of strictures on the
thing as presented, so don't hesitate to loosen the full tempest of your
criticism.[19]

Thinking over what he should do next in a letter a few days later,
John recognised that he could easily write a whole book by way of
introduction, but had been unable even to start on that, 'owing to
proofs of footnotes & new text of corrections of old text' descending
on him. And he had, at one time, hoped to finish everything by
the end of June 1958. While he would have liked another year 'for
leisurely titivating & polishing & improving footnotes', he was

---

*   Powles had been New Zealand High Commissioner in Western Samoa since
       1949, charged with guiding the country from international trusteeship to
       self-government.

conscious of the feelings of the subscribers, impatient for their next volume.[20] In fact, the introduction was finished and revised by the end of September and enthusiastically received by Skelton: 'Your introduction as it stands, is I think a triumph – very well-balanced, very readable (needless to say this), & particularly successful in presenting in humane terms a lot of rather technical material (e.g. Herdman's stuff).'[21] John had told him that Herdman's paper had been invaluable, though he had found it tough 'working him into the texture'.[22] John's mood, when he wrote to me at this time, was equally positive: 'Finishing the volume is quite an event; I feel as if I had been tramping for a long while with a heavy swag & had just dropped it, & have that difficulty in regaining balance; I also think now that I have a fair chance of finishing the whole thing before I die, as long as I continue to cross the road on the white lines.'[23] In the same letter he reported that he was almost through the fourth (and last) volume of Boswell's *Life of Johnson*, which he had not looked at since he read it by the gas fire in Brunswick Square in 1928.

By Christmas 1958 John had got all his Cook proofs corrected and ready to send back, except for some cross references that could not be filled in until he had the proofs of the introductions. In sending Skelton his 'best possible' Christmas wishes, he thanked him 'from the bottom of my soul' for all he had done for him, was doing and 'will no doubt do in the future':

I should be nowhere without you. Or to be more accurate, I should be where I am now, in Wellington, gnashing my teeth. You should have heard my eloquent plea yesterday, in my character of member of the Univ. Research Grants Committee, to the . . . Committee, on the necessity of a quadrupled grant for research, so that researchers could rush over to London (or elsewhere) whenever they reached a crisis. I almost had them in tears. I suppose they recovered afterwards.[24]

At the same time the Banks proofs had just begun to arrive. By the following April he had completed the last of the Cook 'revises', in which he found an awful lot of printer's mistakes; more Banks proofs had arrived. In June he wrote to me that he had not heard from Skelton for about six months. 'Poor devil, he is overwhelmed with work'.[25]

It was not the first time that Skelton's extraordinary workload had taken its toll. Early in 1954, while working on the first voyage, he had apologised for his long silences during the previous year – there had been 'just a wall getting higher & higher', but he had got over it by the time of writing.[26] At the end of 1956, three months after John's departure from London, he wrote: 'My deplorable silence since your repatriation doesn't mean that there has been nothing to tell you. It's not news but time to write about it, that is in short supply'.[27] Twelve months later he wrote: 'You are at least a dozen letters (good letters too) up on me, I'm afraid. I've had a tough time this autumn, & Cook's not had his fair share'.[28] He had had the answers to most of John's footnote problems on his desk for weeks, but had not been able to write a letter to go with them. This time the situation never really recovered. There were four letters between November 1957 and the beginning of February 1958, when he reported that the illustrations were 'all buttoned up',[29] one at the end of April (John welcomed the 'rich bunch of enclosures'[30]), one in June and then nothing until October, when, in the letter in which he praised John's introduction, Skelton apologised for his silence. He had had three Hakluyt Society volumes at once to prepare for printing, 'several others on the boil', and lots of British Museum administration (outside the Map Room) arising from the illness or absence at conferences of other members of the staff.[31] Five further letters survive from the period between October and the following February (1959), then there was nothing until November 1960, when he wrote: 'I am deeply ashamed of my long silence which has no excuse at all & no other explanation than a rather severe personal crisis last year (not easy to write about); while this year has been a very difficult & troublesome one. I can assure you that you won't have to complain again about one-way traffic in our correspondence.'[32] John was to see Skelton when he was in London in 1962, 1966 and 1969, but there seem to have been no more letters from him save for one in 1967 and a final one in 1969.

It was an odd situation that was to puzzle John greatly. Probably he never really understood – indeed it is doubtful if anyone did – what had happened.* The correspondence had been so rewarding in scholarly and, it appears, personal terms that Skelton, finding

---

*   What John was not aware of was the additional pressure on Skelton from 1958 arising from his involvement in the preparation of the volume on the Vinland Map for publication by the Yale University Press. Everyone connected with the project had been sworn to secrecy – an unusual step for a reputable university press to take, and in this case thoroughly unfortunate, as it kept the three authors from sufficient consultation with specialists in other fields which could have raised the doubts about its authenticity that were to prevail in the years after publication. Skelton himself appears to have come to regret the unscholarly restrictions imposed during the preparation of the book. Kirsten A. Seaver gives an engrossing scholarly

himself unable to write as he had at an earlier time, may have felt
unable to write at all. But that is only conjecture. In time, John's
feelings of considerable sympathy for the overwhelming workload
that Skelton was carrying turned to exasperation at his failure to
respond to specific questions, or to ensure that John at least knew
how things stood with the production of the second, and later the
third, volume. For some time, it appears, no one in the Hakluyt
Society was fully aware of the breakdown in communications. This
was still an age when effective communication between Wellington
and London depended on letters, and it was only when Professor
Eila Campbell* was appointed as joint secretary of the society in
1962 that a real link with the society was partly restored.

In July 1959 John visited New Caledonia and the New Hebrides
(Vanuatu). He and Elsie flew to Nouméa, where they stayed
with Tom Smith (now Secretary-General of the South Pacific
Commission) and Sylvia. John flew on to Vila, where once again
he was frustrated by the local transport and concluded that he had
been a fool to allow himself only three weeks away from his desk.
Even before he left home he had decided that, of the various places
in the New Hebrides he would like to see, there would be time only
for Tanna, the southernmost of the bigger islands in the group, and
its Port Resolution, where Cook had stayed longest. Getting there
was a challenge. Shipping in the New Hebrides was thoroughly
disorganised – 'One Condominium vessel laid up for repairs, the
other wouldn't work; no British govt vessel, French vessel chartered
elsewhere'[33] – and he had to make the passage to Tanna in the Burns
and Philp ketch, *Moala,* a 'great ugly lump of timber', which was
going to load copra. They ran into a strong head wind, rising to gale
force, and head seas, and instead of the normal time of nineteen
hours the trip took forty-six hours.

John stayed at Tanna with the district agent and his wife, who
were enormously hospitable, and the day after his arrival the district
agent drove him over to Port Resolution in his Land Rover. 'It was
dull, it rained, visibility was nil beyond the bay, but what a day

account of the whole story in her *Maps, Myths, and Men: The Story of
the Vinland Map* (Stanford: Stanford University Press, 2004); on Skelton,
see especially pp.208–10. In addition to everything else, Skelton continued
to publish a stream of scholarly articles and reviews: see the bibliography
of his published work included in his *Maps: A Historical Survey of Their
Study and Collecting,* published by the University of Chicago Press in
1972, after his death.

*   Professor of geography at Birkbeck College, University of London.

we had!' At the time, he wrote that he could not make out exactly what had happened to the bay since Cook's visit, but later, in the biography, he wrote: 'It is a harbour that still speaks vividly of this eighteenth-century visit, although, raised by earthquake just over a hundred years after Cook, and partly silted up, with a population about it that has declined to a few score, it is not the harbour into which he came with hope and caution in that first week of August [1774]'.[34] Another day they climbed the volcano where John Frum, the cargo-cult figure, was said to live. That cult had emptied the Presbyterian missions overnight about 1942 – 'serve them right', John commented, 'because [the missions] set their faces against dancing & kava drinking, & how else were the Tannese to enjoy themselves, except in adultery & hymn singing'. He was there during the French celebration of 14 July, and finally got back to Vila three days later than planned on the French government ketch *Concorde,* which was under charter to the South Pacific Commission for fisheries research. At Vila he dined with the British Resident Commissioner, who told him that he should have come a year later when they would have a brand new ship and would have taken him all around the New Hebrides – 'Why didn't the fatheads say so before, when I first started making enquiries about ways & means'. He also met a diver who had been diving for the La Pérouse remains at Vanikoro, who gave him a piece of lead from the *Astrolabe* that he later used as a paperweight. He caught a bad infection that, together with the sulpha pills he was given, made him feel more like death than he had ever felt before, and arrived back in Nouméa to take to his bed. He recovered in time for a three-day expedition with Elsie and the Smiths to Balade, on the north-east end of the island – 'Cook at Balade & Cook at Port Resn I really think I now know'.

The trip led him to some wry reflections on the annotations he had done for the New Caledonia/New Hebrides portion of Cook's journal.

I drove a cart & horse through a few solemn statements. Not my fault, I must confess, but that of the Standard Authorities I had used. Perhaps my fault for not going to the N.H. or N.C. before. But can one go everywhere before? One or two things even made me laugh bitterly. I have a fn somewhere roughly to this effect, 'Probably some sort of eucalyptus'. I'll say it is a sort of eucalyptus – & the commonest tree in New Caledonia, it grows in its millions. Niaouli. Then copying some solemn ass who can never have seen one in his life, I referred to its thick cork-like bark. Anything more uncorklike you never saw in your life . . . Why did I copy that man? I think it may have been some fool in one of

the Admiralty Handbooks. And where did he get it from? Laugh bitterly
or squirm bitterly – it just goes to show (1) Cook has never been edited
before (2) No one should edit a Pacific voyage who hasn't been all over
the Pacific & become omniscient.[35]

At home after the break, there was still no news of the second
volume of Cook. Aurousseau, who was working on the index, had
been very unwell. The only alternative to a delay until he recovered
would be to have someone else start over again, but that might well
take even longer.[36] In December John reported to Skelton that it
had been a hell of a year: 'Never so many meetings, never so many
problems . . . never so many irritations & silly things to do'.[37] The
Oxford University Press had asked in 1957 if they could publish a
second edition of *The Discovery of New Zealand*; he had agreed
but kept putting it off, not altogether to the pleasure of the press.
When he got around to looking at the volume, he was horrified and
had to 'give it a thorough revision, not to say re-writing, twice over
– with the thought that if ever anybody thought I could write for
sour apples, he merely displayed his own abysmal lack of taste'.[38]
For Banks, a constant worry and drainer of time, he still had only
corrected galley proofs to show. The third volume of Cook had not
got ahead at all. However, he reassured Skelton,

Lest you think I am in a highly nervous state, or in danger of going
round the bend, I assure you I am not; just exasperated with the
multitudinousness & fatuity of things that keep me from getting on with
my work. I have been calming myself down lately by reading Cowper's
letters in the last half-hour before I go to bed. This is a very placid sort of
amusement for the most part, except when he gets on to the subject of his
own despair. Why he should be regarded as the best letter-writer in the
language I don't quite know; but he is a nice flat domesticated English
landscape, charming, comfortable, nothing like Tanna. Queer thing,
religious mania. I wish there were a corresponding number of volumes
of letters of Cook, & Clerke, & Anderson, & Pickersgill . . . no more of
J.R. Forster, thankyou.[39]

In his letter of 2 November 1960, in which he told John of his
'severe personal crisis', Skelton also reported that the final printing
of volume two had just started. John was 'quite knocked over'; he
had been under the firm impression that it had been printed early
in 1959, and had told Aurousseau that it was too late to make the
corrections he had suggested.

Also I mourned bitterly that I couldn't make corrections that I had found
necessary myself, as a result of going to N Caledonia & New Hebrides,

& reading later work. It was agony to know I was wrong, & not be able
to do anything about it . . . In the despairing hope of still being in time
to save some bloomers I send the enclosed 3 pp., assembled hastily but I
hope accurately.[40]

A week after this letter John wrote a further note to Skelton, full of
sympathy: 'I am accustomed to think I have too many jobs to do . . .
but my burden seems to fade into insignificance by the side of yours.
Do for God's sake look after yourself . . .' And he asked whether the
corrections he had sent did 'any good to anybody'.[41] It appears that
Skelton was able to incorporate them, and that Aurousseau had sent
him copies of his letters to John and that he had made the necessary
corrections there too, but in neither case did he let John know.

The volume was published on 29 September 1961. Almost the
first news of it that John had seems to have been a letter from
Williamson in August to say that he had his copy and had read the
introduction.

I need hardly say [Williamson wrote] . . . that it is masterly, with a cool
unexaggerated balance of things that have to be said, Banks, Forster etc,
and a wonderful background of geographic knowledge of the Southern
Ocean. Further north, your islands are real ones, even to those of us who
have never seen them, instead of names on the map . . . Cook of course is
the middle of all, and you are steadily building him up.[42]

IN 1956, NOT LONG AFTER the first volume of Cook appeared,
Skelton had written to John Easton at MacLehose's with a staggeringly
unrealistic prediction, telling him that the copy for volume three was
expected to be ready for printing by June 1958, and that the volume
would be somewhere 'between 500 and 600 pages (certainly not in
excess of 600)'.[43] It was to be more than three years after that date
before even volume two finally appeared: volume three eventually
came out (in two parts) in 1967, and amounted to 1800 pages.

Establishing a text of Cook's journal for the third voyage did not
present the same problems as those arising from the second voyage.
Only one copy of a journal in Cook's hand survives and the form in
which it is cast suggests that Cook, learning from the experience of
the first two voyages, set out deliberately to write a book which would
need a minimum of editing or rewriting before being published.[44]
Cook's last entry, however, was for Sunday, 17 January 1779,
almost a month before his death. For that critical month, as well as
the remainder of the voyage that followed, John had to decide what

should complete the documentation. The 'journal' that he decided on was a composite one, containing, for what seemed sufficient reasons, some repetition. Cook was succeeded by Clerke, who could write, but who was dying from tuberculosis. Clerke was succeeded by Gore, who could not write. To complete the official account, the Admiralty had turned to Lieutenant King, who succeeded Gore as commander of the *Discovery*, the expedition's second ship. King was a careful observer and a conscientious recorder. John drew on his journal as well as Clerke's, but in the period after Clerke's death King's manuscript journal broke down and John turned to the journals of others to complete the account of the voyage. The voyage was also notable for the quality and interest of a number of other surviving journals. Two of these, John decided, should be printed in full: those of William Anderson, surgeon on the *Resolution*, a man of considerable talent and wide-ranging interests (and another victim of tuberculosis), and David Samwell, surgeon's mate on the *Resolution* (later surgeon on the *Discovery*), and a man of literary and social interests rather than scientific. His journal, John wrote, conveyed, 'as did no other word, the more frivolous side of a voyage that had its frivolities as well as its moments of tragedy'.[45] There were also extracts from the journals of five other officers. It was the inclusion of this material that accounted for the greatly increased size of the volume, and its publication was made possible only by the New Zealand government's granting the society a further £2000 for this purpose.

If establishing the text for the journal was relatively straight-forward compared with the first two voyages, there were parts where the job of annotation was formidable. No earlier scholar had carefully plotted Cook's extraordinarily complex route throughout his exploration of the North-west American coast and north through the Bering Sea into the Arctic Ocean. As John was to write in the preface to the volume:

If one adopts again the primary object of deciding precisely where Cook went, where he was at any given moment, why he said what he did by way of description and explanation, then one has a wearing task indeed; but it must be undertaken. I have had to undertake it, except in one particular spot, with the help only of charts and the printed word against which to check the charts and the written words produced on the voyage; and no one knows better than I how many conjectures I have had to make, and how fruitful – how destructive, sometimes, to laborious reconstruction – might be a detailed examination from the sea of that long coast, with the modern chart and modern instruments of navigation at one's hand as well as Cook's journal under one's eye . . . For cold fact one can lean on the *South-East Alaska Pilot*, the *Bering Sea and Strait Pilot*; but they do not explain the accidents of weather, on some particular day in 1778, which made Cook write as he did.[46]

Nor, in a like way, had anyone followed Cook carefully around the Hawai'ian islands, or grappled with the intricate structure of Hawai'ian society at that time, and the complexities of the contact between explorer and the indigenous people. These provided the background and contributed to the drama of Cook's death, an event that John was to seek to reconstruct (first in editing the journal, again in writing the biography), through exhaustively analysing all the surviving documents, and which, inescapably for editor and biographer, cast its shadow on what had gone before in his analysis of Cook's character and behaviour in the preceding months of the voyage.

The seemingly endless worry over the production of the second volume of Cook and of the Banks *Journal* made progress on volume three very slow. Early in 1960 John told Don Marshall that he was endeavouring to be philosophical but that more than once the delays had made him 'feel like jumping off the wharf'. However, he was trying to 'bury [himself] in vol III & forget other things'.[47] A year later he reported that he was still months behind in the work. He had hoped to get to England that year – and to see Hawai'i on the way – so as to finish work on the volume and see it through the press as a 1961–62 job, but he could not see how that was possible. 'Meanwhile', he wrote, 'I seem to have had hundreds of committees, & dozens of books & papers & chapters by other people to edit or revise. For the rest of this year I refuse point-blank, or I shall be round the bend, & I must remain sane, at least until I finish Cook.'[48] To Janet he reported that 'I keep on narrowly clawing off the coasts of utter distraction', but it was not all the fault of others. When he wrote that letter he was immersed in John Wesley's *Journal* and 'absolutely fascinated, by the preaching & conversions & all the rest of it. What a man! . . . What a century.'[49] Slowly, however, he was able to move ahead. 'The others have all gone to the pictures', he wrote one evening some months later,

& I have stayed home to disentangle some awful island in the Bering Sea that Cook thought was three islands . . . The interesting thing is, really, why didn't he clean the wretched business up by sailing round it, as he would have done on his 1st or 2nd voyage? Fact of the matter is . . . that he was losing his grip a bit, & this is what nobody has ever seen about Cook before.[50]

He was corresponding with Margaret Titcomb, the librarian at the Bernice P. Bishop Museum in Honolulu, who steered his questions to the appropriate experts, and in October 1961 he sought her advice on visiting Hawai'i. 'Would March be a good time?' He was now 'well on' with work on the third voyage, 'though a good deal behind my original schedule', and was planning the trip to London to 'clean it all up'. He wanted to have a good look at the museum for anything in his line, to visit all the Cook sites and 'see as much as possible of what Cook saw – anyhow in the way of landscape', to sit at the feet of anybody who could tell him anything, and to have his annotation of the Hawai'ian part of the journals vetted.[51]

He and Elsie left for England on 1 April 1962, flying via Hawai'i and mainland America. John had been given a visitor's grant by the Carnegie Corporation of New York. His links with them went back twenty-five years, to his early work for the Council for Educational Research and then his work on historical publications for Internal Affairs. The corporation's offer of a grant for him to visit the United States was long-standing. He spent the first three weeks in Hawai'i, partly working at the Bishop Museum and 'exploiting everybody who could be exploited'[52] for the work on Cook, and partly visiting the islands of Hawai'i and Kauai. At Kealakekua Bay, where Cook died, he was taken in hand by Amy Greenwell, a long-time resident in the district with a home on the lee slope of Manua Loa, who was a great source of local information, past and present, as well as lavish hospitality. He drew on her knowledge for a memorable, brooding paragraph for his Introduction to volume three:

No place in the eighteenth century Pacific has been more fully described for us than this bay, the northern half of which stands for so much in the history of exploration . . . The line of the bay is still as it was, though the land is covered with a thorny growth of *kiawe* or American acacia and other shrubs, standing here and there on the very lava lip that edges the water round to the high steep cliff of the Pali, impassable where it meets the sea, cutting off Kaawaloa from the short beach running on towards Hikiau. A track zigzagged over it, and still does over parts; but imported forage grasses have supplanted the *pili* that grew upon it of old. Earthquakes have sheared off the face of the Pali that Cook saw and narrowed the beach, seismic waves and the surf of hurricanes have beaten up the cliff and spread the beach with stones and boulders; the spring where the ships watered is found with difficulty among the rubbish of fallen branches on the hillside just above; the pond on the flat ground not far away is silted up with the washings of a cloudburst; the *heiau* with pavement restored is clean and empty of emotion, and about it are the galvanised iron booths, green-painted and neat enough, where shell necklaces are sold. There are a few fishermen. The population is gone; the brilliant feather cloaks, the proud helmets, are no more, the canoes that covered the water, the huts and villages of *pili* grass are gone, and the carved figures of the gods. The imagination, with an effort, can bring it all back, or some of it, for a fraction of a second; blotting out the thorn-trees, perhaps, behind the lava lip; can see two ships in the bay, and the innumerable brown figures of women and of men, hear uncomprehending invocations or the echo of shouting. The place, for all the accidents of time, is there, and above it the great mountain, Mauna Loa; the imagination, after all, is not unaided.[53]

From Hawai'i John and Elsie continued to Vancouver where the Macmillan, Bloedel and Powell River Company flew John to Nootka Sound,* on the western side of Vancouver Island, to study on the ground Cook's harbour there – this was that 'one spot' on the north-west coast of America that John referred to in his preface where he was not entirely dependent on charts and printed accounts for his knowledge of the land. A windy, rainy, near-desolate place, smothered with trees which often seemed to spring from solid rock, it introduced John, as it had Cook, to a continental coast 'very different from that of Cook's other continent, Australia', and to 'a harbour so very different from the warm Polynesian bays'.[54] In Vancouver, too, they met the New Zealand anthropologist, Professor Harry Hawthorn, who, with his colleagues at the University of British Columbia, proved an invaluable source of information on the anthropology and birds and fishes of the north-west coast.

Between the end of April and the end of June John and Elsie travelled across the United States. There were visits to several libraries with material relating to Cook: the Sutro Library in San Francisco, the Huntington Library in Los Angeles, the Yale Library and the Houghton Library at Harvard. But the trip was much more than Cook research. The Carnegie grants were intended to give their recipients the opportunity to follow their broader interests and get to know something of the country. John's itinerary reflected his fascination with American history and literature, which went back to his student days in London, and which had inspired some of his best teaching. He wished also to look at galleries and museums, and to meet certain people. That he found it enormously rewarding is

---

* The flight came about through the good offices of Geoffrey C. Andrew of the Canadian Universities Bureau, earlier at the University of British Columbia, who had been in New Zealand in 1959 as a member of the three man 'Hughes Parry' committee investigating the state of the universities. John had got to know him then, and Andrew put the idea of the flight to the chairman of the company.

clear from his subsequent report to the Carnegie Corporation:

... 18–19 May. *Charleston*, North Carolina. I was here on a sort of pilgrimage to the historic capital of Southern civilization; and walking assiduously about it, found it still one of the loveliest and most touching of cities ...
24 May. *Charlottesville*, Monticello* and the University of Virginia. I am by nature a Jefferson man.

In Washington they stayed with de Kiewiet, who had retired as President of the University of Rochester and settled just outside the city. In his four days there John noted that 'the richness of American art collections began to fall about me, and the generosity of American art collectors'. They then went on to a fortnight in New York, where John's former student, Frank Corner, had just arrived, with his wife Lyn, to take up the position as ambassador and head of the New Zealand mission to the United Nations. In his report John was reduced to a breathless half-page of stream-of-consciousness. After New York, there was a visit to New Haven, and then a weekend staying in Connecticut with Professor Theodore Sizer and his wife (Elsie had gone on to Ottawa to stay with John and Aileen Reid;† John joined her there at the end of his American travels). In Connecticut were 'some of the loveliest houses and villages'[55] he had seen, and he met Wilmarth Lewis, 'the Horace Walpole man'.‡ Theodore Sizer was professor of the history of art at Yale University and had also, between 1920 and 1947, been assistant director and then director of the Yale University Art Gallery. Under his guidance John met and talked to 'some of the greatest of American eighteenth-century scholars'§ and 'found out something about American editing of historical documents'. Those days he judged to have been some of the most memorable he spent in America. In Providence, Rhode Island, he looked at the work of the

---

*   'Having seen Monticello,' he wrote to Janet, 'I have realized one of the ambitions of my life.' (JCB to JEP, 24 May 1962.)
†   John Reid had become New Zealand High Commissioner to Canada.
‡   Wilmarth Sheldon Lewis edited the Yale edition of Walpole's correspondence and himself possessed much the largest collection of Walpoliana in existence.
§   In addition to Lewis, these included Frederick A. Pottle, editor (either singly or in collaboration) of many of the volumes in the Yale edition of the private papers of James Boswell, and biographer of Boswell; and Leonard W. Labaree, the Yale historian and founding editor of the Yale edition of *The Papers of Benjamin Franklin*. When John met him, this great project was in its early stages. Labaree edited the first fourteen volumes; volume 37 appeared in 2003.

Providence Historical Society in restoring old houses (he was already a member of the National Historic Places Trust in New Zealand). And finally there was a week in Boston, the centre of so much of his study of American history and reading of American literature. He visited Concord, and 'the shades of Emerson and Thoreau', and Salem, with the Peabody Museum and the shade of Hawthorne. In Boston itself, he wrote, 'I walked, attended by innumerable shades'.* When he wrote his report, seven months later after getting home, he still found himself moved

to drop all my usual pursuits in favour of renewed study of American history and writing. I find myself, at the moment, deep in Thoreau; and planning, not with great hope, how to find time to re-read Mathiesson's *American Renaissance*. I turn to the books already on my shelves as well as to those newly set up. I find that I have added to the number of my admirations, but not of my dislikes or distrusts . . . I have had, I find, an emotional as well as intellectual experience of considerable dimensions.

At the beginning of July 1962 he and Elsie flew from Ottawa to London. It must have been something of an anticlimax. For most of their time there they greatly enjoyed staying in a flat in the basement of Sam and Liza Williams's house in Markham Square, off King's Road in Chelsea. John had intended to spend the remainder of the year working in the British Museum and the Public Record Office, finishing the work which had to be done in London for volume three. However, he was asked to be a member of the New Zealand delegation to the general conference of Unesco in Paris for four weeks from mid-November† and felt in duty bound to accept. It cut his time in London to four and a half months, but he believed

---

*   One of those 'shades' in Boston did not arise from his historical reading. 'I started off here,' he wrote to Janet from Boston, 'with a severe and depressing blow.' He had hoped to look up Helen Allen, with whom he had had little or no communication since 1929. He rang the house, got her husband, and discovered she had died two years before 'of a quite ghastly sort of cancer. After 33 years,' he wrote, 'I was still very sick at heart. Oddly enough I had never thought of the possibility of her dying; & as I try to remember her face, that sort of cancer, or cancer at all, seems outrageous. "It was unfair", as her poor husband said over the phone. And how many people have said that? I suppose she'd be in her early 50s . . . I went & looked at the outside of her house, in Chestnut Street, one of the best Boston streets – charming . . . Oh dear, I had better stop this sort of reminiscence.' (JCB to JEP, 25 June 1962.) Other than his letter when he heard of his mother's death, this is possibly the saddest among all those that have survived.

†   '. . . the usual maddening waste of time all through this conference.' (JCB to THB, 3 December 1962.)

he had successfully completed what could only be done there. He saw something of Skelton before his colleague left in September for six months at Harvard sorting out their map collection. John also made some revisions to the Banks *Journal* for a second edition, but declined to do any work on a new edition of *The Exploration of the Pacific* for A. & C. Black until he got home.

Soon after arriving in Wellington, he told Bernard Smith that he 'was well on with the 3rd volume' and hoped to get through his work on it by the end of the year, 'bar final proofs'.[56] He was still having trouble with Hawai'ian genealogies: 'What right did the 18th century Hawai'ians have to have so many chiefs with so many names?' he wrote to Margaret Titcomb. 'What is really needed is a wall chart about 40ft square covered with one immense genealogy with photographs attached.'[57] By this time he was working on the annotations to Samwell's journal (Samwell was an unwearying collector of chiefs' names), was surrounded with proofs, and still had the appendix of documents and the introductions to do.

Almost inevitably, he discovered that he had not quite covered everything while he was in London. Helen Wallis, who was later to give him invaluable assistance when he was preparing the new, greatly revised, edition of *The Exploration of the Pacific*, was also able to provide the sort of help that Skelton had been so good at with the first two volumes of Cook. 'Dear Delinquent', John wrote to her in October 1963:

S.O.S. The battered old ship is damn near sinking. Stove in the bows . . . Waves lapping the gunwales. Time keeper rusted up, compass out of action, hope of reaching port very faint.

Look, dearie, here is a little job I meant to do when I was in London, & it vanished from my mind so completely that when I came back on the relevant blank in my proofs I wondered what on earth I was driving at, & it came back very slowly indeed. Psychiatric treatment indicated. Cook Portfolio of Charts & Views, Chart LI, P.R.O Adm 55/120, removed & in PRO Map Room M.P.I, 82: this here chart has at the top the name of an island which has partly disappeared (name, not island). What is left seems to be ' nton Island'. Now is something gone on the block, or is it gone on the original? Can careful scrutiny of the original discover the missing letters? I should like to get them if possible, because the names on this chart are quite fascinating – they represent Gore, of all people, bursting into an Elizabethan extravagance of mind. You wait till you see my footnotes, I enclose a little tracing to show more precisely what I am driving at.

I am labouring on final work on the galleys of these notes. However hard I try to send the printer a settled & final text, & my God I do, dozens of new things always turn up, blatant inconsistencies reveal themselves, one feels an utter fool.[58]

In early November he was 'about 12 words & 3 letters' from being able to send off the corrected galleys;[59] they were looking as if 'they'd been reconstructed after shell-fire', and he did not know how he was going to apologise to the printers – perhaps he would not this time, 'After all, they've hurt my feelings enough.'[60] 'How I am dying to get this stuff away',[61] he wrote a little later; it was finally posted at the end of November.

He was then ready to begin work on the introduction, but had been invited to deliver the presidential address to the history section of the Australian and New Zealand Association for the Advancement of Science (ANZAAS) Congress being held in Canberra in January 1964. He decided to speak on the death of Cook.* This was understandable: as editor and biographer he would soon reach the point where he had to set down the facts and circumstances of Cook's dramatic but sad end, and here was an opportunity for him to focus on that event. For us it provides a vivid picture of him as an historian at work. The facts, John said, by which he meant the events of that day, 14 February 1779, and the preceding days, were 'fairly simple'. He had read all the journals – there was, unfortunately, no direct account from the Hawai'ian side – and he set down what had happened. There was only one, very brief report, from someone who was actually with Cook at the critical time (Molesworth Phillips, the commander of the marines), and he did not actually see Cook fall. 'The business was now a most miserable scene of confusion', Phillips reported, as events reached their climax. 'The historian's curse is upon us', John wrote, 'we are faced by the old difficulty of seeing clearly the dramatic, the emotional, the critical, swift-moving moments in history'. Notwithstanding this, the problem

---

*   'The Death of Captain Cook', *Australian Journal of Science,* vol.26, no.10 (April 1964), pp.297–304; 'The Death of Captain Cook', *Historical Studies,* vol.11, no.43 (October 1964), pp.289–305 (a revised version of the address); 'The Case of the Needless Death: Reconstructing the Scene – "The Death of Captain Cook"', in *The Historian as Detective: Essays on Evidence,* edited by Robin W. Winks (New York: Harper, 1969), pp.279–302. The paper was printed again in 1979 in two editions designed by Alan Loney. The first edition, limited to fifty copies, was printed on damped handmade paper by Alan Loney at Hawk Press, Eastbourne, New Zealand. The second edition of 1000 copies was printed offset and bound by Whitcoulls Ltd, Christchurch, and published by the Alexander Turnbull Library Endowment Trust.

John grappled with was not what had happened, but why – or, as he put it, what were the circumstances?

At the heart of his discussion of these circumstances is a preoccupation with Cook himself, a conviction that one must understand the man to understand why he died as he did. The death of a hero has fascinated men from antiquity until our own day, and from the moment the news of Cook's death reached London his fate too became part of that enduring tradition. But John's preoccupation with Cook was something quite different, not the uncritical portrayal of the hero but the elusive endeavour to understand the man. Only that, he had come to believe, would answer the question as to why the passage of events at Kealakekua Bay on that February morning was to have its fateful climax. He was led, inexorably, to consider Cook's character, his state of mind, his health, the effects of those seven stressful years of resolute exploration. In his address he suggested that it was these elements that accounted for the misjudgements, the almost inexplicable outbursts on the third voyage, the final fatal loss of temper that precipitated the killing. Studying Cook on the third voyage had led John to conclude that he was a tired man. 'His apprehensions as a discoverer were not so constantly fine as they had been; and he lost his temper more easily and more frequently.' Cook, John believed, should have been forbidden to go on the third voyage, or else the voyage should have been postponed. As it was, in his memorable phrase, 'the hands that signed his commission signed his death-warrant'.

The address is a great set piece. It has a tension and a drama befitting the subject; the sentences are short, the questions and the evidence clearly marshalled, the argument persuasive, not least in its simplicity. John was to publish three accounts of Cook's death: this address, the relevant part of the introduction to volume three of the *Journals,* and finally in his *Life* of Cook. The accounts were essentially the same; we have the same Cook, the same relationship between 'fact' and 'circumstance'.* What the address gives us, in

---

*   When he wrote the *Life,* John went further in one respect when he suggested, in considering Cook's behaviour, that 'a hypothesis of some physical cause is hard to resist'. Later medical research has suggested that there could indeed have been such a cause, that Cook's intestinal problems on the second voyage could have subsequently interfered with his absorption of the B complex of vitamins. The recorded changes in his state of mind and behaviour on the third voyage are all consistent with the symptoms one would expect from such a vitamin deficiency. This can never be more than a hypothesis, though it does accord with all the evidence. See the discussion by Sir James Watt, 'Medical Aspects and Consequences of

a way that complements what we learn from some of his letters, is an idea of how John worked: the initial mastery of the sources, the kind of sustained brooding while, as it were, the past came into focus, and then the imaginative engagement as he sought to understand what had happened. Only then did he start to write, slowly, painstakingly, but with his narrative or argument remarkably complete and polished as it emerged from his pen – it is staggering how little correction one finds in his manuscript pages.

'The Death of Captain Cook' was one of a number of papers on Cook that John completed while he was working on the *Journals*. Some, like this one, represent a first engagement with a subject or problem – reminiscent of Cook sending a small boat ahead of the ship to explore a passage or anchorage, looking for snags or hidden dangers, before the *Endeavour* or *Resolution* followed. His earlier paper 'On the Character of Captain James Cook'* had something of this quality too. Written in 1955, it was both a progress report and a first study for a portrait to come. Others, particularly later on at the time of the Cook bicentennial celebrations, were, rather, reflections on what he had learned, sometimes pulling material together to illuminate a particular topic. The first of these was his paper on 'Some Problems of Editing Cook's Journals',[†] also prepared for an ANZAAS meeting, delivered in Dunedin in January 1957. The October 1965 opening, at the Dominion Museum in Wellington, of an exhibition sent from the Alströmer Collection of the Ethnological Museum of Sweden (which included material collected on Cook's voyages) was the occasion of John's address on 'The Wandering Scholars', an account of Linnaeus and his followers, and especially of those Swedes who sailed with Cook into the Pacific: Solander and Spöring on the first voyage, Sparrman on the second. This lecture was subsequently published in both Sweden and New Zealand.[‡] Two years later, at Victoria University, he lectured on 'Captain Cook and Captain Bligh'.[§]

Cook's Voyages', in *Captain James Cook and His Times*, edited by Robin Fisher and Hugh Johnson (Vancouver: Douglas and McIntyre, 1979).

* 'On the Character of Captain James Cook', *Geographical Journal*, vol.122, part 4 (December 1969), pp.417–29.

† 'Some Problems of Editing Cook's Journals', *Historical Studies*, vol.13 (November 1957), pp.20–31.

‡ 'The Wandering Scholars', *Ethnos*, vol.30 (1965), pp.39–56; *The Wandering Scholars* (Wellington: Dominion Museum, 1966), 15pp.

§ 'Captain Cook and Captain Bligh' (Dr W.E. Collins Lecture, delivered at the university on 3 August 1967). Victoria University of Wellington, 1967, 27pp.

Although, in a sense, these papers were by-products of the work on the *Journals,* they drew on the full range of John's erudition and scholarship, and also showed his growing mastery of the formal lecture. I remember vividly the occasion of the Cook and Bligh lecture, with the lecture hall full, and a quite extraordinary sense of the audience totally engaged by the speaker. His opening was direct:

They were both superb seamen. Is there anything else I can say, to draw parallels, or to define contrasts? . . . They were both able explorers, both excellent hydrographers and marine surveyors. They both sailed the Pacific Ocean. They both had hasty tempers, and swore. They were both exceedingly humane men, careful of the lives of those who served under them. They were both brave . . .

And he went on to sketch the two naval careers, then to a brief discussion of the question of flogging in 'a flogging century' – to conclude that Bligh's reputation as a flogging captain was quite unjust. Strip away the historical myths, John argued, and the two captains had much in common. But there were significant differences: 'the leading characteristic of Bligh was not tyranny but vanity. The contrast here with Cook is complete.' The last pages of the lecture develop that devastating insight, and John sums up in his final paragraph.

Shall I conclude by saying that there is a sort of plain magnanimity of mind in Cook that has no parallel in Bligh; that Cook's character was fundamentally consistent and direct, Bligh's was cursed by paradox; or simply that Cook was a quick-tempered but good-tempered man, and Bligh was a quick- and bad-tempered man? That is a little abrupt. I shall end instead by confessing that when I came to compose this lecture I had thought of a title, and nothing whatever to fill in underneath it. By the time I had felt and fought my way through to this point I found I had – what? Could it be called a study in command?

After returning from the ANZAAS Congress in Canberra in January 1964 John started on the introduction to volume three. By the end of June, he told Janet, he had got Cook to Kealakekua Bay, 'but there are so many things to do before I kill him that I am for the moment quite baffled, & found that last night I was writing a patch not purple but semi-purple, about the bay, & now I don't know how to finish it off, & if I can't finish it off I can't get ahead any way. Nuisance.'[62] A month later it was finished and he had given it to Ilse Jacoby to be typed. In August he was revising the typescript; it had 'turned out the size of a book' (when printed it came to 140 pages) and had exhausted him, but when he saw it in proof he was fairly pleased – 'quite closely reasoned . . . on the whole not badly written. At least I think so.'[63] He still had to do the textual introduction and the calendar of documents. There had been an interminable delay over getting some material for the calendar that a researcher had found in the Public Record Office and the National Maritime Museum. Skelton assured Eila Campbell that he had sent it, but he had not. Eventually, after months had passed, John got in touch with the researcher himself, who sent further copies directly to him. 'Heaven knows when the thing will appear', he wrote in August 1964; he was getting 'furiously impatient' at the printer's slowness in making up pages from what had already been set in galleys.[64] As the page proofs arrived there was further checking – and one disappointment. John had always hoped that there might be one page with one line of text and the rest footnote, but the best he got was seven lines of text and the footnote spilling to the next page: 'A life's ambition denied.'[65] When the Tongan section of the proofs arrived he gave them to a new colleague in the Victoria history department, Dorothy Crozier,[66] to look at. Crozier had worked in Tonga and 'had long genealogical conversations with Queen Salote'. 'Oh dear', John wrote to Janet. 'More counting of spaces. And I say to myself, these bloody Tongans. And none of those bloody reviewers will ever realise how incredibly learned this Tongan annotation is, how truly royal.'[67]

Eila Campbell had begun by being puzzled at the situation with Skelton; she felt that there must have been a dreadful misunderstanding somewhere. She wrote to John that Skelton was as interested in Cook as ever and spoke highly of the work John was doing,[68] but as 1964 passed she became increasingly baffled. 'Quite honestly', she wrote in August, 'I do not understand Peter Skelton',[69] and continued that at every Hakluyt Society council meeting she had declared that it was 'unlikely that Cook III will be published during 1965 or 1966 but Peter has assured the President that he has everything in hand!' Some months later she wrote: 'I just don't understand *why* he doesn't write to you and I have come to believe that he must *dream* that he *has* and so doesn't!!'[70] By the beginning of 1965 she was clearly handling John's queries and looking up things that needed checking. He was also corresponding directly with John Easton, the printer, and on Eila Campbell's suggestion he had sent copies of his introductory material directly to Easton as well as to Skelton.

At the beginning of February Skelton was involved in a car accident when driving from his home to the railway station. He was badly injured, with broken ribs puncturing his lungs, but he made a quick recovery. The enforced absence from the British Museum during this time gave him the opportunity to start work on the illustrations for Cook, but it was not carried through. John Easton, who was a member of the Hakluyt Society council as well as head of MacLehose's, and was increasingly working with Eila Campbell to try to push things along, wrote to John early in 1966 that Skelton's psychological problem had worsened since his accident: 'except that he is too tired to carry on, there is no change in his disposition towards any of us, and especially you. For some reason he has just funked this job, and why I cannot understand!'[71] A separate problem arose over the index. Marcel Aurousseau had planned to do it, but at the last moment was advised by his doctor not to go ahead. Fortunately, Alison Quinn agreed to take on what would be a formidable task.

The delays with Cook had given John a chance to revise *The Exploration of the Pacific* for the third edition. A. & C. Black, the publisher, had proposed a photo-lithographic reprint with minor corrections, but once John started he found he was revising and making corrections on almost every page. There was no choice but to reset the book completely, and Blacks were encouraged by reaching an agreement with the Stanford University Press to bring out an American edition. As always, John was his own hardest critic. As he was reading through the typescript of the revised work he lamented to Janet:

I thought I had revised the writing thoroughly, but keep on coming on bad bits, & have to scrawl in pencil all over it. Every now & again I think Well, this isn't a bad book after all; & then I come on something perfectly dreadful. Why oh why can't one just write down everything perfectly the first time, or if one can't do that why does one want to write at all? . . . Why can't one just be a brilliant young NZ writer, & write stories about drink & lust & Maoris in *Landfall*, & be a credit to one's country? Instead of all this idiotic agonising. And now I'll never be young & brilliant.[72]

'The fact of the matter is', he added a month later, 'it is a young man's book, written when I didn't know anything about the subject, & kidded myself I could write'.[73] He finished the revising just before Christmas 1965 – 'the page proofs look a shambles'[74] – and the book appeared the following year.

There was light relief from the worries over Cook when John was approached by MGM, who were planning a film on the great explorer. He wrote to Helen Wallis:

I've put you down in the Capt Cook movie as the girl in Tahiti that Joe Banks fell for – 'my flame'. I have now had a firm offer from the MGM tycoon. Really they are absurd people. They talk about research. I am inclined to say, Look brother, read the Journals of C.C. & you can have that advice free. They talk about my paying a visit to Los Angeles (=Hollywood, I suppose) later in the year: what for God only knows. But hold yourself ready to leave for Tahiti at any moment clad in a grass skirt & a bottle of sun-tan lotion.[75]

Family plans were made for spending the large fee that we were all sure he would be paid, but nothing came of the project.

At the beginning of 1966, with the printer still waiting on the promised illustrations, Eila Campbell had come to the view that the Hakluyt Society should fly John to London to sort out the remaining problems. 'They owe it to *you* and to the N.Z. Government.'[76] John was already planning a trip, however. He had heard in November that Oxford wished to award him an honorary doctorate, which could be conferred on 4 June. Victoria University agreed to give him three months' leave, and the British Council gave him a grant of £200 towards his return airfare. He welcomed the chance not only to push things along a with volume three, but also 'to scratch round the PRO for traces of Cook before he took on the Pacific Ocean'[77] as a step towards the biography. The period in London was to prove invaluable. 'I seem to have broken the log jam or bottleneck or whatever it was over Cook', he wrote after a month there, '& things are moving a bit, though it means a bit of work for me: still things are moving, & Easton . . . almost weeps with gratitude.'[78] He, Easton and Campbell were in close touch. He and Campbell somehow extracted the note on the graphic records from Skelton ('the light begins to dawn', John wrote), and on hearing the news Easton wrote that 'you are to be congratulated heartily'.[79] They finalised the choice of illustrations. John was immersed in final proofs. He and Elsie bought a Lucie Rie bowl and saw a very good exhibition by Barbara Hepworth before flying home in August, stopping off briefly in New York (where they stayed with the Corners), Chicago and Honolulu: 'swished round in an air-conditioned car in N.Y., retired punch-drunk from the Impressionists in the Art Institute of Chicago, lolled in the water at Honolulu & flew over to Kealakekua Bay again'.[80] It had been hoped that the volumes might appear before the end of 1966, but it was not until the following April that John heard that they were bound and the complimentary copies were about to go out. The volume was officially published on 9 June 1967.

At the end of April, having done so much to see the work

completed, John Easton died. His involvement had been critical in bringing the whole project to a successful conclusion in very difficult circumstances. John recognised the debt he owed him. There was an even greater debt to J.A. Williamson, who had died just over two years earlier, on 31 December 1964. That debt went back to John's student years in London, to the time when Williamson had stood in for A.P. Newton in taking the colonial history seminar at the Institute of Historical Research, and had asked John to write the Pioneer Histories volume on Pacific exploration. Later, he had played a critical role in ensuring John became part of the Hakluyt Society's plans for Cook and finally, he insisted that John take over the editing of volume two and the responsibility for the work on all three voyages.

The publication of the journals of the third voyage marked the completion of a remarkable scholarly undertaking. Williamson had been right when he wrote to John urging 'those three volumes all with your name on the spine – Beaglehole's Cook' and predicted that 'If you never did anything else it would make you memorable'.[81] From the time of their publication, these volumes have been recognised as one of the finest achievements of twentieth-century scholarship, setting a new standard for work of this kind, and providing the foundation for all subsequent work on Cook and his voyages.

PART OF THE HAKLUYT Society's plans for publishing Cook's journals had been a fourth volume, a collection of essays on aspects of his life and achievements. J.W. Davidson, John's former student (and for a brief period, before he went to Cambridge, colleague in the Centennial Branch), had accepted an invitation to edit the volume. When the edition was first planned Davidson had just been appointed lecturer in colonial studies at Cambridge, but in the same year Peter Fraser asked him to advise the New Zealand government on the political situation in Western Samoa. This proved to be the beginning of his long involvement with that island state's approach to self-government and then transition to independence, between 1946 and 1962. In 1949 he was appointed professor of Pacific history at the Australian National University. For Davidson, the Cook volume (among other projected publications) proved to be something of a mirage. It was talked about, some plans were made, a number of scholars were asked to contribute, but little actually happened.

As early as 1952 John wrote to Skelton saying that he was very worried about having Davidson as editor of volume four, and was coming to the point where he was most unwilling to see Davidson's name down as one of the three editors of the edition as a whole.[82] Skelton was more hopeful, and John did not press the point. During 1956 Davidson spent some time in London and 'not only produced a plan & timetable for Vol. IV but also got most of the contributors moving'.[83] He told Skelton that he proposed to have all his copy complete by December 1957, to spend six months editing and revising, and to send it to the printer in June 1958 (the original target date for volume three). Nothing happened. Whenever Davidson visited Wellington to see his mother he always called on John, and their friendship remained warm, but intellectually and emotionally he was involved with Western Samoa, not with Cook. Yet for years he continued to pretend that the work was going ahead. It was only at the beginning of 1964, when John was in Canberra for the ANZAAS conference, that Davidson told him that he wanted to get out of Cook. 'I don't suppose he will write to you himself', John – acting as intermediary – wrote to Skelton, 'however he abandons Vol. IV'.[84,*] Eila Campbell had already told John that he should take over the volume,[85] and after discussions with the Hakluyt Society council, when he was in London in 1966, he 'rather unwisely' let himself be pushed into doing the job.[86]

It proved an impossible project. John clearly felt that his first priority was to complete the biography of Cook that he was about to begin writing. There were considerable distractions during the Cook bicentennial celebrations in 1968 and 1969, when he was called on for lectures in Britain, New Zealand and Australia. Nonetheless he worked closely with Eila Campbell and with Glyndwr Williams[†] (who had been asked by the society to give whatever help was possible from London) to sort out contributors and persuade them to write. At the end of 1970 the only finished essay was that by Professor E.G.R. Taylor on navigation in the age of Cook, which

---

[*]   Davidson did write to Eila Campbell a year later, saying that he was withdrawing from volume 4 and that he had discussed it with John, who had agreed to take it over once he had finished volume 3. (12 March 1965, copy in J.C. Beaglehole Papers. 73-004-09/22. ATL.)

[†]   Williams was a young historian who had completed a London PhD on the search for the North-west Passage. This became his first book, *The British Search for the Northwest Passage in the Eighteenth Century* (London: Longmans, 1962). John had found the thesis very useful when he was working on the introduction to the third voyage. Williams went on to become professor of history at Queen Mary College, to a distinguished career as an historian of exploration, and to a continuing close association with the Hakluyt Society.

she had completed in 1952. Eila Campbell reported to John that the Hakluyt Society council were 'in despair about the continuing delay', but they agreed with him that he could not edit copy until the contributors produced their essays – 'and so the years roll away'.[87] At this time the council were interested in the idea of publishing all of John's Cook lectures, though it is not clear whether they thought of this as a substitute for the planned volume. John had always shared the council's view that the society should keep faith with the original subscribers who had paid for the four volumes – though by any measure they had already had remarkable value for their money. Finally, in May 1971, having finished the first draft of the Cook biography, he suggested that it might take the place of the planned volume. The idea was welcomed, though it was to be more than three years before the *Life* appeared.

IN HIS LECTURE 'SOME Problems of Cook's Biographer',* John dwelt briefly on his predecessors. Of the first, Andrew Kippis, whose work was published in 1788, within ten years of Cook's death, he wrote: 'It must be a comfort to any serious biographer to feel that he can't do any worse than the Rev. Andrew Kippis, on whom was conferred "the pious office of erecting an honourable monument"[88] to Cook's memory, and thus wrote the first and what was for one hundred and nineteen years the standard life'. What John lamented as much as the inaccuracies of Kippis's work were the opportunities he had spurned. He seemed to have had 'no particular interest in Cook' and, although he wrote at a time when there would have been plenty of people alive who had known Cook as a child and a youth, and his married sister and his widow were both alive, Kippis did little or nothing to seek first-hand information. 'When one thinks of his chances as a contemporary, and what he did with them; when one considers how full of positive error is the little that he did gather, one almost weeps as one throws him away.' The Rev. George Young, whose life was published in 1836, 'had some real feeling for the hero, for family history, for the illuminating anecdote', but the years had passed and he discovered very little new information.

The next significant life, which appeared in 1907, was by Arthur Kitson, a businessman rather than a professional writer, but a stickler for accuracy and, in relation to Cook, 'an amateur

---

*   'Some Problems of Cook's Biographer' (Eva G.R. Taylor Memorial Lecture), *Mariner's Mirror,* vol.55, no.4 (November 1969), pp.365–81.

who became devoted'. John found his work useful – though not as useful as did some later writers who had leaned almost entirely on it for numerous short lives. In John's view, however, the book had its defects: Kitson 'apparently saw no reason why he should give any references whatever; his sense of proportion is not impeccable; his style, like his imagination, is rather pedestrian; he had rather a fondness for revising the spelling and punctuation of his extracts; he knew nothing of the Pacific.' The comments are revealing, giving some sense of what John thought was important in writing about Cook. But, for him, knowing what he believed to be important was only the beginning of solving the problems:

> . . . the first task of any serious writer on Cook is to supersede Kitson.
> This means that all the pedestrian virtues are necessary, and also some
> virtues that I don't know how you get hold of. How do you convey
> the sense of greatness and of intimacy, of humdrum efficiency and
> constant battle against the trivial, of practical ability and the growth
> of a mind; how do you render the trivial as the significant and keep the
> significant from being too significant, how do you estimate the influence
> on character of the old immensities of sea and wind and the long swell
> sweeping perpetually into destruction on the reef?

It was not enough to say that Cook was a man of action, and that the biography of a man of action is an account of what he did, for, John asked, 'is not what he thought and felt as well as what he did important to us?' Indeed, could one explain why he did what he did without some understanding of what he thought and felt?

John started writing the biography on 11 July 1967.[89] His heart was already giving him trouble* and he wrote with a keen but stoical awareness of time drawing in. Again he faced what he called 'the awfulness of putting words together to make sense' and, in spite of the years he had been working on Cook, he described how he kept 'falling over all the little bits one knows nothing about, & never thought of before':

> What did Elizabeth Batt's father do? What sort of lodgings did Cook
> get in Shadwell at the end of 1762? Shadwell seems to have been a pretty
> rough & stinking riverside place. If Miss Batts lived at Barking, how did
> Cook meet her? When did he buy the house at Mile End, & what *was*
> Mile End like in those days? – I couldn't find anything even in London
> that told me that. The difficulties of being a biographer.[90]

---

*   This is discussed further in chapter 14.

After a year he had completed chapter eleven (out of a total of twenty-seven), which saw the *Endeavour* reach England at the end of the first voyage.* Just six months later (the date noted, '1 Feb '69 4.30') he had completed chapter seventeen and with it his account of the second voyage. There was then a considerable break while he and Elsie were in England for five months from late April until early October 1969, primarily to take part in events marking the bicentennial of the *Endeavour* voyage. Before he left he sent what he had written to Janet for her 'straight out opinions', commenting that the work 'must have a lot of detail, but the detail must be carried along & not be boring. There must be a lot of quotations from C, but not too much, & only when it illuminates.'[91] Odd comments in letters suggest that he was thinking consciously about biography. Robert Gittings's life of Keats he thought very good, and added, 'curiously enough, the book convinces me that I am tackling the Cook life in the right way'.[92] Later, he found Harold Nicolson's life of George V an 'interesting bit of work as biographical technique'.[93]

John and Elsie flew to London with stops in Australia, Bangkok and Italy. In Canberra and Adelaide, John lectured and met with old friends. They had three weeks in Italy, a marvellous packed week staying with Alister and Doris McIntosh in Rome† and then Siena, Bologna and finally Venice. It was John's first visit to Venice and he was excited and captivated. In London he delivered the E.G.R. Taylor memorial lecture, 'Some Problems of Cook's Biographer', to the Society for Nautical Research; and at a very grand occasion at the Royal Society he lectured on 'Cook the Navigator'.‡ Eila Campbell told him that 'she had heard thousands of lectures, & this one was the best she had ever heard', but John himself would say only he thought he was a better lecturer than the Astronomer Royal.[94] He and Elsie visited the Skeltons at their home in Tilford in Surrey: 'nobody could possibly have been kinder than he & Mrs S. were', John wrote to Helen Wallis, '& it seemed completely spontaneous'. He added that he was still 'completely puzzled', and 'if you are completely puzzled about a friend & contemporary, how on earth

---

*   'I got Cook back to England last night at 11.30, 114,000 words,' he wrote to Janet on 3 July 1968, '& I have started to read the *Golden Bough*. And if anybody else rings me up or writes to me about Cook in the next couple of days I shall probably go off my rocker.'

†   After his retirement as head of the Department of External Affairs, McIntosh was appointed New Zealand ambassador to Italy.

‡   'Cook the Navigator', *Royal Society of London Proceedings*, A314 (1969), pp.27–38. The two lectures were later reprinted in *Employ'd as a Discoverer*, edited by J.V.S. Megaw (Sydney: Reed, 1971), pp.23–41, 117–34.

can you write a biography of a man in the 18th century?'[95],* The
time in London also gave him a chance to do a little further work in
the British Museum and the Public Record Office.

I have finished looking up all the bits & pieces [he wrote to Norman
Richmond], until the next crop arises. I thought I had finished in 1962,
& again in 1966. I am beginning to feel that I may need a special grant
of time from the Lord if ever I am to get this life of Cook finished. Or
if the Lord would simply remove all the people who want me to give
lectures that would be helpful.[96]

When he got back to Wellington in October, he started on
chapter eighteen, 'England 1775–1776' (between the second and
third voyages), but progress was slow. 'I got to the end of the second
voyage a year ago', he told Eric McCormick in February 1970, '&
haven't written a word since, owing to all these damned lectures;
though I admit that writing the lectures made me think & summarize
a bit. I must get it done by the end of this year', he added. 'And then
it will be too long.'[97] He was worrying about working so slowly: 'I
think perhaps my mind is grinding to a stop'.[98] In March he wrote:
'I have begun the next chapter of My Book. I have written 1 page &
1½ lines. The problem is now how to go on, & tomorrow we have
to go to a confounded wedding.'[99] There was a further delay while
he went to Australia from 11 April to 7 May to give more lectures.
When he returned he started on chapter twenty, the beginning of the
third voyage. Three months later he reported to Helen Wallis that he
had got to the end of chapter twenty-one: 'Hero has just left Tonga'.
He 'wanted to get to the end of xxii by end of August, but shan't:
have to go to Auckland for a Historic Places Trust conference. DV
shall finish my draft by Xmas, but maybe D won't V.'[100] He wrote
again to Wallis in December. He was beginning to 'be a bit hopeful'
that he would finish the 'Life of the Capt':

I have written 697 pp., & he is about at the moment to leave Unalaska
on the passage to Hawai'i.† The planning difficulty at the moment is
whether to take two chapters or one to kill him; I think I'll try and do
it in one, it may be longish but it can't be as long as the 56pp. of the last

---

*   Skelton died just over a year later, on 7 December 1970, following another
       car accident. John wrote to Helen Wallis (who succeeded Skelton as
       superintendent of the Map Room) that he was 'a bit distressed', and would
       like to sit down with her and 'talk him all over again'. He added that he
       now 'more than ever' regretted 'whatever it was that put us out of touch . . .
       I didn't cease to admire him, even though my affection waned a bit, alas.'
       (JCB to Helen Wallis, 27 December 1970.)
†   In the *Life* as printed he had reached p.636.

one.* Then one for finishing the voyage, & a last for general reflections. We ought to get done in another hundred pages. But God knows how long rewriting will take.[101]

On 20 January 1971 he completed the chapter on 'Kealakekua Bay': 'I've . . . killed him, for the last time I hope', he wrote to Janet. There were just two more chapters to go: 'It will be incredible to have finished it, even in draft'. He added, 'I do want this book to be a good book . . . of course I shouldn't be thinking about that at all, only about writing a book'.[102] He wrote the final, memorable and moving sentence on 26 March 1971,† and then started on the revision of the typescript.

Completing the draft of the biography had taken nearly four years, but the work on it had really begun when John embarked on editing the *Journals* over twenty years earlier. If the biography rests firmly on the foundation of the *Journals* (and there is a good deal of near repetition from the introductions to those volumes), can it be separated from them? How far does it stand as a coherent work in its own right?[103] For the earlier part of Cook's life the biography gives a much fuller account: the three or four pages in the *Endeavour* volume dealing with his career before 1768 are expanded into four chapters totalling ninety-eight pages, nearly forty of which are devoted to a detailed account of the Newfoundland surveys. Yet the magisterial survey of the intellectual background to the voyages and the pre-Cook history of Pacific exploration, also ninety-eight pages, given in the general introduction in volume one, is reduced in the *Life* to thirty pages. Again, the brief character sketch of the Forsters in the *Life* corresponds to seven pages in the *Journals*, and nearly all the actual phrasing of the shorter version comes from the longer. John's achievement was to write a work which was firmly grounded in that immense scholarly undertaking, but was shaped by the biographer's eye and not by his sources, and stands very successfully on its own.

The *Life* is a long book, 714 pages, but lightened by John's prose, by his vivid portraits of Cook's shipmates, by his wit and power of reflection, the aptness of metaphor or phrase, by his 'splendid gift

---

*   The 'last one', chapter 24, on 'The North-west Coast', came to forty-five printed pages. The chapter on Kealakekua Bay was only thirty-five pages.

†   In his last paragraph John wrote of memorials to Cook. He begins, 'There are statues and inscriptions; but Geography and Navigation are his memorials . . .' The paragraph ends: 'Such things; Geography and Navigation; if we wish for more, an ocean is enough, where the waves fall on innumerable reefs, and a great wind blows from the south-east with the revolving world.'

Right: John and Elsie on their wedding day, 17 February 1930.
Below: Wedding group. Back row: Charlie Holmes, Ern Beaglehole, Elsie, Robert Holmes, Mary Holmes, Peter Holmes, Edith Holmes, Peter's wife Norah, John. Front row: Keith Beaglehole, Marjorie Wiren, Charlie's wife Norah.

Elsie with Robin and Tim, October 1936.

Above: Peter's Farm, 'Kowhai Flat'.
Below: Tim, Giles and Robin, about 1947.

Above: Ivan Sutherland. *Oliver Sutherland collection, Victoria University of Wellington.*
Lower left: Fred Wood.
S.P. Andrew collection, F-43331-1/2, Alexander Turnbull Library, Wellington, NZ.
Lower right: Eric McCormick.
S.P. Andrew collection, F-20080-1/4, Alexander Turnbull Library, Wellington, NZ.

Above: Janet Wilkinson, 1944.
John Pascoe collection, F-1273-1/4, Alexander Turnbull Library, Wellington, NZ.

Below: Joseph Heenan, about 1950.
John Pascoe collection, F-20963-1/4, Alexander Turnbull Library, Wellington, NZ.

Above: John in his study, 1949. *Photograph by Greig Royle.*
Below: Peter Jacoby, John, Ilse Jacoby and Marie Vandewart in the Orongorongo valley, early 1940s.

Right: Keith, 1947.
Below: John and Elsie
with Ester and Helmut
Einhorn, 1962.
Photograph by Jule Einhorn.

Upper: J.A. Williamson
sailing his sloop *Rose* on
the Solent, 1957.
Lower: R.A. Skelton.
Alexa Barrow collection.

Above: Matavai Bay, 1952.
Below: Elsie and John at Kealakekua Bay, 1962.

John's desk as he left it on 9 October 1971. *Photograph by Lyn Corner.*

of rising to the great occasions of the narrative – for instance the striking on Endeavour Reef and the final escape from the clutches of the coral'.[104] In such passages there can be no element of surprise as the story is well known, and yet John contrives to give us the shock, the tension, the reaction when the immediate danger is past, the final lift of the heart when at last they sail through the 'Provedential Channell'. Again, in his account of Cook's death[105] (the fruit, as we have seen, of long deliberation) he leads the reader, with great clarity and mounting tension, through the events of that day, as well as the preceding days. Could there be a reader who did not know what was to happen? And yet Cook's death, when it comes, is almost violently shocking. At that moment the Hawai'ians drew back briefly. Could it have been a chance for the men in the pinnace and the cutter to reclaim the bodies? They did not do so. John closes the chapter: 'The men in the boats may have been shocked out of all awareness of this [chance]. Leaving the dead, Cook and four marines, where they lay, the boats rowed back in silence to the ships; and the ships fell silent.' Looking back over John's account of the third voyage, we can appreciate with what skill he has prepared us for this final tragic act: the brooding sense of unease instilled by repeated low-key references to increasing strain and fatigue, 'that almost imperceptible blurring of the brain',[106] the outbursts of seemingly irrational temper at Moorea and Tonga, precursors of the final loss not of nerve but of judgement at Kealakekua Bay.

The spur to the historical imagination that John gained through visiting many of Cook's anchorages, which led to some of the most memorable passages in the introductions to the *Journals,* can again be seen at work in the biography. He had finally achieved his dream of visiting Dusky Sound – again thanks partly to the New Zealand navy and its survey vessel* – and his description captures that 'remote and wildly magnificent', and virtually unchanged, spot:

The great sheet of water, screened within its entrance from the ocean by an irregular line of islands, and extending into a number of long arms and a vast number of smaller indentations, lies over a bottom anciently

---

*   This visit was in March 1968. The National Film Unit invited John to accompany them (at his own expense) when they were filming in Dusky Sound. They were all accommodated on the *Lachlan.* John's excitement is clear from his description of a visit to Pickersgill Harbour when it poured with rain: 'I was wet to the skin from the toes up, & in the end cold too; but there they were . . . the stumps of the trees that Cook had cut down, & the cascade that Hodges painted, & all the islands, & the rocky ledge where he first saw the Maoris.' Virtually the whole sound was still in virgin bush. (JCB to JEP, 13 March 1968.)

gouged in the land by stupendous glaciers, so that its shores tend to stand up immediately from the sea. The water is almost uniformly deep; only at the head of subordinate stretches have shoals been built up by the quick detritus-laden streams. There is little flat land; the eye is ever carried to immense heights, whether close around or in far misty recession. Except where a prodigious cliff-face falls vertically to the depths, the steep slopes are covered from high water mark up to the limits of growth by forest dense, unbroken, sombre. The scale is so deceptive, as well as so vast, that a full-grown tree, taken as a measure of some less regarded height, becomes insignificant and lost; a tremendous white cataract seems to descend only a few yards, not hundreds of feet, before it plunges hidden under the dark green covering and changes its direction. Low islets are tree-clothed; a rock perhaps will jut out quite bare of earth. Rain falls heavily for days, thick cloud makes invisible the whole landscape; then the sun of an occasional clear day will render the scene sharp as well as heroic. Into this large frame entered the *Resolution*, no larger than she would have seemed amid the waste of the southern ocean.[107]

With all this, one must still ask: how far does John show us the man behind the historical figure? Do we really understand what (to use Cook's own words) brought 'a prentice boy in the Coal Trade to a Commander in the Navy'?[108] John had been unable to add a great deal to the available information about Cook's early life, which remains sketchy; and of his private life, as husband, father, householder, there are the briefest glimpses. Cook's personal correspondence, what there is of it, is unrevealing. His journals tell more about him than his letters; the man was inseparable from the seaman. John's triumph was to read those journals (and the surviving journals of those who sailed with Cook) in a way which drew from them a greater insight into the inner man than anyone had had before. Consider his account of the bloodshed in the immediate aftermath of Cook's first landing in New Zealand: 'The first two days were disastrous, all that Cook deplored and Lord Morton* had warned him against, all with the best intentions . . .'[109] We are immediately engaged in Cook's struggle, as he drafted his journal entry, to explain what had gone wrong. Or in that moment on the second voyage when, having crossed the Antarctic circle for the third time, the *Resolution* faced ice stretching as far as one could see, and Cook wrote:

---

*   The Earl of Morton, president of the Royal Society from 1764 until his death a few weeks after the *Endeavour* sailed, in his *Hints* to Cook and the gentlemen with him, had urged them 'To exercise the utmost patience and forbearance with respect to the Natives of the several Lands where the Ship may touch'.

I will not say it was impossible anywhere to get in among this Ice, but I will assert that the bare attempting of it would be a very dangerous enterprise and what I believe no man in my situation would have thought of. I whose ambition leads me not only further than any other man has been before me, but as far as I think it possible for man to go, was not sorry at meeting with this interruption . . .[110]

It is a measure of John's art as a writer, and his way of humanising the hero, that at such moments he lets Cook, the man of simple direct words, speak for himself.

He shows us the human Cook, as well, in the words of one of the midshipmen on the third voyage. James Trevenen described how at Nootka Sound the captain would go out surveying with a boat's crew of midshipmen and make them row thirty miles, and how they enjoyed the expedition, when Cook would 'relax from his almost constant severity of disposition, & condescend . . . to converse familiarly with us', handing over to the hungry young men the ducks that were shot, and Trevenen breaks into somewhat regrettable verse:

Oh Day of hard labour! oh Day of good living!
When Toote [Cook] was seized with the humour of giving!
When he clothed in good nature his looks of authority,
And shook from his eyebrows their stern superiority.[111]

When finally published in 1974,* *The Life of Captain James Cook* was widely recognised as a masterly study, a brilliantly told story. Brief quotation from three of them give a taste of the reviews.† David Quinn, who had followed John's work closely since the publication

---

*   When John died on 10 October 1971, he had revised the typescript of his draft up to the middle of chapter 19, that is, about two-thirds of the way through the book. In completing the revision and seeing the book through the press, I was helped by a number of his friends who had been involved in his earlier work on the *Journals*. Remarkably little revision was needed: a little tightening of the prose (replacing 'and' with a semi-colon) which he had started doing, and a careful checking of Cook's course through the Aleutian Islands, which he had signalled he intended to do. Had he lived he might well have picked up those very few errors of fact pointed out by readers and reviewers. The bibliography for the book was prepared by Phyllis Mander Jones, the index by Alison Quinn. J.D. Newth, of A. & C. Black, whose friendship with John went back to the publication of *The Exploration of the Pacific*, gave the book meticulous attention in seeing it through the press.

†   The reviews at the time were almost all full of praise, almost adulatory, the notable exception being that by J.H. Plumb in the *New York Review of Books*. This was, however, in Glyndwr Williams's words, 'an object-lesson in ignorance.'

of the first volume of the *Journals,* wrote: 'For someone as fully equipped as John Beaglehole, to write the life of Captain Cook was at once exceptionally easy and supremely difficult. He knew so much about so many episodes in which Cook was concerned that to select and blend together what he knew into the almost flawless narrative of the *Life* was a difficult task of selection, and one that could only succeed by mastery of the narrative art'. It was, he judged, John's 'finest work'.[112] For the American scholar Louis B. Wright, the biography 'deserves that over-used appellation of masterpiece . . . [it] is more than a chronicle of exploration or an account of pioneering scientific observation. It is even more than a remarkably deep and full revelation of the growth of a complex man of many rare and diverse parts. It is, in addition, a literary achievement . . . Only writers who have tried to convey a vast amount of technical information accurately and clearly without being dull can fully realize Beaglehole's remarkable achievement.'[113] And Geoffrey Moorhouse, in the *Guardian,* concluded that 'Cook's biographer has done his subject magnificently proud . . . I suspect that Beaglehole has written one of the great biographies in the English language'.[114]

With such a reception, it is fair to ask how far John's achievement has stood the test of time. The years since he died have seen a great deal of scholarly work related to Cook – much of it drawing on the *Journals* as its starting point – as well as further short biographies of little or no scholarly value. The death of Cook was the subject of a remarkable academic dispute between Marshall Sahlins[115] and Gananath Obeyesekere[116] which, if nothing else, was a reminder of how much there was to learn about the 'discovered' as opposed to the 'discoverers'. Their work has been continued (with less argument) by scholars such as Anne Salmond[117] and Nicholas Thomas[118] who, drawing on a mass of recent research, have greatly increased our knowledge and understanding of Pacific societies at the time of Cook's voyages. Whether this work has given us a Cook significantly different from John's is doubtful. No scholar has attempted a further full biography.

Other researchers, often working on contemporaries of Cook such as Alexander Dalrymple or J.R. Forster, have suggested that John, possibly carried away with the virtues of Cook, could be less than fair to others. John did not care for Forster, the German naturalist who sailed on the *Resolution* on the second voyage: 'there is nothing', he wrote in the *Life,* 'that can make him other than one of the Admiralty's vast mistakes. One does not wish to draw a caricature; but how is one to deny that he was dogmatic, humourless, suspicious, censorious, pretentious, contentious, demanding?'[119] To Rolf du Rietz, the Swedish bibliographical scholar and writer on Bligh and the mutiny on the *Bounty,* John wrote in 1970: 'You said once you hoped I'd modify my view of Forster. The trouble is that the more I find out about him the more it confirms my view. I don't doubt that he was a learned man, & a man of perception in various ways; but he had no perception at all in human relationships. At one time he was arrogant, at another he was crawling. It is his moral – in a general sense – character that worries me, not his brains.'[120] After making a long voyage on the replica of the *Endeavour* and seeing the way in which individual character could resonate through that confined community, I am surprised, even remembering that the *Resolution* was a larger ship, that Forster was not lost overboard one stormy night. But, however convincing John's portrait of Forster might be – and it was one to which he gave great thought – there is the comment he made in a letter to Janet: 'Odd how I have become involved with all these people. I take sides most furiously. Don't tell anybody that, because it might ruin my reputation as a good historian.'[121] He wrote partly in jest (and some years before he started on the biography), but there is a kernel of truth. John believed that in taking sides he was working on the evidence. It is, perhaps, a sign of humanity in a biographer that so often the understanding they reach of their subject leads to admiration. In this question of John's impartiality I, the biographer, defer to the historian.

13

PRIVATE LIFE AND PUBLIC CAUSES

WHEN HE ARRIVED HOME from London in July 1950, after his first leave, John settled into a pattern of life centred on his study at 6 Messines Road that largely persisted until his death just over twenty-one years later. The bookshelves gradually grew higher on the walls, stacks of papers mounted on the floor. If he had a system for keeping anything other than books in an orderly way (he could put his hand on a book he wanted without hesitation), it was not obvious to any observer. On the wall hung Raymond McGrath's watercolour of the East End of London, the portrait of Erasmus that John had sent his father from London in 1927, and a portrait of his grandfather, William Henry Beaglehole, painted by his uncle, George Butler. Later these were joined by one of Janet's drawings. The little bust of Voltaire that he had bought on his first visit to Paris was on one of the shelves. It was about this time that he had a large new desk made, with drawers on each side at the front, and cupboards at the back. The top was always a mass of books, papers and letters waiting to be answered – I have 'recently let down a bucket into the ocean of unanswered correspondence', he wrote on one occasion[1] – but space was made for a photograph of Elsie in a leather frame, a pewter inkstand (which John had found in a second-hand shop in Molesworth Street, bought for ten shillings and got great satisfaction out of cleaning up and polishing), a pottery ashtray for his pipes, and a number of other small things he had collected: a little red lacquer tray to hold pens and pencils, the piece of lead from the *Astrolabe,* a pebble from Matavai Bay, a polished half-coconut shell in which he kept paper clips, and two small pieces of building stone (used as paperweights) whose origins I can no longer remember. From his desk John looked out to the small back garden, to a climbing rose, *Paul Scarlet,* which flowered bravely against an almost sunless wall, and to a crab apple tree – almost every spring he would comment to Janet when it blossomed. A little further away was an old apple tree. When Tommy Hunter died John was given the armchair which had been in his study at Victoria College. It stood next to John's desk; he snoozed in it for half an hour or so after lunch on days when it was not fine enough to lie outside in the sun, and he read there in the evenings.

I think it was about the time of his first leave in London that John gave up beginning his day (once he had helped wash up the breakfast dishes) by playing Bach preludes and fugues on the piano in the sitting room – so clear a part of my childhood memories. This was probably the time, too, when he stopped playing the Town Hall organ for the graduation ceremony. Other habits changed. Now that he was doing only a little teaching, he was walking less regularly to the university; when he needed a break from writing he walked around the neighbourhood, with his pipe and the beret he had bought in Paris when he was at his first Unesco conference, brooding over the next sentence or paragraph. When he was working at his desk he would emerge for morning coffee, which Elsie made, and they would have it together, on the front verandah if it was fine. His afternoon tea he often made himself and drank in the study. When we were very young we had learned that it was sometimes necessary to wait a little for John to appear when a meal was ready – 'Dad's just finishing a sentence' settled the matter.

As the years passed and their finances improved, John and Elsie altered and improved the house,* spurred on, perhaps, by what he recognised as an unrealisable dream: 'I'd still like to be able to build a first-rate, really beautiful house, that one of the kids could live in after me† & that would stand for 2 or 300 years in Wellington as a good thing. And have furniture & books & pictures to go with it.'[2] They worked steadily. The new sitting-room curtains (from the linen fabric found at Heal's in London in 1950) were made and hung. Rooms were lined with Gibraltar board in place of the original scrim, and repapered or painted. John gave the same

---

*   When John was appointed to the Senior Research Fellowship he thought he would celebrate by giving Elsie £50. 'This is for clothes,' he said, 'not stupid things like books', and he suggested she should start with a new nightie. 'Oh thank you, says she, with a kiss, I'll buy a new washing machine. What is the use of a woman like that?' he wrote to Janet. 'She can wear clothes too.' (JCB to JEP, 14 October 1948.) Elsie bought a Bendix, one of the first automatic washing machines, when they were in London the next year. It made life a great deal easier.

†   I am writing this biography in John's study. He and Elsie lived in the house for almost thirty-five years. My wife, Helen, and I have now (in 2005) been here for over thirty years.

painstaking care to decisions on papers and colours that he would give to designing a title page. He did not paint himself but would go to endless trouble stopping nail holes and sandpapering as he took a very gloomy view of the workmanship of New Zealand tradesmen. He spent hours sanding the paint off the frame of a mirror that had belonged to his parents and polishing it, even longer sanding the old tea trolley we used to take meals from the kitchen to the dining room, only to find that the timber was unattractive and he had to repaint it. The kitchen remained a dark and cold room at the back of the house looking out at a steep bank; it had the Cedric Firth wall of cupboards and a large stainless steel bench, and Elsie seemed satisfied. She had become an extremely good cook, not only for her family but for their friends and colleagues and for students and overseas visitors invited to the house.

On the walls of the dining and sitting rooms the Van Gogh and Cézanne prints gave way in time to New Zealand work. Elsie and John's first paintings by T.A. McCormack, Toss Woollaston and Eric Lee-Johnson were joined by more McCormacks, two John Weeks, a number of Evelyn Pages, woodcuts by Mervyn Taylor, a Charles Tole, a second Woollaston and a Frances Hodgkins oil, while the Frances Hodgkins print came home from the university. Other art was not entirely supplanted; two fine Japanese prints hung in the passage, John had the print of Gainsborough's painting of his daughters (from the National Gallery) framed and hung in his and Elsie's bedroom. When in New York in 1962 they acquired a Braque lithograph, and other reproductions were bought when they were overseas, including a Blake which Elsie never cared for and which was hung only briefly. John had the John Basire engraving of William Hodges's portrait of Cook, and Alister McIntosh, who had developed a considerable interest in early prints of New Zealand and the Pacific, gave him a copy of J.K. Sherwin's engraving of Hodges's painting *The Landing at Tanna*. The collection of pewter grew steadily.

A continuing part of John's pattern of life at Messines Road was his books and his reading. Even when he was working hard on Cook, his reading was as wide ranging as ever, and there is hardly a letter among all those he wrote to Janet in which he does not comment on books seen, books bought or books read. In February 1951, for example, he reported to her that he had been reading Boswell's London journal and Byron's letters, which he had bought when on leave in London: 'What extraordinary chaps have committed themselves to paper in the English language; & how they have pushed women around & complained of women'. He felt that he could go on 'reading and reading' the letters, although he considered Byron an 'unpleasant fellow' – 'but what a charm he must have had, & what an intelligence. I must read Don Juan at once; but then there are so many other things I must read at once; & I really keep on meaning to soak myself in the 18th century for Cook & Banks; oh how difficult life is. Why wasn't I born with a single track mind?'³ Read *Don Juan* he did, and then, within a few months, moved on to Henry James:

I've read HJ's *Portrait of a Lady*. The awful thing, the shocking thing about it was that I was so worked up that I had to take part of yesterday morning off to finish it; reckless monster of immorality as I felt myself to be, reading a novel in the daytime, in the morning, yet I was helpless in its grip, the Puritan was vanquished yet again. It's one of those stories with reverberations, so that I can't read anything else except matter of fact until the reverberations have died down a bit within me; oh that chap could write . . . I like his humour – a wonderful line in subdued irony when he likes to let it peep out. And when he really hits you you get it fair in the middle.⁴

A fortnight later he had finished another Henry James, *The Ambassadors*, and wondered, 'Would he have been any better if he hadn't been so frightened of vulgarity? Perhaps, but who knows?'⁵ Later in the year he read the two volumes of *Johnson's England*: 'I call this working up the 18th century background, & find I can thus get away with anything in full view of my conscience.'⁶

ALONGSIDE THE SCHOLAR, comfortable in his study, and increasingly recognised in the university world to which he contributed in a host of ways, was the public man. He did not seek the limelight, indeed in temperament he remained modest and retiring, but if he believed something needed to be done, he was ready to do what he could. The range of his interests is suggested by looking at the period after he returned from London in July 1950, when he quickly resumed his involvement in all sorts of activities in addition to working on Cook. For some months he spent a lot of time on the hopeless struggle to save the historical atlas. Then there was the University of New Zealand Press, and worries over the rising cost of printing. 'It's much easier to lecture on the general principles of book production to the Library School', he wrote to Janet, '& say the art of printing is the art of spacing; when really one should say the art of printing is the art of being a millionaire who doesn't want his money back.'[7] In February 1951 he flew to Christchurch to talk at a refresher course for teachers, organised by the British Council. He wrote a piece on Hunter, marking his retirement, for the *New Zealand Journal of Public Administration*, and a note for *Landfall* on a collection of paintings Helen Hitchings had gathered to be exhibited abroad; he also spent time and energy trying to help her gain government support to do this. In an article for the 1951 *Arts Year Book*, 'A Small Bouquet for the Education Department', he warmly praised the work of School Publications. He reviewed a number of books for the *New Zealand Listener* and gave his views on the Chamber Music concerts of the year for the December *Chamber Music Bulletin*. But the main excitement of 1951 was political, stemming from the struggle between the new National government and the watersiders' union.

Looking back ten years later in *Landfall*, John agreed with those who in 1949 had thought the Labour government should go.[8] Peter Fraser, 'literally myopic and physically exhausted . . . led a party that was, politically speaking, myopic and exhausted also'.* What John found awful, 'however unavoidable it was', was the alternative. 'The naive, the almost childish brutality with which the Chiefs of the National Party fell upon power may seem quite surprising, until one remembers how famished for power they were.' It was almost inevitable that such a government would come into conflict with the waterside workers. Fraser, not without difficulty, had checked the ambitions of a new militant leadership in some of the unions. The National Prime Minister, Sidney Holland, interpreted their challenge as a struggle for power, a struggle that he appeared to welcome and was determined to win. A large part of the country was undoubtedly behind him. What appalled John, and others, was the means that Holland used. Cheered on by the press, the government declared a state of emergency on 21 February 1951; the following day it issued the Waterfront Strike Emergency Regulations. It drew its powers from the Public Safety Conservation Act, enacted in the week following the April 1932 riots in Auckland, giving 'virtually unlimited power to the government of the day to make such regulations as it sees fit'.[9] John was one of several Victoria staff[†] who signed a letter to the *Evening Post* (drafted by Robert Parker)

---

*   Fraser, ill and worn out by his arduous years of leadership, died on 12 December 1950. Walter Nash succeeded him as leader of the Labour Party.

†   The others to sign it were Robert Parker, and John's colleagues in the history department, Fred Wood, Winston Monk, Peter Munz and Bill Oliver.

on the regulations. 'It's a long while since Norman Richmond & I were writing letters to the paper', John wrote to Janet, '& things don't seem to have improved much in the meanwhile. In fact, it was then that the damned emergency regulations started.'[10]

Since then New Zealand had played a significant role in the United Nations' adoption of the Universal Declaration of Human Rights.[11] In 1948 Fraser had appointed John and Fred Wood to a special Human Rights Committee in Wellington to study the draft declaration and covenant carefully, and to send its opinions directly to the United Nations for consideration.* The *Evening Post* had a leader asking what provisions of the declaration had been infringed by the government's actions against the watersiders. The academics' letter suggested that six of its articles were relevant, and quoted them, before asking whether 'the denial of civil liberties, on balance, tended to allay or to exacerbate the present disputes'. The *Post* printed the letter,[12] but as John expected there was a long leader 'denouncing us & saying that this sort of thing should not be discussed'.[13] A reply, drafted by John, was printed a week later;[14] it was summarily dismissed by the editor, and the correspondence was closed. Their arguments fell on deaf ears. It was, perhaps, not a happy coincidence that just at this time John was pressing the Minister of Internal Affairs for a meeting on the future of the Historical Branch and the atlas.[15] The government, deriding Walter Nash's call for a negotiated settlement, portrayed the struggle with the watersiders as part of a worldwide battle against communism, and acted ruthlessly to destroy the Watersiders' Union and the few other militant unions that had supported it. On 14 July, after 151 days, the watersiders acknowledged defeat. As Keith Sinclair wrote, the government's 'stunning victory in the wharf crisis helped it to entrench itself in office'; Holland called an early election, 'seeking a mandate to deal with the Communists', and was returned with an increased majority of seats.[16]

The government's next step was to move to make permanent the extraordinarily repressive powers it had taken under the emergency regulations. The Police Offences Amendment Bill, as introduced on 26 October 1951, was an ill-drafted piece of legislation, in places dangerously vague, that greatly widened the definition of sedition,

---

*   John wrote at the time to Phyllis Mander Jones: 'I have been on a committee working over the draft declaration & convention on Human Rights, & two more dreadfully drafted documents I have never seen. I hope Australia will support our very numerous emendations & drastic reshapings.' (JCB to Mander Jones, 25 March 1948. ML 1709/63. State Library of NSW.)

gave the police extended powers of arrest, and in certain cases put
the onus of proving innocence on an accused person. This time,
however, there was widespread opposition to the government's
move;[17] by the middle of November John reported Wellington to be
'echoing with the attack on the Police Offences Amendment Bill'.[18]
He drafted a further letter to the *Evening Post* which, while not
impugning the government's good intentions, suggested that the
defects of the Bill were such that it should be re-examined:

We do not like the invention of new crimes. We do not like this whittling
away of civil liberties. We do not think that New Zealand can afford
to throw aside any at all of those conservative principles built up so
painfully during the course of British constitutional history, which now
seem in needless and imminent danger from a Government so devoted to
the assertion of constitutional righteousness.[19]

He approached colleagues to sign it – 'amusing to see the visible
wrestling with conscience of some of them who didn't sign'[20] – and
got seven others besides himself. The *Post* printed the letter on 13
November, together with a quite full report of a protest meeting
held on 12 November in the Concert Chamber of the Wellington
Town Hall. The meeting was chaired by the young lawyer Nigel
Taylor (husband of Nan Taylor, John's former student and colleague
in the Historical Branch), and John and Walter Scott were two of
the main speakers. John was reported in the *Post*[21] as saying that he
resented 'the irresponsibility of people in the Government' who had
made the meeting necessary. He continued:

I thought that the dissolution of Parliament and the subsequent election
was the lowest point of irresponsibility we had yet reached in New
Zealand history, but however low we go, there are depths below depths,
and we are plunging into them now. I do not like the prospect of people
being pushed around, and you have heard what this Bill involves in
pushing people around. There are not many safeguards for personal
liberties in it.

He again pointed out the irony that, while New Zealand was
supporting the promulgation of human rights in the wider world, at
home the government was happy to ignore such rights. He concluded
by saying that the Bill 'would be absurd if it were not so vicious and
dangerous'.

John told Janet that he 'let fly' at the meeting,[22] but twenty years
later Walter Scott gave a rather different view. He remembered
particularly John's quotation from Burke's speech on conciliation
with America: 'Magnanimity in politics is not seldom the truest

wisdom; and a great empire and little minds go ill together'. He also remembered that a number of those present rather disapproved of John's address: 'it was less rhetorical, less passionately denunciating, than they wanted. But the knowledge and judgment that guided [John] to Burke for his quotation had disciplined him to be restrained and reasonable even under so great an affront to his strongest beliefs as the Police Offences Amendment Bill.'[23] The newspapers joined the criticism of the Bill – 'even the Dominion', John noted – and he was pleased that the Victoria College law faculty was in the forefront of those making critical submissions to the Statutes Revision Committee: 'they can't say the University isn't doing its part'.[24] There seems little doubt that the outburst of public opinion led to a significant improvement in the Bill before it passed into law on 3 December 1951.

Just over two months later John received his letter from the Minister of Internal Affairs terminating his job with the Historical Branch, as recounted in chapter nine. A number of his friends in the department were 'very distressed'. John saw A.G. Harper, the head of the department, who confirmed the rumour that he had not been consulted until 'after the event', and told John he believed that he was being sacked because of his opposition to the government's Bill.* This time, according to John, 'Elsie was merely highly amused'.[25] He discouraged those who wished to make a public issue of the matter. Bodkin, the minister, denied altogether any political motive in sacking him – 'he just thought apparently it was the natural thing to do'[26] – and John, significantly, in the end thought that he could believe the minister's denial.[27] At the time he appears to have been more upset about the fate of the atlas than his own treatment; he had had enough of the situation in the department and was ready to leave.†

---

*   Fred Wood, writing to Blackwood Paul on 27 February 1952, asked: 'Do you know that J.C.B. was sacked from what remained of his job with Internal Affairs on account of his opposition to the police offences bill?' (F.L.W. Wood Papers. 90-006-07/20. ATL.)

†   That there was some feeling critical of John in the government was shown the following year. When he left Internal Affairs he lost his position as the department's nominee on the National Commission for Unesco. The commission was keen that he should continue. John reported to Janet (14 July 1953): 'I don't think I told you that the Nat. Comm. for Unesco had forced me back on to itself. The Minister refused to appoint me on nomination from University, C.E.R. [Council for Educational Research] etc, but the Nat Comm has the right to nominate three or four the minister must accept, so poor old Algie was caught.' John had had little time for Algie ever since his time at Auckland University College, when Algie was professor of law and one of the more conservative members of staff.

The controversy over the Act led directly to the formation of the New Zealand Council for Civil Liberties,[28] with which John was to be involved for the rest of his life. He had mixed feelings about the inaugural meeting, held on 18 August 1952:

... there were the usual lunatics who wanted more public meetings to rouse Public Enthusiasm. So that I felt impelled to warn my colleague on the Executive Committee, Mr N R Taylor, against too much enthusiasm. I don't know why so many people want to live so constantly in an orgy of enthusiasm. When it comes to the point it's always the unenthusiastic academic who is hoisted up on the platform to assault the govt. Thank God for a few blokes like Walter Scott.[29]

John was elected as president – 'it was thought, unfortunately, it might be a good idea to move down from Tommy Hunter', he wrote to Norman Richmond[30] – with Walter Scott, now vice-principal of the Wellington Teachers' College, as the council's chairman.* It was the beginning of a long partnership that was to continue until John's death. While outwardly mild and gentle, Scott was uncompromising on matters of principle. He was an extremely active chairman, working constantly to build awareness of civil liberties within New Zealand society, and maintaining a structure that would sustain them. The council, having been started following the excitement over the Police Offences Amendment Act, quickly recognised that the danger to civil liberties might be no less real in the restrictive

---

*   The Special Branch of the Police took a close interest in the council's formation. Detective Sergeant D.S. Paterson reported (21 August 1952) that the 'meeting was characterised by the attendance of left-wing, so-called intelligentsia in Wellington including the following who are well-known as Communists or Communist sympathisers', and he named five, beginning with John and Walter Scott. In a record of John's 'attendance at C.P. meetings', the only two listed were this meeting to form the Council for Civil Liberties, and the 1943 annual meeting of the Co-operative Book Society (none of the earlier ones). In his August 1952 report Paterson made no reference to the 'reliable report' received the previous September that, although John 'had been a "leftist" sympathiser in his earlier years he was [now] considered to be not so strong in his sympathies'. The Special Branch continued to take some interest in his activities, as did the Security Service subsequently. The police recorded among other things that he wrote articles for *Landfall*. A Security Service note in 1966 stated that he had 'for years shown a consistent socialist outlook with a strong emphasis on civil liberties – he is President of the NZ Council for Civil Liberties. He is also interested in the nuclear disarmament movement. Though leftist in outlook, he is not regarded as extreme.' Although the Security Service maintained their file on John, he was never the subject of ongoing inquiries, and the latter part of the file consists largely of newspaper clippings referring to him. (J.C. Beaglehole File. New Zealand Security Intelligence Service Papers.)

by-laws of a local authority or in an employer's victimisation of a worker for his or her political beliefs. John was happy to work in the background, drafting statements and joining deputations when called on. But he was also remarkably faithful in attending committee meetings of the council. Scott would ring up to remind him of the meeting and offer him a lift; John would groan quietly at the thought of losing an evening in his study, but always go. Fred Wood described his support for civil liberties as 'patient, wise, restrained, but unfailing'.[31]

During the 1950s, with the shadow of McCarthyism extending to New Zealand, Walter Scott and John led the council in taking up the cases of people who had suffered political discrimination and been victimised for what today would often appear unremarkable opinions. A continuing problem was the difficulty the council had with the press, which generally refused to publish its statements – more often than not drafted or polished by John. The council resorted to other ways of working. John was a member of the deputation on 2 April 1954 (and wrote the case they presented) that persuaded Holland, as Prime Minister, to reprieve the three Niue islanders condemned to death for murdering the resident commissioner.[32] He supported the testing of the 1954 amendments to the Indecent Publications Act through the *Lolita* case,* and was a member of the informal committee that helped the Secretary for Justice, John Robson, frame the new 1963 Act, which created the Indecent Publications Tribunal. Later, he led a delegation from the council that discussed with the Commissioner of Police and his senior officers the better treatment of persons under arrest, and the handling of demonstrations in such a way as to protect, equally and adequately, the rights of all. In Walter Scott's words:

. . . without fuss, or vanity, or any standing on dignity he worked with fellow-citizens to reduce or remove any unwarranted obstacles to freedom of speech and assembly, any interference with the 'liberty to know, to utter, and to argue freely, according to conscience'. He was

---

* In 1960 the Minister of Customs banned Nabokov's novel *Lolita*. As a means of contesting the minister's action the council decided to import copies; these were seized by customs and the council prosecuted for their action. In the Supreme Court Justice Hutchison found that, while the novel had literary merit, it was insufficient to outweigh the emphasis on sex and its tendency to deprave and corrupt young readers. The Appeal Court upheld this view. Although the council lost its case, its action was successful in demonstrating the unsatisfactory, indeed ludicrous, state of censorship in New Zealand, and this played a part in bringing about new legislation.

always the same – cool, unafraid, informed, direct, accurate and honest, treating everyone alike, regardless of rank or reputation.[33]

During John's time the council, which has continued its work to this day, remained a small Wellington-based organisation, though in time it was linked with similar groups in Auckland and Christchurch. Essentially built on a network of friends, colleagues and associates closely associated with Victoria University College (from 1961, Victoria University of Wellington), the council slowly gained credibility and, in an unspectacular way, played a worthwhile role in extending and protecting the civil liberties enjoyed by New Zealanders.

AT THE SAME TIME AS the Council for Civil Liberties was being planned and established, John was also campaigning publicly for the better preservation of New Zealand government archives. The disastrous Hope Gibbons fire on 29 July 1952, which destroyed a substantial part of the (then) Dominion Archives, roused him. 'Ruth Allan [his former student and colleague in the Historical Branch] & I have formed an alliance to shake hell out of somebody or something', he wrote a few days later.[34] His concern about New Zealand's historical records went back to his time in the Centennial Branch. Eric McCormick, when chief archivist in the War History Branch of Internal Affairs, had written a very good report on organising the country's archives,[35] but to John's regret Eric, rather than trying to push his plans through, had taken up a lectureship in English at Auckland University College in 1947, and left that in 1951 to write books. After a further report by Michael Standish, a history graduate and newly appointed archivist,[36] the state of the archives was the subject of a *Listener* editorial and subsequent correspondence in March 1950, when John was still on leave. After he got back he wrote to the professor at each of the four university history departments urging them to throw their weight behind achieving an Archives Act, proper accommodation, and trained staff.[37] The fire provided the opportunity to make this a public issue, one in which, moreover, the press was happy to participate. John had two letters published in the *Evening Post*,[38] each cut by the editor – 'the point carefully filed off the most cutting paragraph, to avoid hurting anybody's feelings'[39] – Ruth Allan wrote to the *Listener*, and the *Dominion* took up the story.

After the anger and frustration of trying to save the atlas, John realised how much better it was 'if you want to raise hell . . . to be outside the public service rather than inside it'.[40] He wrote an article on archives for the *New Zealand Journal of Public Administration*, 'trying to kick senior public servants into some sense of their responsibility',[41] and did not mince his words:

The custom has grown up in civilized countries of regarding national archives as valuable . . . So civilized countries take suitable steps for the preservation of their national records, the by-products of their governmental and administrative activities. They regard them as important. They organize institutions like the Public Record Office in London or the Archives Nationales in Paris . . . We in New Zealand think it preferable to let the records of our national life lie about all over the country, subject to the inroads of dirt and flood and fire; when some stray historian or other eccentric protests that this is not pious, nor economic, nor in any way national, we reply, 'Yes, but where are we to put them?' – and every time a fire occurs eminent public servants congratulate one another and say, Thank God, that lot's gone. [42]

He went on to argue the case for first-rate record clerks – 'in how many Departments is the record-room regarded as the natural home for the dead-beats and the misfits?' – to ensure that the records needed for efficient administration were readily on call; and for first-class archivists, to advise what should be kept and what destroyed, and to see that what was kept was kept properly.

A FURTHER DEMAND ON his time in 1952 was when Fred Wood went on leave in the second half of the year and, as well as everything else, John had to run the history department. 'If Freddy stays away long', he told Janet, 'I shall become dispirited. More & more I thank God I was never made a professor. It's a sovereign specific for frittering away time'[43] – a comment not entirely fair to Wood, who at this time was working on his fine volume in the War History series, *The New Zealand People at War*. John was trying to get the footnotes finished for the first volume of Cook, and complained about how often he was having to go out when he would much rather stay home and get on with what he had come to regard as his real job in life, 'to cultivate my footnotes': 'I feel a bit browned off, & curse public servants, & curse civil liberties, & curse university presses & college calendars & publication funds . . . & history departments'.[44]

In her centennial history of Victoria University, Rachel Barrowman draws a comparison between Fred Wood, the teacher and administrator, and John, the research scholar.[45] This is not quite right. Both men were remarkable teachers. Wood had his limitations as an administrator, not least in his reluctance to make decisions, while his published work, especially his volume on *The New Zealand People at War*, often represents considerable historical scholarship. John, while happy to make decisions, was probably not in the conventional sense a good 'committee man'. His friend Jim Campbell, professor of mathematics, wrote of him: 'His direct and uncomplicated approach could be somewhat disturbing in such gatherings [as the professorial board or a faculty meeting] where, from the nature of their composition, sectional interests and a vagueness about the issues involved make for tiresome desultoriness in the proceedings'. Where he was on university committees, however, such as those dealing with publications, the library or research, his style came into its own and he contributed very fully indeed.[46]

At the end of 1952, with Wood overseas, John had to go to Dunedin to assess examination papers, but his heart was not really in it:

I discussed examination scripts with Willie Morrell [he told Norman Richmond*], who is really interested in that sort of thing; & I tried to show myself as passionately devoted by now & again suggesting that a bloke who had got 58 should get 59, or (by way of variation, & to show what a balanced mind I had) vice versa. And then of course I came home & lay awake at night thinking of the beautiful girls we had failed & whose lives we had blighted. All this was damn silly on my part so far as VUC was concerned, as I didn't know anybody & hadn't done any examining & didn't know enough anyway to pass any of the papers; but I can proudly report that I helped the wheels of the great Machine to turn around.[47]

Examining masters' and doctoral theses, for which he was regularly called, was a more serious matter. It (and the reviewing he did) kept him in touch with research on Pacific and New Zealand history, and he was a careful and sympathetic examiner. He examined the thesis by Bernard Smith, 'long, but exceedingly interesting',[48] which was to become his ground-breaking volume *European Vision and the South Pacific* (1960). He continued to supervise students' research for theses (among these was the work on French exploration in the Pacific by John Dunmore, later to become well-known internationally as an editor and historian in that field) and to

---

*   Richmond by this time was living in Melbourne, where he had been appointed to a lectureship in political science in 1949. The following year he had been forced into early retirement by illness, but he remained in Melbourne, with intermittent institutionalisation, until 1959, when he returned to New Zealand.

read and comment on the work of colleagues, former students and friends. Alan Moorehead wrote asking if John might 'glance through' his typescript (subsequently published as *The Fatal Impact*) and was enormously grateful for the care John took to 'help an amateur in your own subject'.[49] Less welcome were publishers' requests to read – and make good – their latest potboilers on Cook.

EARLY IN 1952 IVAN Sutherland died. He had been on leave for a year to write his long-planned book on race relations in New Zealand, but he had been ill and the book had not progressed as he hoped. When he went missing, and there was what proved to be a false report of his having been seen in Wellington, his friends wondered whether he had had some sort of breakdown and was making his way back to the East Coast and his Ngati Porou friends. John and Elsie went through a period of intense worry which turned to deep gloom when Ivan's body was found in Christchurch. John wrote a warmly evocative note about him for the *Journal of the Polynesian Society*[50] – in Eric McCormick's view 'the finest poem Beaglehole ever wrote'.[51] This recorded Ivan's kindness, his enthusiasm – 'if he had to be cautious, he was even cautious with enthusiasm, he would speak about the necessity for caution with the fervour of the evangelist' – and his single-mindedness – 'whatever he talked about, one felt that for the time being it was the most important thing in the world for him. I think that perhaps there came a time when he found he could be no longer single-minded, and that then too came his time of trouble. But last as well as first I think of his kindness.' Joe Heenan had died a few months before. 'We are all very much grief-struck out here', John told Skelton, '& the contemplation of the present régime does not tend to comfort'.[52] These two, together with Harold Laski, who had died in 1950, were men whom John admired and of whom he had been deeply fond, who had each touched and helped to shape his life in significant ways. He had also to recognise that Norman Richmond, with his illness, could never again be the fellow knight-in-arms of the 1930s, with their shared passion for J.S. Bach, for civil liberties and other great causes.

Finally, in April 1953, it was Tommy Hunter's turn. When it was known that Hunter was dying, John was asked to prepare a talk on him for National Radio; he did this, but could not face pre-recording it, instead broadcasting live on the evening of Hunter's death. At Hunter's direction – he had firm views on the sort of funeral he was to have – John was also called on to speak at the crematorium.

'Lord how the drafting of those few words & of the broadcast took it out of me', he wrote to Janet, 'about nine drafts of each, & then last minute corrections. It makes me realise what a wonderful feat the composition of the Gettysburg address was.'[53] When the two addresses were typed and copies made, John, as always, was critical. But they still impress as well-judged pieces of writing, conveying a vivid sense of Hunter's personality and his impact on others, still deeply moving, even to those who never knew Hunter.

I don't suppose he was a great philosopher or a great psychologist in the academic sense. But he was a great teacher. If you had a mind Hunter led you to use it; you could use it against him if you liked, that didn't matter. But *you* mattered, you were life, you were young, your mind was an individual thing with its individual rights, and he believed in its freedom. He didn't patronise. He really believed in freedom . . . Of course he had his limitations. I wouldn't make him out a solemn paragon of all the virtues. Anyhow, he moved too quickly to be solemn, physically in his young footballing days, mentally always. He wasn't aesthetic or literary. But he never pretended. He could laugh at himself. He knew I liked and admired him, and once asked me why I didn't give him a halo. Well, sanctity wasn't exactly the impression you got from a session with Hunter's reminiscences, but I'd certainly give him a halo before some of our recorded saints.[54]

Hunter and Heenan, John commented more than once, were the two New Zealanders he had known who he believed had real claims to greatness.

John's tributes to the memory of friends reveal more than a little about himself. He believed that affection and loyalty called for the utmost honesty, that what was said should be said (or written) as well as it possibly could be; such acts of piety, which he was increasingly called on to perform, deserved 'the supreme compliment of sympathetic candour'.[55]

What he felt he owed to Heenan was acknowledged, with marked adjectival restraint, in the dedication to the first volume of Cook's *Journals* (the only volume to have a dedication):

TO THE MEMORY OF

JOSEPH WILLIAM ALLAN HEENAN

A CITIZEN OF NEW ZEALAND

A MAN OF MOST VARIOUS MIND

GENEROUS AND LIVELY IN FRIENDSHIP

A SERVANT OF THE PUBLIC

LIBERAL IMAGINATIVE HUMANE

THIS VOLUME IS DEDICATED

It was further recorded and explored in his lecture, *The New Zealand Scholar*, which he gave when he received the Margaret Condliffe Memorial Medal* at Canterbury University College on 21 April 1954. He had first heard of the award nearly eighteen months earlier, and had somewhat irreverently scoffed at it in a letter to Norman Richmond: '[J.H.E.] Schroder who had something to do with it & takes it all very seriously read me the "citation" over the phone. And when I tell you that it finishes up by saying I have inculcated piety towards our ancestors or something you will understand why I swooned away on the spot.'[56] He hoped they would forget all about it, but if he had to deliver an 'oration' he thought 'it would be rather amusing to do Thoughts on Civil Liberties in NZ . . . with Short Historical Notices on Ronald Algie, M. Rocke O'Shea, & other forgotten or to be forgotten Figures'. By September 1953 (when he had almost finished revising the general introduction to the Cook *Journals*) he had decided on the title and had started on the lecture, 'very heavy & painful going, blood & sweat & anguish'.[57] He was reading the American critic F.O. Matthieson's book on T.S. Eliot, which he thought very good and which had given him some ideas for the lecture. He mourned Matthieson's death very much: 'You know a first-rate critic is a very great work of God.' He was also reading, and finding exceedingly interesting, 'a large & good life of Emerson' by Rusk. It was a book he would have liked to send to his father 'with a hearty recommendation'.[58] In early October he had got a draft finished, but when he read it through he thought that he'd 'rarely read a more egotistical, trite, empty, string of words. The only thing worth saying', he reported, 'is the page about Joe Heenan, & I doubt whether people will see the connection between that & anything else.'[59]

John began by drawing a kind of parallel with Emerson's address at Harvard, 117 years before, on the American Scholar – though he hastened to add that he was not setting himself up as a competitor

---

*   The award was endowed by J.B. Condliffe, the eminent New Zealand economist, as a tribute to his mother. He wished it to be given to recognise creative ability, especially in the arts, and hoped it might go to 'a younger man who still had some work left in him'. (Condliffe to JCB, 14 January 1954.) The first award, in 1945, was to Sir James Hight, the former Rector of Canterbury University College, who was seventy-five. The award to John was the second to be made. Whatever he thought about the occasion, John was not thrilled by the medal itself: 'The thing they gave me was dreadful beyond my wildest dreams. Very poor bronze, & shocking design & lettering . . . So much for the late Mr Shurrock, sculptor.' (JCB to JEP, 28 April 1954.)

to Emerson. In that address, hailed by Oliver Wendell Holmes as 'America's, or at least New England's intellectual Declaration of Independence', Emerson had held out a promise: 'We have listened too long to the courtly muses of Europe. We will walk on our own feet; we will work with our own hands; we will speak our own minds.' That John turned to nineteenth-century New England as a starting point for his lecture reflected one of his major scholarly interests of the preceding fifteen years, and also the historical parallels he saw with what came later in New Zealand. 'This process of intellectual growth, of mental change, in a colonial community, this creeping on of self awareness', he wrote, 'I find as an historian endlessly fascinating – even, when we find it among ourselves, exciting.' He did not use the words 'national identity', which he might have seen as unduly narrowing his discussion, and he defined his scholar broadly, using Emerson's term of 'man thinking'.* He was interested both in how an inherited tradition changed over time and in the changing nature of expatriation. He saw New Zealand, in intellectual terms, as having moved from being a colony to a province, suggesting that in one sense what Frances Hodgkins or Katherine Mansfield did when they 'made for the Old World' was simply doing 'what the young Cézanne or the young Arnold Bennett did, they travelled to the fountainhead'.

The heart of the lecture was autobiographical. 'I am bound to confess that I find myself interesting, though only as a sort of case study', John wrote, and he traced his own changing feelings about New Zealand from his time as a postgraduate student in London until the 1950s. His account of his first meeting with Heenan has been noted in chapter nine, together with the role John credited Heenan with in his own growing recognition of what it was to be a New Zealander, of what was or might be worthwhile about life in this country. He ended the lecture on an optimistic note: 'our intellectual culture is beginning to take a new tinge. We are beginning to speak our own minds.' New Zealanders, he suggested, should continue to leave New Zealand:

But a province with a tradition rich enough, with a pattern of life varied enough, with a sense of its own identity and its own time lively enough,

---

*   Some later read this expression as sexist. It would be a mistake, however, to assume that it revealed such views on John's part. That he recognised women as scholars should be clear from his discussion of Frances Hodgkins and Katherine Mansfield in the lecture, and equally from the respect and enthusiasm he had for the work of his former students and colleagues in the Centennial and Historical Branches.

will always bring enough of them back. The time has gone by, I think, when the New Zealander need always be dragging out his cultural nostalgia and brooding over it . . . Am I saying these things too easily? Am I merely whistling to keep my courage up? I am not unaware that my trade as a historian is a school of scepticism. But I venture to hope.

When John finished writing the lecture he sent it to Eric McCormick (whose study of Frances Hodgkins and New Zealand, *The Expatriate*, John was at that time seeing through the university press) for 'some really savage criticism'.[60] He was unsettled by what he considered the 'extravagant praise' of McCormick's reply.* McCormick had read the paper three times on the day it arrived, and he wrote at once to say it was 'extraordinarily good' and 'in many places, very moving – not at all unworthy of its forerunner'.[61] What John had said about Heenan he found 'quite admirable', and the discussion of 'colony', 'province' and 'expatriation' 'profoundly interesting', though he wondered what the audience would make of this, 'some of which presupposes knowledge – and preoccupations – which many of them may not possess'. He ended:

What superb control you have over your material and how beautifully you write! Damn you! But I mustn't end on a note of envy. I feel about this, as I did about the paper in the Tommy Hunter volume,† that it sums up and expresses magnificently ideas and opinions that have been vaguely floating about in a number of inarticulate minds. On this damp mind it has acted as a spark, though there is no danger of any vast conflagration.

The New Zealand Scholar was perhaps the most eloquent expression of John's interest in his own country, an interest that went back to the 1930s, to his *New Zealand: A Short History*, the history of the University of New Zealand, his preoccupation with the Statute of Westminster, and to the work with Heenan. It was reflected in a great number of his activities. The work on Cook, important as it was to him, took its place alongside this rather than taking its place. A few months before delivering the lecture, John opened an exhibition of paintings by Frances Hodgkins with a speech which touched on many of the same points as the lecture.[62] 'We have begun to think', he said, 'as well as to act as New Zealanders. We

---

*   This was more than two years before McCormick's review of the first volume of Cook's *Journals*, which, being public, unsettled John even more.

†   'History & the New Zealander', in *The University & the Community: Essays in Honour of Thomas Alexander Hunter*, edited by Ernest Beaglehole (Wellington: Victoria University College, 1946).

are beginning to think *in* New Zealand.' He talked about Hodgkins in this context, about the ways in which she was important to us, about expatriation: 'Any person who exists by the original use of the mind is bound to be in some way an expatriate, even in the midst of his own people'. Then he drew himself together at the end to remind his audience that their first concern was 'not with social history, nor with a piece of psychological research, but with pictures'. Their duty was 'to examine not the artist but the art'. For himself, it is clear, he was fascinated by both.

He sent a copy of *The New Zealand Scholar* to Ruth Ross, perhaps the most brilliant, and certainly the most forthright, of those former students of his whom he had recruited to the Historical Branch in the early 1940s. She was now living in Auckland but they had kept in touch. Ross matched John's autobiographical digression with twelve pages of her own:

> I very strongly feel that this business of 'being' a New Zealander, of thinking as a New Zealander &c has been and is still being much over-intellectualised. Of course we are New Zealanders, so why bellyache about it? I was born a New Zealander, I am a New Zealander, I behave, and speak and think as a New Zealander, I like being a New Zealander, I shall die a New Zealander – so what? That seems to me a completely normal state of affairs . . . If a few thousand dropped in my lap tomorrow, I would not buy a ticket for London, for concerts and plays and galleries and lectures. I'm damned sure I never want to set foot in the U.S.A. I'd go north again, and look at the bare brown hills of the Bay, and watch from Opononi the sand hills turn golden with rain to come. I'd go to Kaeo and Mongonui [sic] and right up to Reinga. They say there is nothing to see up there, but I'd like to see what nothing is like . . .[63]

Ruth wrote that, for her, John had always been 'the New Zealand scholar'; it had never occurred to her that he did not feel his 'New Zealandness' in the same way as she felt hers.

It was a wonderful letter, and it is clear that Ruth was one of those who believed, almost passionately, that rural New Zealand, the 'country' as opposed to the 'town', was the 'real' New Zealand. This John did not concede: 'I can't see that [rural New Zealand] is any "realer" than urban NZ. My Wellington childhood was just as real as your country one. V.U.C. is just as much NZ as my brother-in-law's farm at Tauherenikau'.[64] This was in a later letter. His reply to her first letter does not appear to have survived, but in her next[65] Ruth noted that the lack of a 'fighting come-back' on John's part suggested that he still had not worked out what he thought and felt about 'some things New Zealand'. It is possibly more likely that he recognised that he simply did not have the time to take Ruth on by letter; Cook and Banks pressed hard. He and Ruth were, for a start, focusing on rather different things. John's very title, 'The New Zealand Scholar', suggests that his primary concern was with high culture, though he defined his scholar very broadly. And in looking ahead at 'seeds sprouting', he wrote, 'I am not sure that the School Publications Branch does not hold the New Zealand future in its hands'. McCormick, who understood and shared so many of John's preoccupations, was very much his age; Ruth belonged to a later generation, which may partly explain their differing views. But there was much more to it than this. While she had grown up in Wanganui, as a girl she had spent much of her free time with her father, who was a stock buyer, hanging around the yards while he drafted sheep, and exploring the country. Taken on a trip to Britain at the age of eleven, she had 'felt like a stranger in a foreign land'.[66]

At the beginning of April 1955 John went to Auckland to open a large retrospective show of paintings by John Weeks. His admiration of Weeks's work went back to their first meeting in 1932, and he gave Weeks an important place in the development of New Zealand painting. He told Ruth Ross that he had been trying to carry their discussion a bit further in the speech he had written for the opening.[67] Unusually, he had made quite extensive notes before he started to write. Once again he was thinking about 'New Zealandness' in terms of a painter: 'The artist, like the community, works in a tradition, thinks in a tradition, exploits a tradition, even if he fights against it. One of his tasks, unconscious perhaps, is to widen a tradition. One of his tasks, in a community like ours, is to discover and make plain a tradition.' John quoted from a letter he had had from Weeks some years before in which he wrote: 'I wish to paint something that embodies the spirit – essence – or whatever else one elects to call it which I feel exists in New Zealand landscape rather than a straight and literal rendering'. The result, John suggested, of this 'sombre struggle to make plain an underlying spirit is not reassuring': 'He is affirmative, certainly, in his finest pictures, with an affirmation that we accept, and draw strength from. Perhaps there is more than one sort of reassurance. Perhaps Mr Weeks' affirmation reassures us of the worth of our position in our own province.'

Ruth was at the opening, in the front row. 'It was nice to catch your eye', John wrote to her, 'in the throng seated so quiescent at my feet, even if said eye was by no means acquiescent, even a bit derisive'. He assured her that Weeks was a 'good bloke' who would measure up to her requirements of a New Zealander – 'Good taste in beer; & you ought to hear him curse people.'[68]

Not long after this Ruth and her family moved north from Auckland when her husband Ian was appointed to teach at the Motukiore Maori School, on the Hokianga Harbour. 'Your move . . . sounds very exciting', John wrote to her. 'You could hardly be closer to the original, autochthonous . . . New Zealand soil. You ought to be very happy'.[69] She saw this as a dig at her reaction to *The New Zealand Scholar*,[70] and made the most of the opportunity the move gave her to learn more about Maori history and to increase her encyclopaedic knowledge of early Northland. She and John were to meet again regularly, and to continue their intellectual sparring, especially between 1963 and 1969, when Ruth joined John as a member of the board of the Historic Places Trust.

JOHN'S ENERGY DURING the 1950s seemed boundless. It is difficult to grasp, let alone convey, the full extent of his activities. As chairman of the university press he was not only involved in what could be lengthy discussions with authors, but also in the design and production of the individual volumes. If that was a continuing responsibility, there was also the host of smaller things that arose. The Council for Educational Research regularly called on him for typographical advice. The week after Hunter died he started on seven lectures to the Library School (two years later he cut it down from seven to two, and when he returned from leave in 1956 he did not give them again). He spent most of a morning writing a memorandum on reorganisation in the Turnbull Library for two new members of staff 'in positions of some authority' (John Reece Cole and Margaret Broadhead). 'They are both nice', he told Janet, '& the prospect of something being done there is brighter than it used to be'.[71] He taught a second-year history tutorial on Puritan New England – 'I am still excited about the Puritans – I am excited every Wednesday, & the kids are nice. I read the book about Increase Mather,* the whole 399 pp. . . . & now', he added, 'I am some way on in *Evelina*'.[72]

Having finished writing *The New Zealand Scholar* John started reading Horace Walpole's letters, late at night, and took only pleasure in the fact that there were eighteen volumes stretched out before him.[73] The following May he read Desmond MacCarthy's

---

*   Kenneth Ballard Murdock, *Increase Mather: The Foremost American Puritan* (Cambridge, Mass.: Harvard University Press, 1926).

Humanities to review for the *Listener* (this was one of five reviews he wrote for the *Listener* in 1954): 'What a delightful civilized mind he had', he told Janet, 'I'm convinced now in late middle-age that the liberal mind is the mind for me, the Desmond MacCarthy-V. Woolf mind; so there is really no hope for me, I'll never be a revolutionary, you'd better wipe me off.'[74] He had been thinking he should acquire 'two or three good standard sets of books to add to the very desirable rows of such things' his father had passed on to him, 'to pass on in due course – no doubt to Tim', and he was able to make a start when he was offered, for £15, the 24-volume 'New York edition' of the novels of Henry James.

He was persuaded to stand for the Victoria College Council as the staff member and was elected unopposed. 'Blast it, blast it, blast it. Only after I had said Yes did Freddy tell me that I should then have to attend the Prof. Board, oh what a curse . . . it wouldn't be so bad if there weren't so many other things.'[75] The same month he was in Dunedin for a three-day meeting of the University Academic Board. He was teaching the history honours paper on American history in place of Winston Monk, who had been killed in an air crash just before the term began – 'his death completely shattered us . . . he was one of the good things in NZ'.[76] Early in 1955, when a 'dreadful hiatus' in the arrival of Cook proofs meant that he could 'plunge into Banks again', he was also giving his last lectures to the Library School and was reading Henry James's letters – 'Even if he talks about the weather it's an education in words & play of mind'.[77]

John could not have achieved everything he did without Elsie; she was extraordinarily capable in running the house and the family, and equally capable in the voluntary work she took on in the community. Domestically he did not get much beyond the washing-up, though he got a certain satisfaction from that: 'I like to finish up a piece of pedantic washing-up sometimes, the sensation of finishing up something properly is always agreeable, & it comes so infrequently in writing books.'[78] That 'pedantic washing-up', however, particularly when he was polishing glasses, drove anyone else involved almost to distraction. He was still cutting the hedges early each summer and the grass when there was not a son around to do it, and there were a number of fuchsia plants which were always referred to as his, though beyond regularly checking their progress he did nothing with them. At this time, in the early 1950s, I was a student at Victoria College and living at home. I do not remember John ever showing more than the mildest impatience with some of the scholarly frustrations he faced – the full extent of which only became clear to me as I read so many of his letters – nor appearing to be weighed down with work he had taken on. While he was trying to tidy all sorts of loose ends before going on leave in 1955, he found the time to read and comment on the MA thesis I was working on. To Janet, he sadly reported that I, unfortunately, had not 'the faintest idea of punctuation'.[79]

For academics in that age before e-mail, not the least of the advantages of going on research and study leave was the opportunity it gave of leaving behind the multifarious distractions of committees and good causes. For the year he was away over 1955 and 1956, John was able to concentrate largely on his work on Cook and Banks. There were still distractions, by no means all unwelcome. He and Elsie looked at lots of paintings. He and Douglas Lilburn (also on leave), acting on instructions from Fred Page, who wrote and told them they could spend £90, bought a painting by Frances Hodgkins for the Victoria staff common room collection:

The picture we bought [he wrote to Page] is entitled 'Kimmeridge Foreshore', or something like that . . . The Redfern had it. We inspected all the Leicester Galleries had, & the Lefèvre . . . This one is quite the best we have seen, bar possibly one. Price – but no, I'll lead up to it gradually. Leicester had a really very fine oil £250, a gouache, Welsh Hills, & a water colour £65 each; & others not considered . . . We wiped the water colour & then Douglas thought he couldn't live with the tree in the gouache. On to the Redfern, where I had been before. Douglas much struck, as I had been. On to the Lefèvre. Some interesting ones, but fantastic prices – £300+, apart from £25, £40, £50 for drawings, not very distinctive, & small water colours. Today we took Elsie & a niece of mine down to the Redfern – verdict favourable. Right, we said, We'll have it. £160 . . . But you say plaintively, like any politician, Where is the money to come from? Simple, we answer; You send all the cash the Common Room has, & you, Douglas, & I put up the rest – & any other mug on the staff you can take down – to be repaid later. If that isn't clear Douglas will explain when he gets back . . . Well, I said to Douglas, as we parted outside Piccadilly Tube, we've done a good day's work. We have, he said. We've done our duty by N.Z., I said. We have, he said. Be seein you, I said. Yup, he said. Thus we parted. And remember, if there is any argument over what the object is in the foreground, we are making it driftwood . . . What a pity I shan't be back till after the first fury of indignation & astonishment is over.[80]

There was a certain amount of debate in the common room when the painting arrived. A young economist suggested that the money might be better spent in providing free tea or coffee, but when the members were told that if they did not wish to keep the painting the Auckland Art Gallery was keen to have it, they decided it should stay. The painting at the Leicester Gallery, *The White Chateau*, John and Elsie had bought for themselves.

WHILE HE WAS IN LONDON on leave the government in 1955 established the National (later New Zealand) Historic Places Trust with John as the representative of the University of New Zealand. His interest in historic buildings and places in New Zealand went back to his work in the Centennial and Historical Branches. At the end of 1942 the government had the opportunity to buy Pompallier House* in Russell. John was sent up to look at it, strongly recommended that it should be bought, and commented – rather rashly, as it turned out – that it was, on the whole, 'excellently preserved'.[81] Cabinet approved its purchase for £2000. Further inspection showed it to be in very bad condition: the woodwork was infested with borer and there were fears that the rammed-earth walls might collapse. Over the next six years more than £9000 was spent on repairs.[†] It was a foretaste of what was involved in conservation. The question of how the building should be used and presented gave a further foretaste of questions the trust would face later. John had firm views:

> . . . it is important to keep the house itself as the main exhibit. That is, it must not be filled up with junk. The interior of the Treaty House on the other side of the Bay is a dreadful warning . . . anything that goes into the house, anyhow the two main lower rooms, should be both interesting & good – whether furniture, pictures, or period knicknacks – & with some period flavour; not necessarily the Pompallier period, for we must remember the place was lived in for nearly 100 years.[82]

When John left the Historical Branch, that was the end of his direct involvement with Pompallier House until it was placed in the care of the trust in 1967.

In its early years the trust's greatest challenge was to save St Paul's Cathedral Church in Wellington (now known as Old St

---

*   In the belief that Bishop Pompallier had at one time lived there, the Pompallier building was known as Pompallier House until the 1980s, when research (building on earlier work by Ruth Ross) which preceded major conservation work by the Historic Places Trust showed clearly that the building was built by the French Marists as a working printery, tannery and book bindery. It was decided then to refer to it simply as 'Pompallier'.

†   John visited the house at the end of 1948 and sent a telegram to Heenan: 'Never mind the cost Pompallier a triumph.' Heenan replied: 'It had better be.' (J.W. Heenan Papers. MS-Papers-1132-16. ATL.)

Paul's) from destruction by the Anglican Church. A timber church designed by the Rev. Frederick Thatcher in the style known as late Early English Gothic, St Paul's had served both the diocese and the parish since the 1860s. Although John had never been drawn to the neo-Gothic style – he wrote on one occasion of the university (now the Hunter) building's 'fake gestures towards the Gothic past'[83] – he became a passionate advocate for St Paul's. 'Many atrocious buildings were raised all over the world under the Gothic name', he wrote, 'occasionally, as with St Paul's, some magic acted and a successful translation in form and spirit was made not merely from one age to another, but from one building material to another'.[84] Although the church had decided in 1937 to build a new cathedral in Molesworth Street, next to Parliament Buildings, and plans were drawn, only in 1954 was the foundation stone laid. A part of the original plan was to incorporate some of the old church in the new building, enclosing in a concrete shell the timber vaulting of the chancel, crossing and part of the nave, to form the cathedral's Lady Chapel. By the time construction started, however, that proposal had its critics; the Wellington Architectural Centre was the first group publicly to criticise the Lady Chapel plan. Before he left for London in August 1955, John was involved with a group, mainly of parishioners, who formed the Society for the Preservation of the Cathedral Church of St Paul and prepared a submission to the newly established Historic Places Trust. A deputation from the trust, led by its chairman, C.M. Bowden, a former National cabinet minister, met with the archbishop, the Most Rev. R.H. Owen. Its reception convinced the trust that it had nothing to hope for, and it concluded, regretfully, that in view of the church's ownership of the building and the trust's lack of statutory power, no purpose would be served by continuing to press for preservation.[85] This, however, was not the end of the matter. Just before he left London to return home, John had a cable 'nailing him down' for a meeting on St Paul's after he got back – 'So I suppose I have got to make a speech & fight the archbishop. I haven't had to fight anybody for a whole year: it's been wonderful.'[86]

For a start he had to persuade the trust to reconsider its view. At his first meeting (on 28 November 1956), he went at once to what was to be the heart of his argument, that ownership of a building of such unique historical and architectural significance should be regarded as a trust. He spoke of the Bishop of London, who had wished to destroy the city churches but had been stopped from doing so by popular outcry. Although the chairman was not inclined to change his view, John was supported by a number of members – the Turnbull Librarian, Graham Bagnall; the Government Architect, Gordon Wilson; Ruth Allan (John's ally in the archives campaign) and others – and after a long debate it was agreed that the trust should support preservation and should prepare a full statement of the reasons for this.[87] John wrote the statement, 'a broadside against the Archbishop',[88] and the *Evening Post* gave it a large part of its leader page. St Paul's, he wrote, should be preserved for its beauty ('a beautiful building in a city remarkably deficient in beautiful buildings and almost entirely deficient in beautiful old buildings'); for its architectural interest ('the design . . . succeeded not merely in enclosing a space for the purposes of ritual and worship, but in translating Gothic forms into the medium and feeling of a new country with astonishing success'); and for its historical significance ('part of the life of Wellington to a unique degree'). The statement responded to points made by the archbishop and, while recognising clearly the church's legal ownership, spelled out John's premiss: some buildings 'by the very facts of their existence and their history pass from the category of private property . . . they become a trust, and a trust maintained not for a portion of the community alone, but for the community as a whole'.[89]

The archbishop would not budge from the inflexible position he had spelled out when he met the trust deputation. There was only one possible way of preserving St Paul's, he asserted, and that was the Lady Chapel proposal. The opponents of his policy he judged 'unable to respect logical argument'.[90] But his claim that the 'best architectural opinion' supported his proposal began to look increasingly shaky. Single-minded in his commitment, which was shared by many Anglicans, to completing the new cathedral, and with an eye to the value of the St Paul's site if it was empty and able to be sold,[91] the archbishop seemed unable to recognise, let alone to understand, the growing support for preservation, and he appeared to view it as impertinence that some of this came from citizens who were not members of the Anglican Church. John, in contrast, told Norman Richmond that it was 'nice to think of the atheists & infidels struggling to preserve an ecclesiastical fabric against the depredations of the Christians'[92] – hardly an accurate view, but a good crack in a letter. He viewed Archbishop Owen, an Englishman who had arrived in New Zealand in 1947, as assuming an authority singularly out of place in mid-twentieth-century New Zealand, and there was a personal edge in the controversy that was more characteristic of John's younger days than his mellower

postwar years. 'Confound the church', he wrote at one point, 'I wish
we could get it saved & done with. That damned archbishop.'[93]

Support for preservation grew steadily. The trust published an
expanded version of John's *Evening Post* statement as a pamphlet in
1958, and a further report on St Paul's as part of its annual report
to parliament the following year.[94] John's eloquent advocacy was
supported when the English architectural historian Nikolaus Pevsner
visited Wellington in 1958 and, having been carefully briefed by
the trust secretary, John Pascoe, made a strong statement to the
newspapers[95] and in a subsequent broadcast.[96] Even in England,
he said, St Paul's interior timber work would be regarded as an
outstanding example of the mid-Victorian period, and he spoke of
'ecclesiastical vandalism' which he hoped would be impossible in his
own country.

With the election of the Labour government in November 1957,
led by the 75-year-old Walter Nash, John's hopes rose that it might
be persuaded to buy St Paul's as a step towards preservation. But
he was sadly disappointed. A deputation from the trust waited
on the Prime Minister; Nash expressed sympathy and support for
preservation, but nothing happened. When the annual report of the
trust was tabled in parliament, the matter of St Paul's was raised
in debate: 'And who were the blokes who were on the right side?'
John wrote to Norman Richmond. 'Nat. Party members. And what
did that great cultural force, the Labour Party, say? Apart from
Walter, nothing, damn all, a blank.'[97] The problem with Nash was
to persuade him actually to do something.* A little later, when John
was waiting to give evidence on civil liberties to a parliamentary
committee, he ran into Nash. The Prime Minister was full of the
difficulties of taking any action to save the church. '"All right" [said
John (as he reported it to Norman)], You said in the House you were
prepared to go with any group of MPs to the church authorities
& talk it over: I'm going to hold you to that". As Walter makes
vague noises, & leaps into a plane & rushes off to Washington or
somewhere, safe for a few weeks from another problem.'[98]

John's mounting frustration – with the church, with the
government, with the Historic Places Trust's lack of power 'except
the power to plaster the country with plaques and accept whatever
it is given, including contumely and contempt from ecclesiastical

---

*   John wrote to Janet on 6 August 1958: 'The Govt can save it if they like,
       but WN is really pretty hopeless, & I'm afraid he's breaking up. He rushes
       round opening things & attending funerals, insists on everything going to
       his desk . . . & gives decisions on nothing.'

quarters'[99] – lay behind his most trenchant statement on preservation, his article 'Private Property or National Interest?', published in the *New Zealand Listener*. He did not mince his words:

I have hanging up at home a very good picture by Frances Hodgkins. It's my property. I bought it, I own it, it's mine, nobody else's. I might of course cut it up into a number of bits, and reframe one or two of them, with a lot of talk about the most precious and best-loved portions. If I did so, I ought to be put in gaol, or a lunatic asylum. I couldn't be, of course, there's no law about it. But if I did so, I hope at least I should be ostracised from the society in which I spend most of my time, the men and women who make life – not just property – precious to me. Is there any chance of our ostracising a cathedral building-committee and diocesan trustees? Alas!

As one of the very few outlets at that time for comment on public issues, the *Listener* was widely noticed and read. John's article rallied further support. The archbishop declined an invitation to reply, and although debate continued – further stirred at one point by the church's extraordinary proposal to transport St Paul's in sections over the Rimutaka ranges to become a chapel at an Anglican private boys' school in Wairarapa – when Owen resigned as archbishop because of illness in February 1960 the way was clear to move forward. Progress was very slow, however. In March 1966 John wrote that he had 'just finished re-drafting a draft by Ormond Wilson [chairman of the trust] of yet another statement on St Paul's', adding, 'I hope that on my dying day I shall not have to drop everything to do still another'.[100] However, by that time the Wellington City Council had thrown its weight behind preservation, the formation of the Friends of Old St Paul's had brought together all those in support, and in November 1966 the government finally announced that it would purchase the site and the building, which had been closed for over two years since the opening of the partially completed new cathedral. There followed several years of painstaking repairs and renovation, carried out by the architects of the Ministry of Works, and the church, administered by the trust through its Old St Paul's Advisory Committee (appointed by cabinet), was restored to a quiet splendour perhaps unmatched in its earlier history.

A great many organisations, groups and individual citizens, particularly in the later years, had come to support its preservation. Successive government architects (*ex officio* members of the trust) included the building in every draft plan of the government centre. John was there from the beginning, passionately committed to a cause which at first found limited backing, steadfast and uncompromising over the years, and ready always to lend his pen, his most effective weapon. Bob Burnett, who, to John's great delight, became secretary of the trust when Pascoe left in 1960, described him as having 'the mana that belongs to those who had often smelt the enemy's powder and who though prepared each time to come home on their shields had returned alive and, in the end, triumphant'.[101]

During the sixteen years John was a trustee, the staff of the Historic Places Trust was tiny. John Pascoe, the first secretary, was assisted by only a typist and a clerk. The first research officer was not appointed until 1964; in 1971 the number of staff had reached only five. Ormond Wilson, who succeeded Bowden as chairman in 1958 and served for twelve years, gave so much time to trust affairs that he almost became an unpaid member of the staff. John, not knowing him well before his appointment, was a little wary of his booming voice and somewhat patrician manner, but they quickly developed a warm respect for each other and a close friendship which extended to their respective families. At this time Ormond and Rosamond Wilson lived at Mount Lees, a 1000-acre farming property at Bulls that Wilson had inherited from his grandfather, J.G. Wilson. There Wilson, with limited interest in farming, was developing a remarkable garden in an unkempt gully of scrub with a few fine surviving totara, kahikatea, titoki and pukatea. John and Elsie became regular visitors. Ormond for his part generally came to stay at Messines Road the night before trust meetings, where he and John could talk over the current business. 'I could always turn to [John]', Ormond later wrote, 'as a friend for wise advice, advice that was never intruded nor dogmatically stated, but weighed thoughtfully.'[102] The glass of whisky they had over agendas and papers marked the first time John and Elsie kept a bottle of spirits in the cupboard.

The trust members, later to be known as the board, generally had five full-day meetings a year; there were also several subcommittees. However, because of the lack of staff, the members could and did become deeply involved in the trust's projects. John's typographical skills were drawn on in the design of trust notice boards, while his historical knowledge – together with that of other members, such as Graham Bagnall, Jim Gardner and, later, Ruth Ross – helped ensure their accuracy. That work was not always straightforward. Certain residents of Mercury Bay were adamant that they knew where Cook in the *Endeavour* had anchored, yet John had a chart that showed the exact spot, which was quite different. Diplomacy was called for. It was a quality John also used at committee meetings. Bob Burnett wrote of 'the sedating effect of his interventions when feelings became prickly, his skill in redrafting resolutions to give coherence to an untidy and occasionally confused debate'.[103]

In 1959 John persuaded the trust to buy the old vicarage at Waimate North to undertake its first major task of preservation and restoration.[104] There had been earlier suggestions that the government should intervene to preserve the building, but these had come to nothing; before John left Internal Affairs he had urged the department to act, saying it would be a 'national disaster' if the house were left to go to ruin.[105] The house had been built during 1831 and 1832 by George Clarke, a Church Missionary Society worker, with a team of Maori helpers; originally one of three houses in the mission station, it was the only one to survive. The fortunes of the mission station declined in the late 1830s. In 1840 George Clarke left Waimate when Governor Hobson appointed him Chief Protector of Aborigines, and two years later the house was rented by Bishop Selwyn on his arrival in New Zealand. For two years it served as a Victorian bishop's palace. In 1844, when Selwyn moved to Auckland, the house (with the rest of the settlement) reverted to the Church Missionary Society. It survived the war in the north, but the field of missionary endeavour was moving to other parts of the country and eventually the house became the local vicarage. When acquired by the trust it was in a sad state of repair.

Was the trust to preserve or to restore the building? And if it was to restore, how far should it go in altering and possibly rebuilding the existing structure? Some answers were at least implicit in the early decision that the building should be called 'the Mission House Waimate North'. 'An awful lot of discussion about exactly what to do in re-doing the Mission House', John wrote about one trust meeting. 'It will be a star turn some day, but oh the time taken over these historic monuments!'[106] In the engaging address he gave when the house finally opened at the end of 1966,[107] John talked about the questions the trust had faced:

Here at Waimate, after painful and prolonged thought, we have been led on to restore. We started, I think I may say with the shingles [to replace the galvanised iron which had replaced the original shingles] . . . From the shingles we seemed to be driven on by a sense of history: back and back, from one thing to another, to what we took to be the original shape and structure of the house . . . Perhaps I should not have used those particular words: because how do we know what *was* the original shape and structure of the house? Also, a house itself is a part of history, it has a history. This house never remained for more than a week, I suppose, exactly as it was when Mr and Mrs Clarke first walked into it in June 1832. Mr and Mrs Clarke and their children were not the last people to live in it. Bishop and Mrs Selwyn and little Willie Selwyn lived in it. Mrs Selwyn objected to various things about it. Bishop Selwyn altered it. Numbers of Maori children were stowed away upstairs. It was a mission station, or rather part of a mission station, and that meant it was a farm house; it was a bishop's palace, a college, a mission station again, a simple vicarage. It was always, one might almost say, being pulled about. Well, exactly what point in history are we to go back to in our restoration – to Clarke in 1832, to Selwyn in 1843, to something in between? And how do we know exactly what the place was like at any particular moment? Only when we begin to study the history of the house do we begin to find out how difficult it is to answer that last question.

The broad objective they had settled on was to restore the interior of the building to a reasonable resemblance of the house lived in by George Clarke and his family in the 1830s. John described the research that had to be done, from contemporary plans and sketches and other historical documents, and from the evidence of the house itself, before the detailed planning and the restoration work could be carried out.

There was lively debate at trust meetings in Wellington; John visited Waimate several times for discussion on the spot. An insight into these discussions is given by a note he wrote after one of the meetings:

. . . Room 6. Controversial door to lobby. Professor Knight says roundly there was no such door. The Chairman feels there cannot have been a door. Mr Burnett feels that, under certain conditions there would be nothing incongruous in such a door . . . Mrs Ross is clear that there must have been a door. I favour an opening for circulation with a statement in the guide book of the problem . . .[108]

John's comment is characteristic, but Ruth Ross, indefatigable in her research, sometimes felt that his suggestions for resolving a difficult issue, rather than arguing it to a conclusion on the evidence, represented a lapse from historical integrity. The trust's files on the Mission House bear witness to her inexhaustible energy and impeccable standards. John, on the whole, thought her very good value, although he once wrote to Janet, 'If only that girl had a sense of proportion: but I suppose I am not the one to reprove anybody for pedantry'.[109] Those two, with Ormond Wilson, Bob Burnett and, in the later stages of the work, John Stacpoole, the Assistant Government Architect in Auckland, were largely responsible for seeing the work through. If the result was not quite the house the

Clarkes occupied in the 1830s, it was, in conservation terms and for its time, a considerable achievement.

The greatest challenges for a body such as the trust are to be an effective advocate and to meet the highest standards in the work of conservation. The role John played in the campaign to save Old St Paul's and in the ground-breaking restoration of the Mission House helped give the trust a credible start, though its work on archaeological sites and waahi tapu was yet to come. Summing up their time together on the trust, Ormond Wilson wrote: 'it would usually be John Beaglehole who pointed to the wise decision, the right choice of words, the balanced judgement. I presided over the Trust but he guided it'.[110] The time-consuming commitment John showed to its work over so many years was a measure of his deep attachment to New Zealand and its future.

JOHN HAD GREETED THE general election in November 1957, which saw Labour scrape in with a two-seat majority, with a marked lack of enthusiasm. 'I never knew a more immoral election for bribery on both sides', he wrote to me in Cambridge, '& damn silly bribes at that'.[111] He and Elsie decided to allow themselves 'the luxury of a personal vote' (in their electorate at that time the National candidate was a certain winner) and voted for the sitting member, Jack Marshall. John thought he had been a good Attorney-General, who had 'even gone as far as to ask the Council for Civil Liberties to come & talk to him about the improvement of one or two things'. But if John did not see 'much hope of sense from the Labour party' at that time and thought them 'just as cowardly as any other party over anything important',[112] the new Labour government, for its part, viewed him with favour. During its three years in office it appointed him to a number of positions, adding to his already considerable activities, and John admitted that he found it pleasant to be appreciated by the party in power.

In January 1958 he was sent by the Department of External Affairs as the New Zealand representative to a Round Table in Bangkok organised by SEATO on 'Traditional Cultures and Technological Progress in South-East Asia'. He seems a slightly odd choice; it was not quite his field. He found the conference 'farcical . . . exasperating almost to the last degree'.[113] He wrote to Janet on the final night that the meeting had been

so silly & so futile, except for a couple of mornings . . . that once or twice I could have screamed. I don't think I have been too popular with the chairman, the wretched phoney poseur Prince Prem (a) because as myself I tried to be flat-footed & force the discussion once or twice on to the alleged subject (b) because as a Nzer I came from NZ, which tried to get the whole thing ditched. But I understand from the Seato boys that in spite of the silliness & futility in terms of the stated subject they still regard it as a great success because it got Asians round the table non-politically & for the first time they didn't fly into quarrels or politics, & they have managed to get joint cultural problems – even if not the problems of technology and culture – seriously discussed. But the capacity for endless statement these chaps have on religion & philosophy & literature! – anything but the point. The most interesting & alive chap here has been Tom Harrison . . . a very cheerful really acute extrovert, now running the museum of ethnology in Sarawak. No respecter of persons.[114]

Fortunately, he had posted off the text and annotation of the second volume of Cook's *Journals* just before Christmas; had he still been trying to finish that work his reaction might have been even stronger. And he had had the chance to 'rush through' some Cook stuff in Sydney on the way to Thailand, as well as having a lively evening with Lascelles Wilson and his family.[115] His feeling of time wasted was tempered by being flown to Ankor Wat after the meeting. He had barely heard of this remarkable complex of Hindu temples in Cambodia and was bowled over: 'Sheer unadulterated naked knock out.'[116]

Not long after his return, he was asked to replace Charles Bowden as chairman of the Historic Places Trust. Tempted to accept and 'tell off the Archbp properly', he reluctantly decided that he could not spare the time for the travelling that would be involved.[117] Two months later he accepted appointment to the Advisory Committee to the State Literary Fund – 'I wish I hadn't: but I suppose I may as well have a go at all the committees I am eligible to be on before I turn things in'.[118] In the middle of all this he was offered the award of the CMG (Companion of the Order of St Michael and St George) in the coming Queen's Birthday honours. Given his long-held attitude to such honours, this put him in a rather awkward position. He consulted Alister McIntosh (in Heenan's view, 'the wisest head on young shoulders') and Nan Taylor. Nan 'said No she wouldn't despise me if I accepted an honour, she would be quite pleased', but he claimed that he decided to accept it to please his sister-in-law Norah and Walter Nash,[119] and also because 'one or two more would be very annoyed'.[120] Many people were pleased – few academics in New Zealand, let alone real scholars, had been honoured in this way – but he particularly liked the reaction of George Currie, the last vice-chancellor of the University of New Zealand, who found John's increasing respectability a little unnerving.

In the latter part of 1958, while he was trying to complete the work on the final proofs of the second Cook volume, and the Banks proofs had at last begun to arrive, he was also very involved in preparations for the Royal Institute of International Affairs Sixth Unofficial Commonwealth Relations Conference, to be held in Palmerston North the following January. As president of the New Zealand Institute since 1954, save for the year when he was away on leave, he was to chair this conference of distinguished delegates from Chatham House and affiliated bodies in many Commonwealth countries. This meant a lot of committee work, and in December he wrote that he was 'sick of meetings . . . beginning to feel a bit tired, & could do with a month of lying in the sun & reading, either in NZ or in some other Pacific island nearer the equator'.[121] However, he found the conference extremely interesting.[122] Among the delegates were Gough Whitlam from Australia and James Callaghan from Britain, both to be prime ministers of their respective countries, as well as Garfield Todd, the New Zealand-born Prime Minister of Southern Rhodesia from 1953 to 1958. For the first time delegates from countries of predominantly European population were outnumbered by those from African and Asian countries, with particularly impressive representatives from India, Ghana and Nigeria. Discussion was largely moderate and liberal – the two Ghanaians and the Nigerian were all Oxbridge graduates – and controversy was largely avoided, a strong defence of apartheid from one of the South Africans being heard 'with attention' though not with approval.[123] John's foreboding about South Africa's future increased and when, some years later, the Southern Africa Defence and Aid Fund started in New Zealand he became one of its earliest supporters.

One more burden was taken on in 1958, when Ruth Allan died in March. In 1951 she had been asked to write the history of Nelson. Despite her knowing that she might not have long to live, her determination to find and to read all the sources, printed and manuscript, meant that the work had grown and grown. As John later wrote:

She dug up records that had been the exclusive home of dirt and the rats for decades upon silent decades; she came to have a detailed and, indeed, quite startling knowledge of the intimacies of the social life in the province. She followed every clue. She was not content to sample. She must assimilate everything . . . hence the slowness and the voluminousness of her drafts, even when they were unfinished.[124]

As a step towards the larger work, in 1954 she had published her little *History of Port Nelson*.

Ruth Allan had been a regular caller at Messines Road, generally for morning coffee, full of enthusiastic talk and guffaws of loud laughter and the latest news on her discoveries. The 250,000 words of drafts, amended drafts and notes that she left took the history up to only the early years of settlement, but a number of her friends felt that this mass could be turned into a publishable volume of real value. John edited the work, Nan Taylor and Pamela Cocks wrote additional chapters, and others helped. There is the occasional reference to this in John's letters. In June 1959 he told Janet that he had spent a week revising one chapter, grappling with the problems of somehow cutting its length. Early in 1962, when he was 'struggling' to get the work on the book done before he left for London,[125] he wrote a biographical introduction, an honest and affectionate picture of Ruth, showing once again his gift for the incisive and sympathetic portrayal of character. *Nelson: a History of Early Settlement* was finally published by A.H. and A.W. Reed in 1965.

FROM THE TIME OF ITS election in 1957 the Labour government was being urged from a number of quarters to provide better funding for the arts,[126] often with the suggestion of a statutory arts council on the British model. The New Zealand Players, a gallant attempt to provide professional theatre to the country, was in a state of near-continuous financial crisis, while the opera and ballet companies were almost equally precarious. Apart from the National Orchestra, administered by the Broadcasting Service, support was generally limited to small grants from Art Union lottery funds under the personal control of the Minister of Internal Affairs, W.F. Anderton, a politician of good intentions but little weight in Cabinet. While men such as Fred Turnovsky and George Swan were both publicly and privately urging Anderton and Walter Nash to action, John (well aware of the problem the Prime Minister presented) was in touch with Ted Fairway, a friend and Deputy Secretary of Internal Affairs, floating the idea of starting with a small advisory body rather than moving to a full arts council straight away. Such a body, he suggested, could be run experimentally for a year or two, to see how it got on; if it was found to fill a real need it could be established permanently, possibly on the model of the Historic Places Trust.[127] Jack Hunn (the energetic troubleshooter in the public service who had been appointed to head Internal Affairs for six months) took up the idea and it slowly moved ahead, with John already giving thought to possible members. It was symptomatic of the Nash government's inability to make decisions, however, that the establishment of the Arts Advisory Council was announced only on 18 November 1960, during the election campaign which led to National's return to power. Its members were the minister, as *ex officio* chairman, the departmental heads of Internal Affairs, Education and Broadcasting, and five others, including John and Fred Turnovsky. There were no women and no one from Auckland. John approved of Turnovsky, having had a lot to do with him over the years in chamber music,[128] and of John Schroder, the Director of Broadcasting. But he was less impressed with the others; and one he deplored, a 'pretentious, silver-voiced smiling useless' man from Dunedin who had already been put on the Historic Places Trust 'as a Labour supporter', and the only 'passenger' they had.[129] There is a certain irony in the way John, with all his experience, still at least half-hoped that such appointments might reflect merit rather than political considerations.

The new council asked John, Turnovsky and Schroder to work on some objectives, and they met for two days at the end of January 1961 to write 'the first paper on arts policy ever attempted in New Zealand'.[130] John optimistically believed that 'some useful work may be in prospect'.[131] The new appointment gave him an excuse to retire from the Literary Fund Advisory Committee; while he was still reading poetry, New Zealand fiction, of which there was still very little, never caught his interest. With the Advisory Council he hoped particularly to do something for the visual arts, and he managed to bring together a visual arts committee comprising Peter Tomory, the lively director of the Auckland Art Gallery, Charles Brasch, Cedric Firth, Fred Page and Bill Sutton, the Christchurch painter who taught at the Canterbury University School of Art. 'How nice it is to have a group of intelligent chaps discussing seriously what can be done about a particular matter', he wrote to Janet after a 'very good meeting', 'when you have a bit of cash to do something with, & know it will not be all talk wasted . . . I've never really had a day's meeting I've enjoyed more.'[132] Brasch later described John chairing one of their meetings 'very coolly & shrewdly'.[133]

An early decision was to attempt to do something for Toss Woollaston, still trying to make ends meet from his painting and job as a Rawleigh's salesman. John, whose admiration for his work went back more than twenty years, had been very impressed with

his show at the Centre Gallery in Wellington in October 1960: 'You
know, the more I see of Woollaston, the more he seems to make
most other people in NZ mere triflers . . . I really think if he keeps
on at this rate he will do some masterpieces. Of course the Nat.
Gallery people treated him with complete ignore, & I just couldn't
find time to do anything about it.'[134] The Arts Advisory Council
offered Woollaston a grant of £1000 to enable him to visit Europe.
John wrote to him explaining their intention:

The idea is to say to a painter (sculptor, musician, what-have-you) 'Look,
you have attained a certain maturity, but you're not dead yet, you're still
capable of development, what about taking £1000 & going away for six
months & just looking at (or listening to) the things you're interested
in & you think will stimulate you? You don't need to paint or draw (or
sculpt or fiddle) though if you want to, by all means do so. There are no
strings attached. All we want you to do is to recreate & shake up your
soul, if you have one, refresh your mind, make this a spring-board for a
fresh jump into the empyrean when you get back.'[135]

This would be the equivalent for the painter, John thought, of
'refresher' or 'sabbatical' leave for the academic. He added that
what he thought Toss needed was 'some solid study of structure &
form' and his advice (if it was asked for) 'would be to go to London
& look hard through the National Gallery . . . & then go to the
Tate, & then to Paris to the Louvre, & then to the modern pictures
in Paris'. Toss, in the midst of a productive spell of painting, seemed
less convinced than John was of the value of going to Europe, and
was rather reluctant to go away at all without his wife Edith.[136]
He tried to get the council to spread the money over three years
to support him painting at home, but John replied that that would
be 'the complete contradiction' of their intentions.[137] Toss began to
plan the trip that would take him overseas for nearly four months in
1962, to Madrid, London and New York.[138] John and Elsie met him
in London the following August, and John gave some more advice:
'look at Cézanne more than at Turner'.[139] Toss looked at both, but
his real discovery seems to have been Goya's paintings in the Prado
in Madrid.

What might appear a straightforward idea could prove extraordinarily complicated to put into effect. It took seven months to arrange
a commission for Evelyn Page to paint a portrait of Walter Nash.
Eventually the Secretary of Internal Affairs took the proposal to
his minister (the council being only an advisory body, all decisions
had to be approved by the minister) and the minister, Leon Götz,
took it to Cabinet, which agreed. The minister then rang Nash,

but he became suspicious of what the government might be up to. John had to go to see Nash and persuade him that this was not a government move to embarrass him somehow but an initiative of the Arts Advisory Council. The visit was successful: Nash moved on to the subject of John's article on 'New Zealand Since the War' which had just been published in *Landfall*. 'I don't know how you know all these things', said Nash, adding that John was 'about ninety per cent right' in what he had written.[140]

The Arts Advisory Council was bedevilled by lack of money. 'I desperately wish we could give [the New Zealand Ballet] more money', John commented on one occasion, 'they want to put on a major production but major productions are a bottomless sink, & their administration isn't good'.[141] The idea of building some sort of infrastructure 'to provide talented artists with the means to create and thrive'[142] proved a chimera; even the hope of consistent policies depended on the minister's accepting the advice he was given.* In September 1963 John wrote that he was 'getting thoroughly fed up with the minister'.[143] By this time legislation had been introduced to create a new statutory Arts Council that would no longer need to make recommendations to the minister, but John recognised that his role might disappear. The more he thought of Götz and his colleagues making the appointments, the more unhappy he became. 'Wouldn't it be awful if the cure was worse than the disease'.[144]

John's fears were largely borne out. The decisions on appointments were made by the government caucus and the new Arts Council consisted largely of good National Party supporters. Neither John nor Fred Turnovsky (widely regarded as the ablest of the old advisory council) was reappointed. The new chairman was G.G.G. Watson, a Wellington lawyer in his late seventies. John 'shuddered at the thought' of him in that position. Turnovsky 'took it very hard indeed', but while John confessed to a 'slight feeling of disappointment' (though my memory is of a rather stronger reaction) he also felt

---

*   John told Janet about one occasion when the minister went back on an agreed policy when he met a drama delegation from Christchurch: 'he completely took our breath away. Now what do you do in a case like that – when you have recovered your breath? Have a row with the minister in the presence of the delegation, & thus make the AAC seem a shambles, or let it go & thus seem fools? Or chase after them after they have left the room & say Don't take this seriously, & leave them wondering what on earth they have come to Wellington for? If I wanted a final proof that the Council should be a statutory body, & not just advisory, this is it – & you know I wasn't too certain when the whole thing started. Ministers – my God.' (JCB to JEP, 10 July 1963.)

'enormous relief (hence 108pp of introd.)'.[145] He reacted also by carrying out his 'long expressed intention' of resigning from what he had come to view as that 'useless & hopeless body', the Board of Trustees of the National Art Gallery and Dominion Museum. John was asked to go on the Visual Arts Advisory Committee of the new statutory council, but 'drunk with . . . new-found freedom' he said, 'No, thank you, not just yet' (he was getting to the end of the introduction to volume three of the Cook *Journals*), though he conceded he might possibly have felt differently about it if they had asked at least one other member of the old committee.[146]

John was never enthusiastic about being on committees, and never had great faith in them as a means of getting things done. Where he believed, however, that there was a vital battle to be fought, as with Old St Paul's, or important work to be tackled, as with the Council for Civil Liberties or the Historic Places Trust, he could be extraordinarily generous with his time and his pen, providing, in Fred Wood's words, 'willing hands for the thankless task which must be done if ideals are to live'.[147]

14

THE PRICE OF EMINENCE

IN THIS FINAL CHAPTER, John the public figure, and the growing recognition he received both in New Zealand and internationally, is set alongside the private man: the loyalties, the quirky humour, the idiosyncrasies and passions that endeared him to so many. The 1960s was a time of new and increasing family involvement. Following his marriage in 1962, my brother Giles and his wife Jenny settled in Feilding. It was conveniently close to Ormond and Rosamond Wilson at Mount Lees, and John and Elsie often combined visits to both families. In 1966 my brother Robin and I both married. John relished his role as father-in-law, and even more that of grandfather. He had always had a remarkable way with small children, who were devoted to him, but was less at ease, at least with his own, when they grew older. There were exceptions to this. For three months in the middle of 1958 the Einhorn daughters, Barbara (sixteen) and Jule (twelve) had stayed at Messines Road while their parents made their first return visit to the much-changed Germany they had left twenty years before. In the two preceding years John and Elsie, their own sons away, had had the student sons of friends to board. Elsie had found them good company, John barely noticed their presence. With Barbara and Jule it was another matter, and he was delighted to be distracted. 'My daughters continue to grow in beauty & knowledge', he told Janet.[1] It was when they left that he hung the print of Gainsborough's daughters – 'as we have lost our flesh & blood daughters, we have to have 18th century ones'.[2]

In 1960 Elsie's health was the cause of some alarm. About July she developed what eventually turned out to be rheumatoid arthritis. She was bed-bound for some weeks and in considerable pain, unalleviated by various treatments. The illness came as a particular blow to one who not only had never been ill but also had always been physically active, tramping every week with her women friends, and for many years attending the classes of Gisa Taglicht, the Viennese refugee and teacher of rhythmical dance and gymnastics. I was due to return from Cambridge at the end of the year and, although John and Elsie were putting a brave face on it, my aunt wrote to warn me that the chances of recovery seemed slight. She also reported on the devoted care John was giving. To me, urging me not to worry, he put it more lightly: he could 'cope with the washing-up & the bed-making, & all the ladies are rallying around'.[3] He seized the opportunity of Elsie being 'safely out of the way . . . to clean up the kettle & the electric kettle & a saucepan or two', which hardly enhanced her equanimity.[4] Fortunately, a new 'wonder drug', cortisone, arrived and had almost miraculous results. When I got home at Christmas Elsie had taken charge again; had I not been told, I would never have suspected that she had been so ill, though it was months before the last pain and discomfort disappeared.

John was pleased with what I had achieved at Cambridge. Typically for someone who was better at telling you these things on paper than face to face, he wrote to tell me this before I left, in case he went 'under a bus' before I got back.[5] He thought that I should return to New Zealand – 'you can lead a pretty full life in NZ now' – and was pleased when I was appointed to a lectureship at Victoria. It did not seem to occur to either of us that having a father and son in the relatively small history department might not always be a comfortable situation. As it turned out, I believe we both enjoyed our six years as colleagues, and I learned a great deal from him. He did give me one piece of advice when I got home: 'You've got your PhD, now it's time you got down to some real reading – you'd better start with Henry James!' For his part, he embarked, once again, on *Paradise Lost* and was 'impressed as never before with what a cold-blooded calculating priggish bastard God is . . . But how wonderful to be pompous & priggish in Miltonic blank verse. Ah well, don't let's read it for the story, just for the style.'[6] Having finished, he felt he had to read 'other stuff' on Milton, including E.M.W. Tilyard's *The Miltonic Setting*.

THE UNIVERSITY OF New Zealand was dissolved on 1 January 1962, a long overdue demise, and on the same day Victoria and the other constituent colleges became independent universities. John, who had found little good to say of it in his 1937 history of the university, now farewelled 'our too-aged academic relative . . . superfluous, useless' without regret, though he conceded that in its last years it had 'used its resources to support real scholarship'.[7] Its passing brought an end to the University of New Zealand Press. John had hoped that the new universities might cooperate to establish a common publishing house, but the will was not there, and eventually most of them, including Victoria, established presses of their own. Independence meant that Victoria for the first time awarded its own degrees, and he designed the new degree certificates, twenty-six different kinds of them, and 'all left far too late'. He did, however, enjoy designing an invitation card for four lectures by a visiting British writer on art, Sir Herbert Read.[8] He became a member of the research committee of the new University Grants Committee, as he was of Victoria's research committee. There was very little money to be distributed, but on the arts side, with which he was particularly concerned, the problem was not money but a failure of staff to apply for it. He had for some time held the view that what was needed in the universities was 'a lot more application & hard work' as well as money.[9]

When John and Elsie were in New York on their way to London later in 1962, John received a letter offering him the Beit Chair in Commonwealth History at Oxford in succession to Vincent Harlow. He suspected, rightly, that Bill Williams had had a hand in this and wrote to him the same day. 'The offer puts me on top of the world & simultaneously bowls me over', he said, but he had 'a devil of a lot of commitments to NZ' and he thought he was too old to take the chair on. 'My principal interest now is in finishing Cook & doing a biography & maybe one or two odds and ends . . . & by the time I am 80 it will be time to die.'[10] Three weeks later he confessed to Janet that, while he found the offer rather hard to turn down, he realised that most of the time he forgot all about it, so he could only conclude he was not really interested.[11] It was not, however, quite as simple as that. He told Fred Wood that it was only after 'an uneasy time of cogitation' that he refused it,[12] and he assured Bill Williams that he 'really did think seriously about it' and hoped to God that he had done the right thing.[13] Four years later, when Oxford awarded him an honorary doctorate, John again suspected the Williams hand – '& if I suspect with justice, well, all I can say is, you seem determined to take my breath away . . . No, I could say more, but if I do so you may suspect me of unmanly sentimentality.'[14]

Had anyone in 1929 suggested to John that thirty-three years later he would turn down a chair at Oxford he would, surely, have been incredulous. It is a measure of how far his feelings about New Zealand and the kind of life that could be lived there had changed.

It was not that he had come to feel, as a conscious New Zealander, that he should necessarily do so – his cultural heritage and the world of scholarship of which he was part made him feel comfortable, if not quite at home, in Britain. The offer was attractive in many ways and he considered it carefully. He was clearly ambivalent about what to do, and uppermost in his mind was concern about finishing the work on Cook, together with what he summed up as 'family and friends'. This is a clear instance of how his letters, with their different emphases to different people, can pose problems for his biographer, and of the care with which those letters, especially where they are to only one recipient, must be read as evidence of what he was thinking.

In 1963 the Victoria history department persuaded him to teach a third-year history course, a teaching load he had not carried since 1947 except for an honours course in 1954. Student numbers had begun to increase dramatically in the late 1950s and early 1960s, and qualified staff were extraordinarily difficult to get and to retain. Looking back, however, I am appalled at the almost cavalier way we added to his work. Yet this gave a new generation of students the chance to hear him on responsible government – the intention had been a fairly broad course on the evolution of the Commonwealth but John, as always, concentrated on what really interested him and got back to some of his favourite historians, Helen Taft Manning on British colonial policy and Chester Martin on responsible government in Canada. He enjoyed meeting students again, often joining the weekly staff/student coffee meetings held at that time, but startled some of them (as well as some colleagues) with the range of his marking, using the full scale when staff were increasingly clustering marks between 45 and 70 per cent.

That same year Victoria University decided that he should be made Professor of British Commonwealth History. John had been very comfortable with the position, and title, of Senior Research Fellow and been paid a professorial salary, but the move was clearly intended as a compliment – 'my colleagues decided that I was a Great Man, & that all Great Men must be Professors, & they got Freddy Wood to turn on the diplomacy', was how he explained it to Bill Williams[15] – so he said yes. For the department it had the added advantage of giving it a second established professorial position. In putting the proposal to the university council, Ian Campbell, the acting vice-chancellor, described the title as more 'consistent with the dignity of the University' and fitting for 'an historian of world eminence'.[16] John suspected he had made a mistake in agreeing to it;

he was sure that he had when told that he would be expected to attend meetings of the professorial board. When the history department moved into the ninth floor of the new Rankine Brown building in June 1966, John left the Hunter building after thirty years. He did not make a great deal of use of the new room, although it had the advantage of having a wall big enough to hang one of the finest pieces of tapa cloth he had brought back from Tonga.

Teaching and the professorial board did little to curb his active interest in what was going on in the wider community. In July 1963 the Wellington Centre Gallery stepped in to show a retrospective exhibition of paintings by Woollaston and McCahon organised by the Auckland City Gallery, after the National Gallery had declined to take it. Because of the number of paintings it had to be shown half at a time in successive weeks. John was enthusiastic about both painters:

Some McCahons very good indeed, I think; a terrific crucifixion; some very good but by Cézanne & Picasso. But certainly he can be very very good. And some of Toss's earlier work comes up marvellously, increases in effect every time I see it. And as Fred Page said, opening the show, it is a crying scandal that neither is in the Nat. Gallery. And how on earth to get them in?[17]

He tried to do this soon after, when I bought my first McCahon painting from the Ikon Gallery in Auckland and arranged with them to send down a series of eight landscape panels that was also in the exhibition, *Landscape Theme and Variations: series A*. John and I took them to the National Gallery and he unsuccessfully urged that they be bought: it proved 'too big a pill to swallow'.[18] It was not long after this that he resigned from the board.

A little later he was embroiled in another controversy, mentioned in chapter thirteen. The government wanted to reform the handling of censorship, 'with a new definition of indecency to give literature a chance'. While applauding the determination of John Robson, the Secretary for Justice, (with the support of his minister) to give the system 'some measure of rationality & publicity', John drafted a statement for the Council for Civil Liberties, 'not wholly favourable to the bill' in all its details. The *Dominion* printed this but the *Evening Post*, which 'had been shrieking about the sacred duty of the Press to give the public the facts', failed to do so.[19] He had barely put down his pen before, two months later, he and Walter Scott were in action again for the Council for Civil Liberties, with a letter John called 'a stinker' to the *Listener* complaining about the Broadcasting Corporation and the government's handling of election broadcasts.[20] In retrospect, his energy seems staggering. Not only was he concerned with these public issues, which involved lengthy meetings and painstaking drafting, but he was trying to finish work on a great mass of galley proofs for the third volume of Cook (finally posted at the end of November). The Waimate Mission House was taking 'an awful lot of discussion' at the trust (with three days in the Bay of Islands in September). He lamented to Janet: 'I saw a couple of new books on Paradise Lost in the library yesterday, but decided I had too much to do to bring them home & read them'. Indeed, he had hardly read anything for some time, 'except snippets' in Roy Parsons' bookshop, and it took him about six weeks to read a Penguin book on polar exploration.[21]

During 1964 and 1965 there was prolonged controversy over the future of the Alexander Turnbull Library following the government's decision to make it a part of a new national library.[22] The argument was fought largely, in Rachel Barrowman's words, 'between those who held to a nostalgic image of the library as the "quiet sequestered retreat" of the scholar-bibliophile, and those who saw its future as part of a properly funded (and properly housed) national library, with resources to sustain academic scholarship'.[23] When John signed a letter to the *Dominion* in March 1965 (along with some other university academic staff) supporting the proposal – 'Only a national collection, with obligations to the whole of society, can afford to devote itself to building a complete record of our own Western civilisation'[24] – he told Janet that he hardly dared to set foot in the library, as feelings were running very high. He had little time for most of those who argued against the national library proposal, being well aware that most of the library's major users (himself and his colleague Joan Stevens prominent among them) shared his view. In October he wrote a further letter in which he appealed for realism and for 'co-ordination of our resources for the sake of scholarship'.[25] The *Evening Post* gave it headlines, cut out only a few sentences, and 'perhaps improved it'.[26] It was an indication of the respect which his opinion now commanded. Whatever fears he might have had, his relationship with the Turnbull remained as close and as congenial as ever.

In the midst of this, his brother Ernest died. He had had major heart surgery some months earlier but his death, on 23 October 1965, was sudden and unexpected. He was only fifty-nine. Pam, Ernest's wife, insisted that the cremation should take place with no ceremonial observance whatever, but for John that was 'overdoing bareness'. 'Brotherly feeling asserted itself', and he slipped into the crematorium '& put a single sprig of Lady Haddington on the coffin & said Ave atque Vale.* Dreadful sentimentality, I admit. And then left'.[27] He had never quite worked out what he felt about Ernest, who, he thought, 'made a thing about cutting away all sentiment, & I was never sure how much that was a pose, or how seriously to take it'.[28] A worse blow came less than six months later when his brother Keith died in London of a heart attack. Keith had spent nearly three months in New Zealand on a business visit just over two years earlier, staying with John and Elsie for part of the time and seeing a lot of them and their friends. John had always greatly loved his brother, and always hoped that when Keith retired he would return to New Zealand or, if not that, when John retired he and Elsie would be able to spend a lot of time with Keith in England. That dream was dashed, and John grieved deeply. The news came just days before he and Elsie left for London on 1 May for the conferment of the Oxford degree. They stayed in Keith's flat in Hampstead, '& while it's a bit harrowing sometimes to be in contact with all Keith's things', John wrote to his nephew Peter, 'it is also a bit consoling, & here is so much visual evidence of what a civilized and humane man he was'.[29] During this time in London he sought to comfort and cheer his niece Betty, a characteristic means being a series of postcards with messages that, like Edward Lear's, gave nonsense formal expression.† The affection could not be disguised.

By this time John's own heart was giving him trouble. Not long before the news of Keith's death, he had been to the East Coast with the Historic Places Trust, and after visiting Gisborne to talk with the harbour board and the city council about the way harbour developments were encroaching on the site of Cook's first landing in New Zealand, they went up to Tolaga Bay. There they 'had a very good walk out to Cook's cove to fix a place to put up a marker

---

*   'Hail and farewell'.

†   An example: on a card with a medieval painting of the animals leaving the ark, sent to his niece Betty (13 July 1966), he wrote: 'I send you this, Enchanting Niece, because although you are no doubt well acquainted with the manner in which the Animals entered the confines of the Ark, you may not know how they left it; & indeed few people are really up to this rather important subject. It has tended to escape proper study. But here you see a flood of light cast on the incident, & one of the dark passages of history revealed with startling clarity. I am glad to see, myself, what is obviously a pair of mermaids sporting in the still abundant waters, because that proves the existence of these interesting creatures, a matter so much doubted in our sceptical time. Do not doubt too much, O Enchanting Niece: have faith, & All shall be revealed to thee, perhaps by thine Uncle, perhaps by some other of the Prophets of GOD.'

& a bronze plaque . . . I was pleased to find that I could still make it', he told Janet, 'with the help of one of my little pills, though it is steep. Blow this hardening artery business. The last time I went I just sprang over, & that was only four years ago.'[30] From the mid-1960s he was noticeably walking more slowly and wrapping up more warmly when it was cold. One was conscious of Elsie, without fuss, carefully watching his well-being. He did not complain, but he generally reported to Janet when he had had a medical check, usually without emotion, and only once in the letters to her does he really show the frustration that he must have felt:

I'm all right. No, I'm not *all* right. I'm not too bad. No that makes me seem far worse than I am. Well, today was a pretty cold day, & I find that I don't like cold days at all . . . What I have the utmost difficulty in doing is taking those pink pills, indoral, oxygen things, regularly, & I keep on forgetting. But I'm all right, more or less, irritated, but all right. According to the doctor, the blood finds another way round in time, & I wish to God it would get a move on.[31]

Towards the end of 1966 he and Elsie had a week 'up north', on Historic Places Trust business. They went first to Mercury Bay on the Coromandel; the spot where Cook had observed the transit of Mercury and where the trust wanted a reserve was threatened by a planned subdivision. From there they went to Northland for the opening of the Waimate Mission House. It had 'come off wonderfully well', John considered, and 'with that & St Paul's saved I suppose we can say the year has had its bright spots'.[32]

I was away on leave at Harvard at that time, and in his Christmas letter to me and my wife, Helen, John reported that he was 'reading here & there' to refresh his mind before he started on Cook's life.

I started off with Doughty's *Travels in Arabia Deserta*, which is a staggering thing, & then did Rousseau's Confessions, & now I have Vienna [by Ilsa Barea] on hand, & Painter's two vols. on Proust in prospect, which I bought in London; oh, & before Rousseau was another Boswell volume remaindered in London, & Pottle's *Boswell The Earlier Years*. I don't know that I shouldn't let Cook go, & spend the rest of my life reading. I might even read some history. I shan't be able to do One Boy's Wellington,* anyhow, until I've finished Cook; I've often thought of it, there are lots of people it would be fun to write about. But crumbs, Daughter-in-law, reading's much easier work than writing.[33]

---

*   I had sent John a copy of the American historian Samuel Eliot Morison's wonderful memoir of his early years, *One Boy's Boston 1887–1907* (Cambridge, Mass.: Houghton Mifflin, 1962) with the comment 'what about one boy's Wellington?'

He got to the George Painter biography of Proust a few weeks later:

I'm not certain that it's as good as they say – 'one of the great biographies' & all that, it's not as good as my life of Cook – but it's pretty good, it keeps on sounding after you've put it down, & when a book keeps on sounding, one really oughtn't to read anything else for a week or two. For extraordinariness Proust really takes the prize. The endless staggering varieties of life on this earth. There is too much to learn about human nature. And what an extraordinary society he lived in. I ought to read his own novel all over again . . . Now I'm reading Harold Nicolson's *Diaries & Letters* – another extraordinary fellow, though not in the same region of extraordinariness as Proust . . .[34]

The beginning of 1967 brought another time-consuming and not very palatable task. Retirement, which otherwise meant little or no difference to the pattern of his life, did mean that he had to clear out his room at the university. Even though his study at home had always been his main base, this was not easy. 'The paper! The odds & ends! A frightful process. I much prefer a straightforward job like cleaning pewter or the copper candlesticks.'[35] And then there were painful decisions on the books; he would have looked at each one carefully, perhaps flicked through it to find a passage he remembered, before putting it down. Some he recognised that he was unlikely to look at again – 'most of that political theory/science stuff' – though he thought he would certainly hang on to some of it for old time's sake. 'The more I look at it the less inclined I am to part with it, but I'll have to part from it some day. Some of these books meant a lot to me once. On the other hand, I'll never read Lenin's *Collected* no it's *Selected Works* now.'[36] It stayed, and he partly solved the wider problem by putting a number of cartons of books in my study at the university for me to find when I returned from leave, and giving others away to colleagues. The tapa cloth remained in place for Mary Boyd, who took over the room.

The Oxford honorary degree was followed by further public recognition. The same year John was awarded the Linnaeus Medal by the Royal Swedish Academy of Sciences and was made a corresponding member of the Royal Historical Society. In 1967 he was made a Fellow of the Royal Society of New Zealand (the first historian to be thus recognised). A year later his own university followed with an honorary doctor of literature. John had his doubts about it all. 'I think these honours spawn one another. And all these letters after one's name, it's very embarrassing . . . [and] very bad for a person like me'. He thought he would like 'just one big honour that swallowed up all the others . . . like J.C. Beaglehole O.M. or J.C. Beaglehole, Grand Master of the Legion of Honour'.[37]

Elsie and John had always been extraordinarily hospitable in having people to stay, family and other relatives, New Zealand friends, and visitors from overseas. They both enjoyed it, and Elsie showed great skill in ensuring as far as possible that John was not too distracted from his work. When he was caught up in work, however, he could be reluctant to go out: 'now the cursed invitations to cocktails start coming in. Why should we go to the American embassy and shake hands with Mr Louis Armstrong & then gas to the usual mob of NZrs? . . . However it may be nice to have dinner with the Director of the British Museum, at least I shall be able to tell him that I know his institution well.'[38] In July and August 1967 David Quinn was a British Council visitor to New Zealand giving lectures at the universities (John had pulled the strings to have him appointed), and he and Alison stayed at Messines Road. Three months later Alan Villiers, square-rigged sailor and writer, stayed with them. A noisy, practical man, he and John were very dissimilar but each had a warm admiration of the other. 'I warm to him more & more', John wrote, '& he is a most racy conversationalist'.[39] The Australian historian, Sir Keith Hancock, was another of their guests. We took him out to walk on the Wellington coast at Makara, and I remember him talking to John about the work on Cook and asking him if he ever 'heard his men talking'. The reply was an enigmatic 'almost'. John and Elsie met frequently with their immediate circle of friends – the Jacobys, Einhorns, Sylvia and Tom Smith, Margaret and Jim Campbell – for meals in one another's homes, for tramping days on the Wellington coast or hills, in Wairarapa, or for holidays further afield. In these years, with their sons off their hands, and partly because of the Historic Places Trust, they saw much more of New Zealand than they had in earlier times. Elsie organised the trips and did all the driving.

Their wider circle of friends in many ways reflected the character of Wellington as a centre of government, education and the arts. It included many colleagues from Victoria, drawn from a wide range of disciplines. In government there was Alister McIntosh, head of the Department of External Affairs, and his wife, Doris; C.E. Beeby, Director of Education, and Beatrice; Dick Powles, who, having returned from Western Samoa and served a term as New Zealand High Commissioner to India, was appointed New Zealand's first Ombudsman in 1962. Other friends representing New Zealand, the Reids and the Corners among them, they kept up with both in Wellington and on the other side of the world. Arthur and Jean Ward (Arthur was now the head of the New Zealand Dairy Board) and Cedric and Bobbie Firth lived close by. In spite of John's view of cocktail parties, they met, and liked, many overseas diplomats posted to Wellington. As John began to slow down as a walker, some of the annual tramps were dropped; other traditions remained, like the after-Christmas family gathering at the McIntoshes' retreat at Te Marua, north of Wellington, where we might do some tree-cutting before a picnic lunch and Mac and John really got down to what was going on in government and the wider world. Every summer there would be a day with tennis or croquet at Bob and Elsie Monro's place (he taught chemistry at Victoria) at Golden Gate on the Porirua Harbour. Here, when my brothers and I were young, Elsie had sometimes taken us to spend a night in the bunkhouse, the one-roomed bach on the very edge of the water below the Monros' house on the hill. A more recent institution was the Wilsons' New Year 'tennis party' at Mount Lees, with Beagleholes, Turnovskys and others, generally including Walter Nash and, after his wife's death, his sister. As the rest of the party shed most of their clothes for tennis or swimming, Walter remained very respectable in a formal suit. Rosamond organised and played tennis and provided copious food; Ormond talked and showed off his garden and bush walk.

Music was flourishing in Wellington. Under John Hopkins as conductor from 1958 to 1963, the National Orchestra reached new heights; the Chamber Music Society was now part of a thriving national federation with many outstanding concerts by overseas and local groups; the opera and ballet companies were making a brave start. John and Elsie went as often as they could. The music department at Victoria, under Fred Page, had established its Thursday lunchtime concerts, remarkable both for their quality and for the programmes performed, which included contemporary work by the young New Zealand composers Douglas Lilburn and David Farquhar; John was a regular attender. In addition to music, Downstage, Wellington's first professional theatre company, which started in 1964, offered a wide range of productions, from Shakespeare to Beckett to the Wellington playwright Bruce Mason. In its early years it was run as a theatre/café and John and Elsie went regularly with friends for a meal followed by the play. Their recent experience of theatre in London gave them a point of comparison and they were often impressed. John judged the *Hamlet* (at the end of 1967) 'quite superb': 'I've never seen a Hamlet as good. Tim Eliott as H. Peter Bland Claudius. Everybody very good except Polonius,

& that's a damned hard part – harder to make good than Hamlet, I think. Ophelia . . . not too good to start with, then heart-breaking when mad.'[40]

As soon as John returned from his trip to Dusky Sound in March 1968, he had to write a speech for the annual meeting of the Chamber Music Federation. In it he looked back to his early years, capturing vividly the musical life both in Wellington and in his own family at that time.[41] But writing it was one more demand on his time:

Why do I never foresee the horrible inconvenience of these things? Well, I do, but some awfully nice bloke rings up, & I think it won't be so bad this time; & then when the time comes it is just as bad. But then the sudden things are just as bad, like Walter Scott ringing up on Sunday night about Mr Muldoon & my having to sit down at once & compose a statement on Mr Muldoon for the C. of Civil Liberties & copy it out twice for the *Dominion* & the Press Association, while Walter waited to take it down in his car . . . There is always some fool like Muldoon popping up to make it necessary to start the fight all over again.[42]

At this time he was rereading Jane Austen, as enthusiastic as ever. 'I don't know why people keep on writing novels. It would be much simpler if we just had J.A., & could keep on reading them. J.A. & Paradise Lost & two or three plays of Shakespeare & Cook's Journals'.[43] At the beginning of the following year, however, he had moved on to Dickens, first *Martin Chuzzlewit* ('in some ways a dreadful book'[44]) and then *Our Mutual Friend*, which he found much better ('a good book, very Victorian but very good'[45]). After that he turned to the Bible, to the Book of Job. 'I got on to Job because he seemed a conveniently short book while I wondered what long book I'd tackle next – another Dickens? – & also because I thought my prose style might be improved for the Royal Soc, England; & you know the prose style is really very good, if only you knew what it meant half the time.'[46]

If it was the Royal Society and their invitation to give a lecture that led him to think of his prose style, their lecture was only one of a number, together with articles and appearances, for which he was called on as the Cook bicentennial was celebrated in England, New Zealand and Australia. He had had to stop work on the biography about the beginning of 1969 to work on the lectures for the Royal Society and the Society for Nautical Research in England, as well as a lecture for the Australian Academy of Science's Cook Bicentenary Symposium, which he was taking part in on his way to England. The *Times* wanted an article on Cook[47] (published just after he and Elsie arrived in London on 28 May) and before they left Wellington

John had written to the *Evening Post* suggesting that New Zealand's memorial for the bicentennial might include a work by the sculptor Henry Moore, to 'celebrate the greatest Yorkshireman of the 18th century by calling to our aid the greatest Yorkshireman of the 20th century – who is also the greatest living sculptor'.[48] The suggestion was not taken up. While he was away John wrote on Cook for the *New Zealand Listener*[49] and also a foreword for Neil and Charles Begg's bicentennial book, *James Cook and New Zealand*.

On arriving home at the beginning of October, John was almost immediately involved in Cook events. On 9 October celebrations at Gisborne marked Cook's first landing. Back in Wellington John had to listen to a lecture, for a change; it was by Basil Greenhill, the Director of the National Maritime Museum at Greenwich, who had been brought out for the celebrations. At the end of October he recorded a broadcast on 'Cook the sailor and his ships', which he then turned into an illustrated lecture given to an almost full Concert Chamber in Wellington on 4 November (this material he used again for lectures in Australia a few months later). Five days after that he was at Mercury Bay for the unveiling of a plaque recording Cook's visit and gave a masterly short address* with an account of Cook's stay in the bay. This was the occasion when he described his and Elsie's first visit to Mercury Bay over thirty years before and his haunting feeling of a ship just outside his vision, of the sound of words just beyond the reach of his ear, and (an echo of his reply to Keith Hancock's question) how he 'almost heard the voices of eighteenth century sailors'. As for the memorial, he confessed that he was rather reluctant to unveil it. 'My idea of a memorial to Cook is a place left as nearly as possible as he found it – so that you can, when conditions are favourable, almost feel his presence. I am not, altogether, in favour of progress, development, more and more people living in more and more houses . . . There is something very satisfactory about a waste of sandhills.' After he had made his speech, he told Janet, 'all the little boys & girls clustered round & wanted my autograph' – 'there was', he decided, 'no further summit to climb'.[50] Returning from Mercury Bay, at Tauranga he met with the Town Clerk to discuss the future of 'Ewelme', an historic missionary home, for the Historic Places Trust.

There was then a break from Cook, first when he went with Elsie to Dunedin to be awarded an honorary doctorate by Otago University on 11 December, and then, a week later, to Doubtless Bay,

---

*   *James Cook and Mercury Bay* (Wellington: Wai-te-ata Press, 1971), 11pp.

in the far north, representing the trust at a commemoration for de Surville, the French seaman who, having narrowly missed meeting Cook off New Zealand's north coast in the stormy weather at the end of 1769, had a brief and unhappy stay at Doubtless Bay. None of this distracted John from his reading. In November he had read Horace Walpole's *Castle of Otranto*: 'it really is priceless . . . it's very short & for us 18th century people life isn't complete till we've read it'.[51] After that he read *Jane Austen and Her Art* by Mary Lascelles, which he found quite superb and could not understand why he had never read it before, as it had appeared in 1938. Over the summer he read the third volume of Bertrand Russell's autobiography ('a bit of a ragbag . . . but can't help be interesting'), he started on Pope's poetry (he had bought the Oxford edition edited by Herbert Davis when he was in London a few months earlier), and read Smollett's *Humphry Clinker* and *Peregrine Pickle*. In the middle of January there was a Cook landing pageant at Ship Cove in Queen Charlotte Sound, at which John was presented with the Australian and New Zealand Association for the Advancement of Science's Mueller Medal. In early February there was a lecture (he recycled an old one) to the Nelson Historical Society, followed the next day by an address (as patron) to the New Zealand Library Association Conference[52] being held in Nelson. After that he and Elsie joined Helen and me and our two-year-old son John for a holiday at Tata Beach in Golden Bay, a part of New Zealand, with the Tasman National Park close by, which they both had come to prize. John still had a lecture to write for his forthcoming visit to Australia* and, although he showed no sign of it on the holiday, was clearly wanting to get back to the Cook biography, of which he had written very little since they left for London nearly eight months before.

A number of John's former students, judging that among all the Cook celebrations John's contribution as the pre-eminent Cook scholar was getting scant recognition in New Zealand,† arranged a dinner for him on 20 March 1970. It was a great success, colleagues

---

*   This was 'Cook the Writer', delivered as the sixth George Arnold Wood Memorial Lecture at the University of Sydney on 15 April 1970. Wood, the father of Fred Wood, was appointed professor of history at Sydney in 1891 at the age of twenty-five and held the chair until his death in 1928, thirty-seven years later. John had agreed to revise Wood's book, *The Discovery of Australia*, first published in 1922, and this new edition was published in 1969.

†   After the dinner had been arranged, the *Dominion*, on 1 January 1970, announced John as 'Man of the Year'. I suspect that those behind the dinner were thinking more of the absence of any government move to honour John's achievement.

and friends coming from all over New Zealand. In John's reply to the toast in his honour, his customary self-deprecating wit was missing; rather, he spoke movingly of just how fortunate a life he had had. The next day his speech took on a new light when we learned that at midday, at Government House in Wellington, he had been conferred with the Order of Merit by Queen Elizabeth II, who was in New Zealand for the Cook bicentennial. John had known of the award since he was told at a reception on the royal yacht, *Britannia*, a week earlier, but had told no one apart from Elsie. It was an honour which clearly delighted him, while leaving him unusually at a loss for words. 'I cannot convince myself that I measure up to the demands of the OM', he wrote to Dan Davin, 'I try damned hard, but am on the point of giving up . . . It is all quite baffling'.[53] Friends, old and new, historians and other fellow scholars, had no such doubts. The flood of messages expressing delight, from all over the world, was overwhelming; John, reluctantly, had to acknowledge many of them with a printed card.

The Order of Merit, founded by King Edward VII in 1902 and limited to twenty-four members at any one time, is intended to recognise men and women of the greatest distinction. For a scientist it is seen as superior even to the Nobel Prize. The award is made directly by the sovereign; governments are not involved in the process of nomination.* John had always, in a joking way, said it was the only honour worth a kettle of fish. After all, it had included among its members Henry James, Bertrand Russell and E.M. Forster, not to mention Winston Churchill, Thomas Hardy and G.M. Trevelyan. The only previous New Zealander to be awarded it was the great scientist Ernest Rutherford.†

Two weeks later John and Elsie flew to Australia for a hectic three weeks. Just how hectic it was is suggested by John's account to Janet:

---

*   The New Zealand Cabinet was apparently told that the award was going to be made and some members were unhappy about it, John still being viewed with displeasure, apparently, by conservative governments. I was told this by John Daniels, former director of the Historic Places Trust, who was told by W.J. Scott (not the same W.J. Scott who worked with John for civil liberties), who had been a member of the government until the election at the end of 1969. Scott then succeeded Ormond Wilson as chairman of the trust. He and John viewed each other with a measure of suspicion at first, which quickly turned to respect.

†   Since John's award a third New Zealander has been made a member of the order: Sir Ronald Syme, the great historian of Rome. Syme, who studied at both Victoria and Auckland University Colleges, went on to Oxford, where he remained for the whole of his distinguished career.

Itinerary; Melbourne, dinner, lecture, shown over Art Gallery by bubbling-over E. Westbrook; Sydney, hon D.Litt, dinner, Wood Mem. Lecture, in costume, God was it hot but I laid aside the hat; Brisbane, dinner, lecture, & v. good cooking at hotel; Townsville, new univ & QUEEN & dinner as univ becomes independent, some Vice-Chancellor sings my praises; Cooktown, Endeavour River & all that, extremely interesting . . . saw reefs from air at low tide on flight back; Townsville again, lecture; Brisbane again for a night . . . by train to Grafton NSW to stay weekend with Richardsons late VUW . . . back to Sydney by air . . . tonight lecture again, & tomorrow Tuesday fly to Bathurst, lecture, then to Canberra, back to airport on Saturday, fly home.

I am still well & hearty.[54]

After Australia he was able at last to make progress on the biography. He was 'beginning to think' he had a reasonable chance of finishing it if he could be left alone for the rest of the year.[55] But he was not. He accepted invitations to talk to the New Zealand Booksellers Jubilee Conference,[56] and to give a jubilee address at the Turnbull Library on 30 June.[57] In the latter, which was largely autobiographical and almost nostalgic in tone, he looked back with affection to his childhood in that Hopper Street home where books 'were as much part of the intimate family environment as my mother's brown scones or the round piano stool that went up and down, so that when you got tired of practising you could twirl round and round on it'. He drew on his memories of literary life in colonial Wellington, of the Turnbull Library during the years in which he had known it – almost inseparable from his own scholarly career. He was apologetic at having no certainties to offer, no grand plan for the future. But no one listening could have missed the sense that libraries, and especially the Alexander Turnbull Library, have a unique role to play in a community aspiring to some sort of civilised existence. A little later the University Tramping Club celebrated its fiftieth anniversary; John was asked to write something on the early days for the jubilee publication, but found it hard and suggested they reprint his account of that far-off trip through the Urewera in 1925, which had been published in *Rata*.[58] By the end of March 1971 the draft of the biography was finished. He realised that he had to rewrite the first chapter entirely (its scale did not match the rest of the book, which had grown in the writing), and feared that when he came to look at it he would have to do the same for 'a good deal of the rest'. Somewhat gloomily, he told Ruth Ross, that 'maybe in another year I'll have finished it. I dunno. Perhaps I should retire from everything else.'[59] After the first chapter, however, remarkably little revision was needed and most of the changes he made were matters of style.

Early in 1970 Janet Paul moved to Wellington. After Blackwood Paul died in February 1965 she had endeavoured to keep their publishing business going, but Blackwood had provided the business acumen; without that, and lacking capital, she found the task impossible. Her move brought to an end the remarkable series of letters that John had written over the preceding twenty-five years. One can only conjecture how he felt. Writing had enabled a kind of communion – 'inter-assured of the mind' was the quote from Donne that he came back to time after time – which would be almost impossible to sustain when their meetings became a part of everyday social life. Without the letters, we no longer have the lively accounts of what he was up to. The last in the collection was written after her move, when he was away in Christchurch, having his portrait painted by W.A. Sutton. Victoria University had commissioned it to mark the award of the Order of Merit; John had been reluctant to lose the time but liked Sutton and, as the painting progressed, thought it should turn out 'fairly well'. 'A pity the OM has to go in,' he told Janet, 'but I'll bet it is the first portrait in which the OM & a pipe have appeared together'.[60]

His pocket diaries, in which he recorded engagements, show that the round of activities continued as ever. The Historic Places Trust ate up a lot of time; in August 1970 there was a three-day regional conference in Auckland, and there were now meetings as well of the Old St Paul's Advisory Committee. The same month he heard the Labour party leader, Norman Kirk, talk to a meeting of the Institute of International Affairs on New Zealand's place in the world, the next month it was Sir Con O'Neill, on the British negotiations (in which he had led the British team) to join the European Union. The Council for Civil Liberties met regularly. There were concerts, lectures and art exhibitions to go to. Friends and family were regularly invited for meals, grandchildren looked after, new ones admired. There are many occasions noted when he and Elsie were invited out by friends. There are also more frequent appointments with his heart specialist. At this time too there was fresh anxiety about Elsie's health; she was in hospital twice for brief periods in 1971, but quickly restored to her customary fitness (she was to outlive John by twenty-five years). On 23 September 1971 John went to the opening of an exhibition of paintings from the university collection, held at the National Gallery. It was a wonderful reminder of what had grown from those first purchases by the staff common room twenty-five years before.

On 9 October he and Elsie went to a New Zealand Opera Company performance of *Aida*. John slept badly that night, and died of a heart attack the next morning.

OF JOHN'S LASTING STATURE as a scholar there can be little doubt; his edition of the journals and the biography of Cook represent one of the great achievements of twentieth-century historical scholarship.[61] If its foundation was the meticulous study of the historical sources, he brought to it a creative imagination that was part of the wider man, a lively human being, deeply involved with his fellow men and women. In part, this is reflected in his reading, both in its range, and in his critical – though not solemn – approach to what he read. He never lost that passionate belief, inherited from his parents, of books being a key to civilised existence, a belief which for him went beyond their contents to their physical being. But his engagement with his fellow men and women, as we have seen, took him far beyond his book-lined study. Making his career in New Zealand, rather than being (as he once feared) a fate to be dreaded, enabled him with his scholarly achievement and his wide-ranging interests to combine an involvement with the wider world and an intimate identification with a small society. If the responsibilities at times threatened to distract from his main work, he used the opportunities he was given to live a remarkable life full of rich accomplishment.

This achievement owed much to what has been characterised as his 'disciplined imperturbability',[62] which one might also characterise as an extraordinary capacity to concentrate on the job at hand. If this suggests a cloistered scholar, it would be to miss an essential part of his being. Fred Wood wrote of his 'warm human qualities – compassion, sensitivity, a basic humility combined with spiritual toughness, and a rare quality of humour, which can sometimes see round the corners of an argument and help reach the heart of men and problems',[63] while Eric McCormick described him as 'a man of profound, even passionate loyalty. . . . a lively human being, deeply caught up with his fellow men'. 'Just as in our anti-heroic age', McCormick continued, 'Beaglehole the writer gave monumental form to his hero, so in his personal relations he reminded the unfashionable terms – "loyalty", "piety", "duty" – and supplied them with fresh meaning.'[64] If that sounds grand, there was, indeed, something grand about his willingness to stand up with sharpness and tenacity for what he believed was right. He never lost his capacity for righteous indignation. But those same qualities found a more discreet and intimate expression in the vagaries of everyday life, in his relations with family, students, fellow scholars and friends. He was as interested in people as in the world of ideas and, showing what Fred Wood called 'his genial skill in human situations', always found time to discuss their plans or their problems. In quoting generously from his letters, I have hoped to illustrate the warmth and sparkle of his mind, the resolute disinclination to confine himself to the main point when there is so much else in life that deserves a comment. There were his cheerful preambles on the phone before getting around to the business of the day, the imagination he brought to a message on a postcard, or the inscription on one of his publications, the verses he wrote for anniversaries and farewells to friends, the twitch of his mouth preceding a genially barbed observation, the thoughtfulness for friends in need. He found no conflict between speaking the truth as he saw it and a simple courtesy to other people.

John was a modest man. He was never quite convinced that his scholarship fully deserved the praise it received, always felt that his prose needed one more critical revision, never quite understood why his advice was sought so often and on such a range of matters. Whatever it was that for the moment engaged him received his concentrated attention. He had a meticulous eye and took pains to get things right, whether a footnote to Cook, the design of a title page or boiling the billy on a family tramp. There was something reminiscent of Cook in this (and *his* shipmates suffered their share of exasperation), the patient tenacity that underlay his greatest work. Looking back on his life, John was struck by how fortunate he had been, and in this there is a large measure of truth. He was fortunate in his parents, in the friends of his student years and later; he was remarkably fortunate in having Elsie as his partner for over forty years and for the loving support and family life she gave him; fortunate to have worked with Heenan, to have had Fred Wood as a colleague, to have had the chance to edit Cook and Banks . . . I could go on. However, it was not simply luck. One must also recognise how far he was the maker of that good fortune, 'the fierce integrity with which he sought out knowledge, down to the most minute detail, and faced truth as he found it',[65] and recall the spirit with which he had faced misfortune and the passionate dedication he brought to the opportunities he was given.

Notes

ABBREVIATIONS

Institutions

ANZ	Archives New Zealand, Te Rua Mahara o te Kāwanatanga
ATL	Alexander Turnbull Library, National Library of New Zealand, Te Puna Matauranga o Aotearoa
HPT	National [New Zealand] Historic Places Trust
MONZPT	Museum of New Zealand, Te Papa Tongarewa
UNZ	University of New Zealand
VUC	Victoria University College
VUW	Victoria University of Wellington

People

DEB	David Ernest Beaglehole
EMB	Elsie Mary Beaglehole
EMH	Elsie Mary Holmes
JCB	John Cawte Beaglehole
JEP	Janet Elaine Paul
JSB	Joseph Samuel Beaglehole
RAS	R.A. Skelton
RMC	R.M. (Dick) Campbell
THB	Timothy Holmes Beaglehole

Unless indicated otherwise, all referenced letters and documents are in the author's possession. The one exception to this are the letters from J.C. Beaglehole to Janet Paul. These are in the Alexander Turnbull Library, in MS-Papers-5738-01 (the 1945 letters), in one folder for each year until MS-Papers-5738-26 which includes the letters from 1970–71. These letters are closed until 2020 and I am grateful to Janet Paul for allowing me to read and use them.

INTRODUCTION

1   Address to the Chamber Music Federation annual general meeting, 23 March 1968, typescript. An edited version of this was published in *Theme* (Chamber Music Federation of New Zealand), no.13 (October 1968), pp.14–15; 'The Library and the Cosmos', *Turnbull Library Record*, vol.3(n.s.), no.2 (August 1970), pp.65–77; 'From Bookshop Assistant to O.M.: Eminent Ex-bookseller talks to N.Z. Jubilee Conference', Bookseller, no.3418 (26 June 1971), pp.2594–7

2   E.H. McCormick, 'J.C. Beaglehole 1901–71: A Biographical Sketch', *Landfall*, vol.25, no.4 (December 1971), p.423

3   Michael Holroyd, *Works on Paper: The Craft of Biography and Auto-biography* (London: Little, Brown and Company, 2002), p.17

4   Frances Spalding, *Duncan Grant* (London: Chatto and Windus, 1997) p.384

1 FOREBEARS

1   Register of baptisms in Breage, 12 September 1805. Cornwall Record Office. William's occupation is given on the register of John's first marriage.

2   John Rowe, *Cornwall in the Age of the Industrial Revolution* (Liverpool: Liverpool University Press, 1953), pp.158–9

3   ibid., p.162

4   St Austell marriage register, 1826. Cornwall Record Office

5   This paragraph draws on Rowe, *Cornwall in the Age of the Industrial Revolution*, pp.151–6

6   Eric Richards, ed., *The Flinders History of South Australia Social History* (Netley: Wakefield Press, 1986), p.126

7   ibid., p.117

8   Claude Berry, *Cornwall* (London: Robert Hale, 1949), pp.146–7

9   Absalom to Joe Beaglehole, 10 March 1907. J.S. Beaglehole Papers. MS-Papers-2068-10. ATL

10   ibid.

11   The following three paragraphs owe a great deal to Margaret H. Alington, *Unquiet Earth: A History of the Bolton Street Cemetery* (Wellington: Wellington City Council and Ministry of Works and Development, 1978), pp.233–52

12   This is taken from an autobiographical fragment which Ernest wrote in his old age.

13   Alington, *Unquiet Earth*, p.244

14   For this account of the Society I have drawn on J.C. Dakin, 'Mutual Improvement Societies: The Way They Worked', in *New Zealand Journal of Adult Learning*, vol.19, nos.1, 2 (May/October 1987), and the records of the society. MS-Papers-1185. ATL

15   *Leader*, vol.5, no.186 (19 April 1889)

16   *Citizen*, vol.1, no.1 (September 1895), p.1

17   ibid., p.2

18   Charles Stubbs to DEB, 8 December 1894

19   *New Zealand Methodist*, 20 February 1892

20   *Citizen*, vol.1, no.8 (1896)

21   Typescript copy of a diary kept by Joseph Butler on the *Ionic*

22   Amy Ward to JCB, undated (c.1961)

2 CHILDHOOD AND YOUTH

1   Amy Ward interview. LC, MSC 430. Oral History Centre, ATL

2   ibid.

3   JCB to JSB, 21 January 1909. J.S. Beaglehole Papers. MS-Papers-2068-8. ATL

4   DEB to JSB, 28 March 1909. J.S. Beaglehole Papers. MS-Papers-2068-7. ATL

5   Annie to JSB, 21 February 1910. ibid.

6   DEB to JSB, 28 March 1909. ibid.

7   G.W. von Zedlitz, *The Search for a Country* (Hamilton: Paul's Book Arcade, 1963), p.10

8   Cecil and Celia Manson, *Doctor Agnes Bennett* (Wellington: Whitcombe and Tombs, 1960)
9   ibid., p.xiii
10   Margaret H. Alington, *Unquiet Earth: A History of the Bolton Street Cemetery* (Wellington: Wellington City Council and Ministry of Works and Development, 1978), p.244
11   ibid.
12   Annie to JSB, 23 November 1909. J.S. Beaglehole Papers. MS-Papers-2068-7. ATL
13   Ward to JCB, undated (c.1961)
14   Keith to JCB, 4 November 1948
15   Ward to JCB, undated (c.1961)
16   Ward interview. LC, MSC 430. Oral History Centre, ATL
17   Allan Thomas, 'The Savage Clubs: A Spirit of "Bohemian" Comradeship', *Turnbull Library Record*, vol.31 (1998), pp.43–62
18   Ward to JCB, undated (c.1961)
19   ibid.
20   Records of Mount Cook School at this time are held in both the ATL and the J.C. Beaglehole Room in the VUW Library. See also the short history by Don Brown, *Mount Cook School 1875–1975* (Wellington: Mount Cook School Centennial Committee, 1975)
21   JCB in *Smudge*, 1 November 1913
22   *Supplement to the New Zealand Gazette*, 1914, vol.1, pp.131–7
23   *Smudge*, 1913, no.1
24   'The Library and the Cosmos', *Turnbull Library Record*, vol.3, no.2 (August 1970), p.65
25   *Smudge*, 1915, no.4
26   Paragraph based on Ward to JCB, undated (c.1961), and Ward interview, LC, MSC 430. Oral History Centre, ATL
27   Annie to JSB, 21 February 1910. J.S. Beaglehole Papers. MS-Papers-2068-7. ATL
28   Ward interview. LC, MSC 430. Oral History Centre, ATL
29   *Spike*, no.41 (June 1922), p.49. The 'welcome' to Tomlinson as assistant to the professor of English at Victoria was almost certainly written by JCB, who was the magazine's editor.
30   JCB to JEP, 8 August 1968
31   JCB to DEB, 26 April 1931
32   A.W. Beasley, *The Light Accepted: 125 Years of Wellington College* (Wellington: Board of Trustees of Wellington College, 1992), p.78
33   JCB, address to the Chamber Music Federation Annual General Meeting, 23 March 1968, typescript. The following three paragraphs draw on this talk.
34   'Choral Music: Some suggestions', *Evening Post*, 29 July 1921
35   Newspaper report of service, 12 November 1905. Quoted in John Maindonald, *A Radical Religious Heritage* (Auckland: Auckland Unitarian Church, 1991), p.10
36   Wellington Unitarian Free Church, *Calendar*, April 1906
37   Annie to JSB, 23 November 1909. J.S. Beaglehole Papers. MS-Papers-2068-7. ATL
38   Annie to JSB, 21 February 1910. ibid.
39   JCB, 'Verses for my father', 1918. Handbound manuscript volume
40   Johann Nikolaus Forkell, *Johann Sebastian Bach: His Life, Art, and Work*, with notes and appendices by Charles Sanford Terry (London: Constable and Co, 1920); C. Hubert H. Parry, *Johann Sebastian Bach: The Story of the Development of a Great Personality* (New York and London: G.P. Putnam's Sons, 1909)

41 JCB, 'The Parson – Some Meditations', *Calendar*, no.181 (July 1922)
42 Heathcote, report of a speech at the Unitarian Church, *New Zealand Times*, 3 August 1922
43 Unitarian Church leaflet, 1923, R.H. Hooper scrapbook, R.H. Hooper Papers. QMS-0998. ATL
44 Report of the management committee for the year ended 30 September 1924, *Calendar*, November 1924
45 Frank Sargeson, *Collected Stories 1935–1963* (Auckland: Blackwood and Janet Paul, 1964), pp.26–7
46 The following paragraphs draw on Challis Hooper interview. OHInt-0221/2. Oral History Centre, ATL, and the Scrapbook of R.H. Hooper. R.H. Hooper Papers. QMS-0998. ATL
47 Phrase from Hooper interview
48 JCB to EMH, 19 August 1926
49 J.C. Beaglehole Papers. 73-004-01/07. ATL
50 JCB to Sophia Hooper, 28 February 1922. ibid.
51 JCB notebook
52 ibid.
53 JCB to EMH, 19 August 1926
54 ibid.
55 'The Library and the Cosmos', *Turnbull Library Record*, vol.3, no.2 (August 1970), p.67
56 The following three paragraphs draw extensively on JCB's address to the Booksellers Association, 21 April 1971, 'From Bookshop Assistant to O.M.: Eminent ex-bookseller talks to N.Z. Jubilee Conference', *Bookseller*, no.3418 (26 June 1971), pp.2594–7
57 Sydney J. Shep, '"Touching the Mind of the Country": J.C. Beaglehole and the Design of the Centennial Publications', in *Creating a National Spirit: Celebrating New Zealand's Centennial* edited by William Renwick (Wellington: Victoria University Press, 2004), p.198
58 Janet Paul, 'J.C. Beaglehole as Typographer: A Background to the Design of the 1940 Centennial Publications', typescript. Janet Paul Papers. MS-Papers-5640-100. ATL
59 JCB, 'From Bookshop Assistant to O.M.'

3 VICTORIA UNIVERSITY COLLEGE

1 JCB, *Victoria University College: An Essay Towards a History* (Wellington: New Zealand University Press, 1949), pp.181–2
2 The results of college examinations are given in the VUC *Calendar* for the subsequent year.
3 English: 50, 76; Latin: 65, 55; French: 36, 59. University of New Zealand Papers. AAMJ W3119, Box 9. ANZ
4 JCB, *Victoria University College*, pp.34–7
5 Eric McCormick to JCB, undated [14 October 1950]
6 JCB, *Victoria University College*, pp.31–4
7 In the University examinations his results for history were less impressive, with marks of 50 and 63. Mental and moral philosophy was worse, with 50 and 40. The first year of the advanced course in English did not have a university examination, advanced courses being examined only at the end of the second year.
8 JCB, 'The Library and the Cosmos', *Turnbull Library Record*, vol.3, no.2 (August 1970), p.70
9 JCB, notebook, 'books read 1920'

10   Norman and Jeanne Mackenzie, *The Time Traveller: The Life of H.G.Wells* (London: Weidenfeld and Nicolson, 1973), p.323

11   ibid.

12   *University of New Zealand Calendar 1922–23*

13   JCB, 'The Library and the Cosmos', *Turnbull Library Record*, vol.3, no.2 (August 1970), p.71

14   JCB, 'An Old Diary', *New Nation*, vol.11, no.5 (1 June 1925), pp.25–6

15   Quoted by W.H. Oliver, 'J.C. Beaglehole & F.L.W. Wood', in *Eminent Victorians*, edited by Vincent O'Sullivan (Wellington: Stout Research Centre, Victoria University of Wellington, 2000), p.168

16   *Spike*, no.35 (June 1919), p.10

17   JCB, *Victoria University College*, p.186

18   Oliver, 'J.C. Beaglehole & F.L.W. Wood', p.167

19   JCB, 'The Library and the Cosmos', p.68

20   H.N. Parton, 'Bickerton, Alexander William 1842–1929', *Dictionary of New Zealand Biography*, vol.2 (all references to the *Dictionary of New Zealand Biography* are to the five volumes published between 1990 and 2000)

21   C.E. Beeby, *Biography of an Idea: Beeby on Education* (Wellington: New Zealand Council for Educational Research, 1992), p.5

22   JCB, 'Harry Espiner', *Spike*, no.58 (October 1930), pp.35–7

23   'To H.G.S.', *New Nation*, vol.1, no.6 (20 December 1924), p.7. John was awarded second prize for this poem in the *New Nation* poetry competition. He also gained the first prize for his 'Sonnet to a friend'.

24   Brian O'Brien, 'Pope, Charles Quentin Fernie 1900–1961', *Dictionary of New Zealand Biography*, vol.4

25   Beryl Hughes, 'Nicholls, Marjory Lydia 1890–1930', *Dictionary of New Zealand Biography*, vol.3

26   JCB, *Victoria University College*, p.194

27   *Spike*, no.43 (June 1922), pp.33–6

28   JCB, *Victoria University College*, p.194n

29   'A Note on Joseph Conrad', *Spike*, no.46 (September 1924), pp.19–22

30   'On Piracy as a Profession for Young Gentlemen', *Spike*, no.47 (June 1925), pp.13–16

31   John's letter is included in the report on 'The Discussions Club', *Spike*, no.48 (September 1925), pp.55–8

32   '"Devolution or Revolution". Consideration of *Report of Royal Commission on University Education in New Zealand* (Wellington, 1925)', *Spike*, no.48 (September 1925), pp.22–6

33   JCB, *Victoria University College*, p.197

34   *Spike*, no.40 (September 1921), p.52

35   JCB, *Victoria University College*, p.198

36   An indication of Sutherland's views at this time is given in his article 'War and Human Nature', *New Nation*, vol.1, no.1 (15 November 1924)

37   JCB to de la Mare, 23 September 1924

38   JCB, *Victoria University College*, p.185

39   ibid., pp.201–2

40   S.A. Wiren, 'Through the Urewera. A Wellington Party on the Tramp. "Swagging it Over the Ranges"', *New Zealand Free Lance*, 4 and 11 February 1925

41   JCB, 'On Foot Through the Urewera', in *Rata New Zealand Annual*, edited by C.A. Marris, 1931

42   ibid.

43   ibid.

44   S.A. Wiren, 'Kaimatau', *New Zealand Alpine Journal*, vol.3, no.15 (December 1926)

45 *Spike*, no.49 (June 1926), p.21. It was also published in *New Zealand Alpine Journal*, vol.3, no.15 (December 1926), pp.311–12
46 JCB to EMH, 25 August 1925
47 Robert Stout et al. to JCB, 31 May 1926
48 Testimonial for JCB by Sir Robert Stout, 6 June 1923
49 'The Butcher Shop', *Spike*, no.49 (June 1926), pp.38–41
50 'A Departure', *Spike*, no.50 (September 1926), p.30

4 *LONDON, 1926–27*

1   JCB to EMH, 12 August 1926
2   JCB to parents, 12 August 1926
3   JCB to parents, [19 August 1926]
4   ibid.
5   JCB to EMH, 19 August 1926
6   JCB to EMH, 24 August 1926
7   JCB to EMH, 25 August 1926
8   ibid.
9   JCB to parents, 28 August 1926
10 Quoted by Hazel Rowley in *Christina Stead: A Biography* (Melbourne: Heinemann, 1993), p.75
11 JCB to parents, 30 August 1926
12 JCB to parents, 18 September 1926
13 JCB to EMH, 25 August 1926
14 Henning to family, 29 August 1926. Quoted by Kenneth R. Dutton in *Ian Henning (1905–1975): A Man and His Times* (Mt Nemo: Boombana Publications, 2002), p.53
15 JCB to parents, 22 August 1926
16 JCB to parents, 7/8 September 1926
17 JCB to parents, 30 August 1926
18 JCB to parents, 22/24 August 1926
19 JCB to EMH, 25 August 1926
20 JCB to parents, 30 August 1926
21 JCB to parents, 7/8 September 1926
22 This paragraph is based on John's letter to his parents, 18 September 1926
23 Donal O'Donovan, *God's Architect: A Life of Raymond McGrath* (Bray: Kilbride Books, 1995), p.43
24 JCB to parents, 28 September 1926
25 JCB to EMH, 17 September 1926
26 JCB to parents, 18 September 1926
27 JCB to EMH, 30 September 1926
28 ibid.
29 The last sentence of JCB to parents, 28 September 1926
30 JCB to EMH, 3 October 1926
31 Kenneth Clark, *The Gothic Revival* (revised edition) (London: Constable, 1950), p.260
32 JCB to EMH, 3 October 1926
33 JCB to parents, 3 October 1926
34 JCB to parents, 7 February 1927
35 JCB to parents, 12 October 1926
36 JCB to Challis Hooper, 13 November 1926. J.C. Beaglehole Papers. 73-004-01/07. ATL
37 JCB to parents, 27 December 1926
38 JCB to parents, 12 October 1926

39　JCB to Hooper, 13 November 1926
40　JCB to EMH, 28 November 1926
41　JCB to parents, 27 November 1926
42　JCB to parents, 2 November 1926
43　JCB to parents, 15 November 1926
44　JCB to parents, 27 November 1926
45　JCB to parents, 8 March 1927
46　Benjamin Haydon, *Autobiography and Memoirs 1786–1846*, edited by T. Taylor, published in 2 volumes (London: Davies, 1926)
47　JCB to parents, 15 November 1926
48　JCB to parents, 27 November 1926
49　JCB to parents, 23 January 1927
50　JCB to parents, 2 November 1926
51　JCB to parents, 12 October 1926
52　ibid.
53　J.P. Kenyon, *The History Men: The Historical Profession in England since the Renaissance* (London: Weidenfield and Nicolson, 1983) p.196
54　A.L. Rowse, *Historians I Have Known* (London: Duckworth, 1995), p.78
55　Kenyon, *The History Men*, p.206
56　JCB to parents, 15 November 1926
57　JCB to EMH, 12 November 1926
58　JCB to parents, 15 November 1926
59　JCB to EMH, 28 November 1926
60　W.G.K. Duncan to THB, 26 November 1980
61　JCB to parents, 27 November 1926
62　JCB to parents, 13 December 1926
63　Duncan to THB, 26 November 1980
64　JCB to RMC, 2 March 1927. R.M. Campbell Papers. MS-Papers-1900-7. ATL
65　JCB, review in *Parsons Packet*, no.23 (July 1953), pp.8–10
66　JCB to parents, 27 November 1927
67　JCB review in *Parsons Packet*, no.23 (July 1953), pp.8–10
68　JCB to parents, 13 December 1926
69　JCB to parents, 12 October 1926
70　JCB to RMC, 2 March 1927. R.M. Campbell Papers. MS-Papers-1900-7. ATL
71　JCB to parents, 15 November 1926
72　JCB to parents, 27 November 1926
73　*New Zealand Times*, 8 January 1927
74　*New Zealand Times*, 14 December 1926
75　JCB to parents, 15 November 1926
76　JCB to RMC, 2 March 1927. R.M. Campbell Papers. MS-Papers-1900-7. ATL
77　ibid.
78　JCB to parents, 27 December 1926
79　JCB to parents, 8 January 1927
80　JCB to parents, 27 December 1926
81　ibid.
82　JCB to parents, 8 January 1927
83　JCB to EMH, 17 September 1926
84　JCB to EMH, 12 November 1926
85　JCB to parents, 23 January 1927
86　ibid.
87　JCB to parents, 16 May 1927
88　JCB to EMH, 28 November 1926

89 JCB to parents, 27 January 1927
90 JCB to parents, 7 February 1927
91 JCB to EMH, 30 May 1927
92 JCB to parents, 22 March 1927
93 JCB to parents, 4 April 1927
94 JCB to parents, 10 April 1927
95 JCB to parents, 3 May 1927
96 JCB to parents, 16 May 1927
97 JCB to parents, 7 February 1927
98 JCB to parents, 22 March 1927
99 JCB to parents, 16 May 1927
100 JCB to parents, 16 June 1927
101 JCB to parents, 10 April 1927
102 JCB to parents, 16 June 1927
103 JCB to parents, 10 July 1927
104 JCB to parents, 23 January 1927
105 JCB to parents, 10 July 1927
106 JCB to EMH, 14 July 1927
107 JCB to parents, 10 July 1927
108 JCB to parents, 20 July 1927
109 JCB to EMH, 22 July 1927
110 JCB to parents, 20 July 1927
111 DEB to JCB, 4 September 1927
112 JCB to parents, 20 July 1927
113 JCB to parents, 8 August 1927
114 JCB to EMH, 3 August 1927
115 JCB to parents, 8 August 1927
116 JCB to EMH, 3 August 1927
117 JCB to parents, 8 August 1927
118 ibid.
119 ibid.
120 JCB to parents, 23 August 1927
121 JCB to parents, 9 September 1927
122 JCB to parents, 7 October 1927
123 JCB to EMH, 4 October 1927
124 JCB to parents, 17 October 1927
125 JCB to parents, 22 September 1927
126 JCB to parents, 7 October 1927
127 JCB to parents, 13 December 1927
128 JCB to EMH, 4 October 1927
129 JCB to parents, 3 November 1927
130 JCB to parents, 13 December 1927
131 JCB to parents, 7 October 1927
132 'War Disabilities: Plea for Tolerance: A Night in Neustadt', *Evening Post*, 21 December 1927
133 *New Zealand Worker*, 4 January 1928
134 *Spike*, no.53 (June 1928)
135 Peter Fraser to JCB, 21 December 1927
136 Eric McCormick to JCB, 3 November 1970
137 JCB to parents, 17 October 1927
138 JCB to parents, 23 December 1927
139 JCB to parents, 13 December 1927
140 JCB to parents, 23 December 1927
141 JCB to parents, 9 September 1927
142 JCB to parents, 13 December 1927

143 JCB to parents, 17 November 1927
144 JCB to EMH, 16 November 1927
145 DEB to JCB, 1 January 1928
146 JCB to parents, 17 November 1927
147 JCB to parents, 8 January 1928

5 *LONDON, 1928–29*

1   JCB to parents, 7 February 1927
2   JCB to parents, 17 October 1927
3   T.A. Hunter to JCB, 12 December 1927
4   JCB to EMH, 28 April, 17 May 1927
5   JCB to EMH, 12 August 1927
6   JCB to EMH, 20 September 1927
7   JCB to EMH, 17 October 1927
8   JCB to EMH, 3 August 1927
9   JCB to EMH, 12 December 1927
10   JCB to EMH, 26 August 1927
11   DEB to JCB, 2 January 1928
12   JCB to parents, 17 November 1927
13   JCB to EMH, 6 February 1928
14   JCB to parents, 23 January 1928
15   JCB to EMH, 6 February 1928
16   JCB to EMH, 29 November 1927
17   JCB to parents, 21 February 1928
18   JCB to parents, 7 February 1928
19   JCB to parents, 23 January 1928
20   JCB to parents, 21 February 1928
21   JCB to parents, 6 March 1928
22   JCB to parents, 20 March 1928
23   JCB to EMH, 14 March 1928
24   DEB to JCB, 6 May 1928
25   JCB to parents, 3 May 1928
26   JCB to Challis Hooper, 4 May 1928. J.C. Beaglehole Papers. 73-004-01/07. ATL
27   JCB to parents, 3 May 1928
28   Raymond McGrath, 'Spanish Moonshine: Some Fragments of a Travel Diary', *Architectural Review*, vol.64, no.381 (August 1928)
29   Ian MacKillop, *F.R. Leavis: A Life in Criticism* (London: Penguin, 1997) p.61
30   JCB to parents, 17 May 1928
31   JCB to EMH, 20 May 1928
32   JCB to parents, 30 May 1928
33   JCB to Hooper, 4 May 1928. J.C. Beaglehole Papers. 73-004-01/07. ATL
34   JCB to parents, 12 July 1928
35   JCB to mother, 10 July 1928
36   JCB to parents, 12 July 1928
37   JCB to parents, 18 July 1928
38   ibid.
39   JCB to parents, 30 July 1928
40   ibid.
41   JCB to parents, 8 August 1928
42   JCB to parents, 20 August 1928
43   JCB to parents, 19 October 1928

44 Henning, quoted in McGrath to JCB, 16 August 1928
45 JCB to Hooper, 15 October 1928. J.C. Beaglehole Papers. 73-004-01/07. ATL
46 JCB to parents, 15 June 1928
47 McGrath to JCB, 7 June 1928
48 JCB to Hooper, 4 March 1929. J.C. Beaglehole Papers. 73-004-01/07. ATL
49 JCB to parents, 28 June 1928
50 McGrath to JCB, 7 August 1928
51 JCB to parents, 23 December 1928
52 JCB to parents, 21 September 1928
53 JCB to parents, 21 November 1928
54 JCB to parents, 20 August 1928
55 JCB to parents, 8 January 1929
56 JCB to parents, 29 June 1927
57 JCB to parents, 17 November 1927
58 JCB to parents, 13 December 1927
59 JCB to parents, 21 February 1928
60 JCB to parents, 6 March 1928
61 W.H. Oliver, 'J.C. Beaglehole & F.L.W. Wood', in *Eminent Victorians*, edited by Vincent O'Sullivan (Wellington: Stout Research Centre, Victoria University of Wellington, 2000), p.173
62 JCB to parents, 20 August 1928
63 JCB to parents 7 September 1928
64 JCB to parents, 2 November 1928
65 James Ritchie and Jane Ritchie, 'Beaglehole, Ernest 1906–1965', in *Dictionary of New Zealand Biography*, vol.5
66 JCB to parents, 21 September 1928
67 Ernest to JSB, 3 October 1928. Ernest Beaglehole Papers. J.C. Beaglehole Room, VUW Library
68 JCB to EMH, 20 May 1928
69 Keith Sinclair, *A History of the University of Auckland 1883–1983* (Auckland: Auckland University Press and Oxford Univeristy Press, 1983), p.153
70 JCB to Hooper, 4 March 1929. J.C. Beaglehole Papers. 73-004-01/07. ATL
71 JCB to parents, 19 October 1928
72 JCB to parents, 2 November 1928
73 JCB to parents, 19 October 1928
74 ibid.
75 JCB to parents, 27 November 1928
76 JCB to Hooper, 4 March 1929. J.C. Beaglehole Papers. 73-004-01/07. ATL
77 JCB to parents, 21 September 1928
78 JCB to parents, 5 October 1928
79 JCB to parents, 7 September 1928
80 McGrath to JCB, 8 September 1928
81 JCB to parents, 11 December 1928
82 JCB to parents, 27 November 1928
83 Ernest to JSB, 5 January 1929. Ernest Beaglehole Papers. J.C. Beaglehole Room, VUW Library
84 JCB to parents, 27 November 1928
85 JCB to parents, 13 November 1928
86 ibid.
87 JCB to parents, 4 February 1929
88 JCB to parents, 27 November 1928
89 JCB to parents, 11 December 1928
90 JCB to parents, 8 January 1929

91 JCB to parents, 23 December 1928
92 JCB to EMH, 31 December 1928
93 JCB to parents, 23 December 1928
94 JCB to parents, 8 January 1929
95 JCB to parents, 4 February 1929
96 ibid.
97 JCB to parents, 8 January 1929
98 JCB to parents, 4 February 1929
99 JCB to Hooper, 4 March 1929. J.C. Beaglehole Papers. 73-004-01/07. ATL
100 JCB to parents, 4 February 1929
101 JCB to parents, 19 February 1929
102 JCB to Hooper, 4 March 1929. J.C. Beaglehole Papers. 73-004-01/07. ATL
103 JCB to parents, 5 April 1929
104 ibid.
105 ibid.
106 JCB to parents, 18 April 1929
107 ibid.
108 McGrath to JCB, 16 August 1928
109 ibid.
110 McGrath to JCB, 23 September 1928
111 JCB to parents, 18 April 1929
112 JCB to parents, 5 April 1929
113 JCB to parents, 2 May 1929
114 JCB to parents, 16 May 1929
115 JCB to Hooper, 4 March 1929. J.C. Beaglehole Papers. 73-004-01/07. ATL
116 The 'private note' with the news does not survive. His parents' replies, expressing their delight, are dated 10 February 1929.
117 JCB to EMH, 4 April 1929
118 L.M. Holmes to EMH & JCB, 7 May 1929
119 Ernest to JSB, 23 March 1929. Ernest Beaglehole Papers. J.C. Beaglehole Room, VUW Library
120 Ernest to JSB, 26 July 1929. ibid.
121 JCB to parents, 16 May 1929
122 Ernest to JSB, 15 June 1929. Ernest Beaglehole Papers. J.C. Beaglehole Room, VUW Library
123 JCB to DEB, 31 May 1929
124 JCB to DEB, 14 June 1929
125 JCB to DEB, 12 July 1929
126 JCB to DEB, 3 August 1929
127 Ernest to DEB, 15 June 1929. Ernest Beaglehole Papers. J.C. Beaglehole Room, VUW Library
128 JCB to Hooper, 11 July 1929. J.C. Beaglehole Papers. 73-004-01/07. ATL
129 Ernest to DEB, 11 July 1929. Ernest Beaglehole Papers. J.C. Beaglehole Room, VUW Library
130 Ernest to DEB, 26 July 1929. ibid.
131 JCB to DEB, 28 June 1929
132 Ernest to DEB, 11 July 1929. Ernest Beaglehole Papers. J.C. Beaglehole Room, VUW Library
133 JCB to Hooper, 11 July 1929. J.C. Beaglehole Papers. 73-004-01/07. ATL
134 JCB to DEB, 26 July 1929
135 Ernest to DEB, 7 August 1929. Ernest Beaglehole Papers. J.C. Beaglehole Room, VUW Library
136 JCB to DEB, 3 August 1929
137 JCB to DEB, 12 September 1929
138 JCB to Hooper, 11 July 1929. J.C. Beaglehole Papers. 73-004-01/07. ATL

139 C.W. de Kiewiet to THB, 4 June 1984
140 JCB to parents, 4 February 1929
141 JCB to parents, 17 November 1927
142 JCB to parents, 29 June 1927
143 JCB to JEP, 22 October 1958
144 *Architectural Review*, vol.72, no.429 (August 1932)
145 Kenneth R. Dutton, *Ian Henning (1905–1975): A Man and His Times* (Mt Nemo: Boombana Publications, 2002)
146 McGrath to JCB, 20 April 1950
147 JCB to parents, 20 August 1928

6 *DUNEDIN, HAMILTON, AUCKLAND, 1930–32*

1 JCB to EMH, 20 October 1929
2 Ada Paterson died on 13 November 1928
3 JCB to Kathleen McKay, 9 February 1930
4 ibid.
5 ibid.
6 JCB to DEB, [5 March? 1930]
7 JCB to RMC, 21 March 1930. R.M. Campbell Papers. MS-Papers-1900-7. ATL
8 Roy Shuker, *Educating the Workers? A History of the Workers' Education Association in New Zealand* (Palmerston North: Dunmore Press, 1984) p.12. I draw on Shuker for the following paragraph.
9 'In the Open: Education under Canvas. W.E.A. Summer School', *Evening Post*, 31 January 1923, p.9
10 JCB to DEB, 12 March 1930
11 JCB to DEB, 23 March 1930
12 JCB to RMC, 21 March 1930. R.M. Campbell Papers. MS-Papers-1900-7. ATL
13 JCB to DEB, 4 April 1930
14 ibid.
15 JCB to DEB, 6 September 1930
16 ibid.
17 JCB to DEB, 18 April 1930
18 JCB to DEB, 27 June 1930
19 JCB to DEB, 14 June 1930
20 JCB to DEB, 18 May 1930
21 JCB to DEB, 14 June 1930
22 JCB to Sophia Hooper, 16 June 1930. J.C. Beaglehole Papers. 73-004-01/07. ATL
23 JCB to DEB, 13 July 1930
24 JCB to McKay, 20 July 1930
25 ibid.
26 JCB to DEB, 4 October 1930
27 ibid.
28 JCB to McKay, 5 December 1930
29 Fisher to JCB, 13 November 1930
30 Nothing came of the planned volume. A note in John's hand enclosed in his father's copy of *New Zealand: A Short History*, giving the dates of writing and revision of that book, makes it clear that the essay of December 1930 eventually grew into the *Short History*.
31 JCB to Registrar, Auckland University College, 7 January 1931
32 Christopher Horton, 'Richmond, Norman McDonald 1897–1971', *Dictionary*

of New Zealand Biography, vol.4. Other material in this paragraph is drawn from this source.

33 JCB to DEB, 3 March 1931
34 G.P. Barton, 'de la Mare, Frederick Archibald 1877–1960', *Dictionary of New Zealand Biography*, vol.3
35 JCB to DEB, 3 March 1931
36 JCB to DEB, 8 March 1931
37 ibid.
38 WEA, Waikato District. Annual Report, 1931, p.1
39 JCB to DEB, 3 March 1931
40 JCB to DEB, 8 March 1931
41 JCB to DEB, 15 March 1931
42 JCB to DEB, 26 April 1931
43 JCB to DEB, 8 March 1931
44 JCB to DEB, 15 March 1931
45 JCB to DEB, 29 March 1931
46 JCB to DEB, 5 April 1931
47 JCB to DEB, 20 April 1931
48 ibid.
49 ibid.
50 Ward to EMB, 6 November 1971
51 JCB to DEB, 19 June 1931
52 WEA, Annual Report, p.3
53 ibid., p.2
54 JCB to DEB, 19 June 1931
55 WEA, Annual Report, p.1
56 JCB to DEB, 23 July 1931
57 WEA, Annual Report, p.3
58 JCB to McKay, 1 August 1931
59 JCB to DEB, 6 August 1931
60 JCB to DEB, 8 July 1931
61 WEA, Annual Report, p.2
62 JCB to DEB, 30 July 1931
63 JCB to DEB, 14 August 1931
64 JCB to DEB, 31 August 1931
65 JCB to editor, *New Zealand Herald*, 29 August 1931 (unpublished)
66 JCB to DEB, 31 August 1931
67 JCB to DEB, 14 October 1931
68 JCB to DEB, 30 October 1931
69 JCB to DEB, 25 November 1931
70 Richmond, testimonial for JCB, 8 December 1932
71 'Workers' Educational Association (Auckland University District) Programme for Country Members, 1932', Auckland, 18 April 1932. This programme gives the titles of the lectures.
72 Richmond, testimonial for JCB, 8 December 1932. He was comparing it not only with other courses prepared in Auckland but also with a number prepared by the Canterbury WEA and used by Auckland.
73 JCB to DEB, 3 March 1932
74 JCB to editor, *Evening Post*, 27 February 1932 (published with cuts, 3 March 1932)
75 Abrams v. U.S. 250 U.S. 616(1919). I have made a minor correction in John's quote where, most uncharacteristically, he had dropped a phrase.
76 JCB to DEB, 17 March 1932
77 ibid.
78 'Verse Competition', *Art in New Zealand*, vol.4, no.15 (March 1932), p.200

79 Keith Sinclair, *A History of the University of Auckland 1883–1983* (Auckland: Auckland University Press and Oxford Univeristy Press, 1983), p.149
80 JCB to DEB, 18 March 1932
81 JCB to DEB, 27 March 1932
82 JCB to DEB, 10 April 1932
83 JCB to McKay, 10 April 1932
84 JCB to DEB, 7 April 1932
85 JCB to DEB, 9 May 1932
86 Sinclair, *University of Auckland*, pp.152–3
87 Keith Sinclair, *A History of New Zealand* (Harmondsworth: Penguin, 1959), p.258
88 Finance Act 1932, section 59
89 Sinclair, *A History of New Zealand*, p.258
90 Sinclair, *University of Auckland*, p.152
91 JCB to DEB, 9 May 1932
92 Masters to Registrar, 28 April 1932. Keith Sinclair Papers. Auckland University Library. Quoted in Ingrid Horrocks, 'Communism and Hysterics: Academic Freedom and Auckland University's Retrenchment of J.C. Beaglehole 1932' (BA Hons research essay in history, VUW, 1996), p.15
93 JCB to DEB, 9 May 1932
94 Registrar to Masters, 5 May 1932. Keith Sinclair Papers. Auckland University Library. Quoted in Ingrid Horrocks, 'Communism and Hysterics', p.15
95 JCB to DEB, 9 May 1932
96 The letter quoted by Keith Sinclair, *University of Auckland*, p.153, is not the one shown to Fowlds but the revised version. The two versions are in F.A. de la Mare, *Academic Freedom in New Zealand, 1932–34* (Auckland: Unicorn Press, 1935), pp.13–15
97 JCB to DEB, 9 May 1932
98 de la Mare, *Academic Freedom*, pp.16–17
99 JCB to DEB, 9 May 1932. Mulgan later wrote to de la Mare, 30 March 1935: 'You say the newspapers refused "Communism and Hysterics" because they disagreed with its opinions. That is only a half truth . . . I refused this letter because I thought publication against public policy. Please bear in mind the nature of the times.' F.A. de la Mare Papers. MS-Papers-3865-2/3/6C. ATL
100 Sinclair, *University of Auckland*, p.154
101 ibid.
102 JCB to DEB, 9 May 1932
103 de la Mare, *Academic Freedom*, pp.18–20
104 Fowlds to JCB, 26 May 1932
105 JCB to DEB, 6 June 1932
106 JCB to DEB, 18 July 1932
107 JCB editors, *Auckland Star* and *New Zealand Herald*, 24 May 1932
108 Editor, *New Zealand Herald* to JCB, 26 May 1932. The managing editor of the *Auckland Star* wrote some time later, on 6 June, also declining to print the letter, and saying: 'The state has surely the right to forbid the Communist to preach the theory as well as the practice of violence.'
109 Editor, *New Zealand Herald* to JCB, 30 May 1932
110 Editor, *New Zealand Worker* to JCB, 15 June 1932
111 JCB to DEB, 6 June 1932
112 Hunter to JCB, 18 July 1932
113 Fisher to JCB, 9 July 1932
114 JCB to DEB, 20 June 1932
115 JCB to DEB, 18 July 1932
116 J.C. Beaglehole File. New Zealand Security Intelligence Service Papers

117 JCB to DEB, 20 June, 4 July, 11 July 1932
118 JCB to DEB, 18 July 1932
119 JCB to DEB, 18 August 1932
120 JCB to DEB, 16 September 1932
121 JCB to DEB, 18 August 1932
122 de la Mare to Fowlds, 13 August 1932. F.A. de la Mare Papers. MS-Papers-3865-2/3/4A. ATL
123 JCB to DEB, 18 August 1932
124 Airey to Fowlds, 14 September 1932; Belshaw to Fowlds, 15 September 1932. Both cited in Sinclair, *University of Auckland*, p.157
125 de la Mare, *Academic Freedom*, pp.25–26
126 ibid., pp.29–30
127 Richmond to de la Mare, 24 September 1932. F.A. de la Mare Papers. MS-Papers-3865-2/3/4A. ATL
128 Richmond to de la Mare, 24 September 1932. F.A. de la Mare Papers. MS-Papers-3865-2/3/4A. ATL. In this letter Richmond tells de la Mare of what he had learned of the council meeting from a long conversation with Mahon.
129 ibid.
130 de la Mare to H.R. Bannister, 2 September 1932. F.A. de la Mare Papers. MS-Papers-3865-2/3/4A. ATL. Bannister was the editor of *Spike*. De la Mare sent him material on the case to be used for an article.
131 Richmond to de la Mare, 7 September 1932. ibid.
132 Richmond to de la Mare, 24 September 1932. ibid.
133 Burbidge to de la Mare, 28 October 1932. ibid.
134 Sinclair, *University of Auckland*, p.158
135 ibid.
136 O'Shea to Hackett, 26 May 1932 Quoted in Sinclair, *University of Auckland*, p.158
137 O'Shea once said that he would like to 'close up' Richmond because of his political views. As Sinclair says, 'It is difficult not to suppose, what Beaglehole's friends suspected in 1933 [sic], that he [O'Shea] had wanted to close Beaglehole up too.' Sinclair, *University of Auckland*, p.159
138 'Academic Freedom, the Case of Dr Beaglehole'. This paper grew to be de la Mare's *Academic Freedom*. O'Shea's comment is recorded in an annotation on p.4 of the draft made in John's handwriting. F.A. de la Mare Papers. MS-Papers-3865-2/3/4B. ATL
139 JCB, *Victoria University College: An Essay Towards a History* (Wellington: New Zealand University Press, 1949), p.214
140 Hunter to de la Mare, 10 October 1932; Richmond to de la Mare, 4 October 1932. F.A. de la Mare Papers. MS-Papers-3865-2/3/4A. ATL. Writing to John on 8 November 1932, Hunter did say: 'I must confess that some members of the Auckland Council, not unfavourable to you, believe the case was decided on the basis of economy, though in their opinion a mistaken conclusion was reached'. He went on to say that his 'feeling' was 'that in the whole Auckland business the sinister figure is O'Shea'.
141 *New Zealand Truth*, 5 October 1932
142 Sinclair, *University of Auckland*, pp.159–68
143 JCB to DEB, 2 November 1932
144 JCB to DEB, 25 November 1931
145 JCB to DEB, 2 November 1932. There is a note on this show in *Art in New Zealand*, vol.4, no.15, (March 1932), pp.219–20
146 JCB to EMB, 23 December 1932
147 JCB to DEB, 5 December 1932
148 ibid.
149 JCB to EMB, 23 December 1932

150 JCB to DEB, 22 December 1932
151 This para draws on JCB to EMB, 27, 29, 29 December 1932 and 1 January
     1933
152 *Evening Post*, 23 October 1971

7 *'UNEMPLOYED AND ODD JOBS', 1933–35*

1   JCB to Norman Richmond, 7 February 1933
2   JCB to Richmond, 9 March 1933
3   JCB to Richmond, 18 January 1933
4   See, for example, his review of John Strachey, *The Coming Struggle for
    Power*, in *Phoenix*, vol.2, no.2 (June 1933)
5   JCB to Richmond, 5 December 1933
6   Unfortunately, Richmond's letters to John for 1933 do not seem to have
    survived. Copies survive of many of those he wrote from March 1934 on.
7   JCB to Richmond, 20 February 1933
8   JCB to Richmond, 9 March 1933
9   ibid.
10 JCB to Richmond, 12 February 1933
11 JCB to Richmond, 18 January 1933
12 JCB to Kathleen Mckay, 6 February 1933
13 JCB to Richmond, 12 February 1933
14 ibid.
15 *Phoenix*, vol.2, no.2 (June 1933)
16 JCB to Richmond, 25 May 1933
17 JCB to Richmond, 7 November 1933
18 *Art in New Zealand*, vol.7, no.1 (September 1934)
19 JCB to Richmond, 18 April 1934
20 This section was published in *New Zealand Best Poems of 1934*, edited by
    C.A. Marris (Wellington: Harry H. Tombs, n.d.(?1935))
21 JCB to Richmond, 12 February 1933
22 Roger Robinson and Nelson Wattie, eds., *The Oxford Companion to New
    Zealand Literature* (Melbourne: Oxford University Press New Zealand,
    1998) p.49
23 *Tomorrow*, 29 August 1934, reprinted in *A Book of New Zealand Verse
    1923–45*, edited by Allen Curnow (Christchurch: Caxton, 1945)
24 Robinson and Wattie, *Oxford Companion*, p.45
25 ibid.
26 Denis Glover, 'Pointers to Parnassus', *Tomorrow*, 30 October 1935, p.17.
    Quoted in Lawrence Jones, *Picking Up the Traces: The Making of a New
    Zealand Literary Culture 1932–1945* (Wellington: Victoria University Press,
    2004), p.154
27 Christchurch *Press*, 18 June 1936
28 JCB to Richmond, 6 April 1933
29 JCB to Richmond, 25 May 1933
30 ibid.
31 JCB to McKay, 15 June 1933
32 JCB to Richmond, 18 July 1933
33 JCB, *Victoria University College: An Essay Towards a History* (Wellington:
    New Zealand University Press, 1949), pp.213–19; Rachel Barrowman,
    Victoria University of Wellington 1899–1999 (Wellington: Victoria
    University Press, 1999), pp.92–4
34 JCB, *Victoria University College*, p.215
35 Barrowman, *Victoria University*, p.93

36   [JCB], 'Academic Memoirs 1934'. unpublished typescript
37   JCB, *Victoria University College*, p.217
38   James's letter, together with other material on the controversy, is reprinted in
     F.A. de la Mare, *Academic Freedom in New Zealand, 1932–34* (Auckland:
     Unicorn Press, 1935), pp.40–5
39   JCB to editor, *Evening Post*, 17 July 1933
40   JCB to Richmond, 25 July 1933
41   JCB, 'Academic Memoirs 1934'
42   JCB to Richmond, 7 November 1933
43   JCB, 'Academic Memoirs 1934'
44   JCB, *Victoria University College*, p.217
45   JCB to Richmond, 7 November 1933
46   JCB to Richmond, 25 July 1933
47   JCB to Richmond, 7 November 1933
48   JCB to de la Mare, 3 November 1933
49   JCB to Richmond, 7 November 1933
50   JCB to Richmond, 25 July 1933
51   ibid.
52   JCB to Richmond, 7 November 1933
53   It appeared on 19 October, 2 November, 16 November, 30 November and 14
     December 1933, 18 January, 1 February, 15 February, 1 March, 15 March,
     29 March, 12 April, 26 April, 10 May, 24 May and 7 June 1934
54   JCB to Richmond, 7 November 1933
55   Chris Hilliard, 'Island Stories: The Writing of New Zealand History 1920–
     1940' (MA thesis, University of Auckland, 1997), p.105
56   JCB to DEB, 6 October 1933
57   JCB to Richmond, 5 February 1934
58   JCB to Richmond, 13 March 1934
59   JCB to Richmond, 14 March 1934
60   JCB to Richmond, 1 July 1934
61   JCB to EMB, 15 July 1934
62   JCB to DEB, 31 July 1934
63   JCB to Richmond, 5 February 1934
64   JCB to Richmond, 27 February 1934
65   JCB to Richmond, 30 July 1934
66   JCB to Registrar, Auckland University College, 6 September 1933
67   JCB to DEB, 16 November 1933
68   Keith Sinclair, *A History of the University of Auckland 1883–1983*
     (Auckland: Auckland University Press and Oxford Univeristy Press, 1983),
     p.159
69   JCB to Richmond, 15 November 1933
70   JCB to McKay, 14 December 1933
71   JCB to Richmond, 5 December 1933
72   JCB to Richmond, 5 February 1934
73   JCB to McKay, 14 December 1933
74   Sinclair, *University of Auckland*, p.159
75   JCB to McKay, 14 December 1933
76   JCB to Richmond, 5 February 1934
77   JCB to Richmond, 1 July 1934
78   JCB to Richmond, 27 July 1934
79   JCB to Richmond, 5 September 1934
80   JCB to DEB, 31 October 1934
81   ibid.
82   JCB to Richmond, 31 October 1934
83   ibid.

84　von Zedlitz to JCB, 2 November 1934
85　*New Zealand Parliamentary Debates*, vol.240 (18 September–10 November, 1934), pp.1076–87
86　*Dominion*, 6 November 1934, p.10; *Evening Post*, 6 November 1934, p.8.
87　JCB to DEB, 7 November 1934
88　JCB to Richmond, 31 October 1934
89　JCB to Richmond, 6 March 1935
90　R.M. Campbell, 'In the name of national security', *New Zealand Listener*, 23 February 1974, p.9
91　JCB to Richmond, 18 February 1935
92　JCB to Richmond, 6 March 1935
93　C.E. Beeby, *The Biography of an Idea: Beeby on Education* (Wellington: New Zealand Council for Educational Research, 1992), p.93
94　J.A. Williamson to JCB, 5 January 1935
95　JCB to Richmond, 18 February 1935
96　ibid.
97　ibid.
98　JCB to McKay, 13 April 1935
99　JCB to Richmond, 6 March 1935. John thought that the Sydney Vice-Chancellor might have had that information from a council member called Forsyth, who was 'bitterly opposed' to John and at the time of the council meeting was in Sydney (ibid. and also JCB to Richmond, 18 February 1935)
100　JCB to Airey, 9 May 1935. Willis Airey Papers. MSS and Archives, A-201, box 25, file 61. Auckland University Library
101　Hunter to de la Mare, 11 March 1935. F.A. de la Mare Papers. MS-Papers-3865-2/3/5B. ATL
102　Peter Munz, 'Wood, Frederick Lloyd Whitfield 1903–1989', *Dictionary of New Zealand Biography*, vol.5
103　JCB to Richmond, 18 February 1936
104　Review by F. Kingdon Ward, *Sunday Times* (UK), 9 December 1934
105　*Sydney Morning Herald*, 5 January 1935
106　ibid.
107　*New York Times*, 10 February 1935
108　*Spectator*, 2 November 1934
109　JCB, *The Exploration of the Pacific* (London: A. & C. Black, 1934), p.373
110　ibid., p.374
111　ibid., p.375
112　ibid., pp.380–1
113　David Mackay, 'Exploring the Pacific, Exploring James Cook', in *Pacific Empires: Essays in Honour of Glyndwr Williams*, edited by Alan Frost and Jane Sampson (Melbourne: Melbourne University Press, 1999), p.254
114　JCB to Richmond, 18 February 1935
115　James Ritchie, 'Sutherland, Ivan Lorin George 1897–1952', *Dictionary of New Zealand Biography*, vol.4
116　Jane Garrett, *An Artist's Daughter: With Christopher Perkins in New Zealand 1929–34* (Auckland: Shoal Bay Press, 1986), p.73
117　JCB to Richmond, 31 July/1 September 1935
118　*Tomorrow*, 28 August 1935, pp.5–7; *Pacific Affairs*, vol.9, no.3 (September 1936), pp.481–3. The quotes which follow are all taken from the review in *Tomorrow*
119　JCB to Richmond, 31 July/1 September 1935
120　JCB to DEB, 12 November 1935
121　JCB to Registrar, 27 August 1934
122　JCB to Richmond,17 December 1935
123　JCB to DEB, 12 December 1935

124 Boyd-Wilson to JCB, 2 December 1935
125 JCB to Richmond, 27 January 1936
126 'James Cook and Mercury Bay' (address delivered at the unveiling of the Cook Memorial at Mercury Bay on 9 November 1969), pp.1–2
127 JCB to DEB, 18 September 1934
128 Williamson to JCB, 28 August 1935
129 Williamson to JCB, 23 December 1935
130 JCB to Duncan, 28 June 1936
131 My discussion of JCB's *New Zealand: A Short History* (London: Allen & Unwin, 1936) draws on Chris Hilliard, 'Island Stories', especially pp.102–7
132 *New Zealand Herald*, 22 August 1936
133 *Tomorrow*, 22 July 1936
134 Jock Phillips, 'Of Verandahs and Fish and Chips and Footie on Saturday Afternoon', *New Zealand Journal of History*, vol.24, no.2 (October 1990), p.124
135 JCB, *New Zealand: A Short History*, pp.57–8
136 ibid., p.59
137 ibid., p.73
138 ibid., p.84
139 ibid., p.125
140 ibid., p.94
141 ibid., p.114
142 ibid., p.115
143 ibid., p.152
144 ibid.
145 ibid., p.157
146 JCB, *New Zealand: A Short History*, p.159
147 Chris Hilliard, 'Island Stories', p.106
148 JCB, 'The New Zealand Scholar', in *The Feel of Truth: Essays in New Zealand and Pacific History*, edited by Peter Munz (Wellington: A.H. & A.W. Reed, 1969), p.244

8 VICTORIA UNIVERSITY COLLEGE, 1936–49

1 Downie Stewart to JCB, 17 November 1938
2 Greg Bowron, 'Firth, Cedric Harold 1908–1994', *Dictionary of New Zealand Biography*, vol.5; JCB to Richmond, 6 August 1936
3 JCB to Richmond, 6 August 1936
4 JCB to DEB, 16 August 1936
5 JCB to McKay, 7 September 1936
6 JCB to Richmond, 29 December 1936
7 ibid.
8 ibid.
9 ibid.
10 ibid.
11 JCB to DEB, 19 July 1936
12 C.E. Beeby, *The Biography of an Idea: Beeby on Education* (Wellington: New Zealand Council for Educational Research, 1992), p.93
13 'The Beginnings of the NZCER', reminiscences of C.E. Beeby at the New Zealand Council for Educational Research 50th Anniversary Dinner, Wellington, 19 May 1984, typescript, pp.10–11. I am grateful to W.L. Renwick who drew this to my attention.
14 ibid.
15 JCB to Richmond, 29 December 1936

16 ibid.
17 JCB, *The University of New Zealand: An Historical Study* (Wellington: New Zealand Council for Educational Research, 1937), pp.viii–x
18 ibid., p.13
19 ibid.
20 ibid., p.388
21 ibid., pp.388–9
22 *Evening Post*, 10 April 1937
23 *New Zealand Free Lance*, 5 May 1937
24 *Evening Star* (Dunedin), 17 April 1937
25 Christchurch *Press*, 17 April 1937
26 *Craccum*, 29 July 1937
27 JCB, *The University of New Zealand*, p.406
28 ibid., p.407
29 E.H. McCormick, 'J.C. Beaglehole 1901–71: A Biographical Sketch', *Landfall*, vol.25, no.4 (December 1971), p.417
30 JCB to Richmond, 29 December 1936
31 Rachel Barrowman, *Victoria University of Wellington 1899–1999: A History* (Wellington: Victoria University Press, 1999) pp.60–1
32 JCB to Richmond, 29 December 1936
33 JCB to DEB, 16 August 1936
34 JCB, *Victoria University College: An Essay Towards a History* (Wellington: New Zealand University Press, 1949), p.228
35 ibid., p.227
36 Susan Skudder, in '"Bringing It Home": New Zealand Responses to the Spanish Civil War 1936–1939' (PhD thesis, Waikato Univerity, 1982), states (p.302) that John was chairman of the Wellington Spanish Medical Aid Committee (SMAC). However, a letter from the Wellington SMAC to the Auckland SMAC, dated June 1938, on its official letterhead gave his position as vice-president (along with Professor Kirk). (George Jackson Papers. MS-Papers-90-234, box 6, folder 2. ATL)
37 JCB, *Victoria University College*, p.230
38 JCB to DEB, 4 October 1937
39 JCB to DEB, 27 January 1938
40 JCB to DEB, 4 February 1938
41 ibid.
42 J.W. Davidson, 'The New Zealand Scholar: A Note on J.C.Beaglehole, 1901–1971', *Journal of Pacific History*, vol.7 (1972), p.153
43 In the above paragraph I have drawn on the institute's booklet, *The New Zealand Institute of International Affairs: Origins, Developments, Prospects* (2002)
44 JCB to Richmond, 10 December 1939
45 An undated cutting of the review, signed C.R.A., which appears to be from the *Otago Daily Times*, was in the copy of *Contemporary New Zealand* owned by Joe Beaglehole
46 JCB, 'New Zealand in the Commonwealth: An Attempt at Objectivity', in *Contemporary New Zealand: A Survey of Domestic and Foreign Policy*, edited by G.R. Powles (Wellington: New Zealand Institute of International Affairs, 1939), p.5
47 Colin Aikman, 'Powles, Guy Richardson 1905–1994', *Dictionary of New Zealand Biography*, vol.5
48 JCB, 'New Zealand in the Commonwealth', p.3
49 Peter Munz, 'A Personal Memoir', in *The Feel of Truth: Essays in New Zealand and Pacific History*, edited by Peter Munz (Wellington: A.H. & A.W. Reed, 1969), p.23

50   JCB to Richmond, 10 December 1939
51   *Evening Post*, 26 February 1940, quoted in Nancy M. Taylor, *The New Zealand People at War: The Home Front*, vol.1 (Wellington: Department of Internal Affairs, 1986), p.191
52   W.J. Scott, 'Civil Liberties in New Zealand', *Landfall*, vol.10, no.1 (March 1956), pp.36–7
53   The draft survives in his papers. It is not clear from the papers I have seen whether it was part of the final submission; it does, however, give a very clear expression of his reaction to the regulations.
54   JCB to Richmond, 21 December 1941
55   JCB to Richmond, 10 December 1939
56   JCB to Richmond, 10 January 1938
57   JCB to Richmond, 14 June 1938
58   Linda Tyler, 'The Urban and Urbane: Ernst Plischke's Kahn House', in *Zeal and Crusade: The Modern Movement in Wellington*, edited by John Wilson (Wellington: Te Waihora Press, 1997)
59   Linda Tyler, 'Plischke, Ernst Anton 1903–1992, *Dictionary of New Zealand Biography*, vol.5
60   Brigitte Bönisch-Brednich, *Keeping a Low Profile: An Oral History of German Immigration to New Zealand* (Wellington: Victoria University Press), p.42
61   JCB to JEP, 16 December 1948
62   JCB to Heenan, 13 February 1939; Heenan to JCB, 1 March 1939. J.C. Beaglehole Papers. 73-004-01/10. ATL
63   JCB to DEB, 16 January 1940
64   JCB to Richmond, 10 December 1939
65   JCB to Downie Stewart, 23 November 1944. Downie Stewart Papers. MS-985-1/1/15. Hocken Library
66   Davidson, 'The New Zealand Scholar', p.153
67   Mary Boyd, 'Lecturer in History', in *J.C. Beaglehole Some Personal Recollections: Supplement to the [VUW] Gazette*, no.11, 1971
68   Noeline Hall to THB, 13 June 2003
69   F.H. Corner, 'Extracts from notes on FHC's university days' (given to the author by Frank Corner, 2003)
70   Boyd, 'Lecturer in History'
71   Munz, 'A Personal Memoir', in *The Feel of Truth* edited by Peter Munz, pp.20–1
72   ibid., p.20
73   ibid.
74   Davidson, 'The New Zealand Scholar', p.153
75   Boyd, 'Lecturer in History'
76   Corner, 'Extracts from notes on FHC's university days'
77   Hall to THB, 13 June 2003
78   Davidson, 'The New Zealand Scholar', p.153
79   JCB, 'History and the New Zealander', in *The University & the Community: Essays in honour of Thomas Alexander Hunter* (1946), p.124
80   ibid.
81   JCB to Vivienne Rich, 6 May 1950
82   JCB, *Victoria University College*, p.232
83   JCB to Richmond, 21 December 1941
84   JCB to JEP, 14 March 1946
85   JCB to Richmond, 21 December 1941
86   Davidson, 'The New Zealand Scholar', p.153
87   JCB to Richmond, 21 December 1941. Fred Wood's file on Elder's threatened libel action is in his history department papers. Exams (correspondence and

related material), Box 1, 1934–42. J.C. Beaglehole Room, VUW Library

88   Burnett to THB, 7 October 1996
89   Munz, 'A Personal Memoir', p.24
90   E.T. Williams to JCB, 6 February 1940
91   E.T. Williams, 'The Colonial Office in the Thirties', *Historical Studies Australia and New Zealand*, vol.2, no.7 (May 1943), pp.141–60
92   Williams to JCB, 14 August 1947
93   *Historical Studies Australia and New Zealand*, vol.2, no.6 (November 1942), pp.95 113
94   JCB to Richmond, 21 December 1941
95   JCB to Downie Stewart, 7 February 1942. Downie Stewart Papers. MS-985-1/1/15. Hocken Library
96   *Historical Studies Australia and New Zealand*, vol.2, no.7 (May 1943), pp.129–40
97   JCB to Downie Stewart, 23 November 1944. Downie Stewart Papers. MS-985-1/1/15. Hocken Library
98   *New Zealand Listener*, 25 May 1945, p.7
99   W.J. Lewis Parker to JCB, 21 June 1946
100   JCB to JEP, 13 June 1946
101   JCB to JEP, 4 December 1946
102   JCB to JEP, 5 November 1946
103   JCB to Ida Leeson, 19 November 1946. carbon copy
104   JCB to JEP, 6 March 1947
105   JCB, draft memo to Sir Thomas Hunter, undated [late November–early December 1947]. J.C. Beaglehole Papers. 73-004-02. ATL
106   JCB to JEP, 22 October 1947
107   Williamson to JCB, 29 October 1947. J.C. Beaglehole Papers. 73-004-02. ATL
108   Edward Lynam to JCB, 12 November 1947. ibid.
109   JCB to Phyllis Mander Jones, 4 December 1947. ML 1709/63. State Library of NSW
110   JCB to Lynam, 19 December 1947, carbon copy. J.C. Beaglehole Papers. 73-004-02. ATL
111   Lynam to JCB, 7 February 1948. ibid.
112   JCB to Mander Jones, 4 February 1948. ML 1709/63. State Library of NSW
113   Chifley to Fraser, 6 February 1948, copy. J.C. Beaglehole Papers. 73-004-02. ATL
114   JCB to Mander Jones, 25 March 1948. ML 1709/63. State Library of NSW
115   JCB to JEP, 20 May 1948
116   Williamson to JCB, 10 June, 12 June 1948
117   JCB to JEP, 24 June 1948
118   JCB to JEP, 14 July 1948
119   JCB to JEP, 8 August 1948
120   ibid.
121   ibid.
122   Fraser to Chifley, 29 July 1948, copy. ML 1709/63. State Library of NSW
123   JCB to Richmond, 4 October 1948
124   JCB to Mander Jones, 4 February 1948. ML 1709/63. State Library of NSW
125   JCB to JEP, 26 June 1947
126   JCB to JEP, 14 August 1947
127   JCB to Richmond, 4 October 1948
128   JCB to JEP, 1 July 1948
129   JCB to JEP, 18 November 1948

130 L.C. Webb, review in *Education*, vol.2, no.5 (November 1949), p.62
131 *NZ Listener*, 2 September 1949, pp.12–13
132 JCB, 'A College Jubilee', *NZ Listener*, 13 May 1949, pp.6–7
133 *Landfall*, vol.4, no.3 (September 1950), pp.253–7
134 JCB to JEP, 9 October 1950
135 JCB to McCormick, 8 October 1950. E.H. McCormick Papers. MS-Papers-5484-08. ATL
136 McCormick to JCB, 'Saturday' [14 October 1950(?), envelope postmarked 16 October]
137 JCB to JEP, 19 May 1949
138 Editorial, *NZ Listener*, 13 May 1949, p.5
139 JCB, 'A College Jubilee', *NZ Listener*, 13 May 1949, p.6
140 JCB, untitled typescript, 27 May 1949 [broadcast?]

9 *'A PECULIAR SORT OF . . . PUBLIC SERVANT', 1939–52*

1   JCB to W.A. Bodkin, Minister of Internal Affairs, 2 November 1950. IA 1, 62/94/39. ANZ
2   JCB, 'The New Zealand Scholar', p.245. First published by Canterbury University College in 1954, the lecture was reprinted in 1969 in *The Feel of Truth: Essays in New Zealand and Pacific History*, edited by Peter Munz (Wellington: A.H. & A.W. Reed, 1969). My page references are to the latter (more accessible) source.
3   JCB to Richmond, 14 June 1938
4   JCB, 'Memorandum for the Under-Secretary of Internal Affairs on the duties of the research adviser to the Turnbull Library', undated. J.C. Beaglehole Papers. 73-004-01/16. ATL
5   Registrar to JCB, 24 June 1938
6   Heenan to JCB, 1 July 1938
7   JCB, Memorandum for the Under-Secretary of Internal Affairs, 7 August 1950. JCB sent a copy of this, which gives an account of his role in the department, to Heenan. J.W. Heenan Papers. MS-Papers-1132-16. ATL
8   Rachel Barrowman, '"Culture-organising": Joe Heenan and the Beginnings of State Patronage of the Arts', *New Zealand Studies*, vol.6, no.2 (July 1996), p.5
9   Keith Sinclair, *Walter Nash* (Auckland: Auckland University Press, 1976), p.208
10   Barrowman, 'Culture-organising', p.5
11   Michael Bassett, *The Mother of All Departments: The History of the Department of Internal Affairs* (Auckland: Auckland University Press and Department of Internal Affairs, 1997), p.111
12   Heenan to R.M. Campbell, 25 June 1937. IA 1, 62/8/1, Part 1. ANZ
13   McCormick to Heenan, 11 October 1937. ibid.
14   JCB to Heenan, 8 November 1937. ibid.
15   E.H. McCormick, *An Absurd Ambition: Autobiographical Writings*, edited by Dennis McEldowney (Auckland: Auckland University Press, 1996), p.141
16   Minutes of standing committee, 8 October 1937. IA 1, 62/8/1, pt 1. ANZ
17   Memorandum from the editor to Under-Secretary, 23 March 1938
18   J.T. Paul, when in Wellington, met with the standing committee to convey their views, not only on this issue, but also on the proposed survey of women, which Dunedin considered 'unnecessary and illogical'. Memorandum on meeting, 14 April 1938. IA 1, 62/8/1, pt 1. ANZ
19   JCB to Richmond, 10 December 1939

20 Minutes of standing committee meeting, 18 May 1938. IA 1, 62/8/1, pt 1. ANZ

21 Barrowman, 'Culture-organising', p.5

22 McCormick, *An Absurd Ambition*, p.145

23 ibid.

24 ibid., p.148

25 Sydney J. Shep, '"Touching the Mind of the Country": J.C. Beaglehole and the Design of the Centennial Publications', in *Creating a National Spirit: Celebrating New Zealand's Centennial*, edited by William Renwick (Wellington: Victoria University Press, 2004), p.199

26 C.E. Beeby, *Biography of an Idea: Beeby on Education* (Wellington: New Zealand Council for Educational Research, 1992), p.93

27 Heenan took the credit for this as one of his 'original ideas'. Heenan to Leicester Webb, 23 July 1940. J.W. Heenan Papers. MS-Papers-1132-250. ATL

28 JCB to Heenan, 15 February 1939. J.C. Beaglehole Papers. 73-004-10/10. ATL

29 McCormick, *An Absurd Ambition*, p.140

30 JCB to Heenan, 30 March 1939. IA 1, 62/9/2. ANZ

31 R.I.M. Burnett, 'John Beaglehole', *Turnbull Library Record*, vol.5 (n.s.), no.1 (May 1972), p.6

32 McCormick to Heenan, 13 October 1939. IA1, 62/9/2. ANZ

33 The draft letter is in ibid.

34 JCB to Heenan, 15 February 1939. J.C. Beaglehole Papers. 73-004-01/10. ATL

35 JCB to Richmond, 10 December 1939

36 ibid.

37 Janet Paul, 'J.C. Beaglehole as Typographer: A Background to the Design of the 1940 Centennial Publications', typescript. Janet Paul Papers. MS-Papers-5640-100. ATL

38 As noted in Janet Paul, 'Draft Lecture on J.C. Beaglehole: His Influence on Book Production in New Zealand 1936–71'. Janet Paul Papers. MS-Papers-5640-028. ATL

39 'Mothers, Sisters and Wives: The Work of Women During Our First Century', *New Zealand Listener*, 12 April 1940, p.34. Shep believes the reviewer to have been Duff, who, during the centennial year, 'unabashedly used the columns of the *New Zealand Listener* to voice his difference of design opinion'.

40 Shep, 'Touching the Mind of the Country', p.196

41 JCB, 'Typography of Centennial Surveys'. Letter to the editor, *NZ Listener*, 26 April 1940, p.34

42 JCB to Heenan, 30 July 1940. J.C. Beaglehole Papers. 73-004-01/10. ATL

43 Burnett, 'John Beaglehole', p. 5

44 Shep, 'Touching the Mind of the Country', p.203

45 JCB to Richmond, 10 December 1939

46 JCB, *The Discovery of New Zealand* (Wellington: Department of Internal Affairs, 1939), p.vii

47 JCB, *The Discovery of New Zealand*, 2nd edition (London: Oxford University Press, 1961) p.vii

48 Chris Hilliard, 'Stories of Becoming: The Centennial Surveys and the Colonization of New Zealand', *New Zealand Journal of History*, vol.33, no.1 (April 1999), p.12

49 A good brief account of the affair is given by Chris Hilliard in 'Stories of Becoming', pp.6–7. A longer account is given by A.J. Booker, 'The

Centennial Surveys of New Zealand, 1936–41' (BA Hons research essay, Massey University, 1983), pp.35–49. The relevant departmental file is IA 1, 62/110/5. ANZ. John gave a brief and forthright account in his letter to Norman Richmond, 21 December 1941.

50 Hilliard, 'Stories of Becoming', p.6
51 Heenan to Nash, 5 March 1941. J.W. Heenan Papers. MS-Papers-1132-296. ATL
52 Heenan to McCormick, 4 July 1941. J.W. Heenan Papers. MS-Papers-1132-134. ATL
53 JCB to Richmond, 21 December 1941
54 JCB to David Hall, 22 January 1941. IA1, 62/110/3. ANZ
55 Michael Bassett is, I think, misleading when he writes in his biography of Fraser that the Prime Minister 'conclud[ed], as did Eric McCormick, J.C. Beaglehole and McIntosh, that [Sutch's book] was a shoddy piece of work and should not form part of the series'. (Michael Bassett and Michael King, *Tomorrow Comes the Song: A Life of Peter Fraser* (Auckland: Penguin, 2000), p.206)
56 JCB to Richmond, 21 December 1941
57 JCB to Heenan, 30 July 1940. J.C. Beaglehole Papers. 73-004-01/10. ATL. The quotations in the following three paragraphs are all from this paper.
58 JCB, 'The New Zealand Scholar', pp.243–4
59 JCB, 'Centennial Meditations', *Spike*, no.68 (1940), p.18
60 JCB, 'The New Zealand Mind', *Australian Quarterly*, vol.12, no.4 (December 1940), p.49
61 ibid.
62 ibid., p.50
63 J.W. Davidson, 'The New Zealand Scholar: A Note on J.C. Beaglehole, 1901–1971', *Journal of Pacific History*, vol.7 (1972), p.152
64 The best account we have of Heenan is that of Rachel Barrowman, 'Culture-organising', pp.3–10
65 JCB, 'The New Zealand Scholar', pp.245–6
66 Heenan to Leicester Webb, 16 August 1940. J.W. Heenan Papers. MS-Papers-1132/250. ATL
67 Memorandum [from Heenan] to the Minister of Internal Affairs, 15 January 1941. IA 1, 62/163. ANZ
68 JCB [to Heenan], 'Comment on Mr McCormick's Memorandum, 19th November, 1940', 21 November 1940. ibid.
69 JCB to Heenan, 10 November 1941. ibid.
70 Mary Boyd, 'Ross, Ruth Miriam 1920–1982', *Dictionary of New Zealand Biography*, vol.5
71 JCB to Heenan, 5 August 1942. IA 1, 62/163. ANZ
72 This and the following paragraph paragraph draw heavily on recollections written for me in April 2003 by Mary Boyd.
73 JCB, 'The New Zealand Scholar', p.246
74 JCB to DEB, 26 July 1941
75 Heenan to J.W. Davidson, 13 April 1942. J.W. Heenan Papers. MS-Papers-1132/48. ATL. Photographs of the volumes are in J.C. Beaglehole Papers. 73-004-01/10. ATL
76 Heenan to R.M. Campbell, 5 May 1943. J.W. Heenan Papers. MS-Papers-1132/30. ATL
77 JCB to Richmond, 21 December 1941. John's review of Curnow's *Island and Time* was reprinted from the *Press* in *Book: A Miscellany*, no.3 (August 1941), p.17
78 JCB to Heenan, 13 April 1942. IA 1, 158/292/1. ANZ

79 Heenan to Campbell, 5 May 1943. J.W. Heenan Papers. MS-Papers-1132/30. ATL

80 Barrowman, 'Culture-organising', p.6

81 Glover to JCB, 18 June 1943

82 An extract from the letter and the other relevant papers are in IA 1, 158/292, pt.1. ANZ

83 JCB to Heenan, 21 February 1940. IA 107/11, pt.1. ANZ. Cited in Frances Porter, *A Sense of History: A Commemorative Publication for John Cawte Beaglehole, O.M., about James Cook's Landing Sites in New Zealand* (Wellington: Government Printer, 1978), p.24. Archives New Zealand could not locate this file in 2003.

84 Porter, *A Sense of History*, p.28

85 JCB to Heenan, 12 December 1941. IA 107/11, pt.2. ANZ. The letter and the photograph are reproduced in Porter, *A Sense of History*, p.29, and the later history of the monument is given on p.30.

86 *Nelson Evening Mail*, 24 October 1942. A cutting is in IA 1, 158/292, pt.1. ANZ

87 The quotation is from the leaflet produced for the occasion.

88 The Internal Affairs file relating to this, volume, IA 1, 126/8/72 pt.3, could not be located in July 2003

89 R. Hawthorne to A.D. McIntosh, 3 February 1948, copy

90 Heenan to Campbell, 13 February 1945. J.W. Heenan Papers. MS-Papers-1132-30. ATL

91 Heenan to Campbell, 20 February 1945. ibid.

92 Heenan to Campbell, 6 April 1945. ibid.

93 Heenan to Campbell, 13 February 1945. ibid.

94 Janet Paul, 'Hints of Becoming', in *Beyond Expectations: Fourteen New Zealand Women Write about Their Lives*, edited by Margaret Clark (Wellington: Allen & Unwin/Port Nicolson Press, 1986), pp.12–13

95 Anthony Dreaver, *An Eye for Country: The Life and Work of Leslie Adkin* (Wellington, Victoria University Press, 1997), pp.185–91

96 Adkin Diary, 5 July 1944, Adkin Collection, MONZPT. Quoted in Dreaver, *Adkin*, p.191

97 JCB to Adkin, 2 November 1944. Quoted in Dreaver, *Adkin*, p.191

98 Dreaver, *Adkin*, p.199

99 Dreaver, *Adkin*, p.211

100 Held in the Downie Stewart Papers. MS-985-1/1/15. Hocken Library

101 JCB to Downie Stewart, 10 March 1946

102 Bassett and King, *Peter Fraser*, p.283

103 JCB to JEP, 10 July 1947

104 Frank Corner in *An Eye, an Ear and a Voice: 50 Years in New Zealand's External Relations 1943–1993*, edited by Malcolm Templeton (Wellington: Ministry of Foreign Affairs and Trade, 1993), p.77

105 JCB to JEP, 2 October 1946

106 JCB to JEP, 7 May 1947

107 JCB to JEP, 19 August 1948

108 Heenan to Fraser, 24 May 1949. J.W. Heenan Papers. MS-Papers-1132-316. ATL

109 JCB to Heenan, 18 July 1949. J.W. Heenan Papers. MS-Papers-1132-016. ATL

110 The relevant file in the National Archives is IA 1, 62/94/39. In the J.C. Beaglehole Papers the relevant folder is 73-004-01/10. I have also found two letters of John's especially useful: JCB to W.H. Shepardson (Carnegie Corporation of New York), 23 May 1952, and JCB to Dan Davin (Oxford

University Press), 5 August 1953. In both of these he gives an account of the winding up of the atlas.

111 JCB to Davin, 5 August 1953, carbon copy
112 JCB to O'Halloran, 20 September 1950. IA 1, 62/94/39. ANZ
113 JCB to Bodkin, 30 November 1951
114 Bodkin to JCB, 14 February 1952. J.C. Beaglehole Papers. 73-004-01/10. ATL
115 JCB to Bodkin, 18 February 1952. IA 1, 62/94/39. ANZ
116 JCB to Shepardson, 23 May 1952, carbon copy
117 Heenan to Glover, 3 December 1948. J.W. Heenan Papers. MS-Papers-1132-82. ATL. Quoted by Barrowman, 'Culture-organising', p.9. Also Heenan to Leicester Webb, 16 August 1940. J.W. Heenan Papers. MS-Papers-1132-250. ATL
118 JCB to Dan Davin, 5 August 1953
119 JCB to JEP, 22 November 1950

10 PUBLIC LIFE, BOOKS, MUSIC AND ART, 1936–50

1   'Conversation with Allen Curnow', *Islands*, vol.4, no.2 (Winter 1973). Quoted in Lawrence Jones, *Picking Up the Traces: The Making of a New Zealand Literary Culture 1932–1945* (Wellington: Victoria University Press, 2003), p. 204
2   Jones, *Picking Up the Traces*, p.204
3   JCB, review in *Book*, 3 (1941). Quoted in Jones, *Picking Up the Traces*, p.205
4   Jones, *Picking Up the Traces*, p.291
5   JCB, 'Centennial Meditations', *Spike*, no.68 (1940), p.19
6   Jones, *Picking Up the Traces*, p.291
7   Bart Fortune, interviewed by Rachel Barrowman. Quoted in Rachel Barrowman, *A Popular Vision: The Arts and the Left in New Zealand* (Wellington: Victoria University Press, 1991), p.93
8   ibid., p.94
9   Minute Book, 1938–41. Wellington Co-operative Book Society Papers. MS-Papers-1122-37. ATL
10 Bridget Williams, 'Parsons, Roy George 1909–1991', *Dictionary of New Zealand Biography*, vol.5
11 Nash to JCB, 2 February 1939. J.C. Beaglehole Papers. 73-004-01/08. ATL. A draft of John's letter to Nash, 1 December 1938, together with two other letters from Nash on the subject, are in the same folder.
12 Minute Book, 1938–41
13 JCB to Richmond, 10 December 1939
14 JCB to Richmond, 21 December 1941
15 Barrowman, *A Popular Vision*, p.116
16 Minute Book, 1938–41. Wellington Co-operative Book Society Papers. MS-Papers-1122-37. ATL
17 JCB to Richmond, 21 December 1941
18 Nancy M. Taylor, *The New Zealand People at War: The Home Front*, vol.2 (Wellington: Department of Internal Affairs, 1986), p.997
19 ibid., p.1001
20 JCB to Nash, 21 November 1940. PM 25/2/5. ANZ. Quoted in Taylor, *The Home Front*, vol.2, p.1002
21 Fraser, 9 July 1942. *NZPD*, vol.261, p.87. Quoted in Taylor, *The Home Front*, vol.2, p.1007
22 JCB to Richmond, 21 December 1941

23 Parsons to Griffin, 8 June 1942. Wellington Co-operative Book Society Papers. MS-Papers-1122-50. ATL
24 Williams, 'Parsons, Roy George 1909–1991'
25 Barowman gives a good account of the PPS in *A Popular Vision*, chapter 5
26 JCB to Richmond, 21 December 1941
27 Ernest Beaglehole, *Islands of Danger* (Wellington: Progressive Publishing Society, 1944), p.[ii]
28 JCB, 'The Work of the Typographical Committee', *Co-op Books*, vol.1, no.13 (November 1944), p.[2]. Quoted in Barrowman, *A Popular Vision*, p.168
29 JCB, 'Note on Modern Books and Publishing Society, 19 October 1942'. Wellington Co-operative Book Society Papers. MS-Papers-1122-41. ATL
30 Glover to JCB, 18 June 1943
31 JCB to JEP, 19 June 1946
32 JCB to JEP, 7 May 1947
33 JCB to JEP, 1 July 1948
34 JCB to JEP, 1 July, 22 July, 4 August 1948. Tombs to the Registrar, UNZ, 25 June 1948
35 J.E. Traue, 'The University of NZ Press', *New Zealand Libraries*, vol.26, no.1 (January–February 1963), p.22
36 Dennis McEldowney, 'Scholarly Publishing in New Zealand', *Scholarly Publishing* (University of Toronto Press), vol.1, no.1 (October 1969), p.108
37 'Report of the New Zealand University Press Board' (signed by JCB as chairman), in *University of New Zealand. Minutes of Senate . . .* (Wellington, 1961), p.73
38 McEldowney, 'Scholarly Publishing in New Zealand', p.108
39 Mary Ronnie, *Education for Librarianship in New Zealand* (London: Mansell, 1996), p.29
40 JCB to JEP, 4 August 1947
41 Eva B. Ottillinger and August Sarnitz, *Ernst Plischke: Das Neue Bauen und die Neue Welt Das Gesamtwerk* (Munchen: Restel Verlag, 2003) p.350
42 JCB, address to the Chamber Music Federation Annual General Meeting, 23 March 1968, typescript
43 Fred Turnovsky, *Turnovsky: Fifty Years in New Zealand* (Wellington: Allen & Unwin, 1990) p.81
44 Wellington Chamber Music Society, minutes of AGM, February 1946. Wellington Chamber Music Society Papers. MS-Papers-4566-01. ATL
45 J.M. Thomson, *Into a New Key: The Origins and History of the Music Federation of New Zealand 1950–1982* (Music Federation of New Zealand, 1983) p.41
46 Thomson, *Into a New Key*, p.34
47 ibid.
48 Minutes of committee meeting, 26 June 1945. Quoted in Thomson, *Into a New Key*, p.37
49 Thomson, *Into a New Key*, p.44
50 James Bertram, *Capes of China Slide Away: A Memoir of Peace and War 1910–1980* (Auckland: Auckland University Press, 1993), p.267
51 JCB to JEP, 26 July 1946
52 JCB to JEP, 10 July 1947
53 Thomson, *Into a New Key*, p.50
54 Owen Jensen, *The NZBC Symphony Orchestra* (Wellington: A.H & A.W. Reed, 1966), p.16. I draw on Jensen's useful account of the orchestra's beginnings in the paragraphs which follow.
55 These names are given by Bolke Water in his article, 'The Birth of a Nation: J.C. Beaglehole and the National Orchestra'. *Music in New Zealand*, no.40 (Summer 2001–02), p.42

56 JCB to JEP, 1 May 1946
57 JCB to JEP, 14 May 1946
58 JCB to JEP, 1 May 1946
59 JCB to JEP, 14 May 1946
60 Jensen, *The NZBC Symphony Orchestra*, p.26
61 JCB to JEP, 26 March 1947
62 H.J. Finlay, 'Have We an Orchestra? A reply to Dr. Beaglehole', *NZ Listener*, 3 April 1947, pp.6–7
63 Heenan to editor, *NZ Listener*, 3 April 1947
64 JCB to editor, *NZ Listener*, 24 April 1946
65 Ormond Wilson to editor, *NZ Listener*, 18 April 1947
66 This point is made by Water, 'The Birth of a Nation', p.43
67 JCB to JEP, 11 September 1947
68 Jensen, *The NZBC Symphony Orchestra*, p.23
69 Frederick Page, *A Musician's Journal 1905–1983*(Dunedin: John McIndoe, 1986), p.98
70 JCB, 'Lots of Poetry'. Reviews of *Hero and Leander* by Christopher Marlowe; *Lyric Poems of New Zealand 1928–42*, chosen by C.A. Marris; *Poems* by Clyde Carr; *Signs and Wonders* by Basil Dowling; *Beyond the Palisade* by James K. Baxter; *The Wind and the Sand* by Denis Glover; *Poetry: The Quarterly of Australasian Verse* (December 1944), edited by Hexmore Hudson; *Three Essays on Czech Poets* by Frederick Ost. *New Zealand Listener*, 8 June 1945, pp.12–13. Lawrence Jones gives an account of the controversy in *Picking Up the Traces*, pp.67–8
71 *NZ Listener*, 6 July 1945
72 JCB, 'Culture Undefined', review of *Notes Towards the Definition of Culture* by T.S. Eliot. *NZ Listener*, 6 May 1949, pp.16–17
73 JCB, 'The National Orchestra', *Landfall*, vol.3, no.4 (December 1948), pp.307–20
74 JCB, 'History and the New Zealander', in *The University and the Community: Essays in Honour of Thomas Alexander Hunter* (Wellington: Victoria University College, 1946), p.124
75 JCB, 'Grounds for Mild Assurance', *NZ Listener*, 10 January 1947, p.12
76 JCB to JEP, 12 March 1946
77 Janet Paul, 'McCormack, Thomas Arthur 1883–1973', *Dictionary of New Zealand Biography*, vol.4
78 JCB, 'Lunch-hour Art in Wellington', *NZ Listener*, 22 March 1946
79 JCB, 'Colin McCahon's Pictures', *NZ Listener*, 5 March 1948
80 JCB to JEP, 4 February 1948
81 JCB, 'The Artist and the School', *NZ Listener*, 28 May 1948. See also his article 'A Small Bouquet for the Education Department', *Arts Year Book 7* [1951], edited by Eric Lee-Johnson
82 JCB to JEP, 12 March 1946
83 E.H. McCormick, *Eric Lee-Johnson* (Hamilton: Paul's Book Arcade, 1956), p.34
84 JCB to JEP, 19 June 1946
85 JCB to JEP, 3 July 1947
86 JCB, 'Note on a Collection of Paintings', *Landfall*, vol.5, no.3 (September 1951), pp.227–30
87 JCB to JEP, 11 February 1946
88 JCB to JEP, 12 March 1946
89 JCB to JEP, 14 January 1946. The other books mentioned in this paragraph he notes having read in further letters to Janet during 1946.
90 JCB to JEP, 4 July 1947
91 JCB to JEP, 26 August 1948

92   United Nations Educational, Scientific, and Cultural Organization. Report of the New Zealand Delegation to the Fourth Session of the General Conference, Held at Paris from 19 September to 5 October,1949. AJHR, 1950, A-11. Unless otherwise noted, the following two paragraphs are based on the report.
93   JCB to Heenan, 17 May 1950. J.W. Heenan Papers. MS-Papers-1132-016. ATL
94   Report of the New Zealand Delegation, p.21
95   JCB, 1949 Unesco Conference, 'General Subject' speech, typescript, p.2
96   JCB, 'Is International Understanding Possible?', *BBC Listener*, vol.43, no.1102 (2 March 1950)
97   JCB to Richmond, 13 November 1949
98   JCB to sons, 17 October 1949
99   JCB to Richmond, 13 November 1949
100 JCB to sons, 17 October 1949
101 JCB to JEP, 2 December 1949
102 JCB to Mary Beaglehole, 14 November 1949
103 JCB to JEP, 15 November 1949
104 Vincent O'Sullivan, *Long Journey to the Border: A Life of John Mulgan* (Auckland: Penguin, 2003), p.111
105 JCB to JEP, 2 December 1949
106 JCB to family, 13 December 1949
107 JCB to family, 20 December 1949
108 JCB to EMB, 2 January 1950
109 JCB to EMB, 10 January 1950
110 EMB to JCB, 8 February 1950
111 JCB to EMB, 9 February 1950
112 JEP to JCB, 19 March 1950
113 JCB to EMB, 25 February 1950
114 JCB to EMB, 6 March 1950
115 JCB to McKay, 1 February 1950
116 JCB to JEP, 26 January 1950
117 JCB to EMB, 30 March 1950
118 JCB, 'Learning, Law, Politics, Friendship', *Parsons Packet*, no.23 (July 1953), pp.8–10
119 JCB to EMB, 15 March 1950
120 JCB to EMB, 20 April 1950
121 ibid.
122 ibid.
123 JCB to EMB, 27 April 1950
124 JCB to EMB, 4 April 1950
125 JCB to EMB, 23 March 1950
126 For the information on Nan Kivell I have drawn on the essay by John Thompson, 'Self-made: Towards a Life of Rex Nan Kivell', in *Paradise Possessed: The Rex Nan Kivell Collection*, published by the National Library of Australia in 1998, the centenary of Nan Kivell's birth.
127 JCB to EMB, 4 May 1950
128 ibid.
129 JCB to Heenan, 12 May 1950. J.W. Heenan Papers. MS-Papers-1132-016. ATL
130 JCB to EMB, 4 May 1950
131 JCB to Heenan, 12 May 1950. J.W. Heenan Papers. MS-Papers-1132-016. ATL
132 JCB to EMB, 19 May 1950
133 The United Nations Educational, Scientific, and Cultural Organization:

Report of the New Zealand Delegation to the Fifth Session of the General Conference, Held at Florence, Italy, from 22 May to 17 June, 1950, p.7. The other quotes in this paragraph, unless otherwise noted, are from the same introductory section of the report.

134 JCB to EMB, 1 June 1950
135 JCB to EMB, 25 May 1950
136 JCB to EMB, 1 June 1950
137 JCB to EMB, 8 June 1950
138 JCB to EMB, 19 May 1950
139 ibid.
140 ibid.
141 JCB to EMB, 1 June 1950
142 JCB to EMB, 21 June 1950
143 JCB to EMB, 28 June 1950

11 THE SCHOLAR AT WORK: I

1   JCB to RAS, 12 September 1951
2   JCB, 'Some Problems of Editing Cook's Journals', *Historical Studies*, vol.8 (November 1957), p.20
3   ibid.
4   JCB to Kathleen McKay, 1 February 1950
5   JCB to Heenan, 12 May 1950. J.W. Heenan Papers. MS-Papers-1132-016. ATL
6   JCB to McKay, 1 February 1950
7   ibid.
8   JCB to Phyllis Mander Jones, 27 May 1952. ML1709/63. Public Library of NSW
9   ibid.
10 JCB to RAS, 3 January 1953
11 JCB to Mander Jones, 27 May 1952
12 JCB, 'Some Problems of Editing Cook's Journals', p.22
13 ibid., p.24
14 For this paragraph I have drawn heavily on D.B. Quinn, 'R.A. Skelton of the Map Room', in *Compassing the Vaste Globe of the Earth: Studies in the History of the Hakluyt Society 1846–1996*, edited by R.C. Bridges and P.E.H. Hair (London: Hakluyt Society, 1996)
15 JCB to Heenan, 12 May 1950. J.W. Heenan Papers. MS-Papers-1132-016. ATL
16 ibid.
17 Quinn, 'R.A. Skelton of the Map Room', p.205
18 JCB to Mander Jones, 27 May 1952. ML1709/63. State Library of NSW
19 JCB to H.L. White, copy, 12 June 1951. J.C. Beaglehole Papers. 73-004-09/06. ATL
20 JCB, 'Some Problems of Editing Cook's Journals', p.20
21 JCB to RAS, 4 March 1951
22 This paragraph draws on John's note 'On the Annotation' in *The Journals of Captain James Cook on His Voyages of Discovery: The Voyage of the* Endeavour *1768–1771,* vol.1, edited by J.C. Beaglehole (Cambridge: Cambridge University Press for the Hakluyt Society, 1955), pp.cclxxiv–cclxxvii
23 ibid., pp.clxxii_cxcii
24 ibid., p.cclxxvii
25 JCB to RAS, 19 November 1951

26 RAS to JCB, 20 January 1952. J.C. Beaglehole Papers. 73-004-09/06. ATL
27 Marcel Aurousseau to JCB, 19 December 1951. J.C. Beaglehole Papers. 73-004-03/05. ATL
28 RAS to JCB, 2 December 1954. J.C. Beaglehole Papers. 73-004-10/16. ATL
29 JCB to RAS, 12 February 1955
30 JCB to RAS, 23 May 1954
31 JCB to RAS, 13 April 1954
32 Obituary of Averil Lysaght, *Notornis*, vol.29, no.1 (March 1982)
33 JCB to RAS, 25 May 1954
34 JCB to RAS, 15 August 1954
35 JCB to RAS, 12 February 1955
36 JCB to Mander Jones, 11 December 1953. ML1709/63. State Library of NSW
37 JCB, *The Endeavour Journal of Joseph Banks 1768–1771* (Sydney: Trustees of the Public Library of New South Wales in association with Angus and Robertson, 1962), vol.1, p.343, n.1; JCB, *Cook's Journals*, vol.1, p.120, n.7
38 JCB to Mander Jones, 13 May 1952. ML1709/63. State Library of NSW
39 JCB to RAS, 8 June 1952
40 JCB to Mander Jones, 13 May 1952
41 JCB to RAS, 9 July 1952
42 JCB, *Cook's Journals*, vol.1, p.xciii
43 Van Wyck Brooks, 'Prologue', in J. Frank Stimson, *Songs and Tales of the Sea Kings* (Salem, Mass.: Peabody Museum of Salem, 1957), p.xxviii
44 JCB to JEP, 24 July 1952
45 JCB to Don Marshall, 6 March 1960
46 JCB to JEP, 24 July 1952
47 JCB to Suzanne McConnaughey, 30 August 1952. MS Gen Ltr 1.25. Bishop Museum Archives
48 JCB to JEP, 24 July 1952
49 JCB to RAS, 3 January 1953
50 JCB to Marshall, 10 May 1954
51 JCB to JEP, 30 July 1952
52 JCB to Mander Jones, 3 January 1953. ML1709/63. State Library of NSW
53 JCB to RAS, 3 January 1953
54 JCB to JEP, 1 August 1951
55 ibid.
56 JCB to RAS, 3 January 1952
57 ibid.
58 JCB to Mander Jones, 2 January 1952. ML1709/63. State Library of NSW
59 JCB to Mander Jones, 7 April 1952. ibid.
60 JCB to JEP, undated (postmarked 20 November 1952)
61 JCB to Marshall, 11 August 1953
62 JCB to JEP, 22 July 1953
63 JCB to JEP, 30 September 1953
64 JCB to RAS, 19 November 1953
65 JCB to McKay, 19 December 1953
66 JCB to RAS, 7 March 1954
67 RAS to JCB, 23 March 1954. J.C. Beaglehole Papers. 73-004-10/16. ATL
68 RAS to JCB, 29 March 1954. ibid.
69 J.A. Williamson to JCB, 16 April 1954. J.C. Beaglehole Papers. 73-004-10/16. ATL
70 RAS to JCB, 11 May 1954. ibid.
71 JCB to RAS, 23 May 1954
72 JCB to JEP, 9 June 1954
73 JCB to RAS, 11 April 1954

74   JCB to Mander Jones, 25 August 1954. ML1709/63. State Library of NSW
75   JCB, *The Life of Captain James Cook* (London: A. & C. Black, 1974), p.453
76   JCB to RAS, 21 September 1954
77   RAS to JCB, 10 June 1954. J.C. Beaglehole Papers. 73-004-10/16. ATL
78   JCB to RAS, 4 July 1954
79   JCB to RAS, 4 September 1954
80   JCB to RAS, 12 February 1955
81   RAS to JCB, 12 March 1955. J.C. Beaglehole Papers. 73-004-10/17. ATL
82   RAS to JCB, 20 April 1954. J.C. Beaglehole Papers. 73-004-10/16. ATL
83   RAS to JCB, 9 August 1954. ibid.
84   JCB to RAS, 24 April 1954
85   RAS to JCB, 17 July 1954. J.C. Beaglehole Papers. 73-004-10/16. ATL
86   JCB to RAS, 21 September 1954
87   RAS to JCB, 17 July 1954. J.C. Beaglehole Papers. 73-004-10/16. ATL
88   JCB to RAS, 26 July 1954
89   JCB to RAS, 23 May 1954
90   JCB to RAS, 9 May 1955
91   JCB to RAS, 12 February 1955
92   JCB to RAS, 24 April 1954
93   RAS to JCB, 11 May 1954. J.C. Beaglehole Papers. 73-004-10/16. ATL
94   JCB to Helen Wallis, 4 May 1954
95   JCB to RAS, 13 April 1954
96   JCB to RAS, 23 May 1954
97   RAS to JCB, 10 September 1954. J.C. Beaglehole Papers. 73-004-10/16. ATL. See also RAS to JCB, 5 September 1954
98   JCB to RAS, 12 October 1954
99   JCB to RAS, 21 September 1954
100 JCB to RAS, 27 February 1955
101 JCB, *Cook's Journals*, vol.1, p.642
102 JCB to JEP, 20 October 1954
103 RAS to JCB, 7 January 1955. J.C. Beaglehole Papers. 73-004-10/17. ATL
104 RAS to JCB, 1 February 1955. ibid.
105 Michael Strachan, 'Esmond de Beer: Scholar and Benefactor', in *Compassing the Vaste Globe of the Earth,* eds Bridges and Hair, pp.216–17
106 JCB to RAS, 30 March 1955
107 JCB to RAS, 7 April 1955
108 RAS to JCB, 14 April 1955. J.C. Beaglehole Papers. 73-004-10/17. ATL
109 JCB to RAS, 10 April 1955. Mander Jones Papers. MC MSS 4337, Box 1(6). State Library of NSW. John's letter must have been sent on to Mander Jones by Skelton.
110 JCB to RAS, 9 May 1955
111 JCB to RAS, 30 March 1955
112 JCB to RAS, 16 May 1955
113 JCB to RAS, 12 February 1955
114 JCB to Mander Jones, 8 February 1955. ML1709/63. State Library of NSW
115 JCB to RAS, 12 February 1955
116 Averil Lysaght to JCB, 26 February 1960
117 JCB to Mander Jones, 1 June 1955. ML 1709/63. State Library of NSW
118 JCB to RAS, 1 June 1955
119 JCB to RAS, 24 November 1954
120 JCB to Marshall, 29 June 1955
121 JCB to RAS, 2 July 1955
122 JCB to RAS, 15 July 1955
123 JCB to JEP, 6 October 1955

124 JCB to JEP, 25 October 1955
125 JCB to JEP, 1 January 1956
126 JCB to Peter Jacoby, 28 November 1955
127 JCB to Principal, VUC, 25 October 1956
128 *Times Literary Supplement*, 11 January 1956
129 Sir John Squire, 'Round the World with Captain Cook', *Illustrated London News*, 14 January 1956
130 O.D., 'The Endeavour Sails Again', *NZ Listener*, 8 June 1956
131 *Journal of the Polynesian Society*, vol.65, no.2 (June 1956)
132 *Education: A Magazine for Teachers*, vol.6, no.1 (February 1957)
133 JCB to RAS, 27 February 1957
134 JCB to Jacoby, 28 November 1955
135 JCB to Mander Jones, 5 March 1956. ML1709/63. State Library of NSW
136 JCB to Mander Jones, 2 July 1956. ibid.
137 JCB to Mander Jones, 5 July 1956. ibid.
138 JCB to RAS, 10 December 1956
139 JCB to G.D. Richardson, Acting Principal Librarian, Public Library of NSW, undated but received 8 April 1957. ML1709/63. State Library of NSW
140 JCB to THB, 14 October 1957
141 JCB to THB, 29 September 1958
142 JCB to THB, 11 June 1959
143 JCB to A.G. Cousins, Halstead Press, 31 October 1960, carbon copy
144 Cousins to JCB, 10 November 1960
145 JCB to Cousins, 28 June 1961, carbon copy
146 G.D. Richardson, Principal Librarian, Public Library of NSW, to JCB, 23 January 1962
147 JCB to Richardson, 30 January 1962, carbon copy
148 Aurousseau to JCB, 1 March 1962
149 *Meanjin Quarterly*, vol.21, no.2 (June 1962), pp.233–5
150 Russel Ward in *Sydney Morning Herald*, 24 March 1962; Denis Dugan in the *Age Literary Supplement*, 3 March 1962; Max Harris in *Australian Book Review*, March 1962
151 JCB to JEP, 1 March 1962

12 THE SCHOLAR AT WORK: II

1 JCB to Principal, VUC, 25 October 1956, carbon copy
2 'On the Character of Captain James Cook', *Geographical Journal*, vol.122, part 4 (December 1956), pp.417–29
3 JCB to RAS, 9 September 1956
4 JCB to RAS, 10 December 1956
5 ibid.
6 JCB ed., *The Journals of Captain James Cook on His Voyages of Discovery: The Voyage of the* Endeavour *1768–1771* (Cambridge: Cambridge University Press for the Hakluyt Society, 1955) vol.2, p.cxv
7 ibid., p.cxviii
8 JCB to RAS, 10 December 1956
9 RAS to JCB, 13 November 1957. J.C. Beaglehole Papers. 73-004-10/18. ATL
10 JCB to RAS, 18 April 1957
11 JCB, *Cook's Journals*, vol.2, pp.336–60
12 JCB to THB, 16 June 1957
13 JCB to THB, 22 May 1957
14 JCB to THB, 16 June 1957

15 ibid.
16 EMB to JEP, 21 July [1957] (in 1959 folder of JCB to JEP letters)
17 JCB to THB, 16 December 1957
18 RAS to JCB, 28 November–27 December 1957. J.C. Beaglehole Papers. 73-004-10/18. ATL
19 JCB to RAS, 15 April 1958
20 JCB to THB, 20 April 1958
21 RAS to JCB, 9 October 1958. J.C. Beaglehole Papers. 73-004-10/18. ATL
22 JCB to RAS, 4 September 1958
23 JCB to THB, 28 September 1958
24 JCB to RAS, 16 December 1958
25 JCB to THB, 11 June 1959
26 RAS to JCB, 23 March 1954. J.C. Beaglehole Papers. 73-004-10/16. ATL
27 RAS to JCB, 9 November 1956. ibid.
28 RAS to JCB, 13 November 1957. J.C. Beaglehole Papers. 73-004-10/18. ATL
29 RAS to JCB, 1 February 1958. ibid.
30 JCB to RAS, 25 May 1958
31 RAS to JCB, 9 October 1958. J.C. Beaglehole Papers. 73-004-10/18. ATL
32 RAS to JCB, 2 November 1960. ibid.
33 JCB to RAS, 7 December 1959. Unless otherwise noted, all the quotations in this paragraph and the following are from the same letter.
34 JCB, *The Life of Captain James Cook* (London: A. & C. Black, 1974), p.402
35 JCB to RAS, 7 December 1959
36 Marcel Aurousseau to JCB, 23 June 1959
37 JCB to RAS, 7 December 1959
38 JCB to Norman Richmond, 7 December 1959
39 JCB to RAS, 7 December 1959
40 JCB to RAS, 11 November 1960
41 JCB to RAS, 18 December 1960
42 J.A. Williamson to JCB, 2 August 1961
43 RAS to John Easton, 31 October 1956, carbon copy
44 These points are taken from John's textual introduction, *Cook's Journals*, vol.3, pp.clxxi
45 JCB, *The Life of Captain James Cook*, p.500
46 JCB, *Cook's Journals*, vol.3, p.vii
47 JCB to Don Marshall, 6 March 1960
48 JCB to Marshall, 21 April 1961
49 JCB to JEP, 2 February 1961
50 JCB to JEP, 10 May 1961
51 JCB to Margaret Titcomb, 2 October 1961. Ms Grp 53. Bishop Museum Archives
52 This quotation and others not separately referenced in the following paragraphs are from John's report to Stephen H. Stackpole, Director of the Carnegie Corporation, 18 February 1963, carbon copy
53 JCB, *Cook's Journals*, vol.3, pp.cxli-cxlii
54 ibid., p.cxxi
55 JCB to JEP, 25 June 1962
56 JCB to Bernard Smith, 21 February 1963. Bernard Smith Papers. ML MSS 5202. State Library of NSW
57 JCB to Titcomb, 23 June 1963. Ms Grp 53. Bishop Museum Archives
58 JCB to Helen Wallis, 17 October 1963
59 JCB to JEP, 6 November 1963
60 JCB to JEP, 30 October 1963

61 JCB to JEP, 21 November 1963
62 JCB to JEP, 29 June 1964
63 JCB to JEP, 17 November 1965
64 JCB to Titcomb, 30 August 1964. MS Grp 53. Bishop Museum Archives
65 JCB to JEP, 4 February 1965
66 For information on Dorothy Crozier, see Ewan Maidment, 'From the Archives: Crozier Papers', *Journal of Pacific History*, vol.38, no.3 (2003), pp.371–3
67 JCB to JEP, 11 January 1966
68 Eila Campbell to JCB, 18 November 1963. J.C. Beaglehole Papers. 73-004-05/14. ATL
69 Campbell to JCB, 26 August 1964. ibid.
70 Campbell to JCB,13 January 1965. ibid.
71 Easton to JCB, 15 February 1966
72 JCB to JEP, 30 April 1965
73 JCB to JEP, 26 May 1965
74 JCB to JEP, 22 December 1965
75 JCB to Wallis, 20 December 1964
76 Campbell to JCB, 1 January 1966. J.C. Beaglehole Papers. 73-004-05/14. ATL
77 JCB to E.T. Williams, 21 November 1965
78 JCB to Tim & Helen Beaglehole, 12 June 1966
79 Easton to JCB, 15 June 1966
80 JCB to Wallis, 28 September 1966
81 Williamson to JCB, 16 April 1954. J.C. Beaglehole Papers. 73-004-10/16. ATL
82 JCB to RAS, 9 July 1952
83 RAS to JCB, 9 December 1956. J.C. Beaglehole Papers. 73-004-10/18. ATL
84 JCB to RAS, 20 May 1964
85 Campbell to JCB, 11 December 1963. J.C. Beaglehole Papers. 73-004-05/14. ATL
86 JCB to Smith, 16 January 1968. Bernard Smith Papers. ML MSS 5202. State Library of NSW
87 Campbell to JCB, 2 November 1970. J.C. Beaglehole Papers. 73-004-05/14. ATL
88 The phrase John quoted is Boswell's, from his *Life of Johnson*, edited by G.B. Hill and L.F. Powell (Oxford: Clarendon Press, 1934), vol.1, p.6
89 This date, together with those given later, was noted by John on the manuscript
90 JCB to JEP, 19 October 1967
91 JCB to JEP, 20 February 1969
92 JCB to JEP, 30 August 1968
93 JCB to JEP. 19 March 1969
94 JCB to JEP, 16 June 1969
95 JCB to Wallis, 27 December 1970
96 JCB to Richmond, 29 July 1969
97 JCB to Eric McCormick, 24 February 1970. E.H. McCormick Papers. MS-Papers-5292-004. ATL
98 JCB to JEP, 29 January 1970
99 JCB to JEP, 5 March 1970
100 JCB to Wallis, 18 August 1970
101 JCB to Wallis, 4 December 1970
102 JCB to JEP, 24 January 1971
103 This and the following paragraph owe a lot to the review of the biography by Professor O.H.K. Spate in *Journal of Pacific History*, vol.11, nos.3–4 (1976), pp.247–52

104 The quote is from Spate; the pages he refers to in JCB, *The Life of Captain James Cook* are pp.237–47

105 JCB, *The Life of Captain James Cook*, pp.663–72

106 ibid., p.711

107 ibid., p.323

108 ibid., p.471

109 ibid., pp.199–200

110 ibid., p.365

111 ibid., pp.588–9

112 *New Zealand Journal of History*, vol.9, no.2 (October 1975), pp.186, 188

113 *History Book Club*, May 1964, pp.9–10

114 *Guardian*, 3 October 1974

115 Marshall Sahlins, *Islands of History* (Chicago: University of Chicago Press, 1985); and *How 'Natives' Think About Captain Cook for Example* (Chicago: University of Chicago Press, 1995)

116 Gananath Obeyesekere, *The Apotheosis of Captain Cook: European Mythmaking in the Pacific* (Princeton: Princeton University Press, 1992)

117 Anne Salmond, *The Trial of the Cannibal Dog: Captain Cook in the South Seas* (London: Allen Lane/Penguin Books, 2003)

118 Nicholas Thomas, *Discoveries: The Voyages of Captain James Cook* (London: Penguin Books, 2003)

119 JCB, *The Life of Captain James Cook*, p.302

120 JCB to Rolf du Rietz, 4 April 1970

121 JCB to JEP, 10 July 1963

13 PRIVATE LIFE AND PUBLIC CAUSES

1   JCB to E.T. Williams, 23 October 1953

2   JCB to JEP, undated (6? August 1952)

3   JCB to JEP, 14 February 1951

4   JCB to JEP, 26 September 1951

5   JCB to JEP, 10 October 1951

6   JCB to JEP, 7 November 1951

7   JCB to JEP, 21 March 1951

8   JCB, 'New Zealand Since the War: Politics and Culture', *Landfall*, vol.15, no.2 (June 1961), pp.138–52

9   Gordon Orr, 'Some Recent Legislation', *Landfall*, vol.6, no.1 (March 1952), p.55

10 JCB to JEP, 18 April 1951

11 Paul Gordon Lauren, '"A Very Special Moment in History": New Zealand's Role in the Evolution of International Human Rights', *NZ International Review*, vol.23., no.6 (Nov./Dec. 1998), pp.2–9

12 *Evening Post*, 20 April 1951, p.6

13 JCB to JEP, 26 April 1951

14 *Evening Post*, 26 April 1951, p.8

15 JCB to JEP, 18 April 1951

16 Keith Sinclair, *Walter Nash* (Auckland: Auckland University Press, 1976), p.287

17 Sonya Reesby, '"Putting Common Sense into Public Affairs": The Origins of the New Zealand Council for Civil Liberties' (research essay for BA Hons in history, Massey University, 1999), pp.11–14. Reesby's essay has been helpful for my account of the founding of the Council for Civil Liberties.

18 JCB to JEP, 14 November 1951

19 *Evening Post*, 13 November 1951, p.8

20   JCB to JEP, 14 November 1951
21   *Evening Post*, 13 November 1951, p.5. John's very brief notes for his speech, on a number of small cards, are in J.C. Beaglehole Papers. 73-004-01/09. ATL
22   JCB to JEP, 14 November 1951
23   Walter Scott, 'Civil Liberties', in *J.C. Beaglehole Some Personal Reflections: Supplement to the [VUW] Gazette*, no.11, 1971
24   JCB to JEP, 14 November 1951
25   JCB to JEP, 20 February 1952
26   JCB to JEP, 27 February 1952
27   JCB to JEP, 27 March 1952
28   Reesby, 'Putting Common Sense into Public Affairs', pp.15–18
29   JCB to JEP, 20 August 1952
30   JCB to Norman Richmond, 16 December 1952
31   F.L.W. Wood, '"A veritable man is not hidden among many": A Tribute by F.L.W. Wood', *NZ Listener*, 1 November 1971, p.11
32   JCB to JEP, 1 April 1954
33   Scott, 'Civil Liberties', in *J.C. Beaglehole Some Personal Reflections*
34   JCB to JEP, undated (6? August 1952)
35   A copy of McCormick's report, 'Development of the National Archives', is in J.C. Beaglehole Papers. 73-004-01/10. ATL
36   A copy of the Standish report is in J.C. Beaglehole Papers. 73-004-01/06. ATL
37   JCB, 'Memorandum for Professor Rutherford, Professor Wood, Professor Morrell, Professor Phillips' (ms draft), 22 August 1950
38   *Evening Post*, 6 August, 12 September 1952. A folder of newspaper clippings is in the J.C. Beaglehole Papers. 73-004-02/02. ATL
39   JCB to JEP, 6 August 1952
40   JCB to JEP, 13 August 1952
41   JCB to JEP, 25 September 1952
42   JCB, 'Why Archives?', *NZ Journal of Public Administration*, vol.15, no.1 (September 1952), pp.9–16
43   JCB to JEP, 11 September 1952
44   JCB to JEP, 25 September 1952
45   Rachel Barrowman, *Victoria University of Wellington 1899–1999* (Wellington: Victoria University Press, 1999), p.55
46   Jim Campbell, 'Colleague and Friend', in *J.C. Beaglehole Some Personal Recollections: Supplement to the [VUW] Gazette*, no.11, 1971
47   JCB to Richmond, 16 December 1952
48   JCB to JEP, 20 December 1956
49   Alan Moorehead to JCB, 1 March, 26 March, 5 May 1965
50   'I.L.G. Sutherland 1897–1952', *Journal of the Polynesian Society*, vol.61, nos.1 & 2 (March, June 1952), pp.120–1
51   E.H. McCormick, 'J.C. Beaglehole 1901–71: A Biographical Sketch', *Landfall*, vol.25, no.4 (December 1971), p.423
52   JCB to RAS, 19 November 1951
53   JCB to JEP, 23 April 1953
54   JCB, 'Sir Thomas Hunter', typescript of broadcast, 20 April 1953
55   McCormick, 'J.C. Beaglehole', p.423
56   JCB to Richmond, 16 December 1962
57   JCB to JEP, 23 September 1953
58   JCB to JEP, 7 October 1953
59   ibid.
60   JCB to JEP, 28 October 1953
61   McCormick to JCB, 19 October 1953

62   'Frances Hodgkins', *Design Review*, vol.5, no.5 (April 1954), pp.109–11
63   Ruth Ross to JCB, 22 September 1954 (carbon copy). Ruth Ross manuscript collection. MS 1442, Box 90(2). Auckland War Memorial Museum Library
64   JCB to Ross, 30 March 1955. ibid.
65   Ross to JCB, 25 February 1955 (carbon copy). ibid.
66   Mary Boyd, 'Ross, Ruth Miriam 1920–1982', *Dictionary of New Zealand Biography*, vol.5. Ross gives an account of this trip in her letter to John, 22 September 1955.
67   JCB to Ross, 30 March 1955. Ruth Ross manuscript collection. MS 1442, Box 90(2). Auckland War Memorial Museum Library
68   JCB to Ross, 4 April 1955. ibid.
69   JCB to Ross, 2 July 1955. Ruth Ross manuscript collection. MS 1442, Box 90(3). Auckland War Memorial Museum Library
70   R.M. Ross, 'The Autochthonous New Zealand Soil', in *The Feel of Truth: Essays in New Zealand and Pacific History*, edited by Peter Munz (Wellington: A.H. & A.W. Reed, 1969), p.47
71   JCB to JEP, 10 June 1953. A draft of John's memorandum is in J.C. Beaglehole Papers. 73-004-01/15. ATL
72   JCB to JEP, 16 September 1953
73   JCB to JEP, 9 December 1953
74   JCB to JEP, 12 May 1955
75   JCB to JEP, 2 June 1954
76   JCB to JEP, 24 March 1954
77   JCB to JEP, 2 February 1955
78   JCB to JEP, 23 September 1953
79   JCB to JEP, 8 June 1955
80   JCB to Fred Page, 7 February 1956. F.L. Page Papers. MS-Papers-3903-1/1/1. ATL
81   JCB, Memorandum for Under-Secretary, Internal Affairs, 15 February 1943. IA1, 135/37 pt. 1. ANZ. The papers on Pompallier House are in this file and pts. 2 & 3.
82   JCB to Secretary, Internal Affairs, 24 September 1951. IA1, 135/37 pt 3. ANZ
83   JCB to Principal, VUC, 16 June 1952, carbon copy
84   Historic Places Trust, *Annual Report 1959*
85   HPT, minutes, fifth meeting, 23 May 1956
86   JCB to JEP, 28 August 1956
87   HPT, minutes, eighth meeting, 28 November 1956
88   JCB to JEP, 22 February 1957
89   HPT, minutes, ninth meeting, 19 February 1957. The statement appeared in the *Evening Post*, 22 February 1957, p.8
90   *Evening Post*, 25 May 1956, p.10
91   Chris Maclean, *John Pascoe* (Nelson: Craig Potton, 2003), p.143
92   JCB to Richmond, 29 October 1959
93   JCB to JEP, 30 April 1959
94   'The Cathedral Church of St Paul', in Report of the National HPT for the year ended 31 March 1959, *AJHR*, H.27 (1959), pp.15–19
95   *Evening Post*, 2 August 1958. Pevsner's statement was followed by other supporting statements and correspondence.
96   *NZ Listener*, 20 November 1958
97   JCB to Richmond, 29 October 1959
98   ibid.
99   JCB, 'Private Property or National Interest?', *NZ Listener*, 6 March 1959
100 JCB to JEP, 17 March 1966

101 R.I.M. Burnett, 'John Beaglehole', *Turnbull Library Record*, vol.5(n.s.), no.1(May 1972), p.7

102 Ormond Wilson, *An Outsider Looks Back* (Wellington: Port Nicholson Press, 1982), pp.175–6

103 Burnett, 'John Beaglehole', p.7

104 Wilson, *An Outsider Looks Back*, p.177

105 Secretary of Internal Affairs to Director-General, Department of Lands and Survey, 21 February 1952. Waimate Mission House files. HPT records

106 JCB to JEP, 13 November 1963

107 JCB, *A House Renewed: Address at the Opening of the Mission House Waimate North, on 4 December 1966* (New Zealand HPT, 1967)

108 Note by JCB on the Waimate Mission House, 7 November 1964. Waimate Mission House files. HPT records

109 JCB to JEP, 21 August 1968

110 Wilson, *An Outsider Looks Back*, p.175

111 JCB to THB, 16 December 1957

112 JCB to JEP, 28 November 1957

113 JCB, 'Report of the New Zealand Representative, South-East Asian Round Table Bangkok January 27–February 2, 1958', copy

114 JCB to JEP, 1 February 1958

115 JCB to EMB, 26 January 1958

116 JCB to JEP, from a letter probably in March 1958. The first page with the date is missing.

117 JCB to JEP, 23 April 1958

118 JCB to THB, 28 September 1958

119 JCB to THB, 30 May 1958; JCB to JEP, 18 June 1968

120 JCB to Mary Beaven, 22 September 1958

121 JCB to THB, 15 December 1958

122 Papers relating to the conference are in Box 1, files 5, 6 and 7, of the records of the New Zealand Institute of International Affairs. J.C. Beaglehole Room, VUW Library

123 C.E. Carrington, 'The New Zealand Commonwealth Conference and Its Predecessors', *International Affairs*, vol.35, no.3 (July 1959), p.339

124 JCB, 'Introduction', in Ruth M. Allan, *Nelson: A History of Early Settlement* (Wellington: A.H. & A.W. Reed, 1965), p.viii

125 JCB to JEP, 1 March 1962

126 Fred Turnovsky, *Turnovsky: Fifty Years in New Zealand* (Wellington: Allen Unwin, 1990), pp.150–63. I draw on Turnovsky's account in the following six paragraphs.

127 JCB to JEP, 9 April 1959

128 John's feeling was reciprocated. See Turnovsky, *Turnovsky*, pp.136–7

129 JCB to JEP, 9 November 1959

130 Turnovsky, *Turnovsky*, p.159

131 JCB to JEP, 2 February 1961

132 JCB to JEP, 22 June 1961

133 Charles Brasch to Ian Milner, 27 August 1963. Ian Milner Papers. MS-Papers-4599. ATL

134 JCB to JEP, 9 November 1960

135 JCB to Woollaston, 9 August 1961. Toss Woollaston Papers. CA 457/2, Box 2. MONZPT

136 Gerald Barnett, *Toss Woollaston* (Wellington: National Art Gallery and Random House, 1991), p.32

137 JCB to Woollaston, 31 August 1961. Toss Woollaston Papers. See also Jill Trevelyan ed., *Toss Woollaston: A Life in Letters* (Wellington: Te Papa Press, 2004), p.239

138 Toss's letters on his trip are in Trevelyan, *Toss Woollaston*, pp.253–90
139 Toss to Edith Woollaston, 15 August 1962, ibid., p.277
140 JCB to JEP, 4 August 1961
141 JCB to JEP, 19 June 1963
142 Turnovsky, *Turnovsky*, p.160
143 JCB to JEP, 5 September 1963
144 JCB to JEP, 29 August 1963
145 Turnovsky, *Turnovsky*, pp.163–4; JCB to JEP, 25 May 1964
146 JCB to JEP, 29 June 1964
147 Wood, '"A veritable man is not hidden among many": A Tribute by F.L.W. Wood', *NZ Listener*, 1 November 1971, p.11

14 THE PRICE OF EMINENCE

1 JCB to JEP, 5 June 1958
2 JCB to JEP, 27 August 1958
3 JCB to THB, 23 August 1960
4 JCB to JEP, 31 August 1960
5 JCB to THB, 9 September 1960
6 JCB to JEP, 5 July 1961. He comments further in his letters of 15 July, 26 July, 4 August and 20 September 1961
7 JCB, 'Death of a University', *NZ Listener*, 12 January 1962, p.10. Text of a broadcast talk.
8 JCB to JEP, 27 March 1963
9 JCB to Norman Richmond, 17 November 1959
10 JCB to E.T. Williams, 4 June 1962
11 JCB to JEP, 25 June 1962
12 JCB to Wood, 14 August 1962
13 JCB to Williams, 3 July 1962
14 JCB to Williams, 21 November 1965
15 JCB to Williams, 6 January 1964
16 I.D. Campbell, memo for council, 21 May 1963, VC file, quoted in Rachel Barrowman, *Victoria University of Wellington 1899–1999* (Wellington: Victoria University Press, 1999), p.275
17 JCB to JEP, 25 July 1963
18 JCB to JEP, 29 August 1963
19 JCB to JEP, 25 September 1963
20 'Election Broadcasts', *NZ Listener*, 29 November 1963; p.8. JCB to JEP, 13 November 1963
21 JCB to JEP, 18 October 1963
22 Rachel Barrowman, *The Turnbull: A Library and its World* (Auckland: Auckland University Press and the Department of Internal Affairs, 1995), pp.103–9
23 ibid.
24 'Support for National Library proposal', letter signed jointly by JCB and university academic staff, *Dominion*, 2 March 1965, p.17
25 'Amalgamation for Turnbull Library Held Best', letter in *Evening Post*, 12 October 1965, p.26
26 JCB to JEP, 13 October 1965
27 JCB to JEP, 27 October 1965
28 JCB to Peter Beaglehole, 13 May 1966
29 ibid.
30 JCB to JEP, 1 December 1965
31 JCB to JEP, 22 May 1968

32 JCB to Tim and Helen Beaglehole, 13 December 1966
33 ibid.
34 JCB to JEP, 8 February 1967
35 ibid.
36 JCB to THB, 2 February 1967
37 JCB to JEP, 24 May 1967
38 JCB to JEP, 14 March 1963
39 JCB to JEP, 1 November 1967
40 JCB to JEP, 1 November 1967
41 I have drawn on this address in chapter 2, pp.43–4
42 JCB to JEP, 21 March 1968
43 JCB to JEP, 17 April 1968. He mentions reading Jane Austen in his letters of 21 March, 27 March, 17 April and 24 April 1968
44 JCB to JEP, 5 February 1969
45 JCB to JEP, 20 February 1969
46 ibid.
47 'The Study of Cook: A Host of Questions to Ask', *The Times*, 31 May 1969, p.9
48 'Cook Memorial', *Evening Post*, 4 March 1969, p.10
49 'The Unknown Cook', *NZ Listener*, 3 October 1969, pp.2–3
50 JCB to JEP, 18 November 1969
51 JCB to JEP, 27 November 1969
52 'Patron's Address: Not about Captain Cook', *New Zealand Libraries*, vol.33, no.2 (April 1970), pp.40, 45–50
53 JCB to Dan Davin, 3 May 1970. Dan Davin Papers. MS-Papers-5079-061. ATL
54 JCB to JEP, 1 May 1970
55 JCB to Phyllis Mander Jones, 3 May 1970. Phyllis Mander Jones Papers. MC MSS4337, Box 4(6). State Library of NSW
56 'From Bookshop Assistant to O.M.: Eminent Ex-bookseller talks to N.Z. Jubilee Conference', *Bookseller*, no.3418 (26 June 1971), pp.2594–7
57 'The Library and the Cosmos', in *Turnbull Library Record Jubilee Issue 1920–1970*, vol.3(n.s.), no.2 (August 1970), pp.65–77
58 'The Urewera Trip 1925', in *VUWTC'71: A Publication to Mark the 50th Jubilee of the Victoria University Tramping Club*, edited by B.A. Sissons (Wellington, 1971), pp.50–3
59 JCB to Ruth Ross, 1 April 1971. Ruth Ross Papers. MS 1442, Box 98(1). Auckland War Memorial Museum Library
60 JCB to JEP, 22 May 1971
61 For the following three paragraphs I have drawn on four articles about John written soon after his death: R.I.M. Burnett, 'John Beaglehole', in *Turnbull Library Record*, vol.5(n.s.), no.1 (May 1972), pp.4–8; J.W. Davidson, 'The New Zealand Scholar: A Note on J.C. Beaglehole (1901–1971)', in *Journal of Pacific History*, vol.7 (1972), pp.151–4; E.H. McCormick, 'J.C. Beaglehole 1901–71: A Biographical Sketch', in *Landfall*, vol.25, no.4 (December 1971), pp.413–23; and F.L.W. Wood, '"A veritable man is not hidden among many": A Tribute by F.L.W. Wood', *NZ Listener*, 1 November 1971
62 Burnett, 'John Beaglehole', p.6
63 Wood, 'A veritable man', p.11
64 McCormick, 'J.C. Beaglehole 1901–71', p.422
65 Wood, 'A veritable man', p.11

Bibliography

1. A SELECT LIST OF PUBLICATIONS BY J.C BEAGLEHOLE.

A bibliography of J.C. Beaglehole's publications, *John Cawte Beaglehole: A Bibliography* (with 297 entries), was prepared and published by the Alexander Turnbull Library in 1972. Kathleen Coleridge, while librarian in charge of the J.C. Beaglehole Room in the Victoria University of Wellington Library, added to and corrected the bibliography, and a copy of her revised version is held in the J.C. Beaglehole Room, together with further additions I have found in the research for this biography. The J.C. Beaglehole Room also holds copies of everything listed in the bibliography.

1922
Editorial in *Spike*, no.41 (June 1922), pp.[9]–12. Russian relief and the university as centre of social reform and progress.

1923
Editorial in *Spike*, no.43 (June 1923), pp.7–10. The role of the university in the community.
Editorial in *Spike*, no.44 (September 1923), pp.[1]–7. The essence of the university.

1924
'Ode on the Unveiling of the Memorial Window, Good Friday, April 18th, 1924: Mortalitate relicta vivunt immortalitate induti', Poem in *Spike*, Silver Jubilee Number (Easter 1924), pp.5–8.
'The Truth about Tramping', Article (signed Viator), *Spike*, no.45 (June 1924), pp.25–9.
'The "Truth" about Tramping: An Editorial Statement', *Spike*, no.46 (September 1924), pp.10–11.
'A Note on Joseph Conrad', *Spike*, no.46 (September 1924), pp.19–22.
Editorial in *Spike*, no.46 (September 1924), pp.[1]–6. On university reform.

1925
'On Piracy as a Profession for Young Gentlemen', Note (signed Junius Brutus), *Spike*, no.47 (June 1925), pp.13–16.
'The Cinderella of the Syllabus: Some Observations on a History Report', Review of *The Teaching of History in Primary and Secondary Schools* (Special Reports on Educational Subjects no.14). *National Education* (June 1925), pp.165–7.
'Devolution or Revolution', Consideration of *Report of Royal Commission on University Education in New Zealand* (Wellington, 1925). *Spike*, no.48 (September 1925), pp.22–6.
'The Discussions Club', *Spike* no.48 (September 1925), pp.55–8. Includes letter from JCB to the Chairman, Royal Commission on University Education, 'for the Victoria University College Free Discussions Club'.

1926

'The Butcher Shop', Anonymous article reviewing *The Butcher Shop* by Jean Devanny, and the decision of the New Zealand Board of Censors to ban it. *Spike*, no.49 (June 1926), pp.38–41.

'Going Home', *New Zealand Times*, 14 December 1926, p.27.

1927

'Bristol Impressions', *Spike*, no.51 (June 1927), pp.6–8.

'War Disabilities: Plea for Tolerance: A Night in Neustadt', Letter to the editor, *Evening Post*, 21 December 1927, p.17. Reprinted in the *New Zealand Worker*, 4 January 1928, p.8; and in *Spike*, no.53 (June 1928), pp.17–21.

1928

Captain Hobson and the New Zealand Company: A Study in Colonial Administration (Northampton, Mass.: Smith College, 1927), 112pp. (Smith College Studies in History, vol.13, nos.1–3, October 1927–April 1928).

'Molecular Theory', Poem in *The Venture*, edited by Anthony Blunt (Cambridge, 1928). Reprinted on JCB Christmas card, dated from 21 Brunswick Square, Bloomsbury, with a woodcut by Raymond McGrath.

1929

'Historical Research in London', *The Press*, 12 October 1929, p.15.

1930

'Molecular Theory', 'To a Fairy', 'The Climber', 'Despondency', 'The Cathedral', 'British Museum', 'In the Cotswolds', Poems in *Kowhai Gold: An Anthology of Contemporary Verse*, edited by Quentin Pope (London: J.M. Dent, 1930), pp.52–7.

1931

'On Foot Through the Urewera', *Rata: New Zealand Annual* (1931), pp.3–4, 7–8.

1932

'Communism and Hysterics', Letter (signed by N.M. Richmond and J.C. Beaglehole) in *New Zealand Worker*, 18 May 1932, p.6. Reprinted in *Academic Freedom in New Zealand, 1932–34: A Statement of the Facts*, collected by F.A. de la Mare (Auckland: Unicorn Press, 1935), pp.14–15

1933

'Youthful Nation: History of New Zealand', Serial publication in *National Opinion*, 19 October 1933 to 7 June 1934. Subtitle varies. Subsequently revised and published as *New Zealand: A Short History*.

'Considerations on Certain Music of J.S. Bach', poem in *Art in New Zealand*, vol.5, no.20 (June 1933), pp.213–18. Parts 4 and 5 reprinted in *New Zealand Best Poems of 1933*, vol.5, no.20 (Wellington: Harry H. Tombs, 1933), pp.10–12.

'Decline of the West', Poem in *Phoenix*, vol.2, no.2 (June 1933), pp.11–13.

1934

The Exploration of the Pacific (London: A. & C. Black, 1934), 426pp.

'Meditation on Historic Change', Poem in *Art in New Zealand*, vol.7, no.1 (September 1934), pp.18–26. Part 6 reprinted in *New Zealand Best Poems of 1934* (Wellington: Harry H. Tombs, 1934), pp.18–19.

1935

Review of *The Maori Situation* by I.L.G. Sutherland, *Tomorrow*, 28 August 1935, pp.5–7.

1936

New Zealand: A Short History (London: Allen & Unwin, 1936), 164pp.

'A Note on T.A. McCormack', *Art in New Zealand,* vol.8, no.4 (June 1936), pp.197–200.

Review of *The Maori Situation* by I.L.G. Sutherland, *Pacific Affairs,* vol.9, no.3 (September 1936), pp.481–3.

1937

The University of New Zealand: An Historical Study (Wellington: New Zealand Council for Educational Research, 1937), 442pp.

1938

Words for Music (Christchurch: Caxton Press, 1938), 14pp.

A School of Political Studies (Wellington: New Zealand Council for Educational Research, 1938), 24pp.

1939

'New Zealand in the Commonwealth: An Attempt at Objectivity', in *Contemporary New Zealand: A Survey of Domestic and Foreign Policy,* edited by G.R. Powles (Wellington: New Zealand Institute of International Affairs, 1939), pp.1–16.

The Discovery of New Zealand (Wellington: Department of Internal Affairs, 1939), 176pp.

1940

'The New Zealand Mind', *Australian Quarterly,* vol.12, no.4 (December 1940), pp.40–50.

'Centennial Meditations', *Spike,* no.68 (1940), pp.18–19.

1941

'The Colonial Office, 1782–1854', *Historical Studies,* vol.1, no.3 (April 1941), pp.170–89.

Review of *Island and Time* by Allen Curnow, *Book: A Miscellany,* no.3 (August 1941), p.[17]. Reprinted from the *Press.*

'A Few Harsh Words on *Areopagitica* as Printed', *Book,* no.4 (September 1941), pp.[18–20].

1942

Abel Janszoon Tasman and the Discovery of New Zealand, edited and designed by J.C. Beaglehole (Wellington: Department of Internal Affairs, 1942), includes essay by JCB, 'On the Place of Tasman's Voyage in History', pp.11–43.

Meet New Zealand (Wellington: Department of Internal Affairs, 1942), 36pp.

'Some Philosophies of History', *Historical Studies,* vol.2, no.6 (November 1942), pp.95–113.

1943

'Copernicus and His Times', in *Nicholas Copernicus: Quadricentennial Addresses, 1543–1943* (Wellington: Victoria University College, 1943), pp.3–13.

'The Writing of Imperial History', reviews of *The British Empire 1815–1939* by Paul Knaplund, and *A History of South Africa, Social and Economic* by C.W. de Kiewiet, *Historical Studies,* vol.2, no.7 (May 1943), pp.129–40.

1944

'The Old Empire and the New', 'The Statute and Constitutional Change', in *New Zealand and the Statute of Westminster,* five lectures by J.C. Beaglehole, F.L.W. Wood, Leslie Lipson, R.O. McGechan, edited by J.C. Beaglehole (Wellington: Victoria University College, 1944), pp.1–32, 33–64.

1945

Introduction to New Zealand, edited and designed by J.C. Beaglehole (Wellington: Department of Internal Affairs, 1945), 271pp.

'Cycling at Night' (1935), 'Lighting my Pipe' (1934), 'Newspaper Reader, 1934', 'Considerations on Certain Music of J.S. Bach: To N.M. Richmond' (1931). Poems in *A Book of New Zealand Verse 1923–45,* edited by Allen Curnow (Christchurch: Caxton, 1945), pp.97, 98–9, 100–5.

'Draft Song for Victory: To John Mulgan and Other New Zealanders', Poem in *New Zealand Listener,* 25 May 1945, p.7.

1946

'History and the New Zealander', in *The University and the Community: Essays in Honour of Thomas Alexander Hunter* (Wellington: Victoria University College, 1946), pp.98–124.

'The Foreign Ministers of the British Commonwealth: Peter Fraser as Foreign Secretary', *World Affairs,* vol.2, no.2 (June 1946), pp.3–6.

1947

The Exploration of the Pacific, second edition (London: A. & C. Black, 1947), 426pp.

How History Is Written (Wellington: Department of Education, School Publications Branch, 1947), Post-primary School Bulletin, vol.1, no.8

'Discovery and Exploration', 'International and Commonwealth Relations', in *New Zealand,* edited by Horace Belshaw (Berkeley and Los Angeles: University of California Press, 1947), pp.3–19, 292–312.

'Reflections on an Orchestral Performance', *New Zealand Listener,* 21 March 1947, pp.8–9.

'Dr Beaglehole Replies', Letter in *New Zealand Listener,* 24 April 1947, p.22.

1948

Something about the Pacific (Wellington: Department of Education, School Publications Branch, 1948), Post-primary School Bulletin, vol.2, no.11.

'Book Production in New Zealand', *Studio: New Zealand Issue,* vol.135, no.661 (April 1948), pp.130–1.

'Colin McCahon's Pictures', *New Zealand Listener,* 5 March 1948, p.7.

'The National Orchestra: An Article and a Postscript', *Landfall,* vol.2, no.4 (December 1948), pp.307–20.

1949

'A College Jubilee', *New Zealand Listener,* 13 May 1949, pp.6–7.

Victoria University College: An Essay Towards a History (Wellington: New Zealand University Press, 1949), 330pp.

'Professor von Zedlitz', *Education,* vol.2, no.4 (September 1949), pp.2–6.

'Simile' (1921), 'Waimakariri (January 6th, 1926)', 'Interior' (1927), 'The Rata' (1930), 'D.J. Donald: Obit. 23 June 1938. In memoriam' (1938), 'Ode on the Unveiling . . .' (1924), 'The Unreturned' (1920). Poems in *The Old Clay Patch,* third edition (Wellington: New Zealand University Press, 1949), pp.9–13, 123–8, 129.

1950

'Is International Understanding Possible?', *BBC Listener,* vol.43, no.1101 (2 March 1950), pp.367–8. Text of Third Programme broadcast.

1951

'Sir Thomas Hunter', *New Zealand Journal of Public Administration,* vol.13, no.2 (March 1951), pp.1–5.

'A Small Bouquet for the Education Department', *Arts Year Book 7* (Wellington: Wingfield Press, 1951), pp.122–9.

'Note on a Collection of Paintings', *Landfall*, vol.5, no.3 (September 1951), pp.227–30. Paintings exhibited abroad by Helen Hitchings.

1952

The Idea of Kingship (Wellington: Department of Education, School Publications Branch, 1952), Post-primary School Bulletin, vol.6, no.4.

'I.L.G. Sutherland 1897–1952', *Journal of the Polynesian Society*, vol.41, nos.1,2 (March and June 1952), pp.120–1.

'Victorian Heritage: Thoughts on New Zealand's Social History', *Political Science*, vol.4, no.1 (March 1952), pp.29–37.

'Why Archives?' *New Zealand Journal of Public Administration,* vol.15, no.1 (September 1952), pp.9–16.

1953

'Learning, Law, Politics, Friendship', Reviews of *Holmes–Laski Letters*, edited by Mark de Wolfe Howe, and *Harold Laski (1893–1950): A Biographical Memoir* by Kingsley Martin. *Parsons Packet,* no.23 (July 1953), pp.8–10.

'Brilliant Harvest of Patience and Determination: The Nan Kivell Collection of Early New Zealand Pictures . . . ' *New Zealand Listener,* 11 December 1953, p.8.

'Indefinable but Priceless Links with Crown', *Evening Post,* 23 December 1953, p.6. Supplement on occasion of Royal Tour, 1953–54.

1954

The New Zealand Scholar (Margaret Condliffe Memorial Lecture Canterbury College, 21 April 1954), (Christchurch: Canterbury University College, 1954), 24pp. Reprinted in *The Feel of Truth: Essays in New Zealand and Pacific History Presented to F.L.W. Wood and J.C. Beaglehole on the Occasion of Their Retirement,* edited by Peter Munz (Wellington: A.H. & A.W. Reed for Victoria University of Wellington, 1969), pp.237–52.

'The Development of New Zealand Nationality', *Cahiers d'Histoire Mondiale: Journal of World History,* vol.2, no.1 (August 1954), pp.106–23.

'Frances Hodgkins', *Design Review,* vol.5, no.5 (April 1954), pp.109–11.

'Winston Monk', *Landfall,* vol.8, no.2 (June 1954), pp.117–18.

1955

The Journals of Captain James Cook on His Voyages of Discovery: The Voyage of the Endeavour *1768–1771* [vol.l], edited by J.C. Beaglehole (Cambridge: Cambridge University Press for the Hakluyt Society, 1955), 970pp. (Hakluyt Society extra series no.34).

1956

'On the Character of Captain James Cook', *Geographical Journal,* vol.122, part 4 (December 1956), pp.417–29.

1957

'Duty to Future, Present, Past. Preserving St. Paul's as an Historic Place', *Evening Post,* 22 February 1957, p.8. Statement by Chairman of National Historic Places Trust, prepared substantially by JCB.

'Some Problems of Editing Cook's Journals', *Historical Studies,* vol.8 (November 1957), pp.20–31.

1958

'A Note on the Paintings of Evelyn Page', *Landfall,* vol.12, no.4 (December 1958), pp.359–63.

1959

'*The Cathedral Church of St. Paul, Wellington: The Case for Its Preservation* (Wellington: National Historic Places Trust, 1959), 7pp.

'Fraser, Peter', biographical article in the *Dictionary of National Biography 1941–1950* (Oxford: Oxford University Press, 1959), pp.271–2.

'Private Property or National Interest?', *New Zealand Listener*, 6 March 1959, p.4.

'Research in the University', *New Zealand University Journal*, vol.8 (1959), pp.17–24.

1960

'The British Commonwealth of Nations', in *The New Cambridge Modern History*, vol.12 (Cambridge: Cambridge University Press, 1960), pp.529–55.

Foreword to *Doctor Agnes Bennett* by Cecil Manson and Celia Manson, Michael Joseph, London, 1960, pp.vii–xiii.

1961

The Discovery of New Zealand, second edition (London: Oxford University Press, 1961), 114pp.

The Journals of Captain James Cook on His Voyages of Discovery: The Voyage of the Resolution *and* Adventure, *1772–1775* [vol.2], edited by J.C. Beaglehole (Cambridge: Cambridge University Press for the Hakluyt Society, 1961), 1191pp (Hakluyt Society extra series no.35).

'New Zealand Since the War: 4. Politics and Culture', *Landfall*, vol.15, no.2 (June 1961), pp.138–52.

1962

The Endeavour Journal of Joseph Banks 1768–1771, edited by J.C. Beaglehole (Sydney: Trustees of the Public Library of New South Wales in association with Angus and Robertson, 1962), 2 vols, 1005pp.

'Death of a University', *New Zealand Listener*, 12 January 1962, p.10. Text of a broadcast talk.

'On the Duties of a Librarian', *New Zealand Libraries*, vol.25, no.1 (January–February 1962), pp.1–6. Address delivered at a graduation ceremony of the New Zealand Library School, 24 November 1961.

1963

The Endeavour Journal of Joseph Banks 1768–1771, edited by J.C. Beaglehole, second edition (Sydney: Angus and Robertson, 1963).

1964

'The Death of Captain Cook', *Australian Journal of Science*, vol.26, no.10 (April 1964), pp.297–304. Presidential address to ANZAAS Congress (Section E), Canberra.

'The Death of Captain Cook', *Historical Studies*, vol.11, no.43 (October 1964), pp.289–305. Revised version of address.

1965

'The Wandering Scholars', *Ethnos*, vol.30 (1965), pp.39–56. Address at opening of exhibition from the Alströmer Collection of the Ethnological Museum of Sweden, at Dominion Museum, Wellington, 28 October 1965.

Nelson: A History of Early Settlement by Ruth M. Allan, edited by J.C. Beaglehole (Wellington: A.H. & A.W. Reed, 1965). Introduction, with much editorial revision, following the author's death.

'Country Loses a Personality', *Dominion*, 9 December 1965, p.2. Obituary of R.M. Burdon.

1966

The Exploration of the Pacific, third (extensively revised) edition (London and Stanford: A. & C. Black, and Stanford University Press, 1966), 356pp.

The Wandering Scholars (Wellington: Dominion Museum, 1966), 15pp.

Biographical articles in *An Encyclopaedia of New Zealand* (Wellington: Government Printer, 1966). 'Hunter, Sir Thomas Alexander', vol.2, pp.123–4; 'MacLaurin, Richard Cockburn', vol.2, p.369.

1967

Captain Cook and Captain Bligh (Dr W.E. Collins Lecture, delivered at the university on 3 August 1967) (Wellington: Victoria University of Wellington, 1967), 27pp.

A House Renewed (Wellington: New Zealand Historic Places Trust, 1967), 7pp. Address at the opening of the Mission House, Waimate North, 4 December 1966.

The Journals of Captain James Cook on His Voyages of Discovery: The Voyage of the Resolution *and* Discovery, *1776–1780* [Vol.3, Pts 1 and 2], edited by J.C. Beaglehole (Cambridge: Cambridge University Press for the Hakluyt Society, 1967), 1871pp. (Hakluyt Society extra series no.36).

Biographical articles in *Encyclopaedia Britannica* (Chicago: 1967). 'Allen, Sir James', vol.1, p.642; 'Cook, James', vol.6, pp.442–3; 'Dalrymple, Alexander', vol.7, p.11; 'Fraser, Peter', vol.9, p.811; 'Holland, Henry Edmund', 'Holland, Sir Sidney George', vol.11, pp.594, 596; 'Seddon, Richard John', vol.20, p.154; 'Vogel, Sir Julius', 'Ward, Sir Joseph George', vol.23, pp.96, 208.

'Cook, James', biographical article in *Book World Encyclopaedia* (Sydney: 1967), pp.202–3.

1968

The Journals of Captain James Cook on His Voyages of Discovery: The Voyage of the Endeavour *1768–1771*, edited by J.C. Beaglehole. Reprinted with addenda and corrigenda.

'The British Commonwealth of Nations', in *New Cambridge Modern History,* vol.12 (Cambridge: Cambridge University Press, 1968), pp.373–402. Revised text.

'Our Music Through the Years', *Theme,* no.13 (October 1968), pp.14–15. Text of an address to the annual meeting of the Chamber Music Federation of New Zealand.

1969

The Journals of Captain James Cook on His Voyages of Discovery: The Voyage of the Resolution *and* Adventure *1772–1775*, edited by J.C. Beaglehole. Reprinted with addenda and corrigenda.

The Discovery of Australia by G. Arnold Wood, revised by J.C. Beaglehole [second revised edition] (Melbourne: Macmillan of Australia, 1969), 406pp.

'Cook the Navigator', *Royal Society of London Proceedings* A314 (1969), pp.27–38.

'Eighteenth Century Science and the Voyages of Discovery', *New Zealand Journal of History,* vol.3, no.2 (November 1969), pp.107–23.

'Some Problems of Cook's Biographer' (Eva G.R. Taylor Memorial Lecture), *Mariner's Mirror,* vol.55, no.4 (November 1969), pp.365–81.

Foreword to *James Cook and New Zealand* by A.C. Begg and N.C. Begg (Wellington: Government Printer, 1969).

1970

Cook the Writer (Sixth George Arnold Wood Memorial Lecture delivered in the University of Sydney, 15 April 1970) (Sydney: Sydney University Press, 1970), 22pp.

'Captain Cook and Wellington Harbour', in *Wellington Prospect: Survey of a City 1840–1970*, edited by N.L. McLeod and B.H. Farland (Wellington: Hicks Smith and Sons, 1970), pp.13–17.

'Cook the Man', in *Captain Cook, Navigator and Scientist: Papers Presented at* the Cook Bicentenary Symposium Australian Academy of Science, Canberra 1 May 1969, edited by G.M. Badger (Canberra: Australian National University Press, 1970), pp.11–29.

'The Library and the Cosmos', Turnbull Library Record, vol.3(n.s.), no.2 (August 1970), pp.65–77. Jubilee address delivered at the Alexander Turnbull Library, 30 June 1970. Extracts reprinted in Evening Post, 16 October 1971, p.46.

'Patron's Address: Not About Captain Cook', New Zealand Libraries, vol.33, no.2 (April 1970), pp.40, 45–50. Address delivered at New Zealand Library Association Conference, Nelson, 10 February 1970.

1971

James Cook and Mercury Bay (Wellington: Wai-te-ata Press, 1971), 11pp.

'Some Problems of Cook's Biographer', 'Cook the navigator', in Employ'd as a Discoverer, Papers Presented at the Captain Cook Bi-Centenary Symposium Sutherland Shire, 1–3 May, 1970, edited by J.V.S. Megaw (Sydney: A.H. & A.W. Reed, 1971), pp.23–41, 117–34.

'The Urewera Trip 1925', in VUWTC '71: A Publication to mark the 50th Jubilee of the Victoria University Tramping Club, edited by B.A. Sissons (Wellington: 1971), pp.50–3. Reprint of 'On Foot Through the Urewera', 1931.

'From Bookshop Assistant to O.M.: Eminent Ex-bookseller Talks to N.Z. Jubilee Conference', Bookseller, no.3418 (26 June 1971), pp.2594–7.

1974

(Posthumous publications)

The Life of Captain James Cook (London: Hakluyt Society, 1974), 771pp. (Hakluyt Society extra series no.37). Issued as vol.4 of The Journals of Captain James Cook. Prepared for the press by T.H. Beaglehole.

The Life of Captain James Cook (London and Stanford: A. & C. Black, and Stanford University Press, 1974), 771pp.

2. MANUSCRIPT SOURCES

After JCB's death a number of boxes of papers from his study, including a lot of material relating to his work on Cook, were given to the Alexander Turnbull Library. A large amount more, including family letters, remained in the family's keeping. Other important sources for this biography held by the Turnbull Library are the Janet Paul Papers (especially the letters JCB wrote to her between 1945 and 1971), and the papers of R.M. Campbell, F.A. de la Mare, and J.W. Heenan. I have also found material in the Turnbull's holdings of papers of J.S. Beaglehole, Dan Davin, R.H. Hooper, George Jackson, E.H. McCormick, Ian Milner, F.L. Page, Mount Cook School, the Mutual Improvement Societies, the Wellington Co-operative Book Society, and the Wellington Chamber Music Society. From its oral history collection I have used the interviews with Elsie Beaglehole, Challis Hooper, and Amy Ward.

The J.C. Beaglehole Room in the Victoria University Library has a small amount of J.C. Beaglehole manuscript material. It also holds the papers of Ernest and Pearl Beaglehole; of F.L.W. Wood as head of the department of history from 1935 to 1969; further records of Mount Cook School; and the records of the New Zealand Institute of International Affairs. JCB's letters to Downie Stewart are in the Downie Stewart Papers in the Hocken Library, University of Otago, Dunedin; those to Ruth Ross (together with carbon copies of many of hers to him) are in the Ruth Ross Collection in the Auckland War Memorial Museum Library; those to Willis Airey are in the Willis Airey Papers, University of Auckland Library. Jill Trevelyan sent me copies of a number of letters from JCB to Toss Woollaston, from the Woollaston Archive, Museum of New Zealand Te Papa Tongarewa.

From the State Library of New South Wales, I have used material from JCB's correspondence with the library, in its archives, and from the papers of Phyllis Mander Jones, and Professor Bernard Smith. The Bishop Museum in Honolulu kindly sent me copies of a number of Beaglehole letters held in its archives. In the New Zealand National Archives I have made use of the records of the Department of Internal Affairs, and in the New Zealand Historic Places Trust a number of files relating to its early years.

Two collections of letters have been of tremendous value in writing this biography. Mark Richmond sent me copies of the surviving correspondence between his father, Norman Richmond, and JCB. And Professor Glyndwr Williams retrieved and passed on to me a box of Hakluyt Society correspondence, largely consisting of the letters from JCB to R.A. Skelton.

Perhaps not surprisingly, many of JCB's correspondents carefully kept his letters, and I have profited considerably by their willingness to make these available to me. They include members of the family: Giles and Jenny Beaglehole, Diana Beaglehole, Mary Beaven, Peter Beaglehole and Betty Beaglehole (who also sent me copies of JCB's letters to his brother Keith). Others who have given or lent me letters to copy include Vivienne Bogle, Mary Boyd, R.M. Campbell, Professor Kenneth Dutton (letters from JCB to Ian Henning), Jule Einhorn, Natalie Goodall (from Tierra del Fuego), Marsden Horden, Kate Lawler (correspondence with her father, A.G.B. Fisher), Ilse Jacoby, Kathleen McKay, Donald S. Marshall, Rolf du Rietz, Helen Wallis, Professor F.L.W. Wood and Sir Edgar Williams.

3. OTHER WORKS

Alcorn, Noeline, *To the Fullest Extent of His Powers: C.E. Beeby's Life in Education* (Wellington: Victoria University Press, 1999).

Alington, Margaret H., *Unquiet Earth: A History of the Bolton Street Cemetery* (Wellington: Wellington City Council and Ministry of Works and Development, 1978).

Bade, James N., *Out of the Shadow of War: The German Connection with New Zealand in the Twentieth Century* (Melbourne: Oxford University Press, 1998).

Barnett, Gerald, *Toss Woollaston: An Illustrated Biography* (Wellington: National Art Gallery and Random House, 1991.

Barrowman, Rachel, *A Popular Vision: The Arts and the Left in New Zealand 1930–1950* (Wellington: Victoria University Press, 1991).

Barrowman, Rachel, *The Turnbull: A Library and Its World* (Auckland: Auckland University Press and Department of Internal Affairs, 1995).

Barrowman, Rachel, '"Culture-organising": Joe Heenan and the Beginnings of State Patronage of the Arts', *New Zealand Studies*, vol.6, no.2 (July 1996).

Barrowman, Rachel, *Victoria University of Wellington 1899–1999: A History* (Wellington: Victoria University Press, 1999).

Bassett, Michael, *The Mother of All Departments: The History of the Department of Internal Affairs* (Auckland: Auckland University Press and Department of Internal Affairs, 1997).

Bassett, Michael and King, Michael, *Tomorrow Comes the Song: A Life of Peter Fraser* (Auckland: Penguin, 2000).

J.C. Beaglehole Some Personal Recollections: Supplement to the [Victoria University] Gazette (contributions by Tim Beaglehole, Harold Miller, James Bertram, Mary Boyd, W.J. Scott, Fred Page and Jim Campbell), no.11, 1971.

Beasley, A.W., *The Light Accepted: 125 Years of Wellington College* (Wellington: Board of Trustees of Wellington College, 1992).

Beeby, C.E., *The Biography of an Idea: Beeby on Education* (Wellington: New Zealand Council for Educational Research, 1992).

Beeby, C.E., 'The Beginnings of the NZCER', reminiscences of C.E. Beeby at the New Zealand Council for Educational Research 50th Anniversary Dinner, Wellington, 19 May 1984, typescript, NZCER.

Berry, Claude, *Cornwall* (London: Robert Hale, 1949).

Bertram, James, *Capes of China Slide Away: A Memoir of Peace and War 1910–1980* (Auckland: Auckland University Press, 1993).

Birch, D.J. and J.M. Horn, eds., *The History Laboratory: The Institute of Historical Research, 1921–96* (London: Institute of Historical Research, 1999).

Bönisch-Brednich, Brigitte, *Keeping a Low Profile: An Oral History of German Immigration to New Zealand* (Wellington: Victoria University Press, 2002).

Booker, A.J., 'The Centennial Surveys of New Zealand, 1936–41', BA Hons research essay in history, Massey University, 1983.

Brooks, Van Wyck, 'Prologue', in J. Frank Stimson, *Songs and Tales of the Sea Kings* (Salem, Mass.: Peabody Museum of Salem, 1957).

Brown, Don, *Mount Cook School 1875–1975* (Wellington: Mount Cook School Centennial Committee, 1975).

Burnett, R.I.M., 'John Beaglehole', *Turnbull Library Record,* vol.5(n.s.), no.1 (May 1972).

Campbell, R.M., 'In the Name of National Security', *New Zealand Listener,* 23 February 1974.

Carrington, C.E., 'The New Zealand Commonwealth Conference and Its Predecessors', *International Affairs,* vol.35, no.3 (July 1959).

Carter, Ian, *Gadfly: The Life and Times of James Shelley* (Auckland: Auckland University Press, 1993).

Dakin, J.C., 'Mutual Improvement Societies – The Way They Worked', *New Zealand Journal of Adult Learning,* vol.19, nos.1,2 (May/October 1987).

Davidson, J.W., 'The New Zealand Scholar: A Note on J.C. Beaglehole, 1901–1971', *Journal of Pacific History,* vol.7 (1972).

de la Mare, F.A., *Academic Freedom in New Zealand, 1932–34* (Auckland: Unicorn Press, 1935).

Dictionary of New Zealand Biography, vols.3–5 (Auckland: Auckland University Press and the Department of Internal Affairs, 1998, 2000).

Dreaver, Anthony, *An Eye for Country: The Life and Work of Leslie Adkin* (Wellington: Victoria University Press, 1997).

Dutton, Kenneth R., *Ian Henning (1905–1975): A Man and His Times* (Mt Nemo: Boombana Publications, 2002).

Garrett, Jane, *An Artist's Daughter: With Christopher Perkins in New Zealand 1929–34* (Auckland: Shoal Bay Press, 1986).

Highland, Genevieve A., Roland W. Force, Alan Howard, Marion Kelly, and Yosihiko H. Sinoto, *Polynesian Culture History: Essays in Honor of Kenneth P. Emory* (Honolulu: Bishop Museum Press, 1967).

Hilliard, Chris, 'Island Stories: The Writing of New Zealand History 1920–1940', MA thesis, University of Auckland, 1997.

Hilliard, Chris, 'Stories of Becoming: The Centennial Surveys and the Colonization of New Zealand', *New Zealand Journal of History,* vol.33, no.1 (April 1999).

Holroyd, Michael, *Works on Paper: The Craft of Biography and Autobiography* (London: Little, Brown and Company, 2002).

Horrocks, Ingrid, 'Communism and Hysterics: Academic Freedom and Auckland University's Retrenchment of J.C. Beaglehole 1932', BA Hons research essay in history, Victoria University of Wellington, 1996.

Jensen, Owen, *The NZBC Symphony Orchestra* (Wellington: A.H. & A.W. Reed, 1966).

Jones, Lawrence, *Picking Up the Traces: The Making of a New Zealand Literary Culture 1932–1945* (Wellington: Victoria University Press, 2003).

Kenyon, J.P., *The History Men: The Historical Profession in England since the Renaissance* (London: Weidenfeld and Nicolson, 1983).

King, Michael, *Frank Sargeson: A Life* (Auckland: Penguin, 1995).

Lauren, Paul Gordon, '"A very special moment in history": New Zealand's Role in the Evolution of International Human Rights', *NZ International Review*, vol.23, no.6 (November/December 1998).

McCormick, E.H., *Eric Lee-Johnson* (Hamilton: Paul's Book Arcade, 1956).

McCormick, E.H., *An Absurd Ambition: Autobiographical Writings*, edited by Dennis McEldowney (Auckland: Auckland University Press, 1996).

McCormick, E.H., 'J.C. Beaglehole 1901–71: A Biographical Sketch', *Landfall*, vol.25, no.4 (December 1971).

McEldowney, Dennis, 'Scholarly Publishing in New Zealand', *Scholarly Publishing* (University of Toronto Press), vol.1, no.1 (October 1969).

Mackay, David, 'Exploring the Pacific, Exploring James Cook', in *Pacific Empires: Essays in Honour of Glyndwr Williams*, edited by Alan Frost and Jane Samson (Melbourne: Melbourne University Press, 1999).

Mackenzie, Norman and Jeanne, *The Time Traveller: The Life of H.G.Wells* (London: Weidenfeld and Nicolson, 1973).

MacKillop, Ian, *F.R. Leavis: A Life in Criticism* (London: Penguin, 1997).

Maclean, Chris, *John Pascoe* (Nelson: Craig Potton Publishing in association with the Whitcombe Press, 2003).

Maidment, Ewan, 'From the Archives: Crozier Papers', *Journal of Pacific History*, vol.38, no.3 (2003).

Maindonald, John, *A Radical Religious Heritage: Auckland Unitarian Church and Its Wider Connections 1898 (Building 1901)–1991* (Auckland: Auckland Unitarian Church, 1991).

Manson, Cecil and Celia Manson, *Doctor Agnes Bennett* (London and Wellington: Michael Joseph and Whitcombe and Tombs, 1960).

Martin, Kingsley, *Harold Laski (1893–1950): A Biographical Memoir* (London: Gollancz, 1953).

Munz, Peter, 'A Personal Memoir', in *The Feel of Truth: Essays in New Zealand and Pacific History Presented to F.L.W. Wood and J.C. Beaglehole on the Occasion of Their Retirement*, edited by Peter Munz (Wellington: A.H. & A.W. Reed for Victoria University of Wellington, 1969).

New Zealand Institute of International Affairs, *The New Zealand Institute of International Affairs: Origins, Developments, Prospects* (Wellington: New Zealand Institute of International Affairs, 2002).

O'Donovan, Donal, *God's Architect: A Life of Raymond McGrath* (Wicklow: Kilbride Books, 1995).

Oliver, W.H., 'J.C. Beaglehole and F.L.W. Wood', in *Eminent Victorians: Great Teachers and Scholars from Victoria's First 100 years*, edited by Vincent O'Sullivan (Wellington: Stout Research Centre, Victoria University of Wellington, 2000).

Orr, Gordon, 'Some Recent Legislation', *Landfall*, vol.6, no.1 (March 1952).

O'Sullivan, Vincent, *Long Journey to the Border: A Life of John Mulgan* (Auckland: Penguin, 2003).

Ottillinger, Eva B. and August Sarnitz, *Ernst Plischke: Das Neue Bauen und die Neue Welt: Das Gesamtwerk* (Munchen/Berlin/London/New York: Prestel Verlag, , 2003).

Page, Frederick, *A Musician's Journal 1905–1983* (Dunedin: John McIndoe, 1986).

Paul, Janet, 'Hints of Becoming', in *Beyond Expectations: Fourteen New Zealand Women Write about Their Lives*, edited by Margaret Clark (Wellington: Allen and Unwin/Port Nicholson Press, 1986).

Phillips, Jock, 'Of Verandahs and Fish and Chips and Footie on Saturday

Afternoon', *The New Zealand Journal of History,* vol.24, no.2 (October 1990).

Phillips, Jock, 'Our History, Our Selves: The Historian and National Identity', *New Zealand Journal of History,* vol.30, no.2 (October 1996).

Porter, Frances, *A Sense of History: A Commemorative Publication for John Cawte Beaglehole, O.M., about James Cook's Landing Sites in New Zealand* (Wellington: New Zealand Government Printer, 1978).

Quinn, D.B., 'R.A. Skelton of the Map Room', in *Compassing the Vaste Globe of the Earth: Studies in the History of the Hakluyt Society 1846–1996,* edited by R.C. Bridges and P.E.H. Hair (London: Hakluyt Society, 1996).

Reesby, Sonia, '"Putting Common Sense into Public Affairs": The Origins of the New Zealand Council for Civil Liberties', BA Hons research essay in history, Massey University, 1999.

Richards, Eric, ed., *The Flinders History of South Australia. Social History* (Netley, South Australia: Wakefield Press, 1986).

Robinson, Roger and Nelson Wattie, eds., *The Oxford Companion to New Zealand Literature* (Melboune: Oxford Universty Press New Zealand, 1998).

Ronnie, Mary, *Education for Librarianship in New Zealand* (London: Mansell, 1996).

Rowe, John, *Cornwall in the Age of the Industrial Revolution* (Liverpool: Liverpool University Press, 1953).

Rowley, Hazel, *Christina Stead: A Biography* (Melbourne: William Heinemann, 1993).

Rowse, A.L., *Historians I Have Known* (London: Duckworth, 1995).

Scott, W.J., 'Civil Liberties in New Zealand', *Landfall,* vol.10, no.1 (March 1956).

Scudder, Susan, '"Bringing it Home": New Zealand Responses to the Spanish Civil War 1936–1939', PhD thesis, Waikato University, 1982.

Seaver, Kirsten A., *Maps, Myths, and Men: The Story of the Vinland Map* (Stanford: Stanford University Press, 2004).

Shep, Sydney J., '"Touching the Mind of the Country": J.C. Beaglehole and the Design of the Centennial Publications', in *Creating a National Spirit: Celebrating New Zealand's Centennial,* edited by William Renwick (Wellington: Victoria University Press, 2004).

Shuker, Roy, *Educating the Workers? A History of the Workers' Education Association of New Zealand* (Palmerston North: Dunmore Press, 1984).

Sinclair, Keith, *A History of New Zealand* (Harmondsworth: Penguin, 1959).

Sinclair, Keith, *Walter Nash* (Auckland: Auckland University Press and Oxford University Press, 1976).

Sinclair, Keith, *A History of the University of Auckland 1883–1983* (Auckland: Auckland University Press and Oxford University Press, 1983).

Spalding, Frances, *Duncan Grant* (London: Chatto and Windus, 1997).

Strachan, Michael, 'Esmond de Beer: Scholar and Benefactor', in *Compassing the Vaste Globe of the Earth: Studies in the History of the Hakluyt Society,* edited by R.C. Bridges and P.E.H. Hair (London: Hakluyt Society, 1996).

Sutherland, I.L.G., *The Maori Situation* (Wellington: Harry H. Tombs Ltd, 1935).

Taylor, Nancy M., *The New Zealand People at War: The Home Front,* 2 vols (Wellington: Department of Internal Affairs, 1986).

Templeton, Malcolm, ed., *An Eye, an Ear and a Voice: 50 Years in New Zealand's External Relations 1943–1993* (Wellington: Ministry of Foreign Affairs and Trade, 1993).

Terrill, Ross, *R.H. Tawney and his Times: Socialism as Fellowship* (Cambridge, Mass.: Harvard University Press, 1973).

Thompson, John, 'Self-made: Towards a Life of Rex Nan Kivell', in *Paradise*

Possessed: The Rex Nan Kivell Collection (Canberra: National Library of Australia, 1998).

Thomson, J.M., *Into a New Key: The Origins and History of the Music Federation of New Zealand 1950–1982* (Music Federation of New Zealand Inc., 1983).

Thomas, Allan, 'The Savage Clubs: A Spirit of "Bohemian" Comradeship', *Turnbull library Record*, vol.31 (1998), pp.43–62.

Traue, J.E., 'The University of NZ Press', *New Zealand Libraries*, vol.26, no.1 (January-February 1963).

Trevelyan, Jill, ed., *Toss Woollaston: A Life in Letters* (Wellington: Te Papa Press, 2004).

Turnovsky, Fred, *Turnovsky: Fifty Years in New Zealand* (Wellington: Allen and Unwin, 1990).

Tyler, Linda, 'The Urban and Urbane: Ernst Plischke's Kahn House', in *Zeal and Crusade: The Modern Movement in Wellington*, edited by John Wilson (Christchurch: Te Waihora Press, 1996).

Water, Bolker, 'The Birth of a Nation: J.C. Beaglehole and the National Orchestra', *Music in New Zealand*, no.40 (Summer 2001–02).

Watt, James, 'Medical Aspects and Consequences of Cook's Voyages', in *Captain James Cook and His Times*, edited by Robin Fisher and Hugh Johnston (Vancouver: Douglas and McIntyre, 1979).

Wilson, Ormond, *An Outsider Looks Back* (Wellington: Port Nicholson Press, 1982).

Wiren, S.A., 'Through the Urewera: A Wellington Party on the Tramp. "Swagging It over the Ranges"', *New Zealand Free Lance*, 4, 11 February 1925.

Wiren, S.A., 'Kaimatau', *New Zealand Alpine Journal*, vol.3, no.15 (December 1926).

Wood, F.L.W., '"A veritable man is not hidden among many": A Tribute by F.L.W. Wood', *NZ Listener*, 1 November 1971.

Zedlitz, G. W. von, *The Search for a Country: The Autobiography of G.W. von Zedlitz* (Hamilton: Paul's Book Arcade, 1963).

Index

You will recall that Mr James B

Captain James Cook of Mile End

on Dr Johnson to tell him all ab

to go ~~on the captain's~~ *voyaging with the captain.* ~~voyage~~

did have that sort of inclinati

very little we learnt. On an[d] th

had been stirred by the same

infirmities had put him off. Now

with the vision of Dr Johnson

or the beach of Matavai Bay.

the other hand, *frequently* reflected ~~most th~~

been for us if by some miracle o[ne]

one of that ship's company. Ther[e]

amiable, on the voyages, men ju[st]

thinks, Johnson had been enthu[se]

Clerk, had unitedly resolved th[at]

tative, *with one rights,* on this inspection of m[e]

got the Royal Society behind the

First Lord, & the more terrible La[w]